Making Relationship Choices videos take communication t

▶ How would you react to your best friend who's been making some questionable choices and posting about them on Facebook?

▶ What's the deal with the guy in your study group who's always late to meetings and doesn't seem to take the group seriously?

◀ Things have been tense between you and your brother since your grandmother died — and now he's not even speaking to you.

◀ Your cousin Britney crashed her car and dropped out of college. What is going on with her?

▶ You've never been that close with your dad, but things got worse last weekend.

▶ Your friend Karina is back from the Peace Corps, but she's not the same.

Making Relationship Choices by chapter

Chapter 1: Introducing Interpersonal Communication: Kaitlyn's story

Chapter 2: Considering Self: Jonathan's story

Chapter 3: Perceiving Others: Dylan's story

Chapter 4: Experiencing and Expressing Emotions: Sam's story

Chapter 5: Understanding Culture: Mom's story

Chapter 6: Understanding Gender: Derek's story

Chapter 7: Listening Actively: Ana's story

Chapter 8: Communicating Verbally: Britney's story

Chapter 9: Communicating Nonverbally: Dakota's story

Chapter 10: Managing Conflict and Power: Devdas's story

Chapter 11: Relationships with Romantic Partners: Javi's story

Chapter 12: Relationships with Family Members: Dad's story

Chapter 13: Relationships with Friends: Karina's story

Chapter 14: Relationships in the Workplace: Elizabeth's story

Reflect & Relate

An Introduction to
Interpersonal Communication

SIXTH EDITION

STEVEN McCORNACK
The University of Alabama at Birmingham

KELLY MORRISON
The University of Alabama at Birmingham

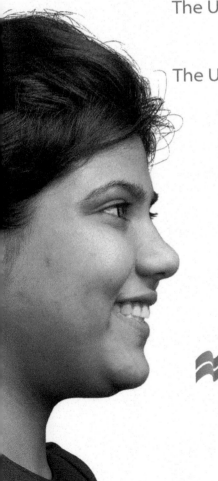

bedford/st.martin's
Macmillan Learning
Boston | New York

For Bedford/St. Martin's

Vice President: Leasa Burton
Senior Program Director, College Success and Communication: Erika Gutierrez
Program Manager, College Success and Communication: Allen Cooper
Director of Content Development, Humanities: Jane Knetzger
Development Manager: Caroline Thompson
Development Editor: Will Stonefield
Assistant Editor: Bill Yin
Director of Media Editorial: Adam Whitehurst
Media Editor: Nicole Erazo
Executive Digital Marketing Manager: Scott Guile
Senior Director, Content Management Enhancement: Tracey Kuehn
Senior Managing Editor: Lisa Kinne
Lead Content Project Manager: Won McIntosh
Lead Workflow Project Manager: Paul Rohloff
Production Supervisor: Robert Cherry
Director of Design, Content Management: Diana Blume
Interior Design: Jerilyn DiCarlo
Cover Design: William Boardman
Director of Rights and Permissions: Hilary Newman
Permissions Associate: Maisie Howell
Photo Researcher: Krystyna Borgen, Lumina Datamatics, Inc.
Director of Digital Production: Keri deManigold
Advanced Media Product Manager: D. Rand Thomas
Composition: Lumina Datamatics, Inc.
Cover Images: (Front cover and back, right; Title Page) Ranta Images/iStock/Getty Images;
(back, left) Eskay Lim/EyeEm/Getty Images
Printing and Binding: LSC Communications

Library of Congress Control Number: 2021937332

ISBN-13: 978-1-319-24758-4 (Student Edition)
ISBN-13: 978-1-319-39576-6 (Loose-leaf Edition)

Printed in the United States of America.
2   3   4   5   6   26   25   24   23   22

Acknowledgments
Acknowledgments and copyrights appear on the same page as the text and art selections they cover; these acknowledgments and copyrights constitute an extension of the copyright page.

At the time of publication all internet URLs published in this text were found to accurately link to their intended website. If you do find a broken link, please forward the information to will.stonefield@macmillan.com so that it can be corrected for the next printing.

For information, write: Bedford/St. Martin's, 75 Arlington Street, Boston, MA 02116

Reflect & Relate, Sixth Edition, connects to the learning outcomes of the National Communication Association (NCA)

In 2018, the National Communication Association (NCA) published learning outcomes for courses within the discipline. Below you can see how these learning outcomes apply to *Reflect & Relate*, Sixth Edition.

NCA Outcome	Relevant Coverage in *Reflect & Relate*, Sixth Edition
Learning Outcome #1: Describe the communication discipline and its central questions.	Foundational communication concepts are discussed in **Chapter 1: Introducing Interpersonal Communication**. After defining communication and describing its main characteristics, a thorough exploration of interpersonal communication reveals the features of this specific communication type, along with the principles and motives embedded within them. Issues surrounding interpersonal communication are also introduced, including culture, gender, sexual orientation, mediated contexts, and challenges in interpersonal relationships.
Learning Outcome #2: Employ communication theories, perspectives, principles, and concepts.	*Reflect & Relate* combines classic and contemporary theory in every chapter, from Knapp's (1984) stages of relationship development (**Chapter 11**) and Orbe's (1998) Co-Cultural Communication Theory (**Chapter 5**) to Blum, Mmari, and Moreau's (2017) research on the impact of varying gender expectations on adolescence around the globe (**Chapter 6**). Each *Making Relationship Choices* case study encourages you to reflect on the concepts you've encountered throughout the chapter, and apply what you have learned to a difficult communication situation.
Learning Outcome #3: Engage in communication inquiry.	In **LaunchPad for *Reflect & Relate***, you'll find bonus content, "Research in Interpersonal Communication," which introduces you to the approaches communication scholars take when conducting research and developing theories, as well as when it is appropriate to employ each method.
Learning Outcome #4: Create messages appropriate to the audience, purpose, and context.	In **Chapter 1**, you'll learn that competent interpersonal communication is tied to *appropriateness*, the degree to which your communication matches the accepted norms for a given audience, purpose, or context. Throughout the rest of the text, you'll learn the necessary skills for communicating appropriately — particularly in the *Skills Practice* feature and *Making Relationship Choices* case studies — whether you are managing a conflict with a family member, offering empathy to a friend, or advocating for yourself with your supervisor at work.
Learning Outcome #5: Critically analyze messages.	One of the primary ways to begin critically analyzing messages is through active listening, which is covered in **Chapter 7**. In this chapter, you'll learn the differences between hearing and listening, as well as how you can improve your listening during each stage of the process, from limiting opportunities for multitasking to paraphrasing what your communication partner has said. In addition, **Chapter 3** is devoted exclusively to perception, where you'll learn how improving your perception-checking skills can also improve your ability to analyze the messages you receive.
Learning Outcome #6: Demonstrate the ability to accomplish communicative goals (self-efficacy).	Each chapter's *Making Relationship Choices* case study feature takes you through a five-step process in which you draw on the communication concepts you've learned throughout the chapter to manage a difficult situation with loved ones, peers, or colleagues. At the end of each case study, you'll measure your self-efficacy by evaluating the appropriateness, effectiveness, and ethics of your communication, and reflect on what you could have done differently to accomplish your goal.
Learning Outcome #7: Apply ethical communication principles and practices.	As with appropriateness, *ethics* is highlighted as one of the key components of competent interpersonal communication. **Chapter 1** defines ethics as the set of moral principles that guide our communicative behaviors. Throughout the text, you'll consider how ethics plays a role in the way you communicate with others and manage difficult situations. The NCA's official "Credo for Ethical Communication" is also included in Chapter 1.
Learning Outcome #8: Utilize communication to embrace difference.	The emphasis of **Chapter 5: Understanding Culture** is on embracing difference in order to dismantle the divisions we perceive with others. This chapter explores the influence of cultural variations on communication, and how understanding these can help us to communicate meaningfully with those who we perceive as different.
Learning Outcome #9: Influence public discourse.	While *Reflect & Relate* focuses on interpersonal communication, rather than public discourse, you can easily purchase access to our public speaking titles at **store.macmillanlearning.com**. Our *Essential Guide to Rhetoric* is available at an affordable price, and will help you create messages capable of impacting audiences and influencing public life.

One of the greatest blessings we all experience as teachers of interpersonal communication is the chance to connect with an array of interesting, complicated, and diverse people. Each term, a new window of contact opens. As we peer through it on that first day, we see the faces of those who will comprise our class. They are strangers to us at that moment, but over the weeks that follow, they become individuated *people*. We learn the names that symbolize their now-familiar faces, as well as their unique identities. And because it's an *interpersonal* class, we also learn their *stories*, as well as the aspirations that urge them to lean forward in knowledge-anticipation. Then the term ends, the window closes, and the shade is drawn. All that remains are the after-images imprinted on the retina of our memories: Alex, who came out of the closet—but only to you; Lourdes, who, as the first in her family to attend college, brought to your class all the hopes and dreams of multiple generations.

The people we come to call *our* students share a common bond that serves to connect them: *they all want to improve their relationships.* They bring to our classes romantic heartbreaks, family rifts, friendship betrayals, and bullying bosses; and they look to us to give them practical, relevant knowledge that will empower them to choose wisely in dealing with these challenges. The legacy of such impact may be found in their emails and social media messages to us months, and even years, later: "I just wanted you to know that your class changed my life!"

Like many of you, we also have had these former students ask, "How do you stay passionate about teaching, after doing it for so many years?" (We've been team-teaching the intro-to-interpersonal class together every semester for more than two decades.) Our answer is always the same. *Our passion for this class stems from its potential for transformative impact.* That is, the skills and knowledge that we *all*—as interpersonal communication instructors—bring to our students have the potential to transform their lives in powerful, positive ways. The idea of *not* being thrilled about sharing this life-changing material is inconceivable! And it's our passion for this content that motivated us to write *Reflect & Relate.*

When Steve wrote the very first edition of *Reflect & Relate,* he wanted to provide his fellow teachers and their students with a textbook that was welcoming, friendly, personal, trustworthy, and practical—a book that was rock-solid in content; represented the finest of new and classic scholarship in our discipline; and provided a clear sense of the field as a domain of scientific endeavor, not just "common sense." He also wanted a book that didn't read like a typical textbook but was so engaging that students might read through entire chapters before they realized they had done so. And, of course, his core mission was creating a book that didn't just tell students what to do but taught students *how* to systematically reason through interpersonal communication challenges. Students could walk away from reading it knowing how to solve their own problems and flexibly adapt to dynamic changes in contexts and relationships.

Starting with the Fifth Edition, Kelly officially joined *Reflect & Relate* as a co-author—but this was really a formal recognition of a role that Kelly had long held as a writer, a thinker, and an adviser on the text. For instance, the very title of the book, *Reflect & Relate,* was Kelly's idea, as was the concept of bolstering students' critical self-reflection abilities by including *Self-Reflection* exercises in the margins, and adding "The Other Side" to the *Making Relationship Choices* feature. And dozens of the most beloved illustrative examples that have given the book its vibrant and engaging readability—such as Gospel for Teens, St. Jude Children's

Research Hospital, and the friendship between Supreme Court justices Ruth Bader Ginsburg and Antonin Scalia—are Kelly's inspirations. Her tireless work ethic and her broad expertise with regard to gender and communication have helped *Reflect & Relate* better fulfill its original mission of engaging students while providing them with the very best scholarship in the field.

The revision of this Sixth Edition of *Reflect & Relate* took place during an unprecedented time in our collective experience: the COVID-19 pandemic. As you know, many instructors (including us) have taught online for the very first time, while others were already teaching online but have found new ways to support their teaching and our students' learning. Some of us have taught synchronously; others asynchronously; others a mix of both. Taking into account this enormous variety of experiences, we decided that what our users would need most in these uncertain times is *stability* in their learning materials. Therefore, we have decided not to make any changes to the organization of our table of contents: our chapters are still in the same order as in the Fifth Edition. What we *have* done in this Sixth Edition is threefold. First, we have thoroughly updated the scholarship and theory cited in every chapter, as you have come to expect from *Reflect & Relate*. But this time, we have gone even further, bringing in over 300 new research citations throughout the text on the most relevant, engaging topics like gender equity and health, the impact of mobile devices on trust and intimacy, the pressure to be constantly "connected" in the workplace, and proven methods to combat anxiety and feelings of isolation (to name just a few!).

Second, we believe it is now more important than ever to emphasize the importance of relational maintenance and staying connected with the people we care about. Research indicates that even before the COVID-19 crisis, loneliness, anxiety, and feelings of social isolation had been increasing in the United States and in many countries worldwide—and that these increases have been especially pronounced among young people. Further, research suggests that these negative experiences—loneliness, anxiety, isolation—are exacerbated by too much time spent on screens. Yet at the same time, screens are also a primary modality that helps us stay connected with our loved ones. In this revision, we recognize that a central challenge going forward will be to balance the use of mediated communication in our relationships—using it to maintain closeness with others while being aware that *too much* screen time can be detrimental. With all this in mind, in this Sixth Edition, we continually return to the idea that *our interpersonal skills cultivate our social connections,* and that these connections in turn allow us to reap the rewards of emotional, mental, and physical well-being. All of the examples and instructional material are designed to give students the skills they need to create and maintain these social connections.

The third major change we have made in the Sixth Edition centers on our Editorial Board for Diversity, Inclusion, and Culturally Responsive Pedagogy. For *Reflect & Relate*, this editorial board consists of seven communication instructors from across the United States, each of whom has brought invaluable experience, insight, and perspective to the revision. The board's mission is to guide our development of the text to ensure that the Sixth Edition welcomes *all* students and instructors, and that the perspectives included in the learning materials truly reflect the diversity of students and instructors in today's classrooms. You will see the results of the board's thoughtful feedback in the text and photos throughout the book. We extend our heartfelt thanks to each of the members; we could not have achieved this revision without their guidance.

We are thrilled about all that *Reflect & Relate,* Sixth Edition, has to offer you and your students, and we would love to hear what you think about this new edition. Please feel free to drop us a line at **smcc911@uab.edu** or **kmmcc@uab.edu** so that we can chat about the book and the course, or just talk shop about teaching interpersonal communication.

What's New in the Sixth Edition?

The sixth edition of *Reflect & Relate* is digital-forward, covering the most important topics in interpersonal communication and connecting them to digital media.

- **The sixth edition has been extensively revised with the guidance of our Editorial Board for Diversity, Inclusion, and Culturally Responsive Pedagogy.** This team of seven communication scholars has advised the authors and editors throughout the revision to ensure that *Reflect & Relate* speaks to *all* students and instructors. With the board's guidance, we have revised coverage and examples throughout the book to ensure that diverse, inclusive perspectives are represented.

- **Updated coverage of culture in Chapter 5 and throughout the text.** The sixth edition has been updated to reflect current conversation surrounding culture, with revised coverage of intersectionality and prejudice in Chapter 5 and an emphasis on embracing cultural difference to dismantle perceived distance. Throughout the text, new examples illustrate the influence of culture on self and perception. This edition includes many new and revised *Focus on Culture* features, which further spotlight the importance of culture—and of communicating competently with a diverse array of people of various identities and cultural backgrounds.

- **Updated coverage of mediated communication** meets students where they are: online. Whether via video call, text, tweet, or note, learning appropriate digital communication skills is vital to competent communication. Specific examples dedicated to mediated communication help students refine and improve their daily use of communication technologies.

Reflect & Relate offers new content in areas that interest students the most.

Topics like *phubbing, workplace telepressure,* and the impact of mobile devices on intimacy and disclosure can be found in every chapter. This content reflects issues of concern for today's students and represents the very best scholarship within the field of interpersonal communication.

- **Current, powerful stories and images hook students' interest.** *Reflect & Relate* is full of new, current, and relatable examples that students will want to read. The text and photo program draw from pop culture—everything from *Outlander* to *Red Table Talk*—as well as current events and real stories from the authors and their students to provide content that resonates and is easy to show and discuss in class.

- **New chapter openers spotlight diverse and compelling stories.** These include a discussion of playwright Lin-Manuel Miranda's use of language to promote inclusion and understanding of U.S. history in his Broadway smash-hit *Hamilton*; a look at Fred Rogers's use of active listening to break down racial barriers in *Mister Rogers' Neighborhood*; and the legend of Zhinu and Niulang (the Cowherd and the Weaver), its significance as a story of romance, and its influence on the modern-day Qixi festival in China.

Flagship Features

Reflect & Relate offers an accessible, innovative look at the discipline.

- *Reflect & Relate* **presents a fresh perspective on interpersonal communication.** Discussions of classic and cutting-edge scholarship from interpersonal communication, psychology, sociology, philosophy, and linguistics are woven together. Unlike other texts, *Reflect & Relate* continues to focus on how these concepts are linked to interpersonal communication and how communication skills can be improved.

- *Reflect & Relate* **balances current topics with classic coverage.** The text integrates coverage of social media, smartphones and intimacy, multitasking online, and other novel topics with foundational subjects like self-awareness, conflict approaches, and nonverbal communication codes.

- **Integrated discussions on culture and gender appear in every chapter.** *Reflect & Relate* treats individual and cultural influences as integral parts of the story by discussing the myths and realities of how gender, ethnicity, race, sexual orientation, religion, and age shape communication.

- *Reflect & Relate* **offers clear explanations, engaging examples, and an attractive art program.** Major concepts are illustrated with examples drawn from pop culture, history, current events, and everyday life — examples that reflect the diversity of students themselves in terms of age, gender, lifestyle, occupation, and culture. Meanwhile, the appealing and pedagogically sound art program works with the examples to grab students' attention and focus them on the subject at hand.

Reflect & Relate helps students look more deeply at themselves — and develop skills for a lifetime.

- *Self-Reflection* **questions foster critical self-awareness.** Self-awareness is essential for competent communication, and carefully placed *Self-Reflection* questions show students how to examine their own experiences and communication in light of theory and research. As a result, students gain a better understanding of concepts — such as emotional intelligence, stereotyping, and relationship ethics — and of themselves.

- *Skills Practice* **exercises strengthen students' abilities.** Every chapter includes three *Skills Practice* exercises — one devoted to online communication — that give step-by-step instruction on practical skills, such as appropriately self-disclosing and interpreting nonverbal codes. *Skills Practice* activities are specifically designed to make it easy for students to implement them in their everyday lives.

- *Focus on Culture* **boxes and** *Self-Quiz* **exercises help students gain knowledge about their own communication.** *Focus on Culture* boxes challenge students to think about how the influence of their own culture shapes their communication. Rooted in research, *Self-Quiz* exercises help students analyze their strengths and weaknesses so that they can focus on how to improve their communication.

Reflect & Relate helps students improve their relationships.

- **Romantic, family, friend, and workplace relationships are explored.** Tailoring communication strategies to specific relationships is both essential and challenging, so *Reflect & Relate* devotes four full chapters to these key communication contexts, giving students in-depth knowledge along with practical strategies for using communication to improve their relationships. Special emphasis is given to relationship maintenance — a key relational concern many students bring to the classroom.

- **Unique *Making Relationship Choices* case studies take application to a new level.** These activities challenge students to draw on their knowledge when facing difficult relationship issues and to create their own solutions. Instead of just asking students, "What would you do?" or offering them solutions, *Making Relationship Choices* walks students step-by-step through realistic scenarios — critically self-reflecting, considering others' perspectives, determining best outcomes, and identifying potential roadblocks — to make informed communication decisions. They then have the opportunity to experience "the other side" of the story by going online to watch a first-person account of the situation. Becoming aware of both sides of the story allows students to broaden their perspective and reevaluate their initial reaction and response.

A Multifaceted Digital Experience Brings It All Together

LaunchPad helps students learn, study, and apply communication concepts.

Digital resources for *Reflect & Relate* are available in LaunchPad, a dynamic platform that combines the e-book with LearningCurve adaptive quizzing; a collection of video clips illustrating key terms and concepts from the text; self-assessments; chapter quizzes; journal activities; and more. LaunchPad comes with pre-built, easy-to-assign units for each chapter in the book that support instructors teaching face-to-face and online — both synchronously and asynchronously. LaunchPad can be packaged with *Reflect & Relate*, or it can be purchased separately.

- **LearningCurve provides adaptive quizzing and a personalized learning program.** In every chapter, call-outs prompt students to tackle the game-like LearningCurve quizzes to test their knowledge and reinforce learning of the material. Based on research on how students learn, LearningCurve motivates students to engage with course materials, while the reporting tools let you see what content students have mastered, allowing you to adapt your teaching plan to their needs.

- *Making Relationship Choices* **videos** help students see "the other side" of the scenario, helping them develop empathy and boost their communication competence.

- **Videos help students see concepts in action and encourage self-reflection.** Accompanying reflection questions help students apply the term or concept illustrated in each video to their own experiences. More than 70 video activities are easily assignable and make useful journal prompts or discussion starters. For ideas on how to integrate videos into your course, see the Instructor's Resource Manual. To access the videos, and for a complete list of available clips, see the last page of this book or visit **macmillanlearning.com /reflectrelate6e**

Digital and Print Formats

Whether it's print, digital, or a value option, choose the best format for you. For more information on these resources, please visit the online catalog at **macmillanlearning .com/reflectrelate6e**.

- **LaunchPad for *Reflect & Relate* dramatically enhances teaching and learning.** LaunchPad combines the full e-book, videos, quizzes and self-assessments, instructor's resources, and LearningCurve adaptive quizzing. Package LaunchPad with the print version of *Reflect & Relate,* or order LaunchPad on its own.

- **The Loose-leaf Edition of *Reflect & Relate*** features the print text in a convenient, budget-priced format, designed to fit into a three-ring binder. The loose-leaf version also can be packaged with LaunchPad.

- ***Reflect & Relate* is available as a print text.** To get the most out of the book, package LaunchPad with the text.

- **E-books.** *Reflect & Relate* is available as an e-book for use on computers, tablets, and e-readers. See **macmillanlearning.com/ebooks** to learn more.

- You want to give your students affordable rental, packaging, and e-book options. So do we. Learn more at **store.macmillanlearning.com**

- **Customize *Reflect & Relate*** to create the ideal textbook for your course. For more information, visit **macmillanlearning.com/curriculumsolutions**

Resources for Instructors and Students

For more information on these resources or to learn about package options, please visit the online catalog at **macmillanlearning.com/reflectrelate6e**

Resources for Instructors

For more information or to order or download the instructor's resources, please visit the online catalog. The Instructor's Resource Manual, Test Bank, Lecture Slides, and iClicker Questions are also available in LaunchPad: **launchpadworks.com**

***Online Instructor's Resource Manual for Reflect & Relate,* Sixth Edition,** by Curt VanGeison (St. Charles Community College), Joseph Ortiz (Scottsdale Community College), and Marion Boyer (Kalamazoo Valley Community College, Emeritus). The comprehensive Instructor's Resource Manual includes teaching notes on managing an interpersonal communication course, organization, and assessment; sample syllabi; advice on teaching multilingual students; and tips for using the pedagogical features of *Reflect & Relate*. In addition, a teaching guide provides suggestions for implementing the book's thorough coverage of cultural issues. Every chapter also includes lecture outlines and class discussion starters, class and group exercises, assignment suggestions, video and music recommendations, and website links.

***Test Bank for Reflect & Relate*, Sixth Edition,** by Charles J. Korn (Northern Virginia Community College). This test bank is one of the largest for the introductory interpersonal communication course, with more than 100 multiple-choice, true/false, and essay questions for every chapter. This easy-to-use test bank also identifies the level of difficulty for each question and includes the section in which the answer may be found.

Lecture slides provide support for important concepts addressed in each chapter. The slides are available for download in LaunchPad and from the online catalog.

iClicker, Active Learning Simplified. iClicker offers simple, flexible tools to help you give students a voice and facilitate active learning in the classroom. Students can participate with the devices they already bring to class using our iClicker Reef mobile apps (which work with smartphones, tablets, or laptops) or iClicker remotes. iClicker is integrated with LaunchPad to make it easier than ever to synchronize grades and promote engagement—both in and out of class. iClicker Reef access cards can also be packaged with LaunchPad for *Reflect & Relate*, Sixth Edition, at a significant savings for your students. To learn more, talk to your Macmillan Learning representative or visit us at **www.iclicker.com**

Communication in the Classroom: A Collection of G.I.F.T.S., by John S. Seiter, Jennifer Peeples, and Matthew L. Sanders (Utah State University). This resource includes a collection of over 100 powerful ideas for classroom activities. Many activities are designed specifically for the interpersonal communication course, and all activities have been submitted by instructors who have tested and perfected them in their classrooms. Each activity includes a detailed explanation and debrief, drawing on the instructor's experiences.

***Teaching Interpersonal Communication*, Second Edition,** by Elizabeth J. Natalle (University of North Carolina–Greensboro) and Alicia Alexander (Southern Illinois University Edwardsville). Written by award-winning instructors, this essential resource provides all the tools instructors need to develop, teach, and manage a successful interpersonal communication course. New and seasoned instructors alike will benefit from the practical advice, scholarly insight, and suggestions for integrating research and practice into the classroom—as well as the new chapter dedicated to teaching online.

Coordinating the Communication Course: A Guidebook, by Deanna Fassett and John Warren. This guidebook offers the most practical advice on every topic central to the coordinator/director role. First setting a strong foundation, this professional resource continues with thoughtful guidance, tips, and best practices on such crucial topics as creating community across multiple sections, orchestrating meaningful assessment, and hiring and training instructors. Model course materials, recommended readings, and insights from successful coordinators make this resource a must-have for anyone directing a course in communication.

The Macmillan Learning Communication Community. This new online space for instructor development and engagement houses resources to support your teaching, such as class activities, video assignments, and invitations to conferences and webinars. Connect with our team, our authors, and other instructors through online discussions and blog posts at **community.macmillan.com/community /communication**

Resources for Students

The Essential Guide Series. This series gives instructors flexibility and support in designing courses by providing brief booklets that begin with a useful overview and then address the essential concepts and skills that students need. Topics that may interest interpersonal communication students include intercultural communication, group communication, and rhetoric. For more information, go to **macmillanlearning.com**

Media Career Guide: Preparing for Jobs in the 21st Century, by Sherri Hope Culver (Temple University). Practical, student-friendly, and revised to include the most recent statistics on the job market, this guide includes a comprehensive directory of media jobs, practical tips, and career guidance for students considering a major in the media industry.

Acknowledgments

We would like to thank everyone at Bedford/St. Martin's who was involved in this project and whose support made it possible, especially Vice President of Humanities Editorial Leasa Burton, Senior Program Director Erika Gutierrez, and Program Manager Allen Cooper. A heartfelt thank you to our Development Editor, Will Stonefield, who optimistically guided our revision process during the uncertainty of the COVID-19 pandemic. You supported us as a sounding board and wizardly word-smith, challenged us to do our very best work, and expanded our community of voices. Thanks to the rest of the editorial team who worked with us throughout the process, including Media Editor Nicole Erazo and Assistant Editor Bill Yin. The book also would not have come together without the efforts of Lead Content Project Manager Won McIntosh, who oversaw the book's tight schedule; and Media Project Manager Training Specialist Allison Hart, who facilitated the production of all components of LaunchPad. The enthusiasm and support from Executive Marketing Manager Scott Guile and the entire Macmillan Learning sales force are particularly appreciated.

On a more personal level, we thank all those who assisted us with the book during its development, and all those who collaborated with us in contributing their extraordinary stories to the text: Melissa Seligman, Vy Higginsen, Jennifer Andrews, Brenda Villa, Eric Staib, Vivian Derr, and Silvia Amaro. We would like to thank our Chair, Tim Levine, and our colleagues and administrators at UAB, for their professional support of this project: we can't begin to tell you how much it means to work at an institution that values the writing of books! And thanks to our three sons—Kyle, Colin, and Conor—who have blessed and enriched our lives more than words on a page could ever express, continuing to inspire us each day, and who fill our lives with laughter, pride, and love.

Throughout the development of this textbook, hundreds of interpersonal communication instructors voiced their opinion through surveys, focus groups, and reviews of the manuscript, and we thank them all. A special thank-you goes to the dedicated members of the Editorial Board for Diversity, Inclusion, and Culturally Responsive Pedagogy (DICR Board): Tim Brown, *Queens University of Charlotte*; Tasha Davis, *Austin Community College*; Danielle Harkins, *Germanna Community College*; Tina Harris, *University of Georgia*; Rody Randon, *Phoenix College*; and Myra Washington, *University of New Mexico*. An extra-special thank-you goes to S. Lizabeth Martin, *Palm Beach State College*, who expertly consulted on changes to particular sections of the manuscript. The DICR Board's thoughtful feedback has allowed us to shape the Sixth Edition of *Reflect & Relate* into an even better, more inclusive, and more useful resource for students and instructors.

We would also like to thank everyone not named above who participated in reviews, surveys, and focus groups from the first edition of *Reflect & Relate* to today.

For the sixth edition: Richard Baca, *Luna Community College*; Lisa Bamber, *Otero Junior College*; Jennifer Becker, *University of Alabama Tuscaloosa*; Angela Blais, *University of Minnesota-Duluth*; Kristin Carlson, *University of Minnesota-Duluth*; Chantele Carr, *Estrella Mountain Community College*; Bethany Chambers, *Southwestern Michigan College*; Wade Cornelius, *Park University*; Rowdy Duncan, *Phoenix College*; Jenny Farrell, *University of Nevada Las Vegas*; Stacy Fitzpatrick, *North Hennepin Community College*; Laura Glasbrenner, *Mineral Area College*; Sally Hastings, *University of Central Florida*; Eric Holmes, *Valencia College*; Anastacia Janovec, *University of Georgia*; Alexis Johnson, *Arkansas Tech University*; Caleb Lamont, *Colby College*; Peter Landino, *Terra State Community College*; Peter Lee, *California State University Fullerton*; Karen McGrath, *The College of Saint Rose*; Rachel Murdock, *Des Moines Area Community College*; Gregory Rickert, *Bluegrass Community and Technical College*; Kelly Rossetto, *Boise State University*; Pamela Sanger, *California State University Sacramento*; Tanika Smith, *Prince George's Community College*; Craig Stark, *Susquehanna University*; Tara Thornton, *Southern Illinois University Edwardsville*; Charlotte Toguchi, *Kapiolani Community College*.

For the fifth edition: Julie Ahasay, *University of Minnesota*; Alicia Alexander, *Southern Illinois University, Edwardsville*; Tenisha Baca, *Glendale Community College*; Laurie Brady, *University of Arkansas*; Kelli Chromey, *South Dakota State University*; Tina Harris, *University of Georgia*; Carrie Kennedy-Lightsey, *Stephen F. Austin State University*; Sharon Martin, *Palm Beach State College*; Susan McDaniel, *Loyola Marymount University*; Marguerite Parker, *Pitt Community College*; Leesha Thrower, *Cincinnati State Community College*.

For the fourth edition: Christine Armstrong, *Northampton County Area Community College, Monroe Campus*; Courtney Atkins, *Union County College*; Diane Badzinski, *Colorado Christian University*; Patrick Barton, *Lone Star College*; Cassandra Carlson, *University of Wisconsin, Madison*; Allison Edgley, *Union County College*; Zach Frohlich, *Tarrant County College, Northwest Campus*; David Fusani, *Erie Community College*; Valerie Manno Giroux, *University of Miami*; Annette Hamel, *Western Michigan University*; Cherlyn Kipple, *Union County College*; Melanie Lea, *Bossier Parish Community College*; Susan McDaniel, *Loyola Marymount University*; Neil Moura, *MiraCosta College*; Ruth Spillberg, *Curry College*; Lindsay Timmerman, *University of Wisconsin, Madison*; Curt VanGeison, *St. Charles Community College*.

For the third edition: Ashley Fitch Blair, *Union University*; Angela Blais, *University of Minnesota, Duluth*; Deborah Brunson, *University of North Carolina, Wilmington*; Cassandra Carlson, *University of Wisconsin, Madison*; Kristin Carlson, *University of Minnesota, Duluth*; Janet Colvin, *Utah Valley University*; Andrew Cuneo, *University of Wisconsin, Milwaukee*; Melissa Curtin, *University of California, Santa Barbara*; Paige Davis, *Cy-Fair College*; Sherry Dewald, *Red Rocks Community College*; Marcia D. Dixson, *Indiana University–Purdue University, Fort Wayne*; Jean Farrell, *University of Maryland*; David Gaer, *Laramie County Community College*; Jodi Gaete, *Suffolk County Community College*; Carla Gesell-Streeter, *Cincinnati State Technical and Community College*; Valerie Manno Giroux, *University of Miami*; Neva Gronert, *Arapahoe Community College*; Katherine Gronewold, *North Dakota State University*; Virginia Hamilton, *University of California, Davis*; Kristin Haun, *University of Tennessee, Knoxville*; Doug Hurst, *St. Louis Community College, Meramec*; Nicole Juranek, *Iowa Western Community College*; Janice Krieger, *Ohio State University*; Gary Kuhn, *Chemekata Community College*; Melanie Lea-Birck, *Bossier Parish Community College*; Myra Luna Lucero, *University of New Mexico*; Sorin Nastasia, *Southern Illinois University Edwardsville*; David Naze, *Prairie State College*; Gretchen Norling, *University of West Florida*; Laura Oliver, *University of Texas, San Antonio*; Lance Rintamaki, *University at Buffalo*; Jeanette Ruiz, *University of California, Davis*; Rebecca Sailor, *Aims Community College*; Alan H. Shiller, *Southern Illinois University Edwardsville*; Mara Singer, *Red Rocks Community College*; Jamie Stech, *Iowa Western Community College*; Deborah Stieneker, *Arapahoe Community College*; Kevin Stoller, *Indiana University–Purdue University, Fort Wayne*; Renee Strom, *St. Cloud State University*; Deatra Sullivan-Morgan, *Elmhurst College*; Marcilene Thompson-Hayes, *Arkansas State University*; Lindsay Timmerman, *University of Wisconsin, Milwaukee*; Curt VanGeison, *St. Charles Community College*; Charles Veenstra, *Dordt College*; Jamie Vega, *Full Sail University*; Judith Vogel, *Des Moines Area Community College*; Thomas Wagner, *Xavier University*.

For the second edition: Michael Laurie Bishow, *San Francisco State University*; Angela Blais, *University of Minnesota, Duluth*; Judy DeBoer, *Inver Hills Community College*; Greg Gardner, *Rollins College*; Jill Gibson, *Amarillo College*; Betsy Gordon, *McKendree University*; Robert Harrison, *Gallaudet University*; Brian Heisterkamp, *California State University, San Bernardino*; Eileen Hemenway, *North Carolina State University*; Yanan Ju, *Connecticut State University*; Beverly Kelly, *California Lutheran University*; Howard Kerner, *Polk Community College*; Karen Krumrey-Fulks, *Lane Community College*; Karen Krupar, *Metro State College of Denver*; Gary Kuhn, *Chemeketa Community College*; Victoria Leonard, *College of the Canyons*; Annie McKinlay, *North Idaho College*; Michaela Meyer, *Christopher Newport University*; Maureen Olguin, *Eastern New Mexico University, Roswell*; James Patterson, *Miami University*; Evelyn Plummer, *Seton Hall University*; Laurie Pratt, *Chaffey College*; Narissra M. Punyanunt-Carter, *Texas Tech University*; Thomas Sabetta, *Jefferson Community College*; Bridget Sampson, *California State University, Northridge*; Cami Sanderson, *Ferris State University*; Rhonda Sprague, *University of Wisconsin, Stevens Point*; Robert Steinmiller, *Henderson State University*; Deborah Stieneker, *Arapahoe Community College*; Anita J. Turpin, *Roanoke College*; Inci Ozum Ucok, *Hofstra University*; Paula Usrey, *Umpqua Community College*; Charles Veenstra, *Dordt College*; Sylvia Walters, *Davidson Community College*; Michael Xenos, *University of Wisconsin, Madison*; Phyllis Zrzavy, *Franklin Pierce University*.

For the first edition: A special thank-you goes to the dedicated members of the editorial board, whose commitment to the project was surpassed only by their help in shaping the book: Kathy Adams, *California State University, Fresno*; Stuart Bonnington, *Austin Peay State University*; Marion Boyer, *Kalamazoo Valley Community College*; Tamala Bulger, *University of North Carolina*; Stephanie Coopman, *San Jose State University*; Susan Drucker, *Hofstra University*; Greg Gardner, *Rollins College*; Kathleen Henning, *Gateway Technical College*; Sarah Kays, *DeVry Institute*; Charles J. Korn, *Northern Virginia Community College*; Karen Krumrey-Fulks, *Lane Community College*; Gary Kuhn, *Chemeketa Community College*; Anna Martinez, *Reedley College*; Elizabeth J. Natalle, *University of North Carolina, Greensboro*; Randall Pugh, *Montana State University*; Marta Walz, *Elgin Community College*; and Cherie White, *Muskingum Area Technical College*.

We would also like to thank everyone else who participated in this process: **Alabama:** Robert Agne, *Auburn University*; Jonathan Amsbary, *University of Alabama*; Angela Gibson Wible, *Shelton State Community College*; Bill Huddleston, *University of North Alabama*; James Vickrey, *Troy State University*. **Arizona:** Anneliese Harper, *Scottsdale Community College*; Douglas Kelley, *Arizona State University, West*; Fred Kester, *Yavapai College, Prescott*; Mark Lewis, *Phoenix College*; Joseph Ortiz, *Scottsdale Community College*. **Arkansas:** Patricia Amason, *University of Arkansas*; Jason Hough, *John Brown University*; Robert Steinmiller, *Henderson State University*. **California:** Katherine Adams, *California State University, Fresno*; Susan Childress, *Santa Rosa Junior College*; Stephanie J. Coopman, *San Jose State University*; Kristin Gatto Correia, *San Francisco State University*; Eve-Anne Doohan, *University of San Francisco*; Jeannette Duarte, *Rio Hondo College*; Anne Duran, *California State University, Bakersfield*; William Eadie, *San Diego State University*; Allison Evans, *California State University, Bakersfield*; G. L. Forward, *Point Loma Nazarene University*; Kimberly Hubbert, *Cerritos College*; Annika Hylmö, *Loyola Marymount University*; Cynthia Johnson, *College of the Sequoias*; Beverly Kelley, *California Lutheran University*; William Kelly, *University of California, Los Angeles*; Randall Koper, *University of the Pacific*; Victoria Leonard, *College of the Canyons*; Ben Martin, *Santa Monica College*; Anna Martinez, *Reedley College*; Lawrence Jerome McGill, *Pasadena City College*; William F. Owen, *California State University, Sacramento*; Laurie Pratt, *Fullerton College*; Catherine Puckering, *University of California, Davis*; Jose Rodriguez, *California State University, Long Beach*; Teresa Turner, *Shasta College*; Jennifer Valencia, *San Diego Miramar College*; Richard Wiseman, *California State University, Fullerton*. **Colorado:** Eric Aoki, *Colorado State University*; Diane Blomberg, *Metropolitan State College of Denver*; Cheryl McFarren, *Arapahoe Community College*; Susan Pendell, *Colorado State University*; Dwight Podgurski, *Colorado Christian University*. **Connecticut:** Yanan Ju, *Central Connecticut State University*; Hugh McCarney, *Western Connecticut State University*; William Petkanas, *Western Connecticut State University*; Terri Toles-Patkin, *Eastern Connecticut State University*; C. Arthur VanLear, *University of Connecticut*; Kathryn Wiss, *Western Connecticut State University*. **Florida:** Kenneth Cissna, *University of South Florida*; Ed Coursey, *Palm Beach Community College*; Susan S. Easton, *Rollins College*; Greg Gardner, *Rollins College*; Katherine Nelson, *Barry University*; Maria Roca, *Florida Gulf Coast University*; Ann Scroggie, *Santa Fe Community College*. **Georgia:** Allison Ainsworth, *Gainesville College*; Marybeth Callison, *University of Georgia*; Michael H. Eaves, *Valdosta State University*; Pamela Hayward, *Augusta State University*; Gail Reid, *University of West Georgia*; Jennifer Samp, *University of Georgia*. **Hawaii:** Chiung Chen, *Brigham Young University, Hawaii*; Cailin Kulp

O'Riordan, *University of Hawaii, Manoa*; Alan Ragains, *Windward Community College*. **Idaho:** Robyn Bergstrom, *Brigham Young University, Idaho*; Marcy Horne, *Lewis-Clark State College*; Annie McKinlay, *North Idaho College*. **Illinois:** Leah Bryant, *De Paul University*; Tim Cole, *De Paul University*; James Dittus, *Elgin Community College*; Katy Fonner, *Northwestern University*; Daena Goldsmith, *University of Illinois, Urbana-Champaign*; Sarah Strom Kays, *DeVry Institute*; Betty Jane Lawrence, *Bradley University*; Jody Littleton, *Parkland College*; Jay Martinson, *Nazarene University*; Lisa Miczo, *Western Illinois University*; Willona Olison, *Northwestern University*; Michael Purdy, *Governors State University*; Lesa Stern, *Southern Illinois University Edwardsville*; Marta Walz, *Elgin Community College*. **Indiana:** Austin Babrow, *Purdue University*; Rebecca Bailey, *Valparaiso University*; Alexandra Corning, *University of Notre Dame*; John Greene, *Purdue University*; Krista Hoffmann-Longtin, *Indiana University–Purdue University, Indianapolis*; Irwin Mallin, *Indiana University–Purdue University, Fort Wayne*; Janet Morrison, *Ivy Tech State College*; James H. Tolhuizen, *Indiana University Northwest*; Ralph Webb, *Purdue University*. **Iowa:** Julie Simanski, *Des Moines Area Community College*; Erik Stroner, *Iowa Central Community College*; Charles Veenstra, *Dordt College*. **Kansas:** David Sherlock, *Independence Community College*; Richard Stine, *Johnson County Community College*. **Kentucky:** Chuck Bryant, *University of Kentucky*; Joy Hart, *University of Louisville*; Mona Leonard, *Jefferson Community College*; Tracy Letcher, *University of Kentucky*; Gregory Rickert, *Bluegrass Community and Technical College*; Kandi L. Walker, *University of Louisville*. **Louisiana:** Terry M. Cunconan, *Louisiana Tech University*; Karen Fontenot, *Southeastern Louisiana University*; Loretta L. Pecchioni, *Louisiana State University*. **Maine:** Julie Zink, *University of Southern Maine*. **Maryland:** Laura Drake, *University of Maryland*; Linda Heil, *Harford Community College*; Audra McMullen, *Towson University*; Susan Ondercin, *Carroll Community College*. **Massachusetts:** Linda Albright, *Westfield State College*; Clea Andreadis, *Middlesex Community College*; Jonathan Bowman, *Boston College*; Elise Dallimore, *Northeastern University*; Joe Klimavich, *Worcester State College*; Michael Milburn, *University of Massachusetts, Boston*; Derrick TePaske, *Framingham State College*; Nancy Willets, *Cape Cod Community College*. **Michigan:** Patricia Amason, *Ferris State University*; Isolde Anderson, *Hope College*; Julie Apker, *Western Michigan University*; Steve Bennett, *Washtenaw Community College*; Marion Boyer, *Kalamazoo Valley Community College*; James Cantrill, *Northern Michigan University*; Robert Loesch, *Ferris State University*; Jennifer Hubbell Ott, *Kalamazoo Valley Community College*; Dennis Patrick, *Eastern Michigan University*; Cami Sanderson-Harris, *Ferris State University*; Sandi Smith, *Michigan State University*; Patricia Sotirin, *Michigan Technical University*. **Minnesota:** Angela Lynn Blais, *University of Minnesota, Duluth*; Christa Brown, *Minnesota State University, Mankato*; Kari Frisch, *Central Lakes College*; Lori Halverson-Wente, *Rochester Community and Technical College*; Ascan Koerner, *University of Minnesota, Twin Cities*; Mariangela Maguire, *Gustavus Adolphus College*; Minda Orina, *University of Minnesota, Twin Cities*; Patricia Palmerton, *Hamline University*; Daniel Paulnock, *Saint Paul College*; Karri Pearson, *Normandale Community College*; R. Jeffrey Ringer, *St. Cloud State University*; Dan West, *Rochester Community and Technical College*. **Missouri:** Leigh Heisel, *University of Missouri, St. Louis*; Lynette Jachowicz, *Maple Woods Community College*; Virgil Norris, *Park University*; Jennifer Summary, *Southeast Missouri State University*. **Montana:** Randall Pugh, *Montana State University, Billings*; Julie Robinson, *Montana State University, Billings*. **Nebraska:** Karla Jensen, *Nebraska Wesleyan University*; Chad M. McBride, *Creighton University*; Lisa Schreiber, *Dana College*. **New**

Hampshire: Phyllis Zrzavy, *Franklin Pierce College*. **New Jersey:** Keith Forrest, *Atlantic Cape Community College*; Rebecca Sanford, *Monmouth University*; Madeline Santoro, *Union County College*. **New Mexico:** Candace Maher, *University of New Mexico*; Virginia McDermott, *University of New Mexico*; Kevin Mitchell, *Eastern New Mexico University*; Pamela Stovall, *University of New Mexico, Gallup*. **New York:** Priya Banerjee, *State University of New York, Brockport*; Rex Butt, *Bronx Community College*; Joseph S. Coppolino, *Nassau Community College*; Susan Drucker, *Hofstra University*; Diane Ferrero-Paluzzi, *Iona College*; Douglas Gaerte, *Houghton College*; Andrew Herman, *State University of New York, Geneseo*; Patricia Iacobazzo, *John Jay College*; Anastacia Kurylo, *Manhattan Marymount College*; Michael Lecesse, *State University of New York, New Paltz*; Linda Reese, *College of Staten Island*; Gordon Young, *Kingsborough Community College*. **North Carolina:** Melissa Atkinson, *Surry Community College*; Alessandra Beasley, *Wake Forest University*; Tamala Bulger, *University of North Carolina, Wilmington*; Allison Carr, *Davidson County Community College*; James Manning, *Western Carolina State University*; Nina-Jo Moore, *Appalachian State University*; Elizabeth J. Natalle, *University of North Carolina, Greensboro*; Chris Poulos, *University of North Carolina, Greensboro*; Melinda Sopher, *North Carolina State University*. **Ohio:** Yemi Akande, *John Carroll University*; Carolyn Anderson, *University of Akron*; Christina S. Beck, *Ohio University*; Kathleen Clark, *University of Akron*; Rozell Duncan, *Kent State University*; David Foster, *University of Findlay*; Stephen Haas, *University of Cincinnati*; William Harpine, *University of Akron*; Kathryn C. Maguire, *Cleveland State University*; Lisa Murray-Johnson, *Ohio State University*; Artemio Ramirez, *Ohio State University*; Deleasa Randall-Griffiths, *Ashland University*; Teresa Sabourin, *University of Cincinnati*; Teresa Thompson, *University of Dayton*; John Warren, *Bowling Green State University*; Cherie White, *Muskingum Area Technical College (now Zane State College)*. **Oklahoma:** Penny Eubank, *Oklahoma Christian University*; Billy Wolfe Jr., *University of Oklahoma*. **Oregon:** Nick Backus, *Western Oregon University*; Cynthia Golledge, *Portland Community College, Sylvania*; Karen Krumrey-Fulks, *Lane Community College*; Gary Kuhn, *Chemeketa Community College*; Paula Usrey, *Umpqua Community College*. **Pennsylvania:** Mary Badami, *Bloomsburg University of Pennsylvania*; Janet Bodenman, *Bloomsburg University of Pennsylvania*; Denise Danford, *Delaware County Community College*; Joseph Donato, *Harrisburg Area Community College, Lebanon*; Karen Lada, *Delaware County Community College*; David Paterno, *Delaware County Community College*; Elaine Zelley, *La Salle University*. **South Carolina:** Merissa Ferrara, *College of Charleston*; Charmaine Wilson, *University of South Carolina, Aiken*. **Tennessee:** Stuart Bonnington, *Austin Peay State University*; Katherine Hendrix, *University of Memphis*. **Texas:** Shae Adkins, *North Harris College*; Richard Bello, *Sam Houston State University*; Ceilidh Charleson-Jennings, *Collin County Community College*; Karen Daas, *St. Mary's University*; Jill Gibson, *Amarillo College*; Marian Houser, *Texas State University, San Marcos*; Shelly D. Lane, *Collin County Community College*; Laurie Metcalf, *Texas A&M University*; Mark Morman, *Baylor University*; John Nicholson, *Angelo State University*; James Pauff, *Tarleton State University*; Frank G. Pérez, *University of Texas, El Paso*; Lori Peterson, *St. Edward's University*; Narissra Punyanunt-Carter, *Texas Tech University*; Juliann Scholl, *Texas Tech University*; Susan Selk, *El Paso Community College*; Barbara Yancy-Tooks, *El Paso Community College*. **Utah:** Matthew Barton, *Southern Utah University*; Brian Heuett, *Southern Utah University*. **Vermont:** Genevieve Jacobs, *Champlain College*. **Virginia:** Melissa Aleman, *James Madison University*; Jill Jurgens, *Old Dominion University*; Charles J. Korn,

Northern Virginia Community College, Manassas; Melanie Laliker, *Bridgewater College*; Michaela Meyer, *Christopher Newport University*; Thomas Morra, *Northern Virginia Community College, Annandale*; Nan Peck, *Northern Virginia Community College, Annandale*; Jeffrey Pierson, *Bridgewater College*; James Roux, *Lynchburg College*. **Washington:** Mara Adelman, *Seattle University*; Margaret Kreiner, *Spokane Community College*; Mark Murphy, *Everett Community College*; Roxane Sutherland, *Clark College*. **Washington, D.C.:** Robert Harrison, *Gallaudet University*; Clay Warren, *George Washington University*. **West Virginia:** Robert Bookwalter, *Marshall University*; Matthew Martin, *West Virginia University*. **Wisconsin:** Cheri Campbell, *University of Wisconsin, Waukesha*; Valerie Hennen, *Gateway Technical College*; Craig Hullett, *University of Wisconsin, Madison*; Rebecca Imes, *Carroll College*; Carol Knudson, *Gateway Technical College*; Lindsay Timmerman, *University of Wisconsin, Milwaukee*.

Finally, no textbook is created by one person. Thank you to the interpersonal communication discipline and its students.

brief contents

4
Experiencing and Expressing Emotions 90

(Image above) Photo by G.N. Miller/MaMa Foundation Gospel for Teens

5
Understanding Culture 120

LaunchPad For LearningCurve adaptive quizzing and videos to help you understand key concepts, go to LaunchPad: launchpadworks.com

6
Understanding Gender 146

   📘 **LaunchPad** For LearningCurve adaptive quizzing and videos to help you understand key concepts, go to LaunchPad: launchpadworks.com

part two / Interpersonal Skills

7
Listening Actively   174

   📘 **LaunchPad** For LearningCurve adaptive quizzing and videos to help you understand key concepts, go to LaunchPad: launchpadworks.com

8
Communicating Verbally 200

9
Communicating Nonverbally 228

(Top to bottom) Sara Krulwich/The New York Times/Redux; Sampson Beaver's family '06 [Leah, Frances Louise, and Sampson Beaver], 1906, Whyte Museum of the Canadian Rockies, Mary Schaffer fonds (V527/ps1-05)

LaunchPad For LearningCurve adaptive quizzing and videos to help you understand key concepts, go to LaunchPad: launchpadworks.com

10
Managing Conflict and Power   254

part three / Interpersonal Relationships

11
Relationships with Romantic Partners   284

(Image above) Imagine China/Newscom

12
Relationships with Family Members   322

13
Relationships with Friends   350

14
Relationships in the Workplace   376

Chapter Review   405

📽 **LaunchPad** For LearningCurve adaptive quizzing and videos to help you understand key concepts, go to LaunchPad: launchpadworks.com

(Image above) Dorien Martin

"We are deeply grateful for the insights gifted to us and this text by the members of the board. Their time, energy, and efforts have resulted in a book expressing not just two voices and perspectives, but a broad and richly diverse plurality."

Steve McCornack grew up in Seattle, Washington, where his love for mountains, the ocean, and grunge/emo music was forged. For as long as he can remember, he has been fascinated with how people create, maintain, and disband close relationships, especially the challenges confronting romantic couples. Steve is currently a Professor at The University of Alabama at Birmingham, where he coordinates the public speaking program, and team-teaches the introductory interpersonal communication course with Kelly. Other than his love of teaching, Steve's principal passions are his family, music (especially spinning vinyl records), meditation, movies, mechanical watches, yoga, karate, Kona coffee, and his 1985 Carrera Targa.

Kelly Morrison grew up in Naperville, Illinois, where she was able to walk across the street to her elementary school, down the block to spend summers swimming at the local pool, and up the road for frequent trips to Dairy Queen (which she still visits). Illustrating a true "circle of life," one of her first jobs after graduating with a business degree from the University of Illinois was in publishing sales for a company that now is part of Macmillan. She is also a Professor and Honors Faculty Fellow at The University of Alabama at Birmingham, where she teaches courses in gender, interpersonal, and health communication, and team-teaches the introductory interpersonal communication course with Steve. When Steve is playing loud music on his stereo, she can be found in another room, crafting or enjoying Hallmark Channel movies and drinking tea. She has been a group fitness instructor since graduating from college, and loves to cook and bake, especially when she can spend time in the kitchen with her three sons.

If you find a wise companion to associate with you—one who leads a virtuous life and is diligent—you should lead a life with that person joyfully and mindfully, conquering all obstacles.

— *The Dhammapada*

the authors

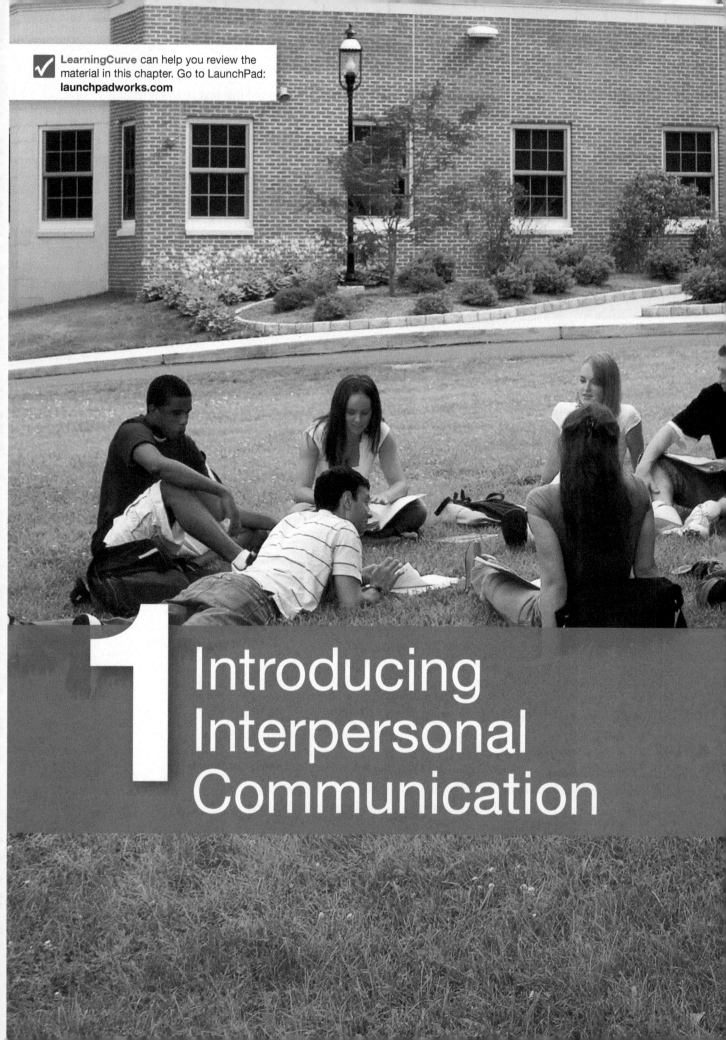

1 Introducing Interpersonal Communication

Interpersonal communication is the bridge that connects us to others.

Rana Faure/Getty Images

"I GOT IN!!!"

This bellowing shout was followed by a thud, and "OOOWWW!!" Our eldest son, Kyle, had just received a congratulatory email notification—complete with virtual confetti—announcing his college admission. His joy and surprise had led him to run and leap high into the air, smacking his hand painfully on the hard ceiling.

Hearing the commotion, the entire family—Kelly, Steve, and their two other sons Colin and Conor—flew into the kitchen, bear-hugging and whooping, beaming with smiles and brimming with tears, and then *immediately* began calling and texting distant family members to share the happy news. Kyle's hand would ache for days. And in a few fleeting months, after Kelly and Steve had held it for years, this same hand would be achingly released.

You hold their hands for a little while, keeping them close, so that you can let them go.

Kelly's mom often referenced this wisdom about raising children, and we have returned to it repeatedly as our sons have grown from toddlers to teens to the men they are today. Our minds are filled with snapshots: the times we held their hands tightly as they crossed the street until they were old enough to cross alone; hugged them goodbye as they left for their first "full" days of school, and then grinned with glee as they eagerly leapt into our arms when we picked them up; visited the mailbox daily, seeking the *promised* letters that were never sent because they were too busy having fun at camp; held our hands and collective breath through games, recitals, and performances; dried their tears and whispered words of comfort to carry them through disappointment

1

until these roles were fulfilled instead by friends and partners.

For Kyle—as for millions of students across the United States each year—getting accepted into college was the culmination of hopes and dreams. Your college admission experience may have been similar to Kyle's, or it may have been different. Like our sons, you may now be far from home. Or you may be reading this book *in* your home, or down the road from home. You may be a first-time college student, or you may be returning to complete your degree. No matter the path that brought you here, your college experience represents a novel chapter in your life, one that is full of fresh opportunities and challenges. This is a time when you will likely meet dozens of new people: friends, acquaintances, perhaps mentors and romantic partners. And as you learn to navigate these relationships and the demands of your college workload, you may at times struggle to keep in touch with the family and friends who have helped you get where you are today.

Although each of our "boys" is now far from us, all living in different states, we have managed to keep them close and sustain our intimate connections with them. How? By using our interpersonal communication knowledge and skills to bridge the distance. In this chapter—and throughout the rest of this book—you will learn how to apply interpersonal communication skills to cultivate closeness with the people you care about.

If you are reading this book, chances are that you are a college student in an introduction to interpersonal communication course. While your sense of home may be a geographic location, it also is a group of people. They may be the people you grew up with, or people you have encountered and collected along the way as you've discovered who you are. Visualize these people and ask yourself: *Why* are they close? Is it because of place—because they live geographically nearby, and proximity has bred familiarity? Is it because of impact—because they live in your thoughts, in carefully tended memories that impart special meaning into your life? Is it because of history—because they have always been there? Or are they close because you communicate with them frequently and intimately?

As we will explore later in this book, all of these experiences can create close ties between people. But the most important way we connect with others is through our interpersonal communication. Think again of the people closest to you, and reflect on the different ways you communicate with them. You may connect from the other side of the country—or from another country—through video calls, which allow you to hear their voices and see their faces. You may frequently text or email. You likely use a variety of social media platforms and apps to share memes, pictures, stories, or videos. You may send cards, letters, or care packages through the mail.

But regardless of how, where, or with whom we communicate, one fact inescapably binds us: *our communication choices powerfully influence the personal, interpersonal, and relationship outcomes that follow.* When we draw on our communication skills to communicate competently, we are more likely to experience desirable outcomes, such as positive emotions, satisfying relationships, and encounters that we like to linger over longer in our minds. When we do not effectively utilize the communication skills we have, we are more likely to experience negative outcomes, such as interpersonal conflict, dissatisfaction with a relationship, and regret over words we wish we could take back. By studying interpersonal communication, you will acquire knowledge and skills that will boost your interpersonal competence, allowing you to build and maintain satisfying relationships and, ultimately, improve your quality of life.

In this chapter, we begin our study of interpersonal communication. You'll learn:

- What communication is and the different models for communication
- The nature of interpersonal communication, the role it plays in relationships, and the needs and goals it helps us fulfill
- How to improve your interpersonal communication competence, both online and off
- Major issues related to the study of interpersonal communication

What Is Communication?

How we create and exchange messages with others] One question students often ask about communication classes and the communication major is "Isn't this all just common sense?" Because communication is something we all do every day, studying communication research and theory in a more formal fashion strikes some students as counterintuitive. Why study something that we already know how to do?

It's true that we all come to communication classes with a lifetime of hands-on experience communicating. But *personal experience provides a different type of knowledge than does guided study.* When you're formally educated about communication, you gain knowledge that goes far beyond your intuition, allowing you to broaden and deepen your skills as a communicator. Communication is like any other form of expertise. Just because you may know how to throw a baseball and may have done it dozens (or even hundreds) of times does not mean that you have the knowledge and skills to pitch for the Chicago Cubs (Kelly's favorite team). Similar to any other type of expertise, competent communication requires knowledge and skills coupled with hard work, self-reflection, and practice.

Our goal for this text is to provide you with knowledge so that you can hone your communication skills, becoming your best version of an interpersonal communicator. This process begins by answering a basic question: What *is* communication?

DEFINING COMMUNICATION

In this text, we define **communication** as the process through which people create messages, using a variety of modalities and sensory channels to convey meanings within and across contexts. This definition highlights the five features that characterize communication.

First, communication is a *process* that unfolds over time through a series of actions that connect the participants. For example, your friend tweets that they[1] are going out to a movie, you text to see if you can join, and so forth. Because communication is a process, everything you say and do affects what is said and done in the present and in the future.

self-reflection

Is good communication just common sense? Does experience communicating *always* result in better communication? When you think about all the communication and relational challenges you face in your daily life, what do you think would help you improve your communication skills?

---

[1]Throughout this book, you will come across the use of the singular pronoun *they.* Singular *they* serves two important roles: first, as a pronoun for people who do not identify as either *he* or *she*; and second, as a more inclusive and less wordy alternative to *he or she* when a person's gender identity is not known or not specified (which is the case in the sentence above on this page).

⬆ Whether we are starting a new romance, visiting with friends, or maintaining our connections with family members (as in this scene from *Black-ish*), communication plays a significant role in our everyday experiences. ABC/ Photofest

Second, those engaged in communication ("communicators") *create* messages to convey meanings. A **message** is the "package" of information that is transported during communication. When people exchange a series of messages, the result is called an **interaction** (Watzlawick et al., 1967).

Third, to convey meanings, communicators choose from many different **modalities**—forms of communication used for exchanging messages. These include the variety used by us (Kelly and Steve) for staying connected with our friends and family members, as we described in our chapter opener: video calls, texting, social media, and email, along with other forms such as handwritten letters and face-to-face interaction. Nowadays, many of us seamlessly integrate digital technologies with more traditional methods of communication, sometimes using multiple forms simultaneously, like when you chat on the phone with a family member while also checking your Instagram (see Figure 1.1 for the most commonly used communication technologies among young adults in the United States).

Fourth, when communicating, people transmit information through various **sensory channels**: perceptual pathways corresponding to our five senses. These include auditory (sound), visual (sight), tactile (touch), olfactory (scent), and oral (taste). For example, your manager at work smiles while complimenting your job performance (visual and auditory channels). A friend who is blind reads a message you left, touching the Braille letters with their fingertips (tactile). Your romantic partner shows up at your house exuding an alluring scent and carrying delicious takeout, which you then share together (olfactory and oral).

Finally, communicators *convey meanings* within and across a seemingly endless assortment of **contexts**, or situations. We communicate with others at sporting events, while at work, and in our homes. In each context, a host of factors influences how we communicate, such as how much time we have, how many people are in the vicinity, and whether the setting is personal or professional. Think about it: you probably communicate with your romantic partner differently when you're in class than when you're watching a movie at home and relaxing on the couch. And if you're communicating through synchronous video calls, you may be blending contexts (e.g., school and home) and may experience fatigue from the additional effort required for sustained attention, eye contact, and verbal focus (Sander & Bauman, 2020).

| Texting | Talking on the phone | Email | Social media posts | Twitter |

figure 1.1 Communication Technologies Used by U.S. Young Adults, Ages 18 to 29
Information from: Newport (2014).

UNDERSTANDING COMMUNICATION MODELS

Think about all the different ways you communicate each day. You text a sibling to find out how they're doing. You give a speech in your communication class to an engaged audience. You exchange a knowing glance with your best friend at the arrival of someone you mutually dislike. Now reflect on how these forms of communication differ from one another. Sometimes messages flow in a single direction, from sender to receiver, as when we create a text and send it to a sibling. The message originates in your phone and arrives at its intended destination: your sibling's phone. In other instances, messages flow back and forth between senders and recipients, as when you deliver a speech to your classmates and they signal to you that they've received and understood your presentation. Still other times, you and another person mutually construct the meaning of a message, as when you and your best friend exchange knowing glances or finish each other's sentences. In such situations, no individual serves as a "sender" or "receiver"; instead, you're both co-communicators. These different ways of experiencing communication are reflected in three models that have evolved to describe the communication process: the linear model, the interactive model, and the transactional model. As you will see, each of these models has both strengths and weaknesses. Yet each also captures something unique and useful about the ways we communicate in our daily lives.

Linear Communication Model According to the **linear communication model**, communication is an activity in which information flows in one direction, from a starting point to an end point (see Figure 1.2). The linear model contains several components (Lasswell, 1948; Shannon & Weaver, 1949), including a *message*, a *modality*, and a *sensory channel* (see the previous section, Defining Communication, for definitions of these terms). Additionally, there must be a **sender** (or senders) of the message—the individual(s) who generates the information to be communicated, packages it into a message, and chooses the modalities and sensory channel(s) for sending it. But the transmission of the message may be hindered by **noise**—environmental factors that may impede messages from reaching their destination. Noise includes anything that causes our attention to drift, such as poor reception during a video call or the smell of fresh coffee nearby. Lastly, there must be a **receiver**—the person for whom a message is intended and to whom the message is delivered.

Interactive Communication Model The **interactive communication model** also views communication as a process involving senders and receivers (see Figure 1.3). However, according to this model, transmission is influenced by two

launchpadworks.com

Noise
Watch this clip online to answer the questions below.

What examples of noise can you identify in this video? On what sensory channels did they occur? What type(s) of sensory channel(s) distract you the most? Why?

Want to see more? Check out LaunchPad for clips on **channel** and the **linear communication model**.

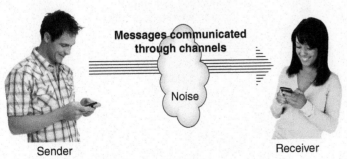

Messages communicated through channels

Noise

Sender   Receiver

figure 1.2 Linear Model of Communication
(left) Flashon Studio/Shutterstock; (right) Elena Elisseeva/Shutterstock

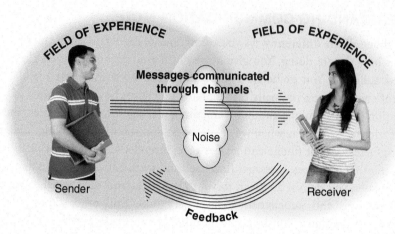

figure 1.3 **Interactive Model of Communication**
Kharidehal Abhirama Ashwin/Shutterstock

additional factors: feedback and fields of experience (Schramm, 1954). **Feedback** is composed of the verbal and nonverbal messages (such as eye contact, utterances such as "Uh-huh," and nodding) that recipients convey to indicate their reaction to communication. **Fields of experience** consist of the beliefs, attitudes, values, and experiences that each participant brings to a communication event. People with similar fields of experience are more likely to understand each other compared to individuals who lack these commonalities.

LaunchPad Video

launchpadworks.com

Transactional Communication Model
Watch this clip online to answer the questions below.

Can you think of situations in which you jointly created meaning with another person? How did this happen? In what ways are these situations different from ones that follow the interactive communication model?

Transactional Communication Model   The **transactional communication model** (see Figure 1.4) suggests that communication is fundamentally multidirectional. That is, each participant equally influences the communication behavior of the other participants (Miller & Steinberg, 1975). From the transactional perspective, there are no "senders" or "receivers." Instead, all the parties constantly exchange verbal and nonverbal messages and feedback, and *collaboratively* create meanings (Streek, 1980). This may be something as simple as a shared look between friends, or it may be an animated conversation among close family members in which the people involved seem to know what the others are going to say before it's said.

These three models represent an evolution of thought regarding the nature of communication, from a relatively simplistic depiction of communication as a linear

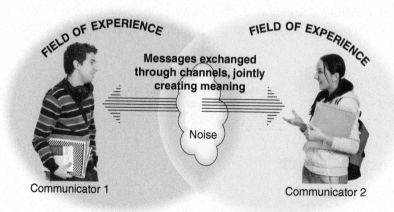

figure 1.4 **Transactional Model of Communication**
Blaj Gabriel/Shutterstock

table 1.1 Communication Models

Model	Examples	Advantage	Disadvantage
Linear	Twitter and Facebook posts, texting, email, scripted public speeches	Simple and straightforward	Doesn't adequately describe most conversations that occur face-to-face, over the phone, or on a video call
Interactive	Classroom instruction, group presentations, team/coworker meetings	Captures a broad variety of communication forms	Neglects the active role that receivers often play in constructing meaning
Transactional	Any encounter (most commonly face-to-face) in which you and others jointly create communication meaning	Intuitively captures what most people think of as interpersonal communication	Doesn't apply to many forms of online communication, such as Twitter and Facebook posts, email, and texting

process to one that views communication as a more faceted and mutually crafted process. Each of these models represents useful ways to depict different forms of communication, rather than "good" or "bad" evaluations of communication. See Table 1.1 for more on each model.

Now that we have defined communication and discussed various models of it, let's look at what is meant by *interpersonal* communication.

What Is Interpersonal Communication?

> Interpersonal communication impacts our relationships

Our students frequently comment that they can't believe how relevant interpersonal communication scholarship is to their everyday lives. After all, we cover (and this book will discuss) self-esteem, jealousy, anger, conflict, betrayal, love, friendship, and healthy close relationships, to name just a few topics. Students often find themselves using this material to analyze everyone they know—sometimes vexing roommates, lovers, friends, and family members who are subjected to their scrutiny!

Of course, interest in interpersonal communication has existed since the dawn of recorded history. In fact, one of the earliest texts ever written—the maxims of the Egyptian sage Ptah Hotep (2200 B.C.E.)—was essentially a guidebook for enhancing interpersonal skills (Horne, 1917). Ptah Hotep encouraged people to be truthful, kind, and tolerant in their communication. He urged active listening, especially for situations in which people lack experience, because "to not do so is to embrace ignorance." He also emphasized mindfulness in word choice, noting that "good words are more difficult to find than emeralds."

DEFINING INTERPERSONAL COMMUNICATION

Why has learning about interpersonal communication always been considered so valuable? One answer is that knowledge of interpersonal skills is essential for maintaining healthy interpersonal *relationships*. For most people, having satisfying relationships with romantic partners, friends, family members, and coworkers is critical in determining overall life happiness (Gustavson et al., 2016). Furthermore, the quality of our relationships directly predicts physical and mental health outcomes, including overall life span (Myers, 2002). For example, research examining the link between loneliness and longevity suggests that feeling socially isolated and disconnected from others has twice the negative impact upon mortality (likelihood

skills practice

Communication Models

❶ Think of someone with whom you engage in both linear and transactional communication.

❷ Identify how your preference for feedback influences when you opt for linear versus transactional communication.

❸ Reflect on how your knowledge of the other person's fields of experience influences your understanding of their feedback.

❹ List several feedback cues you can provide in your next linear and transactional interactions.

❺ Use these cues the next time you text and speak face-to-face, and consider how the feedback cues influenced the creation of meaning.

self-reflection

How do *you* define *interpersonal communication*? Can interpersonal communication happen between more than two people? Can it happen through tweets, texts, or emails? Or is it the content of what is discussed that makes communication interpersonal? What forms of communication are *not* interpersonal?

of death) as does obesity, and four times the negative impact of air pollution (Hawkley & Cacioppo, 2010; Holt-Lunstad et al., 2010).

The connection between relationships and interpersonal communication is clearly illustrated by our definition: **interpersonal communication** is a dynamic form of communication between two (or more) people in which the messages exchanged significantly influence their thoughts, emotions, behaviors, and relationships. This definition has four important implications. First, interpersonal communication differs from some other forms of communication—such as tweets, office memos, email, and formal lectures or speeches—because it's *dynamic* rather than static. That is, communication is constantly in motion and changing over time, unlike carefully planned messages such as advertisements, news articles, or formal public speeches. For example, imagine that you are in a video call with a sibling who lives overseas. The first few moments may be awkward or tense as you strive to reconnect and search for words, demonstrated by long pauses between short sentences. Then one of you cracks a joke, and the whole exchange suddenly feels warmer. Just a few minutes later, as you realize you have to end the encounter, the conversation slows, and the mood shifts yet again to sadness and regret, as each of you tries to delay the impending end of the conversation.

Second, much interpersonal communication is *transactional*, with both parties contributing to the meaning. For example, you and a romantic partner share an intimate dinner, jointly reminiscing about past times together and exchanging expressions and glances of affection fluidly back and forth. But some interpersonal communication isn't transactional. You know that your sister is feeling depressed over a breakup, so you send a consoling text message in the middle of the workday. You don't expect a response, and don't receive one because of your sister's busy schedule. There's no feedback and no interplay between you and your sister. Instead, there is a sender (you), a message (your expression of support), and a receiver (your sister), making it a linear encounter, albeit an interpersonal one.

Third, interpersonal communication is primarily **dyadic**—it involves pairs of people, or *dyads*. You chat with your daughter while driving to school, or you exchange a series of Facebook messages with a long-distance friend. Of course, some interpersonal communication may involve more than just two people. For instance, our family celebration following Kyle's college acceptance—described at the beginning of this chapter—was definitely interpersonal; just as a conversation between you and your three closest friends would be. The (often) dyadic nature of interpersonal communication allows us to distinguish it from **intrapersonal communication**—communication involving only one person, in the form of talking out loud to yourself or having a mental "conversation" inside your own head.

Finally, and perhaps *most* importantly, interpersonal communication creates *impact*: it changes participants' thoughts, emotions, behaviors, and relationships. The impact on relationships is one of the most profound and unique effects created through interpersonal communication, and it stands in sharp contrast to **impersonal communication**—exchanges that have a negligible perceived impact on our thoughts, emotions, behaviors, and relationships. For example, you're watching TV with your partner, and one of you casually comments on an advertisement that is annoying. Within most close relationships, at least some communication has this impersonal quality. But we can shift to interpersonal at a moment's notice. Soon after the ad commentary, you snuggle up to your partner and murmur, "I love you." You're rewarded by warm eye contact, a tender smile, and a gentle hug—all signs that your message has had a significant impact on your partner.

When we interpersonally communicate, we forge meaningful bonds that can help bridge the distance between ourselves and others. Philosopher Martin Buber (1965) argued that we can make this distance seem "thinner" through our communication. Specifically, when we embrace the fundamental similarities that we share with others, strive to see things from others' points of view, treat one another as unique individuals, and communicate in ways that emphasize honesty and kindness, we feel closer to others. We don't have to agree with everything others say or do, but we need to approach each other with an open mind and a welcoming heart, affording everyone the same attention and respect we desire for ourselves. When we do so, using our interpersonal communication skills to reduce distance and orient to the "whole being" of others, we come to perceive them and our relationship as **I-Thou**.

In contrast, when people focus on differences, refuse to accept or even acknowledge others' experiences, and communicate in ways that emphasize perceived superiority, the distance between people "thickens" (in Buber's terms) to the point where it becomes impenetrable. As a consequence, people increasingly perceive their relationships as **I-It**: they regard other people as "objects" that they observe, that are there for "use and exploitation" (Buber, 1965, p. 24). The more that people view others as objects, the greater is the likelihood that they will communicate in disrespectful, manipulative, or exploitative ways. And when people treat others this way, their own relationships deteriorate.

Highlighting the mental, emotional, behavioral, and relational impact of interpersonal communication reinforces the central theme of this text: *our communication choices powerfully influence the personal, interpersonal, and relationship outcomes that follow*. You cannot control what others do, but through interpersonal communication, you can change your own feelings and thoughts about both yourself and others; express yourself in a way that contributes to healing or hate; promote heartbreak or happiness; offer hugs or hostility; create, maintain, or dissolve relationships; and move from I-It to I-Thou. This power means it is critically important that you practice your interpersonal communication skills, which allow you to communicate competently and increase the likelihood that you will experience positive outcomes.

PRINCIPLES OF INTERPERSONAL COMMUNICATION

Now that you know the definition of interpersonal communication, we can expand our understanding of how it functions in our daily lives by exploring several principles suggested by scholars, based on decades of research and theory development. These four principles are affirmed repeatedly throughout our text, and each one suggests practical insights into how you can improve your interpersonal communication skills and, by extension, your relationships.

Interpersonal Communication Conveys Both Content and Relationship Information
During every interpersonal encounter, people simultaneously exchange two types of information (Watzlawick et al., 1967). *Content information* is the actual meaning of the words we utter. *Relationship information* indicates how each person views the relationship: whether you consider yourself superior, equal, or inferior to the other person and whether you see the relationship as casual, intimate, or estranged.

We convey content information directly through spoken or written words, but we primarily use nonverbal cues to communicate relationship information. These

When we interpersonally communicate, we forge meaningful bonds with others.

cues can include vocal tone, and how high or low or loud or soft we speak; facial expression and eye contact; hand gestures; position in relation to the listener; and posture. For instance, imagine that you're on a video call with other students from your class, discussing a project you're all working on. One of your classmates says to you, "Do you think you could have your research done by next Monday?" with a friendly tone, smile, and rising pitch on the word *Monday*. Now imagine the exact same situation—except this time your classmate is frowning and uses a downward pitch and volume emphasis on the last word (*Monday!*). In both scenarios, the content information is identical—they use exactly the same words—but very different relationship information is conveyed. In the first scenario, your classmate conveys both equality and affection, whereas in the second, they communicate hostility and a demand.

Relationship information strongly influences how people interpret content information (Watzlawick et al., 1967). In the preceding example, you likely will look more to how your classmate delivered their message, rather than simply considering their words to decipher the meaning. During most interpersonal encounters, however, people aren't consciously aware of the relationship information being delivered. We don't usually sit there thinking, "Gee, what's this person trying to convey to me about how they see our relationship?" Relationship information

◁ Whether an encounter is interpersonal depends on those people participating in it. Some only consider an encounter interpersonal if they gain new knowledge, make different decisions, or forge an I-Thou connection. Others consider an encounter interpersonal if information is conveyed. When do you think an encounter is interpersonal? Tyler Olson/ Shutterstock

becomes most obvious when it's unexpected or when it suggests that the sender's view of the relationship is different from the receiver's. For example, if a peer at work starts ordering you around like a boss, you are likely to experience anxiety or annoyance ("You're my coworker, not my boss!"). That's why it's important to communicate relationship information in ways that are sensitive to and respectful of others' impressions of the relationship while staying true to your own relationship feelings.

Because relationship information influences how people interpret content information, it can be considered a specific form of **meta-communication**—communication about communication (Watzlawick et al., 1967). Meta-communication includes any message, verbal or nonverbal, that centrally focuses on how the meaning of communication should be interpreted—everything from discussion of previous comments ("I actually was joking when I sent you that text message") to exchanged glances between friends questioning the intent of a message ("What did they mean when they said that?"). During interpersonal encounters, meta-communication serves as an interpretive guide for how to perceive and understand each other's communication.

Interpersonal Communication Can Be Intentional or Unintentional   During interpersonal encounters, people tend to perceive nearly everything we say and do as having communicative meaning—whether or not we intend to send a message. Scholars express this with the axiom "One cannot not communicate" (Watzlawick et al., 1967, p. 51). Most of the time we intend, and people interpret, specific meanings. Sometimes, however, people perceive meanings from behaviors that we didn't intend to be meaningful. In such instances, interpersonal communication *has* occurred, even though it was unintentional. For example, imagine that you greet a friend of yours, "Hey, how's it going?" Your friend greets you back, "Hi, good to see you!" So far so good—both messages were intentional, and both were interpreted as intended. But then, as your friend tells you about their new romantic partner, your contact lens becomes displaced. It's the third time this has happened that day, so

self-
reflection

Consider an instance in which you didn't intend to communicate a message but someone saw your behavior as communicative. How did this person misinterpret your behavior? What were the consequences? What did you say and do to correct the individual's misperception?

self-reflection

Think of an encounter in which you said something and then immediately regretted it. What effect did your error have on you? On the other person or people involved? On your relationship? How could you have expressed the same information differently to avoid negative outcomes?

self-reflection

Recall an interaction that took a sudden turn for the worse. How did each person's communication contribute to the change in the interaction's quality? What did you say or do to deal with the problem?

you sigh loudly in frustration and move your eyes to try to get it back into position. Your friend, seeing this, thinks you're sighing and rolling your eyes *as a message* about their partner, and gets angry, "Oh, so you disapprove? Why!?" Whether you like it or not, interpersonal communication *has* occurred, even though it was unintentional. To avoid such misunderstandings, keep this simple rule in mind: when you're communicating with others, most of what you say and do will be perceived as communication. At the same time, this does *not* mean that you're *responsible* for the inferences that others may make from your unintentional behavior. So, for instance, in the preceding example, it is *not* your fault that your friend thought you disapproved of their new partner. Instead, it was a simple misunderstanding. When such misunderstandings arise, it is useful to quickly clarify the meaning, such as explaining, "This is the third time today my contact lens has slipped." We will discuss interpersonal communication misunderstandings, and how you can resolve them, in more detail in Chapter 8.

Interpersonal Communication Is Irreversible   Every time we communicate interpersonally, we weave together words that influence the current and future conversations and relationship. Take the way you answer your cell phone when your brother calls. The ringtone prompts you to look at the incoming number. Your warm and enthusiastic "Hi!" or terse "Yeah?" depends on how you feel about him. Your answer, in turn, influences his response, which then influences your next comments.

This interconnectedness of action makes all interpersonal communication *irreversible*. By tweeting, posting a message on someone's Facebook timeline, sending a text, leaving a voicemail message, or expressing a thought out loud during a face-to-face encounter, you set in motion the series of outcomes that follow. Simply put, once you've said something, you can't take it back. Because we cannot rewind and edit our conversations, it's important to think carefully before we communicate. Ask yourself, is what I'm about to say going to lead to outcomes I want? If the answer is no, revise your message accordingly.

Interpersonal Communication Is Dynamic   When we interact with others, our communication and all that influences it—perceptions, thoughts, feelings, and emotions—are constantly in flux. This has several practical implications. First, no two interactions with the same person will ever be identical. People with whom we once interacted effortlessly and joyfully can seem difficult to talk with during our next encounter. Those we once felt awkward around may become our closest confidants.

Second, no two moments within the *same* interaction will ever be identical. The complex combination of perceptions, thoughts, moods, and emotions that fuels our interpersonal communication is constantly changing. For instance, you meet your long-distance romantic partner at the airport, and for the first few minutes after reuniting, you both feel joyous. But half an hour later, while driving home, you suddenly find yourselves at a loss for things to talk about. As the silence stretches, the tension mounts and you both silently ponder, "Why don't we have anything to say to each other?"

Now that we have reviewed both the definition of interpersonal communication and four defining principles, let's turn our focus to different motives for communicating interpersonally.

MOTIVES FOR INTERPERSONAL COMMUNICATION

Barry Jenkins's Academy Award–winning 2016 drama *Moonlight* follows Chiron, a Black boy in Miami, through different stages of his life as he comes to embrace his identity and sexuality. Chiron spends most of his childhood and teen years quiet and withdrawn, unwilling to fully open up and connect with other people. But near the end of the film, Chiron—now an adult—meets his childhood friend Kevin, who greets him warmly and tells him all about his life since they last saw each other. Finally, Chiron shares his thoughts and feelings with Kevin, allowing himself to be emotionally vulnerable for the first time. Their encounter represents a breakthrough in Chiron's personal growth, and opens the door for the two to forge a romantic relationship.

Each of us brings our own unique experiences to every communication encounter, but one thing we *all* have in common—as Chiron's story in *Moonlight* reveals—is that we, as human beings, are fundamentally communicative creatures. As we discuss in the next part of this chapter, we *need* to communicate with others to be happy and healthy. Consequently, interpersonal communication isn't trivial or incidental; it fulfills a profound human need for connection that we all possess. Of course, it also helps us achieve a broad range of personal needs and practical goals. Let's look at the needs, goals, and motives that compel us to communicate interpersonally with others.

In the movie *Moonlight*, Chiron experiences a profound moment of interpersonal connection when he meets Kevin, his estranged friend. Have you ever experienced a similar moment of connection with a friend or loved one you hadn't seen in a while?
Atlaspix/Alamy

Interpersonal Communication and Human Needs   Psychologist Abraham Maslow (1970) suggested that we seek to fulfill a hierarchy of needs in our daily lives. When the most basic needs (at the bottom of the hierarchy) are fulfilled, we turn our attention to pursuing higher-level ones. Interpersonal communication allows us to develop and foster the interactions and relationships that help us fulfill these needs. At the foundational level are *physical needs,* such as air, food, water, sleep, and shelter. If we can't satisfy these needs, we prioritize them over all others. Once physical needs are met, we concern ourselves with *safety needs*—such as job stability and protection from violence. Then we seek to address *social needs*: forming satisfying and healthy emotional bonds with others.

Next are *self-esteem* needs, the desire to have others' respect and admiration. We fulfill these needs by contributing something of value to the world. Finally, we strive to satisfy *self-actualization needs* by articulating our unique abilities and giving our best in our work, family, and personal life.

Interpersonal Communication and Specific Goals   In addition to enabling us to meet fundamental needs, interpersonal communication helps us meet three types of goals (Clark & Delia, 1979). During interpersonal interactions, you may pursue one or a combination of these goals. The first—**self-presentation goals**—are desires you have to present yourself in certain ways so that others perceive you as being a particular type of person. For example, you're conversing with a roommate who just did poorly on an exam. You want your roommate to know that you're a supportive friend, so you ask what happened, commiserate, and offer to help them study on future tests.

You also have **instrumental goals**—practical aims you want to achieve or tasks you want to accomplish through a particular interpersonal encounter. If you want to borrow your best friend's car for the weekend, you might mention your solid driving record and your sense of responsibility to persuade your friend to lend you the car.

Finally, you use interpersonal communication to achieve **relationship goals**—building, maintaining, or terminating bonds with others. For example, if you succeed in borrowing your friend's car for the weekend and a stone accidentally chips the windshield, you likely will apologize profusely and offer to pay for repairs to save your friendship.

Interpersonal Communication and Relational Connection   Beyond the needs and goals that lead us to interpersonally communicate with others lies a more fundamental drive compelling our communication: the desire for connection, as illustrated by Chiron and Kevin in *Moonlight*. As social beings, our natural state is to be surrounded by other humans—our families and friends, partners and peers, enemies and allies (Parks, 2007). These social and personal connections buffer us from the stress of daily life and enhance our overall well-being. They also aid our resilience, allowing us, for example, to recover more quickly from significant setbacks at work or from difficult romantic breakups (Zimmerman, 2020). Research confirms that interacting with close partners is associated with less loneliness (Hall & Merolla, 2020) and that romantic relationships, in their many forms, may aid in protecting our mental well-being (Whitton et al., 2020). In simple terms, we *need* to interact and communicate with others.

Now that we've considered some of the reasons why we communicate, let's explore how to become more competent interpersonal communicators.

What Is Interpersonal Communication Competence?

Competence matters the most during difficult situations

As we discuss later in this book (Chapters 11 through 14), the greatest challenge to sustaining closeness with friends, family members, coworkers, and lovers isn't when everything is going great. Instead, it's when things are going *badly*: during conflicts, in the wake of betrayals, or when terrible circumstances disrupt our capacity to stay connected. Similarly, it's easy to communicate competently when people are pleasant and agreeable. *That's* no challenge! What's *hard* is sustaining effective communication in the face of opposition or offense: listening to someone express beliefs with which you vehemently disagree, collaborating at work with a combative colleague, or spending an evening with a family member who delights in belittling you.

Research shows that competent communication pays off: competent communicators report more relational satisfaction (including happier marriages), better psychological and physical health, and higher levels of educational and professional achievement than others (Spitzberg & Cupach, 2002). However, competent communicators don't all communicate in exactly the same way. In other words, *no one single recipe for competence exists*. And while communicating competently will help you better achieve your interpersonal goals, it doesn't guarantee that all your relationship problems will be solved.

This book aims to teach you the knowledge and skills necessary for strengthening your interpersonal competence. In later chapters, we examine how you can communicate more competently across various situations and within romantic, family, friendship, and workplace relationships. But first we need to explore what competence means. We will define competence, reflect on three specific characteristics of competence, and then investigate what it means to be competent during interactions mediated by technology.

UNDERSTANDING COMPETENCE

Interpersonal communication competence means *consistently* communicating in ways that are *appropriate* (your communication follows accepted norms), *effective* (your communication enables you to achieve your goals), and *ethical* (your communication treats people fairly; Spitzberg & Cupach, 1984; Wiemann, 1977). Although these three characteristics are necessary for competence, competence is not a static one-size-fits-all concept. Rather, it varies according to the goals, settings, topics, and participants in the communication interaction.

Acquiring knowledge of what it means to communicate competently is the first step in developing interpersonal communication competence (Spitzberg, 1997). The second step is learning how to translate this knowledge into **communication skills**—repeatable goal-directed behaviors and behavioral patterns that you routinely practice in your interpersonal encounters and relationships (Spitzberg & Cupach, 2002). Both steps require motivation to improve your communication. If you are strongly motivated to do so, you can master the knowledge and skills necessary to develop competence along these three dimensions.

Appropriateness The first characteristic of competent interpersonal communication is **appropriateness**—the degree to which your communication matches situational, relational, and cultural expectations regarding how people should communicate. In any interpersonal encounter, norms exist regarding what people should and shouldn't say or do. Part of developing your communication competence is refining your sensitivity to norms and adapting your communication accordingly. People who fail to do so are less likely to be perceived by others as competent communicators. While communicating appropriately is a key part of competence, overemphasizing appropriateness can backfire. If you focus exclusively on appropriateness and always adapt your communication to what others want, you conform to peer pressure or fears of being perceived negatively by others (Burgoon, 1995).

One of the most important choices you make related to appropriateness is when to use mobile devices and when to put them away. Certainly, cell phones and tablets allow us to quickly and efficiently connect with others (Goodman-Deane et al., 2016).

🔺 Dolores Huerta and César Chávez used their communication competence to transform the lives of thousands, by persuading powerful people to enact new laws ensuring better working conditions and higher wages for field laborers. Both received the U.S. Presidential Medal of Freedom. Their legacy is about justice, nonviolence, and help for the needy. It's also proof that communicating appropriately, effectively, and ethically can bring about profound, real-world change. Arthur Schatz/The LIFE Picture Collection/Getty Images

However, when you're interacting with people face-to-face, the priority should be your conversation with them. Even the mere presence of a device in such settings may be seen as inappropriate. For instance, research reveals that simply having cell phones out on a table—but not using them—during face-to-face conversations significantly reduces perceptions of relationship quality, trust, and empathy compared to having conversations with no phones present (Przybylski & Weinstein, 2012).

Although the mere presence of devices during face-to-face encounters undermines a sense of connection, far worse in terms of inappropriateness is "phone snubbing" or **phubbing**: ignoring conversational partners during interactions by focusing instead on one's phone. Phubbing arises in part from the mistaken belief that "if one isn't on their phone, they're missing out on important information" (Schneider & Hitzfield, 2019); consequently, people who report being addicted to social media are more likely to phub than others (Błachnio & Przepiorka, 2019). (To test your own fear of missing out—commonly abbreviated as "FOMO"—take the *Self-Quiz* below.) Phubbing isn't just perceived as inappropriate—it creates a profound sense of exclusion on the part of people being phubbed, causing stress and undermining feelings of belonging and well-being. Ironically, people who are phubbed often respond by turning to their *own* devices for attention. The result is conversational partners who are physically present, but completely disengaged from any type of meaningful interaction (David & Roberts, 2017).

Given all this, what's the bottom line when it comes to device usage, appropriateness, and competence? *When you're in an interpersonal encounter of any importance, put your mobile devices away (meaning, out of sight) at the beginning of the interaction, and only retrieve them when the encounter has ended.* This will signal to your conversational partners that you are prioritizing them, your relationship with them, and what they have to say, above and beyond all else in that moment.

Effectiveness   The second characteristic of competent interpersonal communication is **effectiveness**: the ability to use communication to accomplish the three types of interpersonal goals discussed earlier (self-presentation, instrumental, and

self-QUIZ

Test Your Fear of Missing Out (FOMO)

Read each item below and select the number that best describes how you feel.

1. I worry that my friends are having more fun than me.
   Not at all   1   2   3   4   5   Very much

2. I often wonder what my friends are doing.
   Not at all   1   2   3   4   5   Very much

3. I frequently check my devices to see what others are doing.
   Not at all   1   2   3   4   5   Very much

4. I am bothered if I miss out on an opportunity to have fun.
   Not at all   1   2   3   4   5   Very much

5. I check my devices while I am in class to see what my friends are doing.
   Not at all   1   2   3   4   5   Very much

6. I spend a lot of time keeping up on what my friends do.
   Not at all   1   2   3   4   5   Very much

7. I feel bad if I don't know what my friends are up to.
   Not at all   1   2   3   4   5   Very much

Information from the "Fear of Missing Out Scale" in Przybylski, Murayama, DeHaan, & Gladwell (2013).

Scoring: 7–10, Low FOMO; 11–20, Moderate FOMO; 21–35, High FOMO

relationship). A single communicative path for achieving all these goals rarely exists, and sometimes you must pursue trade-offs. For example, a critical part of maintaining satisfying close relationships is the willingness to occasionally sacrifice instrumental goals to achieve important relationship goals. Suppose you badly want to see a movie tonight, but your romantic partner needs your emotional support to handle a serious family problem. Would you say, "I'm sorry you're feeling bad—I'll call you after I get home from the movie" (emphasizing your instrumental goals)? Or would you say, "I can see the movie some other time—tonight I'll hang out with you" (emphasizing your relationship goals)? The latter approach is more competent because it facilitates relationship health and happiness.

Ethics   The final defining characteristic of competent interpersonal communication is **ethics**—the set of moral principles that guide our behavior toward others (Spitzberg & Cupach, 2002). At a minimum, we are ethically obligated to avoid intentionally hurting others through our communication. By this standard, communication that's intended to erode a person's self-esteem, that expresses intolerance or hatred, that intimidates or threatens others' physical well-being, or that expresses violence is unethical and therefore incompetent (Parks, 1994).

To truly be an ethical communicator, however, we must go beyond simply doing no harm. During every interpersonal encounter, we need to strive to treat others with respect, and communicate with them honestly, kindly, and positively (Englehardt, 2001). For additional guidelines on ethical communication, review the "Credo for Ethical Communication" below.

self-reflection

Is the obligation to communicate ethically absolute or situation-dependent? That is, are there circumstances in which it's ethical to communicate in a way that hurts someone else's feelings? Can one be disrespectful or dishonest and still be ethical? If so, in what kinds of situations?

Credo of the National Communication Association

The National Communication Association (NCA) is the largest professional organization representing communication instructors, researchers, practitioners, and students in the United States. In 2017, the NCA Legislative Council revised and reaffirmed this "Credo for Ethical Communication," originally adopted in 1999 (National Communication Association, 2017).

- We advocate truthfulness, accuracy, honesty, and reason as essential to the integrity of communication.

- We endorse freedom of expression, diversity of perspective, and tolerance of dissent to achieve informed and responsible decision making.

- We strive to understand and respect other communicators before evaluating and responding to their messages.

- We promote access to communication resources and opportunities as necessary to fulfill human potential and contribute to the well-being of individuals, families, communities, and society.

- We promote communication climates of caring and mutual understanding that respect the unique needs and characteristics of individual communicators.

- We condemn communication that degrades people through distortion, intimidation, coercion, and violence, or expression of intolerance and hatred.

- We are committed to the courageous expression of personal convictions in pursuit of fairness and justice.

- We advocate sharing information, opinions, and feelings when facing significant choices while also respecting privacy and confidentiality.

- We accept responsibility for the short- and long-term consequences for our own communication and expect the same of others.

IMPROVING YOUR MEDIATED COMMUNICATION COMPETENCE

Over the last 20 years, technological advances have completely changed how we communicate with each other (Sullivan et al., 2020). Much of our interpersonal interaction now is mediated through devices such as mobile phones, laptops and desktops, and tablets (Goodman-Deane et al., 2016); and we use these devices to connect with others through social media, email, texting, or in massively multiplayer online video games.

These various forms of mediated communication enable us to forge collaborative work relationships and romances with people we wouldn't encounter otherwise, and stay in touch with friends and family easily and quickly (Goodman-Deane et al., 2016). This is especially important for people who are geographically separated (Howard et al., 2001). For example, friends who are thousands of miles apart can routinely text each other and maintain a sense that they are actually nearby (Baym et al., 2012). And although face-to-face communication plays a central role in most relationships, it is not the "deciding factor" for the caliber of a long-distance romantic relationship (Wang et al., 2019, p. 615). Instead, what's most important is that couples separated by geography make frequent use of multiple modalities to sustain closeness, including phone, text, email, *and* (when possible) face-to-face interaction. In fact, we can predict the quality and strength of interpersonal relationships by the frequency of technology use: relational partners who talk for longer periods of time on their cell phones and text each other more often typically have stronger, closer relationships (Licoppe, 2003).

Given how often we use devices to interpersonally communicate, building mediated competence becomes extremely important. A host of factors—including comfort with mobile devices and beliefs about their usefulness for achieving goals—impact whether or not someone will be a competent mediated communicator. For instance, people who are confident learning new apps tend to be better mediated communicators because they use new media frequently and have fun doing it (Bakke, 2010).

But beyond these factors, what can you do to improve your mediated communication competence? Based on years of research, scholar Malcolm Parks offers five suggestions (see also Table 1.2).

1. *Choose your medium wisely.* An essential part of competent mediated communication is carefully considering your chosen modality, and knowing when to opt for *technologically mediated communication*, or TMC for short. For many interpersonal goals, TMC is more effective than face-to-face communication (FtF). Texting a friend to remind them of a coffee date makes more sense than dropping by their workplace, and it's probably quicker and less disruptive than calling. Email may be best when dealing with problematic people or certain types of conflicts. That's because you can take time to think and carefully draft and revise responses before sending them—something that isn't possible during face-to-face interactions.

   But TMC is not the best choice for giving in-depth, lengthy, and detailed explanations of professional or personal dilemmas, or for conveying weighty relationship decisions. Despite the ubiquity of TMC, many people still expect

table 1.2 **Mediated Communication Competence**

TMC Competence Suggestion	Best Practices Suggestion
1. Choose your medium wisely.	TMC is best for quick reminders, linear messages, or messages that require time and thought to craft. FtF is best for important information: engagements, health issues, and so on.
2. Don't assume that TMC is always more efficient.	If your message needs a quick decision or answer, a form of synchronous communication may be best, such as a phone call or a quick FtF conversation (if you are physically located in the same place). Use asynchronous TMC if you want the person to have time to respond.
3. Presume that your posts are public.	If you wouldn't want a message published for public consumption, don't post it or send it.
4. Remember that your posts are permanent.	Even after you delete something, it still exists on servers and may be accessible.
5. Practice the art of creating drafts.	Don't succumb to the pressure to respond to text messages or emails immediately. Taking your time will result in a more competent message.

important news to be shared in person. Most of us would be surprised if a spouse revealed a long-awaited pregnancy through email, or if a friend disclosed a cancer relapse through a text message. And research clearly suggests that despite the plethora of technology available, *people still consider face-to-face communication to be the most intimate and satisfying modality* (Goodman-Deane et al., 2016).

2. *Don't assume that TMC is always more efficient.* Matters of relational significance or issues that evoke strong emotional overtones are more effectively and ethically handled in person or synchronously over the phone. But so, too, are many simple things—like deciding when to meet and where to go to lunch. Many times, a one-minute phone call or a quick, face-to-face exchange can save several minutes of texting.

3. *Presume that your posts are public.* You may be thinking of the laugh you'll get from friends when you post the funny picture of you drunkenly hugging the houseplant on Instagram or Facebook. But what about family members, future in-laws, or potential employers who see the same picture? That clever joke you made about friend A in an email to friend B—what if B forwards it to C, who then forwards it to A? Even if you have privacy settings on your personal page, what's to stop authorized-access friends from downloading your photos and posts and distributing them to others? Keep this rule in mind: anything you've sent or posted on social media is by definition *social* and can potentially be seen by anyone.

4. *Remember that your posts are permanent.* Old texts, tweets, emails, photographs, videos, and blogs—all these may still be accessible years later. As just one example, everything you have ever posted on Facebook is stored on its server, whether you delete it from your profile or not. And Facebook legally reserves the right to sell your content, as long as it deletes personally identifying

information (such as your name) from that content. One of our students learned this the hard way upon discovering that a personal family photo they had uploaded to Facebook had been packaged as the sample photo in a gift frame at a local store. Think before you post.

5. *Practice the art of creating drafts.* Get into the habit of saving text and email messages as "drafts," then revisiting them later and editing them as needed for appropriateness, effectiveness, and ethics. Because TMC makes it easy to flame, many of us impetuously fire off messages that we later regret. Sometimes the most competent mediated communication is none at all—the result of a process in which you compose a text, save it as a draft, but delete the draft after reviewing it and realizing that it's incompetent.

Issues in Interpersonal Communication

Adapting to influences on interpersonal communication

As we move through the twenty-first century and all the challenges we collectively face, scholars and students alike increasingly appreciate how important interpersonal communication is in our daily lives and relationships. Moreover, they recognize how interpersonal communication can influence societal changes, and how societal changes, such as increasing diversity and technological innovation, impact interpersonal communication. Many communication scholars focus their research on the relationship between communication and the specific issues of culture, gender, and technology. Additionally, many interpersonal communication researchers examine challenging issues in interpersonal relationships.

CULTURE

In this text, we define *culture* broadly and inclusively as an established, coherent set of beliefs, attitudes, values, and practices shared by a large group of people (Keesing, 1974). Culture includes many different types of large-group influences, such as nationality, ethnicity, religion, gender, sexual orientation, physical and mental abilities, and even age. We learn our cultural beliefs, attitudes, and values from parents, teachers, religious leaders, peers, and the mass media (Gudykunst & Kim, 2003). As our world becomes more diverse, scholars and students must consider cultural differences when discussing interpersonal communication theory and research, and how communication skills can be improved.

Throughout this book, and particularly in Chapter 5, we examine similarities and differences across cultures and consider their implications for interpersonal communication. As we cover this material, critically examine the role that culture plays in your own interpersonal communication and relationships.

GENDER AND SEXUAL ORIENTATION

One way to define **gender** is as the social, psychological, and cultural traits generally associated with a person's biological sex (Canary et al., 1997). Unlike biological sex, which we're assigned at birth, gender is largely learned, and it is influenced—or socially constructed—by your culture. You may have read in popular magazines or heard on TV that women are more "open" communicators than men, and that men

⬤ Understanding how culture, gender, and sexual orientation can influence interpersonal communication will help you communicate more effectively. Top Left: Danny Lehman/Getty Images; Top Right: Heiko Meyer/laif/Redux; Bottom Left: Kelvin Murray/Getty Images; Bottom Right: Carl De Keyzer/Magnum Photos

"have difficulty communicating their feelings." However, the research and theory on gender and interpersonal communication indicate that people communicate in more nuanced ways than what is portrayed by simple stereotypes. Throughout this book, and particularly in Chapter 6, we discuss such stereotypes in gender and explore the scholarly research on gender and interpersonal communication.

Many of us also possess a **sexual orientation**: emotional, romantic, and/or sexual feelings toward other people (PFLAG, 2020). Much like common misconceptions about gender, people may also have misconceptions about sexual orientation. However, research documents that people of all sexual orientations form, maintain, and dissolve interpersonal relationships in very similar ways. We discuss this research in greater depth throughout this text.

TECHNOLOGICALLY MEDIATED COMMUNICATION

As noted earlier, radical changes in communication technology have had a profound effect on our ability to interpersonally communicate. Devices keep us in almost constant contact with friends, family members, colleagues, and romantic partners. Our ability to communicate easily and frequently, even when separated by

focus on CULTURE

What Does Culture Mean to You?

In December 2014, Merriam-Webster dictionary declared *culture* to be "the Word of the Year," based on frequency of searches on their website. Why the sudden uptick in interest? Because debates over culture came to a head in 2014 in vivid ways that endure today. For instance, Black Lives Matter first gained prominence in 2014, spotlighting cultural and systemic oppression in the wake of multiple police killings of unarmed Black men. And the concept of "rape culture"—long recognized by scholars—crossed over into popular consciousness that same year, triggered by multiple college campus sexual assault scandals. Since 2014, many other kinds of "cultures" have made headlines, such as "callout culture" and "cancel culture."

As you can see from these examples, the meaning of *culture* is complex and multilayered. Think about it: culture can refer to ethnic or national identities (Argentinian, Ghanaian, Kashmiri) as well as religion (Buddhist, Christian, Sikh). Culture can represent sexual orientations and gender identities, such as LGBTQ+ cultures. Culture also can include passionate interest groups, such as sports teams (fans of the Pittsburgh Steelers or Cleveland Cavaliers) or music genres (K-pop stans or country fans).

But despite its complexity, culture also represents aspiration. Many of us long to be both "more cultured" and "more culturally aware." As the *New Yorker* ideas editor Joshua Rothman (2014) describes, "Culture . . . represents, in its way, a wish: that a group of people might discover, together, a good way of life that expresses itself in their habits, institutions, and activities; and that those, in turn, might help individuals flourish in their own ways. Maybe, in such a world, the meaning of culture would be more obvious, and we wouldn't have to look it up."

discussion questions

- What does the word *culture* mean to you?
- What cultures do you embrace as your own, and how do they shape your communication?

geographic distance, is further enhanced through *technologically mediated communication* (TMC). In this book, we treat such technologies as tools for connecting people interpersonally—tools that are thoroughly integrated into our lives. In each chapter, you'll find frequent mention of these technologies as they relate to the chapter's specific topics.

CHALLENGING ISSUES IN INTERPERSONAL RELATIONSHIPS

Interpersonal communication strongly influences the quality of our interpersonal relationships, and the quality of those relationships, in turn, affects how we feel about our lives. When our involvements with lovers, family, friends, and coworkers are satisfying and healthy, we feel happier in general (Myers, 2002). But the fact that relationships can bring us joy obscures the fact that relationships, and the interpersonal communication that occurs within them, can often be destructive.

In studying interpersonal communication, you can learn much by looking beyond constructive encounters to the types of damaging exchanges that occur all too frequently in life. Throughout the text, we will discuss many of the complicated situations that you may experience, as well as recommendations for how to deal with them.

 **LaunchPad**

Online Self-Quiz: The Challenging Side of Interpersonal Relationships. To take this self-quiz, visit LaunchPad: **launchpadworks.com**

The Journey Ahead

Studying communication is the first step toward improving it

Interpersonal communication is our primary vehicle for exchanging meaning, connecting emotionally, and building relationships with others. This makes it essential that we base our interpersonal decisions on the best knowledge to which we have access. No one would consider making choices about collegiate majors, future careers, or monetary interests without first gathering the most trustworthy information available. Interpersonal communication should be no different.

This chapter—which introduces key definitions and important principles—will start you on your journey into the study of interpersonal communication. As we travel together through interpersonal essentials, skills, and relationships, the transformative potential of your interpersonal communication will become apparent.

◁ We began this chapter with a story about our son Kyle as he began his college journey. What new interpersonal connections have you made on your collegiate journey?
Courtesy of Kelly Morrison

Dealing with a Difficult Friend

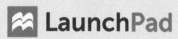 **LaunchPad** For the best experience, complete all parts of this activity in LaunchPad: **launchpadworks.com**

1 Background

Communicating competently is challenging, especially when close relationship partners provoke us. When problematic encounters happen online, it makes dealing with them even more difficult. Read the case study in Part 2; then, drawing on all you know about interpersonal communication thus far, work through the problem-solving model in Part 3.

 Visit LaunchPad to watch the video in Part 4 and assess your communication in Part 5.

2 Case Study

Kaitlyn, Cort, and you have been best friends for years. The three of you are inseparable, and people joke that you're more like triplets than friends. After high school, you and Cort become college housemates. Kaitlyn can't afford tuition yet, so she stays in your hometown to work and save money. Despite the distance, the three of you stay in daily contact.

Recently, however, things have changed. Kaitlyn has been hanging out with people you consider shady. She's been drinking heavily and boasting about her all-night binges. You try to be supportive, but you're worried.

You awake one Sunday to find that one of Kaitlyn's new friends has tagged her in a series of Facebook photos documenting their latest party adventure. Kaitlyn has added a comment that reads, "A new low is reached—I LUV it!!" Surfing through the pictures, you see Kaitlyn drinking until she passes out. Several photos show her friends laughing and posing with her while she's unconscious. In one image, they've drawn a smiley face on her forehead with a Sharpie. Looking at these photos, you're heartsick with humiliation for your friend. Why

would Kaitlyn hang with people like that? But you also can't understand why she would comment on these pictures, rather than insist on having them deleted. What if her family saw them? Or her employers? You email her, telling her she should have the photos deleted, and saying that you're worried about her behavior and her choice of new friends. She doesn't respond.

That night, you're studying with Cort. When Cort steps out to get some food, a message alert sounds on his phone. It's a text from Kaitlyn. You know you shouldn't read it, but your curiosity gets the best of you. It's a rage message, in which Kaitlyn blasts you for prying into her business, for judging her, for thinking you're better than her, and for telling her what to do. It's personal, profane, and very insulting.

You feel sick to your stomach. You love Kaitlyn, but you're also furious with her. How could she say such horrible things when all you were trying to do was help? As you sit there stewing, another text to Cort from Kaitlyn comes in. "Where r u? Text me back! I want to talk w/u about our nosy, o-so-perfect friend!"

Your Turn

Think about all you've learned thus far about interpersonal communication. Then work through the following five steps. Remember, there are no "right" answers, so think hard about what is the *best* choice! (P.S. Need help? See the *Helpful Concepts* list.)

step 1

Reflect on yourself. What are your thoughts and feelings in this situation? What assumptions are you making about Kaitlyn and her communication? Are your assumptions accurate?

step 2

Reflect on your partner. Put yourself in Kaitlyn's shoes. How is she thinking and feeling? Are her views valid?

step 3

Identify the optimal outcome. Think about your relationship and communication with Kaitlyn and all that has happened. What's the best, most constructive relationship outcome possible? Consider what's best for you and for Kaitlyn.

step 4

Locate the roadblocks. Taking into consideration your own and Kaitlyn's thoughts and feelings and all that has happened in this situation, what obstacles are preventing you from achieving the optimal outcome?

step 5

Chart your course. What can you say to Kaitlyn to overcome the roadblocks you've identified and achieve your optimal outcome?

HELPFUL CONCEPTS

I-Thou and I-It, **9**
Relationship information, **10–11**
The irreversibility of interpersonal communication, **12**
Ethics, **17**
Improving your mediated competence, **18–20**

The Other Side

Visit LaunchPad to watch a video in which Kaitlyn tells their side of the case study story. As in many real-life situations, this is information to which you did not have access when you were initially crafting your response in Part 3. The video reminds us that even when we do our best to offer competent responses, there is always another side to the story that we need to consider.

Interpersonal Competence Self-Assessment

After watching the video, visit the Self-Assessment questions in LaunchPad. Think about the new information offered in Kaitlyn's side of the story and all you've learned about interpersonal communication. Drawing on this knowledge, revisit your earlier responses in Part 3 and assess your interpersonal communication competence.

POSTSCRIPT

Rana Faure/Getty Images

We began this chapter with a story of our son and a dream come true. When our oldest son Kyle received the email message of acceptance into college, it wasn't just an individual milestone, it was a family event—shared not just by those closest to us within our kitchen (where life's most important events often occur) but with friends and relatives across the country and around the world. What milestones have marked *your* life's journey? What dreams have you yet to achieve? Who do you seek out to spread the news? Whether these accomplishments are shared face-to-face or through devices, it is interpersonal communication—and your communication choices—that close geographic distance and keep you close to the people that matter most to you.

LaunchPad

LaunchPad for *Reflect & Relate* offers videos and encourages self-assessment through adaptive quizzing. Go to **launchpadworks.com** to get access to:

 LearningCurve
Adaptive Quizzes

▶ Video clips that help you understand interpersonal communication

key terms

▶ You can watch brief, illustrative videos of these terms and test your understanding of the concepts in LaunchPad.

key concepts

What Is Communication?

- The **message** is the basic unit of **communication**. We exchange messages during **interactions** with others, **contexts** shape how we create and interpret messages, and messages are conveyed through a variety of modalities.

- The **linear communication model** describes the components necessary for communication to occur. **Senders** communicate messages to **receivers** that may be misinterpreted due to **noise**. The **interactive communication model** adds **feedback** and **fields of experience**. The **transactional communication model** presents the notion that communication participants collaboratively create meaning.

What Is Interpersonal Communication?

- **Dyadic** communication allows us to distinguish **interpersonal communication** from **intrapersonal communication**.

- Interpersonal communication changes, and is changed by, participants' emotions, thoughts, behavior, and relationships.

- Interpersonal communication is characterized by four principles: it has content and relationship information, it can be intentional or unintentional, it's irreversible, and it's dynamic. It can be used for fulfilling a hierarchy of needs and pursuing **self-presentation**, **instrumental**, and **relationship goals**.

What Is Interpersonal Communication Competence?

- People who demonstrate **appropriateness**, **effectiveness**, and **ethics** in achieving their interpersonal goals are interpersonally competent.

- For competent technologically mediated communication, choose your modality wisely, don't assume mediated communication is always more efficient, presume your posts are public, remember that your posts are permanent, and practice the art of creating drafts.

Issues in Interpersonal Communication

- Relevant topics include culture, **gender** and **sexual orientation**, mediated communication, and challenging issues in interpersonal relationships.

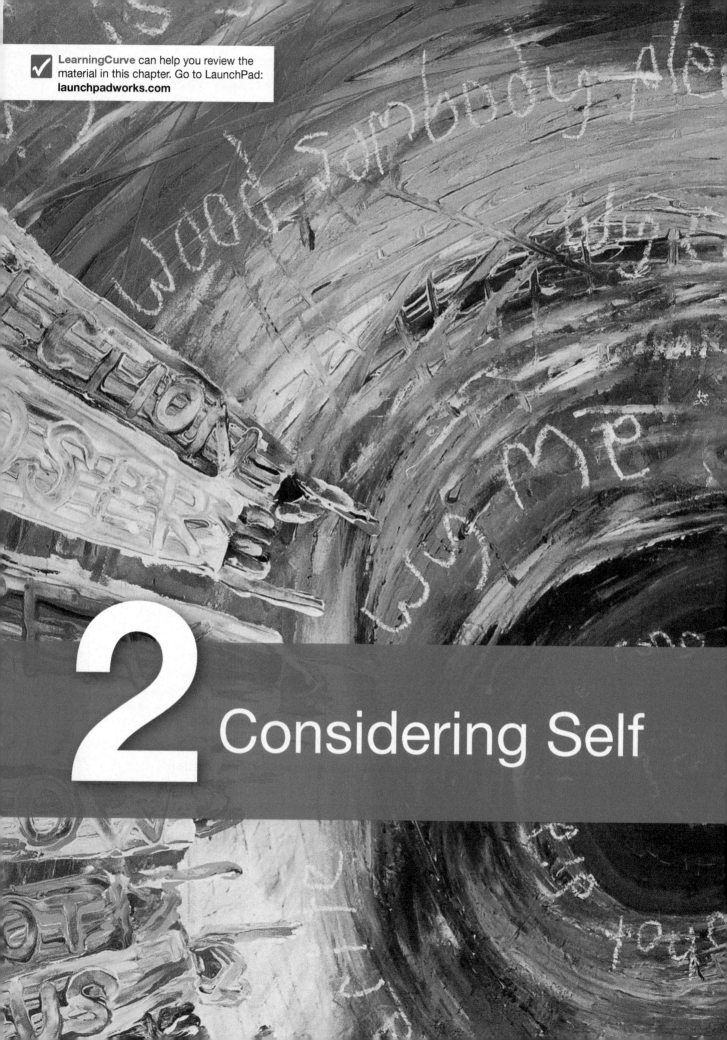

2 Considering Self

By deepening your self-understanding, you can begin to clarify your thoughts and feelings about your self.

Photo by Scott Rosenfeld

Artist Eric Staib describes his 2002 painting *labeled* as a self-portrait. "It depicts my feelings about how my peers saw me when I was growing up. The hands pointing, words said under people's breath. You can tell what they're thinking: you're an idiot, you're stupid, you're a joke."[1]

By the time Eric was in third grade, he knew he was different. Whereas his classmates progressed rapidly in reading and writing, Eric couldn't make sense of words on the written page. But it wasn't until fifth grade that Eric was finally given a label for his difference: learning disabled, or LD. The LD label stained Eric's sense of self, making him feel ashamed. His low self-esteem spread outward, constraining his communication and relationships. "My whole approach was *Don't get noticed!* I'd slouch down in class, hide in my seat. And I would never open up to people. I let nobody in."

Frustrated with the seemingly insurmountable challenges of reading and writing, Eric channeled intense energy into art. By eleventh grade, Eric had the reading and writing abilities of a fifth grader but managed to pass his classes through hard work and artistic ability. He graduated from high school with a D average.

Many of Eric's peers with learning disabilities had turned to substance abuse and dropped out of school, but Eric pursued his education further, taking classes at a local community college. There, something happened that

[1]All information presented regarding artist Eric Staib was provided with his permission, from an interview conducted by the author in February 2005.

29

transformed his view of his self, his self-esteem, and the entire course of his life. While taking his first written exam of the semester, Eric knew the answers, but he couldn't write them down. No matter how hard he focused, he couldn't convert the knowledge in his head into written words. Rather than complete the exam, he wrote the story of his disability on the answer sheet, including his struggles with reading and writing and the pain associated with being labeled LD. He turned in his exam and left. Eric's professor took his exam to the college dean, and the two of them called Eric to the dean's office. They told him, "You need help, and we're going to help you." Their compassion changed Eric's life. Eric's professor arranged for Eric to meet with a learning specialist, who immediately diagnosed him as dyslexic. As Eric explains, "For the first time in my life, I had a label for myself other than 'learning disabled.' To me, the LD label meant I couldn't learn. But dyslexia was different. It could be overcome. The specialist taught me strategies for working with my dyslexia, and gave me my most important tool—my Franklin Spellchecker—to check spellings. But most importantly, I was taught that it was OK to be dyslexic."

Armed with an improving sense of self, Eric went from hiding to asserting himself, "from low self-esteem to being comfortable voicing my opinion, from fear to confidence." That confidence led him to transfer to a Big Ten university, where he graduated with a degree in studio arts, percussion, and horticulture. He subsequently earned a postgraduate degree in K–12 art education, graduating with a straight-A average.

Eric Staib is now an art instructor in the Midwest and was a 2006 recipient of the Robert Rauschenberg Foundation Power of Art Award, given to the top arts educators in the country each year. He also teaches instructors how to use art to engage students with learning disabilities. What means the most to him is the opportunity to pass down the legacy of his personal transformation. "When I think about my dyslexia, it's really incredible. What was my greatest personal punishment is now the most profound gift I have to offer to others."

Every word you've ever spoken during an encounter, every act of kindness or cruelty you've committed, has the same root source—your self. When you look inward, you are peering into the wellspring from which all your interpersonal actions flow. But even as your self influences your interpersonal communication, it is shaped by your communication as well. Through communicating with others, we learn who we are, how others perceive us, and how we should act. This means that the starting point for improving your communication is understanding your self. In this way, you can begin to clarify your thoughts and feelings about your self; comprehend how these are linked to your interpersonal communication; and develop strategies for enhancing your sense of self, your communication skills, and your interpersonal relationships.

In this chapter, we explore the source of all interpersonal communication: the self. You'll learn:

- The components of self, as well as how critical self-reflection can be used to improve your communication skills and your self-esteem

- The ways in which gender, family, and culture shape your sense of self

- How to present and maintain a positive self

- The choices involved in communicating self, including managing self in relationships, and suggestions for successful self-disclosure
- The importance of online self-presentation

The Components of Self

Your self is the driving force of your communication

At Delphi in ancient Greece, the temple of the sun-god Apollo was adorned with the inscription *Gnothi se auton*— "Know thyself." According to legend, when one of the seven sages of Greece, Chilon of Sparta, asked Apollo, "What is best for people?" the deity responded with that simple admonition. More than 2,500 years later, these words still ring true, especially in the realm of interpersonal communication and relationships. To understand our interactions with others and the bonds we forge, we must first comprehend ourselves. But what exactly is "thyself" that we need to know?

The **self** is an evolving composite of self-awareness, self-concept, and self-esteem. Although each of us experiences the self as singular ("*This* is who I am"), it actually is made up of three distinct yet integrated components that continually evolve over time, based on your life experiences.

SELF-AWARENESS

Self-awareness is the ability to view yourself as a unique person distinct from your surrounding environment and to reflect on your thoughts, feelings, and behaviors. That is, you are able to turn a lens on yourself and examine the resulting image that you see. According to sociologist George Herbert Mead (1934), self-awareness helps you develop a strong sense of your self because during interpersonal encounters, you monitor your own behaviors and form impressions of who you are from such observations. As a result, your sense of self may vary by situation, such as home versus school, and relationally, such as close friend versus classmate (Fiske & Taylor, 2017). For example, your best friend texts you that they failed an important exam. You feel bad, so you text a comforting response. Your self-awareness of your compassion and your observation of your kindhearted message lead you to think, "I'm a caring and supportive friend."

When you use your self-awareness to assess how well your communication matches situational norms, you are engaged in **self-monitoring**. Some individuals are keenly self-aware of whether or not their behaviors and communication are well-suited to the situation they are in (Giles & Street, 1994). Known as high self-monitors, these individuals prefer situations in which clear expectations exist regarding how they're supposed to communicate, and they possess both the ability and the desire to alter their behaviors to fit any type of social situation. In contrast, low self-monitors prefer encounters in which they can just "act like themselves" and say what they think and feel, without having to scrutinize their communication to see whether it abides by norms (Oyamot et al., 2010). As a consequence, high self-monitors are often judged as more adaptive and skilled communicators than low self-monitors (Gangestad & Snyder, 2000). However, high self-monitoring may have its drawbacks as well. For instance, people who are chronically lonely tend to suppress their expression of emotions, and research suggests that high self-monitors are more likely than low self-monitors to suppress their emotional expression in this way (Smith et al., 2019).

▨ LaunchPad Video
launchpadworks.com

Self-Monitoring
Watch this clip online to answer the questions below.

Does this video show a low self-monitor or high self-monitor? Please explain your reasoning. Have you ever changed your behavior after self-monitoring? If so, under what circumstances?

This means that high self-monitors may "mask" feelings of loneliness—"putting on a happy face" when in actuality they are profoundly sad—which can make it difficult for others to tell that they are feeling lonely. Consequently, loved ones of high self-monitors may face a wellness challenge: because they can't look to the person's displayed emotions for guidance regarding their true inner states of being, they must instead try to create a context in which it's situationally appropriate to share such feelings, and then ask direct questions about those feelings. Our recommendation is to initiate such encounters face-to-face without other people around in a quiet, private space in which the high self-monitor feels they can safely "let their guard down."

As we're watching and evaluating our own actions, we also engage in **social comparison**: observing and assigning meaning to others' behavior and then comparing it with ours. Social comparison has a particularly potent effect on self when we compare ourselves to people we wish to emulate. When we compare favorably when measured against respected others, we think well of ourselves; when we don't compare favorably, we think less of ourselves.

You can greatly enhance your interpersonal communication by practicing a targeted kind of self-awareness known as *critical self-reflection*. To engage in critical self-reflection, ask yourself the following questions:

- What am I thinking and feeling?
- Why am I thinking and feeling this way?
- How am I communicating?
- How are my thoughts and feelings influencing my communication?
- How can I improve my thoughts, feelings, and communication?

The ultimate goal of critical self-reflection is embodied in the last question: How can I *improve*? Improving your interpersonal communication is possible only when you accurately understand how your self drives your communication behavior. In the remainder of this chapter, and in the marginal *Self-Reflection* exercises you'll find throughout this book, we help you make links between your self and your communication.

SELF-CONCEPT

Self-concept is your overall perception of who you are. If self-awareness is your ability to focus a lens upon yourself, self-concept is the picture taken through that lens. Your self-concept is based on the beliefs, attitudes, and values you have about yourself. *Beliefs* are convictions that certain things are true—for example, "I'm an excellent student." *Attitudes* are evaluative appraisals, such as "I'm happy with how I'm doing in school." *Values* represent enduring principles that guide your interpersonal actions—for example, "I think it's wrong to cheat on schoolwork."

Your self-concept is shaped by a host of factors, including your family, friends, gender, and culture (Vallacher et al., 2002). As we learned in the opening story about Eric Staib, one of the biggest influences on your self-concept is the labels others put on you. How do others' impressions of you shape your self-concept? Sociologist Charles Horton Cooley (1902) argued that it's like looking at yourself in the "looking glass" (mirror). When you stand in front of it, you consider your appearance through the eyes of others. Do they see you as attractive? Confident? Approachable? Seeing yourself in this fashion—and thinking about how others must see you—has a powerful effect on how you think about your physical self. Cooley noted that the same process shapes our broader self-concept: it is based in part on your beliefs about how others see you, including their perceptions and

LaunchPad Video

launchpadworks.com

Social Comparison
Watch this clip online to answer the questions below.

What aspects of your self are you more likely to compare with others? How does this impact your self-awareness?

Want to see more? Check out LaunchPad for a clip on **self-fulfilling prophecies**.

evaluations of you ("People think I'm talented, and they like me") and your emotional response to those beliefs ("I feel good/bad about how others see me"). According to Cooley, when we define our self-concepts by considering how others see us, we are creating a **looking-glass self**.

Some people have clear and stable self-concepts; that is, they know exactly who they are, and their sense of self endures across time, situations, and relationships. Others struggle with their identity, remaining uncertain about who they really are, what they believe, and how they feel about themselves. The degree to which you have a clearly defined, consistent, and enduring sense of self is known as **self-concept clarity** (Campbell et al., 1996), and it has a powerful effect on your health, happiness, and outlook on life. Research suggests that people who have a stronger, clearer, sense of self (i.e., higher self-concept clarity) have higher self-esteem, are less likely to experience negative emotions (both in response to stressful situations and in general), are less likely to experience chronic depression (Lee-Flynn et al., 2011), and are more likely to self-disclose—that is, to reveal personal information about themselves (Tajmirriyahi & Ickes, 2020). In simple terms, high self-concept clarity helps you weather the unpredictability and instability of the world around you.

Keep two implications in mind when considering your self-concept and its impact on your interpersonal communication. First, because your self-concept consists of deeply held beliefs, attitudes, and values, changing it may be challenging. For example, if you've long thought of yourself as "not a creative person," it may take a lot of time and experiences being successfully creative before your self-concept begins to shift (Fiske & Taylor, 1991).

Second, our self-concepts often lead us to create **self-fulfilling prophecies**— predictions about future interactions that lead us to behave in ways that ensure the interaction unfolds as we predicted. Some self-fulfilling prophecies ignite positive events. For instance, you may see yourself as professionally capable and highly skilled at communicating, which leads you to predict job interview success. During an interview, your prophecy of success leads you to communicate in a calm and confident fashion, which impresses the interviewers. In turn, their reaction confirms your

self-reflection

Consider your looking-glass self. What kinds of labels do your friends use to describe you? What kinds of labels does your family use? How do you feel about others' impressions of you? In what ways do these feelings shape your interpersonal communication and relationships?

Self-Fulfilling Prophecies
*Overcoming negative
self-fulfilling prophecies*

❶ Identify a communication problem you experience often (e.g., social anxiety).

❷ Describe situations in which it occurs, including what you think, say, and do.

❸ Use critical self-reflection to identify how your thoughts and feelings shape your communication.

❹ List things you could say and do that would generate positive results.

❺ In similar situations, block negative thoughts and feelings that arise, and focus your attention on practicing the positive behaviors you listed.

prophecy. Other self-fulfilling prophecies elicit negative events. Steve once had a friend who felt unattractive and undesirable, leading him to predict interpersonal failure at social gatherings. When he would accompany Steve to a party, he would spend the entire time in a corner staring morosely into a drink. Needless to say, no one tried to talk to Steve's friend, leading him to complain at the end of the evening, "See, I told you no one would want to talk to me!"

SELF-ESTEEM

After our self-awareness allows us to turn a lens on ourselves, and we develop the picture by defining our self-concepts, **self-esteem** is the overall value, positive or negative, that we assign to what we see. Whereas self-awareness prompts us to ask, "Who am I?" and self-concept is the answer to that question, self-esteem is the answer to the follow-up question: "Given who I am, what's my evaluation of my self?" When your overall estimation of self is negative, you'll have a meager sense of self-worth and suffer from low self-esteem. When your evaluation of self is positive, you'll enjoy high self-esteem.

Your self-esteem strongly shapes your interpersonal communication, relationships, and physical and mental health (Krauss et al., 2020). People with high self-esteem report greater life satisfaction; enjoy more social acceptance; communicate more positively and warmly with others; experience more happiness in their relationships; and exhibit greater leadership ability, athleticism, and academic performance than do people with low self-esteem (Cameron & Granger, 2019). High self-esteem also helps insulate people from stress, anxiety, and depression (Lee-Flynn et al., 2011; Xie et al., 2020).

By contrast, people with low self-esteem are more likely to believe that friends and romantic partners think negatively of them and, as a consequence, are less likely to share their thoughts and feelings with others. This lack of expressivity ultimately undermines their close relationships (Gaucher et al., 2012). In addition, low self-esteem individuals experience negative emotions and depression more frequently (Orth et al., 2009), resulting in destructive feedback loops like the one depicted in Figure 2.1.

Measuring Up to Your Own Standards The key to bolstering your self-esteem is understanding its roots. **Self-discrepancy theory** suggests that one factor influencing your self-esteem, and associated feelings, is how your self-concept compares to two mental standards (Higgins, 1987; Higgins et al., 1985; Mason et al., 2019). The first is your *ideal self*, the characteristics (mental, physical, emotional, material, and spiritual) that you wish to possess—the "perfect you." Kelly describes this as your "fairy godmother" self: that is, if your fairy godmother flew down, and waved her magic wand—instantly transforming you into whoever you dream of being—who would that be? The second is your *ought self*, the person you feel responsible or obligated to be. You can think of this as your "should be" or "supposed to be" self. Importantly, your ideal self and ought self may clash. If you are a perfectionist, for example, you may think that you *should* be "perfect" ("ought self"), but you might *wish* ("ideal self") that you didn't feel this constant pressure. Alternatively, your ideal self and your ought self may match, if the person you wish you were is also the person you feel obligated to be.

Both ideal and ought self standards can be guided by two different perspectives: *your* perspective and the perspectives of *important others*, such as your family, friends,

self-QUIZ

Test Your Ideal and Ought Self-Discrepancies

Think about your self-concept. List three aspects of your self that are central to your self-concept. For **each** of the three aspects, select the number that best describes how you feel for each question below.

For this aspect I am:

very close to 1 2 3 4 5 very far away from who I would ideally like to be

very much like 1 2 3 4 5 not at all like who I aspire to be

exactly like 1 2 3 4 5 completely unlike who I hope to be

very close to 1 2 3 4 5 very far away from who I feel I *should* be

very much like 1 2 3 4 5 not at all like who I feel obligated to be

quite similar to 1 2 3 4 5 quite dissimilar to who I have a responsibility to be

Add up your numbers for the three questions in the left-hand column. This is your ideal self-discrepancy. Then add up your numbers for the three questions in the right-hand column. This is your ought self-discrepancy. Now repeat the questions for *each* of the other two aspects of your self that you listed.

Scoring: For each aspect of your self, a score of 3–5 indicates low self-discrepancy, 6–10 indicates moderate self-discrepancy, and 11 or above indicates high self-discrepancy for that aspect. You can repeat the quiz, rating yourself from an important other person's perspective instead of your own.

colleagues, coaches, or romantic partners. To illustrate this, think about your choice of major—or your thoughts about potential majors, if you haven't yet selected one. How is your thinking influenced by who your parents *wish* you could be—your "ideal self" from their perspective? Or by what they say you're *obligated* to do ("ought self")? Keep in mind these could be different—such as when your parents *wish* you could pursue a career in art or music, but feel that you're *obligated*, given family economic challenges, to major in something more "practical" in terms of future earning power. Now consider: is it what you *wish*, or what you feel you're *supposed* to do? Each of these standards and perspectives can influence your self-esteem.

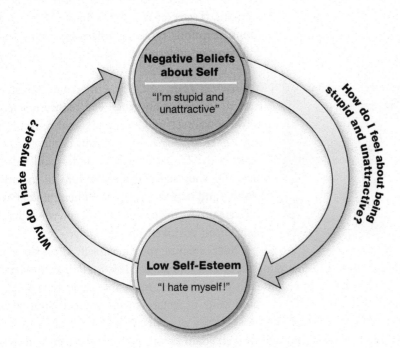

figure 2.1 **Low Self-Esteem: A Vicious Cycle**

According to self-discrepancy theory, you feel happy and content when your self-concept matches both ideal and ought selves (Katz & Farrow, 2000). However, when your self-concept is inferior to both ideal and ought selves, you experience a discrepancy and are likely to suffer low self-esteem (Veale et al., 2003).

Research on self-discrepancy theory documents three interesting facts about discrepancies (Halliwell & Dittmar, 2006; Phillips & Silvia, 2005). First, women report larger ideal self-discrepancies than do men. This isn't surprising, given the degree to which women are deluged with advertising and other media emphasizing unattainable standards for female beauty (see *Focus on Culture* later in this chapter). Second, for both women and men, self-discrepancies impact an array of emotions and feelings linked to self-esteem. For instance, people who feel greater self-discrepancies also experience greater psychological distress, interpersonal stress, negative emotions—such as guilt, shame, and anger—and lower self-esteem, and they are more likely to engage in repeated negative thoughts about self (Liw & Han, 2020; Mason et al., 2019). Finally, self-discrepancies are most apparent and impactful to us when we are consciously self-aware: looking in a mirror, watching ourselves on video, or getting direct feedback from others.

This latter finding suggests an important implication for our relationships. If we surround ourselves with people who constantly criticize, belittle, or comment on our flaws, we are more likely to have wider self-discrepancies and lower self-esteem due to their negative perspectives influencing our standards. Alternatively, if our social networks support us and praise our unique abilities, our self-discrepancies will diminish and self-esteem will rise. Thus, a critical aspect in maintaining self-esteem and life happiness is choosing to reduce contact with people who routinely tear us down, and instead opting for fellowship with those who fortify us.

What's more, it doesn't matter whether or not we *think* we're immune to others' opinions. Research has found that the self-esteem of people who claim they couldn't "care less" about what other people think of them is just as strongly impacted by approval and criticism as the self-esteem of people who report valuing others' opinions (Leary et al., 2003). In short, regardless of your perceptions, receiving others' approval or criticism will boost or undermine your self-esteem.

Improving Your Self-Esteem   Your self-esteem can start to improve only when you reduce discrepancies between your self and ideal and ought selves. How can you do this? Begin by assessing your self-concept. Make a list of the beliefs, attitudes, and values that make up your self-concept. Be sure to include both positive and negative attributes. Then think about your self-esteem. In reviewing the list you've made, do you see yourself positively or negatively?

Next, analyze your ideal self. Who do you wish you were? Is this ideal attainable, or is it unrealistic? If it is attainable, what would you have to change to become this person? If you made these changes, would you be satisfied with yourself, or would your expectations for yourself simply escalate further? Now consider the perspectives of other important people in your life and how they influence your ideal standard, asking yourself these same questions.

Then turn to analyze your ought self, and start with the perspective of important other people. Who do others think you *should* be? Can you ever become

Influencers on social media go to great lengths to present idealized, seemingly perfect versions of their selves—often using filters, airbrushing, and other visual effects. But images like these aren't realistic, and can reinforce an "appearance culture." RossHelen/Shutterstock

focus on CULTURE

How Does the Media Shape Your Self-Esteem?

Korean American comedian Margaret Cho has trailblazed issues of racism and sexism in comedy. In this excerpt from her one-woman show *The Notorious C.H.O.*, she offers her thoughts on self-esteem:

You know when you look in the mirror and think, "Oh, I'm so fat, I'm so old, I'm so ugly"? That is not your authentic self speaking. That is billions upon billions of dollars of advertising—magazines, movies, billboards—all geared to make you feel bad about yourself so that you'll take your hard-earned money and spend it at the mall. When you don't have self-esteem, you will hesitate before you do anything. You will hesitate to go for the job you really want. You will hesitate to ask for a raise. You will hesitate to defend yourself when you're discriminated against. You will hesitate to vote. You will hesitate to dream. For those of us plagued with low self-esteem, improving [it] is truly an act of revolution! (Custudio, 2002)

Cho is right. And it's important to emphasize that this doesn't just apply to women. We live in an "appearance culture," a society that values and reinforces extreme, unrealistic ideals, and glorification of attractiveness, body shape, and physical appearance (Trekels & Eggermont, 2017). In an appearance culture, standards for appearance are defined by the media through digitally enhanced images of bodily perfection (Field et al., 1999), and imposed by peers through conversations and sometimes through bullying (Gattario et al., 2020; Trekels & Eggermont, 2017). When we internalize messages about the perfect body and appearance, we can end up despising our own bodies and craving unattainable perfection (Jones et al., 2004). This can result in low self-esteem, depression, and, in some cases, self-destructive behaviors such as eating disorders (Harrison, 2001). To combat these outcomes, we should do our best to limit consumption of harmful media messages and the destructive comparisons they elicit.

discussion questions

- How would you teach a younger sibling to maintain their self-esteem in an appearance culture? What would be specific tips to help bolster their self-esteem?
- What are some positive ways we can respond to others when their talk seems to be enforcing an appearance culture? How can we help ourselves, and others, focus on our positive qualities and strengths?

the person others expect? What would you have to do to become this person? If you did all these things, would others be satisfied with you, or would their expectations escalate? Then consider your own perspective in terms of who you think you should be, or who you feel that you have an obligation to be, repeating these same questions.

Fourth, revisit and redefine your standards. This step requires intense, concentrated effort over a long period of time. If you find that your ideal and ought selves are realistic and attainable, move to the final step. If you decide that your ideal and ought selves are unrealistic and unattainable, redefine these standards so that each can be attained through sustained work. If you find yourself unable to abandon unrealistic and unattainable standards, from your own or another person's perspective, don't be afraid to consult with a professional therapist or another trusted resource for assistance.

Fifth, create an action plan for resolving any self-discrepancies. Map out the specific actions necessary to eventually attain your ideal and ought selves. Frame your new standards as a list of goals, and post them in your planner, phone, bedroom, or kitchen to remind yourself of these goals. Since self-esteem can't be changed in a day, a week, or even a month, establish a realistic time line. Then implement this action plan in your daily life, checking your progress as you go.

Finally, consider how you can diversify your investments in your self by pursuing multiple interests and activities. For example, if you devoted much of your youth to honing athletic skills and developing that singular aspect of your self, who will you be when you can no longer play your sport? Rather than spending all our time and energy on one aspect of ourselves—putting all our eggs in one basket—we should consider how we can develop across multiple dimensions, building a shield for our self-esteem. Thus, as our self evolves over time, when one dimension diminishes, for whatever reason, another dimension can expand to compensate for it.

The Sources of Self

Outside forces influence your view of self

For most of us, critical self-reflection isn't a new activity. After all, we spend much of our daily lives looking inward, so we feel that we know our selves. But this doesn't mean that our sense of self is entirely self-determined. Instead, our selves are shaped by at least three powerful outside forces: gender, family, and culture.

GENDER AND SELF

One primary outside force shaping our sense of self is our *gender*—the composite of social, psychological, and behavioral attributes that a particular culture associates with an individual's biological sex (American Psychological Association [APA], 2015b). It may strike you as strange to see gender described as an "outside force." Gender is innate, something you're born with, right? Actually, scholars distinguish gender, which is largely learned, or constructed through our social interactions, from *biological sex*, which is a category assigned at birth. Each of us is born with biological sex organs that distinguish us anatomically as female, male, or intersex—that is, a person who is born with or who develops characteristics in reproductive or sexual anatomy that don't seem to fit the typical definitions of female or male (InterACT, 2020). By contrast, our gender is shaped over time through our interactions with others, institutional frameworks, and the culture in which we live.

Immediately after birth, we begin a lifelong process of *gender socialization*. This process may encourage binary—and sometimes stereotypical—distinctions by which we learn from others what it means personally, interpersonally, and culturally to be "male" or "female." Girls may be taught to be aware of their physical appearance and to

▲ The sources of self include your gender, your family, and your culture. (Left to right) Ronnie Kaufman/Getty Images; Caroline Penn/Panos Pictures; age fotostock/Alamy

be more sensitive to their own and others' emotions and needs, such as focusing on domestic chores, while boys may be taught to be tough and competitive, and may be allowed more independence (Kågesten et al., 2016; Lippa, 2002). This process influences our *gender identity*—our innate sense of ourselves as boy, man, or male; girl, woman, or female; or another variation, such as gender-neutral, genderqueer, or gender nonconforming (APA, 2015b). Transgender and gender nonconforming individuals may experience or may outwardly express a gender identity that differs from their sex category assigned at birth (Human Rights Campaign, 2020).

As a result of differing socialization, men and women may end up forming comparatively different self-concepts (Cross & Madson, 1997). In the past, studies showed that women were more likely to perceive themselves as interdependent and connected to others, while men were more likely to see themselves as independent composites of their individual achievements, abilities, and beliefs—separated from others. But scholars also have found contradictory evidence (Foels & Tomcho, 2009; Peker et al., 2018; Pilarska, 2014), and have noted that other factors, such as power, culture, and the communicative situation are important considerations. We will discuss these factors and other topics related to gender in more detail in Chapter 6. Now let's consider the first place most of us are socialized: our families.

self-reflection

What lessons about gender did you learn from your family when you were growing up? From your friends? Based on these lessons, what aspects of your self did you bolster—or bury—given what others deemed appropriate for your gender? How did these lessons affect how you interpersonally communicate?

FAMILY AND SELF

When we're born, we have no self-awareness, self-concept, or self-esteem. As we mature, we become aware of ourselves as unique and separate from our environments and begin developing self-concepts. Research indicates that the family environments we experience in our early years impact our self-esteem in later life (Krauss et al., 2020; Orth, 2018). Our caregivers play a crucial role in this process, providing us with ready-made sets of beliefs, attitudes, and values from which we construct our fledgling selves. We also forge emotional bonds with our caregivers, and our communication and interactions with them powerfully shape our beliefs regarding the functions, rewards, and dependability of interpersonal relationships (Bowlby, 1969; Domingue & Mollen, 2009).

These beliefs, in turn, help shape two dimensions of our thoughts, feelings, and behavior: attachment anxiety and attachment avoidance (Collins & Feeney, 2004). *Attachment anxiety* is the degree to which a person fears rejection by relationship partners. If you experience high attachment anxiety, you perceive yourself as unlovable and unworthy—thoughts that may result from being ignored or even abused during childhood. Consequently, you experience chronic fear of abandonment in your close relationships. If you have low attachment anxiety, you feel lovable and worthy of attention—reflections of a supportive and affectionate upbringing. As a result, you feel comfortable and confident in your intimate involvements.

Attachment avoidance is the degree to which someone desires close interpersonal ties. If you have high attachment avoidance, you'll likely experience little interest in intimacy, preferring solitude instead. Such feelings may stem from childhood neglect or an upbringing that encouraged autonomy. If you experience low attachment avoidance, you seek intimacy and interdependence with others, having learned in childhood that such connections are essential for happiness and well-being.

Four attachment styles derive from these two dimensions (Collins & Feeney, 2004; Domingue & Mollen, 2009), which you can see in Figure 2.2. **Secure attachment** individuals are low on both anxiety and avoidance: they're comfortable with intimacy and seek close ties with others. Secure individuals report warm and

	High Avoidance	**Low Avoidance**
High Anxiety	**Fearful Attachment** *A tendency to fear rejection and shun close relationships*	**Preoccupied Attachment** *A tendency to fear rejection but still desire close relationships*
Low Anxiety	**Dismissive Attachment** *A tendency to view close relationships as unimportant, prioritizing self-reliance instead*	**Secure Attachment** *A tendency to seek close relationships and feel comfortable and confident with intimacy*

figure 2.2 **Avoidance and Anxiety in Attachment Styles**

supportive relationships, high self-esteem, confidence in their ability to communicate, and more resilient attitudes and behaviors (Bender & Ingram, 2018). When relationship problems arise, they move to resolve them and are willing to solicit support from others. In addition, they are comfortable with sexual involvement and are unlikely to engage in risky sexual behavior.

Preoccupied attachment adults are high in anxiety and low in avoidance: they desire closeness but are plagued with fear of rejection. They may use sexual contact to satisfy their compulsive need to feel loved. When faced with relationship challenges, preoccupied individuals react with extreme negative emotion and a lack of trust ("I know you don't love me!"). These individuals often have difficulty maintaining long-term involvements.

People with low anxiety but high avoidance have a **dismissive attachment** style. They view close relationships as comparatively unimportant, instead prizing and prioritizing self-reliance. Relationship crises evoke hasty exits ("I don't need this kind of hassle!"), and they are more likely than other attachment styles to engage in casual sexual relationships and to endorse the view that sex without love is positive.

Finally, **fearful attachment** adults are high in both attachment anxiety *and* avoidance. They fear rejection and tend to shun relationships. Fearful individuals can develop close ties if the relationship seems to guarantee a lack of rejection, such as when a partner is financially or emotionally dependent on them. But even then, they suffer from a chronic lack of faith in themselves, their partners, and the relationship's viability.

CULTURE AND SELF

At the 1968 Summer Olympics, U.S. sprinter Tommie Smith won the men's 200-meter gold medal, and teammate John Carlos won the bronze. During the medal ceremony, as the U.S. flag was raised and "The Star-Spangled Banner" played, both runners closed their eyes, lowered their heads, and raised black-gloved fists. Smith's right fist represented Black power, and Carlos's left fist represented Black unity (Gettings, 2005). The two fists, raised next to each other, created an arch of Black unity and power. Smith wore a black scarf around his neck for Black pride, and both men wore black socks with no shoes, representing Black poverty. These symbols and gestures, taken together, clearly spoke of the runners' allegiance to Black culture and their protest of the poor treatment of Black people in the United States. Nearly 50 years later, in 2016, NFL quarterback Colin Kaepernick mirrored the protests of Smith and Carlos

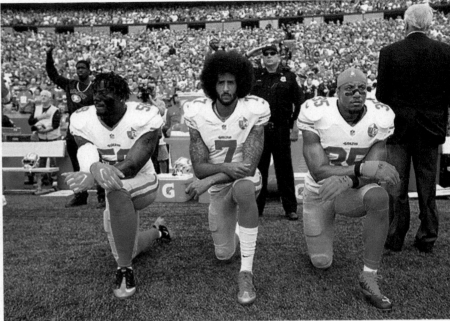

◐ Tommie Smith and John Carlos's protest at the 1968 Summer Olympics, and Colin Kaepernick's protest at NFL games during the 2016 season, showed how they each identified with the Black American culture of their respective eras. AP Images/Anonymous; Michael Zagaris/San Francisco 49ers/Getty Images

by kneeling during the national anthem at games in order to protest police brutality and racial injustice. His symbolic gesture of "taking a knee" subsequently was embraced by many of his teammates—both Black and white—and became a protest emblem used by Black Lives Matter activists and their allies. Kaepernick's protest, like the gesture of Smith and Carlos in 1968, illustrates the powerful connection between culture and self: Kaepernick, Smith, and Carlos each used symbolic gestures to express solidarity with the Black American culture of their respective eras.

As these examples show, in addition to gender and family, our culture is a powerful source of self. *Culture* is an established, coherent set of beliefs, attitudes, values, and practices shared by a large group of people (Keesing, 1974). If this strikes you as similar to our definition of *self-concept*, you're right; culture is like a collective sense of self shared by a large group of people.

Thinking of culture in this way has three important implications. First, culture includes many types of large-group influences, including your nationality as well as your ethnicity, religion, gender, sexual orientation, physical ability, and even age. We learn our cultural beliefs, attitudes, and values from parents, teachers, religious leaders, peers, and the mass media (Gudykunst & Kim, 2003). Second, most of us belong to more than one culture simultaneously and possess the beliefs, attitudes, and values of each. For instance, we may be "American," but also "Latino American" or "Asian American." Third, the various cultures to which we belong sometimes clash. When they do, we sometimes have to choose the culture to which we pledge our primary allegiance.

We'll be discussing culture in greater depth in Chapter 5, where we'll consider some of the unique variables of culture that help to define us and communicate our selves to others, along with the commonalities that connect us across cultures. For example, regarding self-esteem, research has demonstrated that our self-esteem increases from the time we are late adolescents to our middle adult years, and that this finding is consistent across 48 different countries (Bleidorn et al., 2016).

Now that we have defined three of the components comprising self and discussed some external forces shaping self, let's turn our attention to how we communicate self.

self-reflection

When you consider your own cultural background, to which culture do you "pledge allegiance"? How do you communicate this allegiance to others? Have you ever suffered consequences for openly communicating your allegiance to your culture? If so, how?

Communicating Your Self

Presenting your
public self

Rick Welts is one of the most influential people in professional basketball.[2] He created the NBA All-Star Weekend, and he is a cofounder of the women's professional league (the WNBA) and a member of the Basketball Hall of Fame's Class of 2018. For years, he served as the NBA's executive vice president and chief marketing officer, and he is now president of the Golden State Warriors. But throughout his entire sports career—40 years of ascension from ball boy to executive—he lived a self-described "shadow life," publicly playing the role of a straight male while privately being gay. The lowest point came when his longtime partner died and Welts couldn't publicly acknowledge his loss. Instead, he took only two days off from work—telling colleagues that a friend had died—and for months compartmentalized his grief. In early 2011, following his mother's death, he came out publicly. As Welts described, "I want to pierce the silence that envelops the subject of being gay in men's team sports. I want to mentor gays who harbor doubts about a sports career, whether on the court or in the front office. But most of all, I want to feel whole, authentic."

In addition to our private selves, the composite of our self-awareness, self-concept, and self-esteem, each of us also has a public self—the self we present to others (Fenigstein et al., 1975). We actively create our public selves through our interpersonal communication and behavior.

In many encounters, our private and public selves mirror each other. At other times, they seem disconnected. In extreme instances, like that of Rick Welts, we may intentionally craft an inauthentic public self to hide something about our private self we don't want others to know. But regardless of your private self, it is your public self that your friends, family members, and romantic partners hold dear. Most (if not all) of others' impressions of you are based on their appraisals of your public self. People know and judge the "you" who communicates with them, not the "you" you keep inside. Thus, managing your public self is a crucial part of competent interpersonal communication.

LaunchPad Video

launchpadworks.com

Mask
Watch this clip online to answer the questions below.

When, if ever, have you chosen to use a mask to veil your private self or emotions? What motivates you to use a mask? Do you think others use masks for similar reasons?

Want to see more? Check out LaunchPad for a clip on **face**.

MAINTAINING YOUR PUBLIC SELF

Renowned sociologist Erving Goffman (1955) noted that whenever you communicate with others, you present a public self—your **face**—that you want others to see and know. You actively create and present your face through your communication. Your face can be anything you want it to be—"perky and upbeat," "cool and level-headed," or "tough as nails." We create different faces for different moments and relationships in our lives, such as our face as a parent, college student, coworker, or homeless-shelter volunteer.

Sometimes your face is a **mask**, a public self designed to strategically veil your private self (Goffman, 1959). Masks can be dramatic, such as when Rick Welts hid his grief for weeks over the loss of his longtime partner. Or masks can be subtle—the parent who acts calmly in front of an injured child so the youngster doesn't become frightened. Some masks are designed to inflate one's estimation in the eyes of others. One study found that 90 percent of college students surveyed admitted telling at least one lie to impress a person in whom they were romantically interested (Rowatt et al., 1998). Other masks are crafted so that people underestimate us and our abilities (Gibson & Sachau, 2000), like acting

---

[2]All the information that follows regarding Welts is adapted from Barry (2011).

◖ Rick Welts was ultimately able to reconcile his private self with his public self. What parts of your private self do you keep hidden from public view?
Foto AP/The Arizona Republic, Michael Chow

disorganized or unprepared before a debate in the hope that your opponent will let their guard down.

Regardless of the form our face takes—a genuine representation of our private self, or a mask designed to hide this self from others—Goffman argued that we often form a strong emotional attachment to our face because it represents the person we most want others to see when they communicate with and relate to us.

Sometimes after we've created a certain face, information is revealed that contradicts it, causing us to lose face (Goffman, 1955). Losing face provokes feelings of shame, humiliation, and sadness—in a word, **embarrassment**. For example, when we were attending one of our sons' high school symphony performances, the piece they were playing had a brief period of quiet between movements. Mistaking the pause for the end of the song, we both burst into loud applause—only to realize that we were the sole people clapping, as a tide of laughter rippled through the audience and the orchestra.

While losing face can cause intense embarrassment, this is not the only cost. When others see us lose face, they may begin to question whether the public self with which they're familiar is a genuine reflection of our private self. For example, suppose your workplace face is "dedicated, hardworking employee." You ask your boss if there's extra work to be done, help fellow coworkers, show up early, stay late, and so forth. But if you tell your manager that you need your afternoon schedule cleared to work on an urgent report and then they see you bingeing Netflix on your computer, they'll undoubtedly view your actions as inconsistent with your communication. Your face as the "hardworking employee" will be called into question, as will your credibility.

Because losing face can damage others' impressions of you, maintaining face during interpersonal interactions is extremely important. How can you effectively maintain face?[3] Use words and actions consistent with the face you're trying to craft. From one moment to the next and from one behavior to the next, your interpersonal communication and behaviors must complement your face. Make sure your communication and behaviors mesh with the knowledge that others already have about you. If you say or do things that contradict what others know is true about

self-reflection

Recall an embarrassing interpersonal encounter. How did you try to restore your lost face? Were you successful? If you could relive the encounter, what would you say and do differently?

---

[3]All the information that follows regarding how to successfully maintain face is adapted from Goffman (1955).

you, they'll see your face as false. For example, if your neighbor already knows you don't like them, they are likely to be skeptical the next time you warmly greet them and adopt the face of "friendly, caring neighbor."

Finally, for your face to be maintained, realize that your communication and behavior are influenced by factors over which you have only limited control, such as objects and events in the surrounding environment. For example, imagine that your romantic partner—who serves in the military—has recently been deployed overseas. The two of you agree to video chat when you can, and your first scheduled chat is Friday at 5 p.m. But when you're driving home Friday afternoon, your car breaks down. Making things worse, your phone goes dead because you forgot to charge it, so there is no way to contact your partner. By the time you get home and online, your partner has already signed off, leaving a perplexed message regarding your "neglect." To restore face, you'll need to explain what happened.

Of course, all of us fall from grace on occasion. What can you do to regain face following an embarrassing incident? Promptly acknowledge that the event happened, admit responsibility for any of your actions that contributed to the event, apologize for your actions and for disappointing others, and move to maintain your face again. Apologies are fairly successful at reducing people's negative impressions and the anger that may have been triggered, especially when such apologies avoid excuses that contradict what people know really happened (Ohbuchi & Sato, 1994). People who deny their inconsistencies or who blame others for their lapses are judged much more harshly.

DISCLOSING YOUR PRIVATE SELF

In Greta Gerwig's award-winning 2017 film *Lady Bird*, the title character is a teen struggling with who she is and what she wants out of life. Although Christine "Lady Bird" McPherson shares many points of connection with her mother—including their shared loved of their hometown, Sacramento— her mother's relentless criticism causes even casual interactions to escalate into conflict. Their relationship is further fractured when Lady Bird accepts admission to an East Coast university without having told her mom that she applied out-of-state. Heartbroken that her daughter will soon be leaving, her mother struggles to share her feelings with Lady Bird by writing a letter—but ends up throwing multiple failed attempts into the trash. In the closing scenes, Lady Bird's father shares with Lady Bird her mother's discarded letter drafts—which he retrieved from the garbage—and Lady Bird calls her mother, leaving a voice mail. "Hey Mom, did you feel emotional, the first time you drove in Sacramento? I did, and I wanted to tell you, but we weren't really talking when it happened. All those bends I've known my whole life, and stores, and . . . the whole thing. But I wanted to tell you . . . *I love you. Thank you.*"

◢ Lady Bird and her mother continually struggle to communicate their true feelings to each other. Have you ever been in a relationship where you had difficulty expressing yourself? Lifestyle pictures/Alamy

Self-Disclosure   We all can think of situations in which we've struggled with sharing deeply personal feelings, thoughts, or experiences with others, like Lady Bird and her mother. Revealing private information about ourselves is known as **self-disclosure** (Wheeless, 1978), and it plays a critical role in interpersonal communication and relationship development. According to the **interpersonal process model of intimacy**, the closeness we feel toward others in our relationships is created through two things: self-disclosure and the responsiveness of listeners to our disclosure (Reis & Patrick, 1996). Relationships are intimate when *both* partners share private information with each other and each partner responds to the other's disclosures with understanding, caring, and support (Reis & Shaver, 1988).

Four practical implications flow from this model. First, like Lady Bird and her mother, you can't have intimacy in a relationship without disclosure and supportiveness. If you, like Lady Bird, view a friend, family member, or lover as being nonreceptive or nonsupportive, your relationship with that person will be less intimate as a result. Second, if listeners are nonsupportive *after* a disclosure, the impact on intimacy can be devastating. Think about an instance in which you shared something personal with a friend, but they responded by ridiculing or judging you. How did this reaction make you feel? Chances are it substantially widened the emotional distance between the two of you. Third, just because you share your thoughts and feelings with someone doesn't mean that you have an intimate relationship. For example, if you regularly chat with a classmate and tell them all your secrets, but they never do the same in return, your relationship isn't intimate, it's one-sided. In a similar fashion, tweeting or posting personal thoughts and feelings and having people read them don't create intimate relationships. Intimacy only exists when *both* people share with and support each other.

And finally, not all disclosures boost intimacy. Research suggests that one of the most damaging events that can happen in interpersonal relationships is a partner's sharing information that the other person finds inappropriate and perplexing (Planalp & Honeycutt, 1985). This is especially true in relationships where partners are already struggling with a challenging problem or experiencing a painful transition. For example, during divorce proceedings, parents commonly disclose negative and demeaning information about each other to their children. The parents may see this sharing as stress-relieving or "cathartic" (Afifi et al., 2007), but these disclosures only intensify the children's mental and physical distress and make them feel caught between their two parents (Koerner et al., 2002).

Differences in Disclosure   Researchers have conducted thousands of self-disclosure studies over the past 40 years (Tardy & Dindia, 1997). These studies suggest four important facts regarding how people self-disclose.

First, in any culture, people vary widely in the degree to which they self-disclose. Some people are naturally transparent, whereas others are more opaque (Jourard, 1964). Trying to force someone who has a different idea of self-disclosure than yours to open up or be more discreet not only is presumptuous but can damage the relationship (Luft, 1970).

Second, people disclose differently online than they do face-to-face, and such differences depend on the intimacy of the relationship. When people are first getting to know each other, they typically disclose more quickly, broadly, and deeply when interacting online than face-to-face. One reason for this is that online encounters lack nonverbal cues (like tone of voice and facial expressions), so the consequences of such disclosure seem less noticeable, and words take on more importance and intensity than those exchanged during face-to-face interactions (Joinson, 2001). The result is that we often overestimate the intimacy of

launchpadworks.com

Self-Disclosure
Watch this clip online to answer the questions below.

Do you ever find it easier to self-disclose to a stranger? Why or why not? How much self-disclosure do you expect from a close friend, and when, if ever, is it too much?

online interactions and relationships with acquaintances or strangers. However, as relationships mature and intimacy increases, the relationship between the modality of communication and disclosure reverses. Individuals in close relationships typically use online communication for more trivial exchanges (such as coordinating schedules, updating each other on mundane daily events), and reserve their deeper, more meaningful discussions for when they are face-to-face (Ruppel, 2014).

To help ensure competent online disclosure, scholar Malcolm Parks offers the following advice: Be wary of the emotionally seductive qualities of online interaction. Disclose information slowly and with caution. Remember that online communication is both public and permanent; hence, secrets that you tweet, post, text, or email *are no longer secrets*. Few experiences in the interpersonal realm are more uncomfortable than "post-cyber-disclosure panic"—that awful moment when you wonder who else might be reading the innermost thoughts you just revealed in an email or a text message to a friend (Barnes, 2001).

Third, self-disclosure appears to promote mental health and relieve stress (Tardy, 2000). When the information is troubling, keeping it inside can escalate your stress levels substantially, resulting in problematic mental and physical symptoms and ailments (Kelly & McKillop, 1996; Pennebaker, 1997). Of course, the flip side of disclosing troubling secrets to others is that people might react negatively and you might become more vulnerable.

Finally, and importantly, little evidence exists that supports the stereotype that men can't disclose their feelings in relationships. In close same-sex friendships, for example, both men and women disclose deeply and broadly (Shelton et al., 2010). And in cross-sex romantic involvements, men often disclose at levels equal to or greater than their female partners (Canary et al., 1997). At the same time, however, both men and women feel more comfortable disclosing to female than to male recipients (Dindia & Allen, 1992). Teenagers are more likely to disclose to mothers and best female friends than to fathers and best male friends—suggesting that adolescents may perceive females as more empathetic and understanding than males (Garcia & Geisler, 1988).

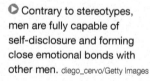

Contrary to stereotypes, men are fully capable of self-disclosure and forming close emotional bonds with other men. diego_cervo/Getty Images

THE RELATIONAL SELF

One of the reasons we carefully craft the presentation of our self is to create inter-personal relationships. We present our self to acquaintances, coworkers, friends, family members, and romantic partners, and through our interpersonal communi-cation, relationships are fostered, maintained, and sometimes ended. Within each of these relationships, how close we feel to one another is defined largely by how much of our self we reveal to others, and vice versa.

Managing the self in interpersonal relationships isn't easy. Exposing our self to others can make us feel vulnerable, provoking tension between how much to reveal versus how much to veil. Even in the closest of relationships, certain aspects of the self remain hidden—from our partners as well as ourselves.

Opening Your Self to Others   In the movie *Shrek*, the ogre Shrek forges a friend-ship with a likable but occasionally irksome donkey (Adamson & Jenson, 2001). As their acquaintanceship deepens to friendship, Shrek tries to explain the nature of his inner self to his companion:

> **SHREK:** For your information, there's a lot more to ogres than people think!
> **DONKEY:** Example . . . ?
> **SHREK:** Example . . . OK . . . Um . . . Ogres . . . are like onions.
> **DONKEY:** They stink?
> **SHREK:** Yes . . . NO!
> **DONKEY:** Or they make you cry?
> **SHREK:** No!
> **DONKEY:** Oh . . . You leave 'em out in the sun and they get all brown and start sprouting little white hairs!
> **SHREK:** No! Layers! Onions have layers—OGRES have layers! Onions have layers! You get it!? We both have layers!
> **DONKEY:** Ooohhhh . . . you both have layers . . . oh. You know, not everybody likes onions . . . CAKE! Everybody loves cakes! Cakes have layers!

Shrek was not the first to use the onion as a metaphor for self. In fact, the idea that revealing the self to others involves peeling back or penetrating layers was first

◐ Shrek at first appears to be a grumpy, unsociable loner—but over the course of his adventure with Donkey, more layers of his personality are revealed. Can you think of a time in your life when someone was not who they initially seemed to be? Dreamworks Llc/ Kobal/REX/Shutterstock

suggested by psychologists Irwin Altman and Dalmas Taylor (1973) in their **social penetration theory**. Like Shrek, Altman and Taylor envisioned the self as an "onion-skin structure," consisting of sets of layers.

At the *outermost, peripheral layers* of your self are demographic characteristics such as birthplace, age, gender, and ethnicity (see Figure 2.3). Discussion of these characteristics dominates first conversations with new acquaintances: What's your name? What's your major? Where are you from? In the *intermediate layers* reside your attitudes and opinions about music, politics, food, entertainment, and other such matters. Deep within the "onion" are the *central layers* of your self—core characteristics such as self-awareness, self-concept, self-esteem, personal values, fears, and distinctive personality traits. We'll discuss these in more detail in Chapter 3.

The notion of layers of self helps explain the development of interpersonal relationships, as well as how we distinguish between casual and close involvements. As relationships progress, partners communicate increasingly personal information to each other. This allows them to mutually penetrate each other's peripheral, then intermediate, and finally central selves. Relationship development is like slowly pushing a pin into an onion: it proceeds layer by layer, without skipping layers.

The revealing of selves that occurs during relationship development involves both breadth and depth. *Breadth* is the number of different aspects of self each partner reveals at each layer—the insertion of more and more pins into the onion, so to speak. *Depth* involves how deeply into each other's self the partners have penetrated: Have you revealed only your peripheral self, or have you given the other person access into your intermediate or central selves as well?

Although social penetration occurs in all relationships, the rate at which it occurs isn't consistent. For example, some people let others in quickly, while others never grant access to certain elements of their selves no matter how long they know a person. The speed with which people grant each other access to the broader and deeper aspects of their selves depends on a variety of factors, including the attachment styles discussed earlier in the chapter. But in all relationships, depth and

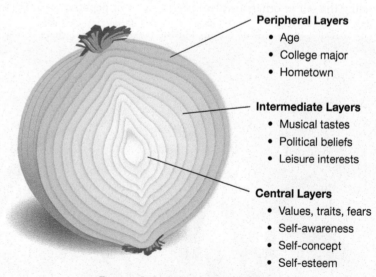

Peripheral Layers
- Age
- College major
- Hometown

Intermediate Layers
- Musical tastes
- Political beliefs
- Leisure interests

Central Layers
- Values, traits, fears
- Self-awareness
- Self-concept
- Self-esteem

figure 2.3 **The Layers of Self**

breadth of social penetration are intertwined with **intimacy**: the feeling of closeness and union that exists between us and our partners (Mashek & Aron, 2004). The more deeply and more broadly we penetrate into each other's selves, the more intimacy we feel; the more intimacy we feel, the more we allow each other access to broad and deep aspects of our selves (Shelton et al., 2010).

Your Hidden and Revealed Self   The image of self and relationship development offered by social penetration theory suggests a relatively straightforward, linear evolution of intimacy, with partners gradually penetrating broadly and deeply into each other's selves over time. But in thinking about our selves and our relationships with others, two important questions arise: First, are we really aware of all aspects of our selves? Second, are we willing to grant others access to all aspects of our selves?

We can explore possible answers to these questions by looking at the model of the relational self called the Johari window (see Figure 2.4), which suggests that some "quadrants" of our selves are open to self-reflection and sharing with other people, while others remain hidden—to both ourselves and others.

During the early stages of an interpersonal relationship and especially during first encounters, our *public area* of self is much smaller than our hidden area. As relationships progress, partners gain access to broader and deeper information about their selves; consequently, the public area expands, and the *hidden area* diminishes. The Johari window provides us with a useful alternative metaphor to social penetration. As relationships develop, we don't just let people "penetrate inward" to our central selves; we let them "peer into" more panes of the window, or parts of our selves, by revealing information that we previously hid from them.

Online Self-Quiz: Discover Your Attachment Style. To take this self-quiz, visit LaunchPad: **launchpadworks.com**

self-reflection

Consider your "blind area" of self. What strengths might you possess that you don't recognize? What character flaws might exist that don't mesh with your self-concept? How can you capitalize on these strengths and mend your flaws so that your interpersonal communication and relationships improve?

Quadrant I	Quadrant II
Public Area	**Blind Area**
Aspects of your self that you and others are aware of. Includes everything you openly disclose— from music and food preferences to religious beliefs and moral values.	Facets of your self that are readily apparent to others through your interpersonal communication but that you're not aware of. Includes strengths that you may not see in yourself or character flaws that don't mesh with your self-concept.
Quadrant III	**Quadrant IV**
Hidden Area	**Unknown Area**
Parts of your self that you're aware of but that you hide from most others. These include destructive thoughts, impulses, fantasies, and disturbing life experiences that don't fit comfortably with your public self or your own self-concept.	Aspects of your self that you and others aren't aware of, such as unconscious motives and impulses that strongly influence your interpersonal communication and relationships. While you can't gain access to your unknown area through critical self-reflection, you can indirectly infer aspects of your unknown area by observing consistent patterns in your own behavior.

figure 2.4 **The Johari Window**

As our interpersonal relationships develop and we increasingly share previously hidden information with our partners, our unknown and blind quadrants remain fairly stable. By their very nature, our unknown areas remain unknown throughout much of our lives. And for most of us, the blind area remains imperceptible. That's because our blind areas are defined by our deepest-rooted beliefs about ourselves—those beliefs that make up our self-concepts. Consequently, when others challenge us to open our eyes to our blind areas, we resist.

To improve our interpersonal communication, we must be able to see into our blind areas and then address the aspects within them that lead to incompetent communication and relationship challenges. But this isn't easy. After all, how can you correct misperceptions about yourself that you don't even know exist or flaws that you consider your greatest strengths? Delving into your blind area means challenging fundamental beliefs about yourself—subjecting your self-concept to hard scrutiny. The goal of this is to overturn your most treasured personal misconceptions. Most people accomplish this only over a long period of time and with the assistance of trustworthy and willing relationship partners.

COMPETENTLY DISCLOSING YOUR SELF

Based on all we know about self-disclosure, how can you improve your disclosure skills? Consider these recommendations for competent self-disclosure:

- **Follow the advice of Apollo: know your self.** Before disclosing, make sure that the aspects of your self you reveal to others are aspects that you want to reveal and that you feel certain about. This is especially important when disclosing intimate feelings, such as romantic interest. When you disclose feelings about others directly to them, you affect their lives and relationship decisions. Consequently, you're ethically obligated to be certain about the truth of your own feelings before sharing them with others.

- **Know your audience.** Whether it's an Instagram post or an intimate face-to-face conversation with a friend, think carefully about how others will perceive your disclosure and how it will impact their thoughts and feelings about you. If you're unsure of the appropriateness of a disclosure, don't disclose. Instead of disclosing, talk more generally about the issue or topic first, gauging the person's level of comfort with the conversation before revealing deeper information.

- **Don't force others to self-disclose.** We often presume it's good for people to open up and share their secrets, particularly those that are troubling them. Although it's perfectly appropriate to let someone know you're available to listen, it's unethical and destructive to force or cajole others into sharing information against their will. People have reasons for not wanting to tell you things—just as you have reasons for protecting your own privacy.

- **Avoid gender stereotypes.** Don't fall into the trap of thinking that because someone is a woman she will disclose freely, or that because he's a man he's incapable of discussing his feelings. Men and women are more similar than different when it comes to disclosure. At the same time, be mindful of the tendency to feel more comfortable disclosing to women. Don't presume that because you're talking with a woman, it's appropriate for you to freely disclose.

- **Be sensitive to cultural differences.** When interacting with people from different backgrounds, disclose gradually. As with gender, avoid stereotypes. Don't presume disclosure patterns based on someone's culture.

- **Go slowly.** Share intermediate and central aspects of your self gradually and only after thorough discussion of peripheral information. Moving too quickly to discussion of your deepest fears, self-esteem concerns, and personal values not only increases your sense of vulnerability but also may make others uncomfortable enough to avoid you.

Now that we have explored how we present our public selves and disclose our private selves, let's consider another facet of how we communicate self, namely, how we present ourselves through social media.

The Social Media Self

Communicating competently on social media

In July 2017, we finally—after several years—tackled the long-delayed project of cleaning out our garage. On the second day of this ordeal, Steve unearthed his long-lost compound bow, which he hadn't shot in years. Steve had never hunted, but for many years had enjoyed the meditative calm of archery. In the days that followed, he snuck away to the backyard, for brief breaks from our garage work, and worked on reclaiming his target-shooting chops. After one particularly successful round, he took a selfie, which he then posted on social media. That's when the fun began. Many people "liked" the post; commenting on how it broadened their view of him ("I didn't know you shot bow!"). Others who saw the photo couldn't figure out what Steve was holding, prompting a lengthy, humorous thread regarding the nature of the "mystery object." Still others expressed criticism: "I didn't know you *hunted*!?" When Steve posted a response indicating that he *didn't* hunt, but that he just liked to target-shoot, his hunter friends pounced, posting, "What have you got against hunting?" Soon a social media scuffle arose on his pages regarding the morality of hunting. Disheartened that a simple selfie had caused such social media drama, Steve deleted the posts and hung his bow back up in the garage.

One of the most common ways we stay connected with each other is through social media, when we produce and share personal content online. Social media includes everything from social networking sites to virtual game worlds and blogs, and it's incredibly widespread: three and a half *billion* people engage in some form of social media (We Are Social, 2019). Thus, social media can be considered an integral part of most people's interpersonal lives, a "way of being" (Kuss & Griffiths, 2017).

SELF-PRESENTATION ON SOCIAL MEDIA

Given the universality of social media, it's no surprise that social networking sites have become *the* principal vehicles people use to express their identities to others. For people under the age of thirty, Instagram is the go-to site for self-presentation; more than 70 percent of young adults ages 18 to 24 years in the United States use Instagram on a regular basis (Smith & Anderson, 2018), and they do so because it's extremely flexible in allowing people to express their identities in multiple ways (Lee & Borah, 2020).

▶ Even seemingly innocent profile photos can cause controversy and drama, depending on how people perceive them. Courtesy of Steve McCornack.

Social media provides us with unique benefits and challenges for self-presentation. When you talk with others face-to-face, people judge your public self based on your words as well as your appearance—your age, gender, clothing, facial expressions, and so forth. Similarly, during a phone call, vocal cues—or how your voice sounds—help you and your conversation partner draw conclusions about each other. But on social media, these visual and vocal cues are radically restricted and more easily controlled. We carefully craft our photos and edit our tweets, texts, emails, and profile descriptions. We selectively self-present in ways that make us look good, without having to worry about verbal slipups or uncontrollable nervous habits (Parks, 2007).

People routinely present themselves on social media, through photos and written descriptions, in ways that amplify positive personality characteristics such as warmth, friendliness, and extraversion (Vazire & Gosling, 2004). Photos posted on social media typically show groups of friends, fostering the impression that the person in the photo is likable, fun, and popular (Ellison et al., 2007). These positive and highly selective depictions of self generally work as intended. Viewers of online profiles tend to form impressions of a profile's subject that match the subject's intended self-presentation (Gosling et al., 2007). So, for example, if you post profile photos and descriptions in an attempt to portray yourself as "entertaining" and "the life of the party," this is the self that others will likely perceive.

Arguably the most impactful and popular means of self-presentation on social media is the **selfie**: a positive photo of oneself taken by oneself (Hong et al., 2020). Selfie-taking and selfie-sharing are among the most frequent social media activities, as they fulfill multiple interpersonal needs simultaneously: self-exploration, attention-seeking, and the gathering of favorable feedback from peers and strangers (Boursier et al., 2020). Because eliciting direct, positive feedback ("You are AWESOME") is crucial, selfie-posting ends up being an interactive and interpersonal activity (Sung et al., 2016). Amongst teens, girls report more frequently sharing selfies, are more likely to use selfies as profile pictures, and experience more anxiety than boys about how selfies will be perceived—and possibly downloaded, altered, and reposted elsewhere (Boursier et al., 2020). This exemplifies the way in which gender socialization for women tends to emphasize appearance, as discussed earlier in this chapter.

The freedom that social media affords us in crafting our selves comes with an associated cost: unless you have met someone in person, you will have difficulty determining whether their social media self is authentic or a mask. Through misleading profile descriptions, fake or altered selfies, and phony screen names, people posting on social media can assume identities that would be impossible for them to maintain in offline encounters (Rintel & Pittam, 1997). On online dating sites, for example, people routinely distort their self-presentations in ways designed to make them more attractive (Ellison et al., 2006).

EVALUATING SOCIAL MEDIA SELF-PRESENTATIONS

Because of the pervasiveness of online masks, people often question the truthfulness of social media self-presentations, especially overly positive or flattering ones. *Warranting theory* suggests that when assessing someone's social media self-descriptions, we consider the **warranting value** of the information presented—that is, the degree to which the information is supported by other people and outside evidence (Walther et al., 2008; Walther & Parks, 2002). Information that was obviously crafted by the person, that isn't supported by others, and that can't be verified offline has *low warranting value*, and most people wouldn't trust it. Information that's created or supported by others and that can be readily verified through alternative sources on- and offline has *high warranting value* and is consequently perceived as valid. So, for example, news about a professional accomplishment that you tweet or post on Facebook will have low warranting value. But if the same information is also featured on your employer's website, its warranting value will increase. Similarly, selfies will have less warranting value than similar photos of you taken and posted by others, especially if the photos are perceived as having been taken without your knowledge, such as candid shots. Not surprisingly, the warranting value of social media self-descriptions plummets when they are directly *contradicted* by others in comment threads or posts.

Research shows that when friends, family members, coworkers, or romantic partners post information on your social media, their messages shape others' perceptions of you *more powerfully than your own posts do*, especially when their posts contradict your self-description. This holds true not just for personality characteristics such as extraversion (how outgoing you are) but also for physical attractiveness. One study of Facebook profiles found that when friends posted things like "If only I was as hot as you" or (alternatively) "Don't pay any attention to those jerks at the bar last night; beauty is on the inside," such comments influenced others' perceptions of the person's attractiveness more than the person's own description did (Walther et al., 2008).

---

self-reflection

Have you ever distorted your self-presentation online to make yourself appear more attractive and appealing? If so, was this ethical? What were the consequences—for yourself and others—of creating this online mask?

The evaluative judgments people make regarding our social media selves extend to selfies as well, as evidenced by the story of Steve's selfie with his compound bow. People view the selfies of others as a gateway into understanding who the person thinks they are (Sung et al., 2016). Selfies that provide information about the person's professional or personal activities and interests—such as while at work, exercising at the gym, or studying at the library—result in stronger positive evaluations and more "likes" than do close-up shots that lack background information. However, when viewers perceive that the selfie was taken with a particular *persuasive* intention—such as creating an impression of the person that isn't authentic—it can trigger strong negative reactions, including the loss of trust. This is especially the case when selfies are altered through the use of enhanced colors or "beauty filters" in an attempt to make the person seem more attractive than they're known to be. Excessive modifications of selfies in these ways can even trigger judgments of narcissism, especially if the person posts such images repeatedly (Hong et al., 2020).

IMPROVING YOUR SOCIAL MEDIA SELF-PRESENTATION

Taken as a whole, research and theory suggest four practices for improving your social media self-presentation. First, keep in mind that social media is dominated by visual information, such as text, photos, and videos. Consider carefully the words and images you select to present your self to others. When you post selfies, try to have them include information about the situation you were in when the photo was taken, to help garner a broader impression of who you are as a person. For example, many women managers know they're more likely than their male peers to be judged solely on appearance, so they post photos of themselves within settings that convey professionalism, such as an office or in front of a book shelf (Miller & Arnold, 2001). And avoid altering your selfies through the use of beauty filters or other digital enhancements that change the way you look.

Second, always remember the important role that warranting value plays in shaping others' impressions of you. The simple rule is that *what others say about you on social media is more important than what you say about yourself.* Consequently, be wary of allowing messages, posts, or links from others on your social media that contradict the self you want to present, or that cast you in a negative light—even if you think such content is cute, funny, or provocative. When friends, family members, coworkers, or romantic partners post information about you that disagrees with how you wish to be seen, you can (politely) ask them to delete it.

Third, subject your social media self-presentation to what we call *the interview test*: Ask yourself, "Would I feel comfortable sharing all elements of this presentation—photos, personal profiles, videos, blogs—in a job interview?" If your answer is no, modify your current social media self-presentation immediately. In a survey of 1,200 human resources professionals and recruiters, 78 percent reported using search engines to screen candidates, while 63 percent reported perusing social networking sites (Balderrama, 2010).

Finally, reflect on the amount of time you spend online, consuming social media, and comparing and curating your self-presentation. Research has found a clear link between how much social media people consume and their likelihood of experiencing loneliness and depression. Consequently, scholars recommend that we limit our time on social media in order to improve our overall well-being (Hunt et al., 2018).

skills practice

Your Social Media Self
Maintaining your desired face on social media

❶ Describe your desired social media face (e.g., "I want to be seen as popular, adventurous, and attractive").

❷ Critically compare this description with your profiles, photos, and posts. Do they match?

❸ Revise or delete content that doesn't match your desired face.

❹ Repeat this process for friends' posts on your personal pages.

❺ In your future social media communication, present yourself only in ways that mesh with your desired face.

Improving Your Self

The self constantly evolves

One of the greatest gifts we possess is our capacity for self-awareness. Through self-awareness, we can ponder the kind of person we are, what we're worth, where we come from, and how we can improve. We can craft face and strive to maintain it. We can openly disclose some aspects of our selves and protect other aspects. And all the while, we can stand apart from our selves, critically reflecting on our interpersonal communication and relationship decisions: Was I right or was I wrong?

At the same time, we're often hampered by the beliefs, attitudes, and values we hold about our selves. Our self-concepts can trap us in destructive self-fulfilling prophecies. Whether imposed by gender, culture, or family, the standards we embrace suggesting who we should be are often unattainable. When we inevitably fall short of these standards, we condemn our selves, destroying our own self-esteem.

But our selves are not static. We constantly evolve, so we always have the opportunity to improve our selves and enhance our interpersonal communication and relationships. Through dedicated and focused effort, we can learn to avoid destructive self-fulfilling prophecies and resolve discrepancies between our self-concepts and standards that damage our self-esteem. We can also maintain face and disclose our selves competently to others. The starting point for improving our selves is the same as it ever was, summed up in the advice mythically offered to Chilon by Apollo: know thyself.

○ A key part of understanding and improving your self is to practice critical self-reflection by analyzing what you are thinking and feeling, why, and how this is influencing your communication. This can help you improve your communication and your relationships. Barack Obama took time for reflection in the Oval Office during his presidency.

White House Photo by Pete Souza

Workplace Self-Disclosure

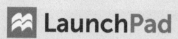 **LaunchPad** For the best experience, complete all parts of this activity in LaunchPad: **launchpadworks.com**

1 Background

Workplace connections are essential to happiness and success on the job. But they can also be tricky, especially when it comes to disclosing personal information. To understand how you might competently manage such a relationship challenge, read the case study in Part 2; then, drawing on all you know about interpersonal communication, work through the problem-solving model in Part 3.

 Visit LaunchPad to watch the video in Part 4 and assess your communication in Part 5.

2 Case Study

You and Jonathan are friendly work rivals. Jonathan is very competitive and always tries to outperform you. At the same time, he has been a reliable workplace friend who goes out of his way to assist you. For instance, several times when you got behind on projects, he stepped in to help you out so that you could make your deadlines. You appreciate Jonathan as a colleague but also as a friend whose company you've come to enjoy.

Your rivalry with Jonathan heated up last year, when you were both up for the same promotion. Jonathan really wanted it; you ended up getting it. In the aftermath, he congratulated you but was visibly upset for several weeks, and your interactions with him during that period were strained.

One of your new job responsibilities is mentoring new hires, and you are assigned to mentor Lennon. Within a few days, it becomes clear that you and Lennon are romantically attracted to each other. This is a problem because your workplace has strict rules about employee romances, particularly across status lines. At the same time, you're not *technically* Lennon's

supervisor, and Lennon will be assigned to a different unit when your mentorship ends.

The two of you start secretly dating. You're nervous because your supervisor Sharon is a stickler about company policies. You two are careful to mask your feelings while you're at work, but it's difficult. You're fairly sure that a few of your colleagues are whispering behind your back. On the other hand, the "forbidden" nature of your affair adds to the passion!

A few days later, you join Jonathan for lunch. He smiles and asks, "So, how long have you been dating Lennon?" When you dodge the question, he says, "Don't worry, I won't say a word!" You decide to disclose the truth because you've been dying to tell someone and you know you can trust him.

The following Monday, Sharon demands to see you in her office. She tells you that she has determined you have violated company policy regarding romantic relationships, and as a result, she is letting you go. Returning to your office in shock, you cross paths with Jonathan, who takes one look at your face and asks what happened. When you tell him, he gives you a hug and says, "This is terrible! How could this have happened?!"

③ Your Turn

Consider all you've learned thus far about interpersonal communication. Then work through the following five steps. Remember, there are no "right" answers, so think hard about what is the *best* choice! (P.S. Need help? See the *Helpful Concepts* list.)

step 1

Reflect on yourself. What are your thoughts and feelings in this situation? What assumptions are you making about Jonathan and his behavior? About your other colleagues? Are your assumptions accurate?

step 2

Reflect on your partner. Put yourself in Jonathan's shoes. What is he thinking and feeling in this situation? What about your other colleagues?

step 3

Identify the optimal outcome. Think about your communication and relationship with Jonathan and all that has happened. What's the best, most constructive outcome possible? Consider what's best for you and for Jonathan.

step 4

Locate the roadblocks. Taking into consideration your own and Jonathan's thoughts and feelings and all that has happened in this situation, what obstacles are preventing you from achieving the optimal outcome?

step 5

Chart your course. What can you say to Jonathan to overcome the roadblocks you've identified and achieve your optimal outcome?

HELPFUL CONCEPTS

Face and masks, **42–44**
Maintaining face, **42–44**
Recommendations for competent
　self-disclosure, **50–51**

④ The Other Side

Visit LaunchPad to watch a video in which Jonathan tells his side of the case study story. As in many real-life situations, this is information to which you did not have access when you were initially crafting your response in Part 3. The video reminds us that even when we do our best to offer competent responses, there is always another side to the story that we need to consider.

⑤ Interpersonal Competence Self-Assessment

After watching the video, visit the Self-Assessment questions in LaunchPad. Think about the new information offered in Jonathan's side of the story and all you've learned about interpersonal communication. Drawing on this knowledge, revisit your earlier responses in Part 3 and assess your interpersonal communication competence.

POSTSCRIPT

Photo by Scott Rosenfeld

Look again at the painting *labeled*. Note that this work of art isn't simply a portrait of the pain and isolation felt by one artist with dyslexia. It embraces all of us. We've all had fingers pointed and names hurled at us.

What metaphorical fingers point at you? Are some of those fingers your own? What names go with them? How do these shape the ways in which you communicate with others and make choices in your relationships?

This chapter began with a self-portrait of suffering—an artist stigmatized in youth by labels. But we can all draw inspiration from Eric Staib's story. Each of us possesses the uniquely human capacity to turn our personal punishments into profound gifts, just as Eric did.

 **LaunchPad**

LaunchPad for *Reflect & Relate* offers videos and encourages self-assessment through adaptive quizzing. Go to **launchpadworks.com** to get access to:

✓ LearningCurve
Adaptive Quizzes

▶ Video clips that help you understand interpersonal communication

key terms

self, 31
self-awareness, 31
 self-monitoring, 31
▶ social comparison, 32
self-concept, 32
looking-glass self, 33
self-concept clarity, 33
▶ self-fulfilling prophecies, 33
self-esteem, 34
self-discrepancy theory, 34
secure attachment, 39
preoccupied attachment, 40
dismissive attachment, 40
fearful attachment, 40
▶ mask, 42
▶ face, 42
embarrassment, 43
▶ self-disclosure, 45
interpersonal process model of intimacy, 45
social penetration theory, 48
intimacy, 49
selfie, 52
warranting value, 53

 You can watch brief, illustrative videos of these terms and test your understanding of the concepts in LaunchPad.

key concepts

The Components of Self

- The root source of all interpersonal communication is the **self**, an evolving composite of **self-awareness**, **self-concept**, and **self-esteem**.

- We make sense of ourselves and our communication by comparing our behaviors with those of others. **Social comparison** has a pronounced impact on our sense of self when the people to whom we're comparing ourselves are those we admire.

- Our **self-concept** is defined in part through our **looking-glass self**. When we have a clearly defined, consistent, and enduring sense of self, we possess **self-concept clarity**.

- And yet, sometimes a clear self-concept can lead us to develop **self-fulfilling prophecies** about our behavior.

- It is challenging to have positive self-esteem while living in a culture dominated by images of perfection. **Self-discrepancy theory** explains the link between these standards and our feelings about our selves, and ways we can overcome low self-esteem.

The Sources of Self

- When our families teach us gender lessons, they also create emotional bonds with us that form the foundation for various attachment styles, including **secure**, **preoccupied**, **dismissive**, and **fearful attachment**.

- Many of us identify with more than one culture and can be thrust into situations in which we must choose a primary cultural allegiance.

Communicating Your Self

- The **face** we present to others is the self that others perceive and evaluate. Sometimes our face reflects our inner selves, and sometimes we adopt **masks**.

- According to **social penetration theory**, we develop relationships by delving deeper and more broadly into different layers of self. The more we reveal, the more **intimacy** we feel with others.

- Revealing private information about ourselves to others is **self-disclosure**, which, along with the responsiveness of listeners to such disclosure, makes up the **interpersonal process model of intimacy**.

The Social Media Self

- Information posted about you online has higher **warranting value** than what you post directly.

3

Perceiving Others

We rely on perception constantly to make sense of everything and everyone in our environment.

Halfpoint/iStock/Getty Images

T he letter arrived just two weeks after we had moved our son into his dorm room at a small liberal arts college. It was from the school's president, and our first, somewhat tongue-in-cheek, thought was "Are they kicking him out already?" The letter wasn't about our son, however—it was about recent campus protests regarding the inclusiveness of the core curriculum. The eloquent note assured us that our son "was not having his educational experience compromised," but of course, the comforting intent of the letter rendered the *opposite* effect upon *us* as parents. We anxiously Googled his school to see what was happening. Sure enough, news outlets and social media were replete with stories detailing "radical student protests" resulting in "canceled classes" and likening our son's school to other campuses and communities where protests had been taking place.

Panicked, we Skyped our son. He surprised us with "Things here are GREAT!" Yes, he said, it was true that protests had erupted and classes *had* been affected. But he viewed the events as educational rather than disruptive: not only was he learning class content, but he also was witnessing, firsthand, transformative cultural change toward greater inclusiveness, through dialog and social activism.

What's more, the situation on campus was more complicated than its portrayal in news and social media. Tensions were being fueled by competing perceptions, and political commentators amplified these tensions by caricaturizing the situation and foisting false narratives upon it. Many pundits were perceptually framing the events as a "spontaneous revolt," pitting "students against faculty," and led by "spoiled

61

children complaining about nothing." Yet our son noted that the protests were led by dedicated students who were deeply concerned about social justice and a required curriculum that favored privileged viewpoints and underrepresented the voices of marginalized groups. Rather than being "students versus faculty," the perceptions of individual faculty and students varied widely. Most supported the protestors' *right* to dissent, but were divided regarding *how* they were doing it. And the issues at play had long been simmering: faculty and students had been working collaboratively to revise the core classes for more than a year. This effort had been triggered by research documenting a deep perceptual divide among students: although 70 percent of straight, white, cisgender male students reported enjoying the required content, only 30 percent of female students described it positively, and 47 percent of students of color and 75 percent of transgender students thought that core texts should be changed (Lydgate, 2017). Our son concluded: "The whole thing has been really cool—I've gotten to see all these different lenses through which people see the same situation!"

No sooner had we closed our Skype session than Steve's phone went off. It was his mother, extremely upset. "Oh, *Steven!*" she lamented, "*How* can you have a son at *that school!*? He's not one of *those protestors,* is he!?" When Steve tried to share his son's views of what was really happening, she interrupted. "There's *no* excuse for disrupting class! These kids today see everything so differently, I just can't understand it!"

People can experience the same events, yet live them in extraordinarily different ways. This is because everything we experience in the world around us is filtered through our own unique perceptual lenses. While information seems to enter our conscious minds clean and clear, what we *actually* see is refracted through our personal experiences and beliefs, and is interpreted based on the meanings we assign to people, their communication, and our relationships. We then look to these *mental creations*—not reality itself—to guide our interpersonal communication and relationship decisions.

These mental creations are shaped by both time and place. The United States, for example, is a culture originally founded upon, and filled with examples of, protest. From college campuses, to local communities and cities, protests have charted the course of the country. In his 1963 *Letter from a Birmingham Jail*, Dr. Martin Luther King Jr. wrote, "we are caught in an inescapable network of mutuality, tied in a single garment of destiny. Whatever affects one directly, affects all indirectly." Call to mind your mental images of social justice protests. Now consider how your mental images illustrate the "network of mutuality" about which King wrote. Each of us has our *direct* experiences—perceiving the world in ways that largely match our own beliefs, attitudes, and unique lived experiences. But *indirect* experiences—our perceptions about other people's beliefs, attitudes and experiences—also mold our mental images. If we focus only on our direct experiences, we can become tethered to our individual perspectives and miss the fact that other people's perceptions may be quite different. In our chapter opener, our son's firsthand campus experience informed his perspective on the student protests, which differed from his grandmother's perspective. To bridge perceptual divides, we first need to realize that we *all* share the flaws of human perceptual biases. Once we recognize our common perceptual limitations, we can move toward overcoming those limitations and understanding the interconnected network of mutuality about which King wrote—a network in which each of us can imagine what other people see, experience, and believe, and can conceive of how other people may be impacted, or impacted differently, by similar experiences.

We begin our studies of perception, and how *our communication behaviors are rooted in our perceptions*, by building on your Chapter 2 knowledge that your capacity for self-awareness can be honed by turning a critical lens inward upon yourself. We now turn the lens outward, examining how we make sense of the world around us, and how improved perception can make you a better interpersonal communicator. You'll learn:

- How the perception process unfolds, and which perceptual errors you need to watch for
- The influence of culture, gender, and personality in shaping your perception of others and your interpersonal communication
- How you form impressions of others, and the benefits and limitations of the methods you use
- Strategies for improving your perceptual accuracy

We begin by defining the components involved in the process of perception.

Perception as a Process

Perception helps us understand our world

The start point for understanding perception is the realization that it isn't one discrete event, but instead, a *process*. Specifically, **perception** is the process of selecting, organizing, and interpreting information from our senses. We rely on perception constantly to make sense of everything and everyone in our environment. Perception begins when we select information on which to focus our attention. We then organize the information into an understandable pattern inside our minds and interpret its meaning. Each activity influences the other: our mental organization of information shapes how we interpret it, and our interpretation of information influences how we mentally organize it. (See Figure 3.1.) Let's take a closer look at the perception process.

SELECTING INFORMATION

It's finals week, and you're in your room studying for a difficult exam. Exhausted, you decide to take a break and listen to some music. You don your headphones, press play, and close your eyes. Suddenly, you hear a noise. Startled, you open your

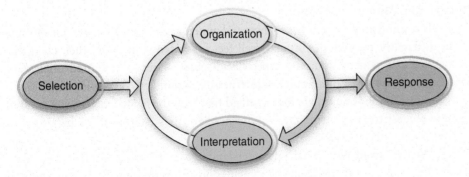

figure 3.1 **The Process of Perception**

eyes and remove your headphones to find that your housemate has just yanked open your bedroom door, snapping, "I've been yelling at you to pick up your phone for the last five minutes! What's going on?!"

The first step of perception, **selection**, involves focusing attention on certain sights, sounds, tastes, touches, or smells in our environment. Consider the housemate example. Once you hear their entry, you would likely select their communication as the focus of your attention. The degree to which particular people or aspects of their communication attract our attention is known as **salience** (Fiske & Taylor, 2017). When something is salient, it stands out relative to the setting you are in and your expectations, and is experienced as especially noticeable and significant. We view aspects of interpersonal communication as salient under three conditions (Fiske & Taylor, 1991). First, communication is salient if the communicator behaves in a visually and audibly stimulating fashion. A housemate yelling and energetically gesturing is more salient than a quiet, motionless housemate. Second, communication becomes salient if our goals or expectations lead us to view it as significant. Even a housemate's softly spoken phone announcement will command our attention if we are anticipating an important call. Last, communication that deviates from our expectations is salient. An unexpected verbal attack will always be more salient than an expected one.

ORGANIZING THE INFORMATION YOU'VE SELECTED

Once you've selected something as the focus of your attention, you take that information and structure it into a coherent pattern in your mind, a phase of the perception process known as **organization** (Fiske & Taylor, 1991). For example, imagine that a cousin is telling you about a recent visit to your hometown. As they share their story with you, you select certain bits of their narrative on which to focus your attention based on salience, such as their sighting of a mutual friend or visiting a favorite old hangout. You then organize your own representation of their story inside your head.

During organization, you engage in **punctuation**, structuring the information you've selected into a chronological sequence that matches how you experienced the order of events (Watzlawick et al., 1967). To illustrate punctuation, think about how you might punctuate the sequence of events in our housemate example. You hear a noise, open your eyes, see your housemate in your room, and then hear them yelling at you. But two people involved in the same interpersonal encounter may punctuate it in very different ways. Your housemate might punctuate the same incident by noting that your ringing phone in the common area disrupted their studying, and despite their efforts to get your attention, you never responded.

If you and another person organize and punctuate information from an encounter differently, the two of you may well feel frustrated with each other. Disagreements about punctuation, and especially disputes about who started unpleasant encounters, are a common source of interpersonal conflict (Watzlawick et al., 1967). For example, your housemate may contend that "you started it" because you ignored their request to get your phone. You may believe they "started it" by barging into your room without knocking.

We can avoid perceptual misunderstandings that lead to conflict by understanding how our organization and punctuation of information differ from those of

LaunchPad Video

launchpadworks.com

Punctuation
Watch this clip online to answer the questions below.

How does punctuation influence each person's perception and communication in the video? How might the previous communication between two people influence how each would punctuate a situation between a parent and a child or between romantic partners?

other people. One helpful way to forestall such conflicts is to practice asking others to share their views of encounters. You might say, "Here's what I saw, but that's my perspective. What do *you* think happened?"

INTERPRETING THE INFORMATION

As we organize information we have selected into a coherent mental model, we also engage in **interpretation**, assigning meaning to that information. We call to mind familiar information that's relevant to the current encounter, and use that information to make sense of what we're hearing and seeing. We also create explanations for why things are happening as they are.

Using Familiar Information We make sense of others' communication in part by comparing what we currently perceive with knowledge that we already possess. For example, when Steve proposed to Kelly, he surprised her after class. He had decorated her apartment with several dozen roses and carnations, was dressed in his best (and only!) suit, and was spinning "their song" on her turntable—the Spinners' "Could It Be I'm Falling in Love" (we LOVE the Spinners!). When she opened the door and he asked her to marry him, she immediately interpreted his communication correctly. But how, given that she had never been proposed to before? Because she knew from friends, family members, movies, and television shows what "a marriage proposal looks and sounds like." Drawing on this familiar information, she correctly figured out what he was up to and accepted his proposal.

The knowledge we draw on when interpreting interpersonal communication resides in **schemata**, mental structures that contain information defining the characteristics of various concepts, as well as how those characteristics are related to each other (Macrae & Bodenhausen, 2001). Each of us develops schemata for individual people, groups of people, places, events, objects, and relationships. In the previous example, Kelly had a schema (the singular form of *schemata*) for "marriage proposal" that enabled her to correctly interpret Steve's actions.

Because we use familiar information to make sense of current interactions, our interpretations reflect what we presume to be true. For example, suppose you're interviewing for a job with a manager who has been at the company for 18 years. You'll likely interpret everything they say in light of your knowledge about "long-term employees." This knowledge includes your assumption that "company veterans generally know insider information." So, when your interviewer talks in glowing terms about the company's future, you'll probably interpret their comments as credible. Now imagine that you receive the same information from someone who has been with the company only a few weeks. Based on your perception of this person as a "new employee" and on the information you have in your "new employee" schema, you may interpret this message as naïve speculation rather than expert commentary, even if their statements are accurate.

Creating Explanations In addition to drawing on our schemata to interpret information from interpersonal encounters, we create explanations for others' comments or behaviors, known as **attributions**. Attributions are our answers to the *why* questions we ask every day. "Why didn't my partner return my text message?" "Why did my best friend share that horrible, embarrassing photo of me on Instagram?"

Consider an example shared with us by a professor friend of ours, Sarah. She had finished teaching for the semester and was out of town and offline for a week.

self-reflection

Recall a conflict in which you and a friend disagreed about "who started it." How did you punctuate the encounter? How did your friend punctuate it? If each of you punctuated differently, how did those differences contribute to the conflict? If you could revisit the situation, what might you say or do differently to resolve the dispute?

table 3.1 **Internal versus External Attributions**

Communication Event	Internal Attribution	External Attribution
Your romantic partner doesn't reply after you send a flirtatious text message.	"My partner doesn't care about me."	"My partner is probably too busy to respond."
Your unfriendly coworker greets you warmly.	"My coworker is friendlier than I thought."	"Something unusual must have happened to make my coworker act so friendly."
Your friend ridicules your taste in music.	"My friend has an unpredictable mean streak."	"My friend must be having a really bad day."

When she returned home and logged on to her email, she found a week-old note from Janet, a student who had failed her course, asking Sarah if there was anything she could do to improve her grade. She also found a second email from Janet, dated a few days later, accusing Sarah of ignoring her:

> **FROM:** Janet [mailto:janet@school.edu]
> **SENT:** Friday, December 14, 2018 10:46 AM
> **TO:** Professor Sarah
> **SUBJECT:** FW: Grade
>
> Maybe my situation isn't a priority to you, and that's fine, but a response email would've been appreciated! Even if all you had to say was "there's nothing I can do." I came to you seeking help, not a handout!—Janet.[1]

Put yourself in Janet's shoes for a moment. What attributions did Janet make about Sarah's failure to respond? How did these attributions shape Janet's communication in her second email? Now consider this situation from Sarah's perspective. If you were in her shoes, what attributions would you make about Janet, and how would they shape how you interpreted her email?

Attributions take two forms, internal and external (see Table 3.1). *Internal attributions* presume that a person's communication or behavior stems from internal causes, such as character or personality. For example, "My professor didn't respond to my email because she doesn't care about students" or "Janet sent this message because she's rude." *External attributions* hold that a person's communication is caused by factors unrelated to personal qualities, such as situational or outside sources: "My professor didn't respond to my email because she's out of town and away from email" or "Janet sent this message because I didn't respond to her first message."

Like schemata, the attributions we make powerfully influence how we interpret and respond to others' communication. For example, if you think Janet's email was the result of her having a terrible day, you'll likely interpret her message as an understandable venting of frustration. If you think her message was caused by her personal rudeness, you'll probably interpret the email as inappropriate and offensive.

self-reflection

Recall a fight you've had with parents or other family members. Why did they behave as they did? What presumptions did they make about you and your behavior? When you assess both your and their attributions, are they internal or external? What does this tell you about the power and prevalence of the fundamental attribution error?

---

[1]This is an example email that a professional colleague contributed to the authors, with all identifying information removed to protect the identity of the student in question.

◁ People are especially susceptible to the fundamental attribution error when communicating electronically, as when texting. PhotoAlto/Eric Audras/Getty Images

Given the dozens of people with whom we communicate each day, it's not surprising that we often form invalid attributions. One common mistake is the **fundamental attribution error**, the tendency to attribute others' behaviors solely to internal causes (the kind of person they are), rather than to the social or environmental forces affecting them (Heider, 1958). For example, communication scholar Alan Sillars and his colleagues found that during conflicts between parents and teens, both parties fall prey to the fundamental attribution error (Sillars et al., 2010). Parents commonly attribute teens' communication to "lack of responsibility" and "desire to avoid the issue," whereas teens attribute parents' communication to "desire to control my life." All these assumptions are internal causes. These errors make it harder for teens and parents to constructively resolve their conflicts, something we discuss in more depth in Chapter 10.

The fundamental attribution error is so named because it is the most prevalent of all perceptual biases (Langdridge & Butt, 2004). Why does this error occur? Because when we communicate with others, they dominate our perception, becoming most salient to us. We often do not see the situational factors, including our own behavior, that may be causing their behavior. Consequently, when we make judgments about why someone is acting in a certain way, we overestimate the influence of the person and underestimate the significance of their immediate environment (Heider, 1958; Langdridge & Butt, 2004). This is especially the case when *we* behave in negative ways that trigger undesirable behavior in other people. In such instances, we often perceptually overlook our own actions, focusing exclusively on the dispositional attributes of the other person (Sillars & McLaren, 2015). For example, one study of university math and science teachers found that professors who engaged in poor teaching practices were more likely to erroneously blame their students' low performance on internal factors such as "lack of work ethic" and "limited intellectual ability" than were professors who were exceptional teachers (Wieman & Welsh, 2016).

The fundamental attribution error is especially common during online interactions (Shedletsky & Aitken, 2004). Because we aren't privy to the rich array of environmental factors that may be shaping our communication partners' messages—all we perceive is words on a screen—we're more likely to interpret others' communication as stemming solely from internal causes (Wallace, 1999). As a consequence, when a text

skills practice

Improving Online Attributions
Critically assessing your attributions while communicating online

❶ Identify a negative text, email, or social media message you've received.

❷ Consider why the person sent the message.

❸ Write a response based on this attribution, and save it as a draft.

❹ Think of and list other possible, external causes for the person's message.

❺ Keeping these alternative attributions in mind, revisit and reevaluate your response draft, editing it as necessary to ensure competence before you send or post it.

message, email, or social media post is even slightly negative in tone, we're very likely to blame that negativity on bad character or personality flaws. Such was the case when Sarah presumed that Janet was a rude person based on her email.

A related error is the **actor-observer effect**, the tendency to attribute other people's behaviors to their dispositions, while explaining our own behaviors according to situational or external factors (Fiske & Taylor, 2017). Because our mental focus during interpersonal encounters is on factors external to us—especially the person with whom we're interacting—we tend to credit these factors as causing our own communication. This is particularly prevalent during unpleasant or negative interactions. Our own impolite remarks during family conflicts, for example, are viewed as "reactions to their hurtful communication" rather than "messages caused by our own insensitivity."

However, we don't always make external attributions regarding our own behaviors. When we take credit for success, but deny responsibility for negative events or failures, we engage in the **self-serving bias**. Suppose you've successfully persuaded a

friend to lend you their car for the weekend. In this case, you will probably attribute this success to your charm and persuasive skill, rather than to luck or your friend's generosity. The self-serving bias is driven by *ego protection*: by crediting ourselves for our life successes, we can feel happier about who we are. Research shows that people have a strong tendency to engage in this bias, regardless of age, gender, or culture (Mezulis et al., 2004).

Clearly, attributions play a powerful role in how we interpret communication. For this reason, it's important to consider the attributions you make while you're interacting with others. Check your attributions frequently, watching for the fundamental attribution error, the actor-observer effect, and the self-serving bias. If you think someone has spoken to you in an offensive way, ask yourself if it's possible that outside forces—including *your own behavior*—could have caused the problem. Also keep in mind that communication (like other forms of human behavior) rarely stems from *only* external *or* internal causes. It's caused by a combination of both (Langdridge & Butt, 2004).

Finally, when you can, check the accuracy of your attributions by asking people for the reasons behind their behavior. When you've made attribution errors that lead you to criticize or lose your patience with someone else, apologize and explain your mistake to the person. After Janet learned that Sarah hadn't responded because she had been out of town and offline, Janet apologized. She also explained why her message was so terse: she thought Sarah was intentionally ignoring her. Upon receiving Janet's apology, Sarah apologized also. She realized that she, too, had succumbed to the fundamental attribution error by wrongly presuming that Janet was a rude person.

◁ When we are uncertain about other people's behavior, we can learn more about them by observing them, by asking their friends about them, or by interacting with them directly. This helps us make decisions about our future communication with them. (Top to bottom) RgStudio/Getty Images; Caiaimage/Robert Daly/Getty Images; David R. Frazier Photolibrary, Inc./Alamy

REDUCING UNCERTAINTY

When intercultural communication scholar Patricia Covarrubias was a young girl, she and her family immigrated to the United States from Mexico. On her first day of school in her adoptive country, Patricia's third-grade teacher, Mrs. Williams, led her to the front of the classroom to introduce her to her new classmates. Growing up in Mexico, her friends and family called her *la chiquita* (the little one) or *mi Rosita de Jerico* (my rose of Jericho), but in the more formal setting of the classroom, Patricia expected her teacher to introduce her as Patricia Covarrubias, or perhaps Patricia. Instead, Mrs. Williams, her hand gently resting on Patricia's shoulder, turned to the class and said, "Class, this is *Pat*."

Patricia was dumbfounded. In her entire life, she had never been Pat, nor could she understand why someone would call her Pat. As she explains, "In one unexpected moment, all that I was and had been was abridged into three-letter, bottom-line efficiency" (Covarrubias, 2000, pp. 10–11). And although Mrs. Williams was simply trying to be friendly—using a shortened name many people in the United States would consider informal—Patricia was mortified. The encounter bolstered her feeling that she was an outsider in an uncertain environment.

In most interpersonal interactions, the perception process unfolds in a rapid, straightforward manner. But sometimes we find ourselves in situations in which people communicate in perplexing ways. In such contexts, we experience *uncertainty*, the anxious feeling that comes about when we can't predict or explain someone else's communication.

Uncertainty is common during first encounters with new acquaintances, when we don't know much about the people with whom we're communicating. According to **Uncertainty Reduction Theory**, our primary compulsion during initial interactions is to reduce uncertainty about our communication partners by gathering enough information about them that their communication becomes predictable and explainable (Berger & Calabrese, 1975). When we reduce uncertainty, we're inclined to perceive people as attractive and likable, talk further, and consider forming relationships with them (Burgoon & Hoobler, 2002).

Uncertainty can be reduced in several ways, each of which has advantages and disadvantages (Berger & Bradac, 1982). First, you can observe how someone interacts with others. Known as *passive strategies*, these approaches can help you predict how someone may behave when interacting with you, thus reducing your uncertainty. Examples include observing them hanging out with friends at a party or checking out someone's Facebook profile. Second, you can try *active strategies* by asking other people questions about someone you're interested in. You might find someone who knows the person you're assessing and ask them to disclose as much information as possible about that individual. Be aware, though, that this approach poses risks: the target person may find out that you've been asking questions. That could embarrass you and upset the target. In addition, third-party information may not be accurate. Third, and perhaps most effective, are *interactive strategies*: starting a direct interaction with the person you're interested in. Inquire where they're from, what they do for a living, and about their interests. You should also disclose personal information about yourself. This enables you to test the other person's reactions to you. Is the person intrigued or bored? That information can help you reduce your uncertainty about how to communicate further.

self-reflection

When do you use passive strategies to reduce your uncertainty? Active strategies? Interactive strategies? Which do you prefer and why? What ethical concerns influence your own use of passive and active strategies?

Influences on Perception

Culture, gender, and personality affect perception

A sense of directness dominates the perceptual process. Someone says something to us, and with lightning speed we focus our attention, organize information, and interpret its meaning. Although this process seems unmediated, powerful forces outside our conscious awareness shape our perception during every encounter, whether we're communicating with colleagues, friends, family members, or lovers. Three of the most powerful influences on perception are culture, gender, and personality.

PERCEPTION AND CULTURE

Your cultural background influences your perception in at least two ways. Recall from Chapter 1 that *culture* is an established, coherent set of beliefs, attitudes, values, and practices shared by a large group of people. Whenever you interact with others, you interpret their communication in part by drawing on information from your schemata. But your schemata are filled with the beliefs, attitudes, and values you learned in your own culture (Gudykunst & Kim, 2003). Consequently, people raised in different cultures have different knowledge in their schemata, so they interpret one another's communication in very different ways. Competent interpersonal communicators recognize this fact. When necessary and appropriate, they check the accuracy of their interpretation by asking questions such as "I'm sorry, could you clarify what you just said?"

Second, culture affects whether you perceive others as similar to or different from yourself. When you grow up valuing certain cultural beliefs, attitudes, and values as your own, you naturally perceive those who share these with you as fundamentally similar to yourself—people you consider **ingroupers** (Allport, 1954). You may consider individuals from many different groups as your ingroupers as long as they share substantial points of cultural commonality with you, such as nationality, religious beliefs, ethnicity, socioeconomic class, or political views (Turner et al., 1987). In contrast, you may perceive people who aren't similar to yourself as **outgroupers**.

Perceiving others as ingroupers or outgroupers is one of the most important perceptual distinctions we make. We often feel passionately connected to our ingroups, especially when they are tied to central aspects of our self-concepts, such as sexual orientation, religious beliefs, or ethnic heritage. Consequently, we are more likely to give valued resources, such as money, time, and effort, to those who are perceived as ingroupers versus those who are outgroupers (Castelli et al., 2008). Basically, we like, and want to support, people who are "like" us.

We also are more likely to form positive interpersonal impressions of people we perceive as ingroupers (Giannakakis & Fritsche, 2011), including perceiving their communication as substantially more trustworthy, friendly, and honest than outgroupers' communication (Brewer & Campbell, 1976). Similarly, when we learn that ingroupers possess negative traits, such as stubbornness or narrow-mindedness, we're likely to dismiss the significance of this revelation, instead ascribing these traits to human nature (Koval et al., 2012). Discovering the same characteristics in outgroupers is likely to trigger a strong negative impression. And in cases where people communicate in rude or inappropriate ways, you're substantially more inclined to form negative, internal attributions if you perceive them as outgroupers (Brewer, 1999). So, for example, if a person wearing a baseball cap with your favorite team's logo says something rude to you, you might perceive them as an ingrouper and make an external attribution to excuse their rudeness. But if a person says something rude while wearing a cap of a rival team, you are more likely to perceive them as an outgrouper and make a negative attribution assigning personal blame.

self-reflection

Consider people in your life whom you view as outgroupers. What points of difference lead you to see them that way? How does their outgrouper status shape your communication toward them? Is there anything you could learn that would lead you to judge them as ingroupers?

How can we bridge these perceptual divides? Research suggests that trust of an outgroup can be enhanced by messages from other ingroup members that present positive information about an outgroup by disavowing negative information, such as one St. Louis Cardinals fan telling another that "Chicago Cubs fans are *not* losers" (Winter et al., 2020). Moreover, recall the limits of our perception and the ease of mistakenly categorizing people as ingroupers or outgroupers. Even if you initially perceive someone to be different from yourself, they may hold beliefs, attitudes, and values similar to your own. If you assume they're outgroupers based on surface-level differences, you may communicate with them in ways that are disrespectful and also prevent you from getting to know them better.

○ Despite popular beliefs, most researchers from communication and psychology argue that men and women are more similar than different in how they interpersonally communicate.
Fox Photos/Getty Images

PERCEPTION AND GENDER

Get your family or friends talking about gender differences, and chances are you'll hear many of them claim that men and women perceive interpersonal communication differently. Even though research across domains informs us that "behavioral differences between men and women have decreased in the last decades" (Krahé & Papakonstantinou, 2020), some people still may insist that "men are cool and logical," while "women see everything emotionally." The scientific relationship between gender and perception is much more complex. Consider research on brain differences between men and women. Historically, researchers have argued that men's and women's brains are substantially different, and that such differences mean that women can more accurately identify others' emotions, and score higher in language comprehension and vocabulary tests, than men (Schlaepfer et al., 1995). But more recent analyses call such sweeping generalizations into question. For example, neuroscience professor Lise Eliot and her colleagues compared 58 studies looking at the size of the amygdala, the portion of the brain responsible for emotion, empathy, aggression, and sexual arousal (Marwha et al., 2017). When controlling for the differential physical size of men versus women, they found little difference between the sexes. Based on these results, Dr. Eliot argues, "Despite the common impression that men and women are profoundly different, large analyses of brain measures are finding far more similarity than difference: there is no categorically 'male brain' or 'female brain,' and much more overlap than difference between genders for nearly all brain measures" (*Science Daily*, 2017, p. 1).

Research in communication and psychology is mostly consistent with this recent brain research. For example, Dan Canary, Tara Emmers-Sommer, and Sandra Faulkner (1997) reviewed data from over 1,000 gender studies and found that if you consider all the factors that influence our communication and compare their impact, only about 1 percent of people's communication behavior is caused by gender. They concluded that when it comes to interpersonal communication, "men and women respond in a similar manner 99% of the time" (p. 9). As linguist Deborah Cameron (2009) summarized, the effect of gender "on most measures of verbal ability is small or close to zero."

Despite the debate over differences, we know one thing about gender and perception for certain: people are socialized to *believe* that men and women communicate differently. Within Western cultures, people tend to believe that women talk more about their feelings than men do, talk about "less important" issues than men do (women "gossip," whereas men "discuss"), and generally talk more than men do (Spender, 1984). But in one of the best-known studies of this phenomenon, researchers found that this was more a matter of perception than real difference (Mulac et al., 1985). Two groups of participants were given the same speech. One group was told that a man had authored and presented the speech, while the other was told that a woman had written and given it. Participants who thought the speech was a woman's perceived it as having more "artistic quality." Those who believed it was a man's saw the speech as having more "dynamism." Participants also described the "man's" language as strong, active, and aggressive, and the "woman's" language as pleasing, sweet, and beautiful, despite the fact that the speeches were identical.

Given the tendency to presume broad gender differences in communication, can we improve the accuracy of our perception? Yes, if we challenge our assumptions about gender and if we remind ourselves that approaches to communication among people of different genders are more similar than different. The next time you find yourself thinking, "Oh, she said that because she's a woman" or "He sees things that way because he is a man," question your perception. Are these people really communicating differently because of their gender, or are you simply perceiving them as different based on *your* beliefs about their gender?

◁ Arthur and his friends exhibit a range of personality traits that influence how they perceive the world around them as well as how we perceive them. © 2000 Marc Brown Studios

PERCEPTION AND PERSONALITY

When you think about the star of a hit television show, a cartoon aardvark isn't usually the first thing to come to mind. But as any one of the millions of weekly viewers in 83 different countries will tell you, the appeal of PBS's *Arthur* is more than just the title character. It is the breadth of personalities displayed across the entire cast, allowing us to link each of them to people in our own lives. Sue Ellen loves art, music, and world culture, while the Brain is studious, meticulous, and responsible. Francine loves interacting with people, especially while playing sports, and Buster is laid-back, warm, and friendly to just about everyone. D.W. drives Arthur crazy with her moods, obsessions, and tantrums, while Arthur—at the center of it all—combines all these traits into one appealing, complicated package.

In the show *Arthur*, we see embodied in animated form the various dispositions that populate our real-world interpersonal lives. And when we think of these people and their personalities, visceral reactions are commonly evoked. We like, loathe, or even love people based on our perception of their personalities and how their personalities mesh with our own.

Clearly, personality shapes how we perceive others, but what exactly is it? **Personality** is an individual's characteristic way of thinking, feeling, and acting, based on the traits—enduring motives and impulses—that they possess (McCrae & Costa, 2001). While several contemporary approaches to assessing personality exist, one of the most prevalent is to describe personality according to five traits using the "Big Five" model (Feher & Vernon, 2020): openness to experience, conscientiousness, extraversion, agreeableness, and neuroticism (see Table 3.2). A simple way to remember them is the acronym *OCEAN*. The degree to which a person possesses each of the Big Five traits determines their personality (McCrae, 2001). These traits are not absolutes, and most people fall somewhere in the middle rather than at the extremes of each trait—for example, many people exhibit a combination of extraverted and introverted behaviors.

Prioritizing Our Own Traits When Perceiving Others Our perception of others is strongly guided by the personality traits we see in ourselves and how we evaluate these traits. If you're an extravert, for example, another person's extraversion becomes

self-reflection

What personality traits do you like in yourself? When you see these traits in others, how does that impact your communication with them? How do you perceive people who possess traits you don't like in yourself? How do these perceptions affect your relationships with them?

table 3.2 **The Big Five Personality Traits (OCEAN)**

Personality Trait	Description
Openness	The degree to which a person is willing to consider new ideas and take an interest in culture. People high in openness prefer novelty to familiarity, and they are more imaginative, creative, and interested in seeking out new experiences than those low in openness.
Conscientiousness	The degree to which a person is organized and persistent in pursuing goals. People high in conscientiousness are methodical, self-disciplined, well organized, and dutiful; those low in conscientiousness are less careful, less focused, and more easily distracted. Also known as *dependability*.
Extraversion	The degree to which a person is interested in regularly interacting with others and actively seeks out interpersonal encounters. People high in extraversion are outgoing and sociable, preferring large groups of people; those low in extraversion are quiet and reserved.
Agreeableness	The degree to which a person is trusting, friendly, unselfish, and cooperative. People low in agreeableness are aggressive, suspicious, and uncooperative. Also known as *friendliness*.
Neuroticism	The degree to which a person experiences negative thoughts about oneself. People high in neuroticism are prone to insecurity and emotional distress; people low in neuroticism are relaxed, less emotional, not easily upset, and less prone to distress. Also known as *emotional stability*.

Information from McCrae & Mõttus (2019).

salient to you when you're communicating with them. Likewise, if you pride yourself on being friendly, other people's friendliness becomes your perceptual focus.

But it's not just a matter of focusing on certain traits to the exclusion of others. We evaluate people positively or negatively in accordance with how we feel about our own traits. We typically like in others the same traits we like in ourselves, and we dislike in others the traits that we dislike in ourselves.

At the same time we perceive people through a filter of our own self-perception, we also tend to perceive our own unique traits more favorably than unique traits possessed by others—even romantic partners—an effect known as the **self-enhancement bias** (El-Alayli & Wynne, 2015). In a series of studies, researchers had partners in close relationships identify characteristics unique to themselves and unique to their partners—and then rate those sets of traits comparatively, in terms of "desirability." Individuals consistently rated their own unique traits as more desirable than their partners'.

To avoid preoccupation with your own traits, and a bias toward perceiving your traits as better than other people's traits, carefully observe how you focus on other people's traits and how your evaluation of these traits reflects your own feelings about yourself. Strive to perceive people broadly, taking into consideration all their traits and not just the positive or negative ones that you share. Then evaluate them and communicate with them independently of your own positive and negative self-evaluations.

Generalizing from the Traits We Know Another effect that personality has on perception is the presumption that because a person is high or low in a certain trait, they must be high or low in other traits. For example, say that we introduce you to a friend of ours, Shoshanna. Within the first minute of interaction, you perceive her as highly friendly. Based on your perception of her high friendliness, you'll likely also presume that she is highly extraverted, simply because high friendliness and high extraversion intuitively seem to go together. If people you've known in the past who were highly friendly and extraverted also were highly open, you may go further, perceiving Shoshanna as highly open as well.

Your perception of Shoshanna was created using **implicit personality theories**, personal beliefs about different types of personalities and the ways in which traits cluster together (Bruner & Taguiri, 1954). When we meet people for the first time, we use implicit personality theories to perceive just a little about an individual's personality and then presume a great deal more, making us feel that we know the person and helping to reduce uncertainty. At the same time, making presumptions about people's personalities is risky. Presuming that someone is high or low in one trait because they are high or low in others can lead you to communicate incompetently. For example, if you presume that Shoshanna is high in openness, you might mistakenly presume she has certain political or cultural beliefs, leading you to say things to her that cut directly against her actual values, such as "Don't you just hate when people mix religion and politics?" However, Shoshanna might respond, "No, actually I think that government should be based on scriptural principles."

Forming Impressions of Others

Perception creates impressions that may evolve over time

When we use perception to size up other people, we form **interpersonal impressions**—mental pictures of who people are and how we feel about them. All aspects of the perception process shape our interpersonal impressions: the information we select as the focus of our attention, the way we organize this information, the interpretations we make based on knowledge in our schemata and our attributions, and even our uncertainty.

Given the complexity of the perception process, it's not surprising that impressions vary widely. Some impressions come quickly into focus—such as meeting a person and immediately liking or disliking them. Other impressions form slowly, over a series of encounters. Some impressions are intensely positive, others neutral, and still others negative. But regardless of their form, interpersonal impressions exert a profound impact on our communication and relationship choices. To illustrate this impact, imagine yourself in the following situation.

It's summer, and you're hanging out at a lake with friends. As you lie on the beach, a friendly-looking man approaches you. He introduces himself as "Ted" and tells you he's waiting for friends who were supposed to help him load his sailboat onto his car. He is easy to talk to, with a nice smile. He mentions injuring his arm playing racquetball, and shows the sling on his left arm. Because his arm is hurting, he asks if you would help him with his boat. You say, "Sure." You walk with him to the parking lot, but when you get to Ted's car, you don't see a boat. When you ask him where his boat is, he says, "Oh! It's at my folks' house, just up the hill. Do you mind going with me? It'll just take a couple of minutes." You tell him you can't go with him because your friends will wonder where you are. "That's OK," Ted says cheerily, "I should have told you it wasn't in the parking lot. Thanks for bothering anyways." As the two of you walk back to the beach, Ted repeats his apology and expresses gratitude for your willingness to help him. He's polite and strikes you as sincere.

Notorious serial killer Ted Bundy was known for adopting a friendly, smiling persona that led his victims to trust him. AP Photo

Think about your encounter with Ted and all that you've perceived. What's your impression of him? What traits besides the ones you've observed would you expect him to have? What do you predict would have happened if you had gone with him to his folks' house to help load the boat? Would you want to play racquetball with him? Would he make a good friend? Does he interest you as a possible romantic partner?

The scenario you've read actually happened. The description is drawn from the police testimony of Janice Graham, who was approached by Ted at Lake Sammamish State Park, near Seattle, Washington, in 1974 (Michaud & Aynesworth, 1989). Graham's decision not to accompany Ted saved her life. Two other women—Janice Ott and Denise Naslund—were not so fortunate. Each of them went with Ted, who murdered them. Friendly, handsome, and polite, Ted was none other than Ted Bundy, one of the most notorious serial killers in U.S. history.

Thankfully, most of the interpersonal impressions we form don't have life-or-death consequences. But all impressions do exert a powerful impact on how we communicate with others and whether we pursue relationships with them. For this reason, it's important to understand how we can flexibly adapt our impressions to create more accurate and reliable conceptions of others.

CONSTRUCTING GESTALTS

One way we form impressions of others is to construct a **Gestalt**, a general sense of a person that's either positive or negative. We discern a few traits and, drawing on information in our schemata, arrive at a judgment based on these traits. The result is an impression of the person as a whole rather than as the sum of individual parts (Asch, 1946). For example, suppose you strike up a conversation with the person sitting next to you at lunch. The person is funny, friendly, and attractive—characteristics associated with positive information in your schemata. You immediately construct an overall positive impression ("I like this person!"), rather than spending additional time weighing the significance of his or her separate traits.

Gestalts form rapidly. This is one reason why people consider first impressions to be so consequential. Gestalts require relatively little mental or communicative effort. Thus, they're useful for encounters in which we must render quick judgments about others with only limited information—a brief interview at a job fair, for instance. Gestalts are also useful for interactions involving casual relationships (contacts with acquaintances or service providers) and contexts in which we are meeting and talking with a large number of people in a small amount of time (business conferences or parties). During such exchanges, it isn't possible to carefully scrutinize every piece of information we perceive about others. Instead, we quickly form broad impressions and then mentally walk away from them. But this also means that Gestalts have significant shortcomings.

The Positivity Bias In 1913, author E. H. Porter published a novel titled *Pollyanna*, about a young child who was happy nearly all the time. Even when faced with horrible tragedies, Pollyanna saw the positive side of things and overlooked the negative. Research on human perception suggests that some Pollyanna exists inside each of us. Examples of *Pollyanna effects* include people viewing their past more positively than it actually was, believing pleasant events are more likely to happen than unpleasant ones, most people deeming their lives "happy" and describing themselves as "optimists," and most people viewing themselves as "better than average" in terms of physical attractiveness and intellect (Matlin & Stang, 1978; Przepiorka & Sobol-Swapinska, 2020; Silvera et al., 2002).

Pollyanna effects come into play when we form Gestalts. When Gestalts are formed, they are more likely to be positive than negative, an effect known as the **positivity bias**. Let's say you're at a party for the company where you just started working. During the party, you meet six coworkers for the first time and talk with each of them for a few minutes. You form a Gestalt for each. Owing to the positivity bias, most or all of your Gestalts are likely to be positive. Although the positivity bias is helpful in initiating relationships, it can also lead us to make bad interpersonal decisions, such as when we pursue relationships with people who turn out to be unethical or even abusive.

The Negativity Effect   When we create Gestalts, we don't treat all information that we learn about people as equally important. Instead, we place emphasis on the negative information we learn about others, a pattern known as the **negativity effect**. Across cultures, people perceive negative information as more informative about someone's "true" character than positive information. Though you may be wondering whether the negativity effect contradicts Pollyanna effects, it actually *derives* from them. How? People tend to believe that positive events, information, and personal characteristics are more commonplace than negative events, information, and characteristics. So when we learn something negative about another person, we see it as unusual. Consequently, that information becomes more salient, and we judge it as more truly representative of a person's character than positive information (Kellermann, 1989).

Needless to say, the negativity effect leads us away from accurate perception. Accurate perception is rooted in carefully and critically assessing everything we learn about people, then flexibly adapting our impressions to match these data. When we weigh negative information more heavily than positive, we perceive only a small part of people, aspects that may or may not represent who they are and how they normally communicate.

Halos and Horns   Once we form a Gestalt about a person, it influences how we interpret that person's subsequent communication and the attributions we make regarding that individual. For example, think about someone for whom you've formed a strongly positive Gestalt. Now imagine that this person discloses a dark secret: they lied to a lover, cheated on exams, or stole from the office. Because of your positive Gestalt, you may dismiss the significance of this behavior, telling yourself instead that the person "had no choice" or "wasn't acting normally." This tendency to positively interpret what someone says or does because we have a positive Gestalt of that person is known as the **halo effect** (see Table 3.3).

table 3.3 **The Halo and Horn Effects**

The Halo Effect		
Impression	**Behavior**	**Attribution**
Person we like :)	Positive behavior	Internal
Person we like :)	Negative behavior	External
The Horn Effect		
Person we dislike :(	Positive behavior	External
Person we dislike :(	Negative behavior	Internal

Note: Information in this table is adapted from Guerin (1999).

self-reflection

Think of someone for whom you have a negative Gestalt. How did the negativity effect shape your impression? Now call to mind personal flaws or embarrassing events from your past. If someone learned of this information and formed a negative Gestalt of you, would their impression be accurate? Fair?

LaunchPad Video
launchpadworks.com

Halo Effect
Watch this clip online to answer the questions below.

When have you made a perceptual error based on the halo effect? How would you suggest reducing the halo effect in hiring practices?

Want to see more? Check out LaunchPad for clips on the **horn effect** and **algebraic impressions**.

The counterpart of the halo effect is the **horn effect**, the tendency to negatively interpret the communication and behavior of people for whom we have negative Gestalts (see Table 3.3). Call to mind someone you can't stand. Imagine that this person discloses the same secret as the individual previously described. Although the information in both cases is the same, you would likely chalk up this individual's unethical behavior to bad character or lack of values.

Do Gestalts—and especially the biasing impact of halo and horn effects—doom us all to perceptual inaccuracy? Not necessarily. Research suggests that these biases can be countered by engaging in analytical thinking—that is, expending effort to slowly form and reflect on impressions as they develop (Wen et al., 2020). One example of such analytical thinking is calculating an *algebraic impression*, which we consider next.

CALCULATING ALGEBRAIC IMPRESSIONS

A second way we form interpersonal impressions is to develop **algebraic impressions** by carefully evaluating each new thing we learn about a person (Anderson, 1981). Algebraic impressions involve comparing and assessing the positive and negative things we learn about a person in order to calculate an overall impression, then modifying this impression as we learn new information. It's similar to solving an algebraic equation, in which we add and subtract different values from each side to compute a final result.

Consider how you might form an algebraic impression of Ted Bundy from our earlier example. At the outset, his warmth, humor, and ability to chat easily strike you as "friendly" and "extraverted." These traits, when added together, lead you to calculate a positive impression: friendly + extraverted = positive impression. But when you accompany Bundy to the parking lot and realize his boat isn't there, you perceive this information as deceptive. This new information—Ted is a liar—immediately causes you to revise your computation: friendly + extraverted + potential liar = negative impression.

When we form algebraic impressions, we don't place an equal value on every piece of information in the equation. Instead, we weigh some pieces of information more heavily than others, depending on the information's *importance* and its *positivity* or *negativity*. For example, your perception of potential romantic partners' physical attractiveness, intelligence, and personal values likely will carry more weight when calculating your impression than their favorite color or breakfast cereal.

As this discussion illustrates, algebraic impressions are more flexible and accurate than Gestalts. For encounters in which we have the time and energy to ponder someone's traits and how they add up, algebraic impressions offer us the opportunity to form refined impressions of people. We can also flexibly change them every time we receive new information about people. But since algebraic impressions require a fair amount of mental effort, they aren't as efficient as Gestalts. In unexpected encounters or casual conversations, such mental calculations are unnecessary and may even work to our disadvantage, especially if we need to render rapid judgments and act on them.

STEREOTYPING

A final way we form impressions is to categorize people into social groups and then evaluate them based on information we have in our schemata related to these groups (Bodenhausen et al., 1999). This is known as **stereotyping**, a term first coined by journalist Walter Lippmann (1922) to describe overly simplistic interpersonal impressions. When we stereotype others, we replace the subtle complexities that make people unique with blanket assumptions based solely on their social group affiliation.

◐ Think of a "banjo-playing bluegrass musician." What image comes to mind? A white musician from Appalachia? Or Rhiannon Giddens (pictured), a multiracial MacArthur Genius Grant recipient who studied opera in college? (See the Focus on Culture feature: Intersectional Stereotyping and U.S. Folk Music for more information about her.) AGE Fotostock

People stereotype because doing so streamlines the perception process. Once we've categorized a person as a member of a particular group, we can apply all the information we have about that group to form a quick impression (Bodenhausen et al., 1999). For example, suppose a friend introduces you to Steve, but all they tell you is that "Steve is Buddhist." Once you perceive Steve as "Buddhist," stereotypes about Buddhists might come to mind: perhaps you assume that Buddhists are quiet and contemplative; that they rarely laugh or joke; or that they speak in slow, solemn, and profound ways. In fact, Steve speaks quickly, laughs frequently, and loves horror movies and emo music. Similarly, say that your friend introduces you to Kelly, but all you're told is that she is a "feminist professor." Depending on your prior views, you might be surprised to discover that she was a marketing rep in industrial sales, loves the Chicago Cubs, and is a group fitness instructor.

As these examples suggest, stereotyping leads us to form flawed impressions of others—impressions that can lead to discriminatory behavior. One study of workplace perception found that male supervisors who stereotyped women as "the weaker sex" perceived female employees' work performance as deficient and gave women low job evaluations, regardless of the women's actual job performance (Cleveland et al., 2000). A separate study examining college students' perceptions of professors found a similar biasing effect for ethnic stereotypes. White students who stereotyped Hispanic people as "laid-back" and "relaxed" perceived Hispanic professors who set high expectations for classroom performance as "colder" and "more unprofessional" than white professors who set identical standards (Smith & Anderson, 2005).

Stereotyping is challenging to overcome, for at least three reasons. First, researchers have documented that categorizing people in terms of their social group affiliation is the most common way we form impressions, more common than either Gestalts or algebraic impressions (Bodenhausen et al., 1999). Why? Social group categories such as race and gender are among the first characteristics we notice about people upon meeting them. As a consequence, we often perceive people in terms of their social group membership before any other impression is even possible (Devine, 1989). The internet provides no escape from this tendency. Without many of the nonverbal cues and additional information that can distinguish a person as a unique individual, people communicating online are even more likely than those communicating face-to-face to form stereotypical impressions when meeting others for the first time (Spears et al., 2001).

Second, most of us presume that our beliefs are valid. As a consequence, we have a high degree of confidence in the legitimacy of our stereotypical impressions, despite the fact that such impressions are flawed (Brewer, 1993). We also continue to believe in stereotypes even when members of a stereotyped group repeatedly behave in ways that contradict the stereotype. In fact, contradictory behavior may actually *strengthen* stereotypes. For example, if you think of yoga instructors as soft-spoken and gentle and you meet a loud and funny yoga teacher, you may dismiss their behavior as atypical. You'll then actively seek examples of behavior that confirm the stereotype to compensate for the uncertainty that the unexpected behavior aroused (Seta & Seta, 1993). As a result, the stereotype is reinforced.

Third, we're often consciously unaware that we even possess such beliefs, especially when the beliefs are negative. Instances in which people possess unrecognized

self-reflection

Think of an instance in which you perceived someone stereotypically based on the information the person posted online (photos, profile information, tweets). How did the information affect your overall impression of them? Your communication with the person? What stereotypes might others form of you, based on *your* online postings?

focus on CULTURE

Intersectional Stereotyping and U.S. Folk Music

Rhiannon Giddens has made it her mission to shatter stereotypes, both about herself and about the roots of U.S. folk music.[2] Growing up in North Carolina, Giddens was stereotyped by peers confused by her interests and by her multiracial background (her father is white; her mother Black and Native American). In middle school, her Black peers labeled her a "hippie" because she was more interested in books than fashion, but she was dubbed "a Black nerd" by white girls when she enrolled in the School of Science and Math. Both groups called her "Pocahontas" when she joined Akwe:kon, a group dedicated to Native American music and dance.

As scholars Christopher Petsko and Galen Bodenhausen (2020) note, people commonly use such stereotypes when perceiving others. But because individuals typically belong to multiple groups simultaneously, the challenge of *intersectional stereotyping*—perceptually labeling complex people in simple ways—often is resolved by perceivers focusing on just one identity or intersection of identities. What determines which identity they focus on? Prominent markers of distinction are based on personal and situational cues. So Rhiannon Giddens was "a hippie" to Black peers because of her white identity and lack of fashion interest; a "Black nerd" to white peers because of

her Black identity and love of math; and "Pocahontas" to both Black *and* white peers because of her Native American ancestry and Akwe:kon membership.

Giddens's lived experience of intersectional stereotyping has helped fuel her passion for correcting musical myths. People often misjudge folk music as "white," despite its Black roots in the United States. Even the banjo—Giddens's favorite instrument—is stereotyped as "white," despite the fact that its origin can be traced, at least in part, to Africa. As Giddens describes, "I grew up thinking the banjo was invented in the mountains, that string band music and square dances were a strictly white preserve and history—that while Black folk were singing spirituals, white folk were do-si-do'ing and fiddling up a storm, which led me to feeling like an alien in what I found is my own cultural tradition." Her career has thus served as a corrective: simultaneously shattering stereotypes about folk music, and reclaiming and transforming what it means to be a bluegrass musician.

discussion questions

- What intersection of identities do you experience? Do you find that people tend to latch onto a specific one of your identities when they perceive you?
- Think of an instance in which you engaged in intersectional stereotyping. How did your narrow perception of the person impact your communication toward them? What could you have done differently to avoid this?

[2]Information from Sullivan (2019) and Mack (2020).

attitudes and stereotypes that are discriminatory are known as *implicit biases* (Greenwald & Banaji, 1995), and such biases have been documented related to a range of issues and identities, including ethnicity, obesity, gender, and sexual orientation (Greenwald et al., 2009).

Knowing these challenges, how can we overcome stereotyping others? Given the speed with which inaccurate stereotypic labeling can occur, perhaps the most important step we can take is to *pause our perceptual process*. Rather than quickly labeling someone based on cursory assessments of outward appearance, stop and ask yourself, "Am I placing this person in a group that prevents me from seeing them as a person?" Then put your self-reflection skills to work. Start by critically assessing your beliefs, reflecting on both the foundation of particular beliefs and your reasons for endorsing these beliefs, as well as what you think it would take to challenge these beliefs. Next, do your homework. Read a variety of materials, from a variety of sources, to increase your knowledge base—using this new, broader knowledge to reexamine your beliefs, rendering the unfamiliar more familiar, and reducing any uncertainty you may have. Finally, when interacting with others, keep in mind that a group is simply a larger collection of individual people, each with unique and varying attitudes, beliefs, and behaviors. Strive to see other people how *you* would like to be seen—as the unique individual you are.

Improving Your Perception

Explore empathy, world-mindedness, and perception-checking

Malcolm X is remembered for his fiery rhetoric denouncing white racism and his rejection of nonviolent protest as a means for dealing with oppression. Less well known is the marked change in his perception and communication that occurred following his visit to Saudi Arabia. He traveled to Mecca for a traditional Muslim hajj, or pilgrimage. During his visit, he worshipped, ate, socialized, and slept in the same room with white Muslims. In doing so, he was shocked to discover that despite their differences in skin color, they all shared similar degrees of religious devotion. The experience was a revelation and led him to reassess his long-standing belief in an unbridgeable racial divide between white and Black people. As he explained in a letter home: "On this pilgrimage, what I have seen and experienced has forced me to rearrange my thought-patterns and toss aside some of my previous conclusions" (Malcolm X, 1964).

Malcolm's transformation suggests important lessons for everyone interested in improving perception and communication. He came to appreciate others' perspectives and feel a strong emotional kinship with those he previously disparaged based on skin color. He also freely called into question his own perceptual accuracy by critically assessing his prior judgments and correcting those found to deviate from "the reality of life." These changes reveal two ways we can improve our perception and interpersonal communication: offering empathy and checking our perception.

OFFERING EMPATHY

Empathy is one of our most valuable tools for communicating competently with others (Campbell & Babrow, 2004). The word *empathy* comes from the Greek word *empatheia*, meaning "feeling into." When we experience **empathy**, we "feel

⬤ Malcolm X's perception changed after 1964, as revealed in this quote: "I believe in recognizing every human being as a human being, neither white, black, brown, nor red—when you are dealing with humanity as one family, it's just one human being marrying another human being, or one human being living around or with another human being." (Left) AP Photo; (right) Bettmann/Getty Images

into" others' thoughts and emotions, making an attempt to both understand their perspectives and be aware of their feelings in order to identify with them (Kuhn, 2001).

Empathy consists of two components. The first is *perspective-taking*—the ability to see things from someone else's vantage point without necessarily experiencing that person's emotions (Duan & Hill, 1996). The second is *empathic concern*—becoming aware of how the other person is feeling, experiencing a sense of compassion regarding the other person's emotional state, and perhaps even experiencing some of their emotions yourself (Stiff et al., 1988).

We often think of empathy as an automatic process beyond our control, something we either feel or don't feel. Consequently, we excuse ourselves from

self-QUIZ

Test Your Empathy

Read these statements, marking the ones with which you agree. Total up your check marks, and interpret your score below.

To take this quiz online, visit LaunchPad: **launchpadworks.com**

Perspective-Taking

_____ Before I criticize a person, I try to imagine how I would view the situation in their place.

_____ I believe there are two sides to every question, and I try to look at both sides.

_____ I find it easy to see things from another person's point of view.

_____ I try to look at everybody's side of a disagreement before I make a decision.

_____ When I am upset with someone, I usually try to put myself in their shoes for a while.

Empathic Concern

_____ When I see a person being taken advantage of, I feel protective toward them.

_____ I often have tender, concerned feelings for people who seem less fortunate than I.

_____ I would describe myself as a fairly softhearted person.

_____ Other people's misfortunes disturb me a great deal.

_____ I am often touched by the things that I see happen to people around me.

Quiz adapted from James B. Stiff, James Price Dillard, Lilnabeth Somera, Hyun Kim, and Carra Sleight (1988). "Empathy, communication and prosocial behavior," Communication Monographs, 55(2). Copyright © 1988.

Scoring: For each section, a score of 0–1 indicates that you have low empathy, 2–3 indicates moderate empathy, and 4–5 indicates high empathy.

being empathic toward outgroupers or people we dislike. But research suggests that whether we feel empathy toward others depends largely on our **empathy mindset**—our beliefs about whether empathy is something that can be developed and controlled (Schumann et al., 2014). People who view empathy as developable and controllable are capable of feeling empathy for a broad range of others—even within interpersonally challenging contexts, such as during conflicts, when arguing about political beliefs, or when asked to listen to a story of tragic loss told by an outgroup member. Those who believe empathy is an uncontrollable, natural response have difficulty experiencing empathy within such challenging encounters.

But experiencing empathy isn't sufficient in itself to improve your interpersonal communication and relationships. You also must convey your empathy to others. To competently communicate the perspective-taking part of empathy, let others know that you're genuinely interested in hearing their viewpoints ("I'd love to get your impression"), and tell them that you think their views are important and understandable ("Seeing it from your side makes a lot of sense"). To communicate empathic concern, disclose to others that you care about them and their feelings ("I hope you're doing OK"). Share with them your own emotions regarding their situation ("I feel terrible that you're going through this"). Competently conveying empathy isn't just something to be strived for as a matter of principle; it's a recommendation packed with practical benefits. Research on perceived perspective-taking, for example, suggests that when others believe that you are taking their perspective, they are more likely to perceive you as relatable, to like you, and to help you when you are in need (Goldstein et al., 2014).

Importantly, avoid using "I know" messages (as in "I know just how you feel"). Even if you make such comments with kind intentions, others will likely view you as presumptuous and perhaps even patronizing, especially if they suspect that you don't or can't feel as they do. For example, when people suffer a great loss—such as the death of a loved one—many don't believe that anyone else could feel the depth of anguish they're experiencing. Saying "I know how you feel" isn't helpful under these conditions.

skills practice

Enhancing Empathy
Improving your ability to experience and express empathy

1 Identify a challenging interpersonal encounter.

2 As the encounter unfolds, consider how the other person is viewing you and the interaction.

3 Think about the emotions they are feeling.

4 Communicate perspective-taking, avoiding "I know" messages.

5 Express empathic concern, letting the person know you value their feelings.

6 Disclose your own feelings.

◁ Empathy is one of the most powerful tools for strengthening interpersonal relationships. Can you think of a time when you used empathy effectively to comfort a friend or family member? Prostock-studio/Alamy

CHECKING YOUR PERCEPTION

The second way to improve your perception is through **perception-checking**, a five-step process in which you apply all that you've learned in this chapter to your perception of others.

1. *Check your punctuation.* People punctuate encounters in different ways, often disagreeing on "who/what started it" or "who/what ended it." When you experience a conflict, be aware of your own punctuation and keep in mind that other people may see things differently. Remember to ask others to share their punctuation with you.

2. *Check your knowledge.* Your perception of others is only as accurate as the information you have in your schemata. Never presume that you know the "truth" about what others "really" mean or what they're "really" like. When in doubt, ask others to explain their meaning to you.

3. *Check your attributions.* Avoid the common temptation to attribute others' communication and behavior exclusively to internal causes, such as character or personality. Remember that all behavior—including interpersonal communication—stems from a complex combination of internal and external forces.

4. *Check perceptual influences.* Reflect on how culture, gender, and personality shape your perception of others. Are you perceiving others as ingroupers or outgroupers? If so, on what basis? How is this perception affecting your communication? Your relationships?

5. *Check your impressions.* Reflect on your impressions as you're forming them. If you find yourself making Gestalts, realize that your Gestalts may bias your perception of subsequent information you learn about a person. Resist stereotyping, but also realize that it's difficult to avoid, given the natural human tendency to categorize people into groups upon first meeting. Strive to create flexible impressions, thoughtfully weighing new information you learn about a person and reshaping your overall impression based on new data.

Perception-checking is an intense mental exercise. Mastering it takes time and effort, but the ability to critically check your own perception goes, as Malcolm X wrote, "hand in hand with every form of intelligent search for truth," whether the truth is personal, interpersonal, or universal. When you routinely perception-check, errors are corrected and perception becomes more accurate, balanced, and objective. As a result, you will make fewer communication blunders, and you will be able to tailor your communication to people as they really are, making your messages more sensitive and effective. The ultimate result will also be perceptual: *others* seeing *you* as a competent communicator.

Practicing Responsible Perception

Perception affects every interpersonal encounter

We experience our interpersonal reality—the people around us, our communication with them, and the relationships that result—through the lens of perception. But perception is a product of our own creation, metaphorical clay we can shape however we want. At each stage of the perception process, we make choices that empower us to mold our perception in constructive or destructive ways. What do I select as the focus of my attention? What attributions do I make? Do I form initial impressions and cling to them in the face of contradictory evidence? Or do I strive to adapt my impressions of others as I learn new information about them? The choices we make at each of these decision points feed directly into how we communicate with and relate to others. When we stereotype people, for example, or refuse to empathize with someone we perceive as an outgrouper, we immediately destine ourselves to incompetent communication.

To improve our interpersonal communication and relationship decisions, we must practice responsible perception. This means routinely perception-checking and correcting errors, resisting stereotypes, and leaning into analytical thinking by striving to adjust our impressions of people as we get to know them better. It means expending the effort that empathy requires—envisioning how others feel; emotionally reaching out to them; and communicating this perspective-taking and empathic concern in open, appropriate ways. Practicing responsible perception means not just mastering the knowledge of perception presented in these pages but also translating this intellectual understanding into active practice during every interpersonal encounter. We all use perception as the basis for our communication and relationship decisions. But when we practice *responsible* perception, the natural result is more competent communication and better relationships.

Balancing Impressions and Empathy

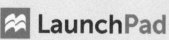 **LaunchPad** For the best experience, complete all parts of this activity
in LaunchPad: **launchpadworks.com**

1 Background

Forging constructive, collaborative work relationships with people whom we judge to be
outgroupers is a challenge, particularly when we've formed negative impressions of them and
they behave in questionable ways. To understand how you might competently manage such a
relationship challenge, read the case study in Part 2; then, drawing on all you know about
interpersonal communication, work through the problem-solving model in Part 3.

 Visit LaunchPad to watch the video in Part 4 and assess your communication in Part 5.

2 Case Study

Your professor assigns a group project that will count for a significant portion of your final course grade.[3] Each group member gets two grades for the project: one for the group presentation and one for the individual contribution. The professor selects you as a group leader. Your responsibilities include making sure that each group member gets his or her work done and telling the professor what grade you think each person deserves. The professor will evaluate you in part based on your skill as group leader.

At your first group meeting, everyone is on time except Dylan. He apologizes and says that "something came up." As everyone introduces themselves, it becomes clear that Dylan's tardiness isn't his only difference from you and the others. He's wearing a shirt emblazoned with extreme political slogans, viewpoints opposed to yours. It quickly becomes clear that his religious beliefs are dissimilar as well. The more you talk with him, the more you dislike him.

Despite your distaste for Dylan, the meeting goes well. The project you all decide on is interesting and provocative. A ton of research needs to be done, but split several ways, you *might* get it done—if everyone does his or her fair share. If even one person fails to follow through, however, it will be a disaster. You exit the meeting excited but anxious.

As the project progresses, Dylan seldom makes it to meetings on time and skips one meeting entirely. At that meeting, two members petition you to remove him from the group, but others argue for keeping him. You decide to give Dylan another chance. A few hours later, Dylan emails you an apology, saying he's been "dealing with family problems." He offers to do extra research to make amends, and you gladly accept his offer, as you're stressed about getting the project done.

It's Thursday afternoon. The group's in-class presentation is next Tuesday. The plan is to rehearse tomorrow afternoon, then use the weekend to complete any final tweaking that needs to be done. Your phone rings, and it's Dylan. He says, "I am so sorry. My family situation has been holding me back. Can I have more time to finish my research?"

---

[3]Information in this situation is from the "Ron" situation developed by O'Keefe (1988).

 **Your Turn**

Think about all you've learned thus far about interpersonal communication. Then work through the following five steps. Remember, there are no "right" answers, so think hard about what is the *best* choice! (P.S. Need help? See the *Helpful Concepts* list.)

step 1

Reflect on yourself. What are your thoughts and feelings in this situation? What attributions are you making about Dylan and his behavior? Are your attributions accurate, or are they shaded by your impressions of him?

step 2

Reflect on your partner. Using perspective-taking and empathic concern, put yourself in Dylan's shoes. What is he thinking and feeling in this situation?

step 3

Identify the optimal outcome. Think about your communication and relationship with Dylan as well as the situation surrounding the group project (including your leadership responsibilities). What's the best, most constructive relationship outcome possible? Consider what's best for you and for Dylan.

step 4

Locate the roadblocks. Taking into consideration your own and Dylan's thoughts and feelings and all that has happened in this situation, what obstacles are keeping you from achieving the optimal outcome?

step 5

Chart your course. What can you say to Dylan to overcome the roadblocks you've identified and achieve your optimal outcome?

HELPFUL CONCEPTS

Attribution errors, **67**
Uncertainty-reducing strategies, **69**
Ingroupers and outgroupers, **70**
Negativity effect, **77**
Algebraic impressions, **78**
Empathy, **81**
Perception-checking, **84**

 The Other Side

Visit LaunchPad to watch a video in which Dylan tells his side of the case study story. As in many real-life situations, this is information to which you did not have access when you were initially crafting your response in Part 3. The video reminds us that even when we do our best to offer competent responses, there is always another side to the story that we need to consider.

 Interpersonal Competence Self-Assessment

After watching the video, visit the Self-Assessment questions in LaunchPad. Think about the new information offered in Dylan's side of the story and all you've learned about interpersonal communication. Drawing on this knowledge, revisit your earlier responses in Part 3 and assess your interpersonal communication competence.

Halfpoint/iStock/Getty Images

We began this chapter with varied views of a campus protest. When students at our son's school called into question the lack of diverse perspectives in their curriculum, people with differing viewpoints clashed over the methods of their dissent.

What perceived injustices have *you* protested in *your* life? When people challenge the validity of your concerns, do your responses to them widen the perceptual gulf between you? Or do you seek to bridge divides by emphasizing the mutual connections we *all* share, and of which Dr. Martin Luther King Jr. so eloquently wrote from his cell in a Birmingham jail?

Social dissent and perception of injustice are the very fabric on which the United States was founded. Rather than perceiving disagreement as divisive, it should remind us of our fundamental commonality: *we all see things through our own lenses*. Although we'll never agree with everyone about everything, we can strive to understand one another's viewpoints. In doing so, we strive to build lives that connect us to others, rather than divide us from them.

 **LaunchPad**

LaunchPad for *Reflect & Relate* offers videos and encourages self-assessment through adaptive quizzing. Go to **launchpadworks.com** to get access to:

 LearningCurve
Adaptive Quizzes

 Video clips that help you understand interpersonal communication

key terms

perception, 63
selection, 64
salience, 64
organization, 64
⊙ punctuation, 64
interpretation, 65
schemata, 65
attributions, 65
fundamental attribution error, 67
actor-observer effect, 68
⊙ self-serving bias, 68
⊙ Uncertainty Reduction Theory, 69
ingroupers, 70
outgroupers, 70
personality, 73
self-enhancement bias, 74
implicit personality theories, 75
interpersonal impressions, 75
Gestalt, 76
positivity bias, 77
negativity effect, 77
⊙ halo effect, 77
⊙ horn effect, 78
⊙ algebraic impressions, 78
stereotyping, 78
⊙ empathy, 81
empathy mindset, 83
perception-checking, 84

⊙ You can watch brief, illustrative videos of these terms and test your understanding of the concepts in LaunchPad.

key concepts

Perception as a Process

- We make sense of our interpersonal world through **perception**, and engage in **selection**, **organization**, and **interpretation** of information received from our senses.
- We interpret the meaning of communication by drawing on known information stored in our mental **schemata**. We make **attributions** regarding why people said and did certain things but sometimes fall prey to the **fundamental attribution error**, the **actor-observer effect**, or the **self-serving bias**.
- According to **Uncertainty Reduction Theory**, we commonly experience uncertainty during first encounters with new acquaintances.

Influences on Perception

- Culture and gender play major roles in shaping our perception of communication.
- **Personality** influences our perception of the traits we possess and how we perceive the traits of others. **Self-enhancement bias** occurs when we view our own unique traits more favorably than the unique traits of others. **Implicit personality theories** guide our perceptions of others' personalities.

Forming Impressions of Others

- When we perceive others, we form **interpersonal impressions**. Sometimes we create general **Gestalts**, which are quite often positive, thanks to the **positivity bias**.
- The **negativity effect** plays a role in shaping how we perceive information we learn about others.
- Forming strong positive or negative Gestalts sometimes leads to a **halo effect** or a **horn effect**, causing us to perceive subsequent information we learn about people in distorted ways.
- The most accurate and refined impressions of others are **algebraic impressions**. When we calculate our impressions based on individual traits, we're more likely to see people as they really are and adapt our communication accordingly.
- The most common form of interpersonal impression is **stereotyping**.

Improving Your Perception

- When you can take the perspective of others and experience empathic concern toward them, your communication becomes more sensitive and adaptive.
- Responsible perception is rooted in **perception-checking**, routinely questioning your perceptions and correcting errors that may lead to ineffective communication.

4 Experiencing and Expressing Emotions

Emotion fills our lives with meaning.

Photo by G.N. Miller/MaMa Foundation Gospel for Teens

When radio personality and producer Vy Higginsen created the nonprofit Gospel for Teens program, her mission was to teach teens gospel music.[1] Higginsen and a group of volunteer instructors met weekly with kids ages 13 to 19, honing their vocal skills and sharing with them the history of gospel. As Higginsen notes, "The lyrics of gospel songs provide courage, inner strength, and hope for a better life in the future." But she quickly found that her program wouldn't only be about introducing gospel to a generation more versed in rap and hip-hop. Instead, Gospel for Teens would become a powerful vehicle for helping teens manage intense and challenging emotions.

Higginsen originally instituted a simple rule governing emotions and program participation: *leave the baggage at the door.* As she describes, "The teen years are a vulnerable time in kids' lives, and they are dealing with shyness, anxiety, trauma, and family dysfunction. Many students are uncomfortable about their physical appearance and self-esteem based on the peers around them. Some are overcome with anxiety from their home life, school, and thoughts of their futures." To keep difficult emotions from hindering performances, Higginsen began each singing session by having participants stand up and shake their hands, arms, legs, and feet, physically purging themselves of emotional constraints. As she instructed, "Any worry, any pain, any problem with your mother, your father, your sister, your brother, the boyfriend, the girlfriend, I want that out now of your consciousness. That's your baggage; leave the bags outside because *this* time is for you!"

---

[1]The information that follows is adapted from a personal interview with the authors, October 2011, and www.mamafoundation.org. Interview content published with permission of Vy Higginsen.

But Higginsen's "no baggage" policy was abandoned when the cousin of one of her most talented students was shot and killed. Higginsen realized that many program participants had suffered similar tragedies, and that her class could provide a forum within which students could safely share their stories, their pain, and their grief with one another—working together to begin healing. As she describes, "Our teens are living a very adult life—their friends and family are getting murdered, dying from diseases and drugs—and it's leaving emotional scars on them. They need something uplifting in their lives. So I decided to allow the students to bring their baggage in. I invited the students to share what was happening in their worlds. I wasn't trying to fix their situations, because I couldn't, but their being heard was a profound step in their being healed. It made our choir realize we are not alone in our experience. We made a connection—emotionally, personally, and interpersonally."

Whereas Higginsen once encouraged students to leave their emotions at the door, she now realizes that the experience of singing and sharing the experience of singing with others provides students with a powerful vehicle for managing negative emotions in positive ways. "I would like the teens to take away the idea that we have emotions yet we are not our emotions. We can recover and thrive by changing our mind and rechanneling our energy through music, art, service, acceptance, meditation, and practice. In simple terms, we can rechannel the negative to the positive and use this as an opportunity for excellence. Gospel music has the power to empower and transform. More than anything, I want my students to know that joy, hope, faith, and goodness are possible."

Emotion fills our lives with meaning (Berscheid & Peplau, 2002).

To experience emotion is to feel alive, and to lack emotion is to view life itself as colorless and meaningless (Frijda, 2005). Because emotion is so important, we feel compelled to express our emotional experiences to others through communication. And when we share our emotions with others, they transition from private and personal to profoundly interpersonal. It's at this point that choice becomes relevant. We may not be able to select our emotions before they arise, but we can choose how to handle and convey them after they occur. These choices impact our relational outcomes. When we intelligently manage and competently communicate emotional experiences, our relationship satisfaction and overall life happiness increase. Conversely, when we don't, our relationships suffer, and these lapses are reflected in relationships and lives torn by anger and sadness.

In this chapter, we examine the most personal and interpersonal of human experiences—emotion. You'll learn:

- The important differences between emotions, feelings, and moods, as well as the best approaches to managing negative moods

- Ways in which gender and personality influence emotion

- Why improving your emotional intelligence can help you more competently manage your experience and expression of emotion

- How to deal with emotional challenges, such as managing anger and grief, communicating empathy online, and handling fading romantic passion

We begin by discussing the nature of emotion and distinguishing it from feelings and moods.

The Nature of Emotion

> Distinguishing between emotions, feelings, and moods

Take a moment and recall the most recent emotion you felt. What comes to mind? For most people, it's a hot emotion—that is, a physically and mentally intense experience, like joy, anger, or grief, during which your palms sweated, your mouth felt dry, and your heart pounded (Berscheid & Regan, 2005). When we are asked to translate these emotions into words, we use vivid physical metaphors. Joy makes "our hearts leap," while anger makes "our blood boil." Grief is "a living hell" (Frijda, 2005). Understanding what emotions are and how they differ from feelings and moods is the first step in better managing our emotions.

DEFINING EMOTION

Scholarly definitions of emotion mirror our everyday experiences. **Emotion** is an intense reaction to an event that involves interpreting event meaning, becoming physiologically aroused, labeling the experience as emotional, managing reactions, and communicating through emotional displays and disclosures (Gross et al., 2006). This definition highlights the five key features of emotion. First, *emotion is reactive*, triggered by our perception of outside events (Cacioppo et al., 1993). A friend telling you that her cancer is in remission leads you to experience joy. Receiving a scolding text message from a parent may trigger both your surprise and your anger. When an emotion-inducing event occurs, we engage in the same perceptual process as we do with other types of interpersonal events—selecting, organizing, and interpreting information related to that event. As we interpret the event's meaning, we decide whether the incident is positive, neutral, negative, or somewhere in between, triggering corresponding emotions (Smith & Kirby, 2004).

A second feature of emotion is that it *involves physiological arousal* in the form of increased heart rate, blood pressure, and adrenaline release. Many researchers consider arousal *the* defining feature of emotion, a belief mirrored in most people's descriptions of emotion as "intense" and "hot" (Berscheid, 2002).

self-reflection

Recall an emotional event in a close relationship. What specific action triggered your emotion? How did you interpret the triggering event? What physical sensations resulted? What does this tell you about the link between events, mind, and body that is the basis of emotional experience?

◁ Emotions are not just internally felt but also expressed through body language, gestures, facial expressions, and other physical behaviors. RAUL ARBOLEDA/Getty Images

Third, to experience emotion, you must become aware of your interpretation and arousal as "an emotion"—that is, you must *consciously label* them as such (Berscheid, 2002). For example, imagine that a friend posts an embarrassing photo of you on Instagram. Upon discovering it, your face grows hot, your breath quickens, and you become consciously aware of these physical sensations. This awareness, combined with your assessment of the situation, causes you to label your experience as the emotion "anger."

Fourth, our emotional experiences and expressions are *constrained by historical, cultural, relational, and situational norms* regarding appropriate behavior (Metts & Planalp, 2002). As a consequence, once we become aware that we're experiencing an emotion, we try to manage that experience and express that emotion in ways we consider acceptable. We may allow our emotion to dominate our thoughts and communication, try to channel it in constructive ways, or suppress our emotion completely. For instance, say that you're at a funeral, and a speaker says something that strikes you as funny regarding your loved one who has passed away. You may momentarily feel joy, and be compelled to laugh out loud. But given the situational constraints for appropriate behavior at a funeral, you'd likely repress the laughter rather than risk being seen by others as heartless. Similarly, if you're sad because your best friend is marrying someone you dislike, you'll likely smile through the ceremony, rather than scowl, because wedding norms suggest that everyone should be joyful. Instances such as these result from the recognition that the unrestrained experience and expression of emotion may lead to negative consequences.

Finally, you *communicate emotion in a variety of ways*. That is, the choices you make regarding emotion management are reflected outward in your verbal and non-verbal displays in the form of word choices, exclamations or expletives, facial expressions, body posture, and gestures (Mauss et al., 2005). The communicative nature of emotion is so fundamental that people developed emoticons to represent emotional expressions in mediated communication, such as social media posts, texts, and email.

Another way we communicate our emotions is by talking about our emotional experiences with others, which is known as **emotion-sharing**. Much of interpersonal communication consists of disclosing emotions, talking about them, and pondering them. Studies show that people share between 75 and 95 percent of their emotional experiences with at least one other person, usually a spouse, parent, or friend (Frijda, 2005). Such sharing occurs through multiple modalities, including face-to-face encounters, phone calls, texting, and social media. Teens, for example, prefer sharing emotions face-to-face. When they share positive emotions through social media, the most popular platforms are Instagram, Snapchat, and status updates on Facebook (Vermeulen et al., 2018). The people with whom we share our emotions generally enjoy being confided in, and often share the incident with others, weaving a socially intimate network of emotion-sharing. The teens in the Gospel for Teens program (described in our chapter opener) use emotion-sharing to connect with one another and collaboratively work together to heal their individual experiences of grief and anger.

What's more, when people share *their* emotions with *us*, we often—without knowing it—mimic or copy their emotional states through our facial expressions, leading us to experience a "pale reflection" of their emotion (Hatfield et al., 2014). Research also suggests that when people are inhibited from facially mimicking the emotions of others, such as when Botox injections paralyze facial muscles from being able to fully move, it is more difficult for those people to identify emotions in others.

This facial mimicry may be connected to **emotional contagion**—when the experience of the same emotion rapidly spreads from one person to others

self-reflection

With whom do you share your emotional experiences? Does such sharing always have a positive impact on your relationships, or does it cause problems at times? What ethical boundaries govern emotion-sharing? How do you choose when to use social media to share emotions?

(Olszanowski et al., 2019). Emotional contagion can be positive, such as when sharing your joy over an unexpected job promotion spreads to your family as you tell them about it. At other times, emotional contagion can be negative. For instance, interacting with people who are anxious can increase your anxiety level—even if you don't share their worries or feel personally concerned about their well-being (Parkinson & Simons, 2012).

Now that we have described the nature of emotions, let's consider how they differ from feelings and moods.

FEELINGS AND MOODS

We often talk about emotions, feelings, and moods as if they are the same thing. But they're not. **Feelings** are short-term emotional reactions to events that generate only limited arousal; they do not typically trigger attempts to manage their experience or expression (Berscheid, 2002). We experience dozens, if not hundreds, of feelings daily—most of them lasting only a few seconds or minutes. An attractive stranger casts you an approving smile, causing you to feel momentarily flattered. A friend texts you unexpectedly when you're trying to study, making you feel briefly annoyed. Feelings are like small emotions. Common feelings include gratitude, concern, pleasure, relief, and resentment.

Whereas emotions occur sporadically in response to substantial events, and feelings arise frequently in reaction to everyday incidents, **moods** are low-intensity arousal states—such as boredom, contentment, grouchiness, or serenity—that typically last longer than feelings or emotions (Fiske & Taylor, 2017). We are almost always "in a mood" of some form or another; they are the slow-flowing currents in our everyday lives. We can think of our frequent, fleeting feelings as ripples, and occasional intense emotions as waves, riding on top of these currents, as displayed in Figure 4.1.

Moods build, dissipate, and shift direction from positive to negative (or vice versa) in response to minor incidents throughout the day or even our own thought processes (Parkinson et al., 1996). So, for instance, you might start the day in a good mood, but during your commute to campus hear a song from Radiohead's *OK Computer*—your ex-partner's favorite album. This leads you to think about your ex, how you two first met at a Radiohead concert, your breakup, the heartache you experienced, and other associated challenges. As these thoughts arise and accumulate, your mood slowly shifts from positive to negative. Later that same day, however, you might arrive at work in a sour mood—only to learn that you've received a

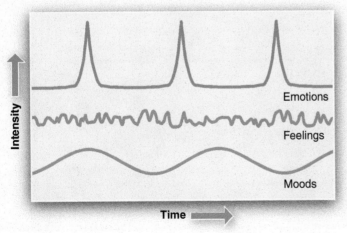

figure 4.1 **The Flow of Emotions, Feelings, and Moods**

promotion. As your workplace friends congratulate you throughout the evening, your negative mood slowly shifts back to positive once more.

Moods powerfully influence our perception (see also Chapter 3). People who describe their moods as "good" are more likely than those in bad moods to form positive impressions of others (Forgas & Bower, 1987); to perceive new acquaintances as "sociable," "honest," "giving," and "creative" (Fiedler et al., 1986); to cast *halo effects* over others, perceiving them positively because of a positive initial impression; and to fall prey to the *fundamental attribution error*—attributing others' behaviors to internal rather than external causes (Forgas, 2011a). Taken together, these findings suggest that people in positive moods aren't especially good perceivers and are more gullible (Forgas, 2019). Why? Because they tend to selectively focus only on things that seem positive and rewarding (Tamir & Robinson, 2007), rather than processing information thoughtfully. In simple terms, when you're happy, you tend to skim along the perceptual surface instead of deeply diving in to ponder things (Hunsinger et al., 2012).

Our moods also influence our communication, including how we talk with partners in close relationships (Cunningham, 1988). People in good moods are significantly more likely to disclose relationship thoughts and concerns to close friends, family members, and romantic partners, regardless of whether those partners welcome such sharing. In contrast, negative moods enhance attentiveness to the communication of others—and as a result, people in bad moods are actually better than those in good moods at matching the intimacy level of their responses to the disclosures that have been shared with them. So, for instance, if you reveal that you're "ashamed of how you treated your parents in the past," a friend who is in a bad mood will be more likely to respond by sharing something similarly intimate about *their* family challenges than a friend who is in a good mood (Forgas, 2011b). At the

self-reflection

How do you behave toward others when you're in a bad mood? What strategies do you use to better your mood? Are these practices effective in elevating your mood and improving your communication in the long run, or do they merely provide a temporary escape or distraction?

▶ Research indicates that exercise is usually the best strategy for improving moods. What strategies have you used to successfully pull yourself out of a bad mood? Rawpixel.com/Shutterstock

focus on CULTURE

Happiness across Cultures

A Chinese proverb warns, "We are never happy for a thousand days" (Myers, 2002, p. 47). Although most of us understand that joy is fleeting, we also tend to presume that greater happiness lies on the other side of various cultural divides. If only we made more money, lived in a different country, or were a different age, *then* we *truly* would be happy. But the science of human happiness has shattered these assumptions, suggesting instead that happiness is more personal and relational than cultural.

Consider economic status. Having enough money to afford health care, housing, food, water, and safety is essential, and people who struggle to make ends meet typically are less happy than those of sufficient means (Fischer & Boer, 2011). At an international level, this means people in wealthier nations tend to be happier than those in impoverished countries (Veenhoven, 2014). At the same time, however, once basic needs *are* met, gaining additional wealth has no impact on happiness. People in the United States, for instance, have tripled their buying power since 1950, and yet their happiness has flatlined during this same period (Myers, 2015).

What about age? A study of 170,000 people in 16 countries found no difference in reported happiness and life satisfaction based on age (Myers, 2002). Gender? No overall differences in happiness between women and men exist, although women living in countries with greater gender equality *are* substantially happier than women in less-equal countries (Veenhoven, 2014).

What *does* predict happiness? People high in optimism, extraversion, and agreeableness tend to be happier; as are people who exercise regularly (Myers, 2015). People with jobs or careers they find fulfilling are happier (Tay & Diener, 2011). Faith also matters: religious people are more likely to report being happy than those who are nonreligious (Myers, 2002). And one of the most potent predictors of happiness is also one of the least recognized: *gratitude*. People who routinely communicate grateful emotions to others, and who notice and appreciate their positive experiences, tend to be happier than those who don't (Portocarrero et al., 2020). But what is *the* most important factor? Relationships. When asked, "What is necessary for your happiness?" people overwhelmingly cite satisfying close relationships with family, friends, and romantic partners at the top of their lists (Berscheid & Peplau, 2002).

discussion questions

- What are your own sources of happiness and life satisfaction?
- Do you agree that interpersonal relationships, spiritual beliefs, and healthy living are the most essential ingredients for happiness? Why or why not?

same time, though people in negative moods may be more "tuned in" to the intimacy level of others' communication, they also often prefer *not* to communicate at all; desiring instead to sit and think, be left alone, and avoid social and leisure activities (Cunningham, 1988).

Despite the perceptual shortcomings associated with positive mood states, most people prefer positive moods because negative moods are so unpleasant. Unfortunately, some of the most commonly practiced strategies for improving bad moods—drinking alcohol or caffeinated beverages, taking recreational drugs, and eating—are also the least effective and may actually *worsen* your bad mood (Thayer et al., 1994). More effective strategies for improving bad moods are ones that involve active expenditures of energy, especially strategies that combine relaxation, stress management, deep breathing, and mind–body awareness. The most effective strategy of all appears to be rigorous physical exercise, with evidence indicating that even just a single exercise session can help shift mood in a more positive direction (Chan et al., 2019). Sexual activity does not seem to consistently elevate mood.

Now that we have distinguished between emotions, feelings, and moods, let's turn to consider different types of emotions, and some forces that shape emotions.

TYPES OF EMOTIONS

Take a moment and look at the emotions communicated by the people in the photos along the top of the following pages. How can you discern the emotion expressed in each picture? One way to distinguish between different types of emotions is to examine consistent patterns of facial expressions, hand gestures, and body postures that characterize specific emotions. By considering these patterns, scholars have identified six **primary emotions** that involve unique and consistent behavioral displays across cultures (Ekman, 1972). The six primary emotions are surprise, joy, disgust, anger, fear, and sadness.

Some situations provoke especially intense primary emotions. In such cases, we often use different words to describe the emotion, even though what we're experiencing is simply a more intense version of the same primary emotion (Plutchik, 1980). For instance, receiving a gift from a romantic partner may cause intense joy that we think of as "ecstasy," just as the passing of a close relative will likely trigger intense sadness that we label as "grief" (see Table 4.1).

In other situations, an event may trigger two or more primary emotions simultaneously, resulting in an experience known as **blended emotions** (Plutchik, 1993). For example, imagine that you borrow your romantic partner's phone and accidentally access a series of flirtatious texts between your partner and someone else. You'll likely experience **jealousy**, a blended emotion because it combines the primary emotions anger, fear, and sadness: in this case, *anger* at your partner or the person sending the texts, *fear* that your relationship may be threatened, and *sadness* at the thought of potentially losing your partner to a rival. Other examples of blended emotions include contempt (anger and disgust), remorse (disgust and sadness), and awe (surprise and fear; Plutchik, 1993).

While people in North America often identify six primary emotions—surprise, joy, love, anger, fear, and sadness (Shaver et al., 1992)—some cultural variation

LaunchPad Video
launchpadworks.com

Blended Emotions
Watch this clip online to answer the questions below.

What blended emotions is the woman in the video experiencing? What type of situation could cause this? What types of communication situations make you experience blended emotions? Why?

Want to see more? Check out LaunchPad for a clip on **emotional contagion**.

table 4.1 **Intense Primary Emotions**

Primary Emotion	High-Intensity Counterpart
Surprise	Amazement
Joy	Ecstasy
Disgust	Loathing
Anger	Rage
Fear	Terror
Sadness	Grief

◀ According to studies performed by psychologist Paul Ekman (1972), people around the world associate the same facial expressions with particular emotional states. Part of improving your interpersonal communication is to recognize others' emotions. Can you identify the ones displayed in each of these photographs? (From left to right, the emotions shown are joy, surprise, anger, disgust, fear, and sadness.)
Kiratsinh Jadeja/Getty Images; michael simons/Alamy; Digital Vision/Getty Images; Howard Kingsnorth/Getty Images; SFIO CRACHO/Shutterstock; Marc Romanelli/Getty Images

exists. For example, in traditional Chinese culture, shame and sad love (an emotion concerning attachment to former lovers) are primary emotions. Traditional Hindu philosophy suggests nine primary emotions: sexual passion, amusement, sorrow, anger, fear, perseverance, disgust, wonder, and serenity (Shweder, 1993).

Forces Shaping Emotion

Personality and gender affect emotion

In the movie *Bridesmaids* (2011), Annie is a woman struggling to overcome the failure of her beloved small business, Cake Baby, as well as her breakup with her boyfriend Ted, who continues to lead her on. Annie's sadness and sense of hopelessness lead her to seek comfort from her best friend Lillian, whose own life is on the upswing because of her recent engagement. Lillian asks Annie to be her maid of honor, but the situation quickly devolves as Annie's anxieties and neuroses cause a series of emotional displays, culminating in her ruining a "girls weekend together" and causing a jealous scene at Lillian's bridal shower.

Surrounding Annie throughout the story are other vivid characters. Becca is perpetually upbeat and perky; Helen—Annie's primary rival for Lillian's affections—is fanatically conscientious; Rita, Lillian's cousin, is always sarcastic and negative.

◀ The characters in *Bridesmaids* display many intense emotions, leading to frequent and sometimes explosive conflicts between them. © Universal Pictures/ Courtesy Everett Collection

Adding to the dispositional mix is Nathan, a warm and friendly state trooper who exempts Annie from a traffic ticket and subsequently tries to romance her. But dominating the group is Megan, who is outgoing to the point of aggressiveness. When Annie succumbs to her sadness, it is Megan who lifts her up:[2]

> **ANNIE:** I can't get off the couch, I got fired from my job, I got kicked out of my apartment, I can't pay any of my bills, I don't have any friends. . . .
>
> **MEGAN:** You know what I find interesting, Annie? That you have no friends. You know why that's interesting? Here's a friend standing directly in front of you trying to talk to you, and you choose to talk about the fact that you don't have any friends. No, I don't think you want any help; you just want to have a little pity party. I think Annie wants a little pity party. I'm life, is life bothering you Annie? . . . Fight back for your life!

As with the characters in *Bridesmaids*, our emotions and their expression just seem to happen: an incident occurs, an emotion arises, and we communicate accordingly. Although emotions seem unfiltered and immediate, powerful forces shape how we experience and express them. Two influential forces are personality and gender.

PERSONALITY

Personality profoundly impacts our emotions. Recall the Big Five personality traits described in Chapter 3—"OCEAN," that is, openness, conscientiousness, extraversion, agreeableness, and neuroticism. Three of these five traits strongly influence our experience and communication of emotion (Pervin, 1993). The first is *extraversion*, the degree to which one is outgoing and sociable versus quiet and reserved. High-extraversion people experience positive emotions more frequently compared to low-extraversion people. This appears to be due to the tendency of high-extraversion people to look for happiness in their everyday lives, and focus their attention more on positive than negative events (Larsen & Ketelaar, 1991). They also are better able to regulate their emotions (Pocnet et al., 2017), and they rate themselves as better able to cope with stress and as more skilled at managing their emotional communication than low-extraversion people (Lopes et al., 2005). In *Bridesmaids*, we see this trait in Megan when she discusses her success in overcoming her challenging high school years by working hard and believing in herself, leading her to land a high-ranking government job (with the "highest possible security clearance").

Another personality trait that influences emotion is *agreeableness*. Like Nathan in *Bridesmaids*, people high in agreeableness (who are trusting, friendly, and cooperative) report being happier in general, better able to manage stress, and more skilled at managing their emotional communication compared to people low in agreeableness. Highly agreeable people also score substantially higher on measures of emotion management, are rated by their peers as having superior emotion management skills (Lopes et al., 2005), and—when combined with high self-esteem—are more likely to engage in the disclosure of negative emotions (McCarthy et al., 2017).

The tendency to think negative thoughts about oneself, known as *neuroticism*, also affects emotional experience and expression. Highly neurotic people, like Annie in *Bridesmaids*, focus their attention primarily on negative events (Larsen & Ketelaar, 1991). Consequently, they report more frequent negative emotions than

---

[2]Information from Mumulo and Wiig (2011).

do low-neurotic people and rate themselves as less happy overall. They also describe themselves as less skilled at emotional communication, and they test lower on scientific measures of emotion management than do people low in neuroticism (Lopes et al., 2005).

Although these findings seem to suggest that highly neurotic people are doomed to lives of negative emotion, this isn't necessarily the case. Psychologist Albert Ellis (1913–2007) dedicated much of his professional life to helping people who were neurotic change their self-defeating beliefs. Ellis believed that much of neurosis and its accompanying emotional states—sadness, anger, and anxiety—are tied to three irrational beliefs: "I must be outstandingly competent or I am worthless," "Others must treat me considerately or they are absolutely rotten," and "The world should always give me happiness or I will die" (Ellis & Dryden, 1997). Ellis developed **Rational Emotive Behavior Therapy (REBT)** as a way for therapists to help patients who are neurotic systematically purge themselves of such beliefs.

If you find yourself frequently experiencing negative thoughts similar to those mentioned above, you can use Ellis's five steps to change your thoughts and the negative emotions that flow from them. First, call to mind common situations that upset you. Second, identify irrational beliefs about yourself and others that are tied to these situations. Third, consider the emotional, behavioral, and relational consequences that you suffer as a result of these beliefs—negative outcomes that you would like to change. Fourth, critically challenge these beliefs, disputing their validity. Is there really any support for these beliefs? What evidence contradicts them? What is the worst thing that can happen if you abandon these beliefs? The best thing that can happen? Finally, identify more accurate and realistic beliefs about yourself, others, and the world at large that lead to more positive emotional, behavioral, and relational outcomes, and embrace these beliefs fully.

Clearly, your degree of extraversion, agreeableness, and especially neuroticism influences how often you experience positive and negative emotions and how effectively you manage and communicate these emotions. At the same time, keep in mind that personality is merely one of many pieces that make up the complex puzzle that is emotion. Part of becoming a competent emotional communicator is learning how your personality traits shape your emotional experience and expression, and treating personality-based emotion differences in others with sensitivity and understanding.

GENDER

Like personality, gender also impacts our experience of emotions, but the way in which it does so is more nuanced than simple binary differences. Scholars once believed that women experienced more sadness, fear, shame, and guilt, and less anger and hostile emotions compared to men (Fischer et al., 2004). But more recent findings suggest that these differences might not hold across cultures, and that we need to consider the influence of other factors, such as age (Gong et al., 2018), sexual identity, and social setting. For example, *gender socialization* (a concept we discussed in Chapter 2 and will discuss in more detail in Chapter 6) creates prescriptive norms and stereotypes that shape how we experience and express our emotions. Women may experience and express certain emotions more than men because they are conforming to the standards that they have been taught to follow in their particular culture. Recent studies suggest that this conformity may dissipate as individuals age, leading to less pronounced gender differences in older people.

self-reflection

To what degree are you extraverted, agreeable, and neurotic? How have these traits affected your emotions? Your relationships? Are these traits, and their impact, enduring and permanent, or can they be changed in ways that will improve your interpersonal communication?

Further, in terms of the intensity of the emotional experience, when women and men experience the same emotions, there is no difference in the intensity of the emotions (Fischer et al., 2004). Whether it's anger, sadness, joy, or disgust, people of all genders experience emotions with equal intensity.

Now that we've covered factors that impact our experience of emotions, let's turn our attention to exploring the concept of emotional intelligence, and the ways we can manage, prevent, and reappraise our emotions.

Managing Your Emotional Experience and Expression

Dealing with emotions after, before, and while they occur

It's arguably *the* most well-known psychology experiment, ever.[3] Over a six-year period, Stanford psychologist Walter Mischel brought 653 young children from the university's Bing Nursery School into a room and offered them a tasty treat of their choice: a marshmallow, an Oreo cookie, or a pretzel stick. But he also presented them with a dilemma. If they could resist eating the treat while he stepped out for several minutes, they would get a second treat as a reward. The children were then left alone. The experiment was a simple test of impulse control: the ability to manage one's emotional arousal, excitement, and desire. Most of the kids gave in and ate the treat, usually in less than three minutes. But about 30 percent held out. Years later, Mischel gathered more data from the same children, who were then in high school. He was stunned to learn that their choices in the experiment predicted a broad range of outcomes. Children who had waited were more socially skilled, were better able to cope with stress, were less likely to have emotional outbursts when frustrated, were better able to deal with temptations, and had closer, more stable friendships than those who hadn't waited. They also had substantially higher SAT scores. Why was "the marshmallow test" such a powerful predictor of long-term personal and interpersonal outcomes? Because it taps a critical skill: the ability to constructively manage emotions. As Mischel notes, "If you can deal with hot emotions in the face of temptation, then you can study for the SAT instead of watching television. It's not just about marshmallows."

⚪ Can you recall a time when you had to resist an emotional impulse or desire, as in the marshmallow study? What was the outcome of this event?
© Quinn Kirk/Terry Wild Stock

EMOTIONAL INTELLIGENCE

Managing your emotions is part of **emotional intelligence**: the ability to interpret emotions accurately and to use this information to manage emotions, communicate them competently, and solve relationship problems (Gross & John, 2002). People with high degrees of emotional intelligence typically possess four skills:

- Acute understanding of their own emotions
- Ability to see things from others' perspectives and to have a sense of compassion regarding others' emotional states (*empathy*)
- Aptitude for constructively managing their own emotions
- Capacity for harnessing their emotional states in ways that create competent decision making, communication, and relationship problem solving (Kotzé & Venter, 2011)

---

[3]Information that follows is from Goleman (2007b); Lehrer (2009); and Shoda et al. (1990).

Given that emotional intelligence (EI) involves understanding emotions coupled with the ability to manage them in ways that optimize interpersonal competence, it's not surprising that people with high EI experience a broad range of positive outcomes. For example, within leadership positions, people with high EI are more likely than low EI people to garner trust, inspire followers, and be perceived as having integrity (Kotzé & Venter, 2011). High EI individuals are less likely than low EI people to bully people or use violence to get what they want (Mayer et al., 2004). Because of their strong empathy and skill at emotion management, high EI people even find it easier to forgive relational partners who have wronged them (Hodgson & Wertheim, 2007). And high EI people have the ability

self-QUIZ

Assessing Your Emotional Intelligence

Consider your emotional experience and communication in your daily life. Then look at the statements listed under each of the four emotional intelligence dimensions, placing a check mark next to each statement that describes your abilities. Follow the directions below to interpret your score.

Perceiving Emotions
Accurately perceiving and interpreting emotional messages as they are communicated by others' facial expressions, vocal tones, and gestures; accurately perceiving your own emotions based on your physiological and mental experiences

_____ I can accurately identify emotions experienced by other people.

_____ I can accurately identify my own emotions by interpreting my physical and psychological states.

_____ I can communicate my emotions accurately to others.

_____ I can discriminate between accurate/ honest feelings and inaccurate/ dishonest feelings in myself and others.

Using Emotions to Facilitate Thinking
Recognizing how emotions and moods influence perception and learning to harness emotional states for more effective problem solving, reasoning, decision making, and creative endeavors

_____ I can redirect and reorganize my thoughts based on emotions I am experiencing.

_____ I can use my emotions to help improve my relationship choices.

_____ I can use my mood changes to help appreciate different points of view.

_____ I can use my emotions to facilitate problem solving and creativity.

Understanding Emotions
Accurately labeling emotions and learning how they blend together and change over time

_____ I understand the similarities and differences between various emotions.

_____ I understand the causes and consequences of emotions.

_____ I understand the differences between feelings, moods, emotions, and blended emotions.

_____ I understand how the experience of emotion changes as time passes.

Managing Emotional Experience and Communication
Learning how to manage the experience and communication of emotions to avoid negative or destructive consequences

_____ I am open to experiencing both pleasant and unpleasant emotions.

_____ I monitor and reflect on my emotions.

_____ I can engage in, prolong, or detach from an emotional state, depending on whether I perceive it as constructive or destructive.

_____ I effectively manage my own emotions.

Note: Information from Mayer and Salovey (1997).

Scoring: Count the number of check marks you made in each dimension. Scores of 0–2 for a particular dimension represent an area of emotional intelligence that needs strengthening; scores of 3–4 represent an area of strength.

to harness the power of positive emotions, savoring them rather than dampening them, thus boosting their overall life satisfaction (Szczygiel & Mikolajczak, 2017) and experiencing better health and well-being (MacCann et al., 2020).

Of the skills that constitute emotional intelligence, emotion management is arguably the most important one to improve because—as demonstrated by Mischel's research—it directly influences your communication, which in turn affects your outcomes (Lopes et al., 2005). How? Put bluntly, *if you can't manage your emotions, you can't communicate competently.* **Emotion management** involves attempts to influence which emotions you have, when you have them, and how you experience and express them (Gross et al., 2006). Because emotions naturally trigger attempts to manage them, the practical issue is not whether you will manage your emotions but how you can do so in ways that improve your interpersonal communication and relationships.

MANAGING EMOTIONS AFTER THEY OCCUR

One strategy for managing emotions is to try to modify or control them *after we become aware of them* (Gross et al., 2006). An event triggers arousal, interpretation, and awareness of an emotion. We then consciously try to modify our internal experience and outward communication of that emotion. If we think of emotional arousal as a flame, these strategies try to regulate a flame that already has been ignited.

The two most common ways people manage emotions after they have been triggered are suppression and venting. **Suppression** involves inhibiting thoughts, arousal, and outward behavioral displays of emotion (Richards et al., 2003), basically damping down the flame. For example, one participant in an emotion management study describes suppressing his communication of happiness and surprise after scoring well on a college paper in which he had invested little effort (Gross et al., 2006):

> I didn't work very hard on this paper so I was surprised. My roommate actually did some work and didn't get a good grade, so he was very down about it. I was very happy inside, but at the same time, I didn't want to show up my roommate because he's my friend. Instead of acting happy and surprised, I kind of put on my academic sad face and said, "Oh, I didn't do well either." (p. 11)

The desire to suppress stems from the recognition that feeling, thinking, and openly communicating certain emotions would be relationally, socially, or culturally inappropriate according to the constraining norms detailed in the "key features of emotion" discussion at the beginning of this chapter. Although people sometimes suppress positive emotions, suppression occurs most commonly with negative emotions, especially anger and sadness (Gross et al., 2006). This is because displays of pleasant emotions elicit favorable responses from others, whereas the expression of negative emotions often drives other people away (Argyle & Lu, 1990; Furr & Funder, 1998).

Suppression is the most widely practiced strategy for managing unavoidable and unwanted emotions. But its effectiveness is marginal because you are trying to modify the intense arousal you are already experiencing, the thoughts you are already thinking, and the body's natural inclination to display this arousal and these thoughts in the form of expressions (Lopes et al., 2005).

The inverse of suppression is **venting**: allowing emotions to dominate our thoughts and explosively expressing them (Fuendeling, 1998; Kostiuk & Fouts, 2002)—fanning the flame of emotional arousal. Venting may be positive, such as when we jump up and shout for joy after learning we got the job we wanted. At other times, we vent negative emotions, such as when we blow up at a spouse or other family member who has been repeatedly pestering us.

An alternative option for managing extant emotions is **acceptance**: allowing emotions to naturally arise without damping or fanning them, and acknowledging that they are an inherent component of human nature rather than judging them as good or bad. This tactic may be especially useful with negative emotions. Research suggests that people who have the ability to engage in acceptance experience better psychological health outcomes, including less brooding, less anxiety, and less negative emotion in response to stress (Ford et al., 2018).

PREVENTING EMOTIONS BEFORE THEY OCCUR

An alternative to managing emotions after they occur is to prevent them from occurring in the first place, so the arousal flame is never ignited. People commonly use four different strategies to prevent emotions, the first of which is **encounter avoidance**: staying away from people, places, or activities that you know will provoke emotions you don't want to experience (Gross et al., 2006). For example, you might purposely avoid a particular class that your ex signed up for because seeing them always provokes intense and unpleasant emotions within you.

A second preventive strategy is **encounter structuring**: intentionally avoiding specific topics that you know will provoke unwanted emotion during encounters with others. For example, over the last many years, as politics in the United States have become increasingly partisan and divisive, many families (including ours!) have forged agreements to simply not talk about politics at all, in an attempt to preserve the family peace.

A third preventive strategy is **attention focus**: intentionally devoting your attention only to aspects of an event or encounter that you know will not provoke an undesired emotion. Imagine that you're sitting in class, listening to a lecture, but the person sitting behind you keeps getting and sending text messages. To use attention focus, you would actively watch and listen to the professor, letting the sound of the text alerts drop beneath conscious awareness so that it doesn't set you off.

A fourth way people preventively manage emotion is through **deactivation**: systematically desensitizing yourself to emotional experience (Fuendeling, 1998). Some people, especially after experiencing a traumatic emotional event, decide that they no longer want to feel anything. The result is an overall deadening of emotion. Though the desire to use this strategy is understandable, deactivation can trigger deep depression.

REAPPRAISING EMOTIONS WHILE THEY OCCUR

An alternative approach to emotion management requires you to realize how you are interpreting an emotion-eliciting event *while* making sense of it. **Reappraisal** entails actively changing how you think about the meaning of emotion-eliciting situations so that their emotional impact is changed (Jackson et al., 2000). Rather than damping or fanning the flame, or keeping it from igniting in the first place, this strategy takes control of what's *fueling* the flame in the first place so that you

skills practice

Using Reappraisal
Managing difficult emotions through reappraisal

❶ Identify a recurring behavior or event that triggers emotions you'd like to manage more effectively.

❷ When the behavior or event happens, focus your thoughts on positive aspects of yourself, the other person, your relationship, and the situation.

❸ Consider ways to communicate that will foster positive outcomes.

❹ Communicate in those ways.

❺ Observe how your positive thoughts and constructive communication affect the relationship.

can adjust the setting of the fire. For example, imagine that your partner tells you that they occasionally receive friendly Facebook messages from former romantic partners. How do you make sense of this information? Perhaps you visualize the previous partner and, with jealousy rising, prepare a snarky retort. Alternatively, you could feel flattered that your partner felt ethically obligated to honestly share these messages with you, and calmly prepare to discuss relational rules for communicating with ex-partners.

As this example illustrates, reappraisal is effective because you employ it at the *onset* of, or immediately before, an emotional reaction, essentially directing the type of emotion that arises according to how you interpret information. This strategy requires little effort compared to trying to suppress or control your emotions after they've occurred. In addition, reappraisal produces interpersonal communication that is partner-focused and perceived as engaged and emotionally responsive (Gross et al., 2006). Across studies, people who manage their emotional communication most effectively report using reappraisal as their primary strategy (John & Gross, 2004).

Reappraisal is accomplished in two steps. First, before or during an encounter that you suspect will trigger an undesired emotion in yourself, *call to mind the positive aspects of the encounter*. If you truly can't think of anything positive about the other person, your relationship, or the situation, focus on seeing yourself as the kind of person who can constructively communicate even during unpleasant encounters with people you ardently dislike. Second, *consider the short- and long-term consequences of your actions*. Think about how communicating positively in the here and now will shape future outcomes in constructive ways.

You can use reappraisal to effectively address *positive* emotional arousal as well. Imagine that you've received a job offer from a company you have long desired to work for. Your roommate, however, hasn't gotten a single interview. Jumping for joy will not help maintain your relationship with them. In this case, reappraisal allows you to focus on your roommate's feelings and perspective; you might respond with "I did receive an exciting offer, but I also know that you're going to land somewhere great. It's a tough market right now, but you have so many desirable skills and qualities; any employer would be lucky to have you."

Thus far, we have described the nature of emotion, factors influencing it, and ways to manage our emotional expression and arousal. Let's now consider four especially challenging emotional states.

Emotional Challenges

Intense emotions are the most difficult to handle

Each day, we encounter a variety of people and settings that trigger emotions and challenge our communication, our relationships, and the quality of our lives. For example, romantic jealousy—which we will discuss in Chapter 11—is toxic to interpersonal communication and must be managed effectively for relationships to survive (Guerrero & Andersen, 1998). Likewise, fear—of emotional investment, vulnerability, or long-term commitment—can prevent us from forming intimate connections with others (Mickelson et al., 1997). In the remainder of this chapter, we focus on four challenges that occur all too frequently in our daily lives: anger, lack of empathy online, passion, and grief.

ANGER

Anger is a negative primary emotion that occurs when you are blocked or interrupted from attaining an important goal by what you see as the improper action of an external agent (Berkowitz & Harmon-Jones, 2004), when someone disparages you, or when you witness another person who is important to you being disparaged (McKasy, 2020). As this definition suggests, anger is almost always triggered by someone or something external to us and is driven by our perception that the interruption or behavior is unfair (Scherer, 2001). So, for example, when your sister refuses to give you a much-needed loan, you're more likely to feel angry if you think she can afford to give you the loan but is simply choosing not to. By contrast, if you think your sister is willing but unable to help you, you'll be less likely to feel anger toward her.

Each of us experiences anger frequently; the average person is mildly to moderately angry anywhere from several times a day to several times a week (Berkowitz & Harmon-Jones, 2004). Perhaps because of its familiarity, we commonly underestimate anger's destructive potential. Anger causes perceptual errors that motivate people to perceive bias, impulsively approach risk in ways they normally wouldn't (McKasy, 2020), and potentially respond in a verbally or physically violent fashion toward others (Lemerise & Dodge, 1993). For instance, both men and women report the desire to punch, smash, kick, bite, or take similar actions that will hurt others when they are angry (Carlson & Hatfield, 1992). The impact of anger on interpersonal communication is also devastating. Angry people are more likely to argue, make accusations, yell, swear, and make hurtful and abusive remarks. Additionally, passive-aggressive communication such as ignoring others, pulling away, giving people dirty looks, and using the "silent treatment" are all more likely to happen when you're angry (Knobloch, 2005).

The most frequently used strategy for managing anger is suppression. You bottle it up inside, rather than let it out. Occasional suppression can be constructive, such as when open communication of anger would be unprofessional, or when anger has been triggered by mistaken perceptions or attributions. But *always* suppressing anger can cause physical and mental problems: you put yourself in a near-constant state of arousal and negative thinking known as **chronic hostility**. People suffering from chronic hostility spend most of their waking hours simmering in a thinly veiled state of suppressed rage. Their thoughts and perceptions are dominated by the negative. They are more likely than others to believe that human nature is innately evil and that most people are immoral, selfish, exploitative, and manipulative. Ironically, because chronically hostile people believe the worst about others, they tend to be difficult, self-involved, demanding, and ungenerous (Tavris, 1989).

A second common anger management strategy is *venting*, which many people view as helpful and healthy; it "gets the anger out." The assumption that venting will rid you of anger is rooted in the concept of *catharsis*, which holds that openly expressing your emotions enables you to purge them. But in contrast to popular beliefs about the benefits of venting, research suggests that while venting may provide a temporary sense of

LaunchPad

Online Self-Quiz: Test Your Chronic Hostility. To take this self-quiz, visit LaunchPad: **launchpadworks.com**

⬇ Anger is our most intense and potentially destructive emotion. Both men and women report the desire to react to anger in similar ways: through verbal outbursts or physical violence. WaveBreak Images/Media Bakery

pleasure, it actually *boosts* anger. One field study of engineers and technicians who were fired from their jobs found that the more individuals vented their anger about the company, the angrier they became (Ebbeson et al., 1975). Another study found that venting anger by hitting a punching bag while mentally focusing on the object of anger was associated with both *more* anger and *more* aggressive behavior (Bushman, 2002).

To manage your anger, it's better to use strategies such as encounter avoidance, encounter structuring, and reappraisal. In cases in which something or someone has already triggered anger within you, consider using the **Jefferson strategy**, named after the third president of the United States. When a person says or does something that makes you angry, count slowly to 10 before you speak or act (Tavris, 1989). If you are very angry, count slowly to 100; then speak or act. Thomas Jefferson adopted this simple strategy for reducing his own anger during interpersonal encounters.

Although the Jefferson strategy may seem silly, it's effective because it creates a delay between the event that triggered your anger, the accompanying arousal and awareness, and your communication response. The delay between your internal physical and mental reactions and your outward communication allows your arousal to diminish somewhat, including lowering your adrenaline, blood pressure, and heart rate. Therefore, you communicate in a less extreme (and possibly less inappropriate) way than if you had not "counted to 10." A delay also gives you time for critical self-reflection, perception-checking, and empathy. These three skills can help you identify errors in your assessment of the event or person and plan a competent response. The Jefferson strategy is especially easy to use when you're communicating by email or text message, two media that naturally allow for a delay between receiving a message and responding.

TEXT-BASED ONLINE COMMUNICATION AND EMPATHY DEFICITS

After giving a lecture about stereotypes, Steve received an email from a student: "Stereotypes are DEMEANING!! People should DENOUNCE them, not TEACH them!!! WHY LECTURE ABOUT STEREOTYPES???" Noting the lack of greeting, capped letters, and excessive punctuation, he interpreted the message as

▽ When we communicate face-to-face, we have the advantage of communicating in real time and having feedback from the person with whom we are interacting. Online communication can cause empathy deficits for which we may need to compensate.
Left: Steve Hix/Getty Images;
Right: Bruno Gori/Cultura/Getty Images

angry. Irritated, he popped back a flippant response, "Uhhhh . . . because people often wrongly believe that stereotypes are true?" Hours later, he received a caustic reply: "I think it's really disrespectful of you to treat my question so rudely!! I'M PAYING YOU TO TEACH, NOT MOCK!!!"

You may have had similar experiences in online text-based encounters—those *lacking* webcams allowing you to see another person's face—in which anger or other emotions were expressed inappropriately, triggering a destructive exchange. In most of these interactions, the messages traded back and forth would never have been expressed face-to-face.

Why are we more likely to inappropriately express our emotions in text-based online encounters? Two features of these interactions—asynchronicity and invisibility—help explain this phenomenon (Suler, 2004). Many of these encounters are *asynchronous*—so rather than interacting with others in real time, we exchange written messages (such as texts, emails, or social media posts) that are read and responded to later. It's almost as if time is magically suspended. We know that there *will* likely be responses to our messages, but we choose when (and if) we view those responses. This predisposes us to openly express emotions that we might otherwise conceal if we knew the response would be immediate.

These encounters also provide us with a sense of *invisibility*. Without sharing a physical context with the people with whom we're communicating, we feel as if we're not really there—that people can't really see or hear us. Consequently, we feel distant from the consequences of our messages.

Brain research suggests that our sense of invisibility when communicating in text-based online encounters may have a neurological basis. Recall from Chapter 1 that *feedback* consists of the verbal and nonverbal messages recipients convey to indicate their reaction to communication. Now remember our definition of *empathy* from Chapter 3: the ability to experience others' thoughts and emotions. Research documents that the same part of the brain that controls empathy—the orbitofrontal cortex—also monitors feedback (Goleman, 2006). This means that our ability to experience empathy is neurologically tied to our ability to perceive feedback (Beer et al., 2006). When communicating face-to-face, over the phone, or on a video call, we constantly track the feedback of others, watching their facial expressions, eye contact, and gestures, and listening to their tone of voice. This enables us to feel empathy for them, to consider what they're thinking and feeling about our communication. When we see or hear people react negatively to something we're saying, we can instantly modify our messages in ways that avoid negative consequences.

Now consider what happens when we lack feedback. Without the ability to perceive others' immediate responses to our communication, it's difficult for us to experience empathy and to adjust our communication in ways that maintain appropriateness (Goleman, 2007a). We're less able to *perspective-take* (see the situation and our communication from another's point of view) and to feel *empathic concern* (experience another's emotions and feelings). Consequently, we're more likely to express negative emotions—especially anger—in blunt, tactless, and inappropriate ways. We may shout at others by using capped letters and exclamation points in our email messages, or we may tweet things we'd never say over the phone or face-to-face. Complicating matters further, people on the receiving end of our communication have the same deficit. Their messages may also be less sensitive, less tactful, and maybe even more offensive than their face-to-face messages. *Without feedback, we have difficulty experiencing empathy and gauging the appropriateness of our emotional expression.*

self-reflection

Recall an online encounter in which you inappropriately expressed emotion. How did lack of empathy shape your behavior? Would you have communicated the same way face-to-face? What does this tell you about the relationship between feedback, empathy, and emotional expression?

skills
practice

Managing Anger in Online Text-Based Encounters
Responding competently during an online encounter in which you're angry

❶ Identify a message or post that triggers anger.

❷ Before responding, manage your anger using one or more of the strategies in this chapter.

❸ Practice perspective-taking and empathic concern toward the message source.

❹ Craft a response that expresses empathy, and save it as a draft.

❺ Later, review your message, revise it as necessary, and then send it.

Moreover, individual differences may influence our empathic abilities. Recall our discussion of attachment styles from our exploration of self in Chapter 2, along with our review of options for managing your emotions in this chapter. Research exploring the impact of these two issues has found that individuals with more secure attachment orientations can reappraise their emotions, rather than suppress or brood over them, allowing for greater empathy (Troyer & Greitemeyer, 2018).

What can you do to experience and express emotions more competently when you can't see the other person? First, compensate for the online empathy deficit by investing intense effort into perspective-taking and empathic concern.

Second, directly communicate these aspects of empathy, following suggestions from Chapter 3. Ask questions that seek the other person's perspectives, such as "What's your view on this situation?" Validate their views when they provide them ("You make a lot of sense") and express empathic concern ("I hope you're doing OK"). If you perceive anger in a message, convey that you recognize the other person is angry and that you feel bad about it ("I feel really terrible that you're so upset").

Third, expect and be tolerant of any aggressive messages you receive, accepting that such behavior is a natural outcome of the online environment, rather than evidence that other people are mean or rude. Finally, avoid crafting and sending angry online messages in the heat of the moment. You might craft a response, wait 24 hours to cool off, revisit it, assess it in terms of empathy, and then modify or even delete the draft if it's inappropriate.

PASSION

Few emotions fascinate us more than romantic passion. Thousands of websites, infomercials, books, and magazine articles focus on how to create, maintain, or recapture passion. Feeling passion toward romantic partners seems almost obligatory, and we often decide to discard relationships when passion fades (Berscheid & Regan, 2005). At the same time, most of us recognize that passion is fleeting and distressingly fragile (Berscheid, 2002).

Passion is a blended emotion, a combination of surprise and joy coupled with a number of positive feelings, such as excitement, amazement, and sexual attraction. People who elicit passion in us are those who communicate in ways that deviate from what we expect (triggering surprise and amazement), whom we interpret positively (generating joy and excitement), and whom we perceive as physically pleasing (leading to sexual attraction).

If passion necessarily involves joy, excitement, and sexual attraction, why would we consider passion a *challenging* emotion? Because passion stems in large part from surprise. Consequently, the longer and better you know someone, the less passion you will experience toward that person on a daily basis (Berscheid, 2002). In the early stages of romantic involvements, our partners communicate in ways that are novel and positive. The first time our lovers invite us on a date, kiss us, or disclose their love are surprising events and intensely passionate. But as partners become increasingly familiar with each other, their communication and behavior do, too. Things that were once perceived as unique become predictable. Partners who have known each other intimately for years may be familiar with almost all the communication behaviors in each other's repertoires (Berscheid, 2002). Consequently, the capacity to surprise partners in dramatic, positive, and unanticipated ways is diminished (Hatfield et al., 1984).

Because passion significantly derives from what we perceive as surprising, you can't engineer a passionate evening by carefully negotiating a dinner or romantic rendezvous. You or your partner might experience passion if an event is truly unexpected, but jointly planning and then acting out a romantic candlelight dinner or weekend getaway cannot recapture passion for both you and your partner. When it comes to passion, the best you can hope for in long-term romantic relationships is a warm afterglow (Berscheid, 2002). However, this is not to say that you can't maintain a happy *and* long-term romance; maintaining this kind of relationship requires strategies that we will discuss in Chapter 11.

self-reflection

How has passion changed over time in your romantic relationships? What have you and your partners done to deal with these changes? Is passion a necessary component of romance, or is it possible to be in love without passion?

GRIEF

In the 2016 movie *Arrival*, linguist Louise Banks (played by Amy Adams) is haunted by grief-stained flashbacks of the years she shared with her daughter—prior to her daughter's untimely death from a terminal illness. The only problem is, she never *had* a daughter. As the film progresses (spoiler alert!), Louise discovers that what she mistook for memories are actually flash-forward visions of *future* events. She then faces a dreadful choice: Does she follow the life and relationship choices that will lead her to *have* her daughter—knowing the eventual outcome and the misery that will result? Or, does she choose a different path, to protect herself? She chooses to have her daughter, knowing that she will have but a short time with her, and keeps this knowledge from her husband. When he later discovers Louise's foreknowledge of the tragedy that transpires, he tells her, "You made the wrong choice," and leaves her.

We all choose whether or not to become intimately attached to others. But when we *do* bond with other mortal beings, the risk of pain through loss arises along with the love, silently waiting in the wings as our love develops. Such pain often takes the form of **grief**: intense sadness following substantial loss. But grief isn't only about mortality. We can experience grief in response to *any* type of major loss. This may include parental (or personal) divorce, physical disability due to injury (as is the case for many returning veterans), breakup of a romantic

◁ In *Arrival*, Louise Banks chooses a life that will allow her to give birth to a daughter, even though she knows she will experience the pain of grief when she loses her child to a terminal illness. Jan Thijs/ © Paramount Pictures/Courtesy Everett Collection

relationship, dismissal from a much-loved job, or even the destruction or loss of a valued object, such as an engagement ring or a treasured family heirloom.

Managing grief is enormously and uniquely taxing. Unlike other negative emotions such as anger, which is typically triggered by a onetime, short-lived event, grief stays with us for a long time—triggered repeatedly by experiences linked with the loss.

Managing Your Grief   No magic pill can erase the suffering associated with a grievous loss. It seems ludicrous to think of applying strategies such as reappraisal, encounter structuring, or the Jefferson strategy to such pain. Grief is a unique emotional experience, and none of the emotion management strategies discussed in this chapter so far can help you.

One strategy that can be effective is *emotion-sharing*: talking about your grief with others who are experiencing or have experienced similar pain, or people who are skilled at providing you with much-needed emotional support and comfort. Participating in a support group for people who have suffered similar losses can encourage you to share your emotions. When you share your grief, you feel powerfully connected with others, and this sense of connection can be a source of comfort. You also gain affirmation that the grief process you're experiencing is normal. For example, a fellow support-group participant who also lost his mother to cancer might tell you that he, too, finds Mother's Day a particularly painful time. Finally, other participants in a support group can help you remember that grief does get gradually more bearable over time.

For those of us without ready access to face-to-face support groups, online support offers a viable alternative. Besides not requiring transportation and allowing access to written records of any missed meetings, online support groups provide a

🔽 This photograph taken by Arko Datta shows a woman mourning a relative who was killed in the 2004 tsunami in South Asia. It won the World Press Photo Foundation Spot News award in 2005. REUTERS/ Arko Datta

certain degree of anonymity for people who feel shy or uncomfortable within traditional group settings (Weinberg et al., 1995). You can interact in a way that preserves some degree of privacy. This is an important advantage, as many people find it easier to discuss sensitive topics online than face-to-face, where they run the risk of embarrassment (Furger, 1996). Indeed, social network sites may help buffer our stress. Research on undergraduate students in Hong Kong found that those who self-disclosed on Facebook experienced less depression, had greater life satisfaction, and perceived more social support (Zhang, 2017).

Comforting Others   The challenges you face in helping others manage their grief are compounded by the popular tendency to use suppression for managing sadness. The decision to use suppression derives from the widespread belief that it's important to maintain a stoic bearing, a "stiff upper lip," during personal tragedies (Beach, 2002). However, a person who uses suppression to manage grief can end up experiencing stress-related disorders, such as chronic anxiety or depression. Also, the decision to suppress can lead even normally open and communicative people to stop talking about their feelings. This places you in the awkward position of trying to help others manage emotions that they themselves are unwilling to admit they are experiencing.

   The best way you can help others manage their grief is to engage in **supportive communication**—sharing messages that express emotional support and that offer personal assistance (Burleson & MacGeorge, 2002). Competent support messages convey sincere expressions of sympathy and condolence, concern for the other person, and encouragement to express emotions. Incompetent support messages tell a person how they *should* feel or indicate that the individual is somehow inadequate or blameworthy. Communication scholar and social support expert Amanda Holmstrom offers seven suggestions for improving your supportive communication.[4]

1. *Make sure the person is ready to talk.* You may have amazing support skills, but if the person is too upset to talk, don't push it. Instead, make it clear that you care and want to help, and that you'll be there to listen when they need you.

2. *Find the right place and time.* Once a person *is* ready, find a place and a time conducive to quiet conversation. Avoid distracting settings such as parties, where you won't be able to focus, and find a time of the day where neither of you has other pressing obligations.

3. *Ask good questions.* Start with open-ended queries such as "How are you feeling?" or "What's on your mind?" Then follow up with more targeted questions based on the response, such as "Are you eating and sleeping OK?" (if not, this could be a potential indicator of depression) or "Have you connected with a support group?" (essential to emotion-sharing). Don't assume that because you've been in a similar situation, you know what someone is going through. Refrain from saying, "I know just how you feel."

   Importantly, *if you suspect a person is contemplating suicide, ask them directly about it.* Say, "Have you been thinking about killing yourself?" or "Has suicide crossed your mind?" Then, if the answer is "Yes," ask, "Do you have a plan?"

LaunchPad Video
launchpadworks.com

Supportive Communication
Watch this clip online to answer the questions below.

What supportive messages are given in this video? How successful are they? If you had to comfort someone who was grieving, how would you convey supportive communication?

---

[4]The content that follows was provided to the authors by Dr. Amanda Holmstrom and published with permission. The authors thank Dr. Holmstrom for her contribution.

This will help you gauge imminent risk. People often mistakenly think that direct questions such as these will push someone over the edge, but in fact it's the opposite. Research suggests that someone considering suicide *wants* to talk about it but believes that no one cares. If you ask direct questions, a suicidal person typically *won't* be offended or lie but instead will open up to you. Then you can intervene, and immediately get the person to a counseling center or emergency room, or direct them to resources like the National Suicide Prevention Hotline (1-800-273-8255). Someone *not* considering suicide will express surprise at the question, perhaps laughing it off with a "What? No way!"

Supportive Communication
Skillfully providing emotional support

❶ Let the person know you're available to talk, but don't force an encounter.

❷ Find a quiet, private space.

❸ Start with general questions, and work toward more specific questions. If you think they might be suicidal, ask directly—and if they indicate that they are, immediately direct them to resources such as the National Suicide Prevention Hotline.

❹ Assure the person that their feelings are normal.

❺ Show that you're attending closely to what is being said.

❻ Ask before offering advice.

❼ Let the person know you care!

4. *Legitimize, don't minimize.* Don't dismiss the problem or the significance of the person's feelings by saying things such as "It could have been worse," "Why are you so upset?!" or "You can always find another lover!" Research shows that these comments are unhelpful. Instead, let the person know that it's normal and OK to feel what they're feeling.

5. *Listen actively.* Show the person that you are interested in what is being said. Engage in good eye contact, lean toward them, and say "Uh-huh" and "Yeah" when appropriate. We will offer more detailed suggestions for active listening in Chapter 7.

6. *Offer advice cautiously.* We want to help someone who is suffering, so we often jump right in and offer advice. But many times that's not helpful or even wanted. Advice is best when it's asked for, when the advice giver has relevant expertise or experience (e.g., is a relationship counselor), or when it advocates actions the person actually can take. Advice is hurtful when it implies that the person is to blame or can't solve their own problems. When in doubt, ask if advice would be appreciated—or just hold back.

7. *Show concern and give praise.* Let the person know you genuinely care and are concerned about their well-being ("I am *so* sorry for your loss; you're really important to me"). Build the person up by praising their strength in handling this challenge. Showing care and concern helps connect you to someone, while praise will help a person feel better.

Living a Happy Emotional Life

Interpersonal connections determine our joy

We all live lives rich in relationships and punctuated with emotion. Lovers arrive, bringing gifts of passion and tenderness, and then exit, marking their passage with anger and sadness. Children flash into being, evoking previously unimaginable exhilaration and exhaustion. Friends and family members tread parallel paths, sharing our emotions, and then pass on, leaving grief and memories in their wake.

Across all our relationship experiences, what balances out our anger and grief is our joy. All human beings share the capacity to relish intense joy and the desire to maintain such happiness in an impermanent and ever-changing world. Also universal is the fact that our personal joy is determined by the quality of our interpersonal connections. We have more fun when we are with others compared to when we

We create joy—through every decision we make and every thought, word, and deed.

pursue solitary enjoyment (Reis et al., 2017). And when our relationships with family, friends, coworkers, and romantic partners are happy, we are happy, and when they're not, we're not.

Yet joy doesn't drop magically from the sky into our hearts and minds and stay there. *We create joy*—through every decision we make and every thought, word, and deed. When we manage our emotional experiences and communication poorly, the interpersonal sorrows we wreak on others reflect back on us in the form of personal unhappiness. When we steadfastly and skillfully manage our emotions, the positive relationship outcomes we create multiply and, with them, our happiness and the joy of those who surround us.

Managing Anger and Providing Support

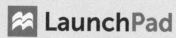 **LaunchPad**   For the best experience, complete all parts of this activity in LaunchPad: **launchpadworks.com**

1 Background

Managing your anger and providing supportive communication are two skills that can clash when you're trying to support someone who is making you angry. To understand how you might competently manage such a relationship challenge, read the case study in Part 2; then, drawing on all you know about interpersonal communication, work through the problem-solving model in Part 3.

 Visit LaunchPad to watch the video in Part 4 and assess your communication in Part 5.

2 Case Study

You're the oldest sibling in a close family in which everyone freely expresses their emotions. Of all your siblings, you share an especially close bond with Sam, the youngest. When Sam accepts a scholarship out of state, you're sad to see him go, but you're excited for his future and take comfort in the daily texts you exchange.

Shortly after Sam moves away, your grandmother (Nana) has a heart attack. Doctors initially think she will make a full recovery, so you text Sam and tell him not to worry. However, her condition suddenly worsens, and she passes away. Everyone is grief-stricken, but Sam is devastated. He is the only one in your immediate family who didn't see her before she died.

When Sam arrives for the funeral, he seems sullen and bitter. But so much is going on that you don't get a chance to talk with him at length. Before you know it, he has left. Following the funeral, Sam rebuffs your attempts to communicate with him. He doesn't return your texts, and after several messages he finally emails you, "Leave me alone!" You become increasingly worried about how he is dealing with his grief. You leave Sam a voice mail telling him that you're coming to visit. Despite receiving no response, you go anyway.

Arriving after several hours of grueling travel, you are shocked to find Sam unwelcoming. Scowling, he says, "What are you doing here? I thought I told you to leave me alone." You start getting angry. After all, you spent a good portion of your savings to get there, and you made the trip out of love and concern. As you try to manage your anger by using the Jefferson strategy, Sam attacks: "Oh, I get it. This is the big 'ease your conscience' trip. You figure that if you comfort me, I'll feel better about you lying to me about Nana's condition. Well, it's not going to work. I didn't get to see her before she died, and it's your fault, so why don't you take your self-serving concern and go home!" He slams the door in your face.

You're left standing on the porch, furious. Do you make the several-hour trip home, heeding Sam's request even though you know he said it out of anger? Or do you pursue your original plan of trying to help Sam deal with his grief?

Your Turn

Think of all you've learned thus far about interpersonal communication. Then work through the following five steps. Remember, there are no "right" answers, so think hard about what is the *best* choice! (P.S. Need help? See the *Helpful Concepts* list.)

step 1

Reflect on yourself. What are your thoughts and feelings in this situation? Are your impressions and attributions accurate?

step 2

Reflect on your partner. Using perspective-taking and empathic concern, put yourself in Sam's shoes. What is he thinking and feeling in this situation?

step 3

Identify the optimal outcome. Think about your communication and relationship with Sam as well as the situation surrounding Nana's death. What's the best, most constructive relationship outcome possible? Consider what's best for you and for Sam.

step 4

Locate the roadblocks. Taking into consideration your own and Sam's thoughts and feelings and all that has happened in this situation, what obstacles are keeping you from achieving the optimal outcome?

step 5

Chart your course. What can you say to Sam to overcome the roadblocks you've identified and achieve your optimal outcome?

HELPFUL CONCEPTS

Gender and emotion, **101**
Emotion management strategies, **102**
Anger, **107**
Grief, **111**
Supportive communication, **113**

The Other Side

 Visit LaunchPad to watch a video in which Sam tells his side of the case study story. As in many real-life situations, this is information to which you did not have access when you were initially crafting your response in Part 3. The video reminds us that even when we do our best to offer competent responses, there is always another side to the story that we need to consider.

Interpersonal Competence Self-Assessment

After watching the video, visit the Self-Assessment questions in LaunchPad. Think about the new information offered in Sam's side of the story and all you've learned about interpersonal communication. Drawing on this knowledge, revisit your earlier responses in Part 3 and assess your interpersonal communication competence.

POSTSCRIPT

Photo by G.N. Miller/MaMa Foundation Gospel for Teens

We began this chapter with the story of a woman committed to transforming the lives of teenagers. Vy Higginsen founded Gospel for Teens in part to create a musical refuge for young people to escape their emotional turmoil. But she quickly learned that her students' emotions couldn't be suppressed, and that through sharing their emotions with one another, they could more quickly heal their wounds of anger and grief.

How do you manage the emotional challenges of your life? Do you leave your baggage at the door, burying your emotions? Or do you let your baggage in, sharing your emotions with others?

The story of Vy Higginsen and her students reminds us that although we have emotions, we are not our emotions. It's our capacity to constructively manage the emotions we experience, and communicate them in positive ways, that makes hope and goodness in our lives possible.

 **LaunchPad**

LaunchPad for *Reflect & Relate* offers videos and encourages self-assessment through adaptive quizzing. Go to **launchpadworks.com** to get access to:

 LearningCurve
Adaptive Quizzes

 Video clips that help you understand interpersonal communication

key terms

You can watch brief, illustrative videos of these terms and test your understanding of the concepts in LaunchPad.

key concepts

The Nature of Emotion

- **Emotion** is the most powerful of human experiences and involves thoughts, physiological arousal, and communication. Emotions are so significant that we feel compelled to engage in **emotion-sharing** with our relationship partners.

- Emotions are rare compared to **feelings**, which occur often and typically arise and decay with little conscious awareness. **Moods** endure longer than feelings or emotions and affect our perception and communication.

- Six **primary emotions** exist based on patterns of nonverbal behavior: surprise, joy, disgust, anger, fear, and sadness. Sometimes we experience more than one primary emotion simultaneously; the result is **blended emotions**. **Jealousy** is an example of a blended emotion, consisting of anger, fear, and sadness.

Forces Shaping Emotion

- Personality plays a powerful role in shaping our experience and expression of emotion.

- Gender contributes to our experience and expression of emotion, often due to the different ways men and women typically orient themselves in interpersonal relationships.

Managing Your Emotional Experience and Expression

- Effective **emotion management** is a critical part of **emotional intelligence**. Emotions are usually managed after they have occurred with **suppression** and **venting**, but we can also learn to practice **acceptance**. Strategies used for preventing emotions before they occur include **encounter avoidance**, **encounter structuring**, **attention focus**, and **deactivation**.

- Of all the strategies available to people for managing emotions, the most effective is **reappraisal**.

Emotional Challenges

- **Anger** is difficult to manage, given its intensity. People who manage anger through suppression can develop **chronic hostility**. Providing a time delay between the onset of anger and your communicative response, known as the **Jefferson strategy**, can be especially effective during online communication.

- Most people experience intense **passion** in the early stages of their involvements, and then a steady decline the longer the relationship endures.

- Managing your own **grief** is best accomplished through emotion-sharing, whereas providing **supportive communication** is the best approach for aiding others in overcoming their grief.

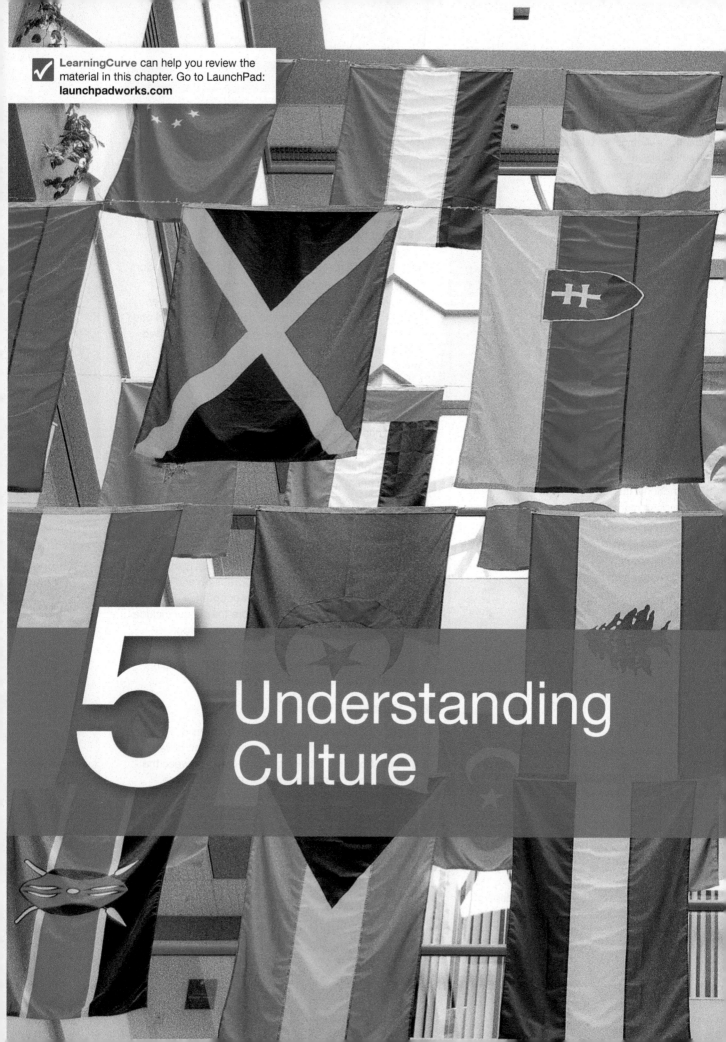

5 Understanding Culture

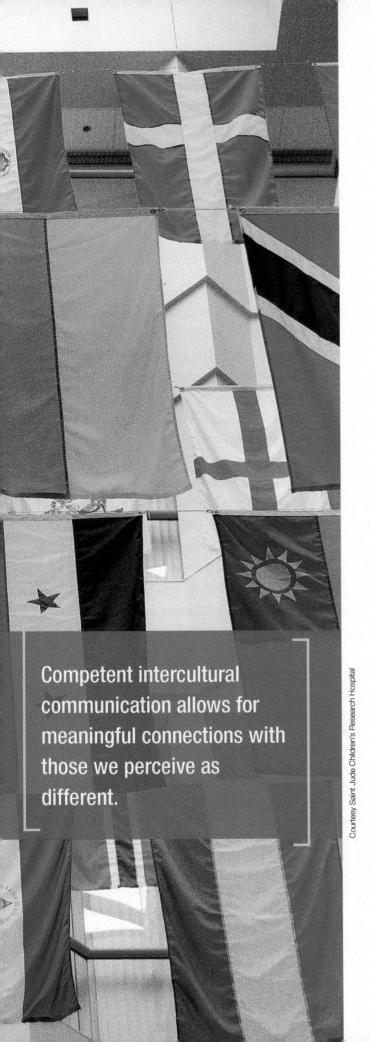

Competent intercultural communication allows for meaningful connections with those we perceive as different.

The most commonplace of objects. A blue telephone, atop a desk in a lobby. Nothing unusual, except perhaps its dated appearance, complete with dual handsets and cords. Yet this seemingly mundane device is significant: if you are picking up this telephone, you are in the lobby of St. Jude Children's Research Hospital in Memphis, Tennessee, likely with a sick child, and you need assistance with language translation. This telephone connects you to the information you need—bridging a language divide and becoming a lifeline—bonding people from different backgrounds into a larger "family" devoted to healing a sick child.

"St. Jude is like heaven on earth," says Crystal, the mother of patient Deuce. "You walk through the doors and everyone is the same. Everyone has a smile. It's like one big family."[1]

Since its inception in 1962, this hospital has focused on treating catastrophic childhood diseases, caring for patients from every state in the union as well as from dozens of countries around the globe. Founder Danny Thomas believed that that "no child should die in the dawn of life" and was committed to inclusion, creating "a hospital for all kids, regardless of race, religion or financial status."

If you visit St. Jude, you will see the many ways that communication and caring combine to create a culture of healing. You may be greeted by the warm smile of Janice in the gift shop, who can tell you how groundbreaking it was in Memphis in 1965 to have Black doctors like

[1]All material in this opener is adapted from information on the St. Jude Children's Research Hospital website: https://www.stjude.org/

121

John Wesley Smith treating white patients. You may see a rainbow of international flags, each representing a country from which members of the St. Jude family have hailed: scientists like Dr. Martine Roussel, born in France, raised in Cameroon, Guinea, Mali and Gabon, and known for her research in molecular-level causes of cancer; and providers like Dr. Gaby Maron Alfaro, a clinician and researcher of infectious diseases and certified translator for patients and families. You may smell the scents of food prepared by sous chef and food service manager Johnny Siv, who fled the 1970s civil war in Cambodia, surviving malnutrition and dehydration, and now cooks for patients. You may see patients holding spiritual intervention boards used by chaplains like Kimberly Russell—two-sided boards that allow patients to communicate nonverbally in English or Spanish by pointing to items on a grid of options.

You may even see adult *former patients* who have returned to work for, and "give back" to, St. Jude— people like Carlos Rodriguez, originally from El Salvador, who was diagnosed with cancer as a

Holly Elmore Images (image taken at the Lambda Alpha International Memphis Land Economics

child and went to St. Jude for treatment. He learned his first English words at St. Jude, to describe the pain he felt during his chemotherapy. Today, now a cancer-free adult, Carlos helps patients and families through *their* pain by driving the St. Jude mail van, delivering packages and awaited messages from friends and family far away.

Walking the hallways of St. Jude may fill you with a sense of awe from witnessing the power of such a diverse family of people working toward a common purpose. Regardless of background, these hallways—and the phone that lies at the intersection of them—unite the people of St. Jude to realize Danny Thomas's dream.

We live in diverse interpersonal worlds. Advances in technology allow us to bridge previously insurmountable distances: if you have shopped on Amazon, you likely have received a package from another part of the world, just as you may regularly have video calls (as we do) with friends, family, or romantic partners in Korea, the Netherlands, China, or Pakistan (although keeping track of the time differences can be a challenge!). In our local communities, too, we regularly interact with people whose cultural traditions are different from our own. Whether it's online, at work, or on campus, a day rarely goes by without being reminded of the diversity of values, beliefs, heritages, and traditions in which we are immersed.

At the same time, as we learned in Chapter 3, things that we perceive as unusual often are more perceptually salient, which means that differences sometimes stand out more than similarities. And when we experience *difference,* we may interpret it as *distance.* So when we sense cultural symbols with which we are unacquainted—whether it's hearing an unfamiliar language or tasting new foods—our minds might hone in on the distinction and lead us to presume that we share little with a stranger. This assumption of distance can lead to a host of negative interpersonal judgments and behaviors, including stereotyping, awkward or incompetent communication, and prejudice.

But with a shift in perspective, we can instead *embrace* difference. Yes, it's true that people differ in their cultural beliefs, traditions, values, and communication—and such differences are deep, not superficial. But *difference doesn't equal distance*. It just means . . . difference! People who are culturally distinct from one another may share profound points of commonality, upon which valuable and impactful encounters and relationships can be built. And, like the blue telephone in the lobby of St. Jude Hospital, you can build bridges if you metaphorically lift the receiver, listen, find common ground, and begin a dialogue.

In this chapter, you'll learn:

- The importance and defining characteristics of culture
- What co-cultures are and their role in communication
- The impact of prejudice on communication and suggestions to reduce it
- The cultural dimensions that influence how people communicate
- How to improve your intercultural communication competence

Understanding Culture

Culture affects
communication ⟩ Communicating competently with people from a variety of cultural backgrounds is an essential skill. Regardless of your own cultural heritage, you will encounter and have opportunities to create interpersonal relationships with people from a broad and diverse range of cultures in college, in the workplace, and in every other context in which you communicate. Additionally, more than 1 million international students enroll in U.S. colleges annually (EducationData, n.d.). You may be such a student yourself—or you may have classmates from various countries and from communities across the United States. Keeping in mind the variety of our backgrounds and experiences, the question arises: What exactly is culture? Understanding the nature of culture, how co-cultures operate within dominant cultures, and how prejudice can impact our interpersonal communication is the starting point for building intercultural communication competence. Let's begin by revisiting our definition of culture from Chapter 1, focusing on four characteristics.

self-
reflection

Recall a childhood memory of
learning about your culture.
What tradition or belief did you
learn about? Who taught you
this lesson? What impact did
this have on your understanding
of your culture?

CULTURE DEFINED

As defined in Chapter 1, **culture** is an established, coherent set of beliefs, attitudes, values, and practices shared by a large group of people (Keesing, 1974). Factors that may impact your perception of culture include your nationality, ethnicity, religion, gender, sexual orientation, physical abilities, and even age. But what really makes a culture feel like a "culture" is that it's *widely shared*. This happens because cultures are learned, communicated, layered, and lived.

Culture Is Learned   You learn your cultural beliefs, attitudes, and values from many sources, including your parents, teachers, religious leaders, peers, and the mass media (Gudykunst & Kim, 2003). This process begins at birth, through customs such as choosing a newborn's name, taking part in religious ceremonies, and selecting godparents or other special guardians. As you mature, you learn from parents or caregivers the deeper aspects of your culture, including the history behind certain traditions: why unleavened bread is eaten during Jewish Passover, for instance, or

⬭ Culture is so integrated into your everyday life, it is easy to overlook how it can inform everything you see, hear, or believe. How do the activities and images shown relate to your culture or not? What other aspects of your culture make you *you*? (Clockwise from top left) J Pat Carter/Getty Images; Hero Images/Getty Images; Chris McGrath/Getty Images; Justin Lane/Epa/REX/Shutterstock

why certain days are more auspicious than others. You also learn how to participate in rituals—everything from blowing out the candles on a birthday cake to lighting Advent candles. In most societies, teaching children to understand, respect, and practice their culture is considered an essential part of child rearing. For example, we (Kelly and Steve) have broad blends of Irish, Scottish, English, Swiss, and German heritage in our ancestry. But our most common *joint* heritage is Celtic/Irish, so we raised our boys as "Irish" by giving them names with traditional Gaelic spellings, and teaching them a number of Irish traditions, such as the myth of the Tuatha de Danaan—a supernatural race in Irish folklore that formed the basis for current and historical belief in "the fairies" (and who regularly would visit our household on special occasions to leave our boys gifts).

self-reflection

Have you ever encountered a situation in which your communication behaviors and those of someone from a different culture clashed? How did you respond? What cultural factors played a role? Were you able to overcome the difficulty?

Culture Is Communicated   Each culture has its own practices regarding how to communicate, and these can widely differ from one another (Whorf, 1952). When you communicate with someone from a different culture, this is called **intercultural communication**. Sometimes intercultural communication is seamless, because similarities exist across cultures that help us stitch together our interactions. You may share a passion for a particular type of music with someone from a different background, for instance, and your joint love of this music quickly connects the two of you. Other times, such interaction can be challenging, especially when cultural communication practices diverge. For example, when Steve was an undergraduate, he and his good friend Amid, who was from Iran, would struggle with how close to stand to one another during their conversations. Amid practiced his cultural tradition of standing less than an arm's length away, whereas Steve had grown up with different expectations regarding appropriate distance. (We'll discuss nonverbal communication, including personal space, in more detail in Chapter 9.) You can imagine how these interactions may have looked to outside observers. Whenever they talked, Amid would constantly sidle closer; Steve would then step back; Amid would then step closer, and Steve would again step back. As their friendship deepened, their culturally based "dance of distance" became a running joke between them, causing shared amusement and laughter.

Culture Is Layered   Many of us belong to more than one culture. This means we experience multiple layers of culture simultaneously, as various traditions, heritages, and practices are recognized and held as important. As noted previously, both of our backgrounds include Scottish and Irish heritage, and Steve's also includes Swiss German. But each of us prioritizes the distinct layers of our ancestry differently. Steve's brother takes the Scottish ancestry *very* seriously, attending the Scottish Highland Games in Washington State every year. Steve's mom, on the other hand, thinks of herself as primarily Swiss German and even made a personal pilgrimage to the hereditary hometown of Breitenbach, Switzerland. In contrast, while Steve celebrates Irish holidays, Kelly doesn't exclusively identify with *any* specific heritage, choosing instead to celebrate as many different cultural holidays as possible!

Culture Is Lived   Culture affects everything about how you live your life. It influences the neighborhoods you live in; the means of transportation you use; the way you think, dress, talk, and even eat. Its impact runs so deep that it is often taken for granted. At the same time, culture is often a great source of personal pride, and a powerful tool for self-expression. Many people consciously live in ways that celebrate their cultural heritage through such behaviors as wearing a Muslim hijab, placing a Mexican flag decal on their car, or greeting others with the Thai gesture of the wai (hands joined in prayer, heads bowed).

Now that we have reviewed four defining characteristics of culture, let's consider another aspect of every culture, the topic of co-cultures.

CO-CULTURES

In most societies, there's usually a group of people who have more *power* than others—that is, the ability to influence or control people and events. (We'll discuss power in more detail in Chapter 10.) Having more power in a society comes from controlling major societal institutions, such as banks; businesses; the government; and legal, health, and educational systems. According to **Co-cultural Communication Theory**, the people who have more power within a society determine the *dominant culture* because they decide the prevailing views, values, and traditions of the society (Orbe, 1998), essentially constructing the social standards. Consider the United States. Throughout its history, wealthy white men have been in power. When the United States was first founded, the only people allowed to vote were landowning males of European ancestry. Now, more than 200 years later, white men still make up the vast majority of U.S. Congress and Fortune 500 CEOs. As a consequence, what is thought of as "American culture" is tilted toward the interests, activities, and accomplishments of these men.

self-
reflection

Which of your co-cultures is most important in shaping your sense of self? Which ones are less important? Why? Are there ever situations in which your different co-cultural identities clash with one another?

Members of a society who don't conform to the dominant culture—by way of language, values, lifestyle, or even physical appearance—often form what are called **co-cultures**: that is, they have their own cultures that *co-exist* within a dominant cultural sphere (Orbe, 1998), as subsets of the larger cultural whole. Co-cultures may be based on age, gender, social class, ethnicity, religion, mental and physical ability, sexual orientation, and other unifying elements (Orbe, 1998). Many U.S. residents who are not members of the dominant culture—including people of color, women, members of the LGBTQ+ community, people with disabilities, and non-Christians—are members of distinct co-cultures, sometimes with their own political lobbying groups, websites, magazines, and television networks.

CO-CULTURES AND COMMUNICATION

When people from co-cultures interact with people from the dominant culture, **co-cultural communication** occurs (Orbe & Roberts, 2012). Because members of co-cultures are (by definition) different from the dominant culture, they develop and use a variety of communication practices that help them interact with people in the culturally dominant group (Ramírez-Sánchez, 2008). These practices include *assimilation*, *accommodation*, and *separation*, and they differ according to the degree to which individuals attempt to suppress their co-cultural identity and fit in with the dominant culture (assimilation); behave in ways that authentically represent their co-culture in an attempt to get members of the dominant culture to accept it (accommodation); or distance themselves from the dominant culture, through bla-

◗ At first glance, Spencer Sleyon of East Harlem, New York, and Rosalind Guttman of Palm Beach, Florida, might seem very different from each other. But they became friends in 2017 when they were paired together in an online game of Words with Friends. After playing hundreds of games and chatting regularly, they finally met in person. Courtesy Amy Butler

tantly challenging its legitimacy and/or isolating themselves socially and interpersonally from it (separation). Each of these practices can be approached with varying degrees of assertiveness (Orbe & Roberts, 2012). For example, say a younger female employee starts working at a new company and finds that her older male supervisors frequently make jokes about her generation's social media use. In response, she might try to excel in all aspects of her professional and personal life, to counteract negative stereotypes about her generational co-culture (assertive assimilation). Alternatively, she might suppress her offended reactions and use more formal and overly polite language with her supervisors (nonassertive assimilation). Or, she might even attempt to act, look, and talk like members of the dominant culture (her supervisors), by even going so far as to openly disparage her own co-culture (aggressive assimilation).

As discussed in Chapter 3, our perceptions of shared attitudes, beliefs, and values based on cultural and co-cultural affiliations can lead us to classify those who are similar to us as *ingroupers* and those who are different as *outgroupers*. This, however, can be a dangerous trap. Just because someone shares a particular co-culture with you (say, your ethnicity or sexual orientation), doesn't mean that you are truly the same. Always remember: perceived similarity is not the same thing as actual similarity (Montoya et al., 2008). For example, you and a classmate might both be Black (the same ethnicity), but you may be Haitian and Catholic, and she may be a Protestant from New York City, with a host of different specific ethnic and religious factors that affect

focus on CULTURE

Is Social Media a Cultural Divide?

Today, the vast majority (about 80 percent) of all U.S. adults use social media. Nevertheless, cultural divides exist—in platform preferences, time spent on social media, and outcomes. Consider platform preferences. An astonishing 91 percent of 18- to 29-year-olds regularly use YouTube, while only 38 percent of people over the age of 65 do. Pinterest is used by three times as many women as men; and WhatsApp is used by three times as many Hispanic people as white people. And when it comes to generational gaps, none is more pronounced than Snapchat and Instagram usage: Snapchat is used by 73 percent of 18- to 24-year-olds but only by 9 percent of 50- to 64-year-olds, and Instagram is used by 75 percent of 18- to 24-year-olds but only by 23 percent of people age 50 to 64 (Perrin & Anderson, 2019).

But the biggest generational culture divide in social media isn't platform preferences—it's *how* people of different ages use social media and corresponding negative impacts. Adults born before 1980 grew up in an era before social media; consequently, they are more likely to balance their usage with offline, face-to-face interactions. In contrast, Millennials and Gen Z are more inclined to prioritize social media over face-to-face interactions.

The negative impacts associated with this preference are pronounced. Millennials and Gen Z are more likely than older people to report anxiety, depression, and social isolation related to their social media consumption (Twenge, 2017). One study of 19- to 32-year-olds found that those who spend two or more hours a day on social media report substantially lower feelings of social support because of reduced face-to-face interaction (Shensa et al., 2016). And the positivity or negativity of the social media experience does little to change these negative effects. In one study, college students who had positive social media experiences (such as having a post repeatedly "liked") experienced no change in their sense of social isolation, whereas students experiencing negative social media incidents (such as conflicts or hostile posts) reported a 13 percent boost in loneliness (Primack et al., 2019).

discussion questions

- How do you balance your time on social media with your time interacting offline?
- Do you feel that your use of social media is isolating you from others? If so, what could you do to change that?

---

your interpersonal communication. In fact, you may be more similar to an Asian American classmate who shares your religious dedication.

It may be helpful at this point to return to the "lens" metaphor we used in Chapter 3. We view ourselves and others through multiple and varied perceptual lenses. If you put them all together, they form a *prism of perception*. Now we are adding two more lenses to the prism—those of culture and co-culture—thereby creating a perceptual kaleidoscope through which we view and are viewed by others. This kaleidoscope is present within all interpersonal encounters, and varies according to the topic being discussed, the person with whom we are communicating, and the desired outcomes related to the interaction (Orbe & Roberts, 2012). Just as *we* turn our kaleidoscope according to our individual fields of experience, others do the same according to *their* experiences.

Each of us is a complex combination of cultural and co-cultural identities and experiences, and each of us speaks and perceives from a specific juncture where all these influences meet. Furthermore, our identities and interactions cannot be detached from the contexts and cultures in which they exist. All cultures create institutional structures and systems of power and privilege, benefiting some people and marginalizing others. One implication is that if your identities involve more

⬆ When we communicate with others, we must consider their complex "kaleidoscope" of experiences as well as our own.

Timothy Fadek/Corbis News/Getty Images

than one underrepresented group, you are likely to face unique degrees of oppression. In her discussion of the experiences of Black women, scholar Kimberlé Crenshaw introduced the term **intersectionality** to describe an experience "greater than the sum of racism and sexism" (Crenshaw, 1989). As she explained in a 2020 interview with *Time* magazine, "We tend to talk about race inequality as separate from inequality based on gender, class, sexuality or immigrant status. What's often missing is how some people are subject to all of these and the experience is not just the sum of its parts" (Steinmetz, 2020).

Now think about this concept as it relates to *you*. You are the unique and particular "you" based on your lived experiences and cultural identities, all of which impact your sense of self and perception, supplying you with a particular kaleidoscope through which you view the world. When you use that kaleidoscope to look outward at others, the challenge is seeing *their* unique experiences and identities while recognizing that different levels of power, privilege, or oppression will be associated with these identities. All too often we may focus our view through just one cultural lens, narrowly spotlighting differences in ethnicity, race, or gender—or we may neglect to note differences in privilege and experience. But if we strive to widen our lens, this shift in perspective may allow a glimpse from another person's kaleidoscope, transforming both our perception and our communication.

PREJUDICE

As we discussed in Chapter 3, people may rely on *stereotypes*—a way to categorize people into a social group and then evaluate them based on prior information related to this group—when interacting with others. People are especially likely to rely on stereotypes about racial and gender characteristics, since these are among the things we are likely to notice first when encountering new people. Research on racial stereotyping suggests that categorizing people in terms of race typically happens within 200 *milliseconds*—that's one-fifth of a second!—and it occurs even when people have been instructed to "focus on people as individuals rather than group members" (Kubota & Ito, 2017).

When stereotypes toward groups and their members are coupled with negative affect (feelings or emotions) and a predisposition to behave negatively toward those people, they become **prejudice** (Dovidio et al., 2010). People can be prejudiced toward any group, and this prejudice can be amplified when people see these groups negatively portrayed by the media (Banas et al., 2020). But whereas stereotypes involve clusters of related *beliefs* about members of social groups, prejudice adds powerful *emotions* to the mix (Amodio, 2014). That is, when someone is prejudiced, they not only harbor negative ideas about a particular group, but they may also feel fear, disgust, contempt, envy, resentment, or anxiety toward members of that group. These experiences may lay the groundwork for discriminatory and destructive behavior (Dovidio et al., 2010), as these emotions have a greater impact on behavior than do stereotyped beliefs alone (Fiske, 2018). This makes prejudice uniquely threatening, depending upon the type and intensity of feelings or emotions involved.

Prejudice, no matter the particular target, is destructive and unethical. Prejudice leads people to communicate in condescending, disrespectful, offensive, and even hostile ways, and it serves as the root for every exclusionary "ism": racism, sexism, ageism, classism, ableism; as well as many "phobias": xenophobia, homophobia, Islamophobia, and so on (Dovidio et al., 2010). Becoming a competent interpersonal communicator requires that we work to overcome prejudices that might influence our communication. Because prejudice is connected to deeply held negative beliefs about particular groups (Ramasubramanian, 2010), one option for working toward overcoming prejudice is to change these viewpoints. In particular, one specific belief set linked to prejudice is the *orientation toward social dominance*—the view that certain groups should rule over other groups—with research indicating that less prejudiced people believe in more equality between social groups (Maunder et al., 2020). You can use the *Self-Quiz* "Test Your Social Equality Orientation" to explore your own views. Then revisit Chapter 3 and review our suggestions for surmounting stereotypes, as well as our recommendations regarding empathy and perception-checking. After reflecting on your beliefs, apply what you know about *emotional intelligence* to uncover the feelings and emotions associated with your beliefs, and revisit the guidance in Chapter 4 on managing emotions. Finally, consider how your beliefs, feeling, and emotions influence your conversations and encounters with others. Research shows that positive interactions with people from different groups reduce prejudice, and this reduction is enhanced when we feel more empathy and less anxiety toward other people by using communication to reduce our uncertainty (Banas et al., 2020; Berger & Calabrese, 1975).

skills practice

Addressing Prejudice
Becoming a less prejudiced communicator

❶ Recognize the differences in power, privilege, and opportunity that exist in your culture.

❷ Commit to bringing an open mind to interactions.

❸ Pause to challenge preconceived beliefs or hasty judgments, striving to see the person as an individual.

❹ Remember that prejudice is the emotional and motivational partner to stereotypical beliefs, and that we can use our communication skills to learn from others and reduce uncertainty and anxiety.

❺ Evaluate your own communication, realizing that your communication influences other people's communication, and that conversations that seek common ground will be more likely to close the distance that many associate with difference.

self-QUIZ

Test Your Social Equality Orientation

Read each item below and circle the number that best represents your beliefs. After you've taken the quiz, refer to the guidelines offered in Chapter 3 for how to overcome stereotypes, offer empathy, and perception-check.

1. Everyone should have the same opportunities available to them in life.
   Strongly disagree 1 2 3 4 5 Strongly agree

2. It is not good for one group of people to be dominant in a society.
   Strongly disagree 1 2 3 4 5 Strongly agree

3. Social equality should be improved in society.
   Strongly disagree 1 2 3 4 5 Strongly agree

4. Societies should strive for income equality.
   Strongly disagree 1 2 3 4 5 Strongly agree

5. More equal treatment of people leads to fewer problems in a society.
   Strongly disagree 1 2 3 4 5 Strongly agree

Information for self-quiz adapted from the Social Dominance Orientation Scale (Pratto et al., 1994).

Scoring: Add your scores across all five questions. 5–10 = low belief in social equality; 11–19 = moderate belief in social equality; 20–25 = high belief in social equality.

Cultural Influences on Communication

Recognizing important cultural factors in communication

Chef Eddie Huang's best-selling memoir *Fresh Off the Boat* takes a humorous look at the cultural differences and challenges Eddie and his family experienced during his childhood. For instance, the first time Eddie saw macaroni and cheese, as a guest at his friend Jeff's house, Eddie mistook the dish for "pig intestines cut into half-moons hanging out in an orange sauce." As he describes it, "Jeff found it incredulous that I didn't know what macaroni and cheese was, but it was formative: he got a taste of macaroni and cheese from *my* eyes, discovering how it felt to be gazed on and seen as exotic instead of being the one gazing." But of all the experiences he had growing up as a first-generation Asian American, the one that stands out most vividly in his memory is an incident that occurred on his first day at a new school. Eddie was standing in the lunch line when the only other student of color at the school called him a racial epithet, pushed him to the ground, and declared, "*You're* at the bottom now!" Eddie still considers the encounter the most impactful moment of his childhood in how it underscored the inescapability of cultural difference and the *prejudice* that often accompanies such perceptions. At the same time, Eddie notes that difference is something we *all* know because it takes so many different forms. As he elaborates, "The feeling of being different is universal, because difference makes us universally human in our individual relationships with society. We're all weirdos. But we've been fixated way too long on universality and monoculture. It's time to embrace difference and speak about it with singularity."[2]

⬇ In *Fresh Off the Boat*, chef Eddie Huang recounts his family's experiences navigating cultural differences as they settle into life in the United States.
AP Images/Blair Raughley

As Eddie Huang's book illustrates, cultural differences are universally experienced, and these differences and the perceptions associated with them can be profound. Scholars suggest that seven dimensions underlie cultural differences in our interpersonal communication: individualism versus collectivism, uncertainty avoidance, power distance, high and low context, emotion displays, masculinity versus femininity, and views of time. To build intercultural communication competence, you need to understand each of these. At the same time, it is crucial to recognize that each dimension is a continuum along which people within a culture will vary according to individual and situational differences (Liu et al., 2019). For example, as we will discuss below, Japan is considered a collectivistic culture, but not every person in Japan has collectivistic cultural attitudes—just as not every person in the United States has individualistic cultural attitudes. As you read through the section that follows, and familiarize yourself with the dimensions, think about how each of them manifests in your *own* culture, interpersonal communication, and relationships.

[2]Information from Huang (2015).

INDIVIDUALISM VERSUS COLLECTIVISM

In **individualistic cultures**, people tend to value independence and personal achievement. Members of these cultures are encouraged to focus on themselves and their immediate family (Hofstede, 2001), and individual achievement is often praised as the highest good (Waterman, 1984). Examples of individualistic countries include the United States, Canada, New Zealand, and Sweden (Hofstede, 2001).

By contrast, in **collectivistic cultures**, people tend to emphasize group identity ("we" rather than "me"), interpersonal harmony, and the well-being of ingroups (Park & Guan, 2006). If you were raised in a collectivistic culture, you were probably taught that it's important to belong to groups or "collectives" that look after you in exchange for your loyalty. In collectivistic cultures, people emphasize the goals, needs, and views of groups over those of individuals, and often define the highest good as cooperation with others rather than individual achievement. Collectivistic countries include Guatemala, Pakistan, Korea, and Japan (Hofstede, 2001).

Differences between individualistic and collectivistic cultures can powerfully influence people's behaviors, including which social networking sites they use and how they use them. For instance, people in collectivistic cultures tend to use sites that emphasize group connectedness, whereas those in individualistic cultures tend to use sites that focus on self-expression (Barker & Ota, 2011). U.S. Facebook users devote most of their time on the site describing their own actions and viewpoints as well as personally important events. They also post controversial status updates and express their personal opinions, even if these trigger debate. Japanese users of mixi, meanwhile, carefully edit their profiles so they won't offend anyone (Barker & Ota, 2011). While U.S. Facebook users often post photos of themselves alone doing various activities, mixi users tend to write in diaries that are shared with their closest friends, boosting ingroup solidarity (Barker & Ota, 2011).

UNCERTAINTY AVOIDANCE

Cultures vary in how much they tolerate and accept unpredictability, known as **uncertainty avoidance**. As scholar Geert Hofstede explains, "The fundamental issue here is how a society deals with the fact that the future can never be known: Should

LaunchPad Video
launchpadworks.com

Individualism
Watch this clip online to answer the questions below.

Do you have higher regard for your personal goals than you do for the needs of your family and community? How might your answer be affected by the culture in which you were raised?

Want to see more? Check out LaunchPad for a clip on **collectivism**.

self-reflection

Consider your own presence on social media. Does how you portray yourself suggest collectivism or individualism? Does your online portrayal match or clash with how you think of yourself offline?

○ How do selfies exemplify the individualistic culture of the United States? How does this differ from the more group-oriented activities seen in a collectivistic culture?
iStock/Getty Images Plus; China Photos/Getty Images

we try to control the future or just let it happen?"[3] In *high-uncertainty-avoidance cultures* (such as Mexico, South Korea, Japan, and Greece), people place a lot of value on control. They define rigid rules and conventions to guide all beliefs and behaviors, and they feel uncomfortable with unusual or innovative ideas. People from such cultures want structure in their organizations, institutions, relationships, and everyday lives (Hofstede, 2001). For example, a coworker raised in a high-uncertainty-avoidance culture would expect everyone assigned to a project to have clear roles and responsibilities, including a designated leader. In his research on organizations, Hofstede found that in high-uncertainty-avoidance cultures, people commit to organizations for long periods of time, expect their job responsibilities to be clearly defined, and strongly believe that organizational rules should not be broken (2001, p. 149). Children raised in such cultures are taught to believe in cultural traditions and practices without ever questioning them.

In *low-uncertainty-avoidance cultures* (such as Singapore, Jamaica, Denmark, Sweden, and Ireland), people tend to put more emphasis on letting the future happen without trying to control it (Hofstede, 2001). They generally care less about rules, tolerate diverse viewpoints and beliefs, and welcome innovation and change. They also feel free to question and challenge authority. In addition, they teach their children to think critically about the beliefs and traditions they're exposed to, rather than automatically following them.

As with each of these cultural distinctions, most countries and people within them fall somewhere between high and low. For instance, both the United States and Canada are moderately uncertainty-avoidant. How does this translate into cultural values? Within both countries, people generally value innovation and new ideas (especially with regard to technology and entrepreneurship) while emphasizing the importance of laws, rules, and clear guidelines governing behavior, particularly within the workplace.

POWER DISTANCE

The degree to which people in a particular culture view the unequal distribution of power as acceptable is known as **power distance** (Hofstede, 1991, 2001). In *high-power-distance cultures*, it's considered normal and even desirable for people of different social and professional status to have different levels of power (Ting-Toomey, 2005). In such cultures, people tend to give privileged treatment and extreme respect to those in high-status positions (Ting-Toomey, 1999). They also expect individuals of lesser status to behave humbly, especially around people of higher status, who are expected to act superior.

In *low-power-distance cultures*, people in high-status positions try to minimize the differences between themselves and lower-status persons by interacting with them in informal ways and treating them as equals (Oetzel et al., 2001). For instance, a high-level marketing executive might chat with the cleaning service workers in the office and invite them to have coffee. See Figure 5.1 for examples of high- and low-power-distance countries.

Power distance affects how people deal with interpersonal conflict. In low-power-distance cultures, people with little power may still choose to engage in conflict with high-power people. What's more, they may do so *competitively*, confronting high-power

---

[3]Hofstede Insights, National Culture, Uncertainty Avoidance Index (UAI). Retrieved from https://hi.hofstede-insights.com/national-culture

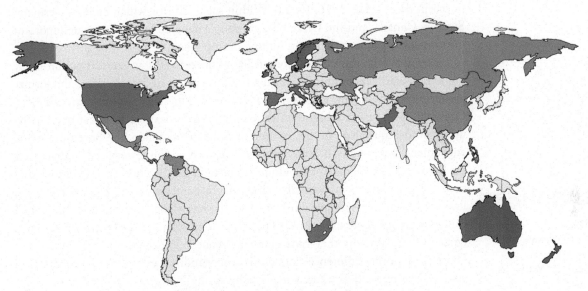

HIGH-POWER-DISTANCE COUNTRIES	**MODERATE-POWER-DISTANCE COUNTRIES**	**LOW-POWER-DISTANCE COUNTRIES**
Russia	Spain	Norway
Panama	Pakistan	Sweden
Guatemala	Italy	Ireland
Philippines	South Africa	New Zealand
Mexico	Hungary	Denmark
Venezuela	Jamaica	Israel
China	United States	Australia

figure 5.1 Power Distance across Countries
Hofstede (2009). Retrieved from https://www.hofstede-insights.com/country-comparison/the-usa/

people and demanding that their goals be met. For instance, employees may question management decisions and suggest that alternatives be considered, or townspeople may attend a meeting and demand that the mayor address their concerns. These behaviors are much less common in high-power-distance cultures (Bochner & Hesketh, 1994), where low-power people are more likely to either *avoid* conflict with high-power people or *accommodate* them when conflict arises. (For more insight on how people approach conflict, see Chapter 10.)

Power distance also influences how people communicate in close relationships, especially families. In traditional Mexican culture, for instance, the value of *respeto* (respect) emphasizes power distance between younger people and their elders (Delgado-Gaitan, 1993). As part of *respeto*, children are expected to defer to elders' authority and to avoid openly disagreeing with them. In contrast, many people in the United States believe that once children reach adulthood, power in family relationships should be balanced, with children and their elders treating one another as equals (Kagawa & McCornack, 2004).

HIGH AND LOW CONTEXT

Cultures can also be described as *high* or *low context*. In **high-context cultures**, such as China, Korea, and Japan, people tend to presume that others within the culture will share their viewpoints and thus perceive situations (contexts) in much the same way. (High-context cultures are often collectivistic as well.) Consequently, people in such cultures often talk indirectly, using hints or suggestions to convey meanings—the

LaunchPad Video
launchpadworks.com

Low Power Distance
Watch this clip online to answer the questions below.

How comfortable would you be offering a manager or professor feedback—particularly negative or constructive feedback? How might your culture affect your response?

Want to see more? Check out LaunchPad for a clip on **high power distance**.

presumption being that because individuals share the same contextual view, they automatically know what another person is trying to say. Relatively vague, ambiguous language—and even silence—is frequently used, and there's no need to provide a lot of explicit information within messages.

In **low-context cultures**, people tend *not* to presume that others share their beliefs, attitudes, and values. So they strive to be informative, clear, and direct in their communication (Hall & Hall, 1987). Many low-context cultures are also individualistic; as a result, people openly express their views and try to persuade others to accept them (Hall, 1976, 1997a). Within such cultures, which include Germany, Sweden, Canada, and the United States, people generally work to make important information obvious, rather than hinting or implying.

How does the difference between high-context and low-context cultures play out in real-world encounters? Consider the experiences of Steve's friend and former graduate student Naomi Kagawa, who is now a Japanese communication professor. Growing up in Japan, a high-context culture, Naomi learned to reject requests by using words equivalent to *OK* or *sure* in order to maintain the harmony of the encounter. These words, however, are accompanied by subtle vocal tones that *imply* no. Because all members of the culture understand this practice, they recognize that such seeming assents are actually rejections. In contrast, in the United States—a low-context culture—people don't share similar knowledge and beliefs, so they spell things out much more explicitly. People often come right out and say no, then apologize and explain why they can't grant the request. When Naomi first visited the United States, this difference caused misunderstandings in her interpersonal interactions. She rejected unwanted requests by saying "OK," only to find that people presumed she was consenting rather than refusing. And she was surprised, even shocked, when people rejected her requests by explicitly saying no.

EMOTION DISPLAYS

In all cultures, norms exist regarding how people should and shouldn't express emotion. These norms are called **display rules**: guidelines for when, where, and how to manage emotion displays appropriately (Ekman & Friesen, 1975). Display rules govern very specific aspects of your nonverbal communication, such as how broadly you should smile, whether or not you should scowl when angry, and the appropriateness of shouting out loud in public when you're excited. (For more discussion of this, see Chapter 9 on nonverbal communication.) Children learn such display rules and, over time, internalize them to the point where following these rules seems normal. This is why you likely think of the way you express emotion as natural, rather than as something that has been socialized into you through your culture (Hayes & Metts, 2008).

Because of differences in socialization and traditions, display rules vary across cultures (Soto et al., 2005). Two of the fastest-growing ethnic groups in the United States are Asian and Hispanic (Chappell, 2017)—so consider, for example, Mexican Americans and Chinese Americans. In traditional Chinese culture, people generally prioritize emotional control and moderation; intense emotions are considered dangerous and are sometimes even thought to cause illness (Wu & Tseng, 1985). This belief shapes communication in close relationships. Chinese American couples tend not to openly express positive emotions toward each other as often as white American couples do (Tsai & Levenson, 1997). Meanwhile, in traditional Mexican culture, people tend to openly express emotion even more so than white Americans (Soto et al., 2005). For many people of Mexican descent, the experience,

---

LaunchPad

Online Self-Quiz: Collectivism, Uncertainty Avoidance, and Power Distance: Where Do You Stand? To take this self-quiz, visit LaunchPad: **launchpadworks.com**

---

skills practice

Negotiating Display Rules
Learning how to competently manage emotions in various situations and encounters

❶ Consider context. Keep in mind that specific contexts also have display rules. For example, some workplaces may demand strict emotional control.

❷ Observe others. Consider how your communication partners regulate emotion, being careful not to judge them as "cold" or "overly emotional."

❸ Adapt accordingly. Ensure that your communication mirrors what is appropriate for the context and your communication partners.

❹ Evaluate your behavior. Consider how your displays of emotion may have helped or hindered achievement of your desired outcomes.

⬤ People don't abide by the display rules of their culture in every situation. In the United States, men are generally socialized not to express vulnerable emotions in public, but this father had a powerful grief response when he saw his son's name at the North Pool of the 9/11 Memorial in New York City. Justin Lane/AFP/Getty Images

expression, and deep discussion of emotions provide some of life's greatest rewards and satisfactions.

When families immigrate to a new society, the move often provokes tension over which display rules to follow. People who are closely oriented to their cultures of origin often continue to communicate their emotions in traditional ways. Others—usually, the first generation of children born in the new society—may move away from traditional forms of emotional expression (Soto et al., 2005). For example, Chinese Americans who adhere strongly to traditional Chinese culture openly display fewer negative emotions than do those who are Americanized (Soto et al., 2005). Similarly, Mexican Americans with strong ties to traditional Mexican culture express intense negative emotion more openly than do Mexican Americans more tied to U.S. culture.

Keep such differences in mind when interpersonally communicating with others. An emotional expression—such as a loud shout of intense joy—might be considered shocking and inappropriate in some cultures but perfectly normal and natural in others. Similarly, openly crying or wailing loudly with grief at a funeral service might be expected within some cultures and prohibited in others. Recalling the concept of co-cultures, we also know not to presume that all people from the same culture share the same expectations. As much as possible, adjust your expression of emotion to match the style of the individuals with whom you're interacting, and according to the communication situation.

MASCULINITY VERSUS FEMININITY

Another cultural dimension that impacts interpersonal communication is the degree to which masculine, versus feminine, values are emphasized. **Masculine cultural values** include the accumulation of material wealth as an indicator of success, assertiveness, and personal achievement. Within highly masculine cultures, people are often taught that competition is the highest good; people who "win" or who are "the best in their field" are often looked up to as heroes. "Beating out the competition" and "having a competitive edge" are emphasized throughout schooling, in politics, and within professional life. So, for example, if you decide not to compete with another coworker for a promotion that will result in a substantial raise—but also increased travel, which you do not want—members of a masculine culture might be perplexed by your choice.

In contrast, **feminine cultural values** emphasize compassion, consensus, and cooperation. Feminine cultures tend to have less distinct gender roles (Mansson & Sigurðardóttir, 2017; Rattrie et al., 2020), and tend to emphasize caring for underrepresented groups and boosting quality of life for all people. To borrow from the previous example, members of a feminine culture might respect and admire a person's decision to bow out of a competition for a promotion, especially if the promotion would reduce the person's quality of life.

Examples of masculine cultures include Japan, Hungary, Venezuela, and Italy; feminine cultures include Sweden, Norway, the Netherlands, and Denmark. The United States rates as a substantially masculine country (62 out of 100 on the masculinity index), whereas Canada is moderately masculine (around 10 points below the United States). See Figure 5.2 for a comparison of the cultural values in the United States and Sweden.

Whether a culture is masculine, feminine, or somewhere in between impacts the people of that culture in very real ways. For example, feminine cultures typically offer lengthy paid or partially paid leaves from work following the birth or

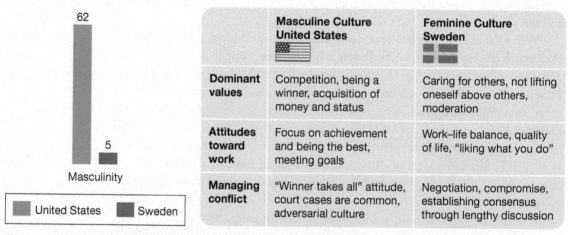

	Masculine Culture United States	**Feminine Culture Sweden**
Dominant values	Competition, being a winner, acquisition of money and status	Caring for others, not lifting oneself above others, moderation
Attitudes toward work	Focus on achievement and being the best, meeting goals	Work–life balance, quality of life, "liking what you do"
Managing conflict	"Winner takes all" attitude, court cases are common, adversarial culture	Negotiation, compromise, establishing consensus through lengthy discussion

figure 5.2 Comparing Masculine and Feminine Cultural Values in the United States and Sweden
The bar graph represents the scores for the United States and Sweden, based on Geert Hofstede's Cultural Survey. According to the Hofstede Centre's website, "The fundamental issue here is what motivates people, wanting to be the best (masculine) or liking what you do (feminine)." As you can see from the graph, the United States has a much higher score on masculinity than Sweden. See the chart for more explanation.
Information from http://geert-hofstede.com/index.php

adoption of a child—in some cases, for more than a year. Within masculine cultures, such extended leaves would be unimaginable. The masculinity or femininity of a culture also shapes very specific aspects of communication. For example, managers in masculine cultures are often expected to be decisive and authoritarian; managers in feminine cultures might be expected to focus more on the process of decision making and the achievement of consensus between involved parties.

VIEWS OF TIME

Cultures also vary in terms of how people view time. Scholar Edward Hall distinguished between two time orientations: monochronic (*M-time*) and polychronic (*P-time*) (1997b). People who have a **monochronic time orientation** tend to view time as a precious resource. It can be saved, spent, wasted, lost, or made up, and it can even run out. If you're an M-time person, "spending time" with someone or "making time" in your schedule to share activities with him or her sends the message that you consider that person—and your relationship—important (Hall, 1983). You may view time as a gift you give others to show your affection, or as a tool for punishing someone ("I no longer have time for you").

People who have a **polychronic time orientation** typically don't view time as a resource to be spent, saved, or guarded. They don't consider time of day (what time it is) as especially important or relevant to daily activities. Instead, they're usually flexible when it comes to time, and they believe that harmonious interaction with others is more important than "being on time" or sticking to a schedule.

Differences in time orientation can create problems when people from different cultures make appointments with each other (Hall, 1983). For example, those with an M-time orientation, such as many Americans, Canadians, Swiss, and Germans, often find it frustrating if P-time people show up for a meeting after the scheduled start time. In P-time cultures, such as those in Arabian, African, Caribbean, and Latin American countries, people think that arriving 30 minutes or more after a meeting's scheduled start is perfectly acceptable and that it's okay to change important plans at the last minute.

You can boost your intercultural competence by understanding other people's views of time. Learn about the time orientation of a destination or country before you travel there. For example, before we traveled as a family to St. Martin in the French West Indies, we learned that it was a P-time culture. So, at the end of our trip, we planned accordingly. When we needed a cab to pick us up at the hotel at 10:30 in the morning, we requested that the cabdriver be there by 9:45. Sure enough, at around 10:25 the cab appeared—almost exactly the amount of lateness that we had anticipated!

Also, respect others' time orientations. If you're an M-time person interacting with a P-time individual, don't suddenly dash off to your next appointment because you feel you have to stick to your schedule. Your communication partner will likely think you're rude. If you're a P-time person interacting with an M-time partner, realize that they may get impatient with a long, leisurely conversation or see a late arrival to a meeting as inconsiderate. In addition, avoid criticizing or complaining about behaviors that stem from other people's time orientations. Instead, accept the fact that people view time differently, and be willing to adapt your own expectations and behaviors accordingly.

skills practice

Understanding Time Orientation
Becoming more mindful of the way you and your communication partners communicate with time

❶ Learn about different time orientations. Perhaps your roommate isn't just a stickler about their bedtime; they may simply be on M-time!

❷ Accommodate others. Don't rush your P-time grandmother off the phone when she's telling you about her week. Call her when your schedule allows for a leisurely conversation.

❸ Avoid criticizing. Time is just one dimension of intercultural communication. Your tendencies toward high- or low-context or individualistic or collectivistic communication styles can confuse someone, as much as you can be frustrated by another's time orientation.

Creating Intercultural Competence

Being mindful of and adapting to cultural difference

In the award-winning movie *Gran Torino*, Clint Eastwood plays Walt Kowalski, a bitter, racist widower who lives alone in Michigan, estranged from his sons. Despite his bigoted attitudes, Walt strikes up a friendship with two Hmong teens who live next door, Sue and Thao, after he saves Thao from a gang beating. To help Walt communicate more competently with the Hmong, Sue teaches him some simple cultural rules: Never touch a Hmong on the head because they believe that the soul resides there. Don't look a Hmong straight in the eye; they consider it rude. Don't be surprised if a Hmong smiles when he or she is embarrassed; that's how they handle that emotion. In return, Walt teaches Thao how to interpersonally interact during a job interview with a U.S. construction foreman: "Look him straight in the eye, and give a firm handshake!" He even instructs Thao on the art of trading teasing insults with U.S. male friends. As these unlikely friendships deepen, Walt (to his astonishment) realizes he has more in common with his neighbors than with his own family.

Like Walt, Thao, and Sue, you will likely form lasting bonds with people who come from cultures vastly different from your own. The gateway to such connections is **intercultural competence**, the ability to communicate appropriately, effectively, and ethically with people from diverse backgrounds. You can strengthen your intercultural competence by applying the following practices: world-mindedness, attributional complexity, and communication accommodation.

WORLD-MINDEDNESS

When you possess **world-mindedness**, you demonstrate acceptance and respect toward other cultures' beliefs, values, and customs (Hammer et al., 2003). You can

In the film *Gran Torino*, Walt realizes that his previous beliefs were racist only when he allows himself to experience his neighbors' culture. How has learning about someone's culture changed or enhanced your impressions for the better? ©Warner Bros./Everett Collection

practice world-mindedness in three ways. First, accept others' expression of their culture or co-culture as a natural element in their interpersonal communication, just as your communication reflects your cultural background (Chen & Starosta, 2005). Second, avoid any temptation to judge others' cultural beliefs, attitudes, and values as "better" or "worse" than your own. Third, treat people from all cultures with respect.

This can be especially challenging when differences seem impossible to bridge or when the other person's beliefs, attitudes, and values conflict with your own. But practicing world-mindedness means more than just tolerating cultural differences you find perplexing or problematic. Instead, treat all people with respect by being kind and courteous in your communication. You can also preserve others' personal dignity by actively listening to and asking questions.

World-mindedness is the opposite of **ethnocentrism**, the belief that one's own cultural beliefs, attitudes, values, and practices are superior to others'. Ethnocentrism is not the same thing as pride in your cultural heritage, or patriotism. You can be culturally proud, or patriotic, and not be ethnocentric. Instead, ethnocentrism is a *comparative evaluation*: ethnocentric people view their own culture or co-culture as the standard against which all other cultures should be judged, and they often have contempt for other cultures (Neuliep & McCroskey, 1997; Sumner, 1906). Consequently, such people tend to see their own communication as competent and that of people from other cultures as incompetent.

ATTRIBUTIONAL COMPLEXITY

When you practice **attributional complexity**, you acknowledge that other people's behaviors have complex causes. To develop this ability, observe others' behavior and analyze the various forces influencing it. For example, rather than deciding that a classmate's reserved demeanor or limited eye contact means they're unfriendly, consider the possibility that these behaviors might reflect cultural differences.

Also, learn as much as you can about different cultures and co-cultures, so you can better understand people's interpersonal communication styles and preferences. Experiencing other cultures through observation, travel, or interaction is a great way to sharpen your intercultural communication competence (Arasaratnam, 2006).

In addition, routinely use *perception-checking* to avoid attributional errors, and regularly demonstrate *empathy* to identify with others. In situations where the cultural gaps between you and others seem impossibly wide, try to see things from their perspective. Consider the motivations behind their communication. Examine how people from diverse backgrounds make decisions; compare their approaches to yours; and when appropriate, politely ask for clarifying information to enhance your understanding. Then thank the other person for sharing their time and information with you.

COMMUNICATION ACCOMMODATION

A final way to enhance your intercultural competence is to adjust your interpersonal communication to mesh with the behaviors of people from other cultures. According to **communication accommodation theory**, people are especially motivated to

self-reflection

Think of an encounter in which you failed to engage in perception-checking while interacting with someone. What happened as a result? What might you have done differently to improve the situation and outcomes?

table 5.1 Creating Intercultural Communication Competence

- Understand the many factors that create people's cultural and co-cultural identities.
- Be aware of the different cultural influences on interpersonal communication: individualism versus collectivism, uncertainty avoidance, power distance, high and low context, emotional displays, masculinity versus femininity, and views of time.
- Embrace world-mindedness to genuinely accept and respect others' cultures.
- Practice attributional complexity to consider the possible cultural influences on your and others' interpersonal communication.
- Use communication accommodation when building and maintaining relationships with people from different cultural backgrounds.

self-reflection

Think of an encounter in which you tried to communicate with someone from a different culture using communication accommodation, but you did so inappropriately. How were you judged as a result? What might you have done differently to improve the encounter?

adapt their communication when they seek social approval, when they wish to establish relationships with others, and when they view others' language use as appropriate (Giles et al., 1991). In contrast, people tend to accentuate differences between their communication and others' when they wish to convey emotional distance and disassociate themselves from others. Research suggests that people who use communication accommodation are perceived as being more competent (Coupland et al., 1991; Giles et al., 1991).

How does this work in practice? Try adapting to other people's communication preferences (Bianconi, 2002). During interpersonal interactions, notice how long a turn people take when speaking, how quickly they speak, how direct they are, and how much they appear to want to talk compared to you. You may also need to learn and practice cultural norms for nonverbal behaviors, including eye contact, head touching, and handshaking, such as those Sue taught Walt in *Gran Torino*. At the same time, avoid imitating other people's dialects, accents, or word choices. Most people consider such imitation inappropriate and insulting. For an overview of ways to create intercultural communication competence, see Table 5.1, which pulls together everything you've learned in this chapter.

Dismantling Divisions

Intercultural communication is a gift

The first day or so we all pointed to our countries. The third or fourth day we were pointing to our continents. By the fifth day, we were aware of only one Earth.

—Sultan bin Salman Al Saud, astronaut

Astronauts experience something few of us ever will: the gift of being able to see the Earth devoid of the boundaries and borders that so often divide us from one another. But given that most of us will never ascend to the altitudes explored by astronauts, we need to alter our perspectives without the aid of rocketry. How? By embracing cultural differences rather than allowing them to create distance, by pulling others closer rather than pushing them away. When we do this, a host of

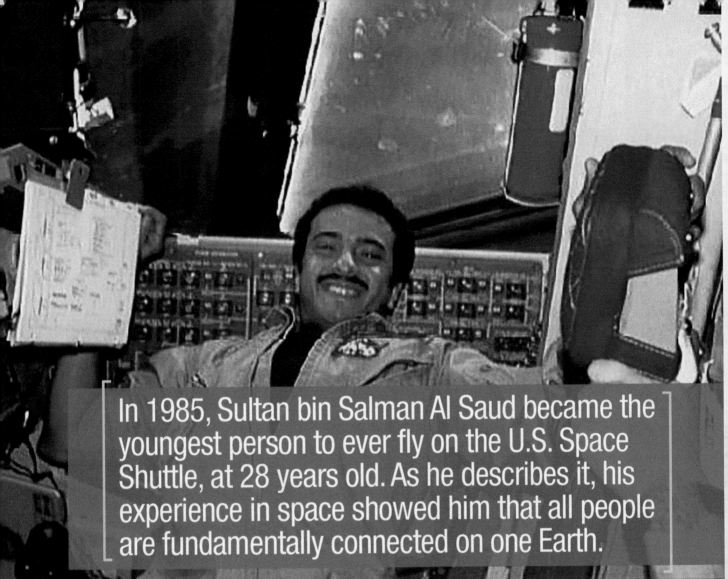

In 1985, Sultan bin Salman Al Saud became the youngest person to ever fly on the U.S. Space Shuttle, at 28 years old. As he describes it, his experience in space showed him that all people are fundamentally connected on one Earth.

NASA

personal and interpersonal doorways immediately open, such as the possibility of new friendships, romances, and professional connections; an enriched understanding of other cultures and co-cultures; and, ultimately, a more refined view of ourselves and how we fit into the rich tapestry that constitutes our human interpersonal world.

Parent–Child Culture Clash

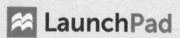 **LaunchPad** For the best experience, complete all parts of this activity
in LaunchPad: **launchpadworks.com**

1 Background

Communicating across cultural boundaries can be challenging, especially when those
boundaries involve differences between children and their elders within the same family. To
understand how you might competently manage such a relationship challenge, read the case
study in Part 2; then, drawing on all you know about interpersonal communication, work
through the problem-solving model in Part 3.

 Visit LaunchPad to watch the video in Part 4 and assess your communication in Part 5.

2 Case Study

You're a first-generation American, the only
child of parents who have deep ties to their
home culture. Your mother was never openly
affectionate, but when you were growing up,
she let you know in many indirect ways that
she loved you. But after your father died, that
changed. She became coldly authoritarian, and
throughout your teen years, she bossed you
around mercilessly.

Your mother's cultural beliefs about parental
power have become triggers for resentment since
you left for college. She chose your major, based
on "your obligation to support her in the future,"
and even scheduled all your classes your
freshman year. You went along with her wishes to
preserve harmony, but you resent the fact that
you are living the life she wants rather than your
own. You've come to believe that she has no
regard for, or interest in, *your* dreams and desires.

This past year, three things happened that
may divide you two further. First, you started
going to a campus church with some of your
American friends, rather than continuing your
culture's religious practices. Although you initially
did this as a secret protest against your mother,
you've enjoyed the experience.

Second, you met Devin. Devin is
Euro-American, and he impresses you by being
outgoing, warm, and funny. You two start
dating, but—like the churchgoing—you don't
tell your mom, because she would never
approve. Third, through hanging out with Devin
and your other American friends, you begin to
question your cultural practices regarding
parental power. This comes to a head when,
with Devin's encouragement, you enroll in a
couple of interesting electives. These classes
make you realize you want to change majors
and pursue a very different career path.

Visiting home one weekend, your mother
abruptly broaches the topic of your future: "You
seem to be drifting from our traditions recently,
and this must stop. You're almost done with
school, and you're no longer a child. The time
has come for you to do what is expected of you.
I have talked with your uncle about hiring you
when you graduate, and he has agreed. And
your grandparents back home have made
arrangements with another family, our long-time
friends, for you to marry one of their children. So,
your future is set, and you will bring great honor
to this family!"

3 Your Turn

Think about all you've learned thus far about interpersonal communication. Then work through the following five steps. Remember, there are no "right" answers, so think hard about what is the *best* choice! (P.S. Need help? See the *Helpful Concepts* list.)

step 1

Reflect on yourself. What are your thoughts and feelings in this situation? Are your impressions and attributions accurate?

step 2

Reflect on your partner. Using perspective-taking and empathic concern, put yourself in your mother's shoes. What is she thinking and feeling in this situation?

step 3

Identify the optimal outcome. Think about your communication and relationship with your mother, as well as the situation surrounding your college experience and future. What's the best, most constructive relationship outcome possible? Consider what's best for you and for your mother.

step 4

Locate the roadblocks. Taking into consideration your own and your mother's thoughts and feelings and all that has happened in this situation and in your home life, what obstacles are keeping you from achieving the optimal outcome?

step 5

Chart your course. What can you say to your mother to overcome the roadblocks you've identified and achieve your optimal outcome?

HELPFUL CONCEPTS

Individualistic and collectivistic cultures, **131**
Uncertainty avoidance, **131**
Power distance, **132**
Display rules, **134**
World-mindedness, **138**
Attributional complexity, **139**
Communication accommodation theory, **139**

4 The Other Side

 Visit LaunchPad to watch a video in which your mother tells her side of the case study story. As in many real-life situations, this is information to which you did not have access when you were initially crafting your response in Part 3. The video reminds us that even when we do our best to offer competent responses, there is always another side to the story that we need to consider.

5 Interpersonal Competence Self-Assessment

After watching the video, visit the Self-Assessment questions in LaunchPad. Think about the new information offered in your mother's side of the story and all you've learned about interpersonal communication. Drawing on this knowledge, revisit your earlier responses in Part 3 and assess your interpersonal communication competence.

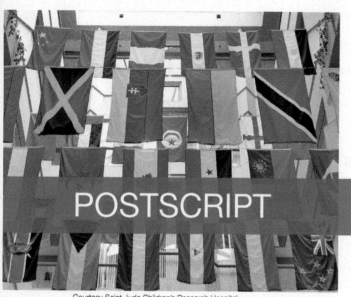

POSTSCRIPT

Courtesy Saint Jude Children's Research Hospital

We began this chapter with a blue telephone in a hospital lobby. When people arrive at St. Jude Children's Research Hospital in Memphis, Tennessee, they find a refuge from the uncertainty and anxiety associated with childhood cancer—one that embraces *all* comers, regardless of economic means, cultural background, or native tongue.

When *you* are confronted with cultural difference, do you double-down on distance, dismissing the possibility of connection? Or, do you offer a "blue telephone," seeking to find a common language that can unite you?

St. Jude Children's Research Hospital was created so that children from all cultures could find a place of light in a time of darkness. The task that *we* face in *our* lives is to mirror that light so it reflects in all directions. When we do so—by treating those who seem different with kindness, fairness, and respect—tolerance triumphs over prejudice. And the world becomes a brighter, more healing place as a result.

LaunchPad for *Reflect & Relate* offers videos and encourages self-assessment through adaptive quizzing. Go to **launchpadworks.com** to get access to:

 LearningCurve
Adaptive Quizzes

 Video clips that help you understand interpersonal communication

key terms

⊙ You can watch brief, illustrative videos of these terms and test your understanding of the concepts in LaunchPad.

key concepts

Understanding Culture

- Our sense of **culture** is deeply influenced by our nationality, ethnicity, religion, gender, and many other factors. When we communicate with those belonging to a different culture, we are engaging in **intercultural communication**.

- According to **Co-cultural Communication Theory**, members of assorted **co-cultures** may engage in **co-cultural communication** to assimilate into the dominant culture, get the dominant culture to accommodate their co-cultural identity, or separate themselves from it entirely.

- **Prejudice** is a uniquely harmful combination of stereotypes and negative emotions related to a particular group of people.

Cultural Influences on Communication

- Whether we grow up within **individualistic cultures** or **collectivistic cultures** strongly influences the extent to which we value personal achievements and independence over group identity. Similarly, the directness or indirectness of our communication is impacted by our experience with **high-** and **low-context cultures**.

- Our level of **uncertainty avoidance** determines our acceptance of life's unpredictability. The **display rules** we learn growing up help us decide when, where, and how to appropriately communicate our emotions.

- Whether and how we will confront people of different social status is affected by the **power distance** of our culture, just as our culture's **masculine cultural values** and **feminine cultural values** impact the importance we place on personal achievement, assertiveness, compassion, and cooperation.

Creating Intercultural Competence

- We demonstrate **world-mindedness** by accepting others' expressions of their culture as part of their interpersonal communication, avoiding the temptation to judge others, and treating others with respect. This is the opposite of **ethnocentrism**, a significant barrier to **intercultural competence**.

- We develop **attributional complexity** by observing others' behavior and analyzing the various forces influencing it.

- **Communication accommodation theory** encourages us to adapt our communication to gain approval and establish relationships, as long as we avoid imitating others' accents or dialects.

6 Understanding Gender

Her mass of red hair is as unruly as she is. We first meet Merida on her birthday, and although she's but a "wee Scottish lass," her father Fergus gifts her with what will become her most treasured possessions: a hand-carved bow and set of arrows. Her mother, Queen Elinor, challenges the gift, but her protest falters in the face of her daughter's joy and immediate attachment to archery. As Merida matures, so does the tension between her fierce spirit and the desire of her mother to constrain her within what's expected of "ladies." Elinor diligently instructs Merida regarding the responsibilities, duties, and expectations of a princess, admonishing her to "remember to smile!" and that "a princess does not put her weapons on the table!" But once a week, free from her royal tutoring, Merida revels in her independence. As the background soundtrack underscores, she is "strong as the seas," honing her archery skills, galloping through the forest astride her horse Angus, with her red curls flying.

The tension between expectation and rebellion peaks when Merida is informed of an upcoming tournament in which the eldest sons of three Scottish clans will compete for her hand in marriage. The constraints placed on her become physical when she is fitted for her princess gown, leading her to protest, "I can't move! It's too tight!" On the day of the event, Merida rebels, opting to compete for her freedom. Unleashing her hair from beneath a tight royal hood, ripping the seams of her fitted gown, and drawing her bowstring determinedly to her cheek, she easily bests her would-be suitors in an archery contest, winning the day, and her independence.

> We are witnessing transformations in how we understand and express gender.

The Disney movie *Brave* opened in theaters in June 2012, celebrating Merida's triumph over gender norms on screens worldwide. But on May 11, 2013, Disney crowned Merida a "Disney Princess" — releasing an assortment of merchandise in support of this labeling — and with their coronation came an extraordinary makeover. What differences do *you* notice in the picture below? Does "Merida the Disney Princess" look older, curvier, and more sparkly? She's sexier too, with an angular face, a tinier waist, and a lower-cut dress. The wide-eyed gaze of childlike wonder has been replaced by eyes adorned by makeup. The tangled red tresses that so energetically blew in the wind as she sped through the woods on horseback are now carefully coifed, yet also more voluminous. But her down-to-earth demeanor and delightful dishevelment are not all that has been stolen from her. Merida's most prized possession — her bow and quiver of arrows — has been replaced by gold, glitter, and a sash that accentuates the hips of a princess. The brave girl has lost the signature symbol of her strength.

A few decades ago, such a metamorphosis for the sake of marketing might have gone unnoticed. But as cultural attitudes about gender continue to shift, a willingness to challenge historical assumptions and constraints, and embrace new norms, has emerged. Consequently, in the wake of Disney's "Merida makeover," over 200,000 angry fans signed a petition on change.org, demanding that Disney return Merida to her original, unbridled state: "Keep Merida Brave!" And fans around the world were not the only ones to defend the strong and courageous girl with her bow. The original creator of the character, Brenda Chapman, fiercely defended Merida's right to be free from the gender constraints of a "princess" label. "I think it's atrocious what they've done to her," declared Chapman. "Merida was created to break that mould: To give young girls a better, stronger, role model; a more attainable role model; something of substance, not just a pretty face that waits around for romance!" (Osborne, 2013). In the end, Disney publicly addressed the backlash and removed images of the redesigned Merida from their website and promotional materials.

To some it might seem silly to ponder the significance of an animated feature film. Yet the fairy tale reveals many themes that we will discuss in this chapter, including the influence that our families and society have on shaping our gender expectations. The outcry over the change in Merida's design also is deeply rooted in our ideas about *gender expression* — how an individual presents their "physical appearance, clothing choice and accessories, and behaviors that express aspects of gender identity or role" (APA, 2015). And lastly, both the movie's narrative and the backlash to Merida's "princess" redesign highlight themes of strength and bravery, which sometimes are required to break down constraints and truly express who we are.

For example, consider Naomi Osaka, the 2020 U.S. Open tennis champion (pictured on the next page), who describes herself as a Black and a multiracial woman, of Haitian and Japanese descent. As sociology professor Robyn Autry notes, "Black women with natural hair that has not been chemically straightened or relaxed can relate to the way Osaka talks about her curls" (Autry, 2020). And in the predominantly white context of professional tennis, Osaka's curls flying in victory — combined with her face masks recognizing Black people who have been killed by police — are bold statements that challenge the dominant culture (see also Chapter 5). In this way, Osaka's self-expression reveals how gender and culture interact to create a unique identity that she presents to the world.

As we journey through this chapter, we will discuss many aspects of gender, including how we learn to *do* gender in our society, how society places gender expectations on us — such as constraints on how we should look — and ultimately how we each can challenge these expectations to bravely write our own stories.

In this chapter, you'll learn:

- How to describe gender and distinguish it from related concepts
- The ways we "do" gender in society
- The influence of gender roles
- The ways gender relates to our communication and relationships
- How to move beyond gender stereotypes

Let's begin by discussing several characteristics of gender.

Understanding Gender

Expanding how we understand gender

In our last chapter, we discussed cultural diversity and the many changes we've welcomed as technological advancements have allowed us to close geographic and social distance. Similar changes occur when people topple walls that previously surrounded historical notions of gender. For example, when we (Kelly and Steve) were young, a female Disney character would *never* have been portrayed as strong and independent as Merida. Instead of skillfully wielding her own weapon while galloping on horseback, she would have sung in a forest surrounded by gentle woodland creatures! As our knowledge, awareness, and understanding expand, our perspectives broaden.

Gradually, we are moving away from a society of constructed **gender polarization**, in which "virtually every other aspect of human experience" is connected to male–female sex distinctions (Bem, 1995, p. 329), to one that recognizes more gradients, or a rainbow of options, for gender. This movement away

Naomi Osaka's natural hair and her face masks in support of the Black Lives Matter movement are powerful expressions in the world of professional tennis. Can you think of a time when you used your self-presentation to make a statement, or to challenge a dominant culture?

Al Bello/Getty Images

from binary male–female categories is illustrated in many ways now in our culture, whether it be "all gender" signs on public restrooms, nonbinary characters in media (such as the character Shep, voiced by Indya Moore, on Cartoon Network's animated series *Steven Universe*), or celebrities who discard binary understandings of gender, and instead describe themselves as **nonbinary**, **gender fluid**, or **genderqueer**. For instance, actress/model Ruby Rose describes gender fluidity as "not really feeling like you're at one end of the spectrum or the other. For the most part, I definitely don't identify as any gender . . ." (Sakiri, 2016). And singer Sam Smith identifies as much as a woman as a man (Petit, 2017). This cultural shift is reflected in our language and interpersonal encounters, such as when a person identifies preferred pronouns as *they/them* or *she/her* or *he/him*, and within public and professional communities, as illustrated by the American Psychological Association and the National Association of School Psychologists' resolution on gender and sexual orientation diversity for public schools, which asserts that "all persons" are entitled to equal opportunity and a safe environment (see Table 6.1).

As stated by the second clause in the APA's resolution (listed in Table 6.1), we are *in the midst* of "rapid cultural and political change" with regard to gender. Because this is a chapter about gender within an introductory textbook on interpersonal communication, our coverage is designed to introduce you to gender as it relates to interpersonal communication and relationships. Thus, our coverage may differ from what you would find in a different discipline, such as sociology or psychology, and may not be as thorough as what you would find in a class specifically on gender. If you find yourself curious about some of the issues we discuss—and we hope that you do!—we encourage you to further your studies by enrolling in a gender and communication course, or a gender class in another discipline.

To begin our introduction to gender and interpersonal communication, we first need to start with some terminology, with the understanding that meanings and understanding of terms are complex, rapidly changing, and still being constructed (Darwin, 2020; Heinz, 2018; Hyde, Bigler et al., 2019). Let's differentiate sex, gender identity, and gender; then we'll consider some characteristics of gender.

GENDER IS DISTINCT FROM SEX AND GENDER IDENTITY

Each of us is born with *anatomical, biological distinctions*, known as our **sex**, which include differences in external genitalia, internal reproductive organs, hormones, and sex chromosomes. At birth we are assigned a "sex category," and in many countries our birth certificates state "male," "female," or "intersex"; the latter category refers to a person who is born with or who develops differences in reproductive or sexual anatomy that don't seem to fit the typical definitions of female or male (InterACT, 2020). We see these distinctions as we grow older: men tend to develop greater height and more upper body strength compared to women, and consequently, we see differences in motor skills, such as men's greater grip strength, as well as throwing velocity and distance (Hyde, 2005).

In contrast, **gender identity** is *internal* to you: it is your deeply felt awareness or inner sense of being a boy, man, or male; a girl, woman, or female; or an alternative,

table 6.1 **Preamble to the Resolution on Gender and Sexual Orientation Diversity in Children and Adolescents in Schools**

WHEREAS people express and experience great diversity in sexual orientation and gender identity and expression;
WHEREAS communities today are undergoing rapid cultural and political change around the treatment of sexual minorities and gender diversity;
WHEREAS all persons, including those who are sexual or gender minority children and adolescents, or those who are questioning their gender identities or sexual orientations, have the right to equal opportunity and a safe environment within all public educational institutions
Adopted by the Council of Representatives, August 2014. Amended by the Council of Representatives, February 2015.

such as genderqueer, gender-nonconforming, or gender-neutral (APA, 2015; APA & National Association of School Psychologists, 2015).

Transgender (trans) people self-label differently than their sex category assigned at birth. *Cisgender* (cis) people self-label the same as their sex category assigned at birth (Hyde et al., 2019). And just like we see multiracial and multicultural diversity, we also see a range of diversity in terms of gender identity and gender expression. The life of Jazz Jennings, a transgender high school girl, is portrayed on the TLC reality show *I Am Jazz*. Danica Roem, who campaigned on the issues of traffic congestion, inadequate teacher salaries, and Medicaid expansion, is the first openly trans person elected to a U.S. state legislature, and is now serving in Virginia's House of Delegates (Bruni, 2017). Kylar Broadus, founder and director of the Trans People of Color Coalition, is the first trans person to testify to the U.S. Senate in support of the Employment Nondiscrimination Act (Abel, 2020). All of these examples illustrate how media representation and policy change accompany shifts in our cultural understanding of gender.

Words also shape our understanding—a topic we will discuss in more detail in Chapter 8—and the words *sex* and *gender* describe very different things. Unlike *sex*

⬥ Jazz Jennings (left), Danica Roem (center), and Kylar Broadus (right) are three of the many figures who are leading the movement toward a more inclusive societal understanding of gender. (Left to Right) Taylor Hill/Getty Images; Paul J. Richards/AFP/Getty Images; © Danielle Levitt/AUGUST

(your assigned category at birth based on anatomical distinctions), or *gender identity* (your inherent knowledge of who you are), **gender** is a broader term encompassing the social, psychological, and behavioral attributes that a particular culture associates with an individual's biological sex (APA, 2015; APA & National Association of School Psychologists, 2015). These attributes may include beliefs about individual characteristics, such as strength, leadership, or emotionality, along with roles in society, such as being a parent, teacher, politician, or CEO. Consider this latter acronym, CEO, for example. When you hear this term, does the image of a chief executive officer who is a man immediately come to mind? If you visualize a man, it would make sense, given that fewer than 8 percent of the CEO positions in Fortune 500 companies are held by women, and this is an all-time high (Ebrahimji, 2020).

Importantly, gender will vary according to culture because different cultures have different standards, or norms, for expected behaviors, roles, and gender expression. So behaviors, roles, or gender expressions that are seen as masculine in one culture may not be regarded as masculine in another culture. Many cultures expect males to display masculine behaviors and females to display feminine behaviors. But as we move away from polarized categories, what constitutes "masculine"? What constitutes "feminine"? Is there overlap between the two? As our chapter opener demonstrates, our society associates "Disney princess" attributes such as beauty with females, or femininity. But beauty is not an attribute we typically associate with males or masculinity. Instead, males and masculinity may be associated with a Disney *prince* character, who likely is described as brave or heroic. This is why many people considered the Disney movie *Brave* to be so revolutionary—it focused on a *courageous young girl*. This also was why they were so quick to defend her, when the attributes marking her strength were stolen from her.

Beyond associating different attributes with masculinity and femininity, we also may describe the *same* attribute by using different words when the attribute is possessed by a male compared to a female. So, if a Disney prince is physically attractive, he is described as "handsome," while a similarly attractive princess would be described as "pretty" or "beautiful." Such gendered associations and assumptions aren't limited to movies, either. When our sons were babies, for example, we experienced this on several occasions. They would be complimented for their "beauty" by complete strangers in the grocery store. Then, after asking for the name of our baby—and realizing they had "mistakenly" characterized a boy as "beautiful"—the strangers would be horrified and apologize profusely for their "error"! But what *was* their "mistake"? Using the wrong gendered term for attractiveness.

GENDER IS LEARNED

Recall Chapter 5, and our discussion of culture as something that is learned from a variety of sources ranging from your family and friends, to schools and the media. Similarly, *gender is learned from a variety of sources,* all of which contribute to the lifelong process of gender socialization. Through the advances of ultrasound imaging technology, many people choose to learn the sex of their baby before birth. This allows parents to begin the gender socialization of their child before the child is even born, through selecting masculine or feminine names, baby clothing, toys, nursery decorations, or even hosting a "gender-reveal party," during which they reveal to family and friends (and sometimes to themselves!) whether their baby will be a boy or a girl. Explore YouTube and you may find more than half a million videos of couples at such parties (Hafner, 2017).

After we are born, this gender socialization process continues and escalates, as parents—like Merida's mother in *Brave*—encourage or discourage behaviors they deem gender "appropriate" or "inappropriate." In one study, parents of 3- to 5-year-old children often encouraged gender nonconformity in young daughters—such as wearing sports-themed clothing or playing with trucks, trains, or building toys—but were less thrilled with gender nonconformity in their young sons. Though they supported their sons playing with kitchen centers to learn domestic skills, parents were more troubled by their sons crying, playing dress-up, or being passive (Kane, 2006).

As they grow, children themselves take a more active role in learning about gender, whether it's voicing their preferences for toys, Halloween costumes, or birthday parties. Think back to when you were quite young and may have been involved in planning your birthday parties. Did you plan pink "dress-up" parties? Sports-themed parties? Disney character parties? How did your parents or caregivers respond to your requests? All these decisions function to bolster gender. But if such decisions run against societal norms for gender, everyone involved feels pressure to conform. For example, when one of our sons decided he wanted to have a "Disney Mulan birthday party," we set out to plan and prepare for the party. We were stunned, however, when we discovered not only that few Mulan decorations were available for purchase, but that salespeople were skeptical about selling them to us when we mentioned the party was for *a boy*! Kelly ended up making most of the decorations for the party, crafting both fans and swords for all the kids to decorate and play with.

🔊 A popular trend for parents-to-be is to host a "gender-reveal party," to celebrate learning the sex of their baby. Some parents will hire party planners to fill a box with balloons. They then "reveal" the sex of the baby to guests by opening the box and watching which balloons—either pink or blue—fly into the air.
Mccallk69/Shutterstock

GENDER IS SOCIALLY CONSTRUCTED

As our experience with the Mulan birthday party illustrates, families are free to make their own choices regarding how their children learn gender, but at some point we all must participate in society. This may entail having a pink, blue, or combination pink-and-blue knit hat placed on a newborn's head in a hospital; hosting a birthday party; sending kids off to their first day of school where there are different public restrooms for boys and girls; or waving a pink, blue, and white striped trans-pride flag while holding your daughter's hand marching in a pride parade (Hassouri, 2020). A central aspect of learning gender is learning the *norms* and *standards* that your society associates with the sex categories.

Gender is *socially constructed* because a primary way we understand gender is by *interacting with other people in society, as well as with societal structures*, such as hospitals, stores, and public restrooms. Because society influences our understandings of gender, as society changes over time, so, too, will our conceptions of gender. To illustrate this, consider the type of career advice you have received thus far in your life. Did it constrain you in ways related to your gender? When Kelly was in high school, for instance, she took multiple classes in typing (on a typewriter!) and shorthand dictation so that she would have strong skills to guarantee continual employment as a secretary (not an "administrative assistant"). Steve, on the other hand, was asked whether he would be a "doctor" or "lawyer." Nowadays, you may see anyone occupying the roles of administrative assistant, attorney, nurse, and physician.

To this point, we've sought to clarify the difference between sex, gender identity, and gender, and we've discussed various aspects of how our culture shapes our gender. But to truly understand how gender is socially constructed, we need to explore more deeply how we "do gender" in our society, and it's this topic to which we next turn.

self-
reflection

Do you remember some of the ways you learned about gender? Was it through the toys you played with, or the toys a friend of a different gender played with? How do you think these early lessons impacted how you conceive of gender now?

Doing Gender

Society expects us to accomplish gender. In one of the most famous articles ever written about gender, entitled "Doing Gender," scholars Candace West and Don Zimmerman (1987, 2009) argued that gender is not a "singular thing" (1987, p. 148); instead, it is something we achieve and are held accountable for every day, emerging from social encounters. This suggests three important implications. First, gender is not a static object or a possession that never changes. It is not something inside of you (like your sense of gender identity). Second, we cannot opt out of doing gender. We are held accountable for doing gender every day, and people expect that we are doing it to the best of our abilities. Third, it is interactional. Because it emerges from social encounters, we achieve it according to the setting, the participants, and the nature of the encounter. Thus, unlike a possession that travels with us, looking and functioning the same way in every context, we accomplish gender by flexibly adapting to our social interactions.

Our understanding of the expected behaviors in a social setting, and the people with whom we are interacting, both influence how we do gender. For instance, when Steve teaches self-defense unarmed combat classes, he talks with a loud voice and uses aggressive movements. But when he's in a different social setting, teaching his yoga students, he speaks more softly, uses different words, and moves more gently. Correspondingly, if you gathered the students from each class, and had them describe Steve's gender expression, they would likely report significant differences. Because gender is something we "do in interaction with others" (Messerschmidt, 2009, p. 86), how we "do" gender changes as the roles, societal expectations, people, and settings change in our daily interactions.

As a deeper illustration of this, consider where Kelly professionally landed after graduating from college with an undergraduate degree in business. Her first job was in industrial sales in the packaging industry. She spent her days interacting with people from many different organizational areas, primarily men, ranging from computer programmers, to die-room employees and their supervisors, to plant and account managers. When she was on the factory-room floors, she pulled from the "tomboy" years of her youth and used much more masculine behaviors to fit in, even though she was wearing a skirt. Many times the men would curse, simply to push her buttons and test how she would respond. When she eventually left her job to move to Michigan, one of the die-room employees gifted her with a button that read, "I'm no lady," and expressed to her that this was his ultimate form of compliment!

People typically expect your gender expression to coincide with your sex, such that girls and women are expected to enact more feminine behaviors, and boys and men are expected to enact more masculine behaviors. This is a central aspect of achieving, or accomplishing, your gender: *behaving in a way that society expects you to, or in a way that typically is consistent with your sex category*. But as the above example illustrates, gender expression and sex category don't always have to coincide: to fit in on the factory floor, Kelly chose to "do" her gender differently, behaving in a more masculine and less feminine fashion.

Additionally, as West and Zimmerman note, a variety of institutional structures, or societal **resources for doing gender**, exist that separate the sexes and instill the idea of *innate* or *natural* differences between girls and boys, and women and men (1987, p. 137), thus further instructing us how to "do gender." Public restrooms are an excellent example of this. Think back to the house you grew up in: Did you share the same bathroom with your brothers and sisters? You might have, but when

self-reflection

In what ways have you adjusted how you "do" gender to match the social setting and people with whom you're interacting? What behaviors or appearances did you alter? Why? Were your adjustments effective?

you were out in public, you were separated into two different restrooms, which may have been labeled with a picture of someone wearing "pants" or a "dress." Biologically, we obviously all need to use restrooms, yet society instructs us to "do gender" by creating physical structures that teach us that we are fundamentally different and need to be separated. Although we now have "family restrooms" in many public spaces, and "all gender" restrooms in some, a variety of these public resources still teach distinct differences that typically are constrained to fit two binary categories, male or female.

Physical spaces aren't the only example of resources for doing gender—we are surrounded by them. In early 2018, PepsiCo received swift public backlash when an interview with its CEO aired, suggesting that different snacks were being considered for women because women and men do not eat Doritos in the same way. Specifically, the CEO claimed that women "don't like to crunch too loudly in public . . . and they don't lick their fingers generously, and they don't like to pour the little broken pieces and the flavor into their mouth" (LaForge, 2018). If PepsiCo had gone forward with its potential product, we would now be choosing between a bag of "Doritos" or "Lady Doritos." Similar to the Merida makeover backlash described in our opener, an angry outcry erupted on Twitter, Facebook, and other social media. PepsiCo quickly backpedaled, stating that the reporting was inaccurate and "We already have Doritos for women—they're called Doritos, and they're enjoyed by millions of people every day . . ." (Bruner, 2018).

◁ Traditionally, many public institutions, such as restrooms, have attempted to separate people into two binary categories. Today, it is common to see public restrooms such as this one that are open to anyone.
Campwillowlake/iStock/Getty Images

skills practice

Recognizing Our Assumptions about Gender

Realizing when institutional structures become internal beliefs

❶ Identify a belief you have regarding gender differences.

❷ Try to recall when you first remember holding this belief.

❸ Is this belief linked to a societal resource for doing gender?

❹ Investigate the teachings of the societal resource. Why do you think this societal resource exists? Is the resource actually based on any real differences between genders?

❺ Revisit your belief about difference, and ponder aspects of similarity and how we can "undo" the binary differences created by this resource.

While "Lady Doritos" may never come to pass, if you keenly observe your surroundings, you'll begin to notice all the rich resources society has created for doing gender according to a binary system in which "male" and "female" are the primary—and polarized—options. We have become accustomed to these binary aspects of society, and actually may take them for granted. For example, do you buy a black razor or pay more money for a pink one? Both products will remove hair, but manufacturers create differences in the products' names and colors, designing different versions of the product for girls/women and boys/men. Additionally, girls and women pay a "pink tax" for the female version of many products (see Table 6.2), spending more money for their purchases, even though they're essentially buying the same items as men (Ngabirano, 2017).

Reflect for a moment on the products you use every week. What color, scent, and price are your shampoo, deodorant, face wash, or T-shirts? Do you choose to pay more money for a "jasmine vanilla-scented body wash," or do you prefer to pay less for one that smells of "spicy freedom"? Have you ever been asked at a drive-through window if you wanted a McDonald's Happy Meal for a "boy" or a "girl"? Perhaps you noticed that boys may receive a "transformer" toy, while girls receive a "my little pony" toy, yet both boys and girls ate the same food. And this is the point. It doesn't really matter if Kelly eats a happy meal and requests a boy's meal, or if Steve shaves with a pink razor—an alarm will not sound. But a key aspect of understanding how we do gender is that we are socialized to believe that we should adhere to these societal expectations and different resources—possibly for fear of being teased or reprimanded. Thus, as West and Zimmerman (1987) note, we are held accountable for accomplishing our gender every day, to the best of our abilities. Thus, one way to alter gender expectations is to challenge the binary resources for doing gender.

table 6.2 The Pink Tax

Products for girls and women cost more than comparable products for boys and men.

Products	Number of Products	Women's Average	Men's Average	Price Difference	Percent Difference
Shampoo and Conditioner (Hair Care)	16	$8.39	$5.68	$2.71	48%
Razor Cartridges	18	$17.30	$15.61	$1.69	11%
Razors	20	$8.90	$7.99	$0.91	11%
Lotion	10	$8.25	$7.43	$0.82	11%
Deodorant	20	$4.91	$4.75	$0.16	3%
Body Wash	18	$5.70	$5.40	$0.30	6%
Shaving Cream	20	$3.73	$3.89	($0.16)	4%
Total	**122**	**$57.18**	**$50.75**	**$6.43**	**13%**

The Pink Tax: Table showing price differences between men's and women's self-care products, excerpted from Candice Elliott, "The Pink Tax—The Cost of Being a Female Consumer," *Listen Money Matters*, https://www.listenmoneymatters.com/the-pink-tax/. Copyright © Listen Money Matters. Reprinted by permission.

Now that we have described gender, and how we do it, let's turn our attention to consider another aspect of how gender is socially constructed: gender roles.

self-reflection

What products do you purchase that are specifically designed for your gender? Have you bought, or would you ever purchase, a product designed for a gender different from your own? Why or why not? If you have bought such a product, did you notice a difference in price?

Considering Gender Roles

How society expects us to behave

Rivals said that they were *too* good; they "moved like boys." One referee suggested they didn't deserve a medal because "they had boys on their team." Opposing-team parents asked them for their names and demanded to see their passports to prove that they were, indeed, *girls*.

If you guessed that these club soccer players were athletes trying to "man up," you would be mistaken. In fact, you could argue that they were trying to "woman up," by imitating the hairstyles of their favorite female role models, including Ellen DeGeneres and Olympic and World Soccer champion Abby Wambach. These comments and criticisms were directed at some of the adolescent girls who were teammates on the Madison, Wisconsin, 56ers youth girls soccer team because they chose to sport short hairstyles to complement their athletic abilities. And the 56ers weren't the only girls to deal with such comments. In June that same year, the Nebraskan soccer team of Milagros "Mili" Hernandez was disqualified from a tournament because she, too, was mistaken for a boy, as a result of her short hairstyle, a typo on the roster, and the related rules violation.

These stories illustrate several issues about gender, including the gender expression displayed by a hairstyle and the way organized sports function as a resource for doing gender by maintaining separate teams and leagues for girl and boy soccer players. But this story also speaks to the broader idea of **gender roles**: shared societal expectations for conduct and behaviors that are deemed appropriate for girls or women and boys or men. At the heart of the story that attracted national news attention (Boren, 2017; Koss, 2017) are the underlying assumptions that "boys play sports better than girls" and "boys wear shorter hairstyles than girls." Therefore, if a girl plays soccer too well, and sports a short hairstyle, she must not be a girl.

As we discussed earlier, we are taught gender roles from a very early age. Think back to the memorable gender messages that may have been communicated to *you* in *your* youth. Were you taught that big boys don't cry? It's not ladylike to curse? Were you teased that you throw like a girl, sound like a girl, look like a boy? Maybe you heard stories about the old "Teen Talk Barbie" doll that lamented, "Math class is tough!" Were you counseled toward or away from particular classes in school or certain careers? All these messages are examples of how we create different expectations, or standards, for girls and boys, and how societies instill gender role beliefs by promoting these personality trait and skill differences (Eagly et al., 2000; Eagly & Wood, 2012).

Research indicates that these beliefs take hold early and impact our aspirations for the future. In one study, both 5-year-old girls and boys were likely to link being smart with their own gender group, whereas in the 6-year-old age group, girls

Mili Hernandez and her teammates were disqualified from a soccer tournament when its organizers believed, incorrectly, that a boy was playing on an all-girls team. Upon learning of their team's disqualification, her teammates also cut their hair short in solidarity. WOWT NBC Omaha/ AP Images

were *less* likely than boys to believe that girls are "really, really smart" (Bian et al., 2017, p. 389). The researchers further suggested that these beliefs may reduce the range of career options girls consider, such as pursuing a job in a mathematics-intensive field.

Beliefs about abilities and intelligence aren't the only differences we see. According to findings from the Global Early Adolescent Study (GEAS; Blum et al., 2017; Chandra-Mouli et al., 2017; Lane et al., 2017), which compiled data on adolescents age 10 to 14 years old from 15 countries (including Belgium, Scotland, the United States, Kenya, Nigeria, Egypt, and India), girls and boys *across the world* encounter unequal gender expectations and stereotypes. The researchers stated that "across all study sites, boys are encouraged to be tough, strong, and brave and to demonstrate heterosexual prowess. Girls are taught to be nice, polite, and submissive and to accentuate their physical beauty while maintaining their modesty" (Chandra-Mouli et al., 2017, p. 56). These gender roles prescribe beliefs that girls are vulnerable and must be protected from boys, who are trouble. Thus, girls' behaviors are often controlled and restricted, while boys are afforded more independence. Notably, these inequities are enforced by parents as well as peers, who sanction or tease each other when straying from such rigid norms.

The GEAS researchers caution us that these prescriptive gender roles have substantial negative outcomes. For instance, their conclusions show that both girls and boys experience fewer cross-sex friendships during adolescence than they did when they were younger. Although girls experience more tolerance when they bend prescriptive gender norms, such as engaging in "tomboy" behaviors or playing sports, boys who engage in feminine behaviors are mocked or bullied. Moreover, girls may leave school early, become pregnant, experience depression, or be victimized by violence. Boys are more prone to suicide, substance abuse, and as adults have a shorter life expectancy compared to women. Transgender youth face increased challenges; they have a higher prevalence of disordered eating; are three times more likely to experience anxiety, depression, and suicidality; and may lack access to supportive health services (Selkie et al., 2020).

The same GEAS researchers further state that these differences are "socially, not biologically determined" (Blum et al., 2017, p. 54) and call for fostering gender equality. Before we contemplate how to promote gender equality and break down these restrictive gender roles, we need to consider how gender influences communication. In the next section of this chapter, we explore some of the ways in which gender is related to both verbal and nonverbal communication.

self-reflection

Recall a situation in which you strayed from the norms for your gender. How did others respond? How did their response make you feel?

skills practice

Resisting Restrictive Gender Roles
Responding when others try to limit your gender role

❶ Identify an instance when another person offers you advice, guidance, or an opinion that limits you because of gender.

❷ Consider the other person's perspective and world experiences.

❸ Reflect on the reasons why this person may have offered this information.

❹ What would happen if you followed the advice, guidance, or opinion given?

❺ In what ways would following this advice constrain you?

❻ Identify how *not* following such advice may impact your relationship with this person.

Gender and Communication

Differing views on gender and communication

Think back to our discussion in Chapter 1 with regard to Watzlawick, Beavin, and Jackson's claim that *you cannot not communicate*. Whether or not we intend to *send* a message, people often interpret our behavior as meaningful, presuming that a message *has* been sent. This idea parallels West and Zimmerman's claim that *we do gender every day*: whether or not we actually speak, or intend to convey meaning, how we present ourselves to others conveys a message about our gender identities. A principal way we do gender, and express our gender identities, is through our verbal and nonverbal communication.

focus on CULTURE

Gender Equity and Health

According to the World Health Organization (WHO), gender inequality is one of the factors damaging the physical and mental health of people around the world. Contributing to this inequality are the differential benefits that typically favor men, such as access to resources, power, and control (WHO, n.d.c). For example, girls and women have reduced access to education, medical care, and nutrition; are more likely to occupy lower-wage jobs; and are less likely to control their sexual and reproductive health. They also lack access to decision making. Consider that over 50 years of reporting, the head of state in 85 of the 153 countries included in the World Economic Forum's global gender gap report has *never* been female (Schwab et al., 2020). These inequities are even more pronounced for people who are members of more than one underrepresented group, such as sexual, racial, and gender minorities and people with disabilities.

To improve the health of all, we need to focus on not just how we socially construct gender and socialize gender roles but also how we can topple existing structural inequities. For instance, women biologically give birth, but it is the social construction of gender and gender roles that teach women they should be the primary caregivers of children, rather than men (Phillips, 2005). Indeed, countries that enact legislation granting paid time off to *both* parents after the birth or adoption of a child create a cultural context in which both parents are encouraged to bond with their child and

participate in caregiving. Other structural improvements to enhance the health of all could include addressing differential career paths for women and men—closing occupational gender gaps, such as having more women represented in engineering, manufacturing, and technology fields, and more men represented in education and care work.

Greater gender equity doesn't simply affect health outcomes: it also affects the status of underrepresented groups. Research indicates that countries with the strongest legislative protections, and most positive attitudes toward lesbians and gay men, also have the greatest gender equality (Henry & Wetherell, 2017). Policies like the WHO's inclusive global health agenda for trans people and commitment to "leave no one behind" as well as institutional and cultural changes, such as those called for to overcome the stalled progress toward gender equality in United States, will be necessary to provide health justice for all (England et al., 2020; WHO, n.d.b).

discussion questions

- What do you think should be done to attract people into careers where they are typically underrepresented?
- How can we influence more women to run for office, so they have more control over decision making and policymaking?
- How does the U.S. Family and Medical Leave Act compare to the parental leave policies of other countries?

GENDER AND VERBAL COMMUNICATION

Pause for a moment, and ponder your beliefs about how women and men communicate. Do you believe that they speak differently? Are men more direct or straightforward, clearly stating exactly what they mean, whereas women take longer to get to the point, speaking more indirectly, politely, or carefully? Does one group talk more than another? Interrupt more? Curse more? Use too much detail?

These beliefs about gender and verbal communication are common. Do a Google search on gender differences in communication and see what comes up. Among the millions of search results, you may discover articles informing you that we are "wired" differently, with women being "emotional" and men "analytical" (Martinez, 2017), and men using more "report" talk and women using "rapport" talk (Rochester Rising, 2018). You may find articles that tell you that we have different "purposes," with men "solving problems" and women "using talk to discover how they feel" (Drobnick, 2017). You may find blog posts stating that "women speak about 20,000 words a day" compared to the "7,000 words that men average a day" (New Media and Marketing, 2017).

Given that we live at a time in which so many resources still exist for doing gender and for teaching gender difference, it naturally follows that many scholars have focused on differences in verbal communication. These scholars have stated that women's verbal communication differs from men's; that they have different styles, purposes, or goals in their communication; that their "lifeblood" runs in different directions (Tannen, 1990, 2006); or that they are socialized to occupy different speech communities (Wood, 2015). These scholars suggest that women focus on intimacy, whereas men focus on status or independence; and that women seek commonality and want to be understood, whereas men interrupt more frequently and want to solve problems (e.g., Tannen, 1990, 2006; Wood, 2015). They describe feminine speech as more disclosive, supportive, and tentative, and masculine speech as more commanding, assertive, and less emotionally responsive (Lakoff, 1973; Mulac et al., 2013; Tannen, 1990, 2006; Wood, 2015).

But other scholars highlight the pronounced *lack* of difference that exists in women's and men's verbal communication. These scholars question why we are even *looking* for differences—as with the paper "Is There Any Reason to Research Sex Differences in Communication?" (Canary & Hause, 1993)—or question the evidence on which generalizations about women's and men's communication are based, as in "You Just Don't Have the Evidence: An Analysis of Claims and Evidence in Deborah Tannen's 'You Just Don't Understand'" (Goldsmith & Fulfs, 1999). Rather than spotlighting differences, these scholars state that women and men are more *similar* than different in their communication behaviors; that actual differences are small; and that when differences do emerge, they likely are due to situational factors related to the interaction rather than gender differences in communication. To put it another way, verbal communication is influenced more by who you are talking to, the type of feedback you are receiving, and the topic you are talking about, than by your gender.

Let's frame this in a personal example. Say that you met us, and we chatted over lunch. You might get the impression that Steve talks way more than Kelly does. This is true in that Steve does talk more than Kelly—when the topics of discussion are music, coffee, cars, or the importance of placing your stereo speakers in precisely the right place to enhance your listening experience when spinning a vinyl record on a turntable! However, if the topic turned to the Chicago Cubs, or the plotlines of Christmas movies on the Hallmark Channel, you suddenly would hear Steve fall silent and Kelly become much more talkative and animated in her communication. So, do we talk differently because Steve is a man and Kelly is a woman? No. We talk differently depending on the topic being discussed, the people we're interacting with, and the context in which the encounter is occurring. Similarly, you may be less comfortable conversing with strangers you are unfamiliar with compared to people you know. The experiences of transgender adults further illustrates this

self-reflection

Recall a recent interaction with someone. In what ways was your communication similar to theirs? In what ways was it different? Do you think these outcomes were due to your gender, or due to the circumstances of the situation?

Communication research suggests that our verbal communication is influenced more by context than by gender. Corepics VOF/Shutterstock

point. Describing their interpersonal interactions with cisgender people—and especially cisgender strangers—trans adults indicated that they experienced stress from fear of judgment, disappointment from not being seen or listened to, and a tendency to withdraw from interactions (Heinz, 2018). But, as one participant in Heinz's research noted, "as long as people are warm and respectful, then I'm not stressed" (p. 12). See the skills practice for more useful tips.

Given the central importance of the communication context, interaction, and participants, it is not surprising that the bulk of research in communication reveals a *lack* of gender differences in verbal communication (Canary & Hause, 1993; Dindia & Allen, 1992; Leaper & Ayres, 2007; Leaper & Smith, 2004). Moreover, this makes sense, given that gender is socially constructed, flexible, and interactional. So in addition to breaking down stereotypical gender roles, we need to foster more accurate beliefs about gender and verbal communication. In Chapter 8, we will review verbal communication in more detail. For now, let's continue our exploration of gender by examining nonverbal communication.

GENDER AND NONVERBAL COMMUNICATION

> "Stop crying." "Stop with the tears." "Don't cry." "Pick yourself up." "Stop with the emotion." . . . "If you never cry then you have all of these feelings stuffed up inside of you, and then you can't get them out. . . ."
>
> —From the movie trailer for *The Mask You Live In* (2015)

These are the opening words to the trailer for the 2015 film *The Mask You Live In*, an award-winning documentary selected for the Sundance Film Festival. The film explores male culture in the United States and how adolescent boys are socialized to "man up" and learn their masculinity. One of the primary ways that they do this is by stifling their emotional displays, or donning a "mask," such that they learn early in their lives not to cry, instead masking their emotional expressiveness. As described by psychologist William Pollack in his book *Real Boys: Rescuing Our Sons from the Myths of Boyhood*, a boy suggests: "It's like I wear a mask. Even when the kids call me names or taunt me, I never show them how much it crushes me inside. I keep it all in" (Pollack, 1999, p. 3).

We experienced the construction and reinforcement of such masks throughout the youths of our boys. We still can recall their first little league soccer matches—they were enormously entertaining! Their skills sets were still in their infancy, their bodies hadn't developed strength and

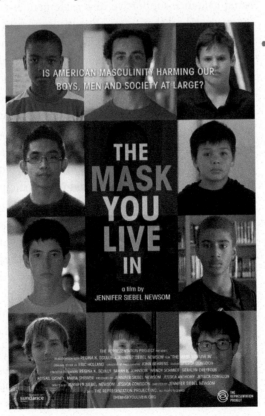

speed, and competition had yet to supersede joy. Positions, strategy, and systematic movements were nowhere to be seen. Instead, the tiny players swarmed the ball wherever it went, like gnats forming clouds. At one particular game, however, a teammate of our son's fell and hurt himself, and began to cry. As he lay on the field right beside where we stood, we were just about to provide comfort, when his mother—who was standing nearby on the sidelines—shouted "SUCK IT UP!" We stood in stunned silence. He was 5 years old.

Now reverse the mask. When do you last recall seeing an adolescent boy, or grown man, smile a face-splitting, jack-o'-lantern-like, *true* smile that goes all the way up his face to his eyes? If you are hard-pressed to come up with examples of both these situations (when a boy or a man could comfortably cry and smile), then you likely have witnessed examples of this emotional "mask."

Combining these examples with the gendered roles we discussed earlier in the chapter, you develop a sense of how deeply intertwined our gender is with our nonverbal communication. The ways in which we use our bodies, voices, facial expressiveness, and personal space; how we choose our clothing, accessories, and personal objects; and how we convey our emotions—these are all key aspects of our gender expression, and how we "do" gender.

As we will review in more detail in Chapter 9 when we discuss *nonverbal communication* (the intentional or unintentional transmission of meaning through an individual's nonspoken physical and behavioral cues), the scientific research suggests several consistent gender differences, unlike the research on verbal communication. For example, and not surprisingly—given our previous discussion of the "mask"—women tend to be *more* facially expressive than men (Hall, 2006; McDuff et al., 2017), often using micro-movements in their faces to communicate their emotions. Although this is a consistent difference, it's also commonly interpreted as being evidence supportive of female gender stereotypes: namely, that "women are more emotional than men." But it's important to ask—given what you now know about gender—does this behavioral difference exist because women are "more emotional" than men, or because women are *allowed*, or even *expected* by society, to be more facially expressive? For instance, when we ask students in our classes if another person—even a complete stranger—has ever directed them to "Smile!", male students rarely recall this happening, whereas female students *frequently* report such an experience. And research supports the idea that we are more likely to expect women to smile and men to be angry. In one study, researchers examined response times (the length of time it took) for participants to categorize gender with happy, angry, or neutral faces. They found that participants took longer to match the unexpected pairs: that is, because we expect women to display happy faces and men to display angry faces, it takes us longer to mentally pair "female" with an angry face, and to pair "male" with a happy face (Smith et al., 2015).

Now, let's pause for a moment to synthesize all you have learned. From our discussion of "doing gender," we know that society tells us to do gender every day and enables this process by creating a variety of resources to mark and reinforce differences between genders. We know from our discussion of gender roles and the GEAS studies that one of the roles boys learn early on is that they are expected to be tough, whereas girls learn to be polite and pretty. If these differences are socialized into you as a set of expectations or rules that you are supposed to follow—and that may lead to teasing, shaming, or bullying if they are *not* followed—who is more likely not to cry and who is more likely to smile? What differences do you

Tatyana Fazlalizadeh is a Brooklyn-based muralist whose series "Stop Telling Women to Smile" attempts to raise awareness around street harassment that women worldwide experience every day. By addressing the act of being told to smile, Fazlalizadeh also opens up a conversation about nonverbal communication norms that women are often expected to adhere to. Dustin Chambers/© The New York Times/Redux

think we would observe if we reversed the rules, expecting boys to be pretty and girls to be tough? If we comforted boys who cried rather than commanding them to "man up"? If girls were given telescopes and challenged to "look up" instead of mirrors teaching them to "look at"?

Much of what we've covered to this point involves the roles of society and family in shaping gender. But to fully answer the questions above, we need to consider two additional and important types of relationships that influence our gender: our same-sex friends and our romantic partners.

Gender and Relationships

Our relationships impact how we do gender.

As mentioned above, and already discussed throughout this chapter, your family plays a central role in shaping your gender and sense of gender identity, as well as in socializing your gender roles. Your family is your first and potentially most impactful instructor on how to do gender. As we mature, however, our attachments tend to broaden from the orbit of our family to our circle of friends, and eventually to romantic partners. And these relationships also play a key role in helping us do gender. Let's first consider our friends.

FRIENDSHIPS

As we'll see in Chapter 13, our friendship relationships differ in many ways from our family connections; one of the most prominent being that we *choose* with whom we are friends, and our choices often are shaped by shared interests and who we like. But friendships do not exist in a vacuum—that is, they are not disconnected from the many institutional structures with which we interact daily, such as school systems, workplaces, and family homes. This means that to understand how gender relates to friendship, we cannot merely focus on the friendship; instead, we also must consider the contexts in which friends interact.

For example, in their examination of communication and friendship networks at summer camp, researchers Traci Gillig and Leila Bighash found that assigning youth to cabins with a diverse group of gender identities led to friendships developing between cabin mates, rather than only between those with similar gender identities. This finding suggests that gender-specific spaces play a powerful role in gender socialization, and that gender-inclusive spaces can play a role in fostering friendships across genders (2019, p. 4910).

So if we create separate spaces, and only focus upon the "separate worlds" (Thorne, 1995, p. 62) occupied by boys and girls within such spaces—ever searching for and spotlighting *differences*—we miss the full picture of gender and friendships because we have overlooked *similarities*. For example, you may have heard or read that men's same-sex friendships are more task-based or activity-oriented and that men like to do things together, compared with the supportive and disclosive same-sex friendships shared by women, in which women often talk about their feelings. Certainly, scholars have described men's friendships as activity-based and women's as communication-based (Aukett et al., 1988; Caldwell & Peplau, 1982; Wright, 1982). But if you carefully reflect on this difference, you may wonder if men engage in activities silently—or if, in fact, they manage to share activities *and* communicate at the same time. As just one example, Steve and his good friend Joe share a love of stereo equipment. Over the last 20 years, they have spent endless hours adjusting speakers, tweaking turntables, playing with cables, and swapping amplifiers and preamplifiers. But every time they get together to "play with audio gear," they *also* talk: sharing their thoughts and feelings about how their families are doing, what's new in their lives, life in general, and the future dreams and plans they each have.

Our culture, and especially our pop culture media, is drawn to documenting gender *differences*. Such differences confirm people's stereotypical beliefs about gender and indeed may be seen as comforting. Often overlooked are the gender similarities and evolving patterns found in the scientific research. For example, regarding same-sex friendships, both men *and* women define intimacy and communicate it in a variety of ways (Monsour, 1992), and desire similar things from their friends, such as friends who are genuine, trustworthy, and loyal (Hall, 2011). In fact, scholars have cautioned us against overemphasizing gender differences (Wright, 1988) and remarked that sometimes greater friendship differences exist *within* a group of girls, or *within* a group of boys, compared to differences *between* girls and boys (Mjaavatn et al., 2016). Finally, some recent studies indicate that men's friendships "are becoming more emotionally nuanced and intimate," evidencing a shift in masculine socialization (Robinson et al., 2018, p. 95).

self-reflection

Think about some of your close friendships. How did you become close friends? How do you stay close friends? Is it through the ways that are traditionally associated with your gender?

ROMANTIC RELATIONSHIPS

Whether HE is athlete, scholar, or just a figment of your imagination at this moment—never let anyone know that you're out date hunting. Every male likes to picture himself the pursuer, likes to think that he's swept the girl off her feet, and while he may very well be flattered to think that a cute number like you has seen fit to single him out of the crowd, he's also apt to be a trifle embarrassed—particularly if his gang takes notice and starts to razz him.

—Bill Gale, "How to Get a Date" (1949)

This is the advice author Bill Gale gave to young girls in an article that appeared in *Calling All Girls* in 1949. This magazine was marketed as "Tops with Teens," and was available for the price of 20 cents. Although we may view his language as outdated ("cute number," "razz"), we actually still adhere to some of the gender assumptions underlying his advice. For instance, Gale presumes that men prefer to be the "pursuers" in romantic relationships, implying that women should wait to be pursued, rather than initiate involvements. He also presumes a *heterosexual bias* regarding sexual orientation: girls are assumed to be romantically and/or sexually attracted *only* to boys, and vice versa; he does not acknowledge same-sex or bisexual romantic relationships.

This bias still permeates much of our culture, from the media to the marriage industry, and even in words used to tease young children, suggesting that they have a "crush" on a friend of a different gender (Thorne, 1995), or to derogate or demean people who do not adhere to this heterosexual bias. As scholars Sharon Scales Rostosky and Ellen Riggle describe, "Same-sex couples form and maintain their relationships in a social context that still stigmatizes their relationships and subjects them to discrimination and minority stress" (2017, p. 10). Same-sex couples tend to experience more stress when they are not surrounded by a supportive network of family and friends (Kennedy et al., 2018). Despite this inequity, research directly comparing same-sex and different-sex romantic relationships reveals more similarities than differences, especially with regard to perceptions of overall relationship quality and satisfaction (Rostosky & Riggle, 2017). Couples describe similar levels of emotional intimacy, commitment, and happiness (Joyner et al., 2019).

More broadly, Bill Gale's advice from 1949 matches both the scientific data on current perceptions about gender roles and popular culture writings on romantic relationships. For instance, the views espoused by Gale mesh with the GEAS report (2017) discussed earlier in this chapter: boys around the world

In 2012, Orlando Cruz, a professional boxer from Puerto Rico, announced he was gay: "I have always been and always will be a proud gay man." In 2016, he dedicated a match to the victims of the Pulse nightclub shooting in Orlando, Florida. Alex Menendez/Getty Images Sport/Getty Images

self-
reflection

How does the media help
promote the *gender differences
hypothesis*? Reflect on the
relationship advice you have
seen on the internet, and in
magazines and books. What
are we learning about gender
and relationships?

still are expected to demonstrate heterosexual prowess, and girls still are expected to exhibit submissiveness and politeness. But it's when we look at contemporary relationship advice books that we most vividly see the similarity in views between present and past regarding romance. Peruse any "self-help/relationship advice" section of a local bookstore, and you'll find dozens of books rooted in the same gender assumptions espoused by Gale back in 1949. Many, and perhaps most, of these books depict women and men as *completely* different from each other with virtually no points of commonality. Also presumed is that men and women are homogenous groups: that is, *all* women are the same in how they view romantic love and sex, and *all* men are the same as well. The differences that purportedly exist between men and women are presumed to be in-born and stable across their life spans — evident in each and every situation, across time and relationships.

Although numerous relationship scholars have debunked the claims offered in popular books like *The Rules* or *Men Are from Mars, Women Are from Venus*, chances are that you haven't heard about *their* works, because they rarely get the same media attention. It bears noting that within the scientific community, little debate exists regarding the issue of gender differences and romantic relationships. As researchers Bobbi Carothers and Harry Reis remarked when interviewed about their study "Men and Women Are from Earth" (2013), "Contrary to the assertions of pop psychology titles like *Men Are From Mars, Women Are From Venus*, it is untrue that men and women think about their relationships in qualitatively different ways" (University of Rochester, 2013, p. 4). As Reis went on to note, heterosexual couples face many of the same issues relating to each other as LGBTQ+ couples do. Thus, rather than homing in on gender as *the* causal factor behind every romantic relationship challenge and experience, *we should consider human character as the source of friction in relationships.* Scholar

▶ Popular books like *Men Are from Mars, Women Are from Venus* attempt to highlight the differences between men and women in relationships. It is important to remember, however, that we bring more to our relationships than just our gender: we bring our individual experiences, culture, and co-cultures, too. Jay Colton/The LIFE Images Collection/Getty Images

Janet Hyde eloquently summed up the view of many social scientists (including us) when she wrote,

> It is time to consider the costs of overinflated claims of gender differences. Arguably, they cause harm in numerous realms, including women's opportunities in the workplace, couple conflict and communication, and analyses of self-esteem problems among adolescents. Most important, these claims are not consistent with the scientific data. (2005 p. 590)

REFLECTING ON GENDER IN OUR RELATIONSHIPS

When reflecting on *your* beliefs about gender and relationships, we encourage you to return once again to the idea that gender is *socially constructed*. We all *do* gender, day in and day out, from the moment we rise to the moment we go to bed. This means that the interactions you have with your friends and romantic partners — and the gender you construct within such encounters — will be the product of the particular person with whom you are communicating, the topic of talk or purpose of the encounter, and the context in which the interaction is occurring. Furthermore, these encounters are positioned in a particular society and culture in which institutional resources for doing gender and for marking power and privilege exist. And finally, gender is just *one* aspect of your self influencing your relationships! It combines with your culture and all the other aspects of your self, as we discussed in Chapter 2, to create the unique mosaic that you are and that you bring to your relationships. Thus, to describe one group of people as all the same and completely different from another group is both overly simplistic and inaccurate.

In Chapters 11 through 14, we will discuss a variety of other concepts that also impact our interpersonal relationships. To conclude our discussion of gender, however, let's ponder some of the ways in which we can move beyond these restrictive gender roles and promote more gender equity.

self-QUIZ

Perceived Social Support Scale

Read each statement below and consider your level of agreement with a rating from 1 (strongly disagree) to 5 (strongly agree). Then total your scores.

_____ My family takes the time to listen to me.

_____ My family is there for me emotionally.

_____ I can depend on my family to be there for me when I need them.

_____ I feel comfortable talking to my family.

_____ My friends take the time to listen to me.

_____ My friends are there for me emotionally.

_____ I can depend on my friends to be there for me when I need them.

_____ I feel comfortable talking to my friends.

Information from the Multi-dimensional Scale of Perceived Social Support, Zimet et al., 1988.

Scoring: Total your scores for the first four items for support from family, and the second four items for support from friends: 4–7: low, 8–14: moderate, 15–20: high.

Moving Beyond Gender Stereotypes

Reflecting on our beliefs about gender moving forward

Differences between males and females has been one of the longest and most comprehensively studied topics in all of psychological science.

—Zell, Strickhouser, Lane, and Teeter, "Mars, Venus, or Earth?" (2016)

Throughout this chapter, we have considered societal stereotypes and scholarly works that promote large distinctions between genders (*gender differences*) and that view men and women as two opposing categories. But research tells us that we are more similar than different (*gender similarities*), illustrating a more nuanced, less dichotomous view of gender, suggesting small, variable, complex distinctions that are more a product of interactions and contexts than of gender. We've contemplated some of the detrimental outcomes of socializing people into restrictive roles: whether it is the shaming of successful soccer players, adolescent boys learning to hide their emotions behind a "mask," or gender disparities in health outcomes that occur globally.

Given all of this, how do we move forward? We offer three suggestions. First, look within; specifically, examine both the attitudes that you hold about women and men, and the beliefs that you have concerning gender differences. Research clearly documents that these two cognitions are connected. A 2016 study by Ethan Zell and his colleagues found that the attitudes we hold about women and men are related to how we perceive gender similarity or difference across a range of issues, such as risk-seeking, self-disclosure, forgiveness, helpfulness, self-esteem, interest in working with other people, and attitudes toward math and science. Specifically, the researchers determined that people with more sexist beliefs also believed that there were *larger* differences between males and females. Investigate the beliefs and attitudes you have about gender, considering how and where you acquired them, and comparing them to the *gender similarities* scientific research presented in this chapter.

Next, look beside you; reflect on the perceived social support you experience from your network of family and friends. As discussed in the section on romantic relationships, we all benefit from supportive networks because these interpersonal relationships buffer us during stressful times. To borrow from our chapter opener, Merida found her strength in her bow and arrows, but a supportive network offers an additional shield of safety. Take the *Self-Quiz* "Perceived Social Support Scale," and then consider how you can use your interpersonal communication skills to cultivate your social support network—topics that we will further explore in Chapters 12 and 13.

Finally, turn your gaze outward. Consider how you communicate with other people and how you interact with societal resources for doing gender. Specifically:

1. Reflect on which resources for doing gender you may use or choose not to use, and ponder why. Examine your artifacts and purchases, considering not just the product but also how it is advertised. Do your choices say anything about gender roles? What would happen if you made changes in this aspect of your life?

In what ways have you moved past gender stereotypes, both in yourself and in your relationships with others?

Photo credit: FatCamera/Getty Images

2. Reflect on the media you consume or choose not to consume, including music, print, and social media. Examine how gender is portrayed. Consider exploring different media literacy or advocacy organizations.

   http://therepresentationproject.org/

   https://seejane.org/

   https://www.about-face.org/

3. Reflect on the words you use and contemplate how they may impact others who might have different identities and beliefs. (See the Skills Practice: Communicating Respectfully earlier in this chapter.)

4. Finally, recall if and when you have spoken out against unfair, unjust, or restrictive gender stereotypes, expectations, or roles; and look for opportunities in the future to do so. What prompts you to speak up? Is it easier to let your voice be heard in defense of someone other than yourself?

Supporting a Gender-Nonconforming Friend

 LaunchPad   For the best experience, complete all parts of this activity in LaunchPad: **launchpadworks.com**

1 Background

People who don't neatly fit into established gender categories often experience extreme pressure to conform. To explore how you might deal with such pressure when it's faced by a friend, read the case study in Part 2; then, drawing on all you know about interpersonal communication, work through the problem-solving model in Part 3.

  Visit LaunchPad to watch the video in Part 4 and assess your communication in Part 5.

2 Case Study

Derek and Daniel have been your neighbors and best friends practically since birth. Although the brothers are only two years apart in age — Derek being the older — they're galaxies apart in personalities and interests. Derek is a fanatical athlete who prides himself on "toughness." He was always the best player of any team in youth leagues, and set high school records in multiple sports. Daniel couldn't be more different. Soft-spoken and gentle, he's a brilliant artist and has never shown *any* interest in athletics — putting him at odds with his entire family.

Although you are close with both brothers, tension between the two of *them* has steadily increased over the years. You blame Derek, as he has always picked on Daniel. When they were young, it was mostly teasing: Derek put Daniel in wrestling holds, called him a "sissy" when he cried, or mocked him for his "girly" interests in fashion, theater, and art. As they aged, the teasing morphed into bullying. Once when you and Daniel were younger and playing "theater," Daniel put on his mother's makeup. When Derek saw him, he put him in a headlock, dragged him to the bathroom, and forcefully scrubbed his face

with soap. You'll never forget the pained look in Daniel's eyes when Derek repeatedly shouted, "Boys don't wear makeup!" It's been a little better since you and Derek left for college, but Daniel is having a tough time being the only one still at home.

You're visiting your family for the weekend, when you get a text from Daniel: "Please help!" Rushing outside, you hear shouting coming from their house. Just then, Daniel rushes out and runs up to you. He is disheveled and crying uncontrollably. "My life is a living hell — I'm leaving!" he sobs. You try to comfort him, but it's no use. "I have a friend who's putting me up for awhile, so I can finish school, but after that who knows," he says. "Don't tell them! I have to get away from him!" And he jumps into his car and leaves.

Furious with Derek, you storm over to the family's house, only to be met by Derek on the porch, looking tired and angry, but also sad. "Oh *great*!" he sarcastically shouts, "This is just the icing on the cake of my weekend! If you know what's good for you, you'll turn around and go back to your house, *NOW*!"

What would you say to Derek?

 **Your Turn**

Consider all you've learned thus far about interpersonal communication. Then work through the following five steps. Remember, there are no "right" answers, so think hard about what is the *best* choice! (P.S. Need help? See the *Helpful Concepts* list.)

step 1

Reflect on yourself. What are your thoughts and feelings in this situation? What attributions are you making about Derek, based on his interpersonal communication? Are your attributions accurate? Why or why not?

step 2

Reflect on your partner. Using perspective-taking and empathic concern, put yourself in Derek's shoes. What is he thinking and feeling in this situation?

step 3

Identify the optimal outcome. Think about all the information you have regarding Daniel, Derek, and their relationship, as well as what role, if any, you should have in this situation. Given all these factors, what's the best, most constructive relationship outcome possible? Be sure to consider not just what's best for you (as their friend) but what's best for Daniel and Derek as well.

step 4

Locate the roadblocks. Taking into consideration your own thoughts and feelings, those of Daniel and Derek, and all that has happened in this situation, what obstacles are keeping you from achieving the optimal outcome?

step 5

Chart your course. What can you say to Derek to overcome the roadblocks you've identified and achieve your optimal outcome?

HELPFUL CONCEPTS

Gender expression, **149**
Gender polarization, **149**
Gender is learned, **152**
Gender roles, **157**
The mask you live in, **161**

 ## The Other Side

📖 Visit LaunchPad to watch a video in which Derek tells his side of the case study story. As in many real-life situations, this is information to which you did not have access when you were initially crafting your response in Part 3. The video reminds us that even when we do our best to offer competent responses, there is always another side to the story that we need to consider.

 ## Interpersonal Competence Self-Assessment

After watching the video, visit the Self-Assessment questions in LaunchPad. Think about the new information offered in Derek's side of the story and all you've learned about interpersonal communication. Drawing on this knowledge, revisit your earlier responses in Part 3 and assess your interpersonal communication competence.

POSTSCRIPT

Courtesy of Stephanie May Kelley

This chapter began with a brave Scottish girl and her beloved bow. The character Merida was created to challenge gender norms regarding how young girls *should* behave, giving them a courageous role model to emulate. And when Disney remade Merida to fit the mold of a princess, fans worldwide protested the robbing of her strength.

What constraining "gowns" of gender expectations have *you* been forced to wear, limiting *your* freedom? What "bows" of strength and courage have been taken from *you*?

The pressure to conform experienced by Merida in *Brave* — and the attempt by Disney to remake her as a princess — are emblematic of cultural tensions we all have experienced between past, present, and future views of gender. Ultimately, however, each of us has the strength to look within ourselves, and — like Merida — embrace the person we find there. As she says in the last line of the film, "You only have to be brave enough to see it."

 **LaunchPad**

LaunchPad for *Reflect & Relate* offers videos and encourages self-assessment through adaptive quizzing. Go to **launchpadworks.com** to get access to:

 LearningCurve
Adaptive Quizzes

key terms

key concepts

Understanding Gender

- We are witnessing a transformation in how our society understands gender. We are moving away from **gender polarization**, which emphasizes a binary male–female construction of gender.

- Some people may identify as **nonbinary**, **gender fluid**, or **genderqueer**, where they don't identify as being either male or female, and their leanings toward one gender or the other may fluctuate.

- When we are born, we are assigned a **sex** category — male, female, or intersex — which is determined by anatomical and biological traits, such as external genitalia, internal reproductive organs, hormones, and sex chromosomes. Sex is distinct from **gender identity**, our inner sense of being male, female, or an alternative gender.

- Sex and gender identity are also distinct from **gender**, a broad term that encompasses the social, psychological, and behavioral attitudes associated with a particular sex. While sex is biological and gender identity is internal, gender is interactional. It is learned beginning at birth and socially constructed.

Doing Gender

- Society creates a number of **resources for doing gender**, such as public restrooms, which teach differences by separating us according to a binary male–female construction of gender.

Considering Gender Roles

- Society also teaches distinct **gender roles**, the shared expectations for conduct and behaviors that are deemed appropriate for men and women. These roles tend to be rigid and further adhere to a binary structure.

7 Listening Actively

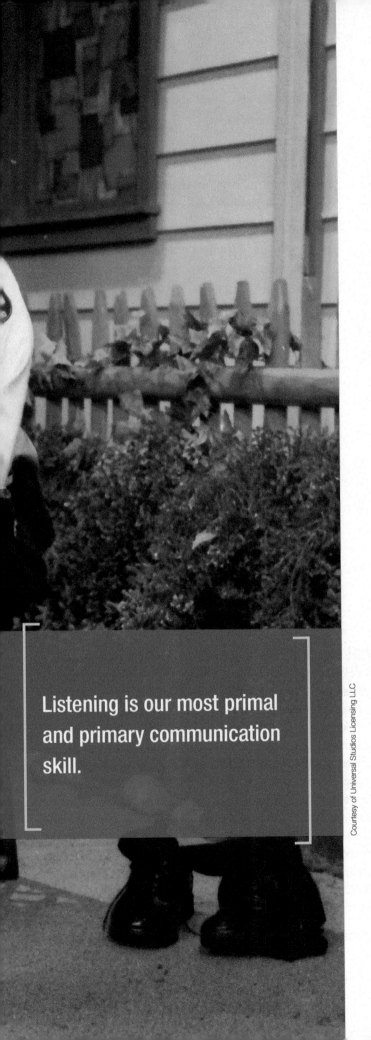

Listening is our most primal and primary communication skill.

Courtesy of Universal Studios Licensing LLC

Fred Rogers began each day by swimming laps in a local pool.[1]

A nonsmoking, nondrinking vegetarian, he was happily married for close to 50 years and helped raise two sons. He also was the most awarded person in television history: two Peabody awards, numerous Emmys, two Lifetime Achievement Awards, the Presidential Medal of Freedom, and a star on the Hollywood Walk of Fame. But Rogers didn't think of himself as a "star" — he viewed himself as a *minister honoring the power of listening*. In his view, the greatest communicative gift people could give was attentive silence that encouraged others — especially children — to openly express themselves.

Rogers originally had planned to enter seminary right out of college, but was sidetracked by the chance to help establish the first public television station in the United States, WQED in Pittsburgh. As he later explained, "I got into television because I hated it so, and I thought there's some way of using this fabulous instrument to nurture those who would watch and listen" (Stimson, 1998). Rogers worked at the station while also attending classes at Pittsburgh Theological Seminary. Ordained in 1963, he decided to minister to children and their families by creating *Mister Rogers' Neighborhood*, a TV program emphasizing affirmation, acceptance, and — most of all — *listening*. In his words, "being a good listener is a vital part of ministry, especially ministry with children. . . . I cultivated my own listening skills in part by integrating silence into my life as a part of my daily spiritual discipline."

---

[1]Biographical information regarding Fred Rogers was obtained from Hohman (2020), Kettler (2020), Millman (1999), Mister Rogers (n.d.), and Stimson (1998).

175

Rogers's gentle listening style belied a fierce devotion to social justice. Responding to civil unrest in 1969 over widespread swimming pool segregation, Rogers filmed an iconic scene of protest. He was cooling his feet in a wading pool when the character Officer Clemmons (played by actor Francois Clemmons) stopped by. Rogers said, "Would you like to join me?" and when Clemmons responded, "I don't have a towel," Rogers suggested, "You can share mine!" The two then proceeded to enjoy the same footbath, while Rogers listened to Clemmons talk about his day. Although the moment was casual — a friend sharing a footbath, a towel, and a listening ear — Clemmons noted, "It was transformative to sit there with him, thinking, something wonderful is happening here. This is not what it looks like. It's much bigger." As Clemmons describes, "Many people, as I've traveled around the country, share what that particular moment meant to them because he was telling them, you cannot be a racist!" Twenty-four years later, the two re-enacted the famous scene during their last episode together — and this time, Rogers didn't just share his towel and his ears, he dried Clemmons's feet.

Mister Rogers' Neighborhood became the longest-running, most-awarded show in television history. But throughout its lengthy, lauded run, Fred Rogers remained committed to the central message of his nondenominational television ministry: *listen* to others and offer them love, respect, and kindness. Two weeks after filming his final episode in 2001, Rogers came out of retirement to film a public service message addressing the 9/11 attacks. Borrowing upon the Hebrew concept of tikkun olam, which literally means "world repair" and connotes concern for social justice, Rogers told viewers, "No matter what our particular job, especially in our world today, we all are called to be 'tikkun olam' — repairers of creation" (Kettler, 2020). He concluded with his characteristic kindness: "Thank you for whatever you do, wherever you are, to bring joy and light and hope and faith and pardon and love to your neighbor and to yourself."

We've all had that experience, whether it was with a parent, a religious leader, a therapist, or a close friend — that moment when another human being listened to us so attentively and compassionately that we felt liberated to bare our souls. *Active listening* does indeed create a safe zone within which we can share our innermost thoughts and feelings with others, an experience akin to coming home. And when we embrace the potential power of active listening for ourselves — taking the time to truly listen to other people — we transcend our own thoughts, ideas, and beliefs, and begin to directly experience their words and worlds (McNaughton et al., 2007). We may even experience such a profound sense of connection, understanding, and immersion while actively listening that we briefly lose our sense of self and time (Geiman & Greene, 2019). By focusing our attention, tailoring our listening to the situation, and letting others know we understand them, we move beyond the personal and create the profoundly *interpersonal*. The result is closer and more satisfying relationships (Bunkers, 2010).

In this chapter, we discuss how to build your active listening skills. You'll learn:

- The five stages of the listening process and strategies for improving your listening skills
- The many functions of listening

- The advantages and disadvantages of different listening styles
- Ways to avoid common forms of incompetent listening

We begin by considering the stages that comprise the complex process of listening.

Listening: A Five-Step Process

Listening draws on auditory and visual cues.

The scares in horror movies almost always begin with sounds. In Steve's favorite scary film of all, *The Babadook* (2014), the stage is set for future fright when a mother and son read a children's story about a monster who announces his arrival with three loud knocks—Dook! Dook! Dook!—only to hear those knocks for real on their own front door. Similar sonic scenes haunt such films as *It Comes at Night* (2017), *The Conjuring* (2013), and *Paranormal Activity* (2007). As we sit in the comfort of movie theaters or living rooms, feeling our blood pressure rising, we listen intently to these sounds, trying to understand them and imagining how we would respond if we were in similar situations.

Horror screenwriters use sounds to trigger fear because they know the powerful role that listening plays in our lives. Listening is our most primal and primary communication skill: as children, we develop the ability to listen long before we learn how to speak, read, or write. As adults, we spend more time listening than we do in any other type of communication activity: research suggests as much as two-thirds of our communication time is spent listening (Bodie et al., 2020). At the same time, the significance of listening often is overlooked, making it a "forgotten dimension of communication" (Jonsdottir & Fridriksdottir, 2020). We often do not realize that listening is a complex *process*. **Listening** involves receiving, attending to, understanding, responding to, and recalling sounds and visual images (Wolvin, 2010). When you're listening to someone, you draw on both auditory and visual cues. In addition to spoken messages, behaviors such as head nodding, smiling, gesturing, and making eye contact affect how you listen to others and interpret their communication. The process of listening also unfolds over time, rather than instantaneously, through the five steps discussed here.

RECEIVING

You're on a video call with your brother, who is in the military, stationed overseas. As he talks, you listen to his words and observe his behavior. How does this process happen? As you observe him, light reflects off his skin, clothes,

In *The Babadook*, Amelia and her son Samuel read about the monster's signature three knocks, which triggers a powerful fear response when they hear the real knocks on their door later. Whenever we hear a sound, we go through a process to help us figure out what we heard and how to respond. ©IFC Midnight/Everett Collection, Inc

Throughout her career, actor Marlee Matlin has advocated for the rights of Deaf people. Her work has helped bring mainstream attention to the Deaf community and has promoted awareness of both signed and spoken communication preferences. Mat Hayward/Getty Images

and hair and travels through the lens of your eye to your retina, which sends the images through the optic nerve to your brain, which translates the information into visual images, such as your brother smiling or shaking his head, an effect called *seeing*. At the same time, sound waves generated by his voice enter your inner ear, causing your eardrum to vibrate. These vibrations travel along acoustic nerves to your brain, which interprets them as your brother's words and voice tone, an effect known as **hearing**.

When seeing and hearing are experienced together, they can create **receiving**, the first step in the listening process. Receiving is critical to listening—you can't listen if you don't see or hear the other person. At the same time, people can receive without experiencing *both* seeing and hearing. Deaf or blind people regularly receive the communication of others through *either* seeing or hearing, rather than both together.

Unfortunately, when it comes to hearing, our ability to receive often is hampered by *noise pollution*, sound in the surrounding environment that obscures or distracts our attention from auditory input. Sources of noise pollution include crowds, road and air traffic, construction equipment, phone alerts, and music. Although we can't escape noise pollution, especially in large cities, some people intentionally expose themselves to intense levels of noise pollution. This can result in *hearing impairment*, the restricted ability to receive sound input across the humanly audible frequency range. The Centers for Disease Control and Prevention estimates that between 6 and 24 percent of U.S. adults under age 70, as well as up to 17 percent of people age 12 to 19, have experienced permanent hearing damage due to exposure to excessive noise (National Institutes of Health, 2019). Twelve percent or more of the global population risks hearing loss from noise (Le et al., 2017); and 75 percent of rock and jazz musicians experience substantial hearing loss (Kaharit et al., 2003). At the same time, people often radically underestimate the negative impact of noise exposure. For instance, more than 40 percent of college students have measurable hearing impairment due to loud music in bars, home stereos, headphones, and concerts, but only 8 percent believe that it is a "big problem" compared with other health issues (Chung et al., 2005).

You can enhance your ability to receive—and improve your listening as a result—by becoming aware of noise pollution and adjusting your interactions accordingly. Practice monitoring the noise level in your environment during your interpersonal encounters, and notice how it impedes your listening. When possible, avoid interactions in loud and noisy environments, or move to quieter locations when you wish to exchange important information with others. If you enjoy live concerts or exercising to music, always use ear protection to ensure your auditory safety. As a lifelong musician, Steve never practices, performs, or attends a concert without earplugs, and as a veteran fitness instructor, Kelly always monitors the sound level of the music in her classes.

ATTENDING

Attending, the second step in the listening process, involves devoting attention to the information you've received. If you don't attend to information, you can't go on to interpret and understand it, or respond to it (Kahneman, 1973). The extent to which you attend to received information is determined largely by its *salience*—the degree to which it seems especially noticeable and significant. As discussed in Chapter 3, we view information as salient when it's *visually or audibly stimulating,* *unexpected*, or *personally important* (Fiske & Taylor, 1991). We have only limited control over salience; whether people communicate in stimulating, unexpected, or important ways is largely determined by them, not us. However, we do control our attention level. To improve your attention, consider trying two approaches: limiting your multitasking and elevating your attention.

Limiting Multitasking   One way to improve attention is to limit the amount of time you spend each day *multitasking*—that is, using multiple forms of technology at once, each of which feeds you an unrelated stream of information (Ophir et al., 2012). An example of such multitasking is Googling content for a class paper on your computer while also tweeting, checking Instagram, surfing Reddit, playing a computer game, or texting family members. Stanford psychologist Clifford Nass has found that habitual multitaskers are extremely confident in their ability to perform at peak levels on the tasks they simultaneously juggle (Glenn, 2010). However, their confidence is misplaced. Multitaskers perform substantially *worse* on tasks compared with individuals who focus their attention on only one task at a time (Ophir et al., 2012). As a specific example, college students who routinely text or post on social media while they are doing their homework suffer substantially lower overall GPAs than do students who limit their multitasking while studying (Juncoa & Cotton, 2012).

Why is limiting multitasking online important for improving attention? Because multitasking erodes your capacity for sustaining focused attention (Jackson, 2008). Cognitive scientists have discovered that our brains adapt to the tasks we regularly perform during our waking hours, an effect known as *brain plasticity* (Carr, 2010). In simple terms, we "train our brains" to be able to do certain things through how we live our daily lives. People who spend much of their time, day after day, shifting attention rapidly between multiple forms of technology train their brains to focus attention only in brief bursts (Jackson, 2008). Consequently, these people lose their ability to focus attention on a singular task for any period of time (Baumgartner et al., 2018). For example, one study of high school and college students found that habitual multitaskers couldn't focus their attention on a single task for more than five minutes at a time without checking social media or text messages (Rosen et al., 2013). And it's not just schoolwork that suffers: the negative impact of multitasking on attention holds for a broad range of everyday tasks, including failure to put important belongings in the right place, grabbing the incorrect item from the refrigerator, and erring in setting one's alarm (Ralph et al., 2013). What's more, habitual multitaskers set themselves up for distraction: they routinely have multiple apps running, which enhances the likelihood of distraction and everyday errors related to poor attention (Rosen et al., 2013).

Not surprisingly, habitual multitaskers have great difficulty listening, as listening requires extended attention (Carr, 2010). Limiting your multitasking and spending at least some time each day focused on just one task (such as reading, listening to music, or engaging in prayer or meditation), without technological distractions, help train your brain to be able to sustain attention. Additionally, if you're in a high-stakes setting in which important information is being shared, and you are using technology (such as taking notes on a laptop), it's essential that you limit access to and use of multiple apps to avoid the attention deficits that accompany distractions (Rosen et al., 2013). To gauge the degree to which multitasking has impacted your attention, take the *Self-Quiz* "Multitasking and Attention."

self-QUIZ

Multitasking and Attention

This quiz gauges how multitasking between various forms of technology can divide your attention and how your ability to focus may suffer as a result. Read each statement below and mark the ones with which you agree. Use your score to assess the degree to which your attention is divided.

To take this quiz online, visit LaunchPad: launchpadworks.com

———— At any one time, I typically have multiple forms of technology turned on, including my phone and computer.

———— If I focus my attention on just one task, I find that my mind quickly starts drifting to other stuff, such as who is messaging me, or what is happening online.

———— Even during class or while I'm at work, I stay connected to and communicate with others through texting, email, or social media.

———— When I spend too much time doing any one thing, I get bored.

———— Text messages, phone calls, email, and social media posts frequently interrupt activities I am trying to focus on.

———— I spend much of my day switching rapidly between multiple activities and apps, including social media, texting, email, games, schoolwork, and web surfing.

———— I feel that I am more easily distracted now than I was just a few years ago.

Information from Bane (2010).

Scoring: If you agree with 0–2 of these, your attention is not divided by multitasking, and you likely find it easy to concentrate on one task for extended periods of time. If you agree with 3–4 of these, you have moderately divided attention and may be experiencing challenges with focusing attention. If you agree with 5–7 of these, you spend much of your time multitasking and likely find it challenging and difficult to focus your attention on just one thing.

skills practice

Elevating Attention
Focusing your attention during interpersonal encounters

❶ Identify an important person whom you find it difficult to listen to.

❷ List factors — fatigue, time pressure — that impede your attention when you're interacting with this person.

❸ Before your next encounter with the individual, address factors you can control.

❹ During the encounter, increase the person's salience by reminding yourself of their importance to you.

❺ As the encounter unfolds, practice mental bracketing to stay focused on your partner's communication.

Elevating Attention   Another way you can try to improve your attention is to elevate it, by following these steps (Marzano & Arredondo, 1996). First, develop awareness of your attention level. During interpersonal interactions, monitor how your attention naturally waxes and wanes. Notice how various factors, such as fatigue, stress, or hunger, influence your attention. Second, take note of encounters in which you *should* listen carefully but that seem to trigger low levels of attention. These might include interactions with parents, teachers, or work managers, or situations such as family get-togethers, classroom lectures, or work meetings. Third, consider the optimal level of attention required for adequate listening during these encounters. Fourth, compare the level of attention you observed in yourself versus the level of attention that is required, identifying the attention gap that needs to be bridged for you to improve your attention.

Finally, and most important, elevate your level of attention to the point necessary to take in the auditory and visual information you're receiving. You can do this in several ways. Before and during an encounter, boost the salience of the exchange by reminding yourself of how it will impact your life and relationships. Take active control of the factors that may diminish your attention. For example, if you sit in the front of the classroom instead of the back, you will be less distracted by other students and better able to attend to the content. When possible, avoid important encounters when you are overly stressed, hungry, ill, fatigued, or under the influence of alcohol; such factors substantially impair attention. If you have higher energy levels in the morning or early in the week, try to schedule attention-demanding activities and encounters during those times. If you find your attention wandering, practice **mental bracketing**—systematically putting aside thoughts that aren't relevant to the interaction at hand. When irrelevant thoughts arise, let them pass through your conscious awareness and drift away, without allowing them to occupy your attention fully.

UNDERSTANDING

While serving with her National Guard unit in Iraq, Army Specialist Claudia Carreon suffered a traumatic brain injury (TBI).[2] The injury wiped her memory clean. She could no longer remember major events or people from her past, including her husband and her 2-year-old daughter. However, because she seemed physically normal, her TBI went unnoticed and she returned to duty. A few weeks later, Carreon received an order from a commanding officer, but she couldn't understand it and shortly afterward forgot it. She was subsequently demoted for "failure to follow an order." When Army doctors realized that she wasn't being willfully disobedient but instead simply couldn't understand or remember orders, her rank was restored, and Carreon was rushed to the Army's Polytrauma Center in Palo Alto, California. Now Carreon, like many other veterans who have suffered TBIs, carries with her captioned photos of loved ones and a special handheld personal computer to help her remember people and make sense of everyday conversations.

Some people who experience long-term memory loss use captioned photos to remember important events and people. Jose Luis Pelaez Inc/Getty Images

The challenges faced by Claudia Carreon illustrate the essential role that memory plays in shaping the third stage of listening. **Understanding** involves interpreting the meaning of another person's communication by comparing newly received information with our past knowledge (Macrae & Bodenhausen, 2001). Whenever you receive and attend to new information, you place it in your **short-term memory**—the part of your mind that temporarily houses the information while you seek to understand its meaning. While this new information docks in your short-term memory, you call up relevant knowledge from your **long-term memory**—the part of your mind devoted to permanent information storage. You then compare relevant prior knowledge from your long-term memory with the new information in your short-term memory to create understanding. In Claudia Carreon's case, her long-term memory was largely erased by her injury. Consequently, whenever she hears new information, she has no foundation from which to make sense of it.

As Claudia's case illustrates, we all have different abilities to temporarily dock and permanently house information. Additionally, we display different abilities in letting people know that they are being listened to; we consider this stage of the listening process next.

RESPONDING

You're spending the afternoon at your apartment discussing your plans for a cross-country road trip with your friends Rishabh and Sarah. You want them to

---

[2]The information that follows is from www.braininjurymn.org/library/archive/NewWarsHallmarkInjury.pdf, retrieved October 12, 2011.

help you with logistical details as well as ideas for interesting places to visit. As you talk, Rishabh looks directly at you, smiles, nods his head, and leans forward. He also asks questions and offers up some goofy Americana attractions, like the Salt and Pepper Shaker Museum in Gatlinburg, Tennessee, and the UFO Watchtower in Hooper, Colorado. Sarah, in contrast, seems completely uninterested. She alternates between looking at the people strolling by your living-room window and texting on her phone. She also sits with her body half-turned away from you and leans back in her chair. You become frustrated because it's obvious that Rishabh is listening closely and Sarah isn't listening at all.

What leads you to conclude that Rishabh is listening and Sarah isn't? It's the way your friends are **responding**—communicating their attention and understanding to you. Responding is the fourth stage of the listening process. When you actively listen, you do more than simply attend and understand. You also convey your attention and understanding to others by clearly and constructively responding through positive feedback, paraphrasing, and clarifying (McNaughton et al., 2007).

Feedback   Critical to active listening is using verbal and nonverbal behaviors known as **feedback** to communicate attention and understanding *while* others are talking. Feedback is crucial not just for conveying attention and understanding, but for creating a sense that a *relationship* exists between the parties involved (Wolvin, 2010). Scholars distinguish between two kinds of feedback: positive and negative (Wolvin & Coakley, 1996). When you use positive feedback, like Rishabh in our earlier example, you look directly at the person speaking, smile, remain largely silent while they speak, position your body so that you're facing them, avoid using electronic devices, and lean forward (Umphrey & Sherblom, 2018). You may also occasionally offer **back-channel cues**, verbal and nonverbal behaviors such as nodding and making comments—like "Uh-huh," "Yes," and "That makes sense"—that signal you've paid attention to and understood specific comments (Duncan & Fiske, 1977). All these behaviors combine to show speakers that you're actively listening and feel a sense of empathy toward them (Wolvin, 2010)—factors that, in turn, facilitate building and sustaining close interpersonal relationships (Umphrey & Sherblom, 2018). In contrast, people who use negative feedback, like Sarah in our example, send a very different message to speakers: "I'm not interested in paying

In many Protestant churches, it is perfectly acceptable for audience members to express their feedback loudly during the minister's sermon by shouting "Amen!" or "Hallelujah!" The same type of positive feedback would be radically inappropriate in a traditional Catholic church. (Left) Godong/UIG/Universal Images Group/ Newscom; (Right) Chris Hondros/Getty Images

attention to you or understanding what you're saying." Behaviors that convey negative feedback include avoiding eye contact, turning your body away, looking bored or distracted, using digital devices, not using back-channel cues, or—on a video call—not even turning on your webcam.

The type of feedback we provide while we're listening has a dramatic effect on speakers (Wolvin & Coakley, 1996). Receiving positive feedback from listeners can enhance a speaker's confidence, generate positive emotions, and create a sense of relationship connectedness (Wolvin, 2010). Negative feedback can cause speakers to hesitate, make speech errors, or stop altogether to see what's wrong and why we're not listening.

To effectively display positive feedback during interpersonal encounters, try four simple suggestions (Barker, 1971; Daly, 1975). First, make your feedback obvious. No matter how actively you listen, unless others perceive your feedback, they won't view you as actively listening. Second, make your feedback appropriate. Different situations, speakers, and messages require more or less intensity of positive feedback. Third, make your feedback clear by avoiding behaviors that might be mistaken as negative feedback. For example, something as simple as innocently stealing a glance at your phone to see what time it is might unintentionally suggest that you're bored or wish the person would stop speaking. Finally, always provide feedback quickly in response to what the speaker has just said.

Paraphrasing and Clarifying   Active listeners also communicate attention and understanding by expressing certain things *after* their conversational partners have finished their turns—statements that make it clear they were listening. One way to do this is by **paraphrasing**, summarizing others' comments after they have finished speaking ("My read on your message is that . . ." or "You seem to be saying that . . ."). This practice can help you check the accuracy of your understanding during both face-to-face and online encounters. Paraphrasing should be used judiciously, however. Some conversational partners may find paraphrasing annoying if you use the technique a lot or if they view it as contrived.

Paraphrasing can also lead to conversational lapses—silences of three seconds or longer that participants perceive as awkward (McLaughlin & Cody, 1982). This occurs because when you paraphrase, you are simply restating what has already been said, rather than advancing the conversational topic forward in new and interesting ways (Heritage & Watson, 1979). Consequently, the only relevant response your conversational partner can provide is a simple acknowledgment, such as "Yeah" or "Uh-huh." A lapse is likely to ensue immediately after, unless one of you has a new topic ready to introduce to advance the conversation. As a result, the conversation may feel awkward rather than smooth. This is an important practical concern for anyone interested in being perceived as interpersonally competent because the more lapses that occur, the more likely your conversational partner is to perceive you as incompetent (McLaughlin & Cody, 1982). To avoid this perception, always couple your paraphrasing with additional comments or questions that usefully build on the previous topic or take the conversation in new directions.

Of course, on some occasions, we simply don't understand what others have said. In such instances, it's perfectly appropriate to respond by seeking clarification rather than paraphrasing, saying, "I'm sorry, but could you explain that again? I want to make sure I understood you correctly." This technique not only helps you clarify the meaning of what you're hearing but also enables you to communicate your desire to understand the other person.

self-reflection

Is the provision of positive feedback limited to face-to-face or phone conversations? How does communicating through mobile devices constrain your ability to provide positive feedback? For example, if a friend shares bad news with you via text message, what can you do to show them that you're actively listening?

skills practice

Responding in a Video Call
Responding effectively during online webcam encounters

❶ Have your camera on, even if it's a large group encounter (e.g., class), so people can see you and your facial expressions.

❷ Look toward the camera, smile, and lean forward while others are speaking.

❸ Avoid multitasking.

❹ Use the chat function to provide partners with positive feedback and signal agreement with things they've said.

❺ Seek clarification regarding messages you didn't understand ("Would you mind explaining that a bit more?").

RECALLING

The fifth stage of listening is **recalling**, remembering information after you've received, attended to, understood, and responded to it. Recalling is a crucial part of the listening process because we judge the effectiveness of listening based on our ability to accurately recall information after we've listened to it (Thomas & Levine, 1994). Think about it: When a romantic partner asks, "Were you listening to me?" how do you demonstrate that you really were actively listening? By recalling everything that was said and reciting it back to your partner. Indeed, practically every scientific measure of listening uses recall accuracy as evidence of listening effectiveness (Janusik, 2007).

Your recall accuracy varies, depending on the situation. When people have no task other than simple memorization, recall accuracy is high. But when people are engaged in activities more complicated than straight memorization, recall accuracy plummets. That's because in such cases, we're receiving a lot of information, which increases the likelihood of perceptual and recall errors. Research on the recall accuracy of criminal eyewitnesses, for instance, has found that people frequently err in their recall of crimes, something most jurors and even the eyewitnesses themselves don't realize (Wells et al., 1980). Our recall of interpersonal and relational encounters is not exempt from error. For negative and unpleasant interactions, such as conflicts, we tend to recall our own behavior as positive and constructive and the behavior of others as comparatively negative, regardless of what actually happened (Sillars et al., 2010).

How can you enhance your recall ability? One way is to use **mnemonics**, devices that aid memory. For example, Kelly can remember and recite the names of the 50 U.S. states without hesitation. How? Because when she was in fifth grade, she learned the song "Fifty Nifty United States"—and the song lingers in her memory to this day.

Because listening is rooted in both visual and auditory information, and memory is enhanced by using all five senses, you can bolster your memory of an interpersonal communication encounter by linking information you've listened to with pleasant or even silly visuals, scents, sounds, or even music—like the "states" song. To create visual images of an interpersonal encounter, you could write detailed notes or doodle diagrams documenting the contents of a conversation. You could also link a new acquaintance's name with one of their characteristics or the place you met. Finally, when you develop mnemonics or notes, review them repeatedly, including reciting them out loud, because repetition reinforces memory.

Now that we have reviewed the five steps in the listening process, let's examine the different reasons for, or functions of, listening.

self-reflection

What's an example of a mnemonic you've created? How did you go about constructing it? Has it helped you more effectively recall important information? If not, what could be done to improve its usefulness?

The Five Functions of Listening

Adapting our listening purposes

On the hit NBC show *The Voice*, the judges (in the fall 2020 season, John Legend, Gwen Stefani, Kelly Clarkson, and Blake Shelton) spend much of each season listening. But they do so in different ways, depending on situational needs. When new contestants audition at the start of the season, the judges listen with their chairs turned away from the singers so that they can carefully assess the quality of the contestants' voices (without being distracted by their appearance) to determine whom to choose

for the competition. Once contestants have been selected, the judges become coaches, and the demands on their listening broaden. They must carefully listen to comprehend what contestants convey about themselves and their life stories to determine the best way to motivate improvement. When contestants argue against their advice, the judges must listen analytically, looking for ways to attack the contestants' reasoning and move them in different directions. When contestants give stunning performances, the judges can listen appreciatively, basking in the vocal talent displayed in that moment. And when contestants break down emotionally, the judges must shift gears yet again, listening supportively and offering encouragement.

The different reasons for listening displayed by the judges on *The Voice* mirror the five common **listening functions**, or purposes for listening, we experience daily: to comprehend, to discern, to analyze, to appreciate, and to support.

LISTENING TO COMPREHEND

Think for a minute about your interpersonal communication class—the course for which this text was assigned. When you're attending class, *why* do you listen to your instructor? The answer is so obvious it's silly: you listen so that you can comprehend (or understand) the information being presented to you. When you listen for this purpose, you work to accurately interpret and store the information you receive, so you can correctly recall it later. Additional examples of this type of listening include listening to a coworker explain how to use a software application at work and listening to a prospective landlord explain your contractual obligations if you sign a lease on an apartment.

LISTENING TO DISCERN

When you listen to discern, you focus on distinguishing one sound from another to help you decipher something. The most common form is to listen carefully to someone's vocal tone to assess mood and stress level. For example, if you're concerned that your romantic partner is angry with you, you might listen carefully to the sound of their voice, rather than the actual words, to gauge how upset they are.

LISTENING TO ANALYZE

When you listen to analyze, you carefully evaluate the message you're receiving, and you judge it. For instance, you might analyze your father's neutral comments about his recent medical checkup, listening for signs of worry so you can determine whether he's hiding serious health problems.

LISTENING TO APPRECIATE

When you listen to appreciate, your goal is simply to enjoy the sounds and sights you're experiencing and then to respond by expressing your appreciation. Common examples include listening to your child excitedly share their story of scoring a soccer goal or listening while a close friend tells a funny story.

---

focus on CULTURE

The Therapeutic Power of Listening to Music

Colleges and universities are reporting unprecedented levels of student mental health challenges. For instance, 95 percent of college counseling center directors report mental health as an increasing concern on their campuses, and 70 percent report that the number of students with serious psychological challenges has increased in recent years (American Psychological Association, 2013a). The top mental health concerns of students? Anxiety and depression. And this prevalence isn't just a U.S. phenomenon: a 2016 Canadian National College Health Assessment found that 65 percent of Canadian students reported "overwhelming anxiety" in the previous year, while the University of Alberta reported that 35 percent of their students had experienced stress-related panic attacks, often triggered by exams (Technology.org, 2020).

Part of this reported increase is due to contemporary college students being "far more conscious of mental health issues — and more able to articulate them — than their parents were," notes Sarah Flower, manager of health promotion for the University of Alberta, in Canada. As she describes, "This generation is much more in tune with what they need. People will say, 'I have anxiety,' or, 'I've been diagnosed with depression' — they are very open to sharing that" (Technology.org, 2020).

Apart from utilizing campus health and wellness services and counseling centers, what can students do to manage their anxiety and depression? One of the most powerful yet unrecognized therapeutic approaches is available to students in the privacy of their own homes: *listening to music*. The largest scientific review to date of the effect that music has upon anxiety — analyzing data from 19 independent studies — found that listening to music substantially reduces college students' self-reported anxiety during stressful episodes and panic attacks, and also lowers students' blood pressure, cortisol (the "stress hormone"), and heart rate (Panteleeva et al., 2018). Listening to music also substantially reduces exam anxiety in the aftermath of important tests, enabling students to more quickly regain a state of calm and emotional well-being (Faus et al., 2019). And regular music listening also reduces depression: data from 26 studies document that people with chronic depression experience significant reductions in their depressive symptoms if they listen to music on a daily basis (Leubner & Hinterberger, 2017).

discussion questions

- How do you use music to help reduce your anxiety, panic attacks, or depression? What types of music do you listen to, to help you manage these challenges?
- What artistic forms other than music might yield similar therapeutic benefits?

LISTENING TO SUPPORT

You're making lunch in your apartment one afternoon when your best friend calls you. You answer only to hear them sobbing uncontrollably. They tell you they have just broken up with their partner, due to the partner's cheating, and say, "I need someone to talk to."

Providing comfort to a conversational partner is another common purpose for listening. To provide support through listening, you must suspend judgment—taking in what someone else says without evaluating it, and openly expressing empathy. Almost by definition, this purpose for listening prioritizes the other person's perspective and needs over your own. Examples include comforting a relative after the death of a spouse or responding with a kind email to a coworker who sends you a message complaining that they were just criticized by their boss at a team meeting.

ADAPTING YOUR LISTENING PURPOSE

The five functions that listening commonly serves are not mutually exclusive. We change between them frequently and fluidly. In fact, many professions require such rapid shifts. For instance, therapists must be able to comprehend what their patients are saying, discern patients' mood states, and supportively listen—often near-simultaneously. The same is true for hair stylists working in beauty salons, who are expected to carefully comprehend technical instructions regarding the desired services, yet also provide "beauty therapy"—listening supportively to the clients' emotional concerns related to personal appearance, relationships, and life events (Hanson, 2019). In fact, for stylists, the degree to which they provide a "supportive ear" is critical in determining their financial survival, as the better they are at listening supportively, the larger the tips they receive (Seiter & Dutson, 2007).

Rapid changes of listening purposes also occur within nonprofessional encounters. For example, you're listening with appreciation at a concert when suddenly you realize one of the musicians is out of tune. You might shift to discerning listening (trying to isolate that particular instrument from the others) and ultimately to listening to analyze (trying to assess whether you are, in fact, correct about the instrument being out of tune). If the musician happens to be a friend of yours, you might even switch to supportive listening following the event, as they lament their performance!

An essential part of active listening is skillfully and flexibly adapting your listening purposes to the changing demands of interpersonal encounters (Bunkers, 2010). To strengthen your ability to adapt your listening purpose, heighten your awareness of the various possible listening functions during your interpersonal encounters. Routinely ask yourself, "What is my primary purpose for listening at this moment, in this situation? Do I want to comprehend, discern, analyze, appreciate, or support?" Then adjust your listening accordingly. As you do this, keep in mind that for some situations, certain approaches to listening may be unethical or simply inappropriate, such as listening to analyze when a relational partner is seeking emotional support.

self-
reflection

Recall a situation in which you listened the wrong way. For instance, a friend needed you to listen supportively, but you listened to analyze. What led you to make this error? What consequences ensued from your mistake? What can you do in the future to avoid such listening mishaps?

LISTENING FUNCTIONS AND MEDIATED LISTENING

Much of our current listening occurs through various digital and mobile devices, including smartphones, tablets, and laptop and desktop computers (Storch & Ortiz

Juarez-Paz, 2018). Although it once was easy to dismiss mediated communication as not involving "listening," this no longer is the case, as much of mediated messaging now involves auditory elements, including video and audio (Vickery, 2018). We use our smartphones to communicate via text messages and video calls (Keaton & Worthington, 2018), which means listening mediated by electronic devices is a key aspect of our everyday lives.

Mediated listening is defined as receiving, attending to, understanding, responding to, and recalling sounds and visual images through mediated, electronic, and social media channels. It is sometimes referred to as "social listening" because so much of it occurs through social media platforms (Stewart & Arnold, 2018). Mediated listening involves the same functions as listening face-to-face or over the phone: that is, mediated listening can be used to comprehend, discern, analyze, appreciate, and support. For example, your best friend knows you're having a rough day, so they send you a text with a funny audio clip attached. As you listen to it, you comprehend the meaning, appreciate the humorous content, and immediately respond with a message of your own, saying how much you value the emotional support that they displayed in sending it.

Beyond the specific functions served by mediated listening, the single most frequent, overarching function of listening through our devices is *creating interpersonal connection*. Researcher Andrea Vickery asked college students to agree or disagree with various descriptions of mediated listening, such as "listening requires active yet silent engagement," "listening requires patience," and "listening should be reciprocal." Although students varied widely in their responses, the top-rated viewpoint regarding mediated listening—with 100 percent of students surveyed endorsing it—was "listening enables me to connect with others" (Vickery, 2018, p. 76).

Now that we've discussed both the nature of listening and the functions it serves, let's turn our attention to the various styles of listening that people display.

Understanding Listening Styles

Culture and gender affect listening styles.

If the person you are talking to doesn't appear to be listening, be patient. It may simply be that he has a small piece of fluff in his ear. —A. A. Milne

In the original Winnie-the-Pooh books, the character of Christopher Robin is a consistently empathic listener to whom all the other characters turn for comfort.[3] Whenever Pooh worries about his own ineptitude ("I am a bear of no brain at all"), Christopher Robin listens and then offers support: "You're the best bear in all the world." In contrast, Owl is Mr. Analytical. He prides himself on being wise and encourages others to bring detailed information and dilemmas to him, even if he often doesn't know the answers. Meanwhile, Rabbit often scurries around and feels very important, critically pondering others' reasoning and decisions. Tigger, though good-natured, seems too impatient to listen. When the group goes adventuring, Tigger urges the others to "Come on!" and then leaves without waiting to hear their responses, bouncing off to his next escapade.

---

[3]The information that follows is adapted from Milne (1926, 1928) and "The Page at Pooh Corner," www.pooh-corner.org/index.shtml

Winnie-the-Pooh is a billion-dollar-a-year industry, and one of the few fictional characters to have a star on the Hollywood walk of fame. Books about him have been translated into 34 languages. But at the heart of A. A. Milne's stories about Edward Bear (Pooh's real name) is a cast of characters who each have very different listening styles.

FOUR LISTENING STYLES

Like the characters in Milne's beloved tales, we all tend to experience habitual patterns of listening behaviors, known as **listening styles** (Barker & Watson, 2000), which reflect our attitudes, beliefs, and predispositions about listening. Graham Bodie and colleagues describe four different listening styles (Bodie et al., 2013). **Task-oriented listeners** see listening as transactional, and prefer brief, to-the-point, and accurate messages from others so they can focus on task completion. Task-oriented listeners, like Tigger, can grow impatient when communicating with people they perceive as disorganized, long-winded, or imprecise. For example, when faced with an upset spouse, a task-oriented listener would want information about what caused the problem so that a solution could be generated, rather than hearing elaborate details of the spouse's feelings.

In contrast, **relational listeners**, like Christopher Robin, view listening as an opportunity to build and maintain relationships with others. They listen to empathically connect with others and understand their viewpoints, feelings, and emotions. Relational listening is useful when others need to communicate in order to better understand a problem or life obstacle. Relational listeners tend to score higher on emotional intelligence (Umphrey & Sherblom, 2018).

Critical listeners, like Rabbit, focus their attention on the accuracy and consistency of what another person says. They have a tendency to critically consider and evaluate another person's message, and focus on discerning mistakes and catching errors in logic. This listening style may be useful to help another person reach a decision or choose between options (Umphrey & Sherblom, 2018), and critical listeners are less likely to experience emotional contagion (Bodie et al., 2013).

Analytical listeners, such as Owl, prefer to withhold their judgment until they have considered all the facts and sides of an issue, taking time to carefully evaluate information and details before forming an opinion about what they've heard. Analytical listeners have strong abilities to take the perspective of others (Bodie et al., 2013).

We learn our listening styles early in life by observation and interaction with parents and caregivers, gender socialization, and cultural values regarding what counts as effective listening (Barker & Watson, 2000). Through constant practice, our listening styles become deeply entrenched as part of our communication routines. As a consequence, most of us use only one or two listening styles in all of our interpersonal interactions (Chesebro, 1999). One study found that 36.1

LaunchPad Video
launchpadworks.com

Task-Oriented Listeners
Watch this clip online to answer the questions below.

How does the manager in this video signal his listening style? Be specific. When have you been a task-oriented listener? Why did you choose that approach?

percent of people reported exclusively using a single listening style across all their interpersonal encounters; an additional 24.8 percent reported that they never use more than two listening styles (Watson et al., 1995). We also resist attempts to switch from our dominant styles, even when those styles are ill-suited to the situation at hand. This can cause others to perceive us as insensitive, inflexible, and even incompetent communicators.

To be an active listener, you have to use all four styles, so you can strategically deploy each of them as needed. For example, in situations in which your primary listening function is to provide emotional support—when loved ones want to discuss feelings or turn to you for comfort—you should adopt a relational listening style. Studies document that when we use our listening to empathically orient to people, this substantially boosts others' perceptions of our interpersonal sensitivity (Chesebro, 1999). In such encounters, use of a task-oriented style would likely be perceived as incompetent.

By contrast, if your dominant listening function is to make an important decision or choose between two or more detailed alternatives, you'll likely want to use both critical and analytical listening styles. If, however, you're talking with someone who is running late for an appointment, you may want to opt for a task-oriented style. For additional tips on how to improve your active listening, see Table 7.1.

GENDER AND LISTENING

Paralleling the lack of major gender differences in communication discussed in Chapter 6, studies have found few (if any) substantial gender differences related to listening. For example, when tasked with listening for and accurately identifying emotions from voice, including sadness, fear, and happiness, women and men perform equally well (Lausen & Schacht, 2018). And scholars Kylie Geiman and John Greene (2019) found no gender differences in their examination of listening and *interpersonal transcendence*—that is, total immersion in an interaction. This means that both women and men are equally likely to "lose themselves" while listening

table 7.1 **Active Listening**

To be a more active listener, try these strategies:

1. Concentrate on important aspects of encounters and control factors that impede your attention.

2. Communicate your understanding to others in competent and timely ways by providing polite, obvious, appropriate, clear, and quick feedback.

3. Improve your recall abilities by using mnemonics or linking new information to other senses, visuals, or features.

4. Develop an awareness of your primary listening functions in various situations.

5. Practice shifting your listening style quickly, depending on the demands of the encounter.

within an intensely meaningful encounter, fully grasp what another person is saying, be genuinely interested in others' perspectives, and feel like they can finish others' statements.

Keeping these similarities in mind during interpersonal encounters is an important part of active listening. When interacting with other people, first observe the listening styles they display with an open mind, and adapt your style accordingly. Be prepared to shift your listening style according to the person, topic, and situation with which you are interacting.

CULTURE AND LISTENING

Because the culture we're immersed in influences our thinking in general (Janusik & Imhof, 2016), it follows that culture also powerfully shapes both how we listen and how we think about listening. Consider, for instance, research comparing U.S. and German students' conceptions of listening. German students were more likely to link listening to relationship building, whereas U.S. students linked listening to the integration and critical reception of information (Imhof & Janusik, 2006). Furthermore, people in individualistic cultures, such as the United States and Canada, often place a high value on time and efficiency, and this may be more pronounced in workplace settings. Consequently, many people in these cultures emphasize task-oriented listening. In contrast, collectivistic cultures tend to emphasize relational listening. In many East Asian countries, for example, Confucian teachings encourage followers to pay close attention when listening, display sensitivity to others' feelings, and be prepared to assimilate complex information (Chen & Chung, 1997). These patterns, taken in tandem, are one reason why studies have found that students from outside the United States view Americans as less willing and less patient listeners than people who come from Africa, Asia, South America, and southern Europe (Wolvin, 1987).

Now that we have considered several factors influencing our listening, including individual styles, gender, and culture, let's consider the ways in which we can improve our listening competence.

Improving Listening Competence

Avoiding the most common listening pitfalls

No one is a perfect active listener all the time. At one time or another, we all make errors during the listening process, fail to identify the right purpose for listening during an interpersonal

encounter, or neglect to use the appropriate listening style. In previous sections of this chapter, we discussed ways to avoid such errors. But being an active listener also means systematically avoiding five notoriously incompetent types of listening.

SELECTIVE LISTENING

A colleague stops by your office to chat and shares exciting news: a coworker to whom you're romantically attracted is similarly interested in you. As your thoughts become riveted on this revelation, the remainder of the conversation fades from your awareness, including important information your colleague shares with you about an upcoming project deadline.

Perhaps the greatest challenge to active listening is overcoming **selective listening**, taking in only those bits and pieces of information that are immediately salient during an interpersonal encounter and dismissing the rest. When we selectively listen, we rob ourselves of the opportunity to learn information from others that may affect important personal or professional outcomes, such as a missed project deadline.

Selective listening is difficult to avoid because it is the natural result of fluctuating attention and salience. To overcome selective listening, you shouldn't strive to learn how to listen to everything all at once. Instead, seek to slowly and steadily broaden the range of information you can actively attend to during your encounters with others. The best way to do this is by improving your overall level of attention through practicing the techniques for enhancing attention discussed earlier in this chapter. By doing so, you boost your chances of noticing information that has important short- and long-term consequences for your personal and professional relationships.

EAVESDROPPING

In *Wuthering Heights*, Emily Brontë's classic tale of romance and vengeance, a major turning point occurs when Heathcliff eavesdrops on a conversation between his lover Catherine and Nelly, the story's narrator. Heathcliff's interpretation of

Catherine's comments causes him to abandon her, setting in motion a tragic series of events that lead to Catherine's death:

> "It would degrade me to marry Heathcliff, now; so he shall never know how I love him; and that, not because he's handsome, Nelly, but because he's more myself than I am. Whatever our souls are made of, his and mine are the same." Ere this speech ended I became sensible of Heathcliff's presence. Having noticed a slight movement, I turned my head, and saw him rise from the bench, and steal out, noiselessly. He had listened till he heard Catherine say it would degrade her to marry him, and then he staid to hear no farther. (Brontë, 1995, p. 80)

We often assume that our conversations occur in isolation and that the people standing, sitting, or walking around the participants can't hear the exchange. But they can. As sociologist Erving Goffman (1979) noted, the presence of other individuals within the auditory and visual range of a conversation should be considered the rule and not the exception. This is the case even with phone conversations, social media posts, email, and texting. Most phone conversations occur with others in the immediate proximity, and social media posts, email, and texts are usually permanent and are not necessarily secure.

When people intentionally and systematically set up situations so that they can listen to private conversations, they are **eavesdropping** (Goffman, 1979). People eavesdrop for a host of reasons: desire to find out if someone is sharing personally, professionally, or legally incriminating information; suspicion that others are talking behind their backs; or even simple curiosity. Eavesdropping is both inappropriate and unethical (hence, incompetent) because it robs others of their right to privacy and disrespects their decision to not share certain information with you. Perhaps not surprisingly, the social norms governing this behavior are powerful. If people believe that you eavesdropped on a conversation, they will typically be upset and angry, and they may threaten reprisals.

Eavesdropping can be personally damaging as well. People occasionally say spiteful or hurtful things that they don't really mean simply to impress others, fit in, or draw attention to themselves. As the *Wuthering Heights* example illustrates, if you happen to eavesdrop on such conversations, the result can be personally and relationally devastating—especially if you take pieces of what you've heard out of context. The lesson is clear: don't eavesdrop, no matter how tempting it might be.

PSEUDO-LISTENING

You stayed up late the night before to finish a course paper, and when you finally got to bed, your apartment roommates were so loud, they kept you up most of the night. Now it's the afternoon and you're sitting in a warm and cozy coffeehouse, listening to your friend tell you a story she's shared with you several times previously. Try as you might, you find yourself fading. But you don't want to embarrass yourself or your friend, so you do your best to play the part of an active listener—maintaining good eye contact, nodding your head, and contributing appropriate responses when needed.

You're engaging in **pseudo-listening**, behaving as if you're paying attention though you're really not. Pseudo-listening is obviously an ineffective way to listen because it prevents you from attending to or understanding information coming

skills practice

Managing Aggressive Listening
Dealing skillfully with an aggressive listener

❶ When someone is using aggressive listening with you, stay calm.

❷ Allow the person to talk, without interruption or challenge.

❸ Express empathy, saying, "I'm sorry you feel that way."

❹ Avoid retaliating with negative comments, as they will only escalate the aggression.

❺ If the person continues to set you up for verbal attacks, end the encounter, saying, "I'm sorry, but I don't feel comfortable continuing this conversation."

from the other person, so you can't recall the encounter later. Pseudo-listening is also somewhat unethical because it's deceptive. To be sure, occasional instances of pseudo-listening to veil fatigue or protect a friend's feelings (such as in our example) are understandable. But if you continually engage in pseudo-listening during your encounters with others, eventually they will realize what's going on and conclude that you're uncaring, dishonest, or disrespectful. Consequently, pseudo-listening should be avoided.

AGGRESSIVE LISTENING

People who engage in **aggressive listening** (also called *ambushing*) attend to what others say solely to find an opportunity to attack their conversational partners. For example, your friend may routinely ask for your opinions regarding fashion and music, but then disparage your tastes when you share them with her. Or your romantic partner may encourage you to share your feelings, but then mock your feelings when you do share them.

The personal, interpersonal, and relational costs of aggressive listening are substantial. People who consistently use listening to ambush others typically think less favorably about themselves (Infante & Wigley, 1986), have lower marital satisfaction (Payne & Sabourin, 1990), and may experience more physical violence in their relationships (Infante et al., 1989).

Some people engage in aggressive listening online. Known as **trolls**, they post messages intentionally designed to annoy, offend, or antagonize others. They wait for people to post responses, and then they attack the responses. If the attacks of a troll are sophisticated enough, naïve group members may side with the troll against participants who seek to oust the instigator from the group. The result can be a flame war that prompts the site manager to shut down the discussion group—the ultimate victory for a troll.

If you find yourself habitually listening in an aggressive fashion, combat this type of incompetent listening by discovering and dealing with the root causes of your aggression. Often, external pressures, such as job stress, relationship challenges, or family problems, can play a role, so be careful to consider all possible causes and solutions for your behavior. Don't hesitate to seek professional assistance if you think it would be helpful. If you're in a personal or professional relationship with someone who uses aggressive listening with you, deal with that person by following the recommendations for addressing verbal aggression outlined in Chapter 8. Limit your interactions when possible, be polite and respectful, and use a relational listening style. Avoid retaliating by using aggressive listening yourself because it will only escalate the aggression.

NARCISSISTIC LISTENING

In Greek mythology, the beautiful nymph Echo falls in love with Narcissus immediately upon seeing him (Bulfinch, 1985). But when she approaches and moves to throw her arms around him, he recoils, telling her that he would rather die than be with her. Heartbroken, Echo flees to the mountains and plots her revenge. She casts a spell on Narcissus, making him fall in love with his own reflected image in a pool. Upon seeing the enchanted image, Narcissus can't tear himself away. He abandons all thought of food and rest, and gazes at himself, entranced, until he finally dies of starvation.

Like its namesake in Greek mythology, **narcissistic listening** is self-absorbed listening: the perpetrators ignore what others have to say and redirect the conversations back to themselves and their own interests. People who engage in narcissistic listening provide positive feedback as long as they are the center of conversational attention, but the moment the topic switches to something other than them, they give negative feedback. In some cases, the negative feedback may be extreme— narcissistic listeners may pout, whine, or even throw tantrums when the conversation switches away from them and onto the other person (Bushman & Baumeister, 1998). To avoid narcissistic listening, allow the conversation to focus on topics other than you and your own interests and offer positive feedback when such topics are discussed.

self-
reflection

How do you feel when people use narcissistic listening with you? Have you ever listened in a narcissistic way? If so, why? Is narcissistic listening always incompetent, or is it acceptable in certain circumstances?

The Gift of Active Listening

Active listening creates interpersonal opportunities.

When we are newborns struggling to make sense of a world filled with mysterious noises, we quickly learn to listen. Long before we recognize written words as having meaning, and long before we can produce our own words, we come to understand the words of others. Our lives as interpersonal communicators begin at that point.

It is ironic, then, that this first communicative gift shared by human beings—the gift of listening—poses so many challenges for us when we reach adulthood. We struggle with listening in part because it is exceptionally demanding. Active listening requires dedication to mastering knowledge, hard work in practicing skills, and the motivation to continually improve.

Yet when we surmount the challenges of active listening by focusing our attention, training our memories, adapting our listening styles, and avoiding preconceived notions about others and incompetent listening, an amazing thing happens. The activity that we originally mistook as passive begins to crackle with the energy of opportunity. For when we actively listen, the words and worlds of others wash over us, providing us with rich and unanticipated opportunities to move beyond the constraints of our own thoughts and beliefs, allowing us to open ourselves to authentic interpersonal connections with others.

Listening When You Don't Want To

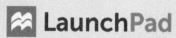 **LaunchPad**   For the best experience, complete all parts of this activity in LaunchPad: **launchpadworks.com**

1 Background

One of the most difficult listening situations you will face occurs when you feel obligated to listen to information that makes you uncomfortable. To understand how you might competently manage such a relationship challenge, read the case study in Part 2; then, drawing on all you know about interpersonal communication, work through the problem-solving model in Part 3.

 Visit LaunchPad to watch the video in Part 4 and assess your communication in Part 5.

2 Case Study

Growing up, you and your twin sister Ana were extremely close. As you've gotten older, however, the differences between the two of you have widened. Ana is a free spirit and never sticks with anything — be it a college major or a romantic interest — for very long. You are much more concerned with conventional notions of success. You plan to finish your degree in four years, have a steady paycheck and a mortgage, and get married before you turn 30.

Lately, you and Ana have been arguing about Ana's friendship with Seneca. You find Seneca to be organized and ambitious, qualities that you hope rub off on Ana. But you still find yourself uncomfortable and awkward around Seneca. Ana says that it's because Seneca is a lesbian and that you have "old-fashioned" values. You get mad at Ana for saying this, but afterward you start to question why you felt defensive against Ana's accusation.

Over the past few months, you've started to wonder if Ana might have a romantic interest in Seneca. On several occasions, it seemed as if she wanted to start a conversation with you about this, but in each case, you've dodged the topic or come up with a reason not to listen.

You and Ana are both home on break. One night, Seneca calls the home phone because Ana's cell-phone battery is dead. You yell upstairs to Ana to pick up the cordless phone in her bedroom, but instead of hanging up the other line, you listen in. You know you shouldn't, but your curiosity gets the best of you. After a few minutes, it becomes clear that Ana and Seneca are lovers. What's more, their conversation centers around their decision to move in together after break.

Coming downstairs after the call, Ana finds you in shock. She says, "You should know that I'm moving into Seneca's apartment next semester. She needs a roommate, and I was looking for a place to live anyway."

A million thoughts race through your mind, including your sister's secrecy in not telling you the truth about her relationship with Seneca. Do you tell her you know the truth, even though it will reveal your eavesdropping, and attack her decision? Offer support, and tell her that you're finally ready to listen to her? Refuse to listen altogether, and change the topic? Seeing your face, Ana scowls and angrily snaps, "Did you hear me? What's your problem!?"

 **Your Turn**

Think about all you've learned thus far about interpersonal communication. Then work through the following five steps. Remember, there are no "right" answers, so think hard about what is the *best* choice! (P.S. Need help? See the *Helpful Concepts* list.)

step 1

Reflect on yourself. What are your thoughts and feelings in this situation? Are your impressions and attributions accurate?

step 2

Reflect on your partner. Using perspective-taking and empathic concern, put yourself in Ana's shoes. What is she thinking and feeling in this situation?

step 3

Identify the optimal outcome. Think about your communication and relationship with Ana and all that has happened in this situation (including your decision

to eavesdrop). What's the best, most constructive relationship outcome possible? Consider what's best for you and for Ana.

step 4

Locate the roadblocks. Taking into consideration your own and Ana's thoughts and feelings and all that has happened in this situation, what obstacles are keeping you from achieving the optimal outcome?

step 5

Chart your course. What can you say to Ana to overcome the roadblocks you've identified and achieve your optimal outcome?

HELPFUL CONCEPTS

Positive and negative feedback, **182**
Listening to analyze, **186**
Relational listeners, **189**
Eavesdropping, **193**
Pseudo-listening, **193**

 The Other Side

 Visit LaunchPad to watch a video in which Ana tells her side of the case study story. As in many real-life situations, this is information to which you did not have access when you were initially crafting your response in Part 3. The video reminds us that even when we do our best to offer competent responses, there is always another side to the story that we need to consider.

Interpersonal Competence Self-Assessment

After watching the video, visit the Self-Assessment questions in LaunchPad. Think about the new information offered in Ana's side of the story and all you've learned about interpersonal communication. Drawing on this knowledge, revisit your earlier responses in Part 3 and assess your interpersonal communication competence.

POSTSCRIPT

Courtesy of Universal Studios Licensing LLC

We began this chapter with a man who dedicated his life to active listening. Fred Rogers brought his ministerial values of love, respect, and kindness to the small screen, and through television he touched the lives of millions of children — and adults. He created a safe space for *all* people, within which children felt simultaneously entertained, educated, and affirmed by an adult who genuinely listened to them.

What values underlie *your* listening? How do you use listening in *your* life, to help "repair the world," as Mr. Rogers did?

The PBS soundstage Fred Rogers once strolled through lies abandoned now, just as his famous cardigan hangs empty in a Smithsonian display case. He'll never again "be back when the day is new." Yet the values he espoused — of bringing "joy and light and hope and faith and pardon and love to your neighbor and to yourself" — will endure as long as people actively, compassionately, and respectfully listen to one another.

LaunchPad

LaunchPad for *Reflect & Relate* offers videos and encourages self-assessment through adaptive quizzing. Go to **launchpadworks.com** to get access to:

 LearningCurve
Adaptive Quizzes

 Video clips that help you understand interpersonal communication

key terms

listening, 177
hearing, 178
receiving, 178
attending, 178
mental bracketing, 181
understanding, 181
short-term memory, 181
long-term memory, 181
responding, 182
feedback, 182
back-channel cues, 182
paraphrasing, 183
recalling, 184
mnemonics, 184
listening functions, 185
mediated listening, 188
listening styles, 189
◉ task-oriented listeners, 189
relational listeners, 189
critical listeners, 189
analytical listeners, 189
◉ selective listening, 192
eavesdropping, 193
pseudo-listening, 193
◉ aggressive listening, 194
trolls, 194
◉ narcissistic listening, 195

◉ You can watch brief, illustrative videos of these terms and test your understanding of the concepts in LaunchPad.

key concepts

Listening: A Five-Step Process

- **Listening** is an active and complex process. The first step of listening is **receiving**, which involves "seeing" or **hearing** the communication of others.

- A critical part of active listening is **attending** to information by being alert to it. To improve your attention skills, you should limit multitasking, control factors that impede attention, and practice **mental bracketing**.

- **Understanding** the meaning of others' communication requires us to compare information in our **short-term memory** and **long-term memory**, using prior knowledge to evaluate the meaning of new information.

- Active listening requires **responding** to the communication of others in clear and constructive ways. Indications of effective responding include positive **feedback** and the use of **back-channel cues**. **Paraphrasing** can also help you convey understanding, but if you use it extensively during face-to-face encounters, your partners may find it annoying.

- Listening effectiveness is often measured in terms of our **recalling** ability.

The Five Functions of Listening

- Even during a single interpersonal encounter, you will likely have multiple purposes for listening, known as **listening functions**.

- The five functions are *listening to comprehend, listening to discern, listening to analyze, listening to appreciate,* and *listening to support.*

Understanding Listening Styles

- Most people have one or two dominant **listening styles**. The four most common styles are **task-oriented**, **relational**, **critical**, and **analytical** listening.

Improving Listening Competence

- **Selective listening** is a natural result of fluctuating attention.

- **Eavesdropping** is an especially destructive form of listening and can have serious consequences.

- If you use **pseudo-listening** deliberately to deceive others, you're behaving unethically.

- Some people use **aggressive listening** to attack others.

- People who engage in **narcissistic listening** seek to turn the focus of the conversation back to themselves.

8 Communicating Verbally

Verbal communication opens doorways to shared understanding, intimacy, and enduring relationships.

I've been reading Common Sense by Thomas Paine. So men say that I'm intense or I'm insane. You want a revolution? I want a revelation! So listen to my declaration: "We hold these truths to be self-evident: That all men are created equal. And when I meet Thomas Jefferson, I'm a compel him to include women in the sequel!"

Composer, lyricist, and actor Lin-Manuel Miranda was traveling to Mexico for a vacation with his wife when he bought a biography of Alexander Hamilton — the first U.S. Treasury Secretary — at an airport bookstore.[1] By the second chapter, Miranda was convinced that Hamilton's story — an immigrant rising from poverty to fortune and fame through the power of his language skills — was perfect for a musical. "As I was reading," he says, "songs were popping out to me. There's the rags-to-riches angle that is very much the American dream. And from the beginning, words were the most important thing to [Hamilton]."

As Miranda's vision for a script solidified, so too did the dominant musical form he would use: hip-hop. "I recognized the arc of a hip-hop narrative in Hamilton's life," explains Miranda, who has compared the Founding Father's childhood to rappers Jay Z and Eminem. The key, though, was hip-hop's exuberant use of language. As Miranda describes, "hip-hop is the language of youth and energy and rebellion. We need a revolutionary language to describe a revolution! This was a war of ideas, and hip-hop's uniquely suited to that, because we get more language per measure than any other musical form." And his completed script would

---

[1]Content that follows uses information from Harding (2017), Paulson (2015a), Paulson (2015b), Simonson (2020), and Zimmer (2016).

201

illustrate hip-hop's power to pack in frenetic prose, boasting more than 20,000 words, delivered at a blistering average of 144 words per minute.

Also revolutionary was Miranda's decision to cast Black and Latino actors as Hamilton, Thomas Jefferson, George Washington, and other historical figures. "Our cast looks like America looks now," he says, "and that's certainly intentional. It's a way of pulling you into the story and allowing you to leave whatever cultural baggage you have about the founding fathers at the door." That choice has resonated deeply with many people of color, including students, who have viewed the show in various productions across the United States and worldwide. But Miranda didn't just want students to listen to the language he had crafted; he wanted them to embrace the power of language for themselves. So he organized a program for low-income high

schools, whereby students could create and perform *their own* raps related to historical figures before matinee performances of *Hamilton*, with Miranda serving as the emcee.

Hamilton has broken every record for musical theater success. Nominated for 16 Tony Awards, it won 11. It also won the Best Musical Theater Grammy and the 2016 Pulitzer Prize for Drama. But at its heart, the show is an homage to the transformative power of language — a force that enabled the immigrant son of a single mother to become one of history's most famous Americans. As Oskar Eustis, artistic director of New York City's Public Theater, describes, "In *Hamilton*, Lin-Manuel Miranda is taking the voice of the people — in rap, rhyme, hip-hop, R&B — and by elevating it to poetry, bringing out what is noble about the common tongue. And that is something that nobody has done as effectively since Shakespeare."

In a life filled with firsts — first kiss, first job, first car — it's a first we don't even remember. But it's celebrated by the people around us, who recognize in that fleeting moment the dawning of a life filled with language. Our first word springs from our mouths as the simplest of monosyllables: "cup," "dog," "ball." But once the sound has left our lips, the path has been irrevocably forged. By age 6, we learn more than 15 new words a day, and our vocabularies have grown to anywhere between 8,000 and 14,000 words (Cole & Cole, 1989). As we master our native tongues, we discover the power of verbal communication. By exchanging words with others through social media, via text message, over the phone, and face-to-face, we share ideas, provide support, influence others, and make relationship choices. We also learn that language can serve both constructive and destructive ends. Used constructively, verbal communication opens doorways to shared understanding, intimacy, and enduring relationships. Used destructively, verbal communication can mislead and injure others and damage our relationships.

In this chapter, we examine the nature and role of verbal communication in our lives. You'll learn:

- The defining characteristics of language
- The important functions that verbal communication serves in our interpersonal encounters and relationships
- Principles you can apply to use verbal communication more cooperatively
- The behaviors and actions that undermine cooperative verbal communication — and how to address them

We begin by describing verbal communication and examining five defining characteristics of language.

Describing Verbal Communication

Understanding how language works

When we think of what it means to communicate, what often leaps to mind is the exchange of spoken or written language with others during interactions, known as **verbal communication**. Across any given day, we use words to communicate with others in our lives in various face-to-face or mediated contexts. During each of these encounters, we tailor our language in creative ways, depending on to whom we're speaking. We shift grammar, word choices, and sometimes even the entire language itself—such as tweeting a message in English and then texting a message to a family member in Spanish.

Because verbal communication is defined by our use of language, the first step toward improving our verbal communication is to deepen our understanding of language. Let's consider five characteristics of language.

LANGUAGE IS SYMBOLIC

Take a quick look around you. You'll likely see a wealth of images: this book, the surface on which it (or your device) rests, and perhaps your roommate or romantic partner. You might experience thoughts and emotions related to what you're seeing—memories of your roommate asking to borrow your car or feelings of love toward your partner. Now imagine communicating all of this to others. To do so, you need words to represent these things: "roommate," "lover," "borrow," "car," "love," and so forth. Whenever we use items to represent other things, these items are considered **symbols**. In verbal communication, words are the primary symbols that we use to represent people, objects, events, and ideas (Foss et al., 1991).

All languages are basically giant collections of symbols in the form of words that allow us to communicate with one another. When we agree with others on the meanings of words, we communicate easily. Your friend probably knows exactly what you mean by the word *roommate*, so when you use it, misunderstanding is unlikely. But some words have several possible meanings, making confusion possible. For instance, in English, the word *table* might mean a piece of furniture, an element in a textbook, or a verb referring to the need to end talk ("Let's table this discussion until our next meeting"). For words that have multiple meanings, we rely on the surrounding context and the conversational participants to help clarify meaning. So if you're in a classroom and the professor says, "Turn to Table 3 on page 47," you aren't likely to search the room for furniture.

LANGUAGE IS GOVERNED BY RULES

When we use language, we follow rules. Rules govern the meaning of words, the way we arrange words into phrases and sentences, and the order in which we exchange words with others during conversations. **Constitutive rules** define word meaning: they tell us which words represent which objects (Searle, 1965). For example, a constitutive rule in the English language is "The word *dog* refers to a

self-reflection

How is the language that you use different when talking with professors versus talking to your best friend or romantic partner? Which type of language makes you feel more comfortable or close to the other person? What does this tell you about the relationship between language and intimacy?

Whether face-to-face or online, we exchange verbal communication daily in our interactions with others.
Ramin Talaie/Bloomberg/Getty Images

L. L. Zamenhof invented Esperanto, a constructed language, in the late nineteenth century. It was intended to be a universal language, one that would permit easy intercultural and international communication. Although Esperanto did not originate with a nationality and remains unaligned with a place or society, it was created in a cultural context that values the goal of universal communication. Chronicle/Alamy

Dr. Zamenhof
Erfind. d. Esperantosprache
geb. 1837

RHEINPERLE
Delikatess-Margarine

Serie Y   Erfinder   No 29.

domestic canine." Whenever you learn the vocabulary of a language—words and their corresponding meanings—you're learning the constitutive rules for that language.

In contrast, **regulative rules** govern how we use language when we verbally communicate. They're the traffic laws controlling language use—the dos and don'ts. Regulative rules guide everything from spelling ("*i* before *e* except after *c*") to sentence structure ("The article *the* or *a* must come before the noun *dog*") to conversation ("If someone asks you a question, you should answer").

To communicate competently, you must understand and follow both the constitutive and regulative rules governing the language you're using. If you don't know which words represent which meanings (constitutive rules), you can't send clear messages to others or understand messages delivered by others. Likewise, without knowing how to form a grammatically correct sentence and when to say particular things (regulative rules), you can't communicate clearly with others or accurately interpret their messages to you.

LANGUAGE IS FLEXIBLE

Although all languages have constitutive and regulative rules, people often bend those rules. If you have traveled to a different country, you may be well aware of this—especially if you discovered that being "conversational" in a second language is a very different thing compared to simply learning vocabulary and grammar rules. Such rule-bending may be even more pronounced in close relationships. For example, intimate partners often create **personal idioms**—words and phrases that have unique meanings to them (Bell et al., 1987). One study found that the average romantic couple created more than a half dozen idioms, the most common being nicknames such as Honeybear or Pookie. This shared linguistic creativity is both reflective and reinforcing of intimacy and relationship satisfaction. For example, greater use of idioms was linked to increased relational satisfaction for college dating couples (Dunleavy & Booth-Butterfield, 2009). Additionally, happily married couples report using more idioms than unhappily married couples, and partners in the early stages of marriage (i.e., the honeymoon phase) use the most idioms of all (Bruess & Pearson, 1993).

LANGUAGE IS CULTURAL

Members of a culture use language to communicate their thoughts, beliefs, attitudes, and values with one another, thereby reinforcing their collective sense of cultural identity (Whorf, 1952). Consequently, the language you speak (English, Mandarin, Spanish, Urdu), the words you choose (proper, slang, profane), and the grammar you use (formal, informal) all announce to others: "This is who I am! This is my cultural heritage!"

Additionally, each language reflects distinct sets of cultural beliefs and values. When a large group of people within a particular culture who speak the same language develop their own variations on that language over time, they create **dialects** (Gleason, 1989). Dialects may include unique phrases, words, and pronunciations (such as accents). Dialects can be shared by people living in a certain region (e.g., midwestern, southern, or northeastern United States), people with a similar socioeconomic status, or people of similar ethnic or religious ancestry (e.g., Amish English, Irish English, or Yiddish English) (Chen & Starosta, 2005). Within the United States, for example, six regional dialects exist (see Figure 8.1), but the two most easily recognizable are New England and the South (Clopper et al., 2005).

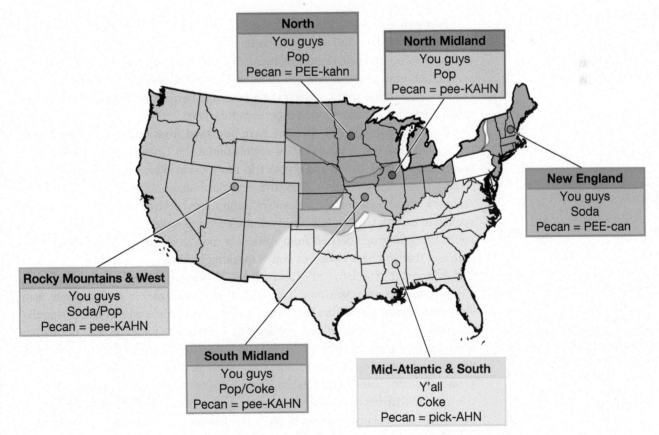

figure 8.1 **Regional Dialects in the United States**

These two dialects are so distinct that most people can accurately identify them after hearing just one spoken sentence, regardless of the speaker's gender (Clopper et al., 2005).

People may perceive others who use dialects similar to their own as *ingroupers*, and may be inclined to make positive judgments about them as a result (Delia, 1972; Lev-Ari & Keysar, 2010). In a parallel fashion, people may perceive those with dissimilar dialects as *outgroupers* and correspondingly make less positive judgments about them. Being aware of this tendency when we communicate with people with whom we don't share a common dialect allows us to approach conversations with an open mind and refrain from hasty judgments. For additional ideas on dealing with ingroup or outgroup perceptions, see Chapter 3.

LANGUAGE EVOLVES

When we learn a new language, the vocabulary and grammar seem (and are taught to us as) stable and static. But in fact, all languages are in a constant state of flux. For example, the American Dialect Society annually selects a "Word of the Year." Recent winners include *fake news*, with the dual definitions of "disinformation or falsehoods presented as real news" and "actual news that is claimed to be untrue" (American Dialect Society, 2018), and "#blacklivesmatter," the first twitter hashtag ever selected (American Dialect Society, 2015). Even the *Oxford English Dictionary*—widely regarded as a defining resource of the English language—annually announces new words. In 2020, this included the word *athleisure* (a noun that refers to comfortable footwear or clothing that can be worn daily and for exercise).

Furthermore, a particular language's constitutive rules—which define the meanings of words—also may shift. As time passes and technology changes, people add new words to their language (*tweet, app, cyberbullying, selfie*) and discard old ones. Sometimes people create new phrases, such as *helicopter parent*, that eventually see wide use. Other times, speakers of a language borrow words and phrases from other languages and incorporate them into their own.

Consider how English-speakers have borrowed from other languages: If you tell friends that you want to *take* a *whirl* around the United States, you're using words derived from Norse; and if your trip takes you to *Wisconsin, Oregon,* and *Wyoming,* you're visiting places with Native American names. If you stop at a café and request a cup of *tea* along the way, you're using a word derived from Amoy (a dialect spoken in eastern China), but if you ask the waiter to spike your coffee with *alcohol,* you're using language derived from Arabic. If you call in sick at work and tell your manager that you have *influenza,* you're speaking Italian.

A language's regulative rules also change. When you learned to speak and write English, for example, you may have been taught that *they* is inappropriate as a singular pronoun. But before the 1850s, people commonly used *they* as the singular pronoun for individuals whose gender was unknown—for example, "the owner went out to the stables, where they fed the horses" (Spender, 1990). In 1850, male grammarians petitioned the British Parliament to pass a law declaring that all gender-indeterminate references be labeled *he* instead of *they* (Spender, 1990), a convention that became widely accepted among teachers of English for over a century. More recently, however, singular *they* has seen a resurgence in popularity, to

self-reflection

Reflect on your use of singular *they* in your speaking, writing, and online communication. What are the advantages of singular *they*? How does it affect perceptions of inclusivity?

the point that the American Dialect Society recently selected it as the Word of the Decade (Goldberg, 2020).

Now that we have described verbal communication and reviewed four characteristics of language, let's turn our attention to the different things we can do with language.

Functions of Verbal Communication

Language guides our interactions.

He was crowned Sportsman of the Century by *Sports Illustrated* and Sports Personality of the Century by the BBC.[2] He was considered by many to be the greatest boxer of all time, a fact reflected in his nickname, the Greatest. He certainly was the most verbal. Muhammad Ali made a name for himself early in his career by poetically boasting about his abilities ("Your hands can't hit what your eyes can't see!") and trash-talking his opponents. "I'm going to float like a butterfly and sting like a bee," he told then-champion Sonny Liston, whom Ali dubbed "the big ugly bear" before defeating him to claim the World Heavyweight title. Ali was just as verbal outside the boxing ring. Early in his professional career, he embraced Islam and subsequently abandoned his birth name of Cassius Clay because the surname came from his ancestors' slave owners. Years before public sentiment joined him, Ali spoke out repeatedly against the Vietnam War. His refusal to participate in the military draft cost him both his world title and his boxing license (both of which were eventually reinstated). Years later, he continued to be outspoken on behalf of humanitarian causes. His work with United Nations hunger relief organizations helped feed tens of millions of people ("Service to others is the rent you pay for your room here on earth"), he lit the torch at the 1996 Olympic Games in Atlanta, and was a United Nations Messenger of Peace and recipient of the Presidential Medal of Freedom. Whether in the boxing ring or on a charity mission, he used his prowess with verbal communication to achieve his goals and dreams.

◯ Muhammad Ali's verbal communication skills served important functions throughout his life, whether intimidating opponents or attracting supporters to his causes.
Michael Cooper/Getty Images

We all use verbal communication to serve many different functions in our daily lives. Let's examine six of the most important of these, all of which strongly influence our interpersonal communication and relationships.

SHARING MEANING

The most obvious function verbal communication serves is enabling us to share meanings with others during interpersonal encounters. When you use language to verbally communicate, you share two kinds of meanings. The first is the literal meaning of your words, as agreed on by members of your culture, known as **denotative meaning**. Denotative meaning is what you find in dictionaries—for example, the word *bear* means "any of a family (Ursidae of the order Carnivora) of large heavy mammals of America and Eurasia that have long shaggy hair" (*Merriam-Webster Dictionary*, n.d.). When Ali called Sonny Liston "the big ugly bear," he knew Liston would understand the denotative meanings of his words and interpret them as an insult.

---

[2]The information that follows is adapted from Hauser (2006).

LaunchPad Video
launchpadworks.com

Connotative Meaning
*Watch this clip online to
answer the questions below.*

In this video, which of the
terms suggested is the most
persuasive to you? The least?
What connotative meanings do
you have for each? How do you
use connotative meanings to
display intimacy or affection with
a family member or a friend?

Want to see more? Check
out LaunchPad for a clip on
denotative meaning.

But when we verbally communicate, we also exchange **connotative meaning**: additional understandings of a word's meaning based on the situation and knowledge we and our communication partners share. Connotative meaning is implied, suggested, or hinted at by the words you choose while communicating with others. Say, for example, that your romantic partner has a large stuffed teddy bear that, despite its weathered and worn appearance, is your partner's most prized childhood possession. To convey your love and adoration for your partner, you might say, "You're *my* big ugly bear." In doing so, you certainly don't mean that your lover is ugly or bearlike in appearance! Instead, you rely on your partner understanding your implied link to their treasured object (the connotative meaning). Relationship intimacy plays a major role in shaping how we use and interpret connotative meanings while communicating with others (Hall, 1997a): people who know each other extremely well can convey connotative meanings accurately to one another.

SHAPING THOUGHT

In addition to enabling us to share meaning during interpersonal encounters, verbal communication also shapes our thoughts and perceptions of reality. Feminist scholar Dale Spender (1990) describes the relationship between words and our inner world in this way:

> To speak metaphorically, the brain is blind and deaf; it has no direct contact with light or sound. The brain has to interpret: it only deals in symbols and never knows the real thing. And the program for encoding and decoding is set up by the language which we possess. What we *see* in the world around us depends in large part on our language. (pp. 139–140)

Consider a conversation Kelly had years ago with one of her younger female cousins, who was about 6 years old at the time. This cousin told Kelly that a female neighbor had helped several children escape a house fire. When Kelly exclaimed that the neighbor was heroic, the cousin stated matter-of-factly, "Girls can't be *heroes*. Only boys can be *heroes*!" In further discussing this assertion, Kelly discovered that her cousin knew of no word representing "brave woman," and had never heard the word *heroine*. Lacking a word to represent "female bravery," she could not conceive of the concept.

The idea that language shapes how we think about things was first suggested by researcher Edward Sapir, who conducted an intensive study of Native American languages in the early 1900s. Sapir argued that because language is our primary means of sharing meaning with others, it powerfully affects how we perceive others and our relationships with them (Gumperz & Levinson, 1996). Almost 50 years later, Benjamin Lee Whorf expanded on Sapir's ideas in what has become known as the *Sapir–Whorf Hypothesis*. Whorf argued that we cannot conceive of that for which we lack a vocabulary—that language quite literally defines the boundaries of our thinking. This view is known as **linguistic determinism**. As contemporary scholars note, linguistic determinism suggests that our ability to think is "at the mercy" of language (Gumperz & Levinson, 1996). We are mentally constrained by language to think only certain thoughts, and we cannot interpret the world in neutral ways because we always see the world through the lens of our languages.

Both Sapir and Whorf also recognized the dramatic impact that culture has on language. Because language determines our thoughts, and people from diverse

self-
reflection

Think about the vocabulary
you inherited from your culture
for thinking and talking about
relationships. What terms
exist for describing serious
romantic involvements, casual
relationships that are sexual,
and relationships that are
purely platonic? How do
these various terms shape
your thinking about these
relationships?

○ We see the world through the lens of our language, yet people from different cultures use different languages. Joshua Dalsimer/Getty Images

cultures use a variety of languages, Sapir and Whorf agreed that people from different cultures would perceive and think about the world in very different ways, an effect known as **linguistic relativity**.

NAMING

A third important function of verbal communication is **naming**, creating linguistic symbols for objects. The process of naming is one of humankind's most profound and unique abilities (Spender, 1984). When we name people, places, objects, and ideas, we create symbols that represent them. We then use these symbols during our interactions with others to communicate meaning about these things. Because of the powerful impact language exerts on our thoughts, the decisions we make about what to name things ultimately determine not just the meanings we exchange but also our perceptions of the people, places, and objects we communicate about. This was why Muhammad Ali decided to abandon his birth name of Cassius Clay. He recognized that our names are *the* most powerful symbols that define who we are throughout our lives, and he wanted a name that represented his Islamic faith while also renouncing the surname of someone who had, years earlier, enslaved his forebears.

As the Muhammad Ali example suggests, the issue of naming is especially potent for people who face historical and cultural prejudice. In the 2000s, the inclusive label of LGBTQ (lesbian, gay, bisexual, transgender, queer or questioning) was created in an effort to embrace the entire community. But this term still doesn't adequately represent many people's self-impressions. One study identified over a dozen different names that individuals chose for their sexual orientation and gender identity, including *pansexual, omnisexual*, and *same-gender loving/SGL* (Morrison & McCornack, 2011). In an effort to be more inclusive, the acronym now often appears in the expanded form LGBTQ+ or LGBTQIA+ (with the latter representing intersex and asexual people). And some people reject names for sexual orientations altogether; as one study respondent put it, "I don't use labels—I'm not a can of soup!" (Morrison & McCornack, 2011).

focus on CULTURE

Adopting Gender-Inclusive Language

In 2012, Sweden introduced the gender-neutral singular pronoun *hen* to complement *hon* (she) and *han* (he),[3] gendered pronouns used in place of names. Though initially received with resistance, the new pronoun has since become more widely accepted. Similarly, in 2011, Pomona College in California removed gender pronouns from its student constitution. "A lot of students do not identify as 'male' or 'female' and aren't using the pronouns 'he' or 'she,' so we are trying to better represent the student body," said Student Commissioner Sarah Applebaum. "Ideally, this will help promote a more supportive campus for gender-nonconforming, queer, and transgender students."

These changes are part of a larger movement across cultures toward gender-inclusive language — one that challenges traditional dichotomous language labels for gender. Scholars have found that gendered languages — those that present male and female versions of nouns, verbs, and pronouns — also exemplify more gender prejudice, such as associating male words with more positive value. Consider the words *salesman*, *chairman*, and *fireman*. Depending on where and when you were born, you may have grown up with these terms, reading and seeing media images of them. You may never have conceived of anyone other than a man filling these roles. But if you have only known the replacements for these gender-marked job titles — *sales representative*, *chairperson*, and *firefighter* — you likely have broader conceptions of what you can do, as well as what you think may be possible. Similarly, inclusive language such as "y'all" addresses everyone present, rather than the gendered expression "you guys." As we continue moving toward gender-inclusive language, we must be thoughtful about our language choices — ever mindful of the power of seemingly small words and phrases.

discussion questions

- Can you think of other examples of job titles that are traditionally gendered? Is the gendered title still often used today? If so, why do you think that is?
- How do you think noninclusive language, such as "you guys" to refer to a group of people of different genders, influences our abilities to be seen and be heard?

[3]Information in Focus on Culture feature from DeFranza et al. (2020); Knutson et al. (2019); and Vergoossen et al. (2020).

PERFORMING ACTIONS

A fourth function of verbal communication is that it enables us to take action. We make requests, issue invitations, deliver commands, or even taunt—as Ali did to his competitors. We also try to influence others' behaviors. We want our listeners to grant our requests or accept our invitations. The actions that we perform with language are called **speech acts** (Searle, 1969). (See Table 8.1 for types of speech acts.)

During interpersonal encounters, the structure of our back-and-forth exchange is based on the speech acts we perform (Jacobs, 1994; Levinson, 1985). When your professor asks you a question, how do you know what to do next? You recognize that the spoken words constitute a "question," and you realize that an "answer" is expected as the relevant response. Similarly, when your best friend texts you and inquires, "Can I borrow your car tonight?" you immediately recognize their message as a "request." You also understand that two speech acts are possible as relevant responses: "granting" the request ("no problem") or "rejecting" it ("I don't think so").

CRAFTING CONVERSATIONS

A fifth function served by language is that it allows us to craft conversations. Language meanings, thoughts, names, and acts don't happen in the abstract; they

table 8.1 Types of Speech Acts

Act	Function	Forms	Example
Representative	Commits the speaker to the truth of what has been said	Assertions, conclusions	"It sure is a beautiful day."
Directive	Attempts to get listeners to do things	Questions, requests, commands	"Can you loan me five dollars?"
Commissive	Commits speakers to future action	Promises, threats	"I will always love you, no matter what happens."
Expressive	Conveys a psychological or emotional state that the speaker is experiencing	Thanks, apologies, congratulations	"Thank you so much for the wonderful gift!"
Declarative	Produces dramatic, observable effects	Marriage pronouncements, firing declarations	"From this point onward, you are no longer an employee of this organization."

Note: Information from Searle (1976).

occur within conversations. Although each of us intuitively knows what a conversation is, scholars suggest four characteristics fundamental to conversation (Nofsinger, 1999). First, conversations are *interactive*. At least two people must participate in the exchange for it to count as a conversation, and participants must take turns exchanging messages.

Second, conversations are locally managed. *Local management* means that we make decisions regarding who gets to speak when, and for how long, each time we exchange turns. This makes conversation different from other verbal exchanges, such as debate, in which the order and length of turns are decided before the event begins, and drama, in which people speak words that have been written down in advance.

Third, conversation is *universal*. Conversation forms the foundation for most forms of interpersonal communication and for social organization generally. Our relationships and our places in society are created and maintained through conversations.

Fourth, conversations often adhere to *scripts*—rigidly structured patterns of talk. This is especially true in first encounters, when you are trying to reduce uncertainty. For example, the topics that college students discuss when they first meet often follow a set script. Communication researcher Kathy Kellermann (1991) conducted several studies looking at the first conversations of college students and found that 95 percent of the topic changes followed the same pattern regardless of gender, age, race, or geographic region (see Figure 8.2). This suggests that a critical aspect of appropriately constructing conversations is grasping and following relevant conversational scripts.

Does the fact that we frequently use scripts to guide our conversations mean this type of communication is inauthentic? If you expect more from an exchange than a prepackaged response, scripted communication may strike you as such. However, communication scripts allow us to relevantly *and* efficiently exchange greetings, respond to simple questions and answers, trade pleasantries, and get to know people in a preliminary fashion without putting much active thought into our communication. This saves us from mental exertion and allows us to focus our energy on more involved or important interpersonal encounters.

skills practice

Ensuring Competent First Encounters

Putting Kathy Kellermann's Research on Conversation Scripts into Action

❶ Identify a new acquaintance with whom you would like to interact.

❷ Greet the person, introduce yourself, and ask how they are doing.

❸ Discuss current surroundings, the weather, and hometowns.

❹ Ask about interests, school, sports, and social activities, all the while looking for points of commonality and ways to compliment the person.

❺ Raise the possibility of future interaction, express gratitude for the current conversation, and exit with a friendly "Goodbye."

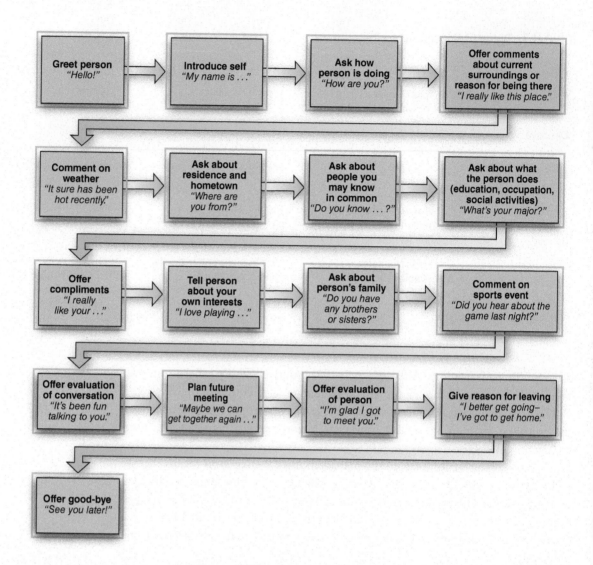

figure 8.2 **Conversational Pattern**

MANAGING RELATIONSHIPS

The 2016 film *Lion* tells the true story of Saroo Brierly, an Indian boy who lost his family at age five when he mistakenly boarded a train transporting him across the country. Too young to explain his identity or hometown to authorities, he was labeled an orphan and adopted by an Australian couple. Haunted by the knowledge that his birth family never knew his fate—coupled with the fact that he only was adopted because Sue, his adoptive mother, couldn't have children—he becomes increasingly emotionally distant. In one of the most powerful scenes of the movie, Sue reveals something that fundamentally redefines their relationship: she *could* have had children, but *wanted* to adopt *him*. "To have a child wouldn't guarantee to make anything better, but to take a child that was suffering, and give it a chance in the world—*that's* something!" The realization that he was adopted from desire, not default, leads to a reconciliation between the two. Sue then supports Saroo in finding his birth family. Eventually he reunites with his birth mother, who thanks Sue for raising her son. Saroo also learns that all these years he has been mispronouncing his name: it actually is *Sheru*, meaning "lion."

○ In *Lion*, Sue creates a deeper, more positive relationship with Saroo when she discloses that she adopted him by choice, not by necessity. See-Saw/Kobal/Shutterstock

Verbal communication's final, and arguably most profound, function in our lives is to help us manage our relationships. We use language to redefine relationships by declaring powerful revelations, such as Sue telling Saroo, "You were wanted." More broadly, verbal communication is *the* principal means through which we maintain our ongoing relationships with family members, lovers, friends, and coworkers (Stafford, 2010). For example, romantic partners who verbally communicate frequently with each other, and with their partners' friends and families, experience less uncertainty in their relationships and are not as likely to break up as those who verbally communicate less often (Parks, 2007). Finally, most of the heartbreaks we'll experience in our lives are preceded by verbal messages that state, in one form or another, "It's over." We'll discuss more about how we forge, maintain, and end our relationships in Chapters 11 through 14. For now, let's examine one of the hallmarks of competent communicators, namely, their ability to use cooperative verbal communication.

self-reflection

Consider a recent instance in which a relationship of yours suddenly changed direction, either for better or for worse. What was said that triggered this turning point? How did the words that were exchanged impact intimacy? What does this tell you about the role that language plays in managing relationships?

Cooperative Verbal Communication

Creating understandable messages

Eager to connect with your teenage son, you ask about his day when he arrives home from school. You receive a grunted "fine" in reply, as he disappears to his bedroom to nap. You invite your romantic partner over for dinner, eager for feedback on your new recipe. But when you ask for an assessment, your partner states, "It's interesting." You text your best friend, asking for their feedback on an in-class presentation you gave earlier that day. They respond, "It went by fast."

Although these examples seem widely disparate, they share an underlying commonality: people failing to verbally communicate in a fully cooperative fashion. To understand how these messages are uncooperative, consider their cooperative counterparts. Your son tells you, "It was all right—I didn't do as well on my chem test as I wanted, but I got an A on my history report." Your partner says, "It's tasty, but I think it'd be even better with a little more seasoning." Your friend's text message reads, "You were enthusiastic, but I thought it could have been presented a little more slowly."

When you use **cooperative verbal communication**, you produce messages that have three characteristics. First, you speak in ways that others can easily understand, using language that is informative, honest, relevant, and clear. Second, you take active ownership for what you're saying by using "I" language. Third, you make others feel included rather than excluded—for example, through the use of "we."

self-reflection

Recall a situation in which you possessed important information but knew that disclosing it would be personally or relationally problematic. What did you do? How did your decision impact your relationship? Was your choice ethical? Based on your experience, is it always cooperative to disclose important information?

UNDERSTANDABLE MESSAGES

In his exploration of language and meaning, philosopher Paul Grice noted that cooperative interactions rest on our ability to tailor our verbal communication so that others can understand us. To produce understandable messages, we have to abide by the **Cooperative Principle**: making our conversational contributions as *informative*, *honest*, *relevant*, and *clear* as is required, given the purposes of the encounters in which we're involved (Grice, 1989).

Attuning ourselves to the encounter is key because in order to apply the Cooperative Principle, we must realize the relevant situational characteristics. For example, while we're ethically bound to share important information with others, this doesn't mean we *always* should. Suppose a friend discloses a confidential secret to you and your sibling later asks you to reveal it. In this case, it would be unethical to share this information without your friend's permission.

Being Informative   According to Grice (1989), being informative during interpersonal encounters means two things. First, you should present all the information that is relevant and appropriate to share, given the situation. When a new coworker passes you in the hallway and greets you with a quick "How's it going?" the situation requires that you provide little information in return—"Great! How are you?"

Oral storytelling is an ancient art, one that creates and passes histories and mythologies down from generation to generation. Seen in almost every society across the world, this tradition continues to take on new forms in the modern era, through media such as podcasts and video essays. © George Rodger/ Magnum Photos

The same question asked by a concerned friend during a personal crisis creates very different demands; your friend likely wants a detailed account of your thoughts and feelings.

Second, you want to avoid being *too* informative—that is, disclosing information that isn't appropriate or important in a particular situation. A detailed description of your personal woes ("I haven't been sleeping well lately, and my cat is sick") in response to your colleague's quick "How's it going?" query would likely be perceived as inappropriate and even strange.

The responsibility to be informative overlaps with the responsibility to be ethical. To be a cooperative verbal communicator, you must share information with others that has important personal and relational implications for them. To illustrate, if you discover that your friend's spouse is having an affair, you're ethically obligated to disclose this information if your friend asks you about it.

Being Honest   **Honesty** is the single most important characteristic of cooperative verbal communication because other people count on the fact that the information you share with them is truthful (Grice, 1989). Honesty means not sharing information that you're uncertain about and not disclosing information that you know is false. When you are dishonest in your verbal communication, you violate standards for ethical behavior, and you lead others to believe false things (Jacobs et al., 1996). For example, if you assure your romantic partner that your feelings haven't changed when, in fact, they have, you give your partner false hope about your future together. You also lay the groundwork for your partner to make continued investments in a relationship that you already know is doomed.

Being Relevant   Relevance means making your conversational contributions responsive to what others have said. When people ask you questions, you provide answers. When they make requests, you grant or reject their requests. When certain topics arise in the conversation, you tie your contributions to that topic. During conversations, you stick with relevant topics and avoid those that aren't. Dodging questions or abruptly changing topics is uncooperative, and in some instances, others may see it as an attempt at deception, especially if you change topics to avoid discussing something you want to keep hidden (McCornack, 2008).

LaunchPad

Online Self-Quiz: Test Your Knowledge of Conversational Patterns. To take this self-quiz, visit LaunchPad: **launchpadworks.com**

Being Clear   Using clear language means presenting information in a straightforward fashion, rather than framing it in obscure or ambiguous terms. For example, telling a partner that you like a recipe but that it needs more seasoning is easier to understand than veiling your meaning by vaguely saying, "It's interesting." But note that using clear language doesn't mean being brutally frank or dumping offensive and hurtful information on others. Competent interpersonal communicators always consider others' feelings when designing their messages. When information is important and relevant to disclose, choose your words carefully to be both respectful *and* clear so that others won't misconstrue your intended meaning.

Dealing with Misunderstanding   Of course, just because you use informative, honest, relevant, and clear language doesn't guarantee that you will be understood by others. When one person misperceives another's verbally expressed thoughts, feelings, or beliefs, **misunderstanding** occurs. Misunderstanding most commonly results from a failure to actively listen. Recall, for example, our discussion in

▶ One downside of our frequent online communication is that it is easy to misunderstand other people's messages and to take them as ruder or less clear than intended. If you need a message to be error-free, consider delivering it face-to-face. HBRH/Shutterstock

skills practice

Using Cooperative Language Online
Using cooperative language during an important online interaction

❶ Identify an important online encounter.

❷ Create a rough draft of the message you wish to send.

❸ Check that the language you've used is fully informative, honest, relevant, and clear.

❹ Use "I" language for all comments that are negative or critical.

❺ Use "we" language throughout the message, where appropriate.

❻ Send the message.

self-reflection

Recall an online encounter in which you thought you understood someone's email, text message, or post, then later found out you were wrong. How did you discover that your impression was mistaken? What could you have done differently to avoid the misunderstanding?

Chapter 7 of task-oriented listeners, who may become impatient or dislike waiting for another person to finish their point (Bodie et al., 2013). This listening style can lead them to misunderstand others' messages. To overcome this source of misunderstanding, practice the active listening skills described in Chapter 7.

Misunderstanding occurs frequently online, owing to the lack of nonverbal cues to help clarify one another's meaning. One study found that 27.2 percent of respondents agreed that email is likely to result in miscommunication of intent, and 53.6 percent agreed that it is relatively easy to misinterpret an email message (Rainey, 2000). The tendency to misunderstand communication online is so prevalent that scholars suggest the following practices: *If a particular message absolutely must be error-free or if its content is controversial, don't use email or text messaging to communicate it.* Whenever possible, conduct high-stakes encounters, such as important attempts at persuasion, face-to-face. Finally, never use emails, social media posts, or text messages for sensitive actions, such as professional reprimands or dismissals, or relationship breakups (Rainey, 2000).

USING "I" LANGUAGE

It's the biggest intramural basketball game of the year, and your team is down by a point when your teammate is fouled—with five seconds left. Stepping to the line for two free throws and a chance to win the game, they miss both, and your team loses. As you leave the court, you angrily snap at them, "You really let us down!"

The second key to cooperative verbal communication is taking ownership of the things you say to others, especially in situations in which you're expressing negative feelings or criticism. You can do this by avoiding **"you" language**, phrases that place the focus of attention and blame on other people, such as *"You* let us down." Instead, rearrange your statements so that you use **"I" language**, phrases that emphasize ownership of your feelings, opinions, and beliefs (see Table 8.2). The difference between "I" and "you" may strike you as minor, but it actually has

table 8.2   **"You" Language versus "I" Language**

"You" Language	"I" Language
You make me so angry!	I'm feeling so angry!
You totally messed things up.	I feel like things are totally messed up.
You need to do a better job.	I think this job needs to be done better.
You really hurt my feelings.	I'm feeling really hurt.
You never pay any attention to me.	I feel like I never get any attention.

powerful effects: "I" language is less likely than "you" language to trigger defensiveness on the part of your listeners (Kubany et al., 1992). "I" language creates a clearer impression on listeners that you're responsible for what you're saying and that you're expressing your own perceptions rather than stating unquestionable truths.

USING "WE" LANGUAGE

It's Thursday night, and you're standing in line waiting to get into a club. In front of you are two couples, and you can't help but overhear their conversations. As you listen, you notice an interesting difference in their verbal communication. One couple expresses everything in terms of "I" and "you": "What do you want to do later tonight?" "I don't know, but I'm hungry, so I'll probably get something to eat. Do you want to come?" The other couple consistently uses "we": "What should we do later?" "Why don't we get something to eat?"

What effect does this simple difference in pronoun usage—"we" rather than "I" or "you"—have on your impressions of the two couples? If you perceive the couple using "we" as being closer than the couple using "I" and "you," you would be right. "We" is a common way people signal their closeness (Dreyer et al., 1987). Couples who use **"we" language**—wordings that emphasize inclusion—tend to be more satisfied with their relationships than those who routinely rely on "I" and "you" messages (Honeycutt, 1999).

An important part of cooperative verbal communication is using "we" language to express your connection to others. In a sense, "we" language is the inverse of "I" language. We use "I" language when we want to show others that our feelings, thoughts, and opinions are separate from theirs and that we take sole responsibility for our feelings, thoughts, and opinions. But "we" language helps us bolster feelings of connection and similarity, not only with romantic partners but also with anyone to whom we want to signal a collaborative relationship. When we (Kelly and Steve) both went through our training to become certified yoga instructors, part of the instruction was to replace the use of "you" with "we" and "let's" during in-class verbal cueing of moves. Rather than saying, "You should lunge forward with your left leg," or "I want you to step forward left," we were taught to say, "*Let's* step forward with *our* left legs." After implementing "we" language in our yoga classes, students repeatedly commented on how they liked the "more personal" and "inclusive" feeling of the class.

Now that we have reviewed ways to improve our cooperative verbal communication, let's investigate some roadblocks, or barriers, to it.

launchpadworks.com

"I" Language
Watch this clip online to answer the questions below.

In this video, how does the partners' use of "I" language affect their interaction? Explain your answer. How might the interaction have been different had they used "you" language? Would it have been a more or less productive discussion?

Want to see more? Check out LaunchPad for clips on **"you" language** and **"we" language**.

Barriers to Cooperative Verbal Communication

Destructive language
can damage
relationships.

Walter White is one of the most complicated, manipulative, brilliant, and disturbing characters to ever grace the TV screen. In the critically acclaimed *Breaking Bad* (one of Steve's favorite shows *ever*), Walter is a high school chemistry teacher who—after being diagnosed with terminal cancer—begins producing methamphetamine to raise money to cover his treatment costs and support his family following his anticipated death. As his involvement with the meth industry increases, his moral and ethical corruption deepens, leading him to lie, steal, aggress, and even murder. In season 4, Walt's marriage to Skyler is instantly devastated by one simple disclosure: Walt has been deceiving Skyler about the degree of his criminality. When she expresses fear for his safety, he makes clear that he is not an innocent "high school teacher trying to help his family" but, instead, the perpetrator of evil:

> Who are you talking to right now? Who is it you think you see? Do you know how much I make a year? Even if I told you, you wouldn't believe it . . . No, you *clearly* don't know who you're talking to, so let me clue you in. I am not "in danger," Skyler. I *am* the danger! A guy opens his door and gets shot, and you think that of *me*? No! *I am the one who knocks!*

When used cooperatively, language can clarify understandings, build relationships, and bring us closer to others. But language also has the capacity to create divisions between people, shatter self-esteem, and damage or destroy relationships. Some people, like Walter White in *Breaking Bad*, use verbal communication to aggress on others, deceive them, or defensively lash out. Others are filled with fear and anxiety about interacting and therefore do not speak at all. In this section, we explore the challenging side of verbal communication by looking at four common barriers to cooperative verbal communication: verbal aggression, deception, defensive communication, and communication apprehension.

VERBAL AGGRESSION

The most notable aspect of Walter White's infamous "I am the one who knocks!" monologue is its ferocity. In fact, he is so scary that his wife Skyler shuns him in its aftermath, out of fear for her life. **Verbal aggression** is the tendency to attack others' self-concepts rather than their positions on topics of conversation (Infante & Wigley, 1986). Verbally aggressive people denigrate others' character, abilities, or physical appearance rather than constructively discussing different points of view—for example, Walt condescendingly snarling at Skyler, "You *clearly* don't know who you're talking to, so let me clue you in." Verbal aggression can be expressed not only through speech but also through behaviors, such as physically mocking another's appearance, displaying rude gestures, or assaulting

◁ In *Breaking Bad*, Walter White's verbal aggression helps him succeed as a drug kingpin but destroys his marriage. Ursula Coyote/© AMC/Everett Collection, Inc

others (Sabourin et al., 1993). And such behaviors negatively impact both the mental health and relational satisfaction of romantic couples (Aloia & High, 2020).

Multiple forms of verbal aggression exist. When such aggression occurs over an extended period of time and is directed toward a particular target, it can evolve into *bullying*. *Cyberbullying* involves repeated and intentional attempts to embarrass or threaten another person through the use of electronic modalities (Chun et al., 2020). When communication stressors that negatively affect others are directed toward people who are members of underrepresented groups, this is known as **microaggression**. Microaggressions can take the form of verbal or nonverbal exchanges, ranging from "microinsults"—such as insensitive communication regarding people's social identities—to "microassaults"—blatant name-calling. Research has documented how microaggressions are especially experienced by people of color, women, and people in the LGBTQ+ community (Lui & Quezada, 2019). Stereotypes and prejudice, such as racism, sexism, homophobia, and heterosexism, underlie microaggressions. All of these forms of verbal aggression are linked with detrimental emotional and mental health outcomes.

Why are some people verbally aggressive? At times, such aggression stems from a temporary mental state. Most of us have found ourselves in situations at one time or another in which various factors—stress, exhaustion, frustration or anger, relationship difficulties—converge. As a result, we lose our heads and spontaneously go off on another person. Some people who are verbally aggressive may, as mentioned above, endorse stereotypical beliefs (see Chapter 3), or may experience chronic hostility (see Chapter 4). Others are frequently aggressive because it helps them achieve short-term interpersonal goals (Infante & Wigley, 1986). For example, people who want to cut in front of you in line, win an argument, or steal your parking spot may believe that they stand a better chance of achieving these objectives if they use insults, profanity, and threats. Unfortunately, their past experiences may bolster this belief because many people give in to verbal aggression, which encourages the aggressor to use the technique again.

If you find yourself consistently communicating in a verbally aggressive fashion, identify and address the root causes behind your aggression. Has external stress (job pressure, a troubled relationship, a family conflict) triggered your aggression? Do you suffer from chronic hostility? Is your aggression rooted in stereotypical beliefs? (If so, refer to the guidelines for overcoming stereotypes in Chapter 3.) If you find that anger management strategies don't help you reduce your aggression, seek out professional assistance.

Responding to verbal aggression is also a daunting challenge. Dominic Infante (1995) offers specific tips for dealing with verbally aggressive people. If you know someone who is chronically verbally aggressive, avoid or minimize contact with that person. For better or worse, the most practical solution for dealing with such individuals is to not interact with them at all. If you can't avoid interacting with a verbally aggressive person, remain polite and respectful during your encounters. Stay calm, and avoid retaliating with personal attacks of your own; these will only further escalate the aggression. Finally, end interactions when someone becomes aggressive, explaining firmly, "I'm sorry, but I don't feel comfortable continuing this conversation."

DECEPTION

Arguably the most prominent feature of Walter White's communication in *Breaking Bad* is his chronic duplicity. For instance, in season 2, Walt is kidnapped by rival drug lord Tuco and consequently goes missing for several days. In the aftermath, he makes up a story about being in a "fugue state" so that his family doesn't suspect the true reason for his absence.

When most of us think of deception, we think of messages like Walt's to his family, in which one person communicates false information to another ("I was in a fugue state!"). But people deceive in any number of ways, only some of which involve saying untruthful things. **Deception** occurs when people deliberately use uninformative, untruthful, irrelevant, or vague language for the purpose of misleading others. The most common form of deception doesn't involve saying anything false at all: studies document that *concealment*—leaving important and relevant information out of messages—is practiced more frequently than all other forms of deception combined (McCornack, 2008).

As noted in previous chapters, deception is commonplace during online encounters. People communicating on online dating sites, posting on social networking sites, and sending messages via email and text message distort and hide whatever information they want, providing little opportunity for the recipients of their messages to check accuracy. Some people provide false information about their background, profession, appearance, and gender online to amuse themselves, to form alternative relationships unavailable to them offline, or to take advantage of others through online scams (Rainey, 2000).

Deception is uncooperative, unethical, impractical, and destructive. It exploits the belief on the part of listeners that speakers are communicating cooperatively—tricking them into thinking that the messages received are informative, honest, relevant, and clear when they're *not* (McCornack, 2008). Deception is unethical because when you deceive others, you deny them information that may be relevant to their continued participation in a relationship, and in so doing, you fail to treat them with respect (LaFollette & Graham, 1986). Deception is also impractical.

Although at times it may seem easier to deceive than to tell the truth (McCornack, 2008), deception typically calls for additional deception. Finally, deception is destructive: it creates intensely unpleasant personal, interpersonal, and relational consequences. The discovery of deception typically causes intense disappointment, anger, and other negative emotions, and frequently leads to relationship breakups (McCornack & Levine, 1990).

At the same time, keep in mind that people who mislead you may not be doing so out of malicious intent. As noted earlier, many cultures view ambiguous and indirect language as hallmarks of cooperative verbal communication. In addition, sometimes people intentionally veil information out of kindness and desire to maintain the relationship, such as when you tell a close friend that her awful new hairstyle looks great because you know she'd be agonizingly self-conscious if she knew how bad it really looked (McCornack, 1997; Metts & Chronis, 1986).

DEFENSIVE COMMUNICATION

A third barrier to cooperative verbal communication is **defensive communication** (or *defensiveness*), impolite messages delivered in response to suggestions, criticism, or perceived slights. For example, at work you suggest an alternative approach to a coworker, who snaps, "We've *always* done it this way." You broach the topic of relationship concerns with your romantic partner, but they shut you down, telling you to "Just drop it!" People who communicate defensively dismiss the validity of what another person has said. They also refuse to make internal attributions about their own behavior, especially when they are at fault. Instead, they focus their responses away from themselves and on the other person.

Four types of defensive communication are common (Waldron et al., 1993). Through *dogmatic messages*, a person dismisses suggestions for improvement or constructive criticism, refuses to consider other views, and continues to believe that their behaviors are acceptable. With *superiority messages*, the speaker suggests that they possess special knowledge, ability, or status far beyond that of the other individual. In using *indifference messages*, a person implies that the suggestion or criticism being offered is irrelevant, uninteresting, or unimportant. Through *control messages*, a person seeks to squelch criticism by controlling the other individual or the encounter (see Table 8.3).

Defensive communication is *interpersonally incompetent* because it violates norms for appropriate behavior, rarely succeeds in effectively achieving interpersonal goals, and treats others with disrespect (Waldron et al., 1993). People who communicate in a chronically defensive fashion suffer a host of negative consequences, including high rates of conflict and lower satisfaction in their personal and professional relationships (Infante et al., 1994). Yet even highly competent communicators behave defensively on occasion.

table 8.3   Examples of Defensive Communication

Message Type	Example
Dogmatic message	"Why would I change? I've always done it like this!"
Superiority message	"I have more experience and have been doing this longer than you."
Indifference message	"*This* is supposed to interest me?"
Control message	"There's no point to further discussion; I consider this matter closed."

Defensiveness is an almost instinctive reaction to behavior that makes us angry—communication we perceive as inappropriate, unfair, or unduly harsh. Consequently, the key to overcoming it is to control its triggering factors. Jennifer Becker and colleagues suggest three triggers of defensive communication: inattentiveness; lack of communicative sharing; and lack of communicative warmth, such as not expressing kindness or affection (Becker et al., 2008). Thus, we can avoid defensive communication by actively listening and attending to others, engaging in self-disclosure, and conveying caring and warmth. Additionally, if a particular person or situation invariably provokes defensiveness in you, practice preventive anger management strategies such as encounter avoidance or encounter structuring (see Chapter 4). If you can't avoid the person or situation, use techniques such as reappraisal and the Jefferson strategy (also in Chapter 4). Given that defensiveness frequently stems from attributional errors—thinking the other person is "absolutely wrong" and you're "absolutely right"—perception-checking (Chapter 3) can also help you reduce your defensiveness.

Using "I" and "we" language appropriately and offering empathy and support for other people can reduce the likelihood that they will communicate defensively with you. However, realize that using cooperative language is not a panacea for managing defensiveness in another person. While we should all strive to maintain ethical communication by treating others with respect, if you sense that a person is escalating a conflict, your best option may be to simply remove yourself from the situation.

COMMUNICATION APPREHENSION

A final barrier to cooperative verbal communication is **communication apprehension**—fear or anxiety associated with interaction, which keeps someone from being able to communicate cooperatively (Daly et al., 2004). People with high levels of communication apprehension experience intense discomfort while talking with others and therefore have difficulty forging productive relationships. Such individuals also commonly experience physical symptoms, such as nervous stomach, dry mouth, sweating, increased blood pressure and heart rate, mental disorganization, and shakiness (McCroskey & Richmond, 1987).

Most of us experience communication apprehension at some point in our lives. The key to overcoming it is to develop **communication plans**—mental maps that describe exactly how communication encounters will unfold—*prior* to interacting in the situations or with the people or types of people that cause your apprehension. Communication plans have two elements. The first is *plan actions*, the "moves" you think you'll perform in an encounter that causes you anxiety. Here, you map out in advance the topics you will talk about, the messages you will deliver in relation to these topics, and the physical behaviors you'll demonstrate.

The second part of a communication plan is *plan contingencies*, the messages you think your communication partner or partners will present during the encounter and how you will respond. To develop plan contingencies, think about the topics your partner will likely talk about, the messages they will likely present, their reaction to your communication, and your response to your partner's messages and behaviors.

When you implement your communication plan during an encounter that causes you apprehension, the experience is akin to playing chess. While you're communicating, envision your next two, three, or four possible moves—your plan actions. Try to anticipate how the other person will respond to those moves and how you will respond in turn. The goal of this process is to interact with enough confidence and certainty to reduce the anxiety and fear you normally feel during such encounters.

In an interview with *Rolling Stone*, Grammy Award–winning artist Adele said she has experienced anxiety before performing, and once had a "full-blown anxiety attack" before meeting Beyoncé. Have you ever felt anxious when communicating? What strategies did you use to deal with your anxiety? Graham Denholm/Getty Images

The Power of Verbal Communication

Language creates our most important moments.

We can't help but marvel at the power of verbal communication. Words are our symbolic vehicle for creating and exchanging meanings, performing actions, and forging relationships. We use language to name all that surrounds us, and in turn, the names we have created shape how we think and feel about these things.

But for most of us, the power of language is intensely personal. Call to mind the most important relationship events in your life. When you do, you'll likely find they were not merely accompanied by verbal communication but were defined and created through it. Perhaps it was the first time you said "I love you" to a partner or posed the heart-stopping query "Will you marry me?" Maybe it was a doctor declaring "You have a healthy baby!" or "It's twins!" Or perhaps the relational events that float upward into memory are sadder in nature, the words bitter remnants you wish you could forget: "I don't love you anymore." "I never want to see you again." "I'm sorry, but the prognosis is grim."

"With great power comes great responsibility," as the saying goes, and our power to shape and use verbal communication is no different. The words we exchange profoundly affect not only our interpersonal communication and relationships but also those of others. The responsibility we bear is to continually strive to communicate cooperatively so that the indelible images left by our language are imprinted with positivity and respect.

Dealing with Difficult Truths

 LaunchPad For the best experience, complete all parts of this activity
in LaunchPad: **launchpadworks.com**

1 Background

Cooperative verbal communicators strive to use appropriate, informative, honest, relevant, and clear language. But in many difficult and complicated relationship situations, deception becomes a tempting alternative. To understand how you might competently manage such a relationship challenge, read the case study in Part 2; then, drawing on all you know about interpersonal communication, work through the problem-solving model in Part 3.

Visit LaunchPad to watch the video in Part 4 and assess your communication in Part 5.

2 Case Study

Since her early youth, your cousin Britney has always gotten her way. Whenever she wanted something, she would throw a tantrum, and your aunt and uncle would give in. Now she's an adult version of the same child: spoiled and manipulative. Thankfully, you see Britney only during the holidays, and she usually ignores you.

Recently, Britney has had troubles. She dropped out of college and lost her license after totaling the new car her parents bought her. Her drug abuse worsened to the point where her folks forced her into rehab. Despite your dislike of Britney, you feel sorry for her because you've struggled with your own substance abuse challenges. Now she has apparently recovered and reenrolled in school.

At Thanksgiving, Britney greets you with a big hug and a smile. "How's my favorite cousin?" she gushes. As she talks, your surprise turns to suspicion. She's acting *too* friendly, and you think she may be high. Sure enough, when the two of you are alone, she pulls out a bag of Vicodin tablets. "Do you want some?" she offers, and, when you refuse, says, "Oh, that's right — you're *in recovery*," in a mocking tone. When you

ask about rehab, she laughs, "It may have been right for you, but I did it just to shut my parents up." Afterward, you corner your folks and disclose what happened. They counsel silence. If you tell Britney's parents, Britney will lie; everyone in the family will have to take sides; and it will ruin the holiday.

Over dinner, your aunt and uncle praise Britney's recovery. Your aunt then announces that she is rewarding Britney by buying her another car. Your blood boils. Although your aunt and uncle are well intentioned, Britney is deceiving and exploiting them! Noticing your sullen expression, your uncle says, "I'm not sure what's bothering you, but I think it might be envy. Not everyone has Britney's strength of character in dealing with adversity. You could learn a lot from her, don't you think?" Seething in anger, you say nothing, and the conversation moves on. Later, Britney corners you and says, "Thanks for covering for me earlier. But my parents noticed that you were acting weird, and they think something is up. I think they might try to ask you about it. If they do, you won't rat me out, will you?"

Your Turn

Consider all you've learned thus far about interpersonal communication. Then work through the following five steps. Remember, there are no "right" answers, so think hard about what is the best choice! (P.S. Need help? See the *Helpful Concepts* list.)

step 1

Reflect on yourself. What are your thoughts and feelings in this situation? Are your impressions and attributions accurate?

step 2

Reflect on your partner. Using perspective-taking and empathic concern, put yourself in Britney's shoes. What is she thinking and feeling in this situation?

step 3

Identify the optimal outcome. Think about all the information you have about your communication and relationship with Britney, your relationship with your other family members, and the situation. What's the best, most constructive relationship outcome possible? Consider what's best for you, Britney, and the family.

step 4

Locate the roadblocks. Taking into consideration your own and Britney's thoughts and feelings and all that has happened in this situation, what obstacles are keeping you from achieving the optimal outcome?

step 5

Chart your course. What can you say to Britney to overcome the roadblocks you've identified and achieve your optimal outcome?

HELPFUL CONCEPTS

Being informative, **214**
Being honest, **215**
Using "I" and "we" language, **216**
Deception, **219**
Defensive communication, **221**

 The Other Side

 Visit LaunchPad to watch a video in which Britney tells her side of the case study story. As in many real-life situations, this is information to which you did not have access when you were initially crafting your response in Part 3. The video reminds us that even when we do our best to offer competent responses, there is always another side to the story that we need to consider.

Interpersonal Competence Self-Assessment

After watching the video, visit the Self-Assessment questions in LaunchPad. Think about the new information offered in Britney's side of the story and all you've learned about interpersonal communication. Drawing on this knowledge, revisit your earlier responses in Part 3 and assess your interpersonal communication competence.

POSTSCRIPT

Sara Krulwich/The New York Times/Redux

We began this chapter with a composer who purchased a historical biography, and consequently created the most award-winning musical in history. When Lin-Manuel Miranda wrote *Hamilton*, he wasn't just honoring the transformative power of language, the rebellious spirit of hip-hop, or the rags-to-riches story of an immigrant who became the first U.S. Treasury Secretary. Instead, he was opening the door for people of all backgrounds, heritages, and histories to see themselves mirrored in the lives of those who helped to found the United States of America.

What history will you create, in your journey through life? How do you harness the power of language to bring about revolutionary change in your life?

Lin-Manuel Miranda's *Hamilton* is more than a musical theater success. It's an homage to the transformative power of language and its ability to engage, entertain, entrance, and *include*.

 **LaunchPad**

LaunchPad for *Reflect & Relate* offers videos
and encourages self-assessment through
adaptive quizzing. Go to **launchpadworks.com**
to get access to:

✓ LearningCurve
Adaptive Quizzes

 Video clips that help you understand
interpersonal communication

key terms

 You can watch brief, illustrative videos
of these terms and test your understanding
of the concepts in LaunchPad.

key concepts

Describing Verbal Communication

- We use **verbal communication** when interacting with others. We employ words as **symbols** to represent people, objects, and ideas.
- Verbal communication is governed by both **constitutive rules** and **regulative rules** that define meanings and clarify conversational structure.
- Partners in close relationships often develop **personal idioms** for each other that convey intimacy. Large groups develop **dialects** that include distinct pronunciations.
- Language constantly changes and evolves.

Functions of Verbal Communication

- When we speak, we convey both **denotative meaning** and **connotative meaning**.
- **Linguistic determinism** suggests that our capacity for thought is defined by our language. People from different cultures experience different realities due to **linguistic relativity**.
- We control language through the power of **naming**.
- Whenever we interact with others, we use language to perform **speech acts**.

Cooperative Verbal Communication

- **Honesty** is the most important characteristic of **cooperative verbal communication**. It requires that you abide by the **Cooperative Principle**. Language should be informative, relevant, and clear to help avoid **misunderstandings**.
- You also should avoid expressing negative evaluations and opinions through **"you" language**; instead, replace it with **"I" language**. **"We" language** is a good means of fostering a sense of inclusiveness.

Barriers to Cooperative Verbal Communication

- When others display **verbal aggression**, it's best to remain polite or to remove yourself from the encounter.
- The most common form of **deception** is concealment.
- People who use **defensive communication** dismiss the validity of what another person says.
- Some people experience **communication apprehension**, which inhibits them from communicating competently. **Communication plans** can help with overcoming apprehension.

chapter review

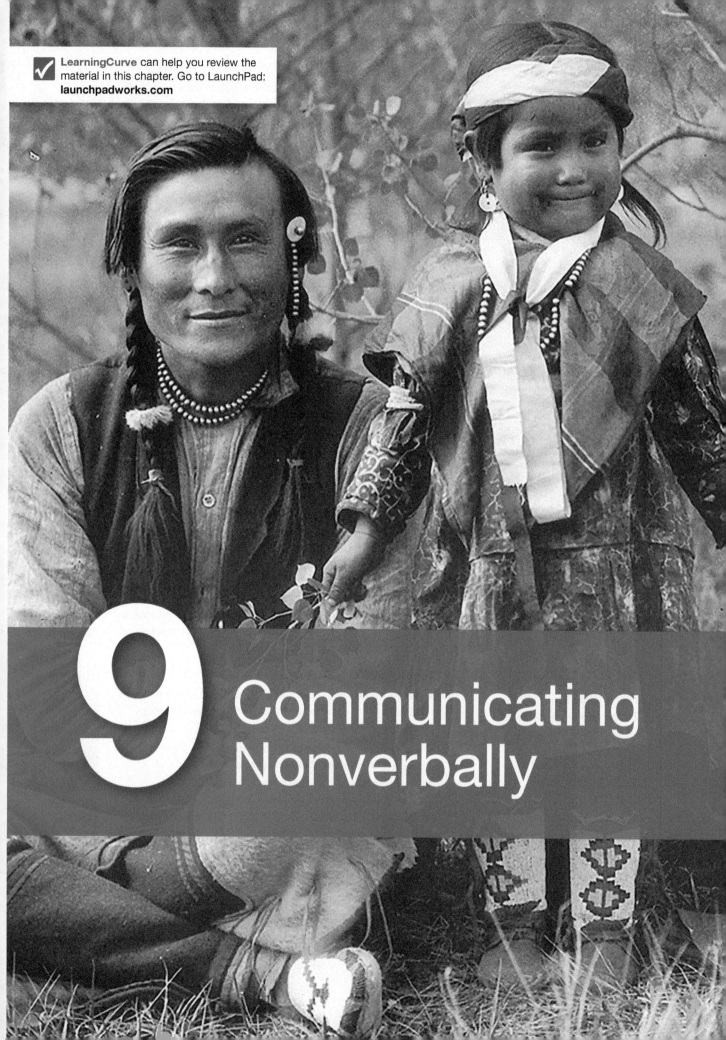

9 Communicating Nonverbally

Nonverbal communication powerfully shapes others' perceptions of you.

Sampson Beaver's family '06 [Leah, Frances Louise, and Sampson Beaver], 1906, Whyte Museum of the Canadian Rockies, Mary Schaffer fonds (V527/ps1-05)

Closely examine this photograph. As you do, try to recall other images of Native Americans from the late 1800s or early 1900s that you've seen. What is different, unique, or interesting about this photo? How does the picture make you feel? What's your impression of the people in it?

We first came upon this image in poster form in our son's preschool classroom, and we were stunned. Intuitively, we found the picture provocative, but we couldn't figure out precisely why. When we asked our son's teacher about it, she clarified our confusion: "They're *smiling*."

By the late 1800s, staged photos of Native American people were being marketed as tourist postcards and magazine illustrations (Silversides, 1994). These photos depicted Native peoples in narrow, stereotypical ways: scowling fearsomely in full ceremonial dress, astride their horses, or posed in front of teepees. Of course, just as people within all cultures did, Native Americans during this time period expressed the full range of human facial expressions, including smiling to express joy. Yet, as Cambridge University professor Maria Tippett (1994) notes, "The image one gets throughout this seventy year period is of a blank-faced, stiff, and unengaged people" (p. 2). When Steve surveyed more than 5,000 photos from this era, he couldn't find a single image portraying Native Americans with smiles — except for this family photo.[1]

This rare portrait, taken by amateur photographer Mary Schaffer (1861–1939), shows people who,

[1]Authors' review of 5,000 photos in the Curtis Archives, http://curtis.library.northwestern.edu/curtis/toc.cgi

229

rather than staring blankly or with faux ferocity into the camera, "communicate with the eyes behind it" (Tippett, 1994). The image has an intriguing history. Schaffer, and her friend Mollie Adams and two guides, were exploring the headwaters of the Saskatchewan and Athabasca Rivers in Canada in late 1907, where they met a band of Stoney Indians who befriended the strangers. Among them were Samson Beaver; his wife Leah; and their young daughter Frances, who invited Mary to dinner. After the meal, Mary asked them if she could take their picture, and they agreed.

The Beaver family photo provides a literal and metaphorical snapshot of an interpersonal encounter: the postures, faces, dress, and use of space during a family meeting with a new friend late one sunny afternoon. You can almost feel the fellowship that infused the conversation, communicated through Samson's smile, his forward lean, and his direct gaze, all cues conveying intimacy and closeness. If you feel an immediate connection and empathy with Samson, you're not alone. This is a typical human reaction to the sight of a smiling person. A scowling face has quite the opposite effect, conveying coldness and distance.

The Beaver family photo reminds us of the universal and transcendent nature of human nonverbal expression and of its powerful role in shaping our impressions of others. Over a hundred years ago, a family joined new friends to share a meal and something of themselves with one another. Although they're all long since passed, the image of their encounter serves as an enduring reminder of the power of human nonverbal expression to shape our interpersonal communication and relationships.

Becoming a skilled nonverbal communicator is essential to competent interpersonal communication (Schlegel et al., 2020). Most of the meaning we exchange during interpersonal encounters comes from our nonverbal expressions (Burgoon & Hoobler, 2002). What's more, skill at managing our nonverbal communication is associated with a host of positive outcomes, including high self-esteem, perceptions of attractiveness and popularity by others, and relationship satisfaction (Hodgins & Belch, 2000).

But being a skilled nonverbal communicator also is incredibly challenging because nonverbal communication involves many different aspects of behavior, all of which must be considered and controlled simultaneously. When you communicate nonverbally, you manipulate your bodily movements, your voice, and — in some situations — the way you touch others. You also decide how to occupy space and craft your appearance. And this is only *half* the challenge because while you're doing all of this, you *also* endeavor to accurately discern the nonverbal communication of *others*. People who are skilled at interpreting *others'* nonverbal expressions report happier relationships, higher levels of mental health and social adjustment, and better academic and workplace performance (Schlegel et al., 2020). To simultaneously — and competently — manage your own nonverbal behavior while monitoring and interpreting that of others requires knowledge of the various means of nonverbal communication, the ability to shape and adapt nonverbal expression, and the motivation to do so.

In this chapter, we discuss nonverbal communication and offer guidelines for strengthening your skills. You'll learn:

- The nature of nonverbal communication, and the characteristics that differentiate it from verbal communication
- How culture, gender, and technology influence our nonverbal communication

- The seven codes of nonverbal communication, and how you can more skillfully use them when interacting with others
- The functions nonverbal communication serves in our everyday lives
- How to competently manage your nonverbal communication

We begin our description of nonverbal communication with a definition and discussion of four characteristics that spotlight its unique nature.

Describing Nonverbal Communication

How nonverbal expression transmits meaning

In this book, we define **nonverbal communication** as the intentional or unintentional transmission of meaning through an individual's nonspoken physical and behavioral cues (Patterson, 1995). This definition embraces both intentional and unintentional nonverbal behaviors as communication. Sometimes we do things like yawn, sigh, or grimace and mean nothing by them, but based on the principle that "one cannot not communicate" from Chapter 1, we know that others may interpret these behaviors as acts of communication. This perception may lead them to respond in ways that affect us, our interpersonal communication, and our relationships. For example, a professor who sees you looking away from the webcam and writing during a remote class may express concern that you're not paying attention, even though you're carefully writing notes. At other times, we intentionally craft nonverbal behaviors to communicate information to others. We add scowling emoji to texts to convey frustration, post smiling photos on Instagram to share joy, or cast confirming looks at coworkers to signal we're ready for meetings. In some situations, we share touch with people we are close to, such as hugging family in holiday greetings, or to comfort a dear friend. We move closer or farther away from communication partners to indicate intimacy or emotional distance. We arrange and light our offices and homes to convey power or peacefulness, dress and groom ourselves to communicate casualness or formality, and don artifacts such as jewelry and watches to display status.

Now that we have defined nonverbal communication, let's consider some characteristics that differentiate nonverbal from verbal forms of expression.

NONVERBAL COMMUNICATION DIFFERS FROM VERBAL COMMUNICATION

Throughout each day, you communicate nonverbally in multiple ways. Sometimes you may carefully consider your nonverbal communication, and other times you may be completely unaware of the nonverbal messages you convey. One way that you can become a more competent communicator is to consider the aspects of nonverbal communication that make it unique, and distinguish it from verbal expression. Let's review four of these key characteristics.

Nonverbal Communication Uses Multiple Sensory Channels   In contrast to verbal communication, which we transmit through a single sensory channel at a time (the human voice when speaking; written text when online), our nonverbal messages are expressed through multiple sensory channels simultaneously—such as auditory, visual, and tactile. When you talk with a good friend, for example, you simultaneously listen to your friend's tone of voice (auditory); watch your friend's facial expressions, use of eye contact, and hand gestures (visual); and perhaps even touch and receive touch from your friend (tactile). What's more, you do this while also listening to and making sense of your friend's verbal communication.

Nonverbal Communication Is More Ambiguous

Nonverbal meanings are more flexible and ambiguous than verbal meanings. A smile can express comfort or contempt, just as a shared glance can convey intimacy or warning—depending on the situation. The ambiguity of nonverbal messages is amplified when using emoji to convey emotional states in email and text messages. For example, one study of emoji interpretation found that although people experienced widespread agreement with regard to "angry" emoji facial expressions, people widely diverged on the meanings of emojis for "calm," "love," "sadness," "surprise," and "relief": some participants perceived the "relieved face" emoji as "love," whereas others saw it as "contempt" (Franco & Fugate, 2020). Needless to say, such wildly varying interpretations create fertile ground for nonverbal miscommunication! To avoid such misunderstandings, try to clearly convey your emotional meanings in text paired with emoji, for example, "I can't believe it!! ☺" to convey surprise, rather than simply relying on emoji alone.

Nonverbal Communication Has Fewer Rules

Nonverbal communication is more ambiguous than verbal communication because it is governed by fewer rules. As we discussed in Chapter 8, you learn literally thousands of constitutive and regulative rules regarding grammar, spelling, pronunciation, and meaning as you master your first and any additional languages. But consider how rarely you've been instructed in the use of nonverbal communication. To be sure, nonverbal rules do exist, such as "Raise your hand if you want to be called on." However, most of these rules are informal norms—for instance, "It's not polite to stare at people."

Nonverbal Communication Has More Meaning

When we interact with others, we often infer more meaning from people's nonverbal communication than from their verbal messages, and we convey more meaning to them through our nonverbal rather than verbal communication. Suppose you meet someone new at a party and find yourself intrigued. Pondering your attraction, you probably gather a lot more information from the person's facial expressions, eye contact, posture, gestures, vocal tone, clothing, and other nonverbal signals than you do from their words. This is particularly true during first encounters because nonverbal communication has a greater impact on our overall impressions of attractiveness than does verbal communication (Zuckerman et al., 1991).

Our reliance on nonverbal communication escalates even higher when people display **mixed messages**, verbal and nonverbal behaviors that convey contradictory meanings (Burgoon & Hoobler, 2002). A friend says that they aren't "sad," but their slumped shoulders and downturned mouth suggest otherwise. In such cases, we almost always trust the nonverbal messages over the verbal ones. In contrast, when verbal and nonverbal messages align ("Yes, I'm sad" coupled with slumped shoulders and frown), the amount of attention we pay to verbal communication rises (Burgoon & Hoobler, 2002).

Despite the differences between verbal and nonverbal forms of expression, and the weight we give nonverbal communication when sending and receiving information, both are essential. When we interact with others, our verbal and nonverbal behaviors combine to create meaning (Jones & LeBaron, 2002). In everyday encounters, verbal and nonverbal communication are not experienced or expressed separately,

We often deduce more meaning from people's nonverbal rather than verbal communication.

© Ian Berry/Magnum Photos

but instead coalesce to create interpersonal communication (Birdwhistell, 1970). Keep this in mind: your skill as a nonverbal communicator goes hand in hand with your skill as a verbal communicator, so you need *both* to communicate competently.

Another way to enhance our competence as nonverbal communicators is to realize the significant influence of culture, gender, and technology, and we consider these issues next.

NONVERBAL COMMUNICATION IS INFLUENCED BY CULTURE

Nonverbal communication and culture are inextricably linked, in ways we will discuss throughout this chapter. You can wrinkle your brow, use a hand gesture, or speak loudly to make a point, but if people in the culture surrounding you don't understand your behavior, you haven't communicated your message. Consider cultural differences in the meaning of eye contact, for example (Chen & Starosta, 2005). Middle Easterners often view direct eye contact as a sign of respect during conversation, but many Cambodians and Thai people see it as insulting and an invasion of privacy.

self-reflection

Call to mind an encounter you've experienced in which cultural differences in nonverbal communication proved challenging. In what ways did your cultural practices contribute to the problem? How was the situation resolved? What could you do differently in the future to avoid such dilemmas?

Some cultural differences in nonverbal communication derive from the dimensions we previously discussed in Chapter 5, especially individualism versus collectivism (independence and personal achievement versus group identity and collective harmony). For example, in one of the largest observational studies ever conducted on facial expressions, involving almost three-quarters of a *million* participants from 12 countries, people from individualistic countries such as the United States, the United Kingdom, and Germany displayed significantly more brow furrowing—an open sign of intense concern or anger—than did people in collectivistic countries, such as China, Peru, and Colombia (McDuff et al., 2017). This likely reflects a concern in collectivistic cultures for preserving the harmony of encounters by veiling concern and anger.

The tight link between culture and nonverbal communication makes cross-cultural communication difficult to master. Sure, the nonverbal symbols used in different cultures are easy enough to learn. But familiarity with the full tapestry of cues—perception of touch, appropriateness of gaze or brow furrowing—takes much longer. Most people need many years of immersion in a culture before they fully understand the meanings of that culture's nonverbal communication (Chen & Starosta, 2005).

NONVERBAL COMMUNICATION IS INFLUENCED BY GENDER

What does communication research tell us about nonverbal communication and gender? The overall findings can be summed up as: *it's complicated*. Consider, for example, ability to accurately perceive the nonverbal communication of others. In a study involving more than 5,000 participants, women and men were equally accurate in identifying both intense and subtle facial expressions of six emotions: happiness, anger, sadness, fear, surprise, and disgust (Fischer et al., 2018). A separate study examining perception of voices found mixed results: women and men were similarly capable of correctly recognizing vocal expressions of anger, fear, sadness, happiness, and disgust, but all participants—regardless of their gender—were more accurate when interpreting the voices of women than those of men (Lausen & Schact, 2018). Taken together, studies suggest that whereas few gender differences exist in the ability to *interpret* nonverbal communication, women may be better at *communicating* nonverbal messages (Hall et al., 2000).

self-reflection

Consider content you've read online regarding gender differences in nonverbal communication. Is this information based on reliable research or stereotypes? Does it match or deviate from your own communication experiences? What does this tell you about the trustworthiness of such information?

What about overall behavioral differences? The study we mentioned previously in our discussion of culture—involving more than 740,000 participants from 12 different countries—found that across cultures, women tend to smile more and furrow their brows less than do men (McDuff et al., 2017). These findings support prior research involving analysis of data from hundreds of gender studies (Hall et al., 2000), and probably reflect the results of gender socialization and differing cultural expectations for people depending on their gender (see Chapter 6 for more information).

NONVERBAL COMMUNICATION IS LIBERATED AND CHALLENGED BY TECHNOLOGY

When our boys were younger, Sunday evenings were family time. We didn't have formal dinners or anything like that, but it was the one night a week when other events and activities didn't intrude, and we could count on being able to eat together, hang out, and chat. As described in Chapter 1, our family is now scattered around the country: we are in Alabama, our oldest son is in Illinois, our middle son is in Missouri, and our youngest is in Oregon. Nevertheless, we *still* see each other and chat every Sunday evening. How? *Video calls.* Technology allows us to not only continue an informal family tradition but also stay emotionally close even as we are geographically distant.

As recently as 20 years ago, our ability to communicate nonverbally was radically restricted by technology. Phone calls limited us to vocal cues, and communicating on the computer meant seeing words on a screen—nothing else. Only one option existed for experiencing the full tapestry of nonverbal communication: face-to-face interaction. Now, nonverbal communication has been liberated through technology. We can upload and download photos and video clips on our devices. We can inter- act "face-to-face" through various apps with loved ones who are separated geographically from us, and we can take college classes remotely with a webcam. We can podcast, stream videos, or post photos of ourselves on social media—then alert all our friends that our content is available for viewing. As of 2020, more than 5 billion videos were viewed each day on YouTube.

This shift from technological restriction to liberation has created two notable outcomes. First, we can choose various forms that let us hear *and* see others when interacting. Second, we can use these modalities to better maintain intimate, long- distance relationships. A generation ago, soldiers stationed overseas waited a week (or more) to receive written letters from loved ones back home. Now they can exchange messages rich with verbal and nonverbal expressions in real time. Like our Sunday video calls with our sons, families, friends, and partners separated by distance—through summer vacations or unanticipated relocations—also can maintain their intimate connections.

At the same time, at least two nonverbal challenges have arisen as we've become increasingly immersed in technology: *Zoom fatigue* and *diminished smiling*. Many of us have experienced emotional and mental exhaustion on video calls—known as **Zoom fatigue** for the webcam platform that rose to prominence during the COVID-19 pandemic (Sander & Bauman, 2020). Why do people find webcam interactions more fatiguing? When people interpersonally communicate via video calls, they tend to smile more animatedly and speak louder than during other conversations, attempting to compensate for the lack of physical presence by being more nonverbally expressive (Croes et al., 2019). As a consequence, these interactions are more energy-consuming than other encounters. And because proximity to faces tends to be closer on video calls than during face-to-face encounters, we must invest more mental effort in monitoring

skills practice

Maintaining Online Friendship
Using nonverbal communication online to maintain a friendship

❶ Identify a long-distance friend with whom you haven't communicated recently.

❷ Think of a story or an update that you want to share with that friend.

❸ Compose a message explaining your story that uses nonverbal cues, such as photos or a video of yourself.

❹ Before sending, review your facial expressions, eye contact, body movement, voice, and appearance; make sure they communicate positively what you want to express.

❺ Email or post the footage, and see how your friend responds.

◖ When taking a job interview online via video call, what would you do differently than in an in-person interview? Why?

our own facial expressions and eye contact, to appear interested and engaged—especially because *we can often see ourselves* during video calls (Sander & Bauman, 2020). These factors, taken together, make video calls uniquely taxing.

A second nonverbal challenge created by our technological immersion is *diminished smiling*. During moments of free time within public settings, people often turn to their cell phones for entertainment. Yet, focusing attention on one's phone—rather than the people in proximity to oneself—has a dramatic effect on smiling: people who have their cell phones out smile at others in their proximity 30 percent less than those without phones (Kushlev et al., 2019). Why is this significant? Because smiling is critical for both initiating encounters and creating a feeling of emotional connection with others (Kunecke et al., 2017). When people smile, others are inclined to "mirror" that expression by smiling themselves, creating an emotional "feedback loop," whereby the original smiler recognizes that their smile has been reciprocated, and feels happier and more connected to others as a result (Kunecke et al., 2017). When people don't smile at others in their proximity, they are substantially less likely to create such emotional connections; and as a result, less likely to interact with people. For instance, one study of cell phones and smiling found that when asked to sit in a waiting room, 78 percent of people with cell phones didn't smile or interact at all with other people in the room, whereas 88 percent of people without cell phones smiled and initiated interaction (Kunecke et al., 2017).

Now that we've described nonverbal communication, let's explore the particular types—or "codes"—of nonverbal communication.

Nonverbal Communication Codes

Explore the variety of nonverbal sensory channels.

One reason nonverbal communication contains such rich information is that during interpersonal encounters, we use many different aspects of our behavior, appearance, and surrounding environment simultaneously to communicate meaning. You can greatly strengthen your nonverbal communication skills by understanding **nonverbal communication codes**, the different means used for transmitting information nonverbally (Burgoon & Hoobler, 2002). Scholars distinguish seven nonverbal communication codes, which are summarized in Table 9.1.

table 9.1 **The Seven Codes of Nonverbal Communication**

Code	Description
Kinesics	Visible body movements, including facial expressions, eye contact, gestures, and body postures
Vocalics	Vocal characteristics, such as loudness, pitch, speech rate, and tone
Haptics	Duration, placement, and strength of touch
Proxemics	Use of physical distance
Physical appearance	Appearance of hair, clothing, body type, and other physical features
Artifacts	Personal possessions displayed to others
Environment	Structure of physical surroundings

COMMUNICATING THROUGH BODY MOVEMENTS

At age 16, Tyra Banks began doing fashion shows in Europe for designers such as Chanel and Fendi. She subsequently appeared in *Elle* and *Vogue*, and was the first African American woman to grace the cover of *GQ*. But what catapulted her to the top of the global modeling industry was not just her beauty; it was her unique self-awareness of, and control over, her body movements. For example, Banks distinguishes 275 different smiles she uses when modeling, and on her show *America's Next Top Model*, she teaches her protégés to practice seven basic smiles. One of these smiles doesn't involve the mouth at all, just the eyes, which Banks calls a *smize*. Another smile uses body posture and movement—shifting her shoulder position sideways and downward, and turning her head toward the listener. These different smiles all reflect specific emotions or situations, from anger to surprise.

Tyra Banks's superlative use of nonverbal skill in her modeling exemplifies the power of **kinesics** (from the Greek *kinesis*, meaning "movement")—visible body movements. Kinesics is the richest nonverbal code in terms of its power to communicate meaning, and it includes most of the behaviors we associate with nonverbal communication: facial expressions, eye contact, gestures, and body postures.

○ Tyra Banks's impeccable control over her posture and facial expressions helped her rise to stardom. What experiences have you had with people who use facial expressions and body movements to communicate traits such as power — or kindness? Robin Marchant/ WireImage/Getty Images

Facial Expression   "A person's character is clearly written on the face." As this traditional Chinese saying suggests, the face plays a pivotal role in shaping our perception of others. In fact, some scholars argue that facial cues rank first among all forms of communication in their influence on our interpersonal impressions (Knapp & Hall, 2002). We use facial expressions to communicate an endless stream of emotions, and we make judgments about what others are feeling by assessing their facial expressions. Our use of emoji (such as ☺ and ☹) to communicate attitudes and emotions online testifies to our reliance on this type of kinesics. The primacy of the face even influences our labeling of interpersonal encounters ("face-to-face") and the names of popular sites and apps ("Facebook," "FaceTime").

Eye Contact   Eye contact serves many purposes during interpersonal communication. We use our eyes to express emotions, signal when it's someone else's turn to talk, and show others that we're listening to them. We also demonstrate our interest in a conversation by increasing our eye contact, or signal relationship intimacy by making

◔ Within a few days of birth, infants can communicate with caregivers through eye contact. AP Photo/Ted S. Warren

eye contact with a close friend or romantic partner. Of course, eye contact can convey hostility as well. One of the most aggressive forms of nonverbal expression is *prolonged staring*—fixed and unwavering eye contact of several seconds' duration.

Gestures   Imagine that you're driving to an appointment and someone is riding right on your bumper. Scowling at the offender in your rearview mirror, you're tempted to raise your middle finger and show it to the other driver, but you restrain yourself. The raised finger is an example of a *gesture*, a hand motion used to communicate messages (Streek, 1993). "Flipping the bird" falls into a category of gestures known as **emblems**, which represent specific verbal meanings (Ekman, 1976). With emblems, the gesture and its verbal meaning are interchangeable. You can say the words or use the gesture, and you'll send the same message.

Unlike emblems, **illustrators** accent or illustrate verbal messages. You tell your spouse about a rough road you recently biked, and as you describe the bumpy road, you bounce your hand up and down to illustrate the ride.

Regulators control the exchange of conversational turns during interpersonal encounters (Rosenfeld, 1987). Listeners use regulators to tell speakers to keep talking, repeat something, hurry up, or let another person talk (Ekman & Friesen, 1969). Speakers use them to tell listeners to pay attention or to wait longer for their turn. Common examples include pointing a finger while trying to interrupt and holding a palm straight up to keep a person from interrupting. During text-based online communication, abbreviations such as *BRB* ("be right back") serve as substitutes for gestural regulators.

Adaptors are touching gestures, often unconsciously made, that serve a psychological or physical purpose (Ekman & Friesen, 1969). They can include touching an object, such as fiddling with a pen, or yourself, such as smoothing your hair to make a better impression before a date, or adjusting a tie before an interview.

Posture   The fourth kinesic is your body posture, which includes straightness of back (erect or slouched), body lean (forward, backward, or vertical), straightness of shoulders (firm and broad or slumped), and head position (tilted or straight up). Your posture communicates two primary messages to others: immediacy and power (Mehrabian, 1972). **Immediacy** is the degree to which you find someone interesting and attractive. Want to nonverbally communicate that you like someone? Lean forward, keep your back straight and your arms open, and hold your head up, facing the person when talking. Conversely, leaning back, closing your arms, and looking away all communicate *dislike*.

Power is the ability to influence or control other people or events (discussed in detail in Chapter 10). Imagine attending two job interviews in the same afternoon. The first interviewer sits upright, with a tense, rigid body posture. The second interviewer leans back in their chair, with their feet up on their desk and their hands behind their head. Which interviewer has more power? Most Americans would say the second. In the United States, high-status communicators typically use relaxed postures (Burgoon et al., 1996), but in Japan, people tend to display power through erect posture and feet planted firmly on the floor.

COMMUNICATING THROUGH VOICE

On February 27, 2019, vocalist T-Pain was declared the winner of the first season of *The Masked Singer*, a show in which celebrities compete anonymously in costumes

LaunchPad Video

launchpadworks.com

Adaptors
Watch this clip online to answer the questions below.

Have you ever been in a situation in which you were influenced by the body movements of another person? Has this mirroring of body language been helpful to you? Are there some situations in which adapting to the physical cues of others hasn't been helpful?

to veil their identities from viewers. This shouldn't have been surprising: he's an *incredible* singer (check out his national anthem performance on YouTube, for example!). Nevertheless, judges, audience members, and even host Nick Cannon were stunned because although T-Pain previously had won a Grammy, and had collaborated with the likes of Bruno Mars, Lil Wayne, Kanye West, and Ludacris, most people weren't familiar with his *actual* singing voice. Instead, people knew him for his pioneering work with the pitch-correction program Auto-Tune. T-Pain was one of the first musicians to realize that Auto-Tune could be used not only to subtly correct singing errors but also to alter one's voice entirely. Running his vocals through the program, his normally full, rich voice becomes thin and reedy sounding, jumping in pitch precisely from note to note without error. The result is a sound that is at once musical yet robotic. His work with Auto-Tune in the early 2000s was so popular that he even released an iPhone app called "I Am T-Pain,"—the best-selling iPhone app of 2009—which allowed fans to record and modify their own voices so that they could sound like him.

The popularity of T-Pain's vocal manipulations illustrates the impact that **vocalics**—vocal characteristics we use to communicate nonverbal messages—has on our impressions. Indeed, vocalics rival kinesics in their communicative power (Burgoon et al., 1996) because our voices communicate our social, ethnic, and individual identities to others. Consider a study that recorded people from diverse backgrounds answering a series of small-talk questions, such as "How are you?" (Harms, 1961). People who listened to these recordings were able to accurately judge participants' ethnicity, gender, and social class, often within only 10 to 15 seconds, based solely on their voices. Vocalics strongly shape our perception of others when we first meet them. If we perceive a person's voice as calm and smooth (rather than nasal or shrill), we are more likely to form a positive impression and judge the person as attractive, extraverted, open, and conscientious (Zuckerman et al., 1990).

When we interact with others, we typically experience their voices as a totality—they "talk in certain ways" or "have a particular kind of voice." But people's voices are actually complex combinations of four characteristics: tone, pitch, loudness, and speech rate.

Tone The most noticeable difference between T-Pain's authentic voice and his digitally altered vocals is tone. Tone is the most complex of human vocalic characteristics and involves a combination of richness and breathiness. You can control your vocal tone by allowing your voice to resonate deep in your chest and throat—achieving a full, rich tone that conveys an authoritative quality while giving a formal talk, for example. By contrast, letting your voice resonate through your sinus cavity creates a more whiny and nasal tone—which is often unpleasant to others. Your use of breath also affects tone. If you expel a great deal of air when speaking, you convey sexiness. If you constrict the airflow when speaking, you create a thin and hard tone that may communicate nervousness or anxiety.

English-speakers use vocal tone to emphasize and alter the meanings of verbal messages. Regardless of the words you use, your tone can make your statements

T-Pain stunned both the judges and viewers alike when he revealed himself as the voice behind the "monster" costume on *The Masked Singer*. Because he is widely known as the self-proclaimed "King of Auto-Tune," the judges had been unable to recognize his natural singing voice, preventing them from guessing his identity. FOX Image Collection/ Getty Images

skills practice

Communicating Immediacy
Using kinesics to communicate immediacy during interpersonal encounters

1 Initiate an encounter with someone you want to impress as an attentive and involved communicator (such as a new friend or potential romantic partner).

2 While talking, keep your facial expression pleasant. Don't be afraid to smile!

3 Make eye contact, especially while listening, but avoid prolonged staring.

4 Directly face the person, keep your back straight, lean forward, and keep your arms open and relaxed (rather than crossing them over your chest).

5 Use illustrators to enhance important descriptions, and regulators to control your exchange of turns.

serious, silly, or even sarcastic, and you can shift tone extremely rapidly to convey different emphases. For example, when talking with your friends, you can suddenly switch from your normal tone to a much more deeply chest-resonant tone to mimic a pompous politician, then nearly instantly constrict your airflow and make your voice sound more like SpongeBob SquarePants. In online communication, we use italics to convey tone change ("I can't *believe* you did that").

Pitch   Vocal pitch has to do with the frequency range of your voice—that is, how high or low it is. People oftentimes confuse pitch with tone, such as when someone speaks with very little pitch variation—hitting the same vocal "notes" repeatedly—and others describe them as "monotone." In fact, such "flat" voices are actually mono-*pitch*.

Across studies, people associate lower pitch with trustworthiness, competence, and dominance (McAleer et al., 2014). And although vocal pitch commonly is stereotyped as related to binary gender—women are presumed to use higher pitch than men—the truth is that differences in average pitch across genders are small (Krahé & Papakonstantinou, 2020). One study of conversational recordings involving 2,500 men and women found that the average vocal pitch for men was 111.9 Hz, whereas the average for women was 168.5 Hz (Berg et al., 2017)—meaning that although a small difference exists, *both* fall into the *same* pitch range defining baritone singers, tenor saxophones, and alto trombones.

self-reflection

Think about someone you know whose voice you find comforting, inspiring, or motivating. What is it about this person's voice that fosters your impression? What vocal characteristics differentiate the impressions?

Loudness   Loudness refers to how high or low your vocal volume is. Consider the following sentence: "Will John leave the room" (Searle, 1965). Say the sentence aloud, each time emphasizing a different word. Notice that emphasizing one word over another can alter the meaning from statement to question to command, depending on which word is emphasized ("WILL John leave the room" versus "Will JOHN leave the room").

Loudness affects meaning so powerfully that people mimic it online by USING CAPITAL LETTERS TO EMPHASIZE CERTAIN POINTS. Indeed, people who extensively cap are punished for being "too loud." For example, a member of a music website Steve routinely visits accidentally left his caps lock key on while posting, and all his messages were capped. Several other members immediately pounced, scolding him, "Stop shouting!"

Speech Rate   The final vocal characteristic is the speed at which you speak. Talking at a moderate and steady rate is often considered a critical technique for effective speaking. Public speaking educators urge students to slow down, and people in conversations often reduce their speech rate if they believe that their listeners don't understand them. But MIT computer science researcher Jean Krause found that speech rate is not the primary determinant of intelligibility (Krause, 2001). Instead, it's pronunciation and articulation of words. People who speak quickly but enunciate clearly are just as competent communicators as those who speak moderately or slowly.

COMMUNICATING THROUGH TOUCH

Using touch to communicate nonverbally is known as **haptics**, from the ancient Greek word *haptein*. Touch is likely the first sense we develop in the womb, and receiving touch is a critical part of infant development (Knapp & Hall, 2002). Infants deprived of affectionate touch walk and talk later than others and suffer impaired emotional development in adulthood (Montagu, 1971).

Touch can vary based on its duration, the situation, and the strength of contact, and these varieties influence how we interpret the physical contact (Floyd, 1999). Scholars distinguish between six types of touch. We use **functional-professional touch** to accomplish some type of task. Examples include touch between a physician and their patient, or when a yoga instructor corrects the alignment of a student working on a new pose. **Social-polite touch** derives from social norms and expectations. The most common form of social-polite touch in many cultures is the handshake, which has been practiced as a greeting in one form or another for over 2,000 years (Heslin, 1974). Other examples include light hugging between friends or relatives, and—in some cultures—the light cheek kiss. We rely on **friendship-warmth touch**—for example, gently grasping a friend's arm and giving it a squeeze—to express our liking for another person. **Love-intimacy touch**—cupping a romantic partner's face tenderly in your hands, giving him or her a big, lingering hug—lets you convey deep emotional feelings. **Sexual-arousal touch**, as the name implies, is intended to physically stimulate another person. Finally, **aggressive-hostile touch** involves forms of physical violence, like grabbing, slapping, and hitting—behaviors designed to hurt and humiliate others.

Cultural upbringing has a strong impact on how people use and perceive touch. Researchers in one study monitored casual conversations occurring in outdoor cafés in two different locales: San Juan, Puerto Rico, and London, England. They then averaged the number of touches between conversational partners. The people in San Juan touched each other an average of 180 times per hour. The average in London? Zero (Environmental Protection Agency, 2002).

Because people differ in the degree to which they feel comfortable giving and receiving touch, it's best to adapt your use of touch to others' preferences, employing more or less touch depending on your conversational partner's boundaries. If you are talking with someone who repeatedly touches your arm gently while talking (a form of social-polite touch), they may be comfortable with you reciprocating. When in doubt, ask. If a person offers you no touch at all, not even a greeting handshake, you would be wise to inhibit your touching.

COMMUNICATING THROUGH PERSONAL SPACE

The fourth nonverbal communication code, **proxemics** (from the Latin *proximus*, meaning "near"), is communication through the use of physical distance. Edward T. Hall, one of the first scholars to study proxemics, identified four communication distances: intimate, personal, social, and public (Hall, 1966). **Intimate space** ranges from 0 to 18 inches. Sharing intimate space with someone counts among the defining nonverbal features of close relationships (see Figure 9.1). **Personal space** ranges between 18 inches and 4 feet and is the distance we occupy during encounters with friends. For most people in the United States and Canada, personal space is about

In yoga classes, the boundaries of physical touch can be challenging to navigate for both instructors and students. "Consent cards" — small cards that say "yes" on one side and "no" on the other — have emerged as one solution, allowing students to communicate their touch preferences to their instructor. ©Molly Kitchen Yoga

LaunchPad Video
launchpadworks.com

Proxemics
Watch this clip online to answer the questions below.

When first meeting someone you are romantically interested in, which proxemics zones do you use? Why? In the video, what prompts the woman to place her coat on the empty chair next to her? What message is the man sending as he changes chairs?

Want to see more? Check out LaunchPad for a clip on **haptics**.

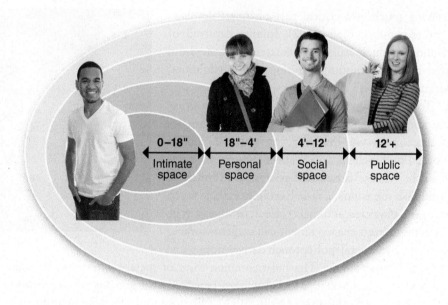

figure 9.1   **Physical Distance in Communication**
(Left to right) Flashon Studio/Shutterstock; Dasha Rusanenko/Shutterstock;
Rido/Shutterstock; Rob Byron/Shutterstock

focus on CULTURE

Touch and Distance

Cultures vary in their norms regarding appropriate touch and distance, some with lots of touching and close distance during interpersonal encounters and others with less (Hall, 1966). Often, these differences correlate with latitude and climate. People living in cooler climes tend to be low contact, and people living in warmer areas tend to be high contact (Andersen, 1997). The effect of climate on touch and distance is even present in countries that have both colder and hotter regions. Cindy, a former student, describes her experience juggling norms for touch and distance[2]:

I'm a Mexican American from El Paso, Texas, which is predominantly Latino. There, most everyone hugs hello and good-bye. And I'm not talking about a short slap on the back — I mean a nice encompassing *abrazo* (hug). While I can't say that strangers greet each other this way, I do recall times where I've done it. Growing up, it just seemed like touching is natural, and I never knew how much I expected it, maybe even relied on it, until I moved.

I came to Michigan as a grad student. My transition here was relatively smooth, but it was odd to me the first time I hung out with friends and didn't hug them hello and good-bye. A couple of times on instinct I did greet them this way, and I'll never forget the strange tension that was created. Some people readily hugged me back, but most were uneasy. Quickly I learned that touching was unacceptable.

Now I find that I hold back from engaging people in this manner. I feel like I'm hiding a part of myself, and it is frustrating. Nonetheless, this is the way things are done here, and I've had to adjust. Fortunately, I now have a few friends who recognize my need to express myself in this way and have opened themselves up to it. I'm grateful for that, and through these people a piece of me and my identity is saved.

discussion questions

- What has your culture taught you about the use of touch and distance? Are you a high- or low-contact person?
- When communicating with people from other cultures, how do you adapt your use of touch and distance?

[2]Cindy's narrative was provided voluntarily to the authors with full permission for publication.

your "wingspan"—that is, the distance from fingertip to fingertip when you extend your arms. **Social space** ranges from about 4 to 12 feet. Many people use it when communicating in the workplace or with acquaintances and strangers. In **public space**, the distance between persons ranges upward from 12 feet, including great distances; this span occurs most often during formal occasions, such as public speeches or college lectures.

In addition to the distance we each claim for ourselves during interpersonal encounters, we also have certain physical areas or spaces in our lives that we consider our turf. **Territoriality** is the tendency to claim physical spaces as our own and to define certain locations as areas we don't want others to invade without permission (Chen & Starosta, 2005). Human beings react negatively to others who invade their perceived territory, and we respond positively to those who respect it (King, 2001). Imagine coming back to your dorm room and finding one of your roommate's friends asleep in your bed. How would you respond? If you're like most people, you would feel angry and upset. Even though your roommate's friend is not violating your personal space (distance from your body), they are inappropriately encroaching on physical space that you consider your territory.

What can you do to become more sensitive to differences in the use of personal space? Keep in mind that North Americans' notions of personal space tend to be larger than those in most other cultures, especially Latin America and the Middle East. When interacting with people from other cultures, adjust your use of space in accordance with your conversational partner's preferences. Realize, also, that if you're from a culture that values large personal space, others will feel most comfortable interacting at a closer distance than you're accustomed to. If you insist on maintaining a large personal space bubble around yourself when interacting with people from other cultures, they may think you're aloof or distant or that you don't want to talk with them.

COMMUNICATING THROUGH PHYSICAL APPEARANCE

Fashion designer Thai Nguyen has crafted couture gowns for celebrities including Laverne Cox, Samira Wiley, Jennifer Lopez, and Katy Perry, but in the Netflix series *Say I Do*, he designs both wedding dresses and tuxedoes for couples who have overcome extraordinary economic and personal challenges to get married. Clothing couples in couture isn't just about superficial allure. Instead, the choice of dress and accessories for the participants conveys powerful communicative messages to others about the couples' identities and emotions. As Nguyen describes, "it's a symbol of their love; it's a symbol of their life story" (Nicolau, 2020).

Although weddings are an extreme example in terms of the emphasis placed on how we look, our **physical appearance** influences all our interpersonal encounters. In simple terms, how you look conveys as much about you as what you say. Standards of physical attractiveness are highly variable—both across cultures and across time periods—but people credit individuals they find physically attractive with higher levels of intelligence, persuasiveness, poise, sociability, warmth, power, and employment success (Hatfield & Sprecher, 1986).

self-reflection

Which locations in your physical spaces at home and work do you consider your most valued territories? How do you communicate this territoriality to others? What do you do when people trespass? Have your reactions to such trespasses caused negative personal or professional consequences?

🔻 On *Say I Do*, a bride's dress is not merely a fashion statement but a statement about who she is as a person. Similarly, your daily physical appearance is a form of nonverbal communication that expresses how you want others to see you. Thai Nguyen Atelier

This effect holds in online environments as well. For example, the physical attractiveness of friends who post their photos on your Facebook page affects people's perceptions of *your* attractiveness (Walther et al., 2008). That is, if you have attractive friends' photos on your page, people will perceive you as more physically and socially attractive.

Your clothing also has a profound impact on others' perceptions of you. Decades of research suggests that clothing strongly influences people's judgments about profession, level of education, socioeconomic status, and even personality and personal values (Burgoon et al., 1996). The effect that clothing has on perception makes it essential that you consider the appropriateness of your dress, the context for which you are dressing, and the image of self you wish to nonverbally communicate. When Steve worked for a Seattle trucking company, he was expected to wear clothes that could withstand rough treatment. On his first day, he "dressed to impress" and was teased by coworkers and management for dressing as if he were an executive at a large corporation. But expectations like this can change in other situations. During job interviews, for example, dress as nicely as you can. Being even moderately formally dressed is one of the strongest predictors of whether an interviewer will perceive you as socially skilled and highly motivated (Gifford et al., 1985).

COMMUNICATING THROUGH OBJECTS

Take a moment to examine the objects that you're wearing and that surround you: your phone case, buttons on a backpack, posters on the wall, accessories like watches or jewelry, and so forth. These **artifacts**—the things we possess that influence how we see ourselves and that we use to express our identity to others—constitute another code of nonverbal communication. As with our use of posture and of personal space, we use artifacts to communicate power and status. For example, by displaying expensive watches, cars, or living spaces, people "tell" others that they're wealthy and influential (Burgoon et al., 1996).

COMMUNICATING THROUGH THE ENVIRONMENT

A final way we communicate nonverbally is through our **environment**, the physical features of our surroundings. Two types of environmental factors play a role in shaping interpersonal communication: fixed features and semifixed features (Hall, 1981). *Fixed features* are stable and unchanging environmental elements, such as walls, ceilings, floors, and doors. Fixed features define the size of a particular environment, and size has an enormous emotional and communicative impact on people. For example, the size of structures communicates power, with bigger often being better. In corporations, it's frequently assumed that larger offices equal greater power for their occupants; and historically, the square footage of homes has communicated the occupant's degree of wealth.

Semifixed features are impermanent and usually easy to change; they include furniture, lighting, and color. We associate bright lighting with environments that are very active and soft lighting with environments that are calmer and more intimate. Color also exerts a powerful effect on our mood and communication: we experience blues and greens as relaxing, yellows and oranges as arousing and energizing, reds and blacks as sensuous, and grays and browns as depressing (Burgoon et al., 1996).

▽ Author, consultant, and Netflix star Marie Kondo helps her clients organize their physical spaces — and in so doing, she helps them organize their lives. She gained international fame for her philosophy which emphasizes that people should only keep items that "spark joy." M. K. Sadler

Now that we've reviewed the different types—or "codes"—of nonverbal communication, let's shift our focus from description to function; specifically, the purposes that nonverbal communication serves in our everyday lives. We will explore how nonverbal communication helps us express emotion, convey meanings, present ourselves to others, manage interactions, and define intimacy.

Functions of Nonverbal Communication

How we use nonverbal behaviors in communication

Triumph. Exultation. Unbridled joy. These meanings are communicated from every aspect of Brandi Chastain's nonverbal expression. On July 10, 1999, Chastain scored the penalty kick that earned the United States the Women's World Cup victory. As tens of millions of viewers watched, she tore off her jersey and dropped to her knees. But even as Chastain celebrated, her decision to communicate in this manner sparked controversy. Although male players routinely removed and waved their jerseys to mark victories, female players weren't supposed to present themselves publicly in this way. As Faye Wattleton, president of the Center for Advancement of Women, notes, a substantial double standard exists: what's acceptable nonverbally for men is often viewed with "collective horror" when women do it. In the aftermath, Chastain's choice would ignite public consternation, influence fashion, and alter athletic rules. Photos appeared on the covers of *TIME*, *Newsweek*, and *Sports Illustrated*. A man on the street confronted Chastain, demanding, "Why did you do that!? I can't let my daughter walk around in a jogging bra!" Some pundits suggested that the gesture was a marketing ploy: the sports bra Chastain wore displayed Nike's trademark "swoosh." In the fashion season that followed, sports-bra sales skyrocketed. And soccer officials banned the "tearing off the jersey" gesture—for women *and* men.

In 2012, ESPN conducted an online poll of the "greatest moment in U.S. women's sports." The Women's World Cup victory was the overwhelming winner. But even though it's been more than two decades since this iconic event, people still question Chastain about her behavior, interpreting it in ways other than what she intended. As she notes, "Everybody is going to have their opinion about it. . . . But it was just a 'YES!' Twenty-something years of playing the game, and this was the most perfect moment."

Like Chastain, when we're caught up in an emotional moment, good or bad, we think of our nonverbal expression as something that just happens, a simple and direct reflection of our inner states. But nonverbal communication serves *many* different functions in our lives. Within interpersonal encounters, nonverbal communication serves at least five functions: it expresses emotions, conveys meanings, presents ourselves to others, helps manage interactions, and defines relationships (Argyle, 1969).

⏷ This photo was taken immediately after Brandi Chastain scored the penalty kick that won the 1999 World Cup. The gesture of tearing off her jersey and falling to her knees communicated many intense emotions and started a media controversy — all without her saying a word.
ROBERTO SCHMIDT/AFP/Getty Images

EXPRESSING EMOTION

When Brandi Chastain described her nonverbal behavior as being "just a 'YES!' " she highlighted arguably the most elemental function of nonverbal communication: the expression of emotion. We communicate emotion nonverbally through

affect displays—intentional or unintentional nonverbal behaviors that display actual or feigned emotions (Burgoon et al., 1996). In everyday interactions, affect displays are presented primarily through the face and voice. Intentional use of the face to communicate emotion begins during late infancy, when babies learn to facially communicate anger and happiness to get what they want (Burgoon et al., 1996). Unintentional affect displays begin even earlier. Infants in the first few weeks of life instinctively and reflexively display facial expressions of distress, disgust, and interest. As adults, we communicate hundreds, if not thousands, of real and faked emotional states with our faces.

People also use vocalics to convey emotions. Consider how you communicate love through your voice. What changes do you make in pitch, tone, volume, and speech rate? How does your "loving" voice differ from your "angry" voice? Most people express emotions such as grief and love through lowered vocal pitch, and hostile emotions—such as anger and contempt—through loudness (Costanzo et al., 1969). Pitch conveys emotion so powerfully that the source of the sound (human voice or other) is irrelevant, and words aren't necessary. Researcher Klaus Scherer (1974) mimicked voice patterns on a music synthesizer and had listeners judge the emotion conveyed. Participants strongly associated high pitch with emotions such as anger, fear, and surprise, and they linked low pitch with pleasantness, boredom, and sadness.

At the same time, keep in mind that cultures have very different *display rules*: guidelines for when, where, and how to manage emotion displays appropriately (discussed in Chapter 5). This means that people unfamiliar with a particular culture's display rules may be less accurate at understanding nonverbal communication among members of that culture. For example, researchers comparing Japanese and Dutch people's ability to perceive nonverbal expressions of anger, fear, disgust, sadness, and surprise found that members of both cultures were substantially better at identifying the expressions of people from their own culture (Yoshie & Sauter, 2019).

CONVEYING MEANINGS

In the wake of her triumph, much of the debate regarding Chastain centered around what she "meant" by her behavior. Was she making a "feminist statement"? Was it a "marketing ploy"?

Just as we use words to signify unique meanings, we often use nonverbal communication to directly convey meanings. Your boss flips you a thumbs-up gesture following a presentation, and you know they mean "Good job!" A friend makes a two-finger *V* at a campus rally, and you recognize it as an emblem for peace.

At other times we use nonverbal communication more indirectly, as a means for accenting or augmenting verbal communication meanings (Malandro & Barker, 1983). We do this in five ways, the first of which is by *reiterating*. Nonverbal communication is used to reiterate or repeat verbal messages, as when you say "Up!" and then point upward. Second, we *contradict* our verbal messages with our nonverbal communication. For example, a friend may ask if you're angry, but you respond by scowling and angrily shouting, "No, I'm not angry!" Third, we use nonverbal communication to *enhance* the meaning of verbal messages, such as when you whisper an intimate "I love you" while smiling and offering a gentle touch to emphasize the point. Fourth, we sometimes use nonverbal communication to *replace* verbal expressions, such as when you shake your head instead of saying no. Finally, we use nonverbal communication to *spotlight* certain parts of verbal messages, such as when you increase the loudness of just one word: "STOP hitting your brother with that lightsaber!"

PRESENTING SELF

Think about your interactions with your manager at work. How do you let them know—without words—that you're a dedicated and hardworking employee? Chances are, you employ almost all the nonverbal codes previously discussed, simultaneously. You convey attentiveness through focused eye contact and a pleasant facial expression, and you communicate seriousness through moderate speech rate and pitch. You also dress appropriately for the office and try to follow workplace norms regarding how you decorate your workspace.

Now imagine that your manager confides in you a recent diagnosis of terminal illness. How would you use nonverbal communication to convey a different self—one who's compassionate and supportive? You'd likely adopt a facial expression conveying sadness and concern. You'd slow your speech rate and lower the pitch of your voice to convey empathy. You'd decrease your interpersonal distance to communicate support.

As these examples suggest, nonverbal communication can help us present different aspects of our self to others. We all use nonverbal communication codes to create our identities during interpersonal encounters. An important part of being a competent nonverbal communicator is recognizing the need to shift our nonverbal communication quickly to present ourselves in different ways when the situation demands—for example, dedicated employee one moment, concerned fellow human being another.

MANAGING INTERACTIONS

Nonverbal communication also helps us manage interpersonal interactions. For example, during conversations, we use regulators, eye contact, touch, smiling, head nods, and shifts in posture to signal who gets to speak and for how long (Patterson, 1988). While chatting with a friend, you probably look at them anywhere from 30 to 50 percent of your talk time. Then when you're approaching the end of your conversational turn, you invite your friend to talk by decreasing your pitch and loudness, stopping any gestures, and focusing your gaze on the other person. As your friend begins speaking, you now look at your partner almost 100 percent of their talk time, nodding your head to show you're listening (Goodwin, 1981).

During conversations, we also read our partners' nonverbal communication to check their level of interest in what we're saying—watching for signals like eye contact, smiles, and head nods. Yet we're usually unaware that we're doing this until people behave in unexpected ways. For example, if a partner *fails* to react to something we've said that we consider provocative or funny, we may narrow our eyes or frown to express our displeasure nonverbally.

Nonverbal communication also helps us regulate others' attention and behavior. For example, a sudden glance and stern facial expression from a parent or babysitter can stop a child from reaching for the forbidden cookie jar. When our sons were young, their elementary school principal gained students' attention by clapping

For romantic couples, the level of nonverbal involvement is a direct indicator of the relationship's health.
Drazen_/Getty Images

loudly and holding up her hand with the request to "give me five." Students responded by holding up their "high five" hands as they fell silent to hear the announcement.

DEFINING INTIMACY

One crucial function nonverbal communication serves is to create **intimacy**, the feeling of closeness and "union" that exists between us and our partners (Mashek & Aron, 2004). For example, in her novel *Written on the Body*, acclaimed British author Jeanette Winterson (1993) offers a vivid and poignant description of how the nonverbal code of touch defines intimacy:

Articulacy of fingers, the language of the deaf. Who taught you to write on my back? Who taught you to use your hands as branding irons? You have scored your name into my shoulders, referenced me with your mark. The pads of your fingers have become printing blocks, you tap a message on to my skin, tap meaning into my body. Your Morse code interferes with my heart beat. I had a steady heart before I met you, I relied upon it, it had seen active service and grown strong. Now you alter its pace with your rhythm, you play upon me, drumming me taut. (p. 89)

But intimacy isn't defined solely through touch. Physical closeness; shared gaze; soft voices; relaxed postures; sharing of personal objects; and, of course, spending time together—each of these nonverbal behaviors highlights and enhances intimacy. Consider just a few specifics. Smiling and gazing are associated with intimacy (Floyd & Burgoon, 1999), something vividly illustrated in the Beaver family photo in our chapter opening. Individuals share more personal space with intimates and liked others than with strangers, and use proximity to convey affection (Floyd & Morman, 1999). Studies that have instructed people

self-QUIZ

Test Your Nonverbal Intimacy

Each of these nonverbal behaviors is commonly used between relational partners to communicate intimacy. The more of them that regularly are shared, the more intimate the relationship! Read each item and count the number you share with your partner.

_____ Sharing mutual gaze

_____ Smiling at one another

_____ Warm vocal tones

_____ Close physical proximity

_____ Positive touch

_____ Giving and exchanging gifts

_____ Spending time together

_____ Sharing laughter

_____ Leaning forward

_____ Affirming head nods

Information in this self-quiz from Andersen et al. (2006).

Scoring: 0–3: low intimacy, 4–6: moderate, 7–10: high

to communicate liking to others have found that the primary way people do so is through increasing gaze, smiling, and leaning forward (Palmer & Simmons, 1995). Conversely, one can communicate lack of intimacy and greater formality through distance, lack of eye contact, decreased vocal expressiveness, precise articulation, and tense postures (Burgoon & Hoobler, 2002).

Research documents that when it comes to expressing affection and intimacy, people rely more upon nonverbal than verbal communication. As a consequence, more intimate relationships—particularly romantic bonds—show higher levels of nonverbal involvement across all the codes (more eye contact, more touch, more smiling, closer distance, etc.), and the level of nonverbal involvement is a direct indicator of the relationship's health (Andersen et al., 2006).

Competently Managing Your Nonverbal Communication

Ways to improve your nonverbal expression

As you interact with others, you use various nonverbal communication codes naturally and simultaneously. Similarly, you take in and interpret others' nonverbal communication instinctively. Look again at the Beaver family photo at the beginning of this chapter. While viewing this image, you probably don't think, "What's Samson's mouth doing?" or "Gee, Frances's arm is touching Samson's shoulder." When it comes to nonverbal communication, although all the parts are important, the overall package delivers the message.

Given the nature of nonverbal communication, we think it's important to highlight some general guidelines for how you can competently manage your nonverbal communication. In this chapter, we've offered very specific advice for improving your use of particular nonverbal codes. But we conclude with three principles for competent nonverbal conduct, which reflect the three aspects of competence first introduced in Chapter 1: effectiveness, appropriateness, and ethics.

First, when interacting with others, remember that people view your nonverbal communication as at least as important as what you say, if not more so. Although you should endeavor to build your active listening skills (Chapter 7) and use of cooperative language (Chapter 8), bear in mind that people will often assign the greatest weight to what you do nonverbally.

Second, be sensitive to the demands of interpersonal situations. For example, if an interaction seems to call for more formal or more casual behavior, adapt your nonverbal communication accordingly. Remind yourself, if necessary, that being interviewed for a job, sharing a relaxed evening with your roommate, and deepening the level of intimacy in a love relationship all call for different nonverbal messages. You can craft those messages through careful use of the many different nonverbal codes available to you.

Finally, remember that verbal communication and nonverbal communication flow with each other. Your experience of nonverbal communication from others and your nonverbal expression to others are fundamentally fused with the words you and they choose to use. As a consequence, you cannot become a skilled interpersonal communicator by focusing time, effort, and energy on only verbal or only nonverbal elements. Instead, you must devote yourself to both because it is only when both are joined as a union of skills that more competent interpersonal communication ability is achieved.

Dealing with Mixed Messages

 **LaunchPad** For the best experience, complete all parts of this activity
in LaunchPad: **launchpadworks.com**

1 Background

Receiving mixed messages — when verbal and nonverbal communication clash — is a common dilemma in relationships. To explore ways to deal with mixed messages, read the case study in Part 2; then, drawing on all you know about interpersonal communication, work through the problem-solving model in Part 3.

 Visit LaunchPad to watch the video in Part 4 and assess your communication in Part 5.

2 Case Study

You, Dakota, and Tad are good friends. On the occasions that the three of you are not hanging out together, you're in touch through text messages, Instagram, and so on. Despite your collective closeness, romance has never arisen. This is partly because the three of you have always been involved with other people.

Over the past six months, however, you've all been through breakups. In the wake of this, things have started to get weird. It began a few weeks ago, when the three of you met for lunch. Dakota was all dressed up, and when you asked, "What's the occasion?" she was evasive. She kept leaning toward Tad, making extensive eye contact, smiling, touching his arm and leg (although each instance seemed accidental), and even suggested that she and he take more classes together next semester. You're pleased, because you like the two of them immensely and think they'd make a good couple. Tad, however, seems completely clueless, which is not surprising; it has long been a joke between the three of you that Tad can't tell when someone is hitting on him.

After lunch, you corner Tad and say, "Dakota is totally crushing on you!" Tad is shocked and adamantly denies it. He is so persuasive that you begin to doubt your own observations. You decide to email Dakota. The two of you have always been honest and open with each other, so you tell Dakota what you saw. She responds with a teasing, "As if I'd ever crush on Tad ;)!" Now you're *really* confused.

In the days that follow, you increasingly sense that Dakota wants a romantic involvement with Tad. Everything about her nonverbal communication suggests intimacy. But whenever you raise the issue, Dakota denies it, responding, "You've got an overactive imagination." You begin to become irked by the mixed messages. Are you really imagining things? Should you push her to tell you the truth? Making matters worse, Tad has finally clued into her behavior, and he confides to you that although he's worried about getting burned again (his breakup with his ex, Jessica, was ugly), he is starting to fall for Dakota.

Later that evening, you get a call from Dakota. After chatting for a few minutes, the issue of Tad comes up. Dakota says, "I know I've been dodging your questions about Tad, but . . . do you think he likes me?"

Your Turn

Consider all you've learned thus far about interpersonal communication. Then work through the following five steps. Remember, there are no "right" answers, so think hard about what is the *best* choice! (P.S. Need help? See the *Helpful Concepts* list.)

step 1

Reflect on yourself. What are your thoughts and feelings in this situation? What attributions are you making about Dakota, based on her interpersonal communication? Are your attributions accurate? Why or why not?

step 2

Reflect on your partner. Using perspective-taking and empathic concern, put yourself in Dakota's shoes. What is she thinking and feeling in this situation?

step 3

Identify the optimal outcome. Think about all the information you have regarding Dakota, Tad, and their relationship, as well as what role, if any, you should

have in this situation. Given all these factors, what's the best, most constructive relationship outcome possible? Be sure to consider not just what's best for you (as their friend) but what's best for Dakota and Tad as well.

step 4

Locate the roadblocks. Taking into consideration your own thoughts and feelings, those of Dakota and Tad, and all that has happened in this situation, what obstacles are keeping you from achieving the optimal outcome?

step 5

Chart your course. What can you say to Dakota to overcome the roadblocks you've identified and achieve your optimal outcome?

HELPFUL CONCEPTS

The ambiguity of nonverbal communication, **232**
Mixed messages, **232**
Immediacy, **238**
Friendship-warmth touch, **241**
Intimacy, **248**

The Other Side

Visit LaunchPad to watch a video in which Dakota tells her side of the case study story. As in many real-life situations, this is information to which you did not have access when you were initially crafting your response in Part 3. The video reminds us that even when we do our best to offer competent responses, there is always another side to the story that we need to consider.

Interpersonal Competence Self-Assessment

After watching the video, visit the Self-Assessment questions in LaunchPad. Think about the new information offered in Dakota's side of the story and all you've learned about interpersonal communication. Drawing on this knowledge, revisit your earlier responses in Part 3 and assess your interpersonal communication competence.

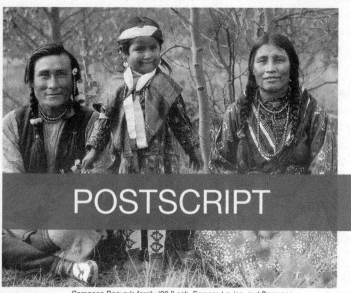

POSTSCRIPT

Sampson Beaver's family '06 [Leah, Frances Louise, and Sampson Beaver], 1906, Whyte Museum of the Canadian Rockies, Mary Schaffer fonds (V527/ps1-05)

Reflect on the postures, dress, use of space, eye contact, and facial expressions depicted in the Beaver family photo. Then think about how nonverbal communication shapes your life. What judgments do you make about others, based on their scowls and smiles? Their posture? Their appearance and voice? Do you draw accurate conclusions about people based on their nonverbal communication? How do others see you? As you communicate with others throughout a typical day, what do your facial expressions, posture, dress, use of space, and eye contact convey?

We began this chapter with a family of smiles. The smile is one of the simplest, most commonplace expressions. Yet like so many nonverbal expressions, the smile has the power to fundamentally shift interpersonal perceptions. In the case of the Beaver family, seeing the smiles that talking with a friend evoked more than 100 years ago helps, in a small way, to diminish more than a century of stereotypes about Native American people. But the power of the Beaver family's smiles goes beyond simply remedying historical prejudice. It highlights the power that even your simplest nonverbal communication has in shaping and shifting others' perceptions of you.

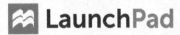 **LaunchPad**

LaunchPad for *Reflect & Relate* offers videos and encourages self-assessment through adaptive quizzing. Go to **launchpadworks.com** to get access to:

✓ LearningCurve
Adaptive Quizzes

 Video clips that help you understand interpersonal communication

key terms

 You can watch brief, illustrative videos of these terms and test your understanding of the concepts in LaunchPad.

key concepts

Describing Nonverbal Communication

- **Nonverbal communication** includes all unspoken behavioral displays and generally carries more meaning than verbal communication.
- Both culture and gender shape people's perceptions and use of nonverbal communication.

Nonverbal Communication Codes

- Although seven different **nonverbal communication codes** exist, the behaviors that most people associate with nonverbal communication — such as facial expressions, gestures, and body posture — are **kinesics**. Four different forms of gestures are commonly used: **emblems**, **illustrators**, **regulators**, and **adaptors**.
- Something as seemingly simple as body posture can communicate substantial information regarding **immediacy** and **power** to others.
- Different features of the voice contribute to the nonverbal code of **vocalics**.
- People vary their duration, placement, and strength of touch (known as **haptics**) to communicate a range of meanings, including **functional-professional touch**, **social-polite touch**, **friendship-warmth touch**, **love-intimacy touch**, **sexual-arousal touch**, and **aggressive-hostile touch**.
- Forms of physical distance, or **proxemics**, include **intimate**, **personal**, **social**, and **public space**. All human beings experience **territoriality** and resent perceived invasions of personal domains.
- Like it or not, our **physical appearance** strongly molds others' impressions of us.
- We use personal **artifacts** to portray who we are to others and to communicate information regarding our worth, status, and power.
- Features of our physical **environment** — such as furnishings — also send distinct messages about status and mood.

Functions of Nonverbal Communication

- Our nonverbal communication serves many purposes. One of the most common is **affect displays**, which function to show others how we are feeling.
- We can harness all the nonverbal communication codes to send powerful messages of **intimacy** to others.

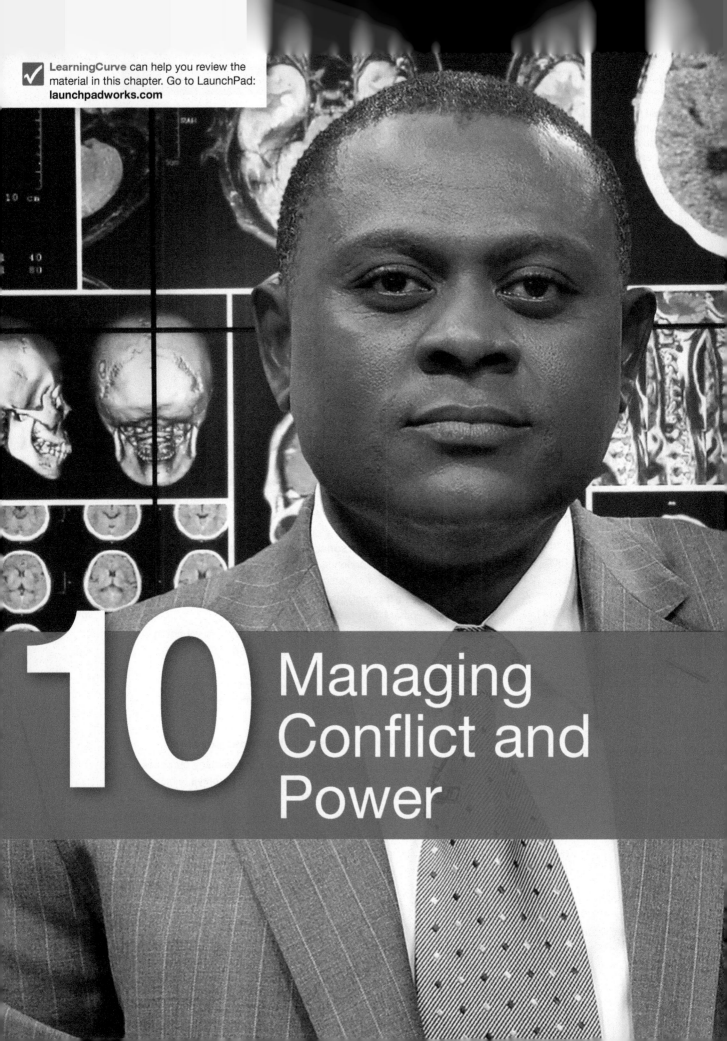

10

Managing Conflict and Power

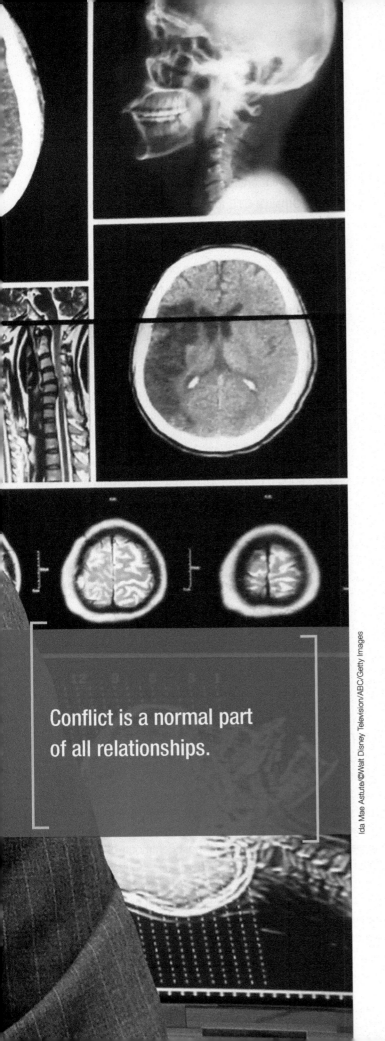

Conflict is a normal part of all relationships.

Ida Mae Astute/©Walt Disney Television/ABC/Getty Images

When forensic pathologist

Bennet Omalu examined a deceased football player's brain, he had no idea that his story would soon become the Hollywood movie *Concussion*, or that his findings would place him in conflict with professional peers and a multibillion-dollar sports industry.[1] Omalu didn't even really know what football was: "I grew up in Africa, in Nigeria. I thought football players were extraterrestrials, going to Mars or something, with headgears and shoulder pads!"

Omalu was in his office late on a Friday night in the fall of 2002, munching on an apple, when he made his initial discovery: the deceased player's brain tissue was deeply damaged, in ways similar to, yet distinct from, Alzheimer's disease, as well as another form of dementia suffered by professional boxers commonly called punch drunk syndrome. What he saw was CTE: *chronic* ("long-term") *traumatic* ("associated with trauma") *encephalopathy* ("a bad brain"). But diagnosing CTE in a professional football player (along with his colleague Dr. Julian Bailes) immediately placed Omalu in conflict with those supportive of football, including his professional peers and the NFL. As he describes, "I was excited. I thought the football industry would be happy. I thought naïvely that they would embrace it to enhance the game and the lives of the players." Instead, a battle began: they perceived him as attacking the game itself.

---

[1]Information in this chapter opener is from M. Kirk (March 25, 2013), Interview with Bennet Omalu, PBS Frontline, https://www.pbs.org/wgbh/pages/frontline/sports /league-of-denial/the-frontline-interview-dr-bennet-omalu/; and from J. M. Laskas (September 14, 2009), Bennet Omalu, concussions, and the NFL: How one doctor changed football forever, *GQ*, https://www.gq.com/story/nfl-players-brain -dementia-study-memory-concussions.

When Omalu submitted his results to a scientific journal for publication, he expected it to be critiqued by two reviewers—the standard practice—but the journal had more than *eighteen* scholars criticize his paper. Reviewers offered comments such as, "Correct me if I'm wrong, but this threatens the very heart of football!" and "You're attacking the American way of life!" And although scientific review is supposed to be "blind" (critics do not know the author's identity), several reviewers snooped Omalu's identity and personally attacked him: "How dare you, a foreigner from Nigeria? Who do you think you are to come to tell us how to live our lives?" Omalu ended up writing *hundreds* of pages of rebuttals to their criticisms before the article was published.

And yet, publication still didn't resolve the conflict. A group of NFL doctors publicly denounced his research as "fraud," and demanded retraction of his article. One even implied that Omalu was practicing "voodoo" instead of science. As he fought to defend his integrity, Omalu grew weary: "I told my younger sister that I'm getting tired, and she called me out immediately, saying, 'No, Bennet. You think it's by chance that this is happening? Everybody has a calling, and God gives you a cross to bear because he knows you can bear that cross. With your knowledge, you can help these people!'"

Soon thereafter, numerous scholars corroborated Omalu's CTE football findings, and he was vindicated. In the aftermath, CTE gained visibility worldwide as a condition affecting athletes across a broad range of sports, and everyone from little leagues to the NCAA began taking steps to combat it. As neuropathologist and Alzheimer's researcher Peter Davies noted, "The credit must go to Bennet Omalu, because he first reported this and nobody believed him, and I'm included in that. But when I looked at the stuff, he was absolutely right."

Omalu himself always believed that the goal should be collaboration toward forging a cooperative solution, rather than adversarial competition. His goal now is to work with the football industry to cure CTE. "Why not? You pop a pill before you play, a medicine that prevents the damage. This is how we now need to talk. Not this back-and-forth of human selfishness. Anybody still denying CTE is out of his mind. The issue now is treatment. That is my next step, now that I understand the disease."

The story of Bennet Omalu echoes conflicts we all have encountered in our own lives. Each of us has experienced situations in which our goals or actions were perceived by others as attacking their interests, provoking a clash. Many of us have also had to interact with people who lashed out at us defensively, or wielded power in an attempt to get us to give up what we want. And in such situations, we often end up feeling a sense of deep despair just as Bennet Omalu did before his sister inspired him to persevere. The words people most commonly associate with interpersonal conflict are *destruction*, *heartache*, and *hopelessness* (Wilmot & Hocker, 2010).

Yet conflicts don't have to be hopeless, because we're not helpless. Each of us has the ability to choose constructive approaches to managing conflicts that will help create positive outcomes for everyone involved—finding a mutually satisfactory "cure," as with Bennet Omalu's current quest.

In this chapter, we explore interpersonal conflict and how best to manage it. You'll learn:

- The nature of conflict
- The role power plays in conflict
- Different approaches for handling interpersonal conflict
- The impact of gender, culture, and technology on conflict
- Resolutions and long-term outcomes of conflict
- The challenges to resolving conflict in close relationships, and how to overcome them

We begin by exploring the nature of conflict.

Conflict and Interpersonal Communication

Most conflicts occur between people who know each other

We like to think of conflict as unusual, an unpleasant exception to the normal routine of our relationships. Each conflict seems freshly painful and unprecedented. "I can't believe it!" we text, "We had a *terrible* fight last night!" Friends reply back supportive messages echoing our shock: "OMG, really?!" Observing other couples, we judge their relationships by how much they fight: couples who argue too much are "doomed to fail," whereas those who rarely disagree must be "blissfully happy."

But such beliefs are mistaken. Conflict is a normal part of *all* relationships (Canary, 2003). Dealing with other human beings (and their unique goals, preferences, and opinions) means regularly having your wants and needs run up against theirs, triggering disputes (Malis & Roloff, 2006). On average, people report seven conflicts a week, mostly with relatives, friends, and romantic partners with whom they've argued before (Benoit & Benoit, 1990). Thus, the challenge you face is not how to avoid conflict, or how to live a conflict-free life, but how to constructively manage the conflicts that *will* arise in your interpersonal relationships. To learn how to do this, let's begin by defining conflict and examining four characteristics that most conflicts share.

WHAT IS CONFLICT?

Almost any issue can spark conflict—money, time, sex, religion, politics, love, chores, and so on—and almost anyone can get into a conflict: family members, friends, lovers, coworkers, or casual acquaintances. Despite such variations, all conflicts share similar attributes. **Conflict** is the process that occurs when people perceive that they have incompatible goals or that someone is interfering in their ability to achieve their objectives (Wilmot & Hocker, 2010). Four features characterize most conflicts: they begin with perception, they involve clashes in goals or behaviors, they unfold over time as a process, and they are dynamic.

Conflict Begins with Perception   Conflict occurs when people perceive incompatible goals or actions (Roloff & Soule, 2002). Because conflict begins with perception, perceptual errors (see Chapter 3) shape how our conflicts unfold.

As we'll discuss later in this chapter, we blame others more than ourselves during conflicts, and perceive others as uncooperative and ourselves as helpful. These self-enhancing errors can lead us to manage conflict in ways that create unsatisfying outcomes.

Conflict Involves Clashes in Goals or Behaviors   At the heart of conflicts are clashes in goals or behaviors (Zacchilli et al., 2009). Some conflicts revolve around incompatible goals, ranging from everyday leisure activity disputes ("I want to go out dancing" versus "I want to stay home and play video games") to serious arguments regarding personal values ("I want our children to be raised Jewish!" versus "I want them to be Catholic!"). Other disputes arise when one person's actions clash with another's. A friend texts you repeatedly while you're studying, and you hastily text a snarky reply; your manager demands that you work over a holiday weekend, and you refuse.

Conflict Is a Process   Although people often describe conflict as a series of unrelated events ("I sent them this carefully crafted email, and for no reason, they went off on me!"), conflict is a process that unfolds over time. Its course is determined by the communication choices we make: everything we say and do during a conflict influences everything our partner says and does, and vice versa.

Moreover, most conflicts proceed through several stages, each involving decisions and actions that affect the conflict's direction and consequences for the individuals involved. In its most basic form, the process of conflict involves people perceiving that a conflict exists, choosing an approach for handling the conflict, and then dealing with the subsequent conflict resolutions and outcomes. Conflict is not a singular, independent event: how you handle a conflict with someone will influence your future interactions and relationship with that person.

Conflict Is Dynamic   Because conflict typically unfolds over a series of exchanged messages, it is ever changing and unpredictable. Research looking at the dynamic nature of conflict finds that in 66.4 percent of disputes, the focus shifts substantially as the conflict progresses (Keck & Samp, 2007). A fight over your father's snide remark regarding your job quickly becomes a battle about his chronic disapproval of you. Or a dispute regarding your roommate eating your leftovers becomes an argument about their failure to be a supportive friend. When a conflict shifts topic, it can devolve into **kitchen-sinking** (from the expression, "throwing everything at them but the kitchen sink"), in which combatants hurl insults and accusations at each other that have little to do with the original disagreement. For example, a couple fighting over whether one of them was flirting with their server at a restaurant may say things like: "What about the time you completely forgot our anniversary?!" and "Oh yeah?! Well, at least my family is intelligent!"

Since conflict often dynamically branches out into other troublesome topics, managing conflict is extremely challenging—you can never fully anticipate the twists and turns that will occur. But remember: you have total control over what *you* say and do, and that can influence how someone responds. If you think a conflict is getting completely off track, choose your communication carefully to help bring it back on topic, or take a time-out until you can attempt to do so.

CONFLICT IN RELATIONSHIPS

Most conflicts occur between people who know each other and are involved in close relationships, such as romantic partners, friends, family members, and coworkers (Benoit & Benoit, 1990). Unlike people who don't know each other well, people in close relationships experience prolonged contact and frequent interaction, which set the stage for disagreements over goals and behaviors.

In close relationships, conflicts typically arise from one of three issues (Peterson, 2002): *irritating partner behaviors* (e.g., a family member has an annoying personal habit, or your partner interrupts you while you're working), *disagreements regarding relationship rules* (e.g., you and your partner disagree about texting with ex-partners, or family members disagree about inviting friends on family vacations), and *personality clashes* (e.g., you have a sunny disposition but your friend is a complainer, or you're ambitious and organized but your partner is carefree and cluttered).

Relationship partners often develop consistent patterns of communication for dealing with conflict that either promote or undermine their happiness. For example, happily married couples are more likely than unhappily married couples to avoid personal attacks during conflicts and instead focus their discussion on the differences at hand (Peterson, 2002). Such patterns are self-perpetuating: happy couples remain motivated to behave in ways guaranteed to keep them happy, and because they believe they can solve their problems, they are more likely to work together to resolve conflict (Caughlin & Vangelisti, 2000). In contrast, dissatisfied couples often choose to avoid important conflicts. Their failure to deal directly with their problems further fuels their unhappiness (Afifi et al., 2009).

Managing conflicts in close relationships presents unique challenges. We feel connected to our intimate partners, and disputes threaten that sense of connection (Berscheid, 2002). *Your conflicts with loved ones are guaranteed to be intense and emotionally draining experiences.* Conflicts also powerfully affect your *future* encounters and relationships. For example, if you and a sibling fight via text message, this conflict will shape not only how the two of you will communicate when you meet again, but also how you'll feel about your relationship moving forward. As scholar Donald Peterson (2002) notes, "Every conflict and every resolution, as well as every failure at resolution, becomes a part of your overall relationship history" (p. 363).

Now that we've discussed the nature of conflict, let's delve into the issue of power, and how it's related to conflict, gender, and culture.

self-
reflection

Think of a relational partner with whom you have the same conflict over and over again. What effect does this conflict have on your relationship? In what ways do you contribute to its continuance? How might you change your communication to end this repetitive cycle?

Power and Conflict

> Power influences who will prevail in conflicts

In the *Kill Bill* movies (2003, 2004), Beatrix Kiddo (played by Uma Thurman) is one of *the* most iconic film characters ever: a cinematic symbol of female empowerment (Dowd, 2018). But even as Beatrix fought on-screen against antagonists seeking her demise, Thurman herself was suffering real-world abuses of power by *Kill Bill* producer Harvey Weinstein and director Quentin Tarantino. In the years prior to filming, Weinstein had repeatedly tried to sexually coerce Thurman; he even physically attacked her at one point. When she threatened to go public about his behavior, Weinstein countered that he would ruin her career. It wasn't until the 2017 #MeToo movement—and Weinstein's downfall—that Thurman finally felt safe enough to disclose her experiences. Additionally, she endured a near-fatal abuse of power on the set of *Kill Bill*. Prior to filming one of the final scenes in which Beatrix races her convertible toward a climactic showdown with Bill, Thurman realized that driving the car would be unsafe. The driver's seat wasn't properly bolted down and the road itself was unstable sand. Thurman refused to do the drive—telling Tarantino that she wanted a stunt driver to handle it. Furious, Tarantino responded, "You need to hit 40 miles an hour or your hair won't blow the right way; and I'll make you do it again!" Thurman gave in, and subsequently lost control of and crashed the car—pinning her legs in the wreckage, giving her a concussion, and permanently damaging her neck and knees. It took 15 years of subsequent legal wrangling before Miramax studios released the crash footage, documenting what she had endured. And although Tarantino subsequently apologized, Thurman is still bitter. "Harvey assaulted me but that didn't kill me. But the crash was dehumanization to the point of death. Quentin finally atoned by giving the footage to me after 15 years? Not that it matters now, with my permanently damaged neck and my screwed-up knees!"

Like so many women whose voices combined to forge the #MeToo movement, the abuses that Uma Thurman suffered were all about **power**: the ability to influence or control people and events (Donohue & Kolt, 1992). Understanding power is critical for constructively managing conflict, because people in conflict often wield whatever power they have to overcome the opposition and achieve their goals. In conflicts in which one party has more power than the other—like Tarantino as

▶ In 2018, when Uma Thurman came forward with her story of abuse during the filming of *Kill Bill*, she became one of the hundreds of women in the #MeToo movement to describe a traumatic encounter with a male superior in the workplace. At the heart of these encounters were issues of power embedded in cultural and professional contexts. Moviestore Collection/Alamy

the director telling Thurman what she had to do—the more powerful tend to get what they want.

POWER'S DEFINING CHARACTERISTICS

Uma Thurman's experience on set during the filming of *Kill Bill* illustrates an abuse of power in a professional or workplace setting, where supervisors have formalized, or legitimate power over employees. But power permeates our nonprofessional lives as well, and is an integral part of interpersonal communication and relationships. Power determines how partners relate to each other, who controls relationship decisions, and whose goals will prevail during conflicts (Dunbar, 2004). Let's consider four defining characteristics of power, suggested by scholars William Wilmot and Joyce Hocker (2010).

Power Is Always Present   Whether you're talking on the phone with a parent, texting your best friend, or spending time with your romantic partner, power is present in all your interpersonal encounters and relationships. Power may be balanced, resulting in **symmetrical relationships** (e.g., friend to friend), or imbalanced, resulting in **complementary relationships** (e.g., manager to employee, parent to young child).

Although power is always present, we're typically not aware of it until people violate our expectations for power balance in the relationship, such as giving orders or talking down to us. Your roommate tells you (rather than asks you) to give them a ride after class. Your work supervisor grabs inventory you were stocking and says, "No—do it *this* way!" even though you were doing it properly. According to **Dyadic Power Theory** (Dunbar, 2004), people with only moderate power are most likely to use controlling communication. Because their power is limited, they can't always be sure they're going to get their way. Hence, they feel more of a need to wield power in noticeable ways (Dunbar, 2004). In contrast, people with high power feel little need to display it; they *know* that their words will be listened to and their wishes granted. This means that you're most likely to run into controlling communication and power-based bullying when dealing with people who have moderate amounts of power over you, such as mid-level managers, team captains, and class-project group leaders, as opposed to people with high power (in such contexts), like vice presidents, coaches, and faculty advisers.

Power Can Be Used Ethically or Unethically   Power itself isn't good or bad—it's the way people use it that matters. Many happy marriages, family relationships, and long-term friendships are complementary: one person controls more resources and has more decision-making influence than the other. Yet the person with more power uses their power to benefit both people and the relationship. In other relationships, a powerful person may wield their power unethically or recklessly. For example, when one of our sons worked at a sporting goods store, a kayak was stolen—a theft made possible by the store manager forgetting to lock up the kayaks displayed outside the store. The next morning the manager frantically demanded that all employees not mention the mistake to the regional manager, who was visiting the store, to avoid being blamed for the loss—an unethical use of power.

Power Influences Conflicts   If you strip away the particulars of what's said and done during most conflicts, you'll find power struggles underneath. Who has more

self-reflection

Think of a complementary personal relationship of yours in which you have more power than the other person. How does the imbalance affect how you communicate during conflicts? Is it ethical for you to wield power over the other person during a conflict to get what you want? Why or why not?

influence? Who controls the resources, decisions, and feelings involved? People struggle to see whose goals will prevail, wielding whatever power they have in pursuit of their own goals. But power struggles rarely lead to mutually beneficial solutions. As we'll see, the more constructive approach is to set aside your power and work collaboratively to resolve the conflict.

Power Is Often Granted   In interpersonal relationships, power doesn't reside within people. Instead, it can be granted by individuals or groups who allow another person or group to exert influence over them. For example, a friend of ours invited his parents to stay with him and his family for the weekend. His parents had planned on leaving Monday, but come Monday morning, they announced that they had decided to stay through the end of the week. Our friend accepted their decision even though he could have insisted that they leave at the originally agreed-on time. In doing so, he willingly granted his parents the power to decide their departure date without his input or consent. One factor influencing a person's willingness to grant power to another is the degree to which others control, or are perceived to control, resources that are valuable—a concept we turn to next.

POWER CURRENCIES

Given that power is not innate but something that some people grant to others, what can we do to obtain power? To acquire power, you must possess or control some form of **power currency**, a resource that other people value (Wilmot & Hocker, 2010). Possessing or controlling a valued resource gives you influence over individuals who value that resource. Likewise, if individuals have resources you value, you will grant power to them.

Five power currencies are common in interpersonal relationships. **Resource currency** includes material things such as money, property, and food. If you possess material things that someone else needs or wants, you have resource power over them. Parents have nearly total resource power over young children because they control all the money, food, shelter, clothing, and other items their children need and want. Managers have high levels of resource power over employees, as they control employees' continued employment and salaries.

Forbes considers Pope Francis to be one of the most powerful people in the world. What kinds of power currency does he have? How do you know? Abaca Press/Vandeville Eric/Sipa USA/Newscom

Expertise currency comprises special skills or knowledge. The more highly specialized and unique your skill is, the more expertise power you possess. A Stuttgart-trained Porsche mechanic commands a substantially higher wage and choicer selection of clients than a franchise-trained oil change attendant.

A person who is linked with a network of friends, family, and acquaintances with substantial influence has **social network currency**. These people may be valued because they can help you meet potential employers who may offer you a job, look better to prospective romantic partners, or garner invitations to exclusive parties.

Personal characteristics that people consider desirable—beauty, intelligence, charisma, communication skill, sense of humor—constitute **personal currency**. Even if you lack resource, expertise, and social network currency, you can still achieve a certain degree of influence and stature by being attractive, funny, or smart, if others value these qualities.

Finally, you acquire **intimacy currency** when you share a close bond with someone that no one else shares. If you have a unique intimate bond with someone—a romantic partner, friend, or family member—you possess intimacy power over them, and they may do you a favor "only because you are my best friend."

POWER AND GENDER

To say that power and gender are intertwined is an understatement. Throughout history and across cultures, *the* defining distinction between the genders has been men's power over women. Through patriarchy, which means "the rule of fathers," men have used cultural practices to maintain their societal, political, and economic power (Mies, 1991). Men have built and sustained patriarchy by denying women access to power currencies.

Although many people presume that the gender gap in power has narrowed, the truth is more complicated. Since 2006, the World Economic Forum has reported an annual global gender gap index that examines four aspects of gender equality: economic opportunity, educational access, political representation,

LaunchPad Video
launchpadworks.com

Expertise Currency
Watch this clip online to answer the questions below.

What types of expertise currency do you have? When are they beneficial to you? Have there been times when your expertise worked to your disadvantage? If so, how?

Want to see more? Check out LaunchPad for clips illustrating all the **power currencies**, including **resource currency**, **social network currency**, **personal currency**, and **intimacy currency**.

◀ The United States has held a total of 59 presidential elections since 1789. To this day, no woman has been elected president. And only one woman—Kamala Harris— has been elected vice president, in the 2020 election. How does this disparity reflect the wider difference between women's and men's political influence in the United States?
Ethan Miller/Getty Images

and health (World Economic Forum, 2019). In the preface for the 2020 report, Klaus Schwab stated, "At the present rate of change, it will take nearly a century to achieve parity . . ." (p. 4). Across 153 countries, women's participation in the labor market has stalled. Women are less likely to enter high-wage professions, such as in the technology fields, and lack access to capital. Although women are close to equality along the education and health dimensions, the political representation dimension continues to have the most pronounced gender gaps: women make up approximately half of the global population but hold less than one-quarter of ministerial positions and 25.2 percent of parliamentary (lower house) seats across all countries surveyed. Iceland, Norway, and Finland continue to top the list of the most gender-equal nations on the planet. Where do Canada and the United States rank? Nineteenth and 53rd overall, but in terms of political empowerment, the United States ranks 86th and Canada, 25th. At the same time, the United States has at long last elected a woman, Kamala Harris, to the second-highest office in the land: the vice presidency.

How does lack of power affect women's interpersonal communication? As gender scholar Cheris Kramarae (1981) notes, women with little or no power "are not as free or as able as men are to say what they wish, when and where they wish. . . . Their talk is often not considered of much value by men" (p. 1). Oxford linguist Deborah Cameron echoes this concern, describing how many women "still experience language as an instrument of male power over women, used to silence, misrepresent, belittle, and harass them" (p. 29, 2020).

Consider the specific example of negotiating for career advancement or salary raises. A widespread belief is that women don't ask for promotions or raises as often as men do (Babcock & Laschever, 2007). And yet, as we know from our Chapter 6 discussion of the social construction of gender, when it comes to communication differences between people, the topic and context matter. In one of the largest analyses of individual differences in negotiation, summarizing findings across 13 countries and 17,504 participants, psychologist Katharina Kugler and her colleagues found that women were only *slightly* less likely to initiate negotiations compared to men, and that these differences depended on the context (2018). In less ambiguous settings—where salary negotiations were seen as perfectly appropriate to discuss—women did not hesitate to initiate negotiations.

But in a world where a pronounced pay gap exists between women and men—estimates indicate that the average pay of U.S. women is about 82 percent of that of U.S. men (Bleiweis, 2020)—the *outcomes* of negotiations are significant. Simply asking for a raise doesn't guarantee receiving one. Research indicates that although women are about as likely as men to ask for a raise or promotion, they are less likely to receive what they requested (Artz et al., 2018). So what can be done? Research suggests that people should broaden their image of a "good" negotiator to include cooperative as well as competitive negotiation techniques. In addition, employers should openly and explicitly indicate to *all* employees which issues can be negotiated, and what settings are appropriate for such discussions (Kugler et al., 2018).

Now that we've considered the nature of power, the next step in managing conflict more constructively is to familiarize yourself with the different approaches to handling conflict.

self-reflection

In your experience, how does power affect people's decisions about whether or not to ask for what they want? How do the topic and context influence the likelihood that someone will ask for what they want? When you think of an effective negotiator, what qualities come to mind? What can you do to become a more confident negotiator?

Handling Conflict

How you approach conflict affects the outcomes

Steve was flying home after spending spring break with his folks. The jet provided so little space between seats that if someone in front of you leaned back, you couldn't have your tray table out. Across the aisle sat "Mike," a businessman typing furiously on his laptop. An hour into the flight, the man sitting in front of him, "Tom," suddenly leaned his seat back and began reading a book. Of course, the moment he did so, the tray table on the back of his seat jammed into Mike's stomach, and the seat back forced his laptop closed.

"*Excuse* me!" snapped Mike, "I'm using my computer—can you lean your seat forward?"

"But I want to lean back," said Tom, staying where he was.

"But I'm trying to use my computer, and I can't if you're leaning back!" snarled Mike.

"Your computer isn't my problem! I have the right to lean back if I want!" exclaimed Tom. Mike then buzzed the flight attendant, who approached Tom.

"Sir, if you could just move your seat forward a little, he can use his computer."

Tom went berserk. "*Why does it have to be me who compromises? I'm not moving!*" he shouted. The attendant then offered a different seat to Mike, who proceeded to shove Tom's seat back when exiting so that it hit him in the head.

What would you have done in this situation? Would you have avoided the conflict by pretending that you weren't being inconvenienced or demanded that your desires be met? Would you have freaked out or attempted to work collaboratively, seeking an agreeable compromise or a solution that met both of your needs?

In situations in which others are interrupting your goals or actions, your most important decision is how to handle the conflict (Sillars & Wilmot, 1994). *Your choice about what you'll say and do will shape everything that follows—whether the situation will go unresolved, escalate, or be resolved.* Your communication choices also influence whether your relationship with the other person (if one exists) will be damaged or grow stronger.

In this section, we examine five approaches people use for handling conflict, along with the impact that gender, culture, and technology have on the selection of these approaches.

APPROACHES TO HANDLING CONFLICT

People generally handle conflict in one of five ways: avoidance, accommodation, competition, reactivity, or collaboration (Lulofs & Cahn, 2000; Zacchilli et al., 2009). Before reading about each approach, take the *Self-Quiz* online to find out how you typically approach conflict.

Avoidance   One way to handle conflict is **avoidance**: ignoring the conflict, pretending it isn't really happening, or communicating indirectly about the situation. One common form of avoidance is **skirting**, in which a person avoids a conflict by changing the topic or joking about it. You suspect your partner may have a crush on a coworker and raise the issue, but your partner just laughs and replies, "Don't you know we'll always be together, like Noah and Allie from *The Notebook*?" Another form of avoidance is **sniping**—communicating in a

Online Self-Quiz: How Do You Approach Conflict? To take this self-quiz, visit LaunchPad: **launchpadworks.com**

self-reflection

Recall a conflict in which you chose avoidance. Why did you make this choice? What consequences ensued? Were there any positive outcomes? If you could relive the encounter, what, if anything, would you say and do differently to obtain more positive results?

negative fashion and then abandoning the encounter by physically leaving the scene or refusing to interact further. You're fighting with your brother on a video call, when he pops off a nasty comment ("I see you're still a spoiled brat!") and signs off before you have a chance to reply.

Avoidance is the most frequently used approach to handling conflict (Sillars, 1980). People opt for avoidance because it seems easier, less emotionally draining, and lower risk than direct confrontation (Afifi & Olson, 2005). But avoidance poses substantial risks (Afifi et al., 2009). One of the biggest is **cumulative annoyance**, in which repressed irritation grows as the mental list of grievances we have against our partner builds (Peterson, 2002). Eventually, cumulative annoyance overwhelms our capacity to suppress it and we suddenly explode in anger. For example, you constantly remind your teenage son about his homework, chores, personal hygiene, and room cleanliness. This bothers you immensely because you feel these matters are his responsibility, but you swallow your anger because you don't want to make a fuss or be seen by him as nagging. One morning you walk past his bathroom to find his bath towel, still damp, left on the floor, something you repeatedly have asked him not to do. You go off on a tirade, listing all the things he has done to upset you in the past month.

A second risk posed by avoidance is **pseudo-conflict**, the perception that a conflict exists when in fact it doesn't. For example, you mistakenly think your partner is about to break up with you because you see tagged photos of them arm in arm with someone else on Instagram. You decide to preemptively end your relationship, even though your partner actually has no desire to leave you (the photos show your partner posing with a cousin).

Despite the risks, avoidance can be a wise choice for managing conflict in situations in which emotions run high (Berscheid, 2002). If everyone involved is angry, yet you choose to continue the interaction, you run the risk of saying things that will damage your relationship. It may be better to avoid greater conflict by taking a time-out to let tempers cool, and respectfully letting others know that you are doing so before you withdraw from the interaction or conversation.

Accommodation   Through **accommodation**, one person abandons their own goals and acquiesces to the desires of the other person. For example, your supervisor at work asks you to stay an extra hour tonight because a coworker is coming in late. Although you had plans for the evening, you cancel them and act as if it's not a problem.

If you're like most people, you probably accommodate those who have more power than you. Why? If you don't, they might use their power to control or punish you. This suggests an important lesson regarding the relationship between power and conflict: people who are more powerful than you probably won't accommodate your goals during conflicts.

Another factor that influences people's decision to accommodate is love. Accommodation reflects a high concern for others and a low concern for self; you want to please those you love (Frisby & Westerman, 2010). Hence, accommodation is likely to occur in healthy, satisfied close relationships, in which selflessness is characteristic (Hendrick & Hendrick, 1992). For example, your partner is accepted into a summer study-abroad program in Europe. Even though you had planned on spending the summer together, you encourage your partner to accept the offer.

LaunchPad Video

launchpadworks.com

Accommodation
Watch this clip online to answer the questions below.

In this video, how does one partner accommodate the other? When have you found it most wise to accommodate in a conflict situation?

Want to see more? Check out LaunchPad for clips illustrating **avoidance**, **sniping**, **competition**, and **collaboration**.

Competition   Think back to the airline conflict. Each of the men involved aggressively challenged the other and expressed little concern for the other's perspective or goals. This approach is known as **competition**: an open and clear discussion of the clash between goals that exists and the pursuit of one's own goals without regard for others' (Sillars, 1980).

The choice to use competition is motivated in part by negative thoughts and beliefs, including a desire to control, a willingness to hurt others in order to gain, and a lack of respect for others (Bevan et al., 2008; Zacchilli et al., 2009). Consequently, you'll be less likely to opt for competition when you are in a conflict with someone whose needs you are interested in and whom you admire. Conversely, if people routinely approach conflict by making demands to the exclusion of your desires, they likely do not respect you (Hendrick & Hendrick, 2006).

At a minimum, competitive approaches can trigger *defensive communication* (described in Chapter 8)—someone refusing to consider your goals or dismissing them as unimportant, acting superior to you, or attempting to squelch your disagreement by wielding power over you (Waldron et al., 1993). But the primary risk of choosing a competitive approach is **escalation**, a dramatic rise in emotional intensity and increasingly negative and aggressive communication, just like in the airplane dispute. If people in conflict both choose competition, and neither is willing to back down, escalation is guaranteed. Even initially trivial conflicts can quickly ignite into intense exchanges.

Reactivity   A fourth way people handle conflict is by not pursuing any conflict-related goals at all; instead, they communicate in an emotionally explosive and negative fashion. This is known as **reactivity,** and it is characterized by accusations of mistrust, yelling, crying, and becoming verbally or physically abusive. Reactivity is decidedly nonstrategic. Instead of avoiding, accommodating, or competing, people simply flip out. For example, one of Steve's former dating partners was intensely reactive. When he noted that they weren't getting along and suggested taking a break, she screamed, "I *knew* it! You've been cheating on me!" and threw a vase of roses at him. Her behavior had nothing to do with managing their conflict. She simply *reacted*.

Similar to competition, reactivity is strongly related to a lack of respect (Bevan et al., 2008; Zacchilli et al., 2009). People prone to reactivity have little interest in others as individuals and do not recognize others' desires as relevant (Zacchilli et al., 2009).

Collaboration The most constructive approach to managing conflict is **collaboration**: treating conflict as a mutual problem-solving challenge rather than something that must be avoided, accommodated, competed over, or reacted to. Often the result of using a collaborative approach is *compromise*, in which everyone involved modifies their individual goals to come up with a solution to the conflict. (We'll discuss compromise in more detail later in the chapter.) You're most likely to use collaboration when you respect the other person and are concerned about their desires as well as your own (Keck & Samp, 2007; Zacchilli et al., 2009). People who regularly use collaboration feel more trust, commitment, and overall satisfaction with their relationships than those who don't (Smith et al., 2008). Whenever possible, opt for collaboration.

To use a collaborative approach, try these suggestions from Wilmot and Hocker (2010). First, *attack problems, not people.* Talk about the conflict as something separate from the people involved, saying, for instance, "This issue has really come between us." This frames the conflict as the source of trouble and unites the people trying to handle it. At the same time, avoid personal attacks while being courteous and respectful, regardless of how angry you may be. This is perhaps the hardest part of collaboration, because you likely *will* be angry during conflicts (Berscheid, 2002). Just don't let your anger cause you to say and do things you shouldn't. If someone attacks you and not the problem, don't get sucked into trading insults. Simply say, "I can see you're very upset; let's talk about this when we've both had a chance to cool off," and end the encounter before things escalate further.

Second, *focus on common interests and long-term goals.* Keep the emphasis on the desires you have in common, not the issue that's driving you apart. Use "we" language (see Chapter 8) to bolster this impression: "I know we both want what's best for the company." Arguing over positions ("I want this!" versus "I want that!") endangers relationships because the conflict may quickly devolve into a destructive contest of wills.

skills practice

Collaborating

Using collaboration to manage a conflict

❶ During your next significant conflict, openly discuss the situation, emphasizing that it's an understandable clash between goals rather than people and remembering to take a time-out to cool tempers if needed, so that the conversation can be broached respectfully.

❷ Highlight common interests and long-term goals.

❸ Create several options, or steps toward a solution, for resolving the conflict that are satisfactory to both of you.

❹ Combine the best elements of these ideas into a single, workable solution.

❺ Evaluate the solution you've collaboratively created, ensuring that it's fair and ethical.

table 10.1 **Competitive versus Collaborative Conflict Approaches**

Situation	Competitive Approach	Collaborative Approach
Roommate hasn't been doing their share of the housework	"I'm sick and tired of you never doing anything around here! From now on, you are doing all the chores!"	"We've both been really busy, but I'm concerned that things are not getting done. Let's make a list of all the chores and figure out how to fairly divide them up."
Coworker is draining large blocks of your work time by socializing with you	"It's obvious that you don't care about your job or whether you get fired. But I need this job, so stop bugging me all the time and let me get my work done!"	"I enjoy spending time with you, but I'm finding I don't have enough time left to get my work done. Let's figure out how we can better balance hanging out and working."
Partner wants you to abandon a beloved pastime because it seems too dangerous	"I've been racing dirt bikes long before I met you, and there's no way I'm giving them up. If you really loved me, you'd accept that instead of pestering me to quit!"	"I'm sorry my racing worries you; I know the reason you're concerned is because you care about me. Let's talk about what we can both do so I don't worry you so much."

Third, *create options before arriving at decisions.* Be willing to negotiate a solution rather than insisting on one. To do this, start by asking questions that will elicit options: "How do you think we can best resolve this?" or "What ideas for solutions do you have?" Then propose ideas of your own. Be flexible. Most collaborative solutions involve some form of compromise, so be willing to adapt your original desires, even if it means not getting everything you want. Then combine the best parts of the various suggestions to come up with an agreeable solution. Don't get bogged down searching for a "perfect" solution—it may not exist.

Finally, *critically evaluate your solution.* Ask for an assessment: "Is this equally fair for both of us?" The critical issue is livability: Can everyone live with the resolution in the long run? Or is it so unfair or short of original desires that resentments are likely to emerge? If anyone can answer yes to the latter question, go back to creating options (step 3) until you find a solution that is satisfactory to everyone.

CULTURE AND HANDLING CONFLICT

Scholars have long suggested that in general, people from more collectivistic cultures (which tend to value group identity and interpersonal harmony) prefer to avoid conflict, whereas people in more individualistic cultures (which tend to value individual achievement and independence) may engage in more direct approaches (Zhang et al., 2014). But similar to our discussion of gender and power earlier in the chapter, current research on culture highlights the importance

focus on CULTURE

Accommodation and Radical Pacifism

You're walking down the street, and a man approaches you and demands your wallet. You immediately give it and then ask him whether he also wants your coat. Or you badly want an open position at work. When you find out that a coworker also wants it, you inform your supervisor that you no longer want the job and encourage them to give it to your colleague instead.

As the biblical verse "When a man takes your coat, offer him your shirt as well" (Luke 6:29) suggests, one way to deal with conflict is an extreme form of accommodation known as *radical pacifism.* Although it is often associated with antiwar movements (Bennett, 2003), radical pacifism embodies a broader philosophy about the nature of interpersonal connections between human beings and how conflict is best resolved. Those practicing radical pacifism believe in a moral obligation to behave in selfless and self-sacrificial ways that quickly end conflicts and assist others. During interpersonal conflict, this means discovering what someone else wants and needs, then aiding that person in attaining those goals, even if it means sacrificing your own.

The practice of radical pacifism cuts across countries, ethnicities, and social classes; it is primarily rooted in the religion of cultures. For example, in the Buddhist text *Kakacupama Sutta* ("The Simile of the Saw"), the Buddha entreats his followers, "Even if bandits were to sever you savagely limb by limb with a two-handled saw, he who gave rise to a mind of hate towards them would not be carrying out my teaching. . . . [Instead] you should abide with a mind of loving kindness" (Bodhi & Nanamoli, 1995). Amish church elders embracing radical pacifism share a similar view: "Even if the result of our pacifism is death at the hands of an attacker during a violent conflict, so be it; death is not threatening to us as Christians. Hopefully the attacker will have at least had a glimpse of the love of Christ in our nonviolent response" (Pennsylvania Dutch Country Welcome Center, n.d.).

discussion questions
- What are your beliefs regarding radical pacifism?
- Do you have an ethical obligation to accommodate others when their interests clash with yours? At what point, if any, does this obligation end?

of context in shaping how individuals across cultures handle conflict. Factors such as the severity of the conflict and the power balance between partners play pivotal roles in shaping people's conflict decisions. Consider, for instance, research comparing Chinese and American collegiate dating couples. Chinese partners tended to withhold critical or negative feedback from their partners more than American couples, which likely stemmed in part from Chinese cultural concern for partners' face and preserving the harmony of the relationship. At the same time, *both* Chinese and American dating partners tended to avoid voicing criticisms when they had comparatively less power than their partners in the relationship—a cross-cultural *similarity* (Li & Samp, 2019).

A comparable pattern was found for African international students interacting with U.S. students on college campuses: African students displayed a preference for avoiding conflict (Adegbola et al., 2018). This tendency was driven by their perceived lack of power: since they were "visiting students from a different country," the African students stressed the need to "be careful" rather than assertive (Adegbola et al., 2018). What's more, substantial differences in conflict approaches existed amongst the African students, leading the researchers to caution that "international students cannot be viewed as a homogeneous whole" (p. 487). The findings from these studies suggest that conflicts—and how people choose to handle them—tend to be context- and topic-specific; consequently, one should avoid making sweeping cultural assumptions regarding how people will handle conflict.

HANDLING TEXT-BASED CONFLICT

Given how much of our daily communication occurs via technology, it's no surprise that conflicts occur through—and because of—texting, email, and social media posts. For instance, 26 percent of teens report that a text or online incident led to conflict with a friend (Lenhart, 2015). Nearly two-thirds of college students (61.2 percent) report using mediated channels to engage in conflicts, the most popular form being text-messaging (Frisby & Westerman, 2010). When asked why they choose mediated channels rather than face-to-face contact, respondents report "geographical distance" as the most common reason. Without the means for immediately seeing someone, texting becomes a tempting alternative for handling conflict.

Unfortunately, text-based messages are not well suited for resolving conflicts. The inability to see nonverbal reactions makes people less aware of the consequences of their communication (Joinson, 2001). As a result, people are more likely to prioritize their own goals, minimize a partner's goals, and use hostile personal attacks in pursuit of their goals compared to when they engage face-to-face (Shedletsky & Aitken, 2004).

The first and most important step in managing conflict constructively is to prioritize a modality that allows you to see or hear nonverbal cues. Doing so may dramatically reduce the likelihood of attributional errors and substantially boost empathy. When college students were asked which channel should be used for handling conflict, they noted that "face-to-face is so much better" because it allows you "to know how the other person feels with their facial expressions" (Frisby & Westerman, 2010, p. 975). If meeting face-to-face isn't an option at the time, you can try to stall the encounter by saying, "I think this is best handled in person. When can we get together and talk?" If you can't (or don't want to) meet, then

skills practice

Managing Text-Based Conflict

Effectively working through text-based conflict

❶ Wait before responding to a message or post that provokes you.

❷ Reread and reassess the message. Ask yourself if you are perceptually adding a "tone of voice" to the message that may not be intended or accurate.

❸ Consider all the factors that may have caused the other person to communicate this way.

❹ Discuss the situation with someone you trust.

❺ Craft a competent response that begins and ends with supportive statements, uses "I" language, expresses empathy, and emphasizes mutuality rather than just your own perspective and goals.

switch to a video call or phone call. That way, you'll at least have nonverbal cues to help gauge a partner's reaction and enhance your empathy.

If, however, you're in a situation in which you must deal with the conflict through text-based communication, try these suggestions (Munro, 2002):

1. *Wait and reread.* All conflict begins with a triggering event: something said or done that elicits anger, challenges goals, or blocks desired actions. When you receive a message that provokes you, don't respond right away. Instead, wait for a while, engage in other activities, and then reread it. This helps you avoid communicating when your anger is at its peak. It also provides the opportunity for reassessment: often, in rereading a message later, you'll find that your initial interpretation was mistaken.

2. *Assume the best and watch out for the worst.* When you receive messages that provoke you, presume that the sender meant well but didn't express themselves competently. Give people the benefit of the doubt. Keep in mind all you know about the challenges of text-based communication: anonymity and online disinhibition, empathy deficits, and people's tendency to express themselves inappropriately. At the same time, realize that some people enjoy conflict, and sending a snappish retort may be exactly what they want.

3. *Seek outside counsel.* Before responding, discuss the situation, ideally face-to-face, with someone who knows you well and whose opinion you trust and respect. Having an additional viewpoint will enhance your ability to perspective-take and will help you make wise communication decisions.

4. *Weigh your options carefully.* Choose cautiously between engaging or avoiding the conflict. Consider the consequences associated with each option, and which is most likely to net you the long-term personal and relationship outcomes you desire. Ask yourself: Will responding at this time help resolve the conflict or escalate things further?

5. *Communicate competently.* When crafting your response, draw on all you know about competent interpersonal communication. That is, use "I" language, incorporate appropriate emoticons, express empathy and use perspective-taking, encourage the other person to share relevant thoughts and feelings, and make clear your willingness to negotiate mutually agreeable solutions. Perhaps most important, start and end your message with positive statements that support rather than attack the other person's viewpoints.

Conflict Endings

Learn about short-term and long-term conflict outcomes

Prince T'Challa, played by the late Chadwick Boseman in the 2018 smash hit *Black Panther*, is a powerful person. Not only is he the heir to the throne of Wakanda—a prosperous and technologically advanced kingdom—he also is the "Black Panther," gifted with superhuman strength and speed. And he has seen more than his share of conflict. When his father, the king, is killed, T'Challa faces multiple challengers who want to seize the throne for themselves: first M'Baku, the leader of the Jabari tribe; and then the ruthless Erik Killmonger,

In *Black Panther*, Chadwick Boseman plays the title character—a superhero who defeats the villainous Killmonger and restores peace to Wakanda. But such methods for resolving conflict aren't always possible in real life. What methods do you use to end conflict in *your* relationships?
Pictorial Press Ltd/Alamy

T'Challa's cousin. Unfortunately, T'Challa has only one choice for dealing with these challengers, given the traditions of Wakanda regarding how to resolve succession disputes: ritual combat. That is, T'Challa must physically fight each claimant to the throne, one-on-one, beneath a sacred waterfall—and whoever prevails will be crowned king. Ultimately, he succeeds, securing the safety of his people and preserving their way of life.

Few (if any) of us will ever face a situation in which we must compete with rivals for succession to a royal throne. Nor can we call upon superheroes like Black Panther to assist us to ensure that our daily conflicts end in fairness. Nevertheless, our conflicts do end—albeit not always in the ways we wish. For instance, call to mind the most recent serious conflict you experienced, and consider the way it ended. Did one of you "win" and the other "lose"? Were you both left dissatisfied, or were you each pleased with the resolution? More important, were you able to resolve the underlying issue that triggered the disagreement in the first place, or did you merely create a short-term fix?

Given their emotional intensity and the fact that they typically occur in relationships, conflicts conclude more gradually than many people would like. You may arrive at a short-term resolution leading to the immediate end of the conflict. But afterwards, you'll experience long-term outcomes as you remember, ponder, and possibly regret the incident. These outcomes will influence your relationship health and happiness long into the future.

SHORT-TERM CONFLICT RESOLUTIONS

The approach you and your partner choose to handle a conflict usually results in one of five short-term conflict resolutions (Peterson, 2002). First, some conflicts end through **separation**, the sudden withdrawal of one person from the encounter. This resolution is characteristic of approaching conflict through avoidance. For example, you may be having a disagreement with your mother when she suddenly hangs up on you. Or you're discussing a concern with your roommate, when they unexpectedly get up, walk into their bedroom, and shuts the door behind them. Separation ends the immediate encounter, but it does nothing to solve the underlying incompatibility of goals or the interference that triggered the dispute in the first place.

However, separation isn't always negative. In some cases, short-term separation may help bring about long-term resolution. For example, if you and your partner have both used competitive or reactive approaches, your conflict may have escalated so much that any further contact may result in irreparable relationship damage. In such cases, temporary separation may help you both cool off, regroup, and consider how to collaborate. You can then come back and work together to better resolve the situation.

Second, **domination**—akin to the Black Panther eventually besting Erik Killmonger—occurs when one person gets their way by influencing the other to engage in accommodation and abandon goals. Conflicts that end with domination are often called *win-lose solutions*. The strongest predictor of domination is the power balance in the relationship. In cases in which one person has substantial power over the other, that individual will likely prevail.

In some cases, domination may be acceptable. For example, when one person doesn't feel strongly about achieving their goals, then abandoning those goals may have few costs. However, domination is destructive when it becomes a chronic pattern and one individual always sacrifices their goals to keep the peace. Over time, the consistent abandonment of goals can spawn resentment and hostility. While the accommodating "losers" are silently suffering, the dominating "victors" may think everything is fine because they are accustomed to achieving their goals.

Third, during **compromise**, both parties change their goals to make them compatible. Often, both people abandon part of their original desires, and neither feels completely happy about it. Compromise typically results from people using a collaborative approach and is most effective in situations in which both people treat each other with respect, have relatively equal power, and don't consider their clashing goals especially important (Zacchilli et al., 2009). In cases in which the two parties do consider their goals important, however, compromise can foster mutual resentment and regret (Peterson, 2002). Suppose you and your partner want to spend a weekend away. You planned this getaway for months, but your partner now wants to attend a two-day workshop that same weekend. A compromise might involve you cutting the trip short by a night and your partner missing a day of their workshop, leaving both of you with substantially less than you originally desired.

Fourth, through **integrative agreements**, the two sides preserve and attain their goals by developing a creative solution to their problem. This creates a *win-win solution* in which both people, using a collaborative conflict approach, benefit from the outcome. To achieve integrative agreements, the parties must remain committed to their individual goals but be flexible in how they achieve them (Pruitt & Carnevale, 1993). An integrative agreement for the weekend-away example might involve rescheduling the weekend so that you and your partner could enjoy both the vacation and the workshop.

Finally, in cases of especially intense conflict, **structural improvements**—people agreeing to change the basic rules or understandings that govern their relationship to prevent further conflict—may result. In cases of structural improvement, the conflict itself becomes a vehicle for reshaping the relationship in positive ways—rebalancing power or redefining expectations about who plays what roles in the relationship. Structural improvements are only likely to occur when the people involved control their negative emotions and handle the conflict collaboratively. Suppose your partner keeps in touch with an ex via Facebook. Although you trust your partner, the thought of an ex chatting with your partner on a daily basis, and tracking your relationship through updates and posted photos, drives you crazy. After a jealousy-fueled fight, you and your partner might sit down and collaboratively hash out guidelines for how often and in what ways each of you can communicate with ex-partners.

skills practice

Resolving Conflict
Creating better conflict resolutions

❶ When a conflict arises in a close relationship, manage your negative emotions and check your perception.

❷ Before communicating with your partner, call to mind the consequences of your communication choices.

❸ Employ a collaborative approach, and avoid kitchen-sinking.

❹ As you negotiate solutions, keep your original goals in mind but remain flexible about how they can be attained.

❺ Revisit relationship rules or agreements that triggered the conflict, and consider redefining them in ways that prevent future disputes.

LONG-TERM CONFLICT OUTCOMES

After the comparatively short-term phase of conflict resolution, you may begin to ponder the long-term outcomes. In particular, you might consider whether the conflict was truly resolved, and what the dispute's impact was on your relationship. Research examining long-term conflict outcomes and relationship satisfaction has

We may try to end a conflict through a "peace offering"—a gift or favor to smooth things over. However, it is important to ensure that the parties involved have all reached a resolution so that no lingering conflict remains. Allen Donikowski/Moment /Getty Images

found that certain approaches for dealing with conflict—in particular, avoidant, reactive, and collaborative approaches—strongly predict relationship quality (Smith et al., 2008; Zacchilli et al., 2009).

The most commonly used conflict approach is avoidance. But because avoidance doesn't address the goal-related clash or actions that sparked the conflict, tensions will likely continue. People who use avoidance have lower relationship satisfaction and endure longer and more frequent conflicts than people who don't avoid (Smith et al., 2008). Consequently, try not to use avoidance unless you're certain the issue is unimportant. This is a judgment call; sometimes an issue that seems unimportant at the time ends up eating away at you over the long run. When in doubt, communicate directly about the issue.

Far more poisonous to relationship health, however, is reactivity. Individuals who handle conflict by (in effect) throwing tantrums end up substantially less happy in their relationships (Zacchilli et al., 2009). If you or your partner habitually uses reactivity, seriously consider more constructive ways to approach conflict. If you do not adjust your approach, you will likely experience dissatisfaction in your relationship.

In sharp contrast to the negative outcomes of avoidance and reactivity, collaborative approaches generally generate positive long-term outcomes (Smith et al., 2008). People using collaboration tend to resolve their conflicts, report higher satisfaction in their relationships, and experience shorter and fewer disputes. The lesson from this is to always treat others with kindness and respect, and strive to deal with conflict by openly discussing it in a way that emphasizes mutual interests and saves your partner's face.

If collaborating yields positive long-term outcomes, and avoiding and reacting yield negative ones, what about accommodating and competing? This is difficult to predict. Sometimes you'll compete and get what you want, the conflict will be resolved, and you'll be satisfied. Or you'll compete, the conflict will escalate wildly out of control, and you'll end up incredibly unsatisfied. Other times you'll accommodate, the conflict will be resolved, and you'll be content. Or you'll accommodate, and the other person will exploit you further, causing you deep discontent. Accommodation and competition are riskier because you can't count on either as a constructive way to manage conflict for the long term (Peterson, 2002).

Challenges to Handling Conflict

Conflicts can spark destructive communication

You and your mother suffer a disagreement that threatens to tear your family apart. So you text her and schedule a lunch date. Sitting down face-to-face, you both express love and admiration for each other, and you agree that the conflict should be resolved in a mutually satisfying fashion. You then collaboratively brainstorm ideas, and voila!—the perfect solution is discovered! You smile, hug, and part ways, each feeling satisfied with the relationship and contented with the resolution as a rainbow appears in the sky.

Yeah, right. If only resolving conflict could be so easy! Unfortunately, conflict in close relationships is rarely (if ever) as streamlined and stress-free as cooperative partners joining forces to reconcile surmountable differences. Instead, close relationship conflict is typically fraught with challenges. Let's take a look at some of the most potent: self-enhancing thoughts, destructive messages, serial arguments, physical violence, and unsolvable disputes.

SELF-ENHANCING THOUGHTS

Arguably the biggest challenge we face in constructively managing conflict is our own minds. During conflicts, we think in radically self-enhancing ways. In a detailed study of conflict thought patterns, scholar Alan Sillars and his colleagues found that during disputes, individuals selectively remember information that supports them and contradicts their partners, view their own communication more positively than their partners', and blame their partners for failure to resolve the conflict (Sillars et al., 2000).

Sillars and his colleagues also found little evidence of complex thought. While conflicts are unfolding, people typically do *not* consider long-term outcomes ("How is this going to impact our relationship?") and do *not* perspective-take ("How are they feeling?"). Instead, their thoughts are locked into simple, unqualified, and negative views: "They're lying and blaming me!" (Sillars et al., 2000, p. 491). In only 2 percent of cases did respondents attribute cooperativeness to their partners and uncooperativeness to themselves. This means that in 98 percent of fights, you'll likely think, "I'm trying to be helpful, and my partner is being unreasonable!" However, your partner will probably be thinking the exact same thing about you.

Self-enhancing thoughts dominate conflict encounters, stifling the likelihood of collaboration. Consequently, *one of the most important things you can do to improve your conflict-management skills is to routinely practice critical self-reflection during disputes.* Although you might not ever achieve objectivity or neutrality in your thoughts, you can work toward this goal by regularly going through this mental checklist:

- Is my partner *really* being uncooperative, or am *I* making a faulty attribution?

- Is my partner *really* solely to blame, or have *I* also done something to cause the conflict?

- Is the conflict *really* due to ongoing differences between us, or is it *actually* due to temporary or external factors, such as stress or fatigue?

DESTRUCTIVE MESSAGES

Think back to the chapter opener when Bennet Omalu tried to get his article published. Reviewers who felt threatened lashed out at him personally, saying horrible things. The same type of thing can happen to you. When conflicts escalate and anger peaks, our minds are filled with negative thoughts of all the grievances and resentments we feel toward others (Sillars et al., 2000). These thoughts often leap out of our mouths, in the form of messages that permanently damage our relationships (McCornack & Husband, 1986).

Sudden-death statements occur when people get so angry that they suddenly declare the end of the relationship, even though breaking up wasn't a possibility before the conflict. When we (Kelly and Steve) had been married for two years, we had a major argument while visiting Kelly's parents. A small dispute over family differences quickly escalated into a full-blown, though short-lived, conflict. After flinging a few kitchen-sink messages at each other, we both exclaimed, "Why are we even together?! We're so different!" Fortunately, this sudden-death statement caused us to calm down. But many couples who blurt out such things during escalation follow through on them.

Perhaps the most destructive messages are **dirty secrets**: statements that are honest in content, have been kept hidden to protect a partner's feelings, and are designed to hurt. Dirty secrets can include acts of infidelity ("I cheated, and it was great!"). They can also include intense criticism of a partner's appearance ("You know how I've always said I like your nose? Well, I hate it!"), and even a lack of feelings ("I haven't been in love with you for years!"). Dirty secrets are designed to hurt, and because the content is true, they can irreparably damage the recipient and the relationship.

Needless to say, destructive messages can destroy relationships. Couples who exchange critical and contemptuous messages during the first seven years of marriage are more likely to divorce than couples who refrain from such negativity (Gottman & Levenson, 2000). Thus, no matter your level of anger or the caustic thoughts that fill your head, it's essential to always communicate toward your partner in a civil, respectful fashion.

self-reflection

Recall a conflict in which you and the other person exchanged destructive messages, such as sudden-death statements or dirty secrets. What led to those statements? What impact did these messages have on the conflict? How did they affect your relationship?

self-QUIZ

Test Your Understanding of Destructive Thoughts

Recall the most recent, serious conflict you've had with another person. Reflect on the thoughts you had *during* the conflict. Then check each statement that fairly represents a thought you had while the conflict was actually happening. When you're done, score yourself using the key at the bottom.

To take this quiz online, visit LaunchPad: **launchpadworks.com**

_____ This isn't all *my* fault.

_____ All my partner cares about is themselves.

_____ My partner just wants to blow the whole thing off and not talk about it anymore.

_____ My partner keeps cutting me off, just like usual.

_____ I'm giving in to what my partner wants, like I always do.

_____ All my partner seems to want to do is verbally attack me, instead of treating me with respect.

_____ I'm just trying to get my point across.

_____ All I'm doing is trying to please my partner.

_____ My partner is just making a lot of excuses about their behavior.

_____ I'm being cooperative, but my partner is being a jerk.

Note: Information in this self-quiz from Table 1 of Sillars et al. (2000, p. 488).

Scoring: 0–3: Few self-enhancing thoughts. The lack of partner-blame and self-praise likely helped you make better communication decisions and collaborate with your partner in solving the conflict. 4–6: Moderate number of self-enhancing thoughts. How you thought about your partner and yourself likely impeded you from approaching the conflict in a collaborative fashion. 7–10: Frequent self-enhancing thoughts. By exclusively blaming your partner while holding yourself faultless, you likely behaved in ways that continued or escalated the conflict. *Note:* If your score is in the "moderate" (4–6) or "frequent" (7–10) range, carefully review the suggested steps for critical self-reflection during conflicts described in the text, to help improve your perspective-taking and empathic abilities.

SERIAL ARGUMENTS

Another conflict challenge we face in close relationships is **serial arguments**: a series of unresolved disputes, all having to do with the same issue (Bevan et al., 2008). Serial arguments typically stem from deep disagreements, such as differing relationship expectations or clashes in values and beliefs. By definition, serial arguments occur over time and consist of cycles in which things "heat up" and then lapse back into a temporary state of truce (Malis & Roloff, 2006). During these "quiet" periods, individuals are likely to think about the conflict, attempt to repair the relationship, and cope with the stress resulting from the most recent fight (Malis & Roloff, 2006).

According to the **serial argument process model**, the course that serial arguments take is determined by the goals individuals possess, the approaches they adopt for dealing with the conflict, and the consequent perception of whether or not the conflict is resolvable (Bevan, 2014). Specifically, when individuals in close relationships enter into serial arguments with positive goals, such as "creating a mutual understanding" or "constructively conveying relationship concerns," they're more likely to use collaborative conflict strategies for dealing with the argument (Bevan, 2014, p. 774). As a result, the conflict is more likely to be perceived as eventually resolvable in the aftermath, and people are less likely to ruminate about it. In contrast, when individuals enter into serial arguments with goals such as "gaining power over the partner" or "personally wounding the partner in order to win," they're more likely to use competitive strategies, the conflict is more likely to be perceived as unresolvable, and they're more likely to stew about it afterwards.

Serial arguments are most likely to occur in romantic and family involvements, in which the frequency of interaction provides ample opportunity for repetitive disagreements (Bevan et al., 2008). They are also strongly predictive of relationship failure: couples who suffer serial arguments experience higher stress levels and are more likely to have their relationships end than those who don't (Malis & Roloff, 2006).

Although many serial arguments involve heated verbal battles, others take the form of a **demand-withdraw pattern**, in which one partner in a relationship demands that their goals be met, and the other partner responds by withdrawing from the encounter (Caughlin, 2002). Demand-withdraw patterns are typically triggered when a person is bothered by a repeated source of irritation, but doesn't confront the issue until they can no longer suppress their anger. At that point, the person explodes in a demanding fashion (Malis & Roloff, 2006).

If you find yourself in a close relationship in which a demand-withdraw pattern has emerged, discuss this situation with your partner. Using a collaborative approach, critically examine the forces that trigger the pattern, and work to generate solutions that will enable you to avoid the pattern in the future.

PHYSICAL VIOLENCE

The most destructive aspect of conflict is violence, "the intentional use of physical force or power, threatened or actual, against oneself, another person, or against a group or community" that may result in psychological harm, injury, or death (World Health Organization, n.d.a). In the National Intimate Partner and Sexual Violence Survey (Smith et al., 2015), 30.6 percent of women and 31 percent of men reported experiencing physical violence from an intimate partner. And physical violence occurs in all types of relationships. More than one-third of lesbians, over half of bisexual women, 24 percent of gay men, and 27 percent of bisexual men have reported physical violence from an intimate partner at some point in their lifetime

(American Psychological Association, 2013b). Both men and women use violence as a strategy for dealing with conflicts. In an analysis of data from 82 violence studies, researcher John Archer found no substantial difference between men and women in their propensity toward violence as a conflict strategy (2000). At the same time, however, women are substantially more likely to be injured or killed, owing to their lesser physical size and strength (Archer, 2000; O'Leary & Vivian, 1990).

One outcome of physical violence in close relationships is the **chilling effect**, whereby individuals stop discussing relationship issues out of fear of their partners' negative reactions (Solomon & Samp, 1998). In these relationships, individuals who are "chilled" constrain their communication and actions to a very narrow margin, avoiding all topics and behaviors they believe may provoke a partner (Afifi et al., 2009). The result is an overarching relationship climate of fear, suppression, anxiety, and unhappiness.

If you find yourself in a relationship in which your partner behaves violently toward you, immediately seek help from family members, friends, and law enforcement officials. We discuss tactics for dealing with relational violence in more detail in Chapter 11.

If you find that you are inclined to violence in relationships, revisit the anger management techniques described in Chapter 4 as well as the suggestions for constructively handling conflict described earlier in this chapter. Most aggression during conflicts stems from people's perception that they have no other options. In reality, however, more constructive alternatives are available. If you are unable to control your impulses toward violence, you should seek professional counseling.

UNSOLVABLE DISPUTES

A final conflict challenge is that some disputes are simply unsolvable, and no degree of wisdom in decision making or competence in communication will resolve them. In an agonizing scene from Greta Gerwig's 2019 brilliant rendition of Louisa May Alcott's *Little Women*, Teddy (portrayed by Timothée Chalamet) declares his love for his friend Jo (played by Saoirse Ronan). He proposes marriage, only to find that his love is unrequited. Jo desperately tries to explain why they shouldn't marry.

> "Teddy, I don't believe I will ever marry. I'm happy as I am. I love my liberty too well to be in any hurry to give it up."
>
> "I think you're wrong about that, Jo . . . I think you will marry. I think you'll find someone and love them and you will live and die for them because that's your way, and you will. And I'll watch."

self-reflection

Think of an unsolvable conflict you've had. What made it unsolvable? How did the dispute affect your relationship? Looking back on the situation, could you have done anything differently to prevent the conflict from becoming unsolvable? If so, what?

▶ Some situations, like Teddy's unrequited love for Jo in *Little Women*, are simply impossible to resolve. Have you ever experienced an unsolvable conflict in your own life?
Album/Alamy

As this scene heartbreakingly illustrates, if one person loves another but the feeling isn't reciprocated, no amount of collaborating will fix things. Part of competently managing conflict is accepting that some conflicts are impossible to resolve. How can you recognize such disputes? Clues include the following: you and the other person aren't willing to change your opinions of each other; your goals are irreconcilable and strongly held; or at least one partner is uncooperative, chronically defensive, or violent. In these cases, the only options are to avoid the conflict, hope that your attitudes or goals will change over time, or abandon the relationship.

Managing Conflict and Power

Conflicts can be opportunities for positive change

Whether it's big or small, when a dispute arises, you may feel that no one else has ever had the same thoughts and emotions. The anger, fear of escalation, pain of hurtful comments that should have been left unsaid, and uncertainty associated with not knowing the long-term relationship outcomes combine to make the experience intense and draining.

But conflicts and struggles over power needn't be destructive. Though they carry risk, they also provide the opportunity to engineer positive change in the way you communicate with others and manage your relationships. Through conflict, you can resolve problems that, left untouched, would have eroded your relationship or deprived you of greater happiness in the future. The key distinguishing feature between conflict and power struggles that destroy and those that create opportunities for improvement is how you interpersonally communicate.

We've discussed a broad range of communication skills that can help you manage conflict and power more competently. Whether it's using collaborative approaches, critiquing your perceptions and attributions, knowing when to take a conflict offline, or being sensitive to gender and cultural differences, you now know the skills necessary for successfully managing the disagreements, disputes, and contests that will erupt in your life. It is up to you to take these skills and put them into practice.

◐ "I think it is something we deserve, while we're going through this trifecta of crises—pandemic, racial inequity, economic crisis—that somehow we can actually still come together in whatever way that we can and feel this music."
—Yo Yo Ma
Tom Williams/CQ Roll Call/Newscom

Dealing with Family Conflict

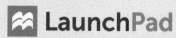 **LaunchPad** For the best experience, complete all parts of this activity in LaunchPad: **launchpadworks.com**

1 Background

Conflict poses complex challenges for interpersonal communication and relationships. Parental expectations, power differences between generations, and the emotional connections within families can make matters even more complex. To understand how you might competently manage such a relationship challenge, read the case study in Part 2; then, drawing on all you know about interpersonal communication, work through the problem-solving model in Part 3.

 Visit LaunchPad to watch the video in Part 4 and assess your communication in Part 5.

2 Case Study

Your parents are old school in their views of parental power: they believe that children should always show deference to their elders. Although you're still in college, your brother Sanjay is much older and has a family of his own, including a teenage son, Devdas. You have always gotten along well with Devdas, but recently he has been going through a rebellious phase in which he shows little respect for all adults, including you. During a recent visit, Devdas sprawled on the sofa all afternoon, playing video games on the big screen. You asked if you could watch a movie, and he snapped, "Find your own &*$%# TV!" You did not mention this incident to the rest of your family to avoid escalating the issue.

Your parents decide to spend a week with Sanjay and his family. You're nervous because your mother delights in picking on Devdas about his hair, clothing, and music, and given Devdas's recent attitude, you're afraid he may strike back. Sure enough, toward the end of the week, you get a phone call from your mother, telling you that she and your father ended their visit early and that she wishes no further contact with your brother or his family. She says that Devdas "swore at her for no reason at all." She says, "I have no interest in associating with children who behave like that." Shortly afterwards, you get a text from your brother. He says that your mother is delusional and "made the whole thing up." When you ask whether Devdas might have sworn at your mom, your brother fires back, "Absolutely not! Devdas doesn't even *know* such words!!!" Since you weren't a witness to the encounter, you try to stay neutral.

As the weeks go by, the rift deepens. Devdas refuses to talk about the issue at all, even with you or his parents. Your mother refuses contact with her grandson until he "admits his wrongdoing!"

Now, with the holidays approaching, you receive an email from your parents. They demand that you side with them, saying, "If you continue to support Devdas in this shameful matter, we will be forced to rethink our financial support for your education." Sitting down at your computer, you write back a message.

Your Turn

Consider all you've learned thus far about interpersonal communication. Then work through the following five steps. Remember, there are no "right" answers, so think hard about what is the *best* choice! (P.S. Need help? See the *Helpful Concepts* list.)

step 1

Reflect on yourself. What are your thoughts and feelings in this situation? What attributions are you making about your mother, Devdas, and their behavior? Are your attributions accurate? Why or why not?

step 2

Reflect on your partner. Using perspective-taking and empathic concern, put yourself in your mother's shoes. Do the same for Devdas. What are they thinking and feeling in this situation?

step 3

Identify the optimal outcome. Think about all the information you have about your communication and relationships with both your mother and Devdas. Consider your own feelings as well as theirs. Given all these factors, what's the best, most constructive relationship outcome possible? Consider what's best for you *and* for your mother and Devdas.

step 4

Locate the roadblocks. Taking into consideration your own thoughts and feelings, those of your mother and Devdas, and all that has happened in this situation, what obstacles are keeping you from achieving the optimal outcome?

step 5

Chart your course. How might you respond to your mother to overcome the roadblocks you've identified and achieve your optimal outcome?

HELPFUL CONCEPTS

Power principles, **261**
Collaboratively managing conflict, **268**
Conflict resolutions and outcomes, **272**
Unresolvable conflicts, **278**

The Other Side

Visit LaunchPad to watch a video in which Devdas tells his side of the case study story. As in many real-life situations, this is information to which you did not have access when you were initially crafting your response in Part 3. The video reminds us that even when we do our best to offer competent responses, there is always another side to the story that we need to consider.

Interpersonal Competence Self-Assessment

After watching the video, visit the Self-Assessment questions in LaunchPad. Think about the new information offered in Devdas's side of the story and all you've learned about interpersonal communication. Drawing on this knowledge, revisit your earlier responses in Part 3 and assess your interpersonal communication competence.

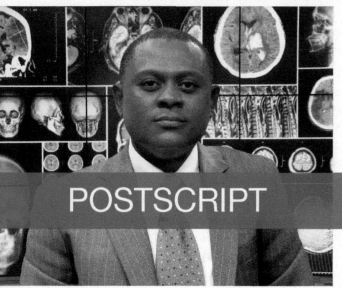

Ida Mae Astute/©Walt Disney Television/ABC/Getty Images

This chapter began with a scientist seeking to help people. When pathologist Bennet Omalu exposed the widespread occurrence of CTE among football players, his goal was to use his research to enhance safety. But many perceived this goal as clashing with their interests, and they subsequently used their power to try to suppress his findings and destroy his reputation.

In what situations have you sought to do what was right, only to be blocked by those whose interests were threatened? Have people in positions of power ever sought to undermine you? Was your response to lash back? Or did you instead seek to collaborate with those antagonizing you, to create a mutually satisfying outcome?

Like Bennet Omalu, we *all* have the power to change the world, in ways large and small. And we do so each and every time we approach a conflict as an opportunity for transformative change, rather than a battle that must be won by denigrating and crushing the opposition.

LaunchPad

LaunchPad for *Reflect & Relate* offers videos and encourages self-assessment through adaptive quizzing. Go to **launchpadworks.com** to get access to:

✓ LearningCurve
Adaptive Quizzes

 Video clips that help you understand interpersonal communication

key terms

conflict,   257
kitchen-sinking,   259
⊙ power,   260
symmetrical relationships,   261
complementary relationships,   261
Dyadic Power Theory,   261
power currency,   262
⊙ resource currency,   262
⊙ expertise currency,   263
⊙ social network currency,   263
⊙ personal currency,   263
⊙ intimacy currency,   263
⊙ avoidance,   265
skirting,   265
⊙ sniping,   265
cumulative annoyance,   266
pseudo-conflict,   266
⊙ accommodation,   266
⊙ competition,   267
escalation,   267
reactivity,   267
⊙ collaboration,   268
separation,   272
domination,   272
⊙ compromise,   273
integrative agreements,   273
structural improvements,   273
sudden-death statements,   275
dirty secrets,   276
serial arguments,   277
serial argument process model,   277
demand-withdraw pattern,   277
chilling effect,   278

⊙ You can watch brief, illustrative videos of these terms and test your understanding of the concepts online in LaunchPad.

key concepts

Conflict and Interpersonal Communication

- **Conflict** arises whenever people's goals clash or they compete for valued resources.
- Avoid **kitchen-sinking**—hurling insults that have little to do with the original dispute.

Power and Conflict

- Conflict and **power** are closely related.
- Friendships are typically **symmetrical relationships**, whereas parent–child relationships are **complementary relationships.**
- Power is granted to you by others, depending on the **power currency** you possess. Types include **resource, expertise, social network, personal**, and **intimacy**.
- Across cultures and time, men have consolidated power over women by strategically depriving women of access to power currencies.

Handling Conflict

- **Avoidance** can lead to damaging behaviors, including **skirting, sniping, cumulative annoyance**, and the inability to overcome **pseudo-conflict**.
- **Accommodation** is often motivated by the desire to please the people we love.
- **Competition** involves the aggressive pursuit of one's own goals at the expense of others' goals.
- **Reactivity** occurs as a negative, explosive response to conflict.
- **Collaboration** is the best approach to conflict, since it reinforces trust in your relationships and builds relational satisfaction.
- If online conflicts arise, it's best to take the encounter offline.

Conflict Endings

- In the short term, conflicts resolve through **separation, domination, compromise, integrative agreements**, or **structural improvements**.
- In the long term, partners consider the conflict's impact on their relationship.

Challenges to Handling Conflict

- **Sudden-death statements** occur when, in anger, people declare the end of the relationship.
- In close relationships, there is a risk of engaging in **serial arguments**, which may lead to **demand-withdraw patterns**.
- When people believe that no other option exists, they may commit acts of violence.
- Some conflicts are impossible to resolve.

11 Relationships with Romantic Partners

Romantic love may not be essential to life, but it may be essential to joy.

Imagine China/Newscom

One meeting of the Cowherd and Weaver amidst the golden autumn wind and jade-glistening dew, eclipses the countless meetings in the mundane world.

— Qin Guan, poet (1049–1100)

The story of their love is literally written in the stars. Zhinu, daughter of the Heaven Goddess, weaves celestial garments from the clouds. Niulang, a human being, is a caretaker of cattle. When Zhinu impulsively ventures to the mortal realm, she meets Niulang, and the two fall in love. Zhinu decides to forgo the heavens, and the two run off together. But the Heaven Goddess discovers Zhinu's desertion and forces her to return home. Distraught, Niulang sneaks to the heavens to free Zhinu, but the Heaven Goddess discovers him, and in a fury casts both lovers into the cosmos as the stars Vega and Altair, separating them for all eternity by the wide celestial river of the Milky Way galaxy. Indeed, if you look to the night sky tonight, you might see the bright blue star Vega (Zhinu), separated from the star Altair (Niulang). Yet once a year, according to the legend, all the magpies in the world fly to the heavens to form a bridge of birds, so that for a single night, Zhinu and Niulang can be reunited.

The Chinese folktale of the cowherd and the weaver dates back more than 2,600 years, and has been celebrated annually since the Han Dynasty (202 B.C.E.–220 C.E.) as the Qixi Festival. Traditional Qixi celebrations included sewing competitions, enjoying fruits or baking,

Today, Qixi celebrations involve a wide range of activities, from dancing in traditional dress (as shown in this photo) to baking and weaving, or simply going on a romantic date.

and adorning the horns of oxen with wildflowers. Today, Qixi is somewhat akin to Valentine's Day, in that many couples enjoy a romantic night out and exchange flowers, chocolates, and jewelry. Festival participants may look skyward to Vega and Altair for blessings of family approval upon their romances, visit the magpie bridge, express their love to others, or even get married. Long-distance couples may offer prayers for happiness and eventual reunion.

Why has the story of the cowherd and weaver resonated so deeply for literally billions of people, across more than two *thousand* years? Because it emphasizes enduring themes of romantic love that people find inspirational and aspirational. As our good friend Xun Zhu, a communication professor who grew up in China, explains, "The story links romantic love to commitment, perseverance, faith, and sacrifice. In the long wait for their annual reunion, the cowherd and the weaver have no means to communicate, support, care, connect, and bond with each other — activities that, in my mind, make romantic relationships sustainable and joyous."

Consider how *you* think about love. Were your views of romance impacted by stories or fairy tales? Did they celebrate ideas of forbidden or star-crossed love, love overcoming any obstacle, soul mates patiently enduring the trials of separation prior to a blissful reunion? Or maybe you think of the hard work of love, the importance of being autonomous yet also connected, and the precious value of interpersonal communication in sustaining closeness. As Professor Zhu puts it, "The story of the weaver and the cowherd affirms my belief in the centrality of communication in romantic relationships. My wife and I were separated for many years, as we each pursued our advanced degrees. But we were committed to collaboratively working toward a long-term goal of being together with the short-term sacrifice of physical separation. Throughout our time apart, we often reminded ourselves of their love, and how they were able to sustain it despite the challenges they faced."

The tale of the cowherd and the weaver is recognized by the Chinese government as one of the four great love legends in China. It has been referenced by sources as diverse as scientist Carl Sagan in his book *Contact*, the anime series *Sailor Moon*, and the J-pop band Supercell. The story exists in dozens of versions throughout Asia. But at the center of it all is an enduring tale of partners who would cross a galaxy to be together — even if only for one day a year.

Throughout time and across cultures, people have fallen in love with each other. When each of us discovers love for ourselves, we honor that legacy, sharing in an experience that is both uniquely and universally human. We also find that romantic love is an assortment of elements, some of which seem contradictory. Initially, our relationships may be all about passion, but they also bring with them the rewards (and costs) of companionship. Our love for others may be selfless and giving, yet we're driven to build and sustain only those relationships that benefit us the most, and to end those that don't. Although romance may be sentimental and seemingly magical, the maintenance of love is decidedly practical. Romantic *relationships* are hard work, entailing constant upkeep to survive the innumerable and unforeseen challenges that threaten them.

In this chapter, the first of four on relationships, you'll learn:

- Defining characteristics of romantic love and relationships
- What drives your attraction to some people and not others
- How communication changes as your romantic relationships come together . . . and fall apart
- How to communicate in ways that keep your love alive
- Some challenges of romantic relationships and how to deal effectively with them

We begin our exploration of love by looking at how loving is different from liking, the different types of romantic love that exist, and what constitutes a romantic *relationship*.

Defining Romantic Relationships

People experience different types of love.

We often think of romantic relationships as exciting and filled with promise—a joyful fusion of closeness, communication, and sexual connection. When researchers Pamela Regan, Elizabeth Kocan, and Teresa Whitlock (1998) asked several hundred people to list the things they associated most with "being in love," the most frequent responses were trust, honesty, happiness, bondedness, companionship, communication, caring, intimacy, shared laughter, and sexual desire. But apart from such associations, what exactly *is* romantic love? How does it differ from liking? The answers to these questions can help you build more satisfying romantic partnerships.

LIKING AND LOVING

Most scholars agree that liking and loving are separate emotional states, with different causes and outcomes (Berscheid & Regan, 2005). **Liking** is a feeling of affection and respect that we typically have for our friends (Rubin, 1973). *Affection* is a sense of warmth and fondness toward another person, while *respect* is admiration for another person apart from how they treat you or communicate with you. **Loving**, in contrast, is a vastly deeper and more intense emotional experience and consists of three components: intimacy, caring, and attachment (Rubin, 1973).

- *Intimacy* is a feeling of closeness and "union" between you and your partner (Mashek & Aron, 2004).
- *Caring* is the concern you have for your partner's welfare and the desire to keep them happy.
- *Attachment* is a longing to be in your partner's presence as much as possible.

The ideal combination for long-term success in romantic relationships occurs when partners both like and love each other.

DIFFERENT TYPES OF ROMANTIC LOVE

Though most people recognize that loving differs from liking, many also believe that to be *in* love, one must feel constant and consuming sexual attraction toward a partner. In fact, many different types of romantic love exist, covering a broad range of emotions and relationship forms. At one end of the spectrum is **passionate love**, a state of intense emotional and physical longing for union with another (Hendrick & Hendrick, 1992). Studies of passionate love suggest six things are true about its experience and expression.

First, passionate love quite literally changes our brains. Neuroimaging studies of people experiencing passionate love suggest substantial activation of brain reward centers, as well as activation of the caudate nucleus—an area associated with obsessive thinking (Graham, 2011). In simple terms, people passionately in love often find the experience intensely pleasurable and may have their thoughts circle constantly around their partners.

Second, people passionately in love often view their loved ones and relationships in an excessively idealistic light. For instance, many partners in passionate love relationships talk about how "perfect" they are for each other. Such beliefs actually function to *increase* commitment and satisfaction within relationships, rather than undermining them through disappointment when real-world partners fail to live up to such idealized expectations (Vannier & O'Sullivan, 2017).

Third, people from all cultures feel passionate love. Studies comparing members of individualist versus collectivist cultures, for example, have found no differences in the amount of passionate love experienced (Hatfield & Rapson, 1987).

Fourth, no gender or age differences exist in people's experience of passionate love, including the frequency and intensity with which it is experienced. Studies using the Juvenile Love Scale (which excludes references to sexual feelings) have found that children as young as age 4 report passionate love toward others (Hatfield & Rapson, 1987). The latter finding is important to consider when talking with children about their romantic feelings. Although they lack the emotional maturity to fully understand the consequences of their relationship decisions, their feelings toward romantic interests are every bit as intense and turbulent as our adult emotions. So if your 6- or 7-year-old child or sibling reveals a crush on a schoolmate, treat the disclosure with respect and empathy rather than teasing or minimizing their experience.

Fifth, for many adults, passionate love is integrally linked with sexual desire (Berscheid & Regan, 2005). In one study, undergraduates were asked whether they thought a difference existed between "being in love" and "loving" another person (Ridge & Berscheid, 1989). Eighty-seven percent of respondents said that there was a difference and that sexual attraction was the critical distinguishing feature of being in love.

Finally, passionate love is *negatively* related to the duration of a relationship. Like it or not, the longer you're with a romantic partner, the less intense your passionate love will feel (Berscheid, 2002).

Although the fire of passionate love dominates media depictions of romance, not all people view being in love this way. At the other end of the romantic spectrum is **companionate love**: an intense form of liking defined by emotional investment and deeply intertwined lives (Berscheid & Walster, 1978). Many long-term romantic relationships evolve into companionate love. As Clyde and Susan Hendrick (1992) explain, "Sexual attraction, intense communication, and emotional turbulence early in a relationship give way to quiet intimacy, predictability, and shared attitudes, values, and life experiences later in the relationship" (p. 48).

self-reflection

Is passion the critical defining feature of being in love? Or, can you fall in love without ever feeling passion? Given that passion typically fades, is romantic love always doomed to fail, or can you still be in love after passion wanes?

◐ In the award-winning romantic drama *Carol,* Therese and Carol are immediately drawn to each other by a powerful attraction that rapidly evolves into a passionate love relationship. Wilson Webb/©Weinstein Company/Everett Collection, Inc

table 11.1 Romantic Love Types

Type	Description	Attributes of Love
Storge	Friendly lovers	Stable, predictable, and rooted in friendship
Agape	Forgiving lovers	Patient, selfless, giving, and unconditional
Mania	Obsessive lovers	Intense, tumultuous, extreme, and all consuming
Pragma	Practical lovers	Logical, rational, and founded in common sense
Ludus	Game-playing lovers	Uncommitted, fun, and played like a game
Eros	Romantic lovers	Sentimental, romantic, idealistic, and committed

Between the poles of passionate and companionate love lies a range of other types of romantic love. Sociologist John Alan Lee (1973) suggested six different forms, ranging from friendly to obsessive and gave them each a traditional Greek name: *storge, agape, mania, pragma, ludus,* and *eros* (see Table 11.1 for an explanation of each). As Lee noted, there is no "right" type of romantic love—different forms appeal to different people.

Although many different types of romantic love exist, powerful binary gender stereotypes, embodied in film, literature, television, and online resources, depict women and men as complete opposites when it comes to love. Specifically, women commonly are stereotyped as "starry-eyed, sentimental, and emotional" lovers, whereas men are depicted as "cool, logical, game-players" (Hill et al., 1976). Neither of these stereotypes is factual. Across decades of scientific research, women score higher than men on measures of *pragma* ("practical love") and both women and men report high levels of disagreement with *ludus*—the idea that love should be "played as a game" (Fehr et al., 2014; Hendrick & Hendrick, 1988, 1992).

Now that we have developed a clearer sense of what romantic love is and the various forms it can take, let's turn our attention to what it means to have a romantic *relationship*.

Online Self-Quiz: Test Your Love Attitudes. To take this self-quiz, visit LaunchPad: **launchpadworks.com**

KEY ELEMENTS OF ROMANTIC RELATIONSHIPS

We know that loving differs from liking and that people experience different types of love. But what exactly does it mean to have a romantic relationship? A **romantic relationship** is a chosen interpersonal involvement forged through communication in which the participants perceive the bond as romantic. Six elements of romantic relationships underlie this definition.

Perception   A romantic relationship exists whenever the partners perceive that it does. As perceptions change, so, too, does the relationship. For example, a couple may consider their relationship "casual dating" but still define it as "romantic" (rather than friendly). Or, a long-term couple may feel more companionate than passionate but still consider themselves "in love." If two partners' perceptions of their relationship differ—for example, one person feels romantic and the other does not—they do not have a romantic relationship (Miller & Steinberg, 1975).

Diversity   Romantic relationships exhibit remarkable diversity in the ages and genders of the partners, as well as in their ethnic and religious backgrounds and sexual orientations. Yet despite this diversity, most relationships function in a similar manner. For example, across sexual orientations, the individuals involved place the same degree of importance on their relationship, devote similar amounts of time and energy to maintaining their bond, and demonstrate similar openness in their communication (Haas & Stafford, 2005). And the exact same factors—honesty, loyalty, commitment, and dedication to maintenance—determine their stability, satisfaction, and marital success (Kurdek, 2005).

Choice   We enter into romantic relationships through choice, selecting not only with whom we initiate involvements but also whether and how we maintain these bonds. Contrary to widespread belief, love doesn't "strike us out of the blue" or "sweep us away." Choice also plays a role in arranged marriages: the spouses' families and social networks select an appropriate partner, and in many cases the betrothed retain at least some control over whether the choice is acceptable (Hendrick & Hendrick, 1992).

Commitment   Romantic relationships often involve **commitment**: the intention to remain in a relationship, based on a strong psychological attachment to a partner and a long-term orientation toward the future of the involvement (Tran et al., 2019). When you forge a commitment with a partner, positive outcomes often result. Commitment leads couples to work harder on maintaining their relationships, resulting in greater satisfaction (Rusbult et al., 2001). Commitment also reduces the likelihood that partners will cheat sexually when separated by geographic distance (Le et al., 2010). These findings hold true across genders, ethnicities, and sexual orientations: data from more than 50,000 diverse participants across 202 different studies revealed that those who were more committed were substantially happier, more

self-
reflection

How much do you desire or
fear commitment? Are your
feelings based on your gender
or other factors? Consider your
friends and acquaintances.
What factors influence their
feelings of commitment? What
does this tell you about the
legitimacy of stereotypes about
gender and commitment?

▶ Depictions of romantic love
are often found in art, movies,
literature, poetry, music, and
other media, but they rarely
detail the everyday interpersonal
communication that makes
successful relationships work.
Erich Lessing/Art Resource, NY

invested, and less attracted to potential alternative partners than less committed partners were (Tran et al., 2019). What's more, comparisons of couples across sexual orientations have found no differences in commitment levels, intimacy, or satisfaction within romantic relationships (Joyner et al., 2019).

Although men are stereotyped in the media as "commitment-phobic," this stereotype is *false*. *Both* men and women view commitment as an important part of romantic relationships (Miller, 2014). Several studies even suggest that men may place a higher value on commitment than do women. For example, when asked which they would choose if forced to decide between a committed romance and an important job opportunity, more men than women chose the relationship (Mosher & Danoff-Burg, 2007). Men also score higher than women on measures of commitment in college dating relationships (Kurdek, 2008).

Tensions When we're involved in intimate relationships, we often experience competing impulses, or tensions, between ourselves and our feelings toward others, known as **relational dialectics** (Baxter, 1990). Relational dialectics take three common forms. The first is *openness versus protection*, the tension between wanting to disclose versus wanting to keep information private. As relationships become more intimate, we naturally exchange more personal information with our partners. Most of us enjoy the feeling of unity and mutual insight created through such sharing. But while we want to be open with our partners, we also want to keep certain aspects of our selves—such as our most private thoughts and feelings—protected. Too much openness provokes an uncomfortable sense that we've lost our privacy and must share *everything* with our lovers.

The second dialectic is *autonomy versus connection*, the tensions between wanting to be independent versus part of a couple. We elect to form romantic relationships largely out of a desire to bond with other human beings. Yet if we come to feel so connected to our partners that our individual identity seems to dissolve, we may choose to pull back and reclaim some of our autonomy.

The final dialectic is when our need for excitement and change clashes with our need for stability—known as *novelty versus predictability*. We all like the security that comes with knowing how our partners will behave, how we'll behave, and how our relationships will unfold. Romances are more successful when the partners behave in predictable ways that reduce uncertainty (Berger & Bradac, 1982). However, predictability often spawns boredom. As we get to know our partners, the novelty and excitement of the relationship wear off, and things seem increasingly monotonous. Reconciling the desire for predictability with the need for novelty is one of the most profound emotional challenges facing partners in romantic relationships.

Communication Romantic involvements, like all interpersonal relationships, are forged through interpersonal communication. By interacting with others through mediated technologies and face-to-face, we build a variety of relationships—some of which blossom into romantic love. Once love is born, we use interpersonal communication to foster and maintain it—and through doing so, increase our happiness and sense of well-being, and reduce our loneliness (Hall & Merolla, 2020).

To this point, we've discussed both romantic love and romantic relationships. But in order to experience love that eventually becomes a relationship, we must first find ourselves attracted to someone. Let's look at the factors that determine whether the seeds for possible love are ever planted in the first place.

Romantic Attraction

Why we are attracted to some people and not others

In our *very* favorite show to binge-watch, *Outlander*, World War II nurse Claire Randall falls through a time portal and is transported back to 1700s Scotland, where she meets James "Jamie" Fraser, a young lord living as an outlaw under British rule. The two quickly develop a fierce and undeniable attraction, partly because they're continually thrown together by circumstances, and because they are both physically attracted to each other. But more important than either of these factors is the fact that, despite the gulf of temporal distance that separates their backgrounds, they share many personality attributes and values in common: they are both principled, practical, compassionate, courageous, and selfless.

You may never meet new people by falling through Scottish time portals, but every day you interact with potential partners in class, while standing in line at the local coffee shop, or at gatherings with friends. Yet few of these individuals make a lasting impression on you, and even fewer strike a chord of romantic attraction. What draws you to those special few? Many of the same factors that drew Claire and Jamie together in *Outlander*: proximity, physical attractiveness, similarity, reciprocal liking, and resources (Aron et al., 2008). These factors influence attraction across genders and sexual orientations (Felmlee et al., 2010; Hyde, 2005).

PROXIMITY

self-reflection

How does proximity influence your attraction? Are you more or less attracted to those with whom you have frequent daily contact? How does the context influence your attraction?

The simple fact of physical proximity—being in each other's presence frequently— exerts far more impact on romantic attraction than many people think. Like Claire and Jamie, you're likely to feel more attracted to those with whom you have frequent contact and less attracted to those with whom you interact rarely, a phenomenon known as the **mere exposure effect** (Bornstein, 1989). At the same time, although you're more likely to be attracted to people you're around a lot, the effect of proximity on attraction depends on your experience with them. Repeated exposure to people you already dislike—such as a rude coworker or noisy neighbor—actually may increase your distaste for them (Bornstein & Craver-Lemley, 2004), just as being repeatedly exposed to the unattractive habits of people in your proximity will increase your disgust, not your attraction (Cunningham et al., 2005).

▶ In *Outlander*, Claire and Jamie are drawn to each other because of their proximity, physical attraction, and shared personality traits and ideals. What factors have led you to become romantically attracted to someone? Mary Evans/AF Archive/ Sony Pictures Television/AGE Fotostock

PHYSICAL ATTRACTIVENESS

It's no secret that many people feel drawn to those they perceive as physically attractive. This may be because we view beautiful people as competent communicators, intelligent, and well adjusted, a phenomenon known as the **beautiful-is-good effect** (Eagly et al., 1991). But although most of us find physical beauty attractive, we tend to form long-term romantic relationships with people we judge as similar to ourselves in physical attractiveness. This is known as **matching** (Feingold, 1988). Research documents that people don't want to be paired with those they regard as substantially "below" or "above" themselves in looks (White, 1980).

At the same time, being perceived as exceptionally physically attractive by others may actually create relationship instability for some people. In a series of four studies, Harvard psychologist Christine Ma-Kellams and her colleagues documented that people who were perceived as more physically attractive by others had shorter marriages and higher divorce rates than their less-attractive counterparts (Ma-Kellams et al., 2017). Why? Because highly attractive people have a broader range of alternative partners who strongly desire them, making their current relationship less unique and necessary (Ma-Kellams et al., 2017). They also are more likely to be on the receiving end of "poaching attempts"—that is, numerous potential partners "hit on" them and try to lure them away from their current lovers (Schmitt & Buss, 2001).

SIMILARITY

No doubt you've heard the contradictory clichés regarding similarity and attraction: "Opposites attract" versus "Birds of a feather flock together." Which is correct? Scientific evidence suggests that we are attracted to those we perceive as similar to ourselves (Miller, 2014). This is known as the **birds-of-a-feather effect**. One explanation for this phenomenon is that people we view as similar to ourselves are less likely to provoke uncertainty. In first encounters, they seem easier to predict and explain than do people we perceive as dissimilar (Berger & Calabrese, 1975). Thus, we feel more comfortable with them.

Similarity means more than physical attractiveness; it means sharing parallel hobbies, attitudes, personalities, values, and likes and dislikes (Markey & Markey, 2007). Having fundamentally different personalities or widely disparate values erodes attraction between partners in the long run. At the same time, differences in mere tastes and preferences have no long-term negative impact on relationship health, as long as you and your partner are similar in other, more important ways. For example, we (Kelly and Steve) have very different tastes in music. Steve is more into angst-filled, sad, and edgy music—such as Radiohead, Chastity Belt, and Sufjan Stevens—whereas Kelly likes up-tempo, happier, danceable music: The Police, Bruno Mars, Frank Sinatra. Steve *loves* Pink Floyd; Kelly *hates* the group. But we have very similar personalities and values, and those foundational points of commonality—along with a shared love for Rush (may Neil Peart rest in peace!), Johnny Hartman, The Spinners, and Led Zeppelin—have kept us happily married for more than 32 years. What's the moral of the story? Differences in tastes don't predict relationship success, so you shouldn't dismiss potential romantic partners because of minor likes and dislikes.

self-reflection

When you find out that someone really likes you, how does this impact your feelings toward them? Have you ever fallen for someone who you knew didn't like you? What does this tell you about the importance of reciprocal liking in shaping attraction?

RECIPROCAL LIKING

A fourth determinant of romantic attraction is one of the most obvious and often overlooked: whether the person we're attracted to makes it clear, through communication and other actions, that the attraction is mutual, known as **reciprocal liking** (Aron et al., 2008). Reciprocal liking is a potent predictor of attraction; we tend to be attracted to people who are attracted to us. Studies examining people's narrative descriptions of "falling in love" have found that reciprocal liking is *the* most commonly mentioned factor leading to love (Riela et al., 2010), and its effect on attraction is stronger than that of similarity (Montoya & Horton, 2012).

RESOURCES

A final spark that kindles romantic attraction is the unique resources that another person offers. Resources include such qualities as sense of humor, intelligence, kindness, supportiveness, and whether the person seems fun to be with. These attributes are viewed as valuable regardless of gender or sexual orientation (Felmlee et al., 2010). But what leads *you* to view a person's resources as desirable?

Social exchange theory proposes that you'll feel drawn to those you see as offering substantial benefits (things you like and want) with few associated costs (things demanded of you in return). Two factors drive whether you find someone initially attractive: whether you perceive the person as offering the kinds of rewards you think you deserve in a romantic relationship (affection, emotional support, money, sex), and whether you think that the rewards the person can offer you are superior to those you can get elsewhere (Kelley & Thibaut, 1978). In simple terms, you're attracted to people who can give you what you want and who offer better rewards than others.

Once you've experienced attraction because of perceived rewards, **equity**—the balance of benefits and costs exchanged by you and the other person—determines whether a relationship will take root (Stafford, 2003). Romantic partners are happiest when the balance of giving and getting in their relationship is equal for both, and they're least happy when inequity exists (Hatfield et al., 1985).

What is *inequity*? People in relationships have a strong sense of proportional justice: the balance between benefits gained from the relationship versus contributions made to the relationship (Hatfield, 1983). Inequity occurs when the benefits or contributions provided by one person are greater than those provided by the other. People who get more rewards from their relationships for fewer costs than their partners are *overbenefited*; those who get fewer rewards from their relationships for more costs than their partners are *underbenefited*. Overbenefited individuals experience negative emotions such as guilt, while underbenefited partners experience emotions such as sadness and anger (Sprecher, 2001).

Equity strongly determines the short- and long-term success of romantic relationships. One study found that during a period of several months, only 23 percent of equitable romances broke up, whereas 54 percent of inequitable romantic relationships ended (Sprecher, 2001).

TECHNOLOGY AND ROMANTIC ATTRACTION

The enormous range of communication technologies available to us refines and enhances the attraction process. You can establish virtual proximity to attractive others by befriending or following them on social media and then exchanging updates and posts. You can assess a prospective partner's similarity to you and the rewards they could offer you by interacting with the person through texting or simply by checking their online profiles. You can assess physical attractiveness by viewing online photo albums and video clips. On dating apps such as OkCupid, Bumble, Hinge, and Coffee Meets Bagel, you can be matched with a broad range of potential partners by entering a set of parameters, such as desired age, interests, gender identity, sexual orientation, and so on. As the dating site eharmony reports, the most important factors that people report seeking are physical features they find appealing and characteristics they share in common (Thottam, n.d.). Thirty percent of people in the United States have used online dating sites to meet new partners, and this percentage increases to 55 percent among lesbian, gay, or bisexual adults (Vogels, 2020). Online dating platforms are pervasive and profitable, with about 8,000 different sites worldwide worth close to $2 billion annually (Bonilla-Zorita et al., 2020). Online dating is so popular, in large part, because it is convenient and allows people to interact with a much broader range of potential partners than they otherwise could.

◁ Although they show you a wide range of potential partners, dating apps have drawn controversy from critics, who claim that the matchmaking system is superficial and often based overwhelmingly on physical appearance. What differences have you found between online dating and asking someone out, in person, on a date?
Predrag Vuckovic/Getty Images

But the rewards of convenience are balanced by risk. While we may ask our friends to help us craft our online profiles, we are now less likely to have our friends or family connect us to potential partners because we can meet through online platforms (Rosenfeld et al., 2019). And this loss of network intermediaries may increase uncertainty. For example, you have to decide not only how honest to be in your online self-presentation (Ellison et al., 2006) but also how honest you think others are in their online self-presentations. Seventy-one percent of online daters think it is very common for people to lie in order to appear more appealing in their profiles (Anderson et al., 2020). And these perceptions are on point. A majority of people *have* lied in their online profiles, with 20 percent of women lying about their appearance and 40 percent of men lying about their jobs (Thottam, n.d.). As one user describes, "Everyone is so wonderful over the internet. What the internet doesn't tell you is that, 'I'm defensive, I talk about my problems all the time, I can't manage my money' " (Ellison et al., 2006, p. 435). Furthermore, people have noted the objectification that can occur on these platforms (Bonilla-Zorita et al., 2020) and have reported troubling encounters, such as continuing to be contacted by someone after indicating a lack of interest (Vogels, 2020).

So how can we approach these relationships? If your goal is to forge an offline romantic relationship, craft your online self-descriptions in a way that accentuates your attractive attributes without resorting to distortion or dishonesty. If you feel you may be crossing the line into deception, ask a trustworthy friend to check your online description and assess its authenticity. And then continue to seek the counsel of your network of friends and family to help reduce your uncertainty through the process, asking for and listening to their perceptions and input.

We now have an understanding of what romantic love and relationships are, and how love sparks in the first place. In the next section, we explore the different stages through which romantic relationships commonly pass.

▼ Ali Stroker (see the Focus on Culture box) is the first actor who uses a wheelchair to appear on Broadway and to be nominated for and win a Tony Award. Scott Gries/Invision/AP Images

Relationship Development and Deterioration

How couples come together and separate

Romantic relationships come together and apart in as many different ways and at as many different speeds as there are partners who fall for each other (Surra & Hughes, 1997). Many relationships are of the "casual dating" variety — they flare quickly, sputter, and then fade. Others endure and evolve with deepening levels of commitment. But all romantic relationships undergo stages marked by distinctive patterns in partners' communication, thoughts, and feelings. We know these transitions intuitively: "taking things to the next level," "kicking it up a notch," "taking a step back," or "taking a break." Communication scholar Mark Knapp (1984) modeled these patterns as ten stages: five of "coming together" and five of "coming apart."

focus on CULTURE

Romance and People with Disabilities in Pop Culture

When you think of people falling in love, what comes to mind? If you are a fan of televised holiday romantic movies, you might think of people who kindle new romances while busy with their jobs and holiday preparations. The Lifetime Channel movie *Christmas Ever After* fits this mold. The movie stars Tony Award–winning actor Ali Stroker as a writer struggling with writer's block who debarks to a favorite holiday resort before Christmas. In a classic example of holiday movie magic, her character befriends the innkeeper's young granddaughter, successfully completes her novel, and falls in love with the innkeeper's son. Discussing how she clears her mind to overcome writer's block, Stroker's character says, "I like to get my body moving. Usually I'll go for a push in my neighborhood."

In December 2020, Stroker became the first lead actor in a Lifetime Channel movie who has a disability — and the first wheelchair user *ever* to star in a lead role in a holiday movie. Notably, *Christmas Ever After* does *not* primarily focus on her character's disability, but rather on her job and her developing romance. *Anyone* could have played the lead character. Unlike many other films and TV shows that have cast actors without disabilities to portray characters with disabilities, or that have focused on characters with disabilities overcoming challenges, this movie is simply about people falling in love.

Recent years have seen increased representation of people with disabilities in the media. Actors with disabilities are actively defining how they are seen and portrayed in the broader entertainment industry, including on television, on Broadway, on streaming services, and — yes — in romantic movies (Harris, 2020). As Esme Mazzeo of *Marie Claire* magazine writes in her review of *Christmas Ever After*, "As a wheelchair user who has all but given up on dating apps. . . . I can finally watch someone who looks like me get their happy ending" (2020). And such media representation has a powerful impact on our perceptions and our communication in real life. Positive portrayals, such as Stroker's character in *Christmas Ever After*, help mainstream audiences understand that people with disabilities are simply *people* who experience romance, friendship, family relationships, and workplace relationships just like everyone else.

discussion questions

- What are some of your favorite media representations of romantic love? How are people represented in these images?
- What lessons have you learned about romantic love from these representations?

COMING TOGETHER

Knapp's stages of coming together illustrate one possible flow of relationship development (see Figure 11.1). As you read through the stages, keep in mind that these suggest turning points in relationships and are not fixed rules for how involvements should or do progress. Your relationships may go through some, none, or all of these stages. They may skip stages, jump back or forward in order, or follow a completely different and unique trajectory.

Initiating　During the **initiating** stage, you size up a person you've just met or noticed. You draw on all available visual information (physical attractiveness, age, clothing, posture) to determine whether you find them attractive. Your primary concern at this stage is to portray yourself in a positive light. You also ponder and present a greeting you deem appropriate. This greeting might be in person or online.

figure 11.1　**Stages of Coming Together**

Experimenting   Once you've initiated an encounter with someone else (online or face-to-face), you enter the **experimenting** stage, during which you exchange demographic information (names, majors, where you grew up). You also engage in *small talk*—disclosing facts you and the other person consider relatively unimportant but that enable you to introduce yourselves in a safe and controlled fashion. As you share these details, you look for points of commonality on which you can base further interaction. This is the "casual dating" phase of romance. For better or worse, *most involvements never progress beyond this stage*. We go through life experimenting with many people but forming deeper connections with very few.

Intensifying   Occasionally, you'll progress beyond casual dating and find yourself experiencing strong feelings of attraction toward another person. When this happens, your verbal and nonverbal communication becomes increasingly intimate. During this **intensifying** stage, you and your partner begin to reveal previously withheld information, such as secrets about your past or important life dreams and goals. You may begin using informal forms of address or terms of endearment (e.g., "honey") and saying "we" more frequently. One particularly strong sign that your relationship is intensifying is the direct expression of commitment. You might do this verbally ("I think I'm falling for you") or online by marking your profile as "in a relationship" rather than "single." You may also spend more time in each other's personal spaces, as well as begin physical expressions of affection, such as hand-holding, cuddling, or sexual activity.

LaunchPad Video

launchpadworks.com

Integrating
Watch this clip online to answer the questions below.

How many of your relationships have progressed to the integrating stage? How did you know when they reached that stage? What verbal and nonverbal behaviors do two people in the integrating stage of their relationship use?

Want to see more? Check out LaunchPad for clips illustrating **experimenting** and **bonding**.

Integrating   During the **integrating** stage, your and your partner's personalities seem to become one. This integration may be reinforced through sexual activity and the exchange of belongings (items of clothing, music, photos, etc.). When you've integrated with a romantic partner, you cultivate attitudes, activities, and interests that clearly join you together as a couple—"*our* song" and "*our* favorite restaurant." Friends, colleagues, and family members begin to treat you as a couple—for example, always inviting the two of you to parties or dinners. Not surprisingly, many people begin to struggle with the dialectical tension of *connectedness versus autonomy* at this stage. As a student of ours once told his partner when describing this stage, "I'm not me anymore; I'm *us*."

Bonding   The ultimate stage of coming together is **bonding**, a public ritual that announces to the world that you and your partner have made a commitment to each other. Bonding is something you'll share with very few people—perhaps only one—during your lifetime. The most obvious example of bonding is marriage.

Bonding formally institutionalizes your relationship. Before this stage, the ground rules for your relationship and your communication within it remain a private matter, to be negotiated between you and your partner. In the bonding stage, you import into your relationship a set of laws and customs determined by governmental authorities and perhaps religious institutions. These laws and customs can make your relationship feel more rigid and structured, as it's now defined not solely by you and your partner, but by historical, social, and legal practices. At the same time, these external factors also function to solidify your relationship—making it "official" to all those in your social network as well

There are many ways for couples to bond, but the key is that both partners agree and make a deep commitment to each other. Mario Tama/Getty Images; Larry Dale Gordon/Getty Images

as the broader public at large. This is especially important for LGBTQ+ couples, in order to offset discrimination they may face regarding their relationships (Kennedy et al., 2018).

COMING APART

Coming together is often followed by coming apart. One study of college dating couples found that across a three-month period, 30 percent broke up (Parks & Adelman, 1983). Similar trends occur in the married adult population in the United States, which has a divorce rate of about 40 to 50 percent (APA, n.d.). According to the Pew Research Center, the marriage rate has been declining, the average age of first marriage has risen to age 30 for men and 28 for women, and the divorce rate among adults ages 65 and older has nearly tripled since 1990 (Barroso et al., 2020).

In some relationships, breaking up is the right thing to do. Partners have grown apart, they've lost interest in each other, or perhaps one person has been abusive. In other relationships, coming apart is unfortunate. Perhaps the partners could have resolved their differences but didn't make the effort or didn't know what to do.

Like coming together, coming apart unfolds over stages marked by changes in thoughts, feelings, and communication (see Figure 11.2). But unlike coming together, these stages often entail emotional turmoil that makes it difficult to negotiate skillfully. Learning how to communicate supportively while a romantic relationship is dissolving is a challenging but important part of being a skilled interpersonal communicator.

Differentiating   Circumscribing   Stagnating   Avoiding   Terminating

figure 11.2 **Stages of Coming Apart**

skills practice

Differentiating
Overcoming the challenge of differentiating

❶ Identify when you and your romantic partner are differentiating.

❷ Check your perception of the relationship, especially how you've punctuated encounters and the attributions you've made.

❸ Call to mind the similarities that originally brought you and your partner together.

❹ Discuss your concerns with your partner, emphasizing these similarities and your desire to continue the relationship.

❺ Mutually explore solutions to the differences that have been troubling you, considering their significance and if they are attitude, personality, or value differences.

Differentiating In all romantic relationships, partners share differences as well as similarities. But during **differentiating**—the first stage of coming apart—the beliefs, attitudes, and values that distinguish you from your partner come to dominate your thoughts and communication ("I can't *believe* you think that!" or "We are *so* different!").

Most healthy romances experience occasional periods of differentiating. These moments can involve unpleasant clashes and bickering over contrasting viewpoints, tastes, or goals. But you can move your relationship through this difficulty—and thus halt the coming-apart process—by openly discussing your points of difference and working together to resolve them. To do this, review the constructive conflict skills discussed in Chapter 10.

Circumscribing If one or both of you respond to problematic differences by ignoring them and spending less time talking, you enter the **circumscribing** stage. You actively begin to restrict the quantity and quality of information you exchange with your partner. Instead of sharing information, you create "safe zones" in which you discuss only topics that won't provoke conflict. Common remarks made during circumscribing include "Don't ask me about that" and "Let's not talk about that anymore." It is like playing a game of Twister with conversational topics: you can only touch this topic or that one, but not any of the others.

Stagnating When circumscribing becomes so severe that almost no safe conversational topics remain, communication slows to a standstill, and your relationship enters the **stagnating** stage. You both presume that communicating is pointless because it will only lead to further problems. People in stagnant relationships often experience a sense of resignation; they feel stuck or trapped. However, they can remain in the relationship for months or even years. Why? Some believe that it's better to leave things as they are rather than expend the effort necessary to break up or rebuild the relationship. Others simply don't know how to repair the damage and revive the earlier bond.

Avoiding During the **avoiding** stage, one or both of you decide that you can no longer be around each other, and you begin distancing yourself physically. Some people communicate avoidance directly to their partner ("I don't want to see you anymore"). Others do so indirectly—for example, by going out when their partner's at home, screening phone calls, ignoring texts, blocking someone from their social media, or changing their social media status from "in a relationship" to "single."

self-reflection

Have most of your romantic relationships ended by avoiding? Or, have you sought the closure provided by terminating? In what situations is one approach to ending relationships better than the other? Is one more ethical?

Terminating In ending a relationship, some people want to come together for a final encounter that gives a sense of closure and resolution. During the **terminating** stage, couples might discuss the past, present, and future of the relationship. They often exchange summary statements about the past—comments on "how our relationship was" that are either accusations ("No one has ever treated me so badly!") or laments ("I'll never be able to find someone as perfect as you"). Verbal and nonverbal behaviors indicating a lack of intimacy are readily apparent, including physical distance between the two individuals and reluctance to make eye contact. The partners may also discuss the future status of their relationship. Some couples may agree to end all contact going forward. Others may choose to maintain some level of physical intimacy even though the emotional side of the relationship is officially over. Still others may express interest in "being friends."

Many people find terminating a relationship painful or awkward. It's hard to tell someone else that you no longer want to be involved, and it is equally painful to hear it. Draw on your interpersonal communication skills to best negotiate your way through this dreaded moment. In particular, infuse your communication with *empathy*—offering empathic concern and perspective-taking (see Chapter 3). Realize that romantic breakups are a form of loss and that it's normal to experience grief, even when breaking up is the right thing to do. Offer supportive communication ("I'm sorry things had to end this way" or "I know this is going to be painful for both of us"), and use grief management tactics (see Chapter 4). Conversations to terminate a relationship are never pleasant or easy. But the communication skills you've learned can help you minimize the pain and damage, enabling you and your former partner to move on to other relationships.

To this point, we've talked a good deal about the nature of love, and we've traced the stages through which many romances progress. Now let's shift focus to a more practical concern: how you can use interpersonal communication to maintain a satisfying, healthy romantic relationship.

Maintaining Romantic Relationships

Strategies to sustain romances over time and across distance

Having been married for more than 32 years now, and having team-taught a class on close relationships for the last 25 of those years, we've occasionally had students tell us about their hopes to have a relationship like ours. We respond by shifting the focus to *our* role models for marriage—our parents. Both of our parents' marriages have lasted for more than 55 years, and both marriages are vital and happy. They always made marriage *look* easy, so when we each entered into our own fledgling romances, we thought love just "happened." People fell in love, got along, and it endured.

But as we've aged, and dealt with the challenges of our own marriage, we've learned that our youthful impressions of our parents' relationships were naïve. The romantic love that Ross and Carol (Kelly's parents) and Connie and Bruce (Steve's parents) have felt for one another hasn't been a magical, mystical union that just

○ Our parents have worked tirelessly to maintain their relationships by staying positive, offering assurances, sharing tasks, and practicing self-disclosure. What strategies have you used to maintain a romantic relationship?
Steven McCornack; Courtesy of Kelly Morrison

existed. Instead, their loves have been *actively maintained*, day in and day out. Across decades, they have consistently gone out of their way to compliment each other, give each other little gifts, and lift each other's spirits through humor. They have assured each other of their feelings and commitment, and they've pitched in to help each other out with daily chores and tasks, regardless of fatigue or mood. They've shared everything with each other—all their hopes, dreams, and vulnerabilities—and they've accepted each other for who they really are. In short, the enduring love between our parents, which looked effortless to us as children, was actually the result of hard work.

MAINTENANCE STRATEGIES

Love is often depicted as just happening—it strikes, and then it endures. A basic rule of romantic love, however, is that maintenance is necessary to keep relationships from deteriorating (Stafford, 2003). **Relational maintenance** refers to using communication and supportive behaviors to sustain a desired relationship status and level of satisfaction (Stafford et al., 2000). Couples who engage in frequent maintenance often possess a "communal" attitude toward their relationships, focusing on their partners' needs out of a sense of loving concern rather than a desire for self-gain (Stafford, 2020). They also experience a host of relational benefits as a result, including increases in happiness, commitment, equality in decision making, love, liking, and relationship longevity (Ogolsky & Bowers, 2012). Investing time and energy into maintenance doesn't just make *relationships* healthier and happier, however; it also impacts *individuals'* well-being. Research documents that investing daily time into sustaining closeness with a romantic partner substantially boosts one's *own* life happiness, increasing the frequency of positive emotions and reducing the experience of negative emotions (Hudson et al., 2020).

Across several studies, communication scholar Laura Stafford has observed seven strategies that satisfied couples routinely use to maintain their romances (Stafford, 2010). (See Table 11.2 for an overview of these categories.)

Positivity   Positivity includes communicating in a cheerful and optimistic fashion, doing unsolicited favors, and giving unexpected gifts. Partners involved in romantic relationships cite positivity as *the* most important maintenance tactic for

table 11.2 Romantic Relationship Maintenance Strategies

Maintenance Strategy	Suggested Actions
Positivity	Be cheerful and optimistic in your communication.
Assurances	Remind your partner of your devotion.
Sharing tasks	Help out with daily responsibilities.
Acceptance	Be supportive and forgiving.
Self-disclosure	Share your thoughts, feelings, and fears.
Relationship talks	Make time to discuss your relationship and really listen.
Social networks	Involve yourself with your partner's friends and family.

ensuring happiness (Ogolsky & Bowers, 2012). This holds true regardless of sexual orientation (Stafford, 2010; Haas & Stafford, 2005). You use positivity when:[1]

- You try to make each interaction with your partner enjoyable.
- You try to build your partner up by giving them compliments.
- You try to be fun, upbeat, and romantic with your partner.

You undermine positivity when:

- You constantly look for and complain about problems in your relationship without offering solutions.
- You whine, pout, and sulk when you don't get your way.
- You criticize favors and gifts from your partner.

Assurances Assurances are messages that emphasize how much a partner means to you, demonstrate how important the relationship is, and describe a secure future together. Similar to positivity, assurances substantially boost relationship satisfaction, and are *the* most powerful maintenance tactic for solidifying and sustaining a sense of commitment (Ogolsky & Bowers, 2012). Assurances are especially impactful for individuals experiencing depression, who often express a greater need for messages of relational affirmation (Fowler & Gasiorek, 2017).

Assurances may be expressed directly and verbally, such as saying "I love you" or "I can't see myself ever being with anyone but you." But they also can be communicated through actions. One of the most powerful ways to convey assurances to a romantic partner is to *prioritize your partner as the focus of your attention, in situations where the principal activity is sharing time together*—such as on a romantic date, or during mutually recognized "quality time" at home. Research on romance and technology usage indicates that couples distinguish between time spent "casually hanging out together" versus "intimate/quality time," and that cellphone usage is acceptable during the former but considered off-limits during the latter (Miller-Ott & Kelly, 2015). More specifically, partners consider phone usage during encounters where attention "should be" focused on them to be a substantial violation of expectations, one that communicates powerful messages about the *lack* of importance placed on the relationship, undermining relational satisfaction (Kelly et al., 2017). And it's not just usage that matters, but *the perception that a partner is dependent on their phone*. Across studies, people who perceive their partners to be obsessively fixated on their phones (even if they're not actively using them) are substantially less happy with their romantic relationships and experience more loneliness (Lapierre, 2020).

You use assurances when:

- You regularly tell your partner how devoted you are to your relationship.
- You talk about future plans and events to be shared together (anniversaries, vacations, marriage, children).
- You prioritize your partner as the sole focus of your attention when sharing "quality time" together.

---

[1]Information that follows is from the revised relationship maintenance behavior scale of Stafford (2010).

You undermine assurances when:

- You flirt with others and talk about how attractive they are in front of your partner.
- You tell your partner not to count on anything long term.
- You always have to have your cell phone with you, and you prioritize it or other electronic devices over your partner during romantic encounters.

Sharing Tasks   The most *frequently* practiced form of maintenance is sharing tasks. This involves taking mutual responsibility for chores and negotiating an equitable division of labor. Although this may sound like something that only serious, cohabiting, or married couples face, sharing tasks is relevant for all couples and includes responsibilities like providing transportation to work or campus, running errands, and making reservations for dinner. You share tasks when:

- You try to pitch in equally on everyday responsibilities.
- You ask your partner how you can help out.
- You make an effort to handle tasks before your partner asks you to do them.

You undermine task sharing when:

- You strategically avoid having to do your share of the work.
- You never ask your partner how you can help out.
- You expect your partner to run errands and do chores for you, without reciprocating.

Acceptance   Part of what builds a strong sense of intimacy between romantic partners is the feeling that partners accept us for who we really are, fully and completely, and forgive us our flaws. Acceptance involves communicating this affirmation and support. You convey acceptance when:

- You forgive your partner when they make mistakes.
- You support your partner in their decisions.
- You are patient with your partner when they are irritable or in a bad mood.

You undermine acceptance when:

- You hold grievances and grudges against your partner.
- You tell your partner that you wish they were different.
- You critique your partner's appearance, personality, beliefs, and values.

Self-Disclosure   An essential part of maintaining intimacy is creating a climate of security and trust within your relationship. This allows both partners to feel that they can disclose fears and feelings without repercussion. To foster self-disclosure, each person must behave in ways that are predictable, trustworthy, and ethical. Over time, consistency in behavior evokes mutual respect and the perception that self-disclosure will be welcomed. You use self-disclosure when:

- You tell your partner about your fears and vulnerabilities.
- You share your feelings and emotions with your partner.
- You encourage your partner to disclose their thoughts and feelings, and offer empathy in return.

LaunchPad Video

launchpadworks.com

Relational Maintenance
Watch this clip online to answer the questions below.

Maintaining a relationship after a conflict can be a challenging situation. How is the couple in the video handling the situation? What maintenance strategies are they using? What maintenance strategies do you think are especially important after a fight? On a daily basis?

You undermine self-disclosure when:

- You disparage your partner's perspective.
- You routinely keep important information hidden from your partner.
- You betray your partner by sharing confidential information about them with others.

Relationship Talks   Romantic maintenance includes occasionally sitting down and discussing the status of your relationship, how you each feel about it, and where you both see it going. Relationship talks allow you to gauge how invested you each are and whether you agree on future plans and goals. They also provide a convenient forum for expressing and resolving concerns, and forestalling future conflict. You encourage relationship talks when:

- You set aside time in your schedule to chat about your relationship.
- You openly and respectfully share your relationship concerns with your partner.
- You encourage your partner to share their feelings about the relationship with you.

You undermine relationship talks when:

- You react defensively and egocentrically whenever your partner shares relationship concerns.
- You avoid or refuse to have relationship talks with your partner.
- You actively ridicule the need to discuss the relationship.

Social Networks   Romances are more likely to survive if important members of a couple's social networks approve of the relationship (Felmlee, 2001). For example, communication scholars Malcolm Parks and Mara Adelman (1983) measured how much support romantically involved individuals received from their partner's friends and family, what percentage of their partner's network they had met, and how often they communicated with these people. Using these factors and others, Parks and Adelman were able to predict with 88 percent accuracy which relationships would survive. What were the strongest determinants of whether couples stayed together? Support from family and friends, and regular communication with one's partner.

Fostering healthy relationships with surrounding friends and family appears especially crucial for those involved in interethnic relationships (Baptiste, 1990), for gay and lesbian couples (Williams et al., 2016), and for transgender people and their romantic partners (Marshall et al., 2020). As professor David Ludden describes, when a marriage lacks support from family, friends, or broader society, this may "tip the scale towards dysfunction and divorce" (2017). Gay and lesbian couples still experience stress from discrimination, despite recent trends toward greater cultural inclusivity and acceptance (Cooper et al., 2020). This makes having supportive environments—such as churches or clubs—and being treated "the same" as straight couples by their friends and family especially important for their relationship stability and satisfaction (Haas & Stafford, 1998). Meanwhile, trans people and their partners find themselves navigating not just disapproval and discrimination behavior, but broader cultural norms emphasizing and enforcing binary gender, as discussed in Chapter 6. Connecting with others who share similar experiences and finding support at the personal and community levels are important factors for these couples (Marshall et al., 2020).

You foster supportive social networks when:

- You tell your partner how much you like their friends and family.
- You invite your partner's friends or family members to share activities with the two of you.
- You willingly turn to family members of both partners for help and advice when needed.

You undermine social networks when:

- You make critical and disparaging remarks regarding your partner's friends and family.
- You intentionally avoid encounters with your partner's friends and family.
- You demand that your partner choose between spending time with you and spending time with friends and family.

MAINTAINING ROMANCE ACROSS DISTANCE

People often think that long-distance relationships are doomed to fail. We (Kelly and Steve) are living proof that this is mistaken. Over the course of our marriage, we have been long-distance for two extended periods because of job demands: once for a year and a half, and once for two years. Although both instances were challenging, the key was compensating for the lack of direct contact by using other available modalities. During our most recent separation, for example, we visited each other every six weeks or so, but texted multiple times daily, sent bitmojis and cards, and chatted via webcam nightly. Our face-to-face conversations when we were proximic were pretty much the same as our technologically mediated interactions when we were apart, in terms of breadth and depth of topics.

Our experience in these instances of geographic separation matches the research, which suggests that the keys to sustaining closeness and satisfaction within long-distance romances are the ability to comfortably and fluidly transition between communication modalities, and to avoid limiting the discussion of certain topics to specific modes (Wang et al., 2019). For instance, couples who reported "experiencing discomfort when transitioning from conversations in person to using only technology to talk" were substantially less happy when they were long distance, as were couples who opted to "delay discussion of certain topics until we're face-to-face" (Wang et al., 2019, p. 609). What's more, over time, long-distance couples come to associate different modalities with different meanings and purposes. Text-only formats such as email, messaging, and texts are most frequently used for daily updates and casual banter; video chat often is viewed as the most intimate and meaningful; and written forms such as letters and postcards convey effort and thoughtfulness (Janning et al., 2018). And although each couple determines what works best for them, the most important thing for *all* long-distance couples is that they use available modalities to create a "shared space" within which they feel emotionally and intimately connected (Janning et al., 2018).

Some research has found that long-distance romantic relationships actually can be *more* satisfying and stable than those that are geographically close

skills practice

Maintaining Romance through Mediated Communication
Using mediated communication to maintain romance

❶ Send your partner a text message or email that has no purpose other than to compliment them.

❷ Post a message on your partner's social media, saying how excited you are about seeing them soon.

❸ During a high-stress day for your partner, send an email or text message that says, "Just thinking of you."

❹ Recall a friend or family member whom your partner has been concerned about, and send an email or text to your partner inquiring about that person.

❺ Think of a task your partner has been wanting you to do, complete it, then text your partner to let them know you took care of it.

◐ Couples who are geographically distant can use video chat to stay emotionally close. Have you ever been in a long-distance relationship? What strategies did you use to stay connected to your partner? PhotoAlto/Frederic Cirou/Getty Images

(Stafford, 2010). On measures of love, positivity, agreement, and overall communication quality, geographically distant couples often score *higher* than local partners (Stafford & Merolla, 2007). Why? Stafford (2010) offers several reasons. Couples separated by distance often constrain their communication to only that which is positive, steadfastly shying away from mundane complaints or criticisms that they might be more inclined to share if they were in the same location. Geographically distant couples also idealize their partners more. When you're not around your partner every day, it's easy to cherish misconceptions about their "perfection." And visits between partners are typically occasional, brief in duration, and passionate. This amplifies the feeling that all their time together is intense and positive—an unsustainable illusion when people see each other regularly (Sahlstein, 2004).

The most difficult maintenance challenge long-distance couples face is not the separation but the eventual reunion. Almost all couples separated by distance express a desire to be near each other again, and they anticipate that being together will result in dramatic relationship improvements (Stafford et al., 2006). But the reality is more complicated. Couples who are reunited following separation are twice as likely to break up, compared with those who remain long distance (Stafford & Merolla, 2007). Rather than being "all bliss, all the time," living locally presents a blend of rewards and costs (Stafford et al., 2006). On the plus side, couples get to spend more time together, savoring each other's company and sharing in the "little" things they missed when apart. On the minus side, partners' cherished illusions about each other are shattered. Reunited couples report realizing for the first time their lover's negative characteristics, such as laziness, sloppiness, immaturity, or failure to invest effort in the relationship. They describe a substantial reduction in autonomy, experienced as a loss of time and space for themselves, loss of interaction with friends and family, and irritation with having to be accountable to their partner. Reunited couples also report increased conflict, as formerly "taboo" topics become regularly discussed and fought over.

Despite the challenges, you can have a happy and enduring long-distance romance. Here are some suggestions to help maintain such relationships:

1. While separated, use a variety of modalities to regularly communicate and create a sense of "shared space" with your partner. Using text messaging, email, and video chat can substantially boost relationship health and happiness (Janning et al., 2018), and reduce the likelihood of loneliness, sleep disruption, anxiety, and depression that often flow from being physically separated from a partner (Yoder & Du Bois, 2020).

2. When communicating with your distant partner, follow the maintenance strategies discussed earlier in this chapter. In particular, focus on the two most important for maintaining satisfaction—positivity and assurances—and try to keep your interactions upbeat, positive, and filled with discussions of shared future plans and dreams.

3. When you permanently reunite, expect a significant period of adjustment— one that is marked by tension (as you rebalance autonomy versus connection), disappointment (as idealistic illusions of your partner are replaced by the reality), and conflict (as you begin talking about topics you shelved during the separation). Avoid expecting everything to be perfect, and use the strategies you've learned in our discussion of conflict (Chapter 10) to manage difficult dilemmas when they arise.

DECIDING WHETHER TO MAINTAIN

In Steve's favorite movie of all time, *Eternal Sunshine of the Spotless Mind* (2004), Joel (Jim Carrey) and Clementine (Kate Winslet) are lovers struggling to maintain a bittersweet romance (Bregman et al., 2004). Clementine, an outgoing self-described "high-maintenance girl," is the opposite of quiet, bookish Joel, who communicates more with his private journal than with her. Following a fight, Clementine impetuously visits a clinic that specializes in memory erasure and has Joel expunged

▶ In *Eternal Sunshine of the Spotless Mind,* Joel and Clementine decide to take another shot at their relationship despite the risks.
© Focus Features/Everett Collection, Inc.

from her mind. Despondent, Joel follows suit. But the two meet again and find themselves attracted to each other. Eventually discovering the truth—that they aren't strangers at all but longtime lovers—they face a momentous decision: Do they invest the time and energy necessary to maintain their romance a second time, knowing that they failed so terribly before that they chose to destroy their memories? Or, do they end it before their history of relational disaster can repeat itself?

Romantic relationships aren't always about happiness and celebration. No matter how much you love your partner, you will still experience unpleasant moments, such as feeling irked, bored, or trapped. In fact, on any given day, 44 percent of us are likely to be seriously annoyed by a close relationship partner (Kowalski et al., 2003). Though such experiences are normal, many people find them disturbing and wonder whether they should end the relationship.

As one way to work through the decision of whether to maintain an involvement or end it, familiarize yourself with the characteristics of couples whose relationship has survived. Four factors, each of which we've discussed, appear to be most important in predicting the survival of a romantic relationship. First is *the degree to which the partners consider themselves "in love."* Couples are more likely to stay together if they think of themselves as in love, are considering marriage or a lifelong commitment, rate their relationship as high in closeness, or date each other exclusively (Hill et al., 1976). In *Eternal Sunshine*, this is the factor that eventually leads Joel and Clementine to decide to stay together: the realization that despite all they've suffered—including the purging of their memories—they still love each other. Second is *equity*. Romantic relationships are happiest and most stable when the balance of giving and getting is equal for both partners (Hatfield et al., 1985). Third is *similarity*. Highly similar couples are more likely to stay together than couples who are dissimilar (Hill et al., 1976). Fourth is *network support*. A romance is more likely to endure when the couple's social networks approve of the relationship (Felmlee, 2001; Parks & Adelman, 1983). To determine how well your relationship meets these criteria, ask yourself the following questions:

- Are you still in love with your partner?
- Is your relationship equitable?
- Do you and your partner share values and personality traits?
- Do your family and friends support your relationship?

If you answer yes to these questions, your relationship may warrant investment in maintenance. But remember: *deciding whether to maintain a struggling relationship or to let it go is a choice only you can make.* Friends, family members, pop-culture relationship experts, and textbooks can't tell you when to keep or when to leave a romantic involvement. Romantic relationships are in many ways practical endeavors. Your decision to maintain or end a struggling romance should be based on a long-term forecast of your relationship. Stacking your relationship up against those four criteria can give you insight into whether your relationship has a solid foundation upon which to invest further effort.

Romantic Relationship Challenges

Addressing challenges related to romance

In Kaui Hart Hemmings's novel *The Descendants* (2008), attorney Matt King is the descendant of native Hawaiian royalty, whose wife Joanie is in an irreversible coma. Suddenly a single parent, Matt must try to reconnect emotionally with two daughters from whom he has long been detached. Complicating matters further, he discovers that Joanie—whom he had considered his best friend, sparring partner, and closest

▶ In *The Descendants,* Matt King is able to move on and come to terms with his wife's betrayal by bonding with his daughters. Have you ever felt betrayed by a romantic partner? If so, what strategies did you use to cope with this betrayal? Merie Weismiller Wallace/TM and copyright ©Fox Searchlight Pictures/Everett Collection

confidante—was cheating on him before the accident and had planned to divorce him. In the climactic scene of the book, he puts the pain of her betrayal to rest:

> I bow my head and speak to Joanie softly. "I'm sorry I didn't give you everything you wanted. I wasn't everything you wanted. You were everything I wanted. Every day. Home. There you are. Dinner, dishes, TV. Weekends at the beach. You go here. I go there. Parties. Home to complain about the party." I can't think of anything else. Just our routine together. "I forgive you," I say. Why is it so hard to articulate love, yet so easy to express disappointment? (Hemmings, 2011, pp. 235–236)

Romantic love inspires us to strive toward a host of ideals, including compassion, caring, generosity, and selflessness. But romance has an intensely challenging side as well. As scholar Robin Kowalski pointedly puts it, "People in romantic relationships do a lot of mean and nasty things to one another" (Kowalski et al., 2003, p. 472). And when they do, the result is often unparalleled pain and despair.

In this section, we explore some of the most troubling issues related to romance—betrayal, jealousy, intrusion, and violence—and discuss communication strategies for addressing them.

BETRAYAL

As illustrated in *The Descendants,* betrayal is one of the most devastating experiences that can occur in a close involvement (Haden & Hojjat, 2006). **Romantic betrayal** is defined as an act that goes against expectations of a romantic relationship and, as a result, causes pain to a partner (Jones et al., 2001). Common examples include *sexual infidelity* (engaging in sexual activity with someone else), *emotional infidelity* (developing a strong romantic attachment to someone else), *deception* (intentional manipulation of information), and *disloyalty* (hurting your partner to benefit yourself). But any behavior that violates norms of loyalty and trustworthiness can be considered betrayal.

self-QUIZ

Do Your Behaviors Betray Your Partner?

Read each statement, and rate how often you have engaged in the activity described: 1 (never), 2 (once), 3 (a few times), 4 (several times), 5 (many times). Tally your score by adding up your answers.

To take this quiz online, visit LaunchPad: **launchpadworks.com**

_____ Snubbing your partner when you are with a group you want to impress

_____ Gossiping about your partner behind their back

_____ Making a promise to your partner with no intention of keeping it

_____ Telling others information given to you in confidence by your partner

_____ Concealing information from your partner

_____ Failing to stand up for your partner when they are criticized or belittled by others

Note: Information in this *Self-Quiz* as adapted for romantic relationships is from Jones and Burdette (1994).

Scoring: 6–14: infrequent betrayal; 15–23: moderate betrayal; 24–30: frequent betrayal. Consider how these behaviors impact your partner and your relationship and revisit the chapter content on maintenance.

In romantic relationships, partners inevitably behave in ways that defy each other's expectations and cause disappointment. But betrayal is different. Betrayal is *intentional*. As a result, it typically evokes two intense, negative reactions in betrayed partners. The first is an overwhelming sense of relational devaluation—the realization that our partner does not love and respect us as much as we thought they did (Leary, 2001). This sense of devaluation, which is triggered most by sexual infidelity and deception, is difficult to overcome and often leads us to abandon our relationships. The second is a profound sense of loss. In the wake of betrayal, we may feel that all the time and effort we invested in our partner and the relationship were a waste, and that intimacy, commitment, and trust have been permanently destroyed (Haden & Hojjat, 2006). Consequently, when you are betrayed by a lover, expect to feel *grief* over the loss of the relationship that was. (See Chapter 4 for more on grief management.)

Infidelity   Whether emotional or sexual, infidelity is one of the most destructive forms of romantic betrayal. A partner who cheats on you has broken a fundamental sacrament—the spoken or unspoken pledge to remain faithful. Simply suspecting your partner of infidelity has been found to negatively impact a person's well-being (Weigel & Shrout, 2020). Not surprisingly, many people react to infidelity with a strong urge to leave their partner (Warach et al., 2019) and may engage in a variety of behaviors, such as attempting to separate joint finances, looking for a way to move out of shared residences, or taking an interest in other potential partners (Walsh et al., 2019). Research suggests that people who have a previous history of infidelity are more likely to cheat on their partners, compared to those without a previous history of cheating. Other traits related to the likelihood to cheat on dating partners include having more positive attitudes about infidelity, lower commitment to your current relationship, and lower relationship satisfaction (Martins et al., 2016).

Cheating is a fairly frequent occurrence across individuals and relationships. Research on North Americans suggests that approximately a quarter of

🔺 Most people discover lies indirectly, through hearing about them from a third party or stumbling across damning evidence. Bojan Milinkov/Shutterstock

self-reflection

Think about Carpenter's research. Which would you find more upsetting: discovering that your romantic partner had formed an emotional attachment outside of the relationship or that they had been sexually unfaithful? If your partner did betray you in one of these ways, how would you respond?

men and between 11.6 and 19.2 percent of women have sexually betrayed a romantic partner at least once in their lives. Further, researchers estimate that between 2.2 and 4.7 percent of married people in the United States sexually betray their spouse *each year* (Warach et al., 2019). The numbers are higher for dating relationships, with between 65 and 75 percent of college students reporting that they have cheated sexually, emotionally, or a combination of both (Weigel & Shrout, 2020).

Although scholars long believed—and taught in classrooms and textbooks—that men are more concerned about their partners *sexually* straying, and women more concerned about partners being *emotionally* unfaithful, the truth is more complicated. In a study of more than 63,000 gay, lesbian, bisexual, and straight individuals that explored reactions to sexual and emotional infidelity, David Frederick and Melissa Fales (2016) found that the gender difference held only for straight couples. Additionally, in an analysis of data from 54 separate studies involving thousands of gay, lesbian, and straight people, communication scholar Chris Carpenter (2012) found that although people were deeply upset by sexual infidelity, when asked to choose which was *more* distressing—emotional or sexual betrayal—most participants agreed that emotional betrayal (a partner "falling in love with someone else") was worse. As Professor Carpenter concludes, people looking to help others work through the devastating emotional aftermath of having been cheated on "would profit from avoiding gender-based assumptions about which aspect of infidelity is likely to be more upsetting" (p. 25).

Deception   As defined in Chapter 8, deception involves misleading your partner by intentionally withholding information, presenting false information, or making your message unnecessarily irrelevant or ambiguous (McCornack, 1997). Despite media images depicting romantic partners catching each other in lies, most people discover lies indirectly, through hearing about them from a third party or stumbling across damning evidence, such as a text message or email (Park et al., 2002). When partners discover a lie, the experience typically is emotionally intense and negative. One study looking at the emotional and relational aftermath of lies found that 16 percent of people who recalled having discovered a lie reported breaking up because of it (McCornack & Levine, 1990). That decision was usually determined by the severity of the lie. If the lie was "important" (e.g., lying about relationship feelings), people were more likely to end their involvement (McCornack & Levine, 1990).

Dealing with Betrayal   The truth about romantic betrayal is that no simple solution or skill set will remedy the sense of devaluation and loss that results. The strongest predictor of what happens afterwards is the seriousness of the betrayal. If a betrayal permanently stains your perception of your partner, the relationship probably won't survive. If you believe you can eventually overcome the pain, then your relationship has a chance.

People struggling to cope with betrayal commonly adopt one of four general communication approaches (Rusbult, 1987). You can actively confront the betrayal, seeking to understand the conditions that led to it and jointly working with your partner to change those causes. You can quietly stand by your partner, choosing to forgive and forget and trusting that, in time, your love will heal the pain you feel. You can stand by your partner but simmer with pain and rage, venting your anger by constantly reminding the person of their transgression or withholding sex or other rewards. Or, you can simply end the relationship, believing that the emotional costs associated with the betrayal are too substantial to surmount.

Regardless of which approach you take, the hard truth is that after a betrayal, your relationship will never be the same, and it will never be "better" than it previously was in terms of trust, intimacy, and satisfaction. You can certainly rebuild a strong and enduring relationship, but it will always be scarred. As our therapist friend Joe says, "You will *never* get over it. You just learn to live with it."

JEALOUSY

A second problem for romantic relationships is **jealousy**—a protective reaction to a perceived threat to a valued relationship (Hansen, 1985). Most scholars agree that jealousy isn't a singular emotion but rather a combination of negative emotions, primarily anger, fear, and sadness (Guerrero & Andersen, 1998).

Jealousy especially plagues users of social media, creating the possibility for people other than your romantic partner to post provocative photos and send alluring messages, which can trigger your partner's jealousy. Imagine how you'd feel if you saw such communication on your partner's page. Studies of Facebook have found that jealousy is one of the most frequent problems reported by users (Morrison et al., 2008). Jealousy can intensify even further if users engage in **wedging**. Through wedging, a person deliberately uses messages, photos, and

skills
practice

Dealing with Jealousy
Communicating more competently when jealousy strikes

❶ Identify a situation in which your jealousy is sparked.

❷ Continue your current activities, not letting the jealousy-evoking event distract you from completing what you are doing.

❸ Avoid immediate communication with your partner.

❹ While you're finishing what you are doing, practice the Jefferson strategy (see Chapter 4), counting to 10 or 100 until you cool off.

❺ Initiate communication with your partner, using your cooperative language skills and explaining to them why the event caused you to feel jealous. Solicit your partner's perspective.

posts to try and "wedge" themselves between partners in a romantic couple because they are interested in one of the partners (Morrison et al., 2008).

The most effective way to deal with jealousy is *self-reliance*: allowing yourself to feel jealous but not letting whatever sparked your jealousy interrupt you. You should continue your current activities and give yourself time to cool off (Salovey & Rodin, 1988). Avoid communicating with your partner until you're able to do so in a cooperative and constructive fashion. When you *are* ready to talk, don't be afraid to candidly acknowledge your own jealousy and discuss your perception of threat with your partner: "I saw that post from your ex, and I'm worried that they want to get back together with you. Am I reading too much into this, or should I really feel threatened?"

RELATIONAL INTRUSION

Sometimes romantic partners try to control you or behave in ways that invade your privacy. In mild cases, they might check up on you—talking with your friends or family to verify your whereabouts. In more extreme instances, they might search your phone, read your email, or check your private social media posts and messages without permission. Such behaviors are known as **relational intrusion**: the violation of one's independence and privacy by a current or former intimate partner (Brownhalls et al., 2019). Intrusion happens in all cultures and across all ethnicities, gender identities, and sexual orientations (Lavy et al., 2009).

Within intact romances, two forms of intrusion are common. The first is *monitoring and controlling*. A partner may text you constantly to ensure that you are always accounted for and instruct you to be home by a certain time. They may put a tracking app on your devices, follow you, or hire a private investigator to conduct surveillance. People who have experienced this behavior say, "My partner wants to know where I am and what I'm doing all the time," and "My partner does not let me meet my family or friends without him being present" (Lavy et al., 2009, p. 995). The second form of intrusion is *invasion of privacy*. This includes nosing or snooping through your belongings, computer, and phone, and asking overly personal and suspicious questions designed to "interrogate" you.

Intrusion is especially common and intense in the wake of bitter breakups initiated unilaterally by one partner, when the other person doesn't wish to end the involvement (Brownhalls et al., 2019). In such instances, when the "dumped" partner feels extreme distress and a longing for reunion, they often respond by engaging in unwanted and persistent behaviors designed to "win" the partner back. Of people who report difficulty in dealing with breakups, 79 percent admit behaving intrusively (Dutton & Winstead, 2006). The most common forms of post-relationship intrusion are leaving gifts and messages for an ex-partner, expressing exaggerated levels of affection (such as giving public serenades or posting love poems), posting malicious or threatening messages to potential new partners online, physically following the ex-partner around, and showing up uninvited at the ex-partner's home or work. If done repeatedly, these latter behaviors may be considered *stalking*, which is a criminal offense.

For its recipients, relational intrusion is decidedly negative and threatening, as everyday life patterns and preferred activities may become disrupted by the unwanted physical presence or mediated messages (e.g., emails, texts, posts) of the intruder (Henry et al., 2020). If the relationship is intact, intrusion generates strong negative impressions, uncertainty, and relational turmoil (Lavy et al., 2009). As one victim describes, "He was acting so unfair; I no longer was sure about our relationship" (Lavy et al., 2009, p. 999). For people dealing with post-relationship intrusion, anger and fear are common responses, and the intrusion may spark a desire to seek revenge against or act violently toward the intruding partner (Lavy et al., 2009).

What makes intrusion tricky, however, is that perpetrators typically perceive their behaviors *positively*, as reflecting love, loyalty, or just the desire to stay in touch (Cupach & Spitzberg, 2004). In fact, most relational intruders rationalize their behaviors as justified and view themselves as "pursuing the one they love" (Brownhalls et al., 2019). Consequently, they tend to minimize or deny the harms created by their undesirable and unethical actions.

How can you best deal with intrusion? Realize first that intrusion is absolutely unacceptable and intolerable. No one has the right to impose themselves on another in an unwanted fashion. If you're on the receiving end of intrusion, talk with your partner or ex directly about their behavior, and firmly express your discontent and discomfort. Use "I" language, avoid "you" language, and make it clear that your privacy is being violated and that the intrusive behavior is unacceptable and needs to stop ("I feel really uncomfortable receiving this gift" or "I am really upset by this, and I feel that my privacy is being invaded"). Most important, keep your language respectful and polite. Avoid lashing out verbally, especially if you're angry, as it will only escalate the situation. If the person's behavior persists, contact local authorities to ask for help. You can find relevant and helpful resources at the Stalking Prevention, Awareness, and Resource Center (SPARC) at www.stalkingawareness.org.

If you find yourself engaging in intrusive behaviors, stop immediately. The fact that *you* view your actions as well intentioned is irrelevant. *If you are making a partner or ex feel uncomfortable, you are behaving unethically and unacceptably.* If you don't know how to stop, seek counseling from a licensed therapist.

INTIMATE VIOLENCE

Intimate violence affects millions of people and knows no demographic boundaries: people of all ages, gender identities, sexual orientations, social classes, ethnicities, and religions experience violence in romantic relationships. As of 2020, the Centers for Disease Control and Prevention (CDC) reports that roughly one in four women and nearly one in ten men have experienced sexual violence, physical violence, and/ or stalking by an intimate partner during their lifetime (CDC, 2020). In addition to physical injuries (and in extreme cases, death), survivors of intimate violence are more likely than others to suffer from substance abuse, low self-esteem, suicidal thoughts, and eating disorders (Ackard & Neumark-Sztainer, 2002). And as scholars note, it's no longer accurate to think of intimate violence solely as encounters involving direct physical or verbal violence (Marganski & Melander, 2018). People often use digital communication technologies to perpetrate violence against intimate partners in the form of malicious and hateful posts and messages, sharing intimate and private content, threats, and cyberstalking (Henry et al., 2020). Such instances are so widespread that nearly three-quarters of college students surveyed reported at least one experience of online intimate violence within the past year. Importantly, occurrences of physical, verbal, and online violence aren't independent from one another, but instead frequently appear in tandem as a "nexus" of intimate violence by abusive partners (Marganski & Melander, 2018).

If you haven't experienced a violent relationship, it's easy to think, "Well, the person should have seen it coming!" But this is false, for at least two reasons (Eisikovits & Buchbinder, 2000). First, violence doesn't happen all at once—it typically escalates slowly over time, not escalating into full-blown physical violence until relationships are firmly established, making victims all that much more vulnerable because of their love and commitment. Second, potential abusers often mask their jealousy, violent anger, and excessive need for control in the early stages of a relationship, making it difficult to discern "warning signs" (see Table 11.3 for a detailed list).

What should *you* do if you find yourself in a relationship with a violent partner? First and foremost, avoid believing that you can "heal" your partner through love, or "save" them by providing emotional support. Relationship repair strategies will not prevent or cure intimate violence. Your only option is to extricate yourself from the relationship. As you move toward ending the involvement, keep in mind that the most dangerous time comes immediately after you end the relationship, when the abuser is most angry. So, make sure you cut all ties to the abuser, change your phone number and delete social media, and have ready a *safety plan*: a road map of action for departing the relationship that provides you with the utmost protection. For information on how to develop such a plan, or for help in dealing with an abusive relationship, call the National Domestic Violence Hotline, 1-800-799-SAFE, or visit www.thehotline.org, where you can chat live with someone who cares.

table 11.3 Five Common Warning Signs of an Abusive Partner

An abusive partner will . . .
(1) isolate you from others Examples: restricting your contact with friends and family, showing extreme paranoid jealousy regarding perceived romantic rivals, or telling you lies about friends and family
(2) use power to control you Examples: insisting that they make all decisions about leisure activities, including sex; exploding into anger when you "disobey"; demanding knowledge of your whereabouts, access to your devices, and your social media passwords; or displaying violence, such as throwing or breaking objects
(3) frequently threaten you in various ways Examples: verbally or digitally threatening to leave you or hurt themselves if you leave, threatening violence against past lovers or perceived romantic rivals, threatening to lie about you to others or file false charges against you, or threatening violence
(4) use emotionally abusive language Examples: criticizing your weight, appearance, intelligence, career, or sexual skill; calling you names; swearing at you; posting malicious or hateful comments about you; or ridiculing your pain when they have hurt you
(5) shift the blame to you Examples: blaming you for their jealousy, violence, and destructiveness, or tricking you into behaving badly so your partner can exploit your guilt

Source: Information from "Symptoms: Indicators of Abusive Relationships," An Abuse, Rape, and Domestic Violence Aid and Resource Collection (AARDVARC). Retrieved from www.aardvarc.org/dv/symptoms.shtml

The Hard Work of Successful Love

Love is not singular, but plural.

Romantic relationships are most satisfying and stand a greater chance of surviving when you and your partner view your bond without illusions and embellishments. When you do this, when you look love squarely in the face, you'll find that it isn't one simple, clear, obvious thing. Instead, love is complex. Love is triumph *and* heartache. It is passion *and* peaceful companionship. It is joy *and* grief. And keeping love alive is hard work. Some days, your love for your partner will take your breath away. On others, everything your partner does will annoy you. Most days, it will fall somewhere in between.

Romantic relationships endure because *partners choose to communicate in ways that maintain their relationship*. It's the everyday communication and effort that you and your partner invest that will most enable you to build a satisfying, intimate bond—and sustain it if that's what you choose to do. Enduring couples succeed at love by working at it day in and day out; they help each other with studying or the dishes, cheer each other with kind words following disheartening days at school or work, nurse each other through illness, and even hold each other close as one partner lets go of life.

Managing Jealousy about a Partner's Ex

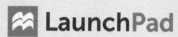 **LaunchPad** For the best experience, complete all parts of this activity in LaunchPad: **launchpadworks.com**

1 Background

Dealing with jealousy in a romantic relationship is challenging, but it becomes even more so when the relationship is rather volatile and you're unsure about your partner's level of commitment. To understand how you might competently manage such a relationship challenge, read the case study in Part 2; then, drawing on all you know about interpersonal communication, work through the problem-solving model in Part 3.

 Visit LaunchPad to watch the video in Part 4 and assess your communication in Part 5.

2 Case Study

Your relationship with Javi is the most passionate you've ever had, and you consider yourself head-over-heels in love. You share a powerful sexual connection, fueled in part by the fact that Javi is extremely physically attractive.

On the down side, Javi is undeniably high-maintenance. Although affectionate and funny, Javi has a volatile temper. You've learned the hard way that if you raise an issue that Javi perceives as problematic, huge drama with lots of yelling, and then sulking, is likely to ensue. More concerning, however, is Javi's flirtatiousness. Javi loves being the center of attention and frequently flirts with others, sometimes right in front of you. Javi also sends mixed signals about commitment, saying "I love you!" one day and "I hope you're not getting too serious on me!" the next.

Your friends think Javi is "ridiculously hot." They also think Javi is "trouble." Nevertheless, you're happy with your relationship because you've never experienced this intensity of connection before, and you think Javi may actually be your soul mate.

Recently, a few incidents have sparked worry. Javi didn't return any of your texts one night and afterwards said, "My phone battery

was dead." The thing is, you borrowed Javi's phone earlier that evening and it was fully charged. There also have been instances in which Javi's phone has gone off but Javi either ignored it or said, "It's a solicitor." You know this latter excuse is bogus because Javi is on a do-not-call list.

Tonight, you and Javi are having fun at a party, when Javi's ex, Pau, shows up. Although you're jealous, you tell Javi that it's fine for him to go talk to Pau because you're busy with your own friends. You keep an eye on the two of them, however, and sure enough, after a few minutes, you see them flirting. Your jealousy escalates as you see them sitting close together and laughing like they're still a couple! What's more, they can't seem to keep their hands off each other. Although the touches are all technically friendly and innocent, they imply a degree of intimacy that further fuels your jealousy.

As you two are driving back to your apartment, you're fuming about Javi and Pau. Noticing your demeanor, Javi explodes: "You know, you can be really annoying sometimes! You tell me to talk to Pau, and then you get all mad when I do! What's your problem?"

3 Your Turn

Consider all you've learned thus far about interpersonal communication. Then work through the following five steps. Remember, there are no "right" answers, so think hard about what is the best choice! (P.S. Need help? See the *Helpful Concepts* list.)

step 1

Reflect on yourself. What are your thoughts and feelings in this situation? What attributions are you making about Javi? Are your attributions accurate? Why or why not?

step 2

Reflect on your partner. Using perspective-taking and empathic concern, put yourself in Javi's shoes. What is Javi thinking and feeling in this situation?

step 3

Identify the optimal outcome. Think about all the information you have about your communication and relationship with Javi and the situation surrounding the encounter with Pau. Consider your own feelings as well as Javi's. Given all these factors, what's the best, most constructive relationship outcome possible? Consider what's best for you and for Javi.

step 4

Locate the roadblocks. Taking into consideration your own and Javi's thoughts and feelings and all that has happened in this situation, what obstacles are keeping you from achieving the optimal outcome?

step 5

Chart your course. What can you say to Javi to overcome the roadblocks you've identified and achieve your optimal outcome?

> **HELPFUL CONCEPTS**
>
> Romantic love types, **287**
> Deciding whether to maintain or end, **308**
> Jealousy, **313**
> Relational intrusion, **314**
> Dating violence, **315**

4 The Other Side

 Visit LaunchPad to watch a video that will expose you to Javi's side of the case study story. As in many real-life situations, this is information to which you did not have access when you were initially crafting your response in Part 3. The video reminds us that even when we do our best to offer competent responses, there is always another side to the story that we need to consider.

5 Interpersonal Competence Self-Assessment

After watching the video, visit the Self-Assessment questions in LaunchPad. Think about the new information offered in Javi's side of the story and all you've learned about interpersonal communication. Drawing on this knowledge, revisit your earlier responses in Part 3 and assess your interpersonal communication competence.

POSTSCRIPT

Imagine China/Newscom

We began this chapter with a love story written in the stars. When the Heaven Goddess cast the weaver Zhinu and the cowherd Niulang into the cosmos, separating them by a celestial river, she thought to put an end to their romance. But their commitment to one another and their dedication to making their love work could not be thwarted, even by galactic separation, and so their romantic relationship endured.

What "rivers" of challenge have kept you from finding or being with the one you love? What bridges have been built, by you or by others, to ford those challenges?

The Chinese folk tale of the cowherd and the weaver, and the Qixi Festival that honors it, have been celebrated by billions of people over thousands of years. But at the heart of this story and related celebrations is the truth observed and experienced by Professor Xun Zhu: it isn't magic or myth that sustains romantic love, but commitment, perseverance, hard work, and sacrifice.

LaunchPad

LaunchPad for *Reflect & Relate* offers videos and encourages self-assessment through adaptive quizzing. Go to **launchpadworks.com** to get access to:

 LearningCurve
Adaptive Quizzes

 Video clips that help you understand interpersonal communication

key terms

liking, 287
loving, 287
passionate love, 287
companionate love, 288
romantic relationship, 289
commitment, 290
▶ relational dialectics, 291
mere exposure effect, 292
beautiful-is-good effect, 293
matching, 293
birds-of-a-feather effect, 293
reciprocal liking, 294
social exchange theory, 294
equity, 294
initiating, 297
▶ experimenting, 298
intensifying, 298
▶ integrating, 298
▶ bonding, 298
▶ differentiating, 300
circumscribing, 300
▶ stagnating, 300
avoiding, 300
terminating, 300
▶ relational maintenance, 302
romantic betrayal, 310
jealousy, 313
wedging, 313
relational intrusion, 314

▶ You can watch brief, illustrative videos of these terms and test your understanding of the concepts in LaunchPad.

key concepts

Defining Romantic Relationships

- **Liking**, **loving**, **passionate love**, and **companionate love** are all distinct.
- A **romantic relationship** often involves **commitment** and **relational dialectics**.

Romantic Attraction

- Attraction is strongly influenced by proximity; this is known as the **mere exposure effect**.
- We often attribute positive characteristics to physically appealing people, known as the **beautiful-is-good effect**. We tend to engage in **matching** when forming long-term romantic relationships.
- **Social exchange theory** suggests that attraction to others is driven in part by the resources they can offer you. For relationships to survive, **equity** must exist.

Relationship Development and Deterioration

- When coming together, couples commonly go through **initiating** and **experimenting**. Some couples move to **intensifying** and **integrating**. Few relationships progress to **bonding**.
- **Differentiating** leads partners to believe that their differences are insurmountable, and they may begin **circumscribing** or even **stagnating**.
- Many relationships end by **avoiding**, although some couples may conduct a **terminating** discussion.

Maintaining Romantic Relationships

- Long-term couples use several **relational maintenance** tactics.
- Long-distance romantic relationships can create unique maintenance issues.

Romantic Relationship Challenges

- **Romantic betrayal** is the gravest threat to relationships.
- **Wedging** occurs when someone deliberately interferes in a relationship.
- If a romantic partner uses behaviors that invade your privacy, it is called **relational intrusion**.
- Intimate violence affects both men and women of all ages and ethnicities. If you experience such abuse, reach out for professional help.

chapter review

12 Relationships with Family Members

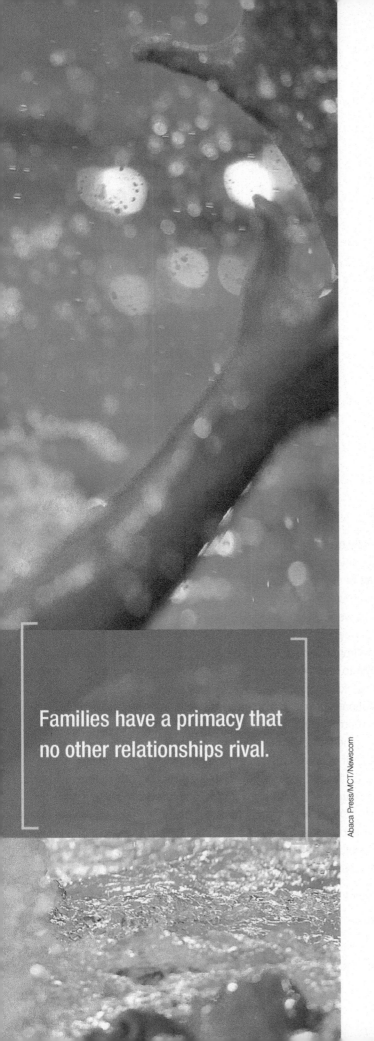

Families have a primacy that no other relationships rival.

Abaca Press/MCT/Newscom

She's one of the greatest water polo players ever.[1] She was FINA *Aquatics World Magazine* player of the decade for 2000–2010 (Elliot, 2020), a 2012 Olympic gold medalist, a three-time world champion, and a World Cup champion. The aquatics center where she learned to swim as a child is now named after her. But when Brenda Villa is asked about her abilities and accomplishments, she is quick to credit her family, especially her mother: "I get my confidence and 'swagger' from my mom. She's one tough woman. She always supports me but is unafraid to tell me when I'm not being humble."

Brenda grew up in Commerce, California, where her mother enrolled her at a young age in swimming classes. Brenda excelled and gravitated to water polo. Although her parents had no experience with the sport, they encouraged Brenda's interest. "They taught me that you should always be open to new things."

Growing up, four themes were foundational in the Villa family: *support*, *honesty*, *sacrifice*, and *love*. As Brenda describes, "Both my parents worked full time. Yet they were at all my swim meets, water polo games, school activity nights, and assemblies. They knew that I was committed to both school and sports, and they supported me in every way so that I could achieve my goals." The Villa family was also always willing to sacrifice for one another. For example, Brenda's training camps for the U.S. team were in Chula Vista, a two-hour commute from Commerce. Her parents drove her, without debate or resentment. As Brenda describes, "I don't remember asking my parents to do

---

[1]Unless otherwise noted, direct quotes that follow are adapted from personal interviews with the authors, July 2011, and published with permission.

323

this—they just did it. And I never realized how hard it was for them. My mother would accompany my dad because she was afraid he would fall asleep on the drive home. I didn't appreciate the depth of their sacrifice at the time, as a kid, but now that I'm older, I'm so thankful that they put me first." The willingness to sacrifice communicated a powerful message of love. "Their love is unconditional. It warms my heart to think that my mom would accompany my dad just to keep him awake. *That's* love!"

The sacrifices that Brenda's family made on her behalf are mirrored in her own desire to give back to her community. As she described in 2020, "For me, my intersectionality of being a woman, being a Latina, being in a small sport, it's 'How can I contribute?'" (Elliot, 2020).

Following her retirement in 2012, she began coaching, and founded a nonprofit called Project 2020 that minimizes costs for kids to play water polo (Elliot, 2020).

Though she's one of America's most talented and celebrated twenty-first-century athletes, Brenda Villa remains humble about her accolades. As the Women's Sports Foundation notes, "[Brenda] seems unaware of the splash she has made as role model and hero to Latina athletes. Maybe she's just too busy and too modest by nature" (Lewellen, 2008). But the truth is, Brenda doesn't think of herself as role model—she thinks of her parents that way. "I look at their 30-plus years of marriage and how they still always put their kids first. I hope to be as selfless as them with my own children."

Families have a primacy that is unparalleled. Across our life spans, our interactions with family members shape our beliefs, values, and communication behaviors more than any other relationship type (Rauscher et al., 2020). This isn't surprising, given that family members are the first people we see, hear, touch, and interact with. As we grow from infancy to childhood, we learn from family the most basic of skills: how to walk, talk, feed, and clothe ourselves. As we develop further, our families teach us deeper lessons about life akin to those learned by Brenda Villa from her parents: the importance of support, honesty, sacrifice, and love. As our relationships broaden to include friendships and romances, we still use kinship as a metaphor to describe closeness: "How close are we? We're like *family*!" (Rubin, 1996). But family relationships are also compulsory. We don't *choose* our families— we are brought into them by birth, adopted into them by law, or integrated into them by remarriage. When problems arise in our family relationships, the stress is unrivaled. One survey of adults found that the greatest source of emotional strain the preceding day was "family" (Warr & Payne, 1982). When the same sample was asked to name the greatest source of pleasure from the previous day, the answer was identical: "family." Day in and day out, family relationships provide us with our greatest joys and most bitter heartaches (Myers, 2002).

In this chapter, we look at the most influential and enduring of our close involvements: family relationships. You'll learn:

- Defining features of family
- The different ways in which families communicate
- Communication strategies to maintain healthy family relationships
- Challenges that families face, and how to manage them

Defining Family

Family identity is
created through
communication

Families today are incredibly diverse. Between 1960 and 2020, the percentage of households composed of married couples with biological children in the United States declined from 44 to 19 percent (Vanorman & Jacobsen, 2020). Partners are increasingly living together rather than getting married: as of 2018, 9 percent of young adults ages 18 to 24 were living with an unmarried partner, whereas 7 percent were living with a spouse (Gurrentz, 2018). Rising divorce rates over the past half century have also decreased the average size of households, as families divide into smaller units and re-form into blended arrangements featuring stepparents and stepchildren. Adding to this complexity, individual families are constantly in flux, as children move out, then lose jobs and move back in with parents; and grandparents merge households with their adult children, to help with day care or receive care themselves. As of 2017, more than one-third of U.S. adults ages 18 to 34 were living with their parents (Vanorman & Jacobsen, 2020), and 20 percent of U.S. households were multigenerational (Cohn & Passel, 2018).

DEFINING CHARACTERISTICS OF FAMILY

The enormous diversity in contemporary families requires a broad, inclusive definition. **Family** is a network of people who share their lives over long periods of time and are bound by marriage, blood, or commitment; who consider themselves as family and communicate with one another as such; and who share a significant history and anticipated future of functioning in a family relationship (Galvin et al., 2004). This definition highlights seven characteristics that distinguish families from other social groups.

First, families possess a strong sense of family identity, created by how they communicate (Braithwaite et al., 2010). The way you talk with family members, the stories you exchange, and even the manner in which members of your family deal with conflict all contribute to a shared sense of what your family is like (Tovares, 2010).

Second, the communication that defines families has a profound impact on individual family members. For example, children's interactions with parents clarify not just their purpose and place within the family, but how much they are appreciated and valued. This, in turn, shapes their self-esteem: multiple studies have documented that parental messages expressing love, support, nurturing, affection, and acceptance substantially boost children's esteem, just as messages conveying rejection, neglect, humiliation, or aggression undermine it (Krauss et al., 2020). And such effects are enduring: psychologist Ulrich Orth tracked more than 8,000 U.S. participants from the time they were 8 years old until they were 27, and found that parental warmth of communication during early childhood substantially influenced the esteem these individuals experienced as adults, decades later (Orth, 2018).

Third, families use communication to define boundaries, both inside the family and to distinguish family members from outsiders (Afifi, 2003; Koerner & Fitzpatrick, 2006). As we'll discuss later, some families constrict information that flows out ("Don't talk about our family problems with anyone else"). Some also restrict physical access to the family—for example, by dictating with whom family members can become romantically involved. Others set few such boundaries: a family may welcome friends and neighbors as unofficial members, such as an "uncle" or "aunt" who isn't really related to your parents (Braithwaite et al., 2010). For instance, our sons grew up knowing and referring to our good friend Tim Levine as "Uncle Tim," even though he isn't a blood relation. A family may even welcome others' children, such as the neighbors across the street you think of as your "family away from home." If remarriage occurs and stepfamilies form, these boundaries are renegotiated (Golish, 2003).

Fourth, the emotional bonds underlying family relationships are intense and complex. Although families commonly are depicted as exclusively loving and supportive (think: Hallmark Channel), being emotionally hurt by others in one's family is surprisingly commonplace (McLaren & Sillars, 2020), leading many family members to hold both warm *and* antagonistic feelings toward one another (Silverstein & Giarrusso, 2010). As author Lillian Rubin (1996) notes, family relationships have "an elemental quality that touches the deepest layers of our inner life and stirs our most primitive emotional responses" (p. 256). Consider the strength of feeling that arises in you when you get into an argument with a parent or sibling, or when you celebrate an important milestone (a graduation, a wedding, a new job) with family members.

Fifth, families share a history (Galvin et al., 2004). Such histories can stretch back for generations and feature family members from a broad array of cultures. These histories often set expectations regarding how family members should behave ("We Ngatas have always been an honest bunch, and we're not about to change that now"). Families also share a common future: they expect to maintain their bonds indefinitely. For better or worse, everything you say and do becomes a part of your family history, shaping future interactions and determining whether your family relationships are healthy or destructive.

Sixth, family members may share genetic material (Crosnoe & Cavanagh, 2010). This can lead to shared physical characteristics as well as similar personalities, outlooks on life, mental abilities, and ways of relating to others. For example, studies suggest that interpersonal inclinations such as shyness and aggressiveness may be influenced by genes (Carducci & Zimbardo, 1995); and research examining twins separated at birth has found strong similarities in their levels of empathy, regardless of differences in the environments within which they grew up (Abramson et al., 2020).

Finally, family members constantly juggle multiple and sometimes competing roles (Silverstein & Giarrusso, 2010). Within your family, you're not just a child, but perhaps a sibling and grandchild as well. By the time you reach middle age, you may simultaneously be a parent, spouse, aunt or uncle, grandparent, *and* sibling—and each of these roles carries with it varying expectations and demands. This makes communicating competently within families challenging.

Now that we understand some of the defining features of families, let's look at the various types of families that exist.

TYPES OF FAMILIES

No "typical" family type exists. Instead, families come in many different forms (Braithwaite et al., 2010). But even these forms are not fixed: you may experience several different family structures as you progress through life and as our larger society evolves. Today the **nuclear family**—a wife, a husband, and

In *This Is Us*, the Pearson family members have differing personality types that often create conflict between them, but in the end, they are a supportive family with a strong bond. Photofest

their biological or adopted children—is in the minority. As we discuss the family types further, keep this in mind: *what matters most is not the "type" of family you have but whom you consider part of your family in terms of love, respect, and communication.*

When relatives such as aunts, uncles, parents, children, and grandparents live together in a common household, the result is an **extended family**. By the year 2060, nearly a quarter of all people in the United States will be over the age of 65 (Vespa et al., 2020), and many of these individuals will be sharing a household with relatives.

Approximately 40 percent of marriages in the United States are remarriages for one or both partners (Geiger & Livingston, 2019). This often creates a **stepfamily** in which at least one of the adults has a child or children from a previous relationship (Ganong & Coleman, 1994). Stepfamilies are often called blended or remarried families. More than 50 percent of children born throughout the twenty-first century will grow up in stepfamilies (Crosnoe & Cavanagh, 2010).

Some couples live together prior to or instead of marriage. These **cohabiting couples** consist of two unmarried, romantically involved adults living together in a household, with or without children. Cohabitation is steadily increasing in Western societies. This is partly due to an increase in cohabitation among middle-aged and older adults, many of whom were formerly married but now want the relational flexibility that cohabitation affords (Silverstein & Giarrusso, 2010).

In a **single-parent family**, only one adult resides in the household, possessing sole responsibility as caregiver for the children. Twenty-three percent of children in the United States and 15 percent of children in Canada were growing up in single-parent households as of 2019 (Kramer, 2019).

A final family type is the **voluntary kin family**: a group of people who lack blood and legal kinship but who nevertheless consider themselves "family." Often such families arise due to distance from, dissatisfaction with, or estrangement from blood and legal relatives. In such cases, three types of voluntary kin families arise (Braithwaite et al., 2010). The most frequent form is the *supplemental family*, in which dissatisfaction with family relationships leads people to begin labeling other close people in their lives as "family," even though they retain contact with their blood and legal

⬥ Although every family possesses its own distinct identity, all families—whether bound together by marriage, blood, or commitment—have a profound shared history made up of the small, everyday moments they spend together.
Ariel Skelley/DigitalVision/Getty Images; JAG IMAGES/Cultura Creative RF/Alamy

self-reflection

What type of family did you grow up with? What makes you collectively a family—the fact that you are biologically related? Live in the same household? Share a strong emotional bond? Now think about other people's families. Are there any that consider you a part of their family? If so, why?

relatives. In contrast, people who create a *substitute family* have no contact whatsoever with blood or legal relatives—either because of estrangement or death—and replace their relatives entirely with a group of individuals considered to be "family." Finally, within a *convenience family*, people may, for a particular time span, come to think of a group of people as their "family," although the ties between them are temporary. For instance, students who study abroad may live in a household in which the residents become "family" for that time period, only to have the relationships splinter after everyone returns home. The same thing may happen within institutionalized settings—for example, during lengthy stays in rehab—when people in an intensive, residential counseling facility bond together, only to have those ties fray upon completion of the therapy.

Characteristics and types define families from the outside looking in. But within a family, how do members create a sense of family identity? We look at this next.

FAMILY STORIES

One of the most powerful ways we define our collective family identity is to share stories (Tovares, 2010). For example, whenever we and our boys (Kyle, Colin, and Conor) reunite, a fair amount of time is spent reliving "classic" stories from our family. These include the time that Kelly and Conor staged an "intervention" to get Steve to stop shouting and clapping so loudly at Conor's school music performances; or Steve discovering an aerosol can, rubber tubing, and potatoes in his car trunk—remnants from Kyle and his friends' makeshift "potato cannon"; or when Kelly labored for several hours to handcraft a Thomas the Tank Engine birthday cake—only to have a 2-year-old Colin scream in horrified terror when he saw it. And each time we relive and retell these stories and others like them, we bolster the bond that this shared sense of family history provides.

Family stories are narrative accounts shared repeatedly within a family that retell historical events and are meant to bond the family together (Stone, 2004). Such stories organize collective memories about significant events in the past, and link those occurrences to the present and future in ways that provide family members with a deep sense of meaning regarding their relationships with one another (Frost, 2012). As family story scholar Jody Koenig Kellas describes, "Telling and hearing significant family stories can have long lasting effects on those involved, often in the form of values, impressions, fears, lessons, and/or beliefs" (2018, p. 62). Importantly, it's not just the content of the stories that bonds families together; it's the activity of storytelling. Family members often collaborate in telling stories: adding details, disagreeing, correcting discrepancies, and confirming perspectives (Kellas, 2005).

When people tell family stories, they typically lace their narratives with opinions and emotions that make clear how they feel about other family members (Vangelisti et al., 1999). These

⬇ The authors' sons (left to right) Kyle, Colin, and Conor, in 2019. Sharing photographs can bring family stories to life by providing lasting, powerful images of family relationships. Do you associate any particular images or other mementos with your favorite family stories?
Courtesy of Steve McCornack

evaluations have a powerful effect on closeness: the regular sharing of stories that cast relational partners in a positive light and that have "happy endings" substantially boosts relationship satisfaction and mental health (Frost, 2012). However, family stories aren't always positive; some criticize family values, condemn specific family members' actions, or discourage dissent. These stories may also involve family histories of abandonment, abuse, or parental oppression, and corresponding lessons about how not to parent (Goodsell et al., 2010).

Family stories come in as many different forms as there are families, and may be told to entertain, tease, show pride, or even rebuke family members (Scharp et al., 2020). But across all the many types of stories that exist, three stand out as especially potent in affirming family identity: *courtship stories*, *birth stories*, and *survival stories* (Stone, 2004).

Courtship Stories   When Steve was growing up, one of the favorite stories told around the family dinner table was how his dad serenaded his mom from the courtyard of her dorm at Pomona College while she stood on her balcony, listening. Forty-five years later, Steve and his parents visited Pomona. While driving around campus, Steve's mom suddenly shouted "Stop!" and leapt from the car. Steve quickly parked the car, and he and his dad followed her into a well-worn building, only to find her standing in the very courtyard that had been described so many times. Steve's mom stood there, gazing at the balcony where she'd listened to his dad's song more than four decades earlier. "There it is," she whispered, "the spot where your father serenaded me," and her eyes filled with tears.

Some families share *courtship stories* about how the parents fell in love. Courtship stories emphasize the solidity of the parents' relationship, which children find reassuring. But perhaps most important, such stories give children a framework for understanding romantic love by suggesting what one should feel about love and how to recognize it when it occurs (Stone, 2004).

Birth Stories   Families may also share *birth stories*, which describe the latter stages of pregnancy, childbirth, and early infancy of a child. Birth stories help children understand how they fit into the family ("You'll always be the baby"), which roles they're expected to play ("Firstborns are always so independent"), and what their parents hope and dream for them ("We knew from the moment you were born that you'd accomplish great things!").

Unlike biological children, adopted children often have little knowledge of their birth or birth parents. Consequently, the stories that adoptive parents create about how and why the children entered their adoptive families—known as *entrance stories*—are important in providing the child with a sense of personal identity and self-esteem (Krusiewicz & Wood, 2001). Entrance stories also help heal the broken bond with birth parents by giving the child an explanation of why the adoption occurred. For example, one of the most common and constructive entrance stories involves framing the birth mother's decision as altruistic: "the loving, painful decision of an amazing, caring woman" (Krusiewicz & Wood, 2001, p. 793).

Survival Stories   *Survival stories* relate the coping strategies family members have used to deal with major challenges. Survival in these stories may be physical, as in the accounts that combat soldiers and disaster victims tell. Or, survival may refer to a family member's ability to prevail by achieving a level of financial stability or other forms of success. Survival stories give children the sense that they come from a tough, persevering family, which prepares them to face their own difficulties. For example, the mother of water polo star Brenda Villa (featured in our chapter opener) emigrated from Mexico when she was only 18, following the death of her father (Brenda's grandfather).[2] She came to the United States to earn money and help support her family back home. This story of struggle and hardship inspired Brenda to work hard and achieve her own goals.

Telling Family Stories   The breadth and depth of your family experiences provide a rich resource to share with family members. But not all shared experiences are ones your family members would like to relive. To ensure that family stories strengthen, rather than erode, family relationships, select experiences that cast the family and individual members in a positive light and that emphasize unity rather than discord. When sharing stories with younger family members, keep in mind that they will learn values from your story (Tovares, 2010). Ask yourself whether the story sends the message you intend about your family's values.

Stories that cast individual family members in a humorous light require special care. Although such stories may be perfectly appropriate to share, make sure that the "target" family member enjoys and agrees to the telling. For example, you might repeatedly revisit the time your brother brought home an eccentric date or recount the day your father accidentally drove the car through the garage wall while miraculously avoiding injury. Avoid sharing stories that breach personal confidences ("John never told any of you what really happened, but here it is!") or that make sport of family members in ways they don't enjoy. When in doubt, simply (but privately) ask the family member whether they want you to share the story. If the answer is no, keep silent.

To this point, we've discussed the defining features of families, the various types that exist, and how families use stories to create a cohesive family identity. We now turn our attention to the various communication patterns that exist within families.

Communicating in Families

Communication patterns reflect how families converse

The award-winning 2014 film *Boyhood* follows the development of its central character Mason across 12 years of actual, real-world time (the movie was filmed with the same actors over more than a decade). As time passes within the story line, Mason's family structure changes again and again, as Mason's mother marries, gets divorced, remarries, and gets divorced again. Mason's first stepfather is authoritarian, abusive, and not at all interested in discussion. He expects everyone to share his viewpoint and enforces it by telling Mason's mother to "back me up!" In contrast, Mason's biological father, Mason Sr., who stays in touch with his kids across the years, emphasizes open communication and diverse opinions. In one scene, Mason Sr. is out driving with Mason and his sister, but when the kids aren't sharing openly enough, Mason Sr. pulls the car to the curb and confronts them:

> **MASON SR.:** No no no! That's *not* how we are going to talk to one another, all right? I will *not* be that guy. You *cannot* put me in that category, you know, the "biological father who I spend every other weekend with, and make polite conversation, while he drives me places and buys me stuff"—no! Talk to me!

---

[2]Excerpted from interview with authors, July 13, 2011. Published with permission.

In *Boyhood*, Mason experiences several different family communication patterns, from his friendly, supportive biological father to his two abusive and controlling stepfathers. What is the dominant communication pattern in your family?
© IFC Films/Photofest

MASON JR.: But, Dad, why is it all on *us*, though? You know, what about *you*? How was *your* week? Who do *you* hang out with? Do *you* have a girlfriend? What have *you* been up to?

MASON SR.: (smiling) I see your point. So, we should just let it happen more natural.

BOTH KIDS: Yeah!

MASON SR.: That's what you're saying. OK, that's what we'll do, starting now.

Like the families depicted in *Boyhood*, our own families' communication is guided by shared beliefs about how families should converse and by interpersonal communication behaviors that reflect those beliefs, known as **family communication patterns** (Koerner & Fitzpatrick, 2002). Family communication patterns allow families to coordinate everyday activities and interactions within and outside the family sphere, as well as to collaboratively create a shared definition of family and its meaning. Family communication patterns often are handed down across generations, with adults teaching their children the patterns that they, themselves, learned as children. One study looking at three generations of families found that grandparents, parents, and grandchildren typically shared the same family communication patterns (Rauscher et al., 2020). Family communication patterns evolve from two communication dimensions, which we'll discuss next.

COMMUNICATION DIMENSIONS

According to *Family Communication Patterns Theory* (Koerner & Fitzpatrick, 2006), two dimensions underlie the communication between family members. The first is **conversation orientation**, the degree to which family members are encouraged to participate in unrestrained interaction about a wide array of topics. Families with a *high conversation orientation* are like Mason's biological father: they believe that open and frequent communication is essential to an enjoyable and rewarding family life. Consequently, they interact often, freely, and spontaneously, without many limitations placed on time spent together and topics discussed. Perhaps not surprisingly, children growing up in *high conversation orientation families* tend to report high levels of satisfaction regarding the quality of their parent–child interactions (Aloia, 2020).

In contrast, families with a *low conversation orientation* are like Mason's stepfather: they view interpersonal communication as something irrelevant and unnecessary for a satisfying, successful family life. Such families interact only infrequently and limit their conversations to a few select topics—weather, daily activities, current events, and the like. Disclosure of intimate thoughts and feelings between family members is discouraged, as is debate of attitudes and perspectives.

The second dimension is **conformity orientation**, the degree to which families believe that communication should emphasize similarity or diversity in attitudes, beliefs, and values. Conformity orientation involves a constellation of interrelated beliefs, including respect for authority, experiences of parental control, pressure to adopt parental values and beliefs, and the inability to question those values and beliefs (Horstman et al., 2018).

Like Mason's stepfather, *high conformity families* use their interactions to highlight and enforce uniformity of thought. Such families are sometimes perceived as more "traditional" because children are expected to obey parents and other elders, who (in turn) are counted on to make family decisions. Members of these families tend to prioritize family relationships over outside connections, such as friendships and romantic involvements. Moreover, they are expected to sacrifice their personal goals for the sake of the family.

Low conformity families, akin to Mason's biological father, communicate in ways that emphasize diversity in attitudes, beliefs, and values, and that encourage uniqueness, individuality, and independence. These families typically view outside relationships as equally important to those within the family, and they prioritize individual over family interests and goals. In low conformity families, children contribute to family decision making, and members view the family as a vehicle for individual growth rather than a collective in which members must sacrifice their own interests for the good of the whole.

FAMILY COMMUNICATION PATTERNS

According to communications scholars Ascan Koerner and Mary Anne Fitzpatrick (2006), conversation and conformity dimensions give rise to four possible family communication patterns: *consensual, pluralistic, protective,* and *laissez-faire*.

Consensual Families   Families high in both conversation and conformity are **consensual families**. In such families, members are encouraged to openly share their views with one another as well as debate those beliefs. Consensual family communication is marked by high disclosure; attentive listening; and frequent expressions of caring, concern, and support toward one another (Rueter & Koerner, 2008). At the same time, consensual family members are expected to steadfastly share a single viewpoint. Parents in such households typically exert strong control over the attitudes, behaviors, and interactions of their children (Rueter & Koerner, 2008). For example, parents may encourage their children to share their thoughts and feelings about important issues ("What do you think we should do?"), but then make clear that only one perspective (the parents') is acceptable. Because of their emphasis on conformity, consensual families perceive conflict as intensely threatening. Consequently, they address conflicts as they occur and seek to resolve them as constructively as possible to preserve family unity.

Pluralistic Families   Families high in conversation but low in conformity are **pluralistic families**. They communicate in open and unconstrained ways, discussing

Online Self-Quiz: What Communication Pattern Does Your Family Have? To take this self-quiz, visit LaunchPad: **launchpadworks.com**

LaunchPad Video

launchpadworks.com

Consensual Families
Watch this clip online to answer the questions below.

How does the family in the video exhibit both high conversation and high conformity orientations? In what types of situations has your own family used a more "consensual" approach to communication? Why?

a broad range of topics and exploring them in depth. Pluralistic families enjoy debating the issues of the day, and judge one another's arguments on their merit rather than on whether they mesh with other members' attitudes. People in pluralistic families typically don't try to control other family members' beliefs or attitudes (Rueter & Koerner, 2008). Since parents don't feel compelled to wield power over their children, children's contributions to family discussions and decision making are treated as relevant and equally valid. For example, parents in a pluralistic family might ask for their children's opinions regarding a job opportunity ("Should Mom accept the offer from TelCo?") or a family vacation ("Where should we go this year?"). Pluralistic families deal directly with conflict, seeking to resolve disputes in productive, mutually beneficial ways. They may, for instance, establish "official" times (such as mealtimes or family meetings) when members can vent their concerns and work collaboratively to settle them. For this reason, pluralistic family members report the highest rates of conflict resolution of any of the four family types.

Protective Families   **Protective families** are low on conversation and high on conformity. Communication in these families functions to maintain obedience and enforce family norms, and little value is placed on the exchange of ideas or the development of communication skills. Parent–child power differences are firmly enforced, and children are expected to quietly obey. Sayings such as "Children should be seen and not heard" and "Children should speak when spoken to" reflect this mindset. Parents invest little effort in creating opportunities for family discussion, and the result is low levels of disclosure among family members (Rueter & Koerner, 2008). Protective families avoid conflict because it threatens the conformity they value and because they often lack the skills necessary to manage conflicts constructively. Members may tell each other "Don't make waves" or "You don't want to cause trouble."

Laissez-Faire Families   Families low in both conversation and conformity are **laissez-faire families**. Few emotional bonds exist between their members, resulting in low levels of caring, concern, and support expressed within the

LaunchPad Video
launchpadworks.com

Protective Families
Watch this clip online to answer the questions below.

In your view, what are the potential advantages and disadvantages of protective families? Do you think family patterns might change as children grow older?
    Want to see more? Check out LaunchPad for clips illustrating **pluralistic families** and **laissez-faire families**.

family (Rueter & Koerner, 2008). Their detachment shows itself in a lack of interaction and a decided disinterest in activities that might foster communication or maintenance of the family as a unit. Similar to parents in pluralistic families, laissez-faire parents believe that children should be independent thinkers and decision makers. But this belief derives from their disinterest in their children's thoughts and decisions. Such parents tend to leave it up to their children to form their own opinions regarding sexual behavior, drug and alcohol use, and educational achievement. Because members of such families interact infrequently, they rarely get embroiled in conflict. If a disagreement does erupt, they either avoid it or (if they feel strongly invested in the issues at stake) compete to "win" the debate.

To this point, our discussion of families and interpersonal communication has been largely descriptive: the various types of families that exist, and how they communicate. Now we turn to a more *prescriptive* focus: how *you* can use interpersonal communication to deepen the bonds within *your* family relationships.

Maintaining Family Relationships

All family relationships need constant maintenance

Camille Geraldi always knew she wanted to care for children with disabilities, ever since she was a young nurse working in a south Florida hospital.[3] In the early 1990s, she and her husband Michael, a pediatrician—who passed away in 2016—began adopting children. Eventually their family grew to dozens of children, with older children and professional staff helping to take care of the younger ones. At the center of their family bond lies Camille's intensely positive, assuring, and disclosive communication. Camille showers the children with compliments ("You look beautiful this morning") and shares feelings that assure the children of their importance to her. And these children finally feel that they're part of a family, as Camille tells them, "It's my dream that we're all together, that we can do this all together and that we all grow old together." The impacts of her constant positivity, assurances, and disclosure are profound. As just one example, her daughter Mariah was brought home from the hospital at age 5 months, completely nonresponsive and judged by experts as being in a coma. Camille's communication literally brought Mariah to life. More than a decade later, Mariah was attending school and her eighth-grade prom. The Geraldi family is now so large that they live on a 30-acre farm in North Carolina. As Camille describes, "The address here is 'Possibility Mountain Trail.' To be on Possibility Mountain Trail means that everything is possible for these children. There is nothing that we can't reach or attain."

The story of the Geraldi family reminds us of a simple truth: *we create our families through how we communicate.* Although you're only one member of your family, the

◆ The Possible Dream Foundation, launched and led by Camille Geraldi, strives to improve the quality of life of children and adults with developmental disabilities by providing a loving home, a caring family, and an understanding environment where individuals can reach their full potential.

---

[3]Information about Camille Geraldi is from *60 Minutes*, The Possible Dream Foundation. Retrieved February 4, 2021, from https://www.youtube.com/watch?v=7Pp1T90M6-s

interpersonal choices you make—and what you say and do as a result—ripple outward. To help boost your family's closeness and happiness, use your interpersonal communication skills to maintain your family relationships, and work carefully to balance ongoing family tensions.

MAINTENANCE STRATEGIES FOR FAMILIES

Many people take their family relationships for granted. Instead of communicating in ways designed to maintain these relationships, people assume that "your family is always there for you" (Vogl-Bauer, 2003). But all family relationships need constant maintenance to be sustained (Aloia, 2020). As illustrated by the communication of Camille Geraldi, three of the most important strategies for maintaining family relationships are positivity, assurances, and self-disclosure (Vogl-Bauer, 2003).

Positivity   The most powerful maintenance tactic in shaping family satisfaction with their communication and relationships is *positivity* (Aloia, 2020; Stafford, 2010). This holds true not just for parents and children, but for grandparents and grandchildren as well (Mansson, 2020). In family settings, positivity means communicating with your family members in an upbeat and hopeful fashion. To implement positivity in your family encounters, start doing favors for other family members without being asked, and unexpectedly gift them in little ways that show you care. Invest energy into making each encounter with family members enjoyable. Avoid complaining about family problems that have no solutions; ridiculing family members; whining or sulking when you don't get your way; and demanding that caregivers, siblings, or other kin give you favored treatment.

Assurances   The second way you can bolster your family relationships is by offering regular *assurances* of how much your family means to you. Let other family members know that you consider your relationship with each of them unique and valuable, and that you are committed to maintaining these bonds well into the future ("I love you," "I will always be here for you," "I miss you," or "I can't wait to be home again so I can spend time with you"). Avoid devaluing family relationships in front of others ("They're *just* my family") and commenting on how other families are superior to yours ("I'd give anything to have other parents"). Similar to positivity, offering regular assurances has a powerful effect in boosting family members' satisfaction with their communication and relationships (Aloia, 2020).

Self-Disclosure   *Self-disclosure* in family relationships means sharing your private thoughts and feelings with family members and allowing them to do the same without fear of betrayal. You do this by treating other family members in ways that are consistent, trustworthy, and ethical. Ways to practice self-disclosure include making time in your schedule to talk with parents, siblings, or children about how they are doing; encouraging them to share their feelings and concerns with you; and offering your perspective in a cooperative, respectful way. It also means avoiding communication practices that undermine disclosure, such as betraying confidences, refusing to make time for family conversation, reacting defensively when family members share their feelings with you, disparaging family members' viewpoints, and hiding things from your family.

Making You Noise
—for my mother
The day before you are deaf completely, I will make you noise. I will bring birds, bracelets, chimes to hang in the wind. We will drive from Idaho to Washington again, and I will read to keep you awake, and I will tap little poems on the backs of your arms, your neck to be sure you hear me. I will play spoons on your body in restaurants, smack my lips, heave you sighs, each one deeper than the rest. We will finally shout. And then, as quiet slips in, settling over, I will speak. I will keep speaking. I will sing you nonsense songs until you go to sleep.
—*Francesca Bell, poet*

TECHNOLOGY AND FAMILY MAINTENANCE

We live in Hoover, a suburb of Birmingham, as we teach at the University of Alabama at Birmingham (UAB). Kelly's parents and brothers all live in the suburbs west of Chicago, but she regularly texts with them, and talks with her parents every weekend. Steve's parents and brother live in Seattle, but they email throughout the week, and video chat on the weekends. And although our sons are scattered around the country—Kyle in Chicago, Colin in St. Louis, and Conor in Portland—we're all *constantly* emailing and texting, and we have a "family get-together" via video chat every Sunday evening.

Although some lament that technology has replaced face-to-face interaction and reduced family intimacy ("Families are always on the computer and never *talk* anymore"), families typically use mediated and face-to-face communication in a complementary, rather than substitutive, fashion. Families who communicate frequently via email, text, and social media *also* communicate frequently face-to-face or on the phone. They typically choose synchronous modes of communication (face-to-face, phone, video call) for personal or urgent matters, and asynchronous modes (email, text, social media) for less important issues (Tillema et al., 2010).

Mobile phones are central to family relationship maintenance, allowing family members to frequently monitor each other's well-being and whereabouts, coordinate mutual activities and events, and express affection and support (Velasquez, 2018). In particular, the convenience and speed of texting enables a state of near-perpetual contact between family members who are geographically separated that's simply not possible with other forms of mediated communication. This is especially important for new college students who are away from home for the first time. Research documents that new students who regularly text with their parents have better mental and physical well-being as a result, and that this is particularly true for students who have difficulty initiating encounters with strangers and making new friends (Ruppel et al., 2018).

Social media also is used by families whose members are geographically separated in order to stay informed and connected. In effect, family members "listen" to the family news of the day by reading each other's posts. Even if family members choose to not post comments in response, the simple reading of personal updates on social media allows family members separated by distance to collaboratively share in the same experiences, sustaining closeness. The flip side is that posting content judged as inappropriate by family members can send emotional shock waves throughout the entire family network, as people repeatedly share and repost the content (Storch & Juarez-Paz, 2017). As scholars Sharon Storch and Anna Ortiz Juarez-Paz (2017) caution, using social media to maintain family connections "creates a history and that history can be damaging to people's reputations within the family system" (p. 123), depending on the nature of the content.

Families also commonly use email to connect. Interpersonal scholar Amy Janan Johnson and her colleagues found that more than half of college students reported interacting with family members via email in the preceding week and that the primary purpose of these emails was relationship maintenance (Johnson et al., 2008). Students used email to maintain *positivity* ("Have a great day!"), provide *assurances* ("I love you and miss you!"), and *self-disclose* ("I'm feeling a bit scared about my stats exam tomorrow").

skills practice

Maintaining Family Ties through Technology
Communicating positivity and assurances to family members

❶ Send an email to a family member with whom you've been out of touch, letting them know you care.

❷ Offer congratulations via text message or email to a family member who has recently achieved an important goal.

❸ Post a message on the Facebook page of a family member with whom you've had a disagreement, saying that you value their opinions and beliefs.

❹ Send an e-card to a long-distance family member, sharing a message of affection.

❺ Post a supportive response to a family member who has expressed concerns via social media.

DEALING WITH FAMILY DIALECTICS

Within all families, tension exists between competing impulses, known as **relational dialectics** (see Chapter 11). Two dialectics are especially pronounced in families: *autonomy versus connection* and *openness versus protection*. As we mature, each of us must balance our desire for autonomy against the connection that we share with our families and the corresponding expectations and obligations regarding who we "should" be as family members. We also face frequent decisions regarding how openly we should communicate with other family members, as well as how much information about our families we should share with those outside the family unit. Balancing these tensions is challenging. However, you can strike a balance by applying the following techniques.

Balancing Autonomy and Connection   Even though you may feel intensely connected to your family, you probably also struggle to create your own separate identity. You may enjoy the feeling of intimacy that connectedness brings, while resenting how your family seems blind to your true abilities: "My family insists on seeing me only as an athlete" or "My family doesn't think I can make mature decisions because I'm the youngest."

The tension between autonomy and connection in families is especially difficult to manage during adolescence (Crosnoe & Cavanagh, 2010). As children move through their teen years, they begin to assert their independence from parents. Their peers eventually replace parents and other family members as having the most influence on their interpersonal decisions (Golish, 2000).

How can you best manage the tension between autonomy and connection in your family? Use two additional relationship maintenance strategies discussed in Chapter 11—sharing tasks and cultivating social networks. In this case, however, it is important to strike a balance between family relationships and outside relationships. First, for sharing tasks, you need to balance your dependence on family members to help you carry out everyday chores with a reliance on yourself and people outside your family. Too much dependence on family members—especially for tasks you could accomplish on your own—can erode your self-reliance, self-confidence, and independence (Strauss, 2006).

Second, examine your social networks (including your family), and assess the degree to which family members constitute the closest people in your life. As with sharing tasks, a balance between family relationships and outside connections is ideal. If you have few or even no close ties with anyone outside of the family sphere, you may feel intensely dependent on your family and experience a corresponding loss of autonomy. Likewise, having no close ties to any family members can create a sense of independence so extreme that you feel little emotional bond with your family.

Balancing Openness and Protection   Families also experience tension between openness and protection. In any close relationship—family bonds included—we want both to share personal information and to protect ourselves from the possible negative consequences of such sharing (Afifi & Steuber, 2010).

⬤ On the Facebook Watch show *Red Table Talk*, Jada Pinkett Smith, her daughter Willow Smith, and Jada's mother Adrienne Banfield-Norris discuss personal stories as well as strategies they have used to overcome challenges relating to family dynamics. DS7/Derrick Salters/WENN/Newscom

self-reflection

Who has more influence in shaping your relationship decisions: your family or your friends? Who do you look to for emotional support in times of need? Has the degree to which you depend on your family versus your friends changed over time? If so, why?

In families, the tension between these two needs is even more pronounced. For example, your family may be extremely close, and as a consequence, almost anything that you tell one family member quickly becomes common knowledge. This creates a dilemma when you want to share something with only one family member. Do you disclose the information, knowing that within a week's time your entire family will also know it, or do you withhold it?

According to **Communication Privacy Management Theory** (Petronio, 2000), individuals create informational boundaries by carefully choosing the kind of private information they reveal and the people with whom they share it. These boundaries are constantly shifting, depending on the degree of risk associated with disclosing information. The more comfortable people feel disclosing, the more likely they are to reveal sensitive information. Inversely, people are less likely to share when they expect negative reactions to the disclosure (Afifi & Steuber, 2010).

focus on CULTURE

Autonomy and Connection: Helicopter and Snowplow Parents

"I gave my kindergarten students a fun Halloween activity that was basically a color by number chart. I hung them up for parents to see, and one of the moms saw her daughter's paper and told me, 'She can color better than that, you just have to push her.' She's five, and it was supposed to be fun" (Cruz, 2020).

Over the last few decades, parents in the United States increasingly have come to view their role as cultivating their children's talents in a highly orchestrated fashion (Lareau, 2003). Driven by a desire for their children to be the best at everything they do, and correspondingly to be seen themselves as "perfect parents" (Segrin et al., 2020), these individuals create and control all activities of their children. In extreme form, children may have little or no autonomy, as parents hover over all aspects of their lives like helicopters or push all perceived obstacles out of their children's paths like snowplows. Technology facilitates such hovering and snowplowing: parents can monitor their kids' academic performance through school websites, follow their children's personal lives and activities through social media, and track their physical whereabouts through text-messaging and location-tracking apps placed on mobile devices.

Public elementary and secondary schools in the United States strongly endorse an intense connection between parents and children, and in the 1990s and early 2000s they structured their curricula and school-related activities accordingly (Lareau, 2003). For instance, homework assignments were created to encourage parent–student collaborative projects; parents were sometimes encouraged to sit in on classes; and online resources were created to allow parents daily oversight of their children's academic performance, as well as teachers' lesson plans. But a growing body of research now suggests that such intense connectedness does a disservice to children, because it robs them of the opportunity and ability to make decisions, achieve goals, and resolve conflicts on their own. Overparenting in a helicopter or snowplow fashion has been documented as increasing the likelihood that children will experience psychological distress, entitlement, low self-efficacy, narcissism, poor academic engagement, delayed or inhibited leadership ability, and alcohol and drug use (Segrin et al., 2020).

discussion questions

- How has your parents' or caregivers' approach to balancing autonomy and connection influenced their relationship with you? Would you describe them as "helicopters," "snowplows," or neither?
- What are the advantages and disadvantages of the way your parents or caregivers balanced your connection with them and your autonomy?

Within families, these boundaries are defined by **family privacy rules**: the conditions governing what family members can talk about, how they can discuss such topics, and who should have access to family-relevant information (Petronio & Caughlin, 2006). In some families, members feel free to talk about any topic, at any time, and in any situation. In other families, discussion of more sensitive topics such as politics and religion may be permissible only in certain settings. Your family might talk about religion immediately after attending services together or debate political issues over dinner, but you might not discuss such matters during breakfast or while watching or playing sports. Or, some topics may be permanently excluded from your family discussion altogether. Breaking a family privacy rule by forcing discussion of a "forbidden" topic can cause intense emotional discomfort among other family members and may prompt the family to exclude the "rule breaker" from future family interactions. Keep this in mind before you force discussion of an issue that other family members consider off-limits.

Family privacy rules govern *how* family members talk about topics as well, including what's considered an acceptable opinion and how deeply family members can explore these opinions. It may be acceptable to talk at any time about the personal lives of your various family members, for instance, but only if your comments are positive. Or, it may be permissible to discuss religion after church, but only if you have a certain viewpoint.

Additionally, family privacy rules identify the people with whom family members can talk. If your family holds a particular religious or political viewpoint that is at odds with surrounding neighbors' views, you might be instructed to avoid these topics when conversing with neighborhood friends ("This stays within the family," or "Don't talk about this at school").

Although family privacy rules help members know how to balance openness and protection, they can also amplify tension within families as people age. When children grow up, the parent–child relationship often shifts from being authority based to being friendship based (Silverstein & Giuarrusso, 2010). As this occurs, people may feel pressure to change long-standing privacy rules. For example, even if your family has never openly discussed severe illness, you may feel compelled to talk about this topic if your mother starts displaying early symptoms of Alzheimer's disease.

How can you improve your family privacy rules and, in doing so, bring about a better balance of openness and protection? First, remember that all families have approved and taboo conversation topics, certain viewpoints they promote over others, and people they include or exclude from receiving information about the family. Effective family privacy rules aren't "one size fits all." Instead, they should strike the balance between openness and protection that best fits your family. Second, be respectful of the varying opinions and preferences individual family members have regarding openness and protection. Keep in mind that if your family communication pattern is low on conversation orientation and high on conformity orientation, any push for a change in privacy rules may strike others as a threat to the family.

Finally, if you believe that your family privacy rules should be altered to allow greater openness or increased protection, avoid abrupt, dramatic, and demanding calls for change. Such pronouncements will likely offend family members and put them on the defensive. Instead, identify a single family member you think might share your views. Discuss your desire for change with them by using your interpersonal competence skills and cooperative language (see Chapters 1 and 8). Ask this

skills practice

Changing Family Communication Rules
Changing communication about an important issue that's being avoided

❶ Identify an important issue that your family currently avoids discussing.

❷ Select one family member who might be open to talking about this concern.

❸ Initiate a discussion with this person, using competent and cooperative language.

❹ Mutually create a plan for how the issue can be raised with other family members and exactly what you both will say.

❺ Implement your plan, perhaps engaging one family member at a time.

self-reflection

What topics, if any, are off-limits for discussion within your family? Why are these topics taboo? What would be the consequences of initiating a discussion on these issues? How does not being able to talk about these things with family members make you feel about your family?

person's opinion on the possibility of modifying your family's privacy rules, and invite them to suggest ideas for implementing the change. If they agree that change is needed, identify an additional family member who might also concur. Then initiate a three-way discussion. Changes in long-standing family privacy rules—especially for low conversation, high conformity families—are best accomplished slowly, through interactions with one family member at a time.

To this point, our focus has been on the positive side of family relationships. In the last part of this chapter, however, we turn our attention to several challenges that people face in their family relationships, and options for how to deal with them.

Family Relationship Challenges

Managing stepfamily transitions, family favoritism, and family conflicts

We like to think of family relationships as simple, straightforward, and uniformly positive. Family consists of the most supportive people in our lives—individuals we like, love, and depend on. For many people this is true. But family relationships also face daunting challenges. Three of the most difficult to navigate are stepfamily transition, parental favoritism, and interparental conflict.

STEPFAMILY TRANSITION

While most people enter into stepfamilies with the best intentions for a new start, not all stepfamily members experience the transition equally. Adolescents tend to have more difficulty transitioning into a stepfamily than do pre-adolescents or young adults. Studies have found that children in stepfamilies have more frequent behavioral problems, turbulent relationships, and lower self-esteem than do children in first-marriage families (Golish, 2003).

The majority of stepfamilies confront very similar challenges, including negotiating new family privacy rules, dealing with discrepancies in conflict-management styles, and building solidarity as a family unit (Golish, 2003). But the most frequent and perplexing challenge is **triangulation**: loyalty conflicts that arise when a coalition is formed, uniting one family member with another against a third family

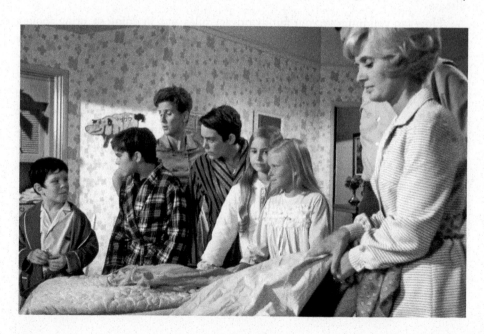

⏵ In the classic TV series *The Brady Bunch*, widowed architect Mike Brady marries Carol Martin, creating a new stepfamily. Mike, Carol, and their children have trouble transitioning at first, but they eventually accept that they are all one family. As Carol tells her new son Bobby, "The only 'steps' in this house are those, the ones that lead up to your bedroom." Everett Collection, Inc

member (Schrodt & Afifi, 2007). Two forms of triangulation are common within stepfamilies: children feeling caught between their custodial and their noncustodial parent, and stepparents feeling caught between the children in their stepfamily (Golish, 2003). Family members caught in triangulation feel torn between different loyalties. As one daughter described her triangulation between her birth parents, "I would carry things from her, she'd say stuff about him, and he'd do the same and talk about her. It's kind of hard to get both sides of it. So I avoided them for a while. . . . I just felt that I was caught in the middle" (Golish, 2003, p. 52). Such triangulation has pronounced negative effects: children who feel "caught between parents" report higher levels of stress and anxiety, and substantially less satisfaction with their parent–child relationships, than do children who aren't triangulated (Schrodt & Shimkowski, 2013). In contrast, supportive co-parenting by former spouses—including relying on one another for parenting advice and assistance when needed—substantially reduces aggression, anxiety, and depression in children of divorce (Herrero et al., 2020).

Given such challenges, how can you help ease the transition to a stepfamily, should you experience it? Try these suggestions:

1. *Go slow, but start early.* Except for the couple getting married, the relationships between other stepfamily members are involuntary. Yet stepfamily members often feel pressure to immediately become intimate (Ganong et al., 1999). This can cause stress and anxiety, as no one enjoys feeling forced to be close to others. To avoid this, *go slow* in building ties with your stepparents, stepchildren, or stepsiblings. Take the time to get to know one another, forging relationships in the same way you would any other interpersonal involvements—by having fun and doing things together. If possible, *start early* in creating these bonds—ideally as soon as it becomes certain that a stepfamily will form. Not doing so can lead to tension and conflict later, when the stepfamily formally becomes a family unit.

2. *Practice daily maintenance.* Research on stepfamilies emphasizes the importance of displaying affection, attending important activities and events, engaging in everyday talk, and sharing humorous stories—the behaviors fundamental to all families (Afifi, 2003). Try to express your support for your new family members by doing at least some of these things every day.

3. *Create new family rituals.* A critical part of building a new family identity is creating *stepfamily rituals*: events or activities shared between stepfamily members that function to define the group as a family. This can be sharing a weekly dinner or attending religious services together. Whatever form it takes, the most constructive stepfamily rituals are those that bring stepfamily members together as a family but still recognize and value what was important from the previous families (Schrodt, 2006).

4. *Avoid triangulating family members.* You may feel it's strategic or even enjoyable to team up and triangulate against a stepparent or stepsibling, but such behavior damages your relationship with them and creates family stress (Schrodt & Afifi, 2007). If you're the one caught in the middle of triangulation, confront the perpetrators. Using your interpersonal skills (cooperative language, competent interpersonal communication), respectfully

self-reflection

Call to mind an instance of triangulation within your family, your stepfamily, or the family of someone you know. Who was involved? Why was the coalition formed? What impact did the triangulation have on the relationships among the triangulated people? The family as a whole?

self-reflection

Does your family or stepfamily have rituals? Which rituals mean the most to you, and why? How does the regular practice of these rituals affect how you feel about your family or stepfamily?

explain to them how their behavior is making you feel and the damage it is doing to the family. Remind them that stepfamilies are difficult enough to maintain without also having to deal with alliances, loyalty struggles, and power battles. Ask them to please stop.

5. *Be patient.* Whenever families experience a major transition, there is always a lengthy period of adjustment. In the case of remarriage, it typically takes anywhere from three to five *years* for a stepfamily to stabilize as a family unit (Hetherington, 1993). Expect that new relationship bonds are going to take a long time to develop, that you will feel uncertain about your new family roles, and that disputes will arise over privacy rules and personal boundaries (Golish, 2003).

PARENTAL FAVORITISM

Few things matter more to children than expressions of affection from parents (Floyd & Morman, 2005). Such displays include verbal statements ("I love you"), nonverbal contact (hugs, cuddling), gifts, favors, and other resources that make children feel adored and appreciated. But when there is more than one child in the family, competition between children for parental affection becomes a natural part of family life (Golish, 2003).

Many parents respond to this age-old dilemma by equally allocating their affection and resources. However, some parents engage in **parental favoritism**, whereby one or both parents allocate an unfair amount of valuable resources to one child over others. This may include intangible forms of affection, such as statements of love, praise, undue patience (letting one child "get away with anything"), and emotional support. Or, it may involve tangible resources, such as cash loans, college tuition, cars, or job offers. For example, when Steve's friend Susan was growing up, her father blatantly favored her sister over her. He bought her sister a BMW for her 16th birthday but refused to loan Susan his car when she needed to get to work. Susan's father paid her sister's out-of-state college tuition but refused to contribute toward Susan's community college education. When she finally confronted him

Some parents manage to equally allocate their resources and affection, while others struggle to disguise their preference for one child over another. What impact might favoritism have on a family's relationship and communication?
Jill Lehmann Photography/Moment/GettyImages

about his lifelong favoritism, his response was clear: "Your sister *deserves* all I've given her because I love her more than you."

Parental favoritism appears to be stable over time: children that are favored by one parent or both in youth typically are favored in adulthood as well (Suitor et al., 2016). And the effects are both profound and enduring. Because favored children garner more of their parents' resources, they are more likely than their siblings to be professionally successful as adults (Hertwig et al., 2002). Favored children also report a greater sense of well-being and life satisfaction in adulthood than do disfavored children (Suitor et al., 2009). In contrast, disfavored children are more likely than their favored siblings to experience loneliness, depression, and anxiety (Stocker et al., 2020).

At the same time, the *relational* consequences are devastating, especially for siblings. Studies show that siblings from households in which favoritism occurred feel and express substantially less warmth and more hostility toward one another than those from households where it did not. Similarly, siblings from favoritism families are substantially less close and report more conflict than those who grew up in equitable families (Suitor et al., 2009). This is true regardless of family size, gender of siblings, or the family's ethnicity. Siblings from favoritism families also communicate far less regularly—whether face-to-face or via phone, email, text, social media, or video chat—than siblings from non-favoritism families (Stocker et al., 2020).

Given the obvious inequity and devastating impacts of parental favoritism, why would parents favor certain children over others in the first place? Two kinds of reasons are prominent: *relational* and *evaluative* (Suitor et al., 2016). *Relational* reasons refer to how well parents and children get along versus how often they disagree and fight. If one child routinely disagrees with their parents' beliefs, attitudes, and values, triggering conflict—whereas other children in the household consistently agree with their parents—over time this can lead to favoritism, as the conflict-prone child becomes labeled "the troublemaker" of the family. *Evaluative* reasons are the degree to which parents feel pride versus disappointment in children's achievements. If one child routinely falls short of parental expectations, whereas others meet or exceed these expectations, favoritism may arise. Sadly, research documents that children's objective achievements during adulthood, in the form of societal, educational, and professional accomplishments, do little to change parental favoritism, which is instead driven by whether the child embodies shared values and exceeds the parents' expectations (Suitor et al., 2016). In simple terms, a disfavored child can become incredibly accomplished, yet still "fall short" in the eyes of disapproving parents. This suggests that disfavored adults seeking to gain parental approval through accumulating accomplishments may be pursuing a fruitless path.

How can we handle parental favoritism? First, realize that favoritism is never the fault of the favored child. The sad truth is that some parents play favorites. If you're a disfavored child, avoid blaming your sibling. If you feel unmanageable resentment toward your favored sibling, seek counseling. Second, carefully consider whether it is worth confronting your parents. Unfortunately, challenging parental favoritism is unlikely to bring about positive outcomes. For one thing, you can't control your parents' behavior. Some parents may not even realize they favor one child over others, especially if their favoritism is subtle (e.g., differential praise, attention, or emotional support). In such cases, challenging parents for being "unfair" will only hurt their feelings and create a rift between you, them, and the favored sibling. Alternatively, if your parents recognize and relish their preferential treatment, confrontation may lead them to defend their behavior in ways that hurt your feelings further.

self-QUIZ

How Much Family Favoritism Exists?

Call to mind a family whose favoritism you would like to assess (yours or someone else's). Then check off the statements with which you agree. Total the number to calculate your score, and use the key to assess the degree of favoritism in that family.

To take this quiz online, visit LaunchPad: launchpadworks.com

Parents, stepparents, or caregivers . . .

_____ punish one child less than others for misbehavior.

_____ openly display more pride in the accomplishments of one child than in those of others.

_____ obviously enjoy sharing time and activities more with one child than with others.

_____ are more sensitive to the thoughts and feelings of one child than to those of others.

_____ give more money and valuable gifts to one child than to others.

_____ are more likely to do favors for one child than for others.

_____ are more supportive of the decisions made by one child than those made by others.

_____ are more likely to give in to the requests and demands of one child over others.

_____ display more affection and love toward one child than toward others.

_____ listen to and respect the opinions of one child more than those of others.

Information in this self-quiz is from the Sibling Inventory of Differential Experience (SIDE), Daniels (1986).

Scoring: 0–2: low favoritism; 3–6: moderate favoritism; 7–10: high favoritism

Instead, focus on maintaining your sibling relationship by regularly practicing positivity, assurances, and self-disclosure. If you're a favored child, realize that your siblings may resent you and all you've gained. Discuss this openly with them, and look for opportunities to "balance things out" between you and them through acts of generosity and support. To repair the relational damage done by their father, for instance, Susan's sister began quietly funneling financial support to Susan to help her pay for nursing school. Although Susan and her father no longer speak, she and her sister are quite close. This is an unusual outcome, only achieved through both sisters' hard work to overcome the bitter wedge driven between them in their youth.

INTERPARENTAL CONFLICT

One of the most potent family challenges is **interparental conflict**: overt, hostile interactions between parents in a household. While such constant fighting is harmful to the parents' relationship, the impact on children in the household is worse. Interparental conflict is associated with children's social problems, including lower levels of play with peers and lower friendship quality (Rodrigues & Kitzmann, 2007). Such children are more likely to imitate their parents' destructive interaction styles and, consequently, are more at risk for aggressive and delinquent behaviors (Krishnakumar et al., 2003).

But the most devastating effects of interparental conflict are relational. Adolescents who perceive a high frequency of interparental conflict are more likely to report feelings of jealousy and fears of abandonment in their romantic relationships (Hayashi & Strickland, 1998). Interparental conflict also negatively impacts late teen and adult perceptions of interpersonal trust, love attitudes, sexual behaviors, relationship beliefs, cohabitation, and attitudes toward marriage and divorce (Rodrigues & Kitzmann, 2007). And in instances in which the interparental conflict is violently aggressive, bearing witness to such hostility can lead to emotional desensitization, in which people experience less negative stress with regard to conflict and are more likely to perceive verbally aggressive behavior as acceptable, especially within romantic relationships (Aloia & Worley, 2019).

Why do children suffer so many profound and negative outcomes from fights between parents? One explanation is the **spillover hypothesis**: emotions, affect, and mood from the parental relationship "spill over" into the broader family, disrupting children's sense of emotional security (Krishnakumar et al., 2003). Children living in households torn by interparental conflict experience a chronic sense of instability—not knowing when the next battle will erupt and if or when their parents will break up. This gives them a deep-seated sense of emotional insecurity related to relationships (Rodrigues & Kitzmann, 2007), which manifests in their own intimate involvements, months and even years later. Of course, the spillover hypothesis works both ways: children growing up in households in which parents actively *support* each other's parenting efforts and *calmly discuss* disagreements are more likely to be satisfied in their relationships with their parents, and report better mental health overall, including lower levels of stress and anxiety (Schrodt & Shimkowski, 2013).

What can you do to manage interparental conflict and its outcomes? If you have parents who fight, encourage them individually to approach their conflicts more constructively. Share with them all you know about conflict from Chapter 10: effective approaches for managing conflict, the negative role of self-enhancing thoughts, the dangers associated with destructive messages, and the trap of serial arguments. If you feel that you are suffering negative outcomes from having grown up in a conflict-ridden household, seek therapy from a reputable counselor. And if you're a parent with children, realize this: everything you say and do within the family realm—including interactions you have with your spouse or partner—spills over into the emotions and feelings of your children.

The Primacy of Family

Family ties run so deep that we often use kinship as a metaphor to describe closeness in other relationships

As with romantic relationships, the day-to-day work of maintaining family bonds isn't especially glamorous. Birth, adoption, marriage, or remarriage may structure your family, but the quality of your family relationships is defined by whether you invest time and energy in your interpersonal communication. Such efforts don't have to be complex: a story told to your child or shared with a sibling, gratitude expressed to a parent, an affectionate email sent to a grandparent—all these simple acts of communication keep your family bonds alive and thriving.

Yet we often neglect to communicate with family members in these ways, in part because such relationships lack the sparkle, excitement, and drama of romances. When we dismiss, look past, or simply take for granted our families, we're like Dorothy in *The Wizard of Oz*—running away from Auntie Em and the farm, thinking we'll do just fine on our own. But life is *not* a skip down the yellow brick road. When we battle metaphorical witches in the form of hardship, disappointment, and even tragedy, often it's our family members who lock arms with us. They're the ones who help us charge forward, even though we're afraid or discouraged. The truth about our family relationships stands like the wizard behind the curtain. When you step forward boldly and pull the curtain back, it's revealed. There is no place like home.

skills practice

Managing Interparental Conflict

Helping parents better manage their conflicts

❶ Following a significant conflict between parents or caregivers, reach out to each person individually, letting them know you're available to talk.

❷ Encourage them to be mindful of how negative emotions and flawed attributions shape their conflict perceptions and decisions, encouraging a time-out when emotions flare.

❸ Remind them of the relational damage wrought by destructive messages.

❹ Help them identify the causes of the conflict.

❺ List goals and long-term interests they have in common.

❻ Use these points of commonality to collaboratively create solutions that will prevent similar conflicts in the future.

❼ Evaluate these solutions in terms of fairness for both of them.

Struggling with Family Transitions

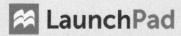 **LaunchPad**   For the best experience, complete all parts of this activity
in LaunchPad: **launchpadworks.com**

 Background

One of the biggest challenges family members face is transitioning from a family to a stepfamily. To understand how you might competently manage such a relationship challenge, read the case study in Part 2; then, drawing on all you know about interpersonal communication, work through the problem-solving model in Part 3.

 Visit LaunchPad to watch the video in Part 4 and assess your communication in Part 5.

2 Case Study

Your parents married young, and it was a bad match. Your dad is cold, authoritarian, and a strict disciplinarian. You respect and fear him more than you love him. In contrast, your mom is affectionate and outgoing. She's your principal source of emotional support, and the two of you are very close.

During your childhood, your dad dominated the family. His decisions were the law, and family discussions were rare. Your parents fought constantly over his need for control, and your mom eventually divorced him and gained custody of you.

Despite the divorce, your dad continued to believe that the family would someday reunite. This fantasy was shattered when your mom married Stephan. Stephan is the opposite of your dad; he is open, funny, and kind. He places enormous value on talking things through as a family and welcomes your opinion, even when it differs from his. Slowly you adjust to having a diversity of views encouraged and your opinion valued. You come to adore Stephan, and relish the warm, witty, and varied discussions of your stepfamily.

Your dad remains bitter about your mom's remarriage. He constantly mocks Stephan in emails to you. He also plies you for personal information about your mother and her marriage. You feel like a spy. When you tell your mom about your dad's prying, she is furious, and a huge fight erupts between them. The tension is resolved when you leave for college because your parents cease contact with each other.

You're home for the weekend, visiting your dad. When the topic of your mom arises, your dad stuns you by confessing that he still loves her. He says he realizes now that they will never be together, and he blames Stephan for "ruining everything!" He demands that you choose between him and Stephan. He threatens to move away and sever ties with you unless you cut off contact with Stephan, saying, "Knowing you've replaced me with another father reminds me of all I've lost!" Later, when you call your mom and tell her what happened, she says, "Good! He *should* leave. I know *I'm* happier without him in my life. You will be, too!" The next day, your dad shoots you a text, asking whether you've made a decision yet.

Your Turn

Consider all you've learned thus far about interpersonal communication. Then work through the following five steps. Remember, there are no "right" answers, so think hard about what is the best choice! (P.S. Need help? See the *Helpful Concepts* list.)

step 1

Reflect on yourself. What are your thoughts and feelings in this situation? What attributions are you making about your dad? Are your attributions accurate? Why or why not?

step 2

Reflect on your partner. Using perspective-taking and empathic concern, put yourself in your dad's shoes. What is he thinking and feeling in this situation?

step 3

Identify the optimal outcome. Think about all the information you have about your communication and relationship with your dad and the situation

surrounding your parents' divorce and your mom's remarriage. Consider your own feelings as well as your dad's. Given all these factors, what's the best, most constructive outcome possible? Consider what's best for you and for your dad.

step 4

Locate the roadblocks. Taking into consideration your own and your dad's thoughts and feelings and all that has happened in this situation, what obstacles are keeping you from achieving the optimal outcome?

step 5

Chart your course. What can you say to your dad to overcome the roadblocks you've identified and achieve your optimal outcome?

HELPFUL CONCEPTS

Protective and pluralistic families, **332**
Maintenance strategies for families, **335**
Balancing openness and protection, **337**
Triangulation, **340**
Interparental conflict, **344**

 The Other Side

Visit LaunchPad to watch a video in which your dad tells his side of the case study story. As in many real-life situations, this is information to which you did not have access when you were initially crafting your response in Part 3. The video reminds us that even when we do our best to offer competent responses, there is always another side to the story that we need to consider.

 Interpersonal Competence Self-Assessment

After watching the video, visit the Self-Assessment questions in LaunchPad. Think about the new information offered in your dad's side of the story and all you've learned about interpersonal communication. Drawing on this knowledge, revisit your earlier responses in Part 3 and assess your interpersonal communication competence.

POSTSCRIPT

W e began this chapter with a world champion and the family that encouraged her to excel. Throughout her life, Brenda Villa's parents have been a source of inspiration and motivation. Through their support, honesty, sacrifice, and love, they created the foundation on which Brenda has built the most successful water polo career in U.S. history.

To whom do you turn to listen—or to provide you with a necessary boost—when you're feeling sorry for yourself? From whom did you get the confidence and swagger to face the challenges that life presents?

The story of Brenda Villa and her parents reminds us of a simple truth regarding the primacy of family. The successes, victories, and medals we achieve in our lives may be won through our own efforts, but they were made possible by the people who raised us.

 **LaunchPad**

LaunchPad for *Reflect & Relate* offers videos and encourages self-assessment through adaptive quizzing. Go to **launchpadworks.com** to get access to:

 LearningCurve
Adaptive Quizzes

 Video clips that help you understand interpersonal communication

key terms

You can watch brief, illustrative videos of these terms and test your understanding of the concepts in LaunchPad.

key concepts

Defining Family

- Given the diversity in contemporary **family** structures, scholars define *family* in very inclusive ways. Families come in myriad forms, including **nuclear**, **extended**, **step-**, **cohabiting couples**, **single-parent**, and **voluntary kin families**.

- Families solidify their sense of identity by sharing **family stories**. These narrative accounts of birth, courtship, and survival bind children, parents, and other relatives together.

Communicating in Families

- Regardless of the structure of a family, *Family Communication Patterns Theory* suggests that most families' communication is determined by two dimensions: **conversation orientation** and **conformity orientation**.

- These two dimensions help describe four family communication patterns: **consensual**, **pluralistic**, **protective**, and **laissez-faire**. Such families have very different communication beliefs and practices, which shape interpersonal relationships among family members.

Maintaining Family Relationships

- Three of the most important strategies for maintaining family relationships are positivity, assurances, and self-disclosure. Technology is making it easier for family members to communicate such maintenance strategies, especially when distance separates them.

- The ways family members deal with dialectical tensions can be understood through **Communication Privacy Management Theory**. These boundaries are defined by **family privacy rules**: the conditions governing what family members can talk about, how they can discuss such topics, and who should have access to family-relevant information.

Family Relationship Challenges

- A common challenge in stepfamily transition is **triangulation**. Such loyalty conflicts can make individuals feel torn between family members.

- **Parental favoritism** can include both intangible and tangible forms of affection and often drives a wedge between siblings, in addition to other long-term effects.

- Dealing with **interparental conflict** is one of the hardest family communication challenges. Such fights can have long-term and devastating effects on both parents and the children, as explained by the **spillover hypothesis**.

13 Relationships with Friends

Our friends keep us grounded and provide us with support in times of crisis.

He was the first animated character in history to have a wax likeness in Madame Tussaud's New York museum. He has inspired albums, video games, theme park rides, and even a Broadway musical. The media franchise controlling his image is an $8 billion global industry. But the story of SpongeBob SquarePants is not one of a solitary sea sponge sitting alone at the bottom of the ocean. Instead, it's a tale of friendship and the deep and recognizable connections that exist between the characters.

SpongeBob is the brainchild of marine biologist and animator Stephen Hillenburg. While working at the Ocean Institute in California, Hillenburg created a comic titled "The Intertidal Zone," to educate students about oceanic animal life. Inspired to expand the characters into an animated feature, he pitched the plan to Nickelodeon executives, accompanied by Hawaiian music and an underwater terrarium. Nickelodeon funded the project, and the series was born.

At the center of the show are the friendships SpongeBob shares with Sandy, Squidward, and Patrick. Sandy is a consistent voice of reason, supporting SpongeBob when he gets into trouble by offering useful advice. In "MuscleBob Buffpants" (season 1, episode 11a), for instance, Sandy helps SpongeBob with his strength training, although her exercise regimen proves too daunting (SpongeBob ends up buying inflatable muscle arms instead). The support goes both ways. In "House Sittin' for Sandy" (season 8, episode 165a), she asks SpongeBob to take care of her Treedome while she is away. When the result is disastrous, Sandy forgives him.

Although Squidward delights in insulting SpongeBob, beneath his gruff exterior he seems to harbor genuine affection for his spongy friend. In the episode "Squidville" (season 2, episode 26b), Squidward becomes so enraged by SpongeBob's reef-blower play that he explodes, "I would rather tear out my brain stem, carry it to the middle of the nearest four-way intersection, and skip rope with it than go on living where I do now!" But when he moves away, he finds himself missing his former neighbor.

SpongeBob's best friend is Patrick. Whether it's chasing jellyfish, selling chocolates, or playing "Robot-Pirate Island" in an empty cardboard box, they do almost everything together. At the core of their friendship is emotional support. In "Big Pink Loser" (season 2, episode 23a), Patrick is heartbroken when he realizes he has never won an award. SpongeBob immediately steps up, coaching Patrick through the task of opening a jar. When Patrick finally (after many failed attempts) succeeds, they mutually celebrate Patrick's triumph.

SpongeBob's friendships are not without challenges, however. He betrays Sandy by mocking squirrels as part of his comedy act ("What's up with that squirrel fur? I guess fleas need a home, too!"). Patrick gets SpongeBob into trouble at school by drawing an insulting picture of the teacher, then allowing SpongeBob to take the blame. SpongeBob is consumed with jealousy when Patrick replaces him as Grandma Sponge's "baby." But despite these difficulties, the friends always manage to maintain their relationships.

SpongeBob SquarePants has won multiple Emmys, Kids' Choice Awards, and BAFTA Children's Awards. Images of SpongeBob have been embraced by groups as diverse as American schoolchildren and Egyptian revolutionaries. But the resonance of the show lies within a text deeper than its silliness. When we watch SpongeBob, we're reminded of the complexities of our own friendships. Our friends are people who are similar to us, but annoy us. They help us and have our backs, but also hurt us. They lift us up but can also tear us down. Ultimately, though, our friends are the people we choose to share our lives with because, beyond everything else, we *enjoy their companionship*.

It may strike you as strange to think of your friendships as similar to those of an animated sea sponge who lives in a pineapple. Nevertheless, the friendships that fill our lives are akin to SpongeBob's in important ways. We are drawn to our friends through the realization of shared interests. We count on our friends to provide support. We build our friendships by disclosing our thoughts, feelings, and vulnerabilities, while trusting our friends to not betray us. At the same time, our friendships can be difficult to define. They lack the permanence of family bonds and the clear constraints and expectations of romantic involvements. This makes them more fragile and confusing than other close relationships.

In this chapter, we look at friendship. You'll learn:

- How friendships are unique and distinct
- The varied types of friendships you'll experience
- Ways you can communicate so that your friendships survive and thrive
- Challenges to friendships and how to overcome them

The Nature of Friendship

Friendships are both
delicate and deep

Like family and romantic bonds, friendship plays a crucial role in our lives. Friendship is an important source of emotional security and self-esteem (Rawlins, 1992). Friendship facilitates a sense of belonging when we're young, helps solidify our identity during adolescence (Miller et al., 2007), and is connected to our academic and professional success (Persich et al., 2020). As we move through adulthood, our friendships impact a range of important personal outcomes. In a study of more than 270,000 people across 100 countries, those with strong friendships reported better physical health, higher degrees of happiness, and greater personal well-being across their life span, compared with those having weak friendships (Chopik, 2017). And these effects were especially pronounced for people over the age of 50, for whom friendships proved to be more powerful predictors of health and happiness than family ties did (Chopik, 2017).

It's clear from these studies that friendships are extremely important. But what exactly *is* friendship? We begin our discussion by defining friendship, and how it differs from other close relationships. Then we'll look at the functions friendship serves; how it changes across our life spans; and the impact of culture, gender, and technology on our friendship relationships.

FRIENDSHIP DEFINED

Friendship is a voluntary interpersonal relationship characterized by intimacy and liking (McEwan et al., 2008). Whether it's casual or close, short or long term, friendship has several distinguishing characteristics.

Friendship Is Voluntary   We have greater liberty in choosing our friends than we do in choosing partners for any other relationship type (Sias et al., 2008). Whether a friendship forms is determined largely by the people involved, based on their mutual desire to create such a relationship. This is different from romantic, workplace, and family involvements. Consider romantic relationships. You may face substantial familial or cultural constraints in your choice of romantic partners. You may be expected (or allowed) to only date people your family approves. In the workplace (discussed in Chapter 14), you are required to work collaboratively with your colleagues, whether you like them or not. And in your family, you're bound to others through birth, adoption, or the creation of a stepfamily. These ties are involuntary, creating social contact that may seem more obligatory (Ermer & Proulx, 2020). As French poet Jacques Delille (1738–1813) put it, "Fate chooses your relations, you choose your friends."

Friendship Is Driven by Shared Interests   Similarity is the primary force that draws us to our friends (Parks & Floyd, 1996), regardless of our age, gender, sexual orientation, or ethnicity. One practical implication of this is that when your interests and activities change, so do your friendships. If you change your political or religious beliefs or suffer an injury that prevents you from playing a beloved sport, friendships related to those things may change as well. Some friendships will endure—the focus of the relationship shifting to new points of commonality—but others will fade away. One of the most common reasons for friendships ending is a change in shared interests and beliefs (Miller et al., 2007).

self-
reflection

What constraints, if any, do you face in whom you can choose as friends? Who puts these limits on you? In your experience, do you have more, or less, freedom in choosing friends than romantic partners? How does this influence your choice of friends?

► A shared love of comedy brought together Tina Fey and Amy Poehler, and they've remained close friends even after their roles on *Saturday Night Live* ended. How did you meet your closest friends?
Michael Buckner/Getty Images

Friendship Is Characterized by Self-Disclosure We consider most people in our lives "acquaintances." Only a select few rise to the level of "friends." What distinguishes the two groups? *Self-disclosure.* People report that being able to freely and deeply disclose is the defining feature of friendship (Parks & Floyd, 1996), and being able to discuss problems and seek advice are primary motivators for friendship formation (Apostolou et al., 2020). Self-disclosure between friends means sharing private thoughts and feelings, and believing that "we can tell each other anything." The relationship between friendship and self-disclosure is reciprocal as well. The more you consider someone a friend, the more you will disclose; and the more you disclose, the more you will consider that person a friend (Shelton et al., 2010).

Friendship Is Rooted in Liking We feel affection and respect for our friends. In other words, we *like* them (Rubin, 1973). We also enjoy their company; pleasure in sharing time together is a defining feature of friendships (Hays, 1988), fulfilling our needs to socialize with others (Apostolou et al., 2020). And although friends do share an emotional connection (Wentzel et al., 2018), because friendships are rooted in liking—rather than love—we're not as emotionally attached to our friends as we are to other intimates, and we're not as emotionally demanding of them. Correspondingly, we're expected to be more loyal to and more willing to help romantic partners and family members than friends (Davis & Todd, 1985).

Friendship Is Volatile Friendships are less stable, more likely to change, and easier to break off than family or romantic relationships (Johnson et al., 2003). Why? Consider the differences in depth of commitment. We're bonded to friends by choice, rooted in shared interests. But we're bonded to families by social and legal

self-reflection

Call to mind your three closest friends in middle school. Then do the same for high school. Now think about your three closest friends today. Are the lists the same? How have they changed? Why? What does this tell you about the volatility of friendships?

commitment, and to our partners by deep emotional and sometimes sexual attachment. These loyalties mean we may choose or forgo professional opportunities to preserve romances or stay close to family. But most of us will choose to pursue our careers over staying geographically close to friends (Patterson, 2007).

FRIENDSHIP FUNCTIONS

Friendships serve many functions in our lives. Two of the most important are that they help us fulfill our need for *companionship*—by doing fun things together—and they help us *achieve practical goals*, such as dealing with problems or everyday tasks (de Vries, 1996).

Companionship   One of the functions friendships serve is enabling us to share life events and activities with others. Compared to family and work relationships, friendship interactions are the least task-oriented and tend to revolve around leisure activities, such as talking or eating (Argyle & Furnham, 1982). For example, you may have played Pokémon Go with your friends, or formed new friends doing so, and research shows that you likely experienced psychological benefits from this activity (Bonus et al., 2018). Scholar William Rawlins (1992) describes friendships that focus primarily on sharing time and activities together as **communal friendships**. These friends may get together as often as possible and provide solidarity, encouragement, and emotional support to one another during times of need. Because emotional support is a central aspect of communal friendship, only when both friends fulfill the expectations of support for the relationship does the friendship endure (Burleson & Samter, 1994).

Achieving Goals   We also look to friends for help in achieving practical goals in both our personal and our professional lives. Friends help us study for exams, fix cars, set up computers, and even complete professional projects. You may have a friend at school with whom you complete projects or homework; studies find that such friendships are linked to better academic performance (Wentzel et al., 2018). Friendships in which the parties focus primarily on helping each other achieve practical goals are known as **agentic friendships** (Rawlins, 1992). Agentic friends value sharing time together—but only if they're available and have no other priorities at the moment. They also aren't interested in the emotional interdependence and mutual sharing of personal information that characterize communal friendships. They're available when the need arises, but beyond that, they're uncomfortable with more personal demands or responsibilities. For example, an agentic friend from work may gladly help you write up a monthly sales report, but they may feel uncomfortable if you ask for advice about your relational problems.

Although friendships have been described as either communal or agentic, these distinctions may strike you as simplistic. Many of our friendships fulfill multiple functions, providing us with someone to spend time with, emotionally support us *and* practically support our abilities to accomplish projects or tasks. And our friendships change as we do—a topic we consider next.

FRIENDSHIP ACROSS THE LIFE SPAN

The importance we attribute to our friendships changes throughout our lives. Up through fourth grade, most children look to their family as their sole source of emotional support (Furman & Simon, 1998). If a child suffers a disappointment at

LaunchPad Video
launchpadworks.com

Communal Friendships
Watch this clip online to answer the questions below.

Why are the men in this video considered communal friends? How much do factors like gender, culture, shared interests, and self-disclosure influence your communal friendships?

Want to see more? Check out LaunchPad for a clip illustrating **agentic friendships**.

self-reflection

Consider your friendships and the types of functions they fulfill. Do you have friends you seek out, or who seek you out, for a particular function? Do you communicate differently with them? How does this impact how you feel about them? Why?

school, has a frightening dream, or just wants to share the events of the day, they will turn to parents or siblings. But during adolescence, children slowly transfer their emotional attachment from their family to friends (Welch & Houser, 2010), and strive for more autonomy from parents (White et al., 2018). As they mature, the quality of teens' friendships evolves, typically decreasing in conflict, and increasing in support and intimacy. If romantic relationships are pursued, these may replace close friendships as the primary source for teens' intimacy and support (Camirand & Poulin, 2019).

By middle adulthood, many people form long-term romantic commitments and start families of their own. Consequently, their romantic partners and children become the primary providers of companionship, affection, and support. Research suggests that during middle adulthood both family and friends are linked to our well-being, yet in older adulthood greater well-being is connected to social time with friends (Ermer & Proulx, 2020). Later in life we may experience the loss of spouses and siblings, children forming their own families, and more time with neighbors. For elderly people, friendships are *the* most important relationships for providing social support and intimacy (Chopik, 2017; Patterson, 2007).

FRIENDSHIP, CULTURE, AND GENDER

Given that friendships center on shared interests and identity support, it's no surprise that people tend to befriend those who are similar demographically (with regard to age, gender, economic status, and so on). But people also regularly defy this norm, forging friendships that cross demographic lines, known as **cross-category friendships** (Galupo, 2009). Such friendships are a powerful way to break down ingroup and outgroup perceptions and purge people of negative stereotypes. Some of the most common cross-category friendships relate to both culture and gender.

Culture   *Intercultural friendships* are those between people from different cultures or countries. Such friendships have become more widespread due to the growing cultural diversity within countries and increasing migration between cultures (Galyapina et al., 2020). These friendships are both challenging and rewarding (Sias et al., 2008). Challenges include overcoming differences in language and cultural beliefs, as well as negative stereotypes. Differences in language alone present a substantial hurdle. Incorrect interpretations of messages can lead to misunderstanding, uncertainty, frustration, and conflict (Sias et al., 2008). Yet these challenges may be outweighed by the substantial benefits, which include reducing prejudice; enhancing language skills, academic performance, and commitment to social justice; and increasing empathy toward people of other racial groups (Gareis et al., 2019; Hudson, 2020). People who develop a close friendship with someone of a different ethnicity become less prejudiced toward people of all ethnicities as a result (Shelton et al., 2009). Moreover, these outcomes benefit other people in the networks of the intercultural friends: that is, if you know someone who has an intercultural friendship, you *also* may experience positive outcomes from their friendship, such as reducing your own prejudice (Gareis et al., 2019).

So how can we cultivate intercultural friendships? Scholar Tara Hudson (2020) suggests several ways we can develop and maintain them. The first important step is "embracing similarity without forgetting difference" (p. 10). We embrace similarity when we focus on what we have in common, such as sharing a sense of humor, beliefs, values, or personality. Simultaneously, differences must be respectfully engaged when they arise. Other steps include fostering trust, exploring and engaging with each other's cultures, and finding a way to see connections through differences rather than letting them lead to conflict. As Hudson states, when we do so "we discover that what we share is greater than what we do not" (p. 3, 2020).

Gender Positive outcomes also arise related to gender and friendship. Even though most of us feel peer pressure to conform to gender roles during middle childhood and our teen years (Schroeder & Liben, 2020), grow up in environments with many sex-segregated settings, and have collegiate social networks largely segregated by sex (Mehta et al., 2017), more than 80 percent of adults nevertheless have had a cross-sex friend whom they identify as close (Reeder, 2017). At the same time, we often lack societal role models for cross-sex friendships. Communication scholar Heidi Reeder suggests that college students commonly construct these relationships using other types of roles as guides. For example, you might orient to a friend like a sibling, or perhaps as "just friends" to clearly label the friendship as *not* modeling a romantic relationship. Reeder suggests that this framing gives people both a means to express and comprehend these friendships. In addition, adopting a "just friends" or "sibling" understanding of these friendships has been linked to more happiness in the relationship.

We also see the importance of roles in friendships for sexual and gender minorities. Lesbian, gay, bisexual, and trans friendships may serve as important communities of support—or voluntary families—for each other. This may be especially true for people who feel that their identities do not conform to societal norms, or do not feel accepted in their biological families, thus increasing the importance of the friendship and the necessity of social support (Boyer & Galupo, 2018). Simply put, friends buffer each other from stress.

◀ In *New Girl*, main character Jess (played by Zooey Deschanel) forms close relationships with her male roommates. Though they all have very different personalities and interests, they bond through shared humor. Adam Taylor/©Fox/courtesy Everett Collection

Despite the diverse ways we negotiate friendships and gender, one thing seems clear: when people need a friend for emotional or social support, they typically seek out female friends, regardless of their own sexual orientation or sex (Willis, 2014). This likely is because of the broad tendency, described in Chapter 2, of people preferring to self-disclose to women.

FRIENDSHIP AND TECHNOLOGY

As with other interpersonal relationships, communication technologies have reshaped the way people orient to friendships. In the past, people forged friendships slowly. They took time to discover the values and interests of their neighbors, coworkers, and acquaintances, often in face-to-face encounters, and then built friendships with those who shared their values and interests. Now, however, you can form friendships quickly and with more people, sometimes without ever meeting them in person. For example, college students using Instagram view it as an easy way to present themselves in a positive light, thereby facilitating friendship development (Lee & Borah, 2020). Information gleaned from social media also aids our friendship decisions, providing a means of "doing homework" about potential friends (Standlee, 2019).

Of course, just because someone is your social media "friend" doesn't necessarily mean that they're a "real" friend. Although we may have hundreds of friends, followers, or people we follow on social media, typically we can only keep track of about 150 relationships. And in terms of our "inner circle," most of us only consider about five to fifteen friends to be intimate or close (Fischetti & Christiansen, 2018). These relationships may include coworkers, acquaintances, neighbors, family, and people we have never even met.

Communication technologies make it possible for friends to stay constantly connected with one another, such that we have access to an always-available network (Okdie & Wirth, 2018). For better or worse, you can now keep your friends updated 24/7 on the latest news in your life through posts and messages. And perhaps not surprisingly, our technological choices for communication are related to

self-reflection

Think of friends you only know and interact with online, and compare them with the friends who populate your offline world. Which friends do you consider closer? When you're confronted with a challenging problem or personal crisis, which friends do you turn to for support? Why?

▶ In *Ready Player One*, Wade and his allies meet in the virtual world OASIS, but in the real world, they must work to meet each other and build their friendships. Jaap Buitendijk/© Warner Bros. Pictures/Courtesy Everett Collection

focus on CULTURE

Broadening Diversity of Friends through Social Media

Using social media lets "people get in touch and get connected with people from different cultures and different civilizations and different countries." In an international study by Laura Silver, Christine Huang, and Kyle Taylor (2019), this is how one woman from Tunisia described the primary benefit of her social media use. These researchers explored mobile technology use in 11 countries with emerging economies: Columbia, India, Jordan, Kenya, Lebanon, Mexico, the Philippines, South Africa, Tunisia, Venezuela, and Vietnam. Across these countries and cultures, social media often function to enhance the diversity of friendship networks. Specifically, Silver, Huang, and Taylor examined four categories of diversity related to people we may encounter through social media: people with different religious, political, and racial backgrounds, and people with different income levels. The researchers found that social media use in developing countries increased the likelihood that people would connect with diverse others across all four of these categories—people they might not otherwise come into contact with in their daily lives.

At the same time, participants in the study also recognized the limitations of social media. As a woman from Mexico described, "Communication is not as it used to be, as social networks are not social. You don't see people in person." The result can be the feeling that social media friendships are less intimate than in-person involvements. As a study participant from Kenya concluded, "You find yourself having 3,000 friends, but in real life, you only know 50, but you kind of know them because you share comments and you like similar things. It's like you know them, but you don't."

discussion questions

- Considering the four categories of diversity described above, how diverse is your social media network? What might you gain by expanding the diversity of your network?
- Are your friendships that exist solely through social media as close as your in-person friendships? How do the two types of involvements differ?

the closeness of our friendships. We tend to call and text our closest friends, whereas with less intimate friends we might instead communicate via instant messaging, online gaming, or social networking sites (Liu & Yang, 2016).

Despite the utility of technology in allowing us to forge and sustain friendships, we also need to ensure that communicating through technology does not replace our time spent interacting face-to-face. Studies show that we are happier when we spend time in person with others, such as loved ones and close friends, compared to when we are alone (Hudson et al., 2020), and that using technology rather than engaging face-to-face may increase loneliness and potentially impact our social skills (Twenge et al., 2019). Just remember, social media is *not*, in actuality, social.

To this point, we've focused on the nature of friendship, and how it's distinct from other relationships. We now turn our attention to different types of friendships that exist.

Types of Friendships

Characteristics and roles of different friends

Across our lives, each of us experiences many different types of friendships. Some are intensely close; others less so. Some become less close over time, and others stand the test of time. In this section we consider some of these different friendship categories.

 LaunchPad

Online Self-Quiz: What Kind of Friend Are You? To take this self-quiz, visit LaunchPad: **launchpadworks.com**

BEST FRIENDS

Think of the people you consider *close* friends—people with whom you exchange deeply personal information and emotional support, with whom you share many interests and activities, and around whom you feel comfortable and at ease (Parks & Floyd, 1996). Or, as friendship scholar William Rawlins describes, people you expect to talk to, enjoy, and rely upon (Beck, 2015). How many come to mind? Chances are you can count them on one, or maybe both, hands.

What makes a close friend a *best* friend? Many things. First, best friendship involves greater intimacy, more disclosure, and deeper commitment than does close friendship (Weisz & Wood, 2005). People talk more frequently and more deeply with best friends about their relationships, emotions, life events, and goals. Second, people count on their best friends to listen to their problems without judging and to "have their back"—provide unconditional support (Pennington, 2009). Third, best friendship is distinct from close friendship in the degree to which shared activities commit the friends to each other in substantial ways. For example, best friends are more likely to join clubs together, participate on intramural or community sports teams together, move in together as roommates, or spend a spring break or another type of vacation together (Becker et al., 2009).

Finally, the *most* important factor that distinguishes best friends is unqualified provision of **identity support**: behaving in ways that convey understanding, acceptance, and support for a friend's valued social identities. **Valued social identities** are the aspects of your public self that you deem the most important in defining who you are—for example, musician, athlete, poet, dancer, teacher, parent. Whoever we are—and whoever we dream of being—our best friends understand us, accept us, respect us, and support us, *no matter what*. Say that a close friend who is a pacifist suddenly announces their intention to join the military because they feel strongly about defending our country. What would you say to your friend? Or, imagine that a good friend tells you about their change in religious beliefs, and this new view clashes with your own beliefs. How would you respond? In each of these cases, *best* friends would distinguish themselves by supporting such identity shifts even if they found them surprising. Research following friendships across a four-year time span found that more than any other factor—including amount of communication and perceived closeness—participants who initially reported high levels of identity support from a new friend were more likely to describe that person as their *best* friend four years later (Weisz & Wood, 2005).

But will you be able to sustain your best friends beyond four years? The answer may depend on several things. We will explore friendship maintenance later in this chapter, but one thing to consider beyond identity support is how well you can predict what your best friend thinks. For example, if you are partnered with your best friend to play a board game where the goal is to have your friend guess a word, and you're only allowed to communicate *one-word clues*, how many words do you think it would take you to succeed? Andrew Ledbetter and colleagues (2007) used the board game Password to see how effectively best friends communicated—and then tracked the survival of the friendships over the years that followed. They found that better performance in the game was related to how close best friends were *19 years* later! This means that friends who had a sense of each other's thoughts (allowing them to communicate more efficiently) were more likely to be close later in life, compared to those who performed poorly in Password.

self-reflection

Call to mind your most valued social identities. Which friends provide the most acceptance, respect, and support of these identities? Which friends do you consider closest, or most intimate? What does this tell you about the importance of identity support in determining friendship intimacy?

ACTIVE, DORMANT, AND COMMEMORATIVE FRIENDS

Our friendships often change as our life circumstances evolve. Based on his interviews of adults about their friends, William Rawlins (1994) described three categories of friendship: active, dormant, and commemorative. *Active friends* are characterized by positive interactions, being readily available when needed for things like emotional support, and enduring across time. *Commemorative friends* are those we have lost touch with and who now exist more as fond recollections in our memories than in our daily lives. *Dormant friends* are essentially "on hold"; friends who have shared an important part of our lives, and who we feel we could resume contact with and would like to hear from, but currently see less frequently (Beck, 2015; LaBelle & Myers, 2016).

Are there ways we can awaken friendships from dormancy or keep them active? We explore these questions next, as we revisit the important topic of maintenance.

Maintaining Friendships

Ways to sustain enduring and happy friendships

The animated series *Avatar: The Last Airbender* follows a group of friends—initially three, Aang, Sokka, and Katara—in their quest to stop the Fire Nation from conquering the world. In their realm, some people have the special ability to manipulate—or *bend*—water, earth, fire, or air, such as stopping the movement of a rock (earthbending) or shooting fire from their hands (firebending). Twelve-year-old Aang is the last person from the Air Nation, and he must learn how to bend the other elements to fulfill his destiny as the Avatar and bring peace to the world.

As Aang and his friends travel together, they learn to trust, support, defend, and depend on one another, forming a friendship that eventually deepens to a family-like bond. This bond is clearly displayed when Katara and Sokka pass up an opportunity to reunite with their father—whom they hadn't seen in years—to continue traveling with the Avatar. Aang, surprised by their decision, asks, "Don't you want to see your father?" Sokka replies, "Of course we do . . . but you're our family too. And right now, you need us more." Katara then sums it up: "And we need you."

It's true. We *need* our friends. Most of us don't need them for survival, as we don't face frequent attacks from firebenders! But our friends do provide a constant and important shield against the stresses, hardships, and threats of our everyday lives. We count on friends to be there when we need them and to provide support; in return, we do the same. This is what bonds us together.

At the same time, friendships don't endure on their own. As with romantic and family involvements, friendships flourish only when you consistently communicate in ways that maintain them.

As Aang, Katara, and Sokka grow to trust, defend, and depend on one another in *Avatar: The Last Airbender*, they realize that friendship is one of the keys to defeating the Fire Nation and restoring balance to the world. Photofest

Two ways that we keep friendships alive are by following friendship rules and by using maintenance strategies.

FOLLOWING FRIENDSHIP RULES

In the second season of *Avatar: The Last Airbender*, a new friend, Toph, joins the group and initially butts heads with the other members—especially Katara. In one episode, Katara tries to instruct Toph on the unspoken rules of pulling her fair share: "Usually when setting up camp, we try to divide up the work." Rules like these allow the group to get along and continue their quest.

In the real world, one of the ways we can help our friendships succeed is by following **friendship rules**—general principles that prescribe appropriate communication and behavior within friendship relationships (Argyle & Henderson, 1984). In an extensive study of friendship maintenance, social psychologists Michael Argyle and Monica Henderson observed 10 friendship rules that people share across cultures, and that distinguish happy from unhappy friendships (Schneider & Kenny, 2000). Not abiding by them may even cost you your friends: people around the globe describe failed friendships as ones that didn't follow these rules (Argyle & Henderson, 1984). The 10 rules for friendship are:

self-reflection

Consider the 10 universal rules that successful friends follow. Which of these rules do you abide by in your own friendships? Which do you neglect? How has neglecting some of these rules affected your friendships? What steps might you take to better follow rules you've previously neglected?

1. *Show support.* Within a friendship, you should provide emotional support and offer assistance in times of need, without having to be asked (Burleson & Samter, 1994). You also should accept and respect your friend's valued social identities. When they change majors, try out for a competitive team, or opt into a different career path, support the decision—even if it's one you yourself wouldn't make.

2. *Seek support.* The flip side of the first rule is that when you're in a friendship, you should not only deliver support but *seek* support and counsel when needed, disclosing your emotional burdens to your friend. Other than sharing time and activities, mutual self-disclosure serves as the glue that binds together friendships (Dainton et al., 2003).

3. *Respect privacy.* At the same time that friends anticipate both support and disclosure, they also recognize that friendships have more restrictive boundaries for sharing personal information than do romantic or family relationships. Recognize this, and avoid pushing your friend to share information that they consider too personal. Also resist sharing information about yourself that's intensely private or irrelevant to your friendship.

4. *Keep confidences.* A critical feature of enduring friendships is trust. When friends share personal information with you, do not betray their confidence by sharing it with others.

5. *Defend your friends.* Part of successful friendships is the feeling that friends have your back. Your friends count on you to stand up for them, so defend them if they are being attacked—whether it's online or off, face-to-face or behind their back.

6. *Avoid public criticism.* Friends may disagree or even disapprove of each other's behavior on occasion. But airing your grievances publicly in a way that makes

a friend look bad will only hurt your friendship. Avoid communication such as questioning a friend's loyalty or offering unsolicited advice in front of other friends.

7. *Make your friends happy.* An essential ingredient to successful friendships is striving to make your friends feel good while you're in their company. You can do this by practicing positivity: communicating with them in a cheerful and optimistic fashion, doing unsolicited favors for them, and buying or making gifts for them.

8. *Manage jealousy.* Unlike long-term romantic relationships, most friendships aren't exclusive. Your close friends will likely have other close friends, perhaps even friends who are more intimate with them than you are. Accept that each of your friends has other good friends as well, and constructively manage any jealousy that arises in you.

9. *Share humor.* Successful friends spend a good deal of their time joking with and teasing each other in affectionate or playful ways. Enjoying a similar sense of humor is an essential aspect of most long-term friendships.

10. *Maintain equity.* In enduring, mutually satisfying friendships, the two people give and receive in roughly equitable proportions (Canary & Zelley, 2000). Help maintain this equity by conscientiously repaying debts, returning favors, and keeping the exchange of gifts and compliments balanced.

MAINTENANCE STRATEGIES FOR FRIENDS

Most friendships are built on a foundation of shared activities and self-disclosure. To maintain your friendships, strive to keep this foundation solid by regularly doing things with your friends and making time to talk.

Sharing Activities Through *sharing activities*, friends structure their schedules to enjoy hobbies, interests, and leisure activities together. But even more

◁ Two important ways you can maintain your friendships are sharing activities and being open in your communication with your friends. Roman Lacheev/Alamy

important than the actual sharing of activities is the perception that each friend is willing to make time for the other. Scholar William Rawlins notes that even friends who don't spend much time together can still maintain a satisfying connection as long as each perceives the other as "being there" when needed (Rawlins, 1994).

Of course, most of us have several friends but only finite amounts of time available to devote to each one. Consequently, we often are put in positions in which we have to choose between time and activities shared with one friend versus another. Unfortunately, given the significance that sharing time and activities together plays in defining friendships, your decisions regarding with whom you invest your time will often be perceived by friends as communicating depth of loyalty (Baxter et al., 1997). In cases in which you choose one friend over another, the friend not chosen may view your decision as disloyal. To avert this, draw on your interpersonal communication skills. Express gratitude for the friend's offer, assure them that you very much value the relationship, and make concrete plans for getting together another time.

Self-Disclosure   A second strategy for friendship maintenance is self-disclosure. All friendships are created and maintained through the discussion of thoughts, feelings, and daily life events (Dainton et al., 2003). To foster disclosure with your friends, routinely make time just to talk—encouraging them to share their thoughts and feelings about various issues, whether online or face-to-face. Keep in mind that how you respond to a friend's disclosure will impact the process. In one study examining how friends reveal mental health issues, for instance, the authors indicated that friends "do not make a singular decision to disclose." Instead, repeated decisions will be made during one encounter, and these decisions are influenced by the responses of the person to whom you are disclosing the information (Venetis et al., 2018, p. 661). Equally important, avoid betraying friends—sharing with others personal information friends have disclosed to you.

As with romantic and family relationships, it's important to balance openness in self-disclosure with protection (Dainton et al., 2003). Over time, most friends learn that communication about certain issues, topics, or even people is best avoided to protect the relationship and preclude conflict. Research suggests that topic avoidance can influence how we feel about the relationship, sometimes leading to feelings of hurt or dissatisfaction (Palomares & Derman, 2019). As a result, friends negotiate communicative boundaries that allow their time together and communication shared to remain positive. Such boundaries can be perfectly healthy as long as both friends agree on them and the issues being avoided aren't central to the survival of the friendship. For example, several years ago a friend of ours began dating someone we thought treated him badly. His partner, who we'll call "Sam," had a very negative outlook, constantly complained about our friend, and belittled him and their relationship in public. We thought Sam's communication was unethical and borderline abusive. But whenever we expressed our concern, our friend grew defensive. Sam just had an "edge" to his personality, our friend said, and we "didn't know the real Sam." After several such arguments, we all agreed that, for the sake of our friendship, the topic of Sam was off-limits. We all respected this agreement—thereby protecting our friendship—until our friend broke up with Sam. After that, we opened the topic once more to free and detailed discussion.

skills practice

Maintaining a Friendship
Using interpersonal communication to maintain a friendship

❶ Think of a valued friendship you wish to maintain.

❷ Make time each week to talk with this person, whether online or face-to-face.

❸ Have fun together and share stories.

❹ Let your friend know that you accept and respect their valued social identities.

❺ Encourage disclosure of thoughts and feelings.

❻ Avoid pushing for information that they consider too personal.

❼ Negotiate boundaries around topics that are best avoided.

❽ Don't share secrets disclosed by your friend with others.

❾ Provide emotional support and assistance when needed, without having to be asked.

❿ Defend your friend online and off.

Friendship Challenges

Dealing with friendship betrayal, geographic distance, and attraction

Ashlee and Rachel were best friends throughout high school.[1] As Ashlee describes, "Rachel was brilliant, confident, blunt, and outgoing. She liked to mock people, but she could make me laugh like nobody else, and she loved the same things I did." After graduation, they were separated by distance, attending universities in different states. Although they regularly texted and emailed, they grew apart. The following summer, they were reunited, this time as a foursome: Rachel was dating Mike (a friend from high school), and Ashlee was dating Ahmed (a Lebanese transfer student). The four hung out regularly, waterskiing, going to movies, and partying.

One day, after Mike bought a new iPhone, he offered his old one to Ashlee. Arriving home, Ashlee found that her SIM card wasn't compatible, so she started manually clearing Mike's information. When she got to his text in-box, she was stunned to see an offensive message from Rachel, insulting and demeaning both Ashlee and Ahmed. As Ashlee describes, "My heart just stopped. I literally sat there, shaking. I thought it was a joke, until I scrolled down and found *hundreds* of similar messages." Text after text slammed her with sexist slurs and mocked Ahmed's ethnicity. Later that night, crying hysterically, Ashlee summoned the courage to text Rachel: "I cleared out Mike's phone and found all your texts about me and Ahmed. You two are *horrible*. I want nothing to do with either of you." Rachel immediately texted back, "How dare you read our messages! Those were private! Whatever, Ashlee—I'm sorry you're angry, but Mike and I were just messing around. You're completely overreacting." In the aftermath, Ashlee returned Mike's iPhone and refused all contact with Rachel. Back at school that fall, Ashlee received an email with the subject line "please don't delete." The message read: "I don't even know where to begin. I know I messed up, but I can't lose you as a friend. We've been best friends forever, and I'd hate to lose you over something this dumb. I know I'm asking a lot of you to forgive me, but please think about it." Ashlee deleted the message.

To this point, we've talked about friendships as involvements that provide us with abundant and important rewards. Although this is true, friendships also present us with a variety of intense interpersonal challenges. Three of the most common are friendship betrayal, geographic distance, and attraction.

BETRAYAL

Given the value friends place on mutual support and defending each other, it's no surprise that betrayal is the most commonly reported reason for ending a friendship (Miller et al., 2007). Acts of friendship betrayal include breaking confidences, backstabbing (criticizing a friend behind their back), spreading rumors or gossip, and lying—all of which violate the friendship rules discussed earlier. When friends violate these rules, it's difficult for friendships to survive. Similar to romantic betrayal, friends who are betrayed experience an overwhelming sense of relationship devaluation and loss (Miller et al., 2007). And—as with the Ashlee and Rachel example—betrayal often leads people to realize things about their friends' characters that simply can't be tolerated.

---

[1] All information in this example is true. The names and personal information of the people in question have been altered for confidentiality. This example is used with permission from "Ashlee."

skills practice

Managing Friendship Betrayal

Dealing with betrayal in a friendship:

1 Manage the intense anger and grief you experience.

2 Avoid seeking revenge or verbal retaliation.

3 Contact others who have experienced similar betrayals, and discuss your experience with them.

4 Evaluate the betrayal, including how serious it is, what caused it, whether it's a one-time event or part of a behavioral pattern, and whether you would have done something similar.

5 Assess the value of your friendship, compared with the damage of the betrayal.

6 End or repair the friendship based on your analysis.

How can you better manage friendship betrayal when it occurs? If it's a friendship of any closeness, expect to experience grief as you suffer the loss of trust, intimacy, and the image of your friend you once held dear. Revisit the suggestions for grief management offered in Chapter 4, especially the value of *emotion-sharing*—talking about your experience directly with people who have gone through the same thing. Avoid lashing out at the betrayer or seeking revenge, both of which will simply make matters worse.

When you're able, ponder whether you can or should repair the friendship. Ask yourself the following questions to help guide your decision. First, how serious was the betrayal? Not all betrayals are of equal standing, so think carefully about whether this incident is something you can learn to live with or not. Second, what was the context preceding and surrounding the betrayal? Did *you* do something to provoke the betrayal? Would you have done the same thing in the same situation—or *have* you done similar things in the past? Be careful about blaming others for behaviors that you caused, holding double standards, and judging friends in ways you wouldn't wish to be judged yourself. Third, do the benefits of continuing the friendship outweigh the costs? Use the friendship rules as a guide: Does your friend follow most of these rules, most of the time? If so, they may actually be a desirable friend. Fourth, is this betrayal a one-time event or part of a consistent pattern? Everyone falls from grace on occasion; what you want to avoid is a person who habitually abuses your trust. Last, and perhaps most important, does this betrayal reveal something about your friend's character that you simply can't live with? Be honest with yourself and realize that some friendships are best left broken following betrayal. In Ashlee's case, despite years of having Rachel as her best friend—and the corresponding energy, time, and emotional investment—the betrayal revealed multiple aspects of Rachel's character that Ashlee simply couldn't tolerate.

GEOGRAPHIC SEPARATION

A contributing factor to Ashlee and Rachel's falling out was their geographic separation, which led them to grow apart. Separation is one of the most common and intense challenges friends face (Wang & Andersen, 2007) and is linked to

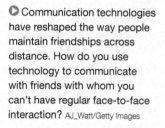

▶ Communication technologies have reshaped the way people maintain friendships across distance. How do you use technology to communicate with friends with whom you can't have regular face-to-face interaction? AJ_Watt/Getty Images

self-QUIZ

Friendship Distance-Durability

This quiz helps you determine whether a friendship is durable enough to survive the challenge of geographic distance. Place a check mark next to each statement with which you agree. Then total your check marks and use the scoring key at the bottom to determine your friendship distance-durability.

To take this quiz online, visit LaunchPad: launchpadworks.com

_____ My friend and I share a great deal of personal history.

_____ I feel a strong sense of warmth and fondness toward my friend.

_____ I have great respect for my friend as a person.

_____ I don't expect my friend to be the exact same person in the future as they are now.

_____ Having this person as my friend makes me happy.

_____ Even if we've been out of touch for a while, my friend and I always seem to be able to pick up where we left off when we communicate again.

_____ I welcome future changes in my friend's beliefs, values, and attitudes—even if they're different from mine—as long as these changes bring them happiness.

_____ My friend is the kind of person I would like to be.

_____ My friend and I enjoy sharing numerous stories from our past that remind us of how close we've been.

_____ I anticipate that as my friend ages, they will develop new and varied interests.

Scoring: 0–3: low durability, friendship may have difficulty surviving geographic separation; 4–6: moderate durability, friendship may be able to handle separation; 7–10: high durability, friendship has strong potential for enduring across time and distance.

the ways friendships change (Becker et al., 2009). Eighty percent of people report having a close friend who lives far away (Rohlfing, 1995). Physical separation may prevent friends from adequately satisfying the needs that form the foundation of their relationship, such as sharing activities, but communication technology has afforded people a wide range of options for maintaining their friendships (Ruppel et al., 2018a).

Although most friends begin long-distance separations with the intention of seeing each other regularly, they rarely visit solely for the sake of reuniting. Instead, they tend to see each other only when there's some other reason for them to be in the same area. This is because long-distance friends often don't have the money or time to travel only to visit a friend (Rohlfing, 1995). Instead, they visit when other commitments, such as professional conferences, visits with relatives, or class reunions, bring them together. Such contacts often leave friends feeling empty because their time together is so limited.

Which friendships tend to survive geographic distance, and which lapse? In friendships that survive, the two people feel a particularly strong *liking*—affection and respect—for each other. Friendships between individuals who "enjoy knowing each other" and "have great admiration for each other" are most likely to endure.

Friends who overcome separation also accept change as a natural part of life and their relationship. If you get together with a good friend you haven't seen in a long while, you both will likely have changed in terms of profession, attitudes, and appearance. Friends who are comfortable with such changes and offer identity support tend to have relationships that survive. Friends who want their friends to "always stay the same" don't.

Moreover, friendships that survive separation involve friends who have a strong sense of shared history. In their conversations, they frequently celebrate the past as well as anticipate sharing events in the future. This sense of shared past, present, and future enables them to "pick up where they left off" after being out of touch for a while. Successful long-distance friendships thus involve feeling a sense of relationship continuity and perceiving the relationship as solid and ongoing.

How can you communicate in ways that foster these qualities in your own long-distance friendships? Use technology (video chats, phone calls, texting, and so on) to regularly communicate with your friends. Focus your communication on activities and interests that you share. Doing this alleviates the feeling of loss that comes with the inability to actually spend time together (Rabby, 1997). So, for example, if a friend who now lives far away used to be your daily workout or jogging buddy, send regular emails or texts updating them on your marathon training and inquiring about their performance in local races.

Also, remind your long-distance friends that you still think of them with affection and hold them in high regard. Look for opportunities to appropriately express your feelings for a friend, such as, "I miss our Thursday night movie! Have you seen any good films lately?" In addition, devote some of your communication to fondly recounting events and experiences you have shared in your past, as well as discussing plans for the future. Such exchanges bolster the sense of relational continuity critical to maintaining friendships.

Finally, when your long-distance friends go through dramatic life changes—as they inevitably will—communicate your continued support of their valued social identities. For instance, a close friend you haven't seen in a while may abandon previously shared religious beliefs, adopt new political viewpoints, or substantially alter their appearance. In making these and other kinds of significant changes, your friend may look to you for identity support, as a friend. A good long-distance friend of Steve's, Vikram, occupied a job for several years that required a fair degree of professional contact with Steve, allowing them the opportunity (and excuse) to communicate regularly. Then Vikram accepted a new position with a different company. This new opportunity represented a dramatic professional advancement for him, but it also meant that he would have far fewer opportunities to interact with Steve. When he broke the news to Steve, he expected a negative reaction. Instead, Steve surprised him by expressing firm support and excitement regarding his decision.

ATTRACTION: ROMANCE AND FWB RELATIONSHIPS

A final challenge facing friends is attraction to each other beyond friendship: romantic, sexual, or both. Given that many friendships begin between people who spend time together and share similar interests, it is not surprising that we may become attracted to our friends. One study found that over 86 percent of college students reported feeling sexually attracted to a friend at some point in their lives (Asada et al., 2003).

But when attraction does blossom between friends, pursuing a relationship beyond friendship often brings its own challenges. Friends who feel attracted to each other typically report high uncertainty as a result, regarding both the nature of their relationship and whether or not their friend feels the same way (Weger & Emmett, 2009).

---

skills practice

Using Technology to Overcome Distance
Maintaining long-distance friendships through online communication

1 Think of a close friend who lives far away.

2 In your online interactions, focus your message on common interests, making sure to ask about your friend's continued participation in these things.

3 Send text messages saying you're thinking of and missing them.

4 Craft emails that fondly recap past shared experiences, and participate in online experiences, such as gaming, together.

5 Set up times to video chat to share coffee or lunch.

6 When your friend discloses major life events, provide support in the quickest fashion possible, whether by text message, email, phone call, or all three.

Friends cope with attraction by doing one of three things. Some friends simply repress the attraction, most commonly out of respect for their friendship (Messman et al., 2000). Friends who seek to repress attraction typically engage in *mental management*—they do things to actively manage how they think about each other so that the attraction is diminished (Halatsis & Christakis, 2009). These may include pacts and promises to not pursue the attraction, a strict avoidance of flirting, and the curtailing of activities (such as going out drinking) that might inadvertently lead to sexual interaction (Halatsis & Christakis, 2009). Alternatively, some friends act on their attraction by either developing a full-fledged romantic involvement or trying to blend their friendship with sexual activity through a "friends-with-benefits" arrangement.

Romance between Friends   Many friends who develop an attraction opt to pursue a romantic relationship. The first and most powerful cue of such desire is a radical increase in the amount of time the friends spend flirting with each other (Weger & Emmett, 2009). Although many of us like to think of friendships and romantic relationships as strictly separate, many enduring and successful romances evolve from friendships. One of the strongest predictors of whether or not a friendship can successfully transition to romance is simply whether the friends already possess romantic beliefs that link friendship with love (Hendrick & Hendrick, 1992).

Although people may believe that pursuing a romantic relationship eventually leads to the loss of both a romance and a friendship, the results are actually mixed. People who were friends prior to a romance are much more likely to be friends following a failed romance than those who were not friends first (Schneider & Kenny, 2000). In unrequited love friendships—those in which the romantic feelings are not reciprocated—people who were more committed to the friendship prior to the romantic feelings emerging tend to be more motivated to continue and maintain the friendship afterward. Common motivations for continuing a friendship include *interpersonal connections*—genuinely caring for the other person—and *investment*—that is, the friends are accustomed to spending time together. These are two of the strongest reported motivations in the wake of unrequited love experiences (Clark et al., 2020). However, postromance friendships tend to be less close than those with friends who have always been platonic.

How can you successfully transition from friendship to romance, or back again? First, *expect difference*. Romantic relationships and friendships are fundamentally different in expectations, demands, commitment, and corresponding emotional intensity. Don't presume that your feelings, those of your partner, or the interplay between you two will be the same. Second, *emphasize disclosure*. Relationship transitions tend to evoke high uncertainty, as partners worry about what the other thinks and feels, and wonder where the relationship is going. To reduce this uncertainty, make sure you are ready to share your feelings in an open and honest fashion, and encourage your partner to do the same. And it may take time to make this decision. One study found that people averaged about two and a half years before they confessed romantic feelings to a friend (Clark et al., 2020). Finally, *offer assurances*. Let your partner know that whether you two remain friends or pursue romance, you stand by them, and your relationship, regardless. This is especially important when transitioning back to friendship from romance, as your partner may believe that your relationship is now over.

⬆ Illustrating how common FWB relationships are, two films with very similar plotlines were released in the same year: *No Strings Attached* and *Friends with Benefits*. In each film, the two main characters develop FWB relationships, but as in many real-life FWB relationships, they eventually have to deal with the romantic impulses that they feel toward each other. Dale Robinette/©Paramount Pictures/ Courtesy Everett Collection; Pictorial Press Ltd/Alamy

Friends with Benefits   Some friends deal with sexual attraction by forming a "friends-with-benefits" (FWB) relationship. In **FWB relationships**, the participants engage in sexual activity without the purpose of transforming the relationship into a romantic attachment (Hughes et al., 2005). FWB relationships are widespread: studies suggest that between 50 and 60 percent of college students have had such a relationship (Bisson & Levine, 2007; Mongeau et al., 2003). And just as there are many types of friendship, there are many ways people approach FWB relationships (Mongeau et al., 2019).

Two common reasons for pursuing an FWB relationship are because people welcome the lack of commitment (and all its attendant sacrifices), and because they want to satisfy sexual needs (Asada et al., 2003). Both men and women cite these same reasons, contradicting stereotypes that women seek only emotional satisfaction in relationships while men want only sex.

Most partners in FWB relationships develop rules regarding emotional attachment, communication, and sex (Hughes et al., 2005). For example, they commonly strike an agreement to not fall in love. And they establish rules governing the frequency of phone calling, emailing, and texting, as well as sex rules regarding safe sex practices, frequency of sex, and sexual exclusivity. But despite these rules, a majority of FWB relationships eventually fail, sometimes costing the participants their original friendship as well as the sexual arrangement. Why? Participants tend to develop romantic feelings despite their best efforts to avoid them, and many decide that the FWB relationship doesn't satisfy them enough emotionally (Hughes et al., 2005).

The Importance of Friends

Friends provide essential emotional security

Friendships are both delicate and deep. On the one hand, they're the most transitory of our close relationships. They come and go across our life span, depending on where we're living, going to school, and working, and how our personal interests shift and evolve. As a simple test of this, make a list of the five closest friends in your life right now, in rank order. Then make the same list based on your

For much of our lives, friendships are *the* most important close relationships we have.

closest friends five years ago. Chances are, at least some of the names and rankings will have changed.

But at the same time, friendships are deep. For much of our lives, friendships are *the* most important close relationships we have. Our friends keep us grounded and provide us with support in times of crisis. If partners hurt us, or family members annoy us, it's our friends we turn to for support. When everything else seems wrong with the world, and our lives seem mired in misadventure, we find solace in the simple truth shared by Clarence the Angel in the movie *It's a Wonderful Life*: "No one is a failure who has friends."

Choosing between Friends

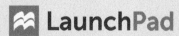 **LaunchPad** For the best experience, complete all parts of this activity in LaunchPad: **launchpadworks.com**

1 Background

Maintaining friendships can be challenging. But when a close friend changes in ways that put her at odds with your other friends, you may be forced to choose between them. To understand how you might competently manage such a relationship challenge, read the case study in Part 2; then, drawing on all you know about interpersonal communication, work through the problem-solving model in Part 3.

 Visit LaunchPad to watch the video in Part 4 and assess your communication in Part 5.

2 Case Study

For years you've hung around with the same group of friends. Your ringleader is Karina. She's brilliant and beautiful. She always dresses immaculately, with perfect hair, nails, and makeup. She has a caustic wit and enjoys mocking other people's fashion sense.

But Karina has another side: she is deeply caring. When your Mom was diagnosed with terminal cancer, your other friends avoided visiting. Not Karina. She hung out with your mom for hours, cracking jokes and sharing funny YouTube videos. After your mother died, it was Karina who supported you in your grief.

One night, Karina gathers everyone together and announces, "Guess what!? I'm joining the Peace Corps!" Your friend John breaks the bewildered silence by joking, "Yeah, right! Who's gonna do your nails!?" Everyone laughs except Karina. She's serious.

Karina serves for two years as a youth development coordinator in Malawi. You hear from her occasionally through email. She shares with you the difficulties of her assignments, the kindness of the people, and the beauty of the landscape. During her absence, you remain close to your other friends—partying, shopping, and taking classes together.

Then Karina is back! Meeting her at the airport, you're staggered by her appearance. She has lost 20 pounds and wears no makeup. She is unusually quiet, and as time passes, it's clear that Karina has changed. Gone is the glam girl who tossed nasty and hilarious remarks at people. Instead, she is thoughtful and pensive. Rather than partying or shopping, she spends her free time volunteering at a homeless shelter.

You're not sure what to make of her. On the one hand, she's a nicer person than before, and always available for support. On the other hand, she is so *serious* all the time! And she seems really uncomfortable around your other friends. Does she still care about *you*? Is she still interested in being *your* friend?

Although you're on the fence, your friends are unanimous: they can't *stand* the "new" Karina. One night John hosts a party, and Karina again opts to skip the get-together. The gathering quickly devolves into a "hate on Karina" fest. One by one, everyone vents their dislike of her "ugly new look" and how "quiet and boring she is." Everyone (except you) agrees the time has come to drop her from the group. You remain silent until John notices and asks, "You're awfully quiet. What do you think?"

3 Your Turn

Consider all you've learned thus far about interpersonal communication. Then work through the following five steps. Remember, there are no "right" answers, so think hard about what is the best choice! (P.S. Need help? See the *Helpful Concepts* list.)

step 1

Reflect on yourself. What are your thoughts and feelings in this situation? What attributions are you making about Karina? About John and your other friends? Are your attributions accurate? Why or why not?

step 2

Reflect on your partner. Using perspective-taking and empathic concern, put yourself in Karina's shoes. Do the same for John and your other friends. What are they thinking and feeling in this situation?

step 3

Identify the optimal outcome. Think about all the information you have about your communication and relationships with both Karina and your other friends. Consider your own feelings as well as everyone else's. Given all these factors, what's the best, most constructive relationship outcome possible? Consider what's best for you and for Karina and the others.

step 4

Locate the roadblocks. Taking into consideration your own and Karina's thoughts and feelings, those of your other friends, and all that has happened in this situation, what obstacles are keeping you from achieving the optimal outcome?

step 5

Chart your course. What can you say to John to overcome the roadblocks you've identified and achieve your optimal outcome?

HELPFUL CONCEPTS

Best friends, **360**
Identity support, **360**
Friendship rules, **362**
Betrayal, **365**

---

4 The Other Side

 Visit LaunchPad to watch a video in which Karina tells her side of the case study story. As in many real-life situations, this is information to which you did not have access when you were initially crafting your response to John in Part 3. The video reminds us that even when we do our best to offer competent responses, there is always another side to the story that we need to consider.

---

5 Interpersonal Competence Self-Assessment

After watching the video, visit the Self-Assessment questions in LaunchPad. Think about the new information offered in Karina's side of the story and all you've learned about interpersonal communication. Drawing on this knowledge, revisit your earlier responses in Part 3 and assess your interpersonal communication competence.

© Paramount Pictures/Photofest

POSTSCRIPT

We began this chapter with an animated sea sponge who lives in a pineapple. Although SpongeBob SquarePants may be an internationally famous kids' cartoon, it also is a tale of friendships and the corresponding complexities, rewards, and challenges that come with such interpersonal involvements.

Which friends of yours support and "coach" you in your times of need? With whom do you share your time and passionate interests? Who can you count on to forgive you when you inevitably let that person down?

Although the relationships between SpongeBob and his friends may be comical, they mirror the friendships we experience in our own lives. Like us, the characters were drawn to each other through shared interests. And like the bonds we forge with our friends, theirs remain cemented through communication, companionship, humor, and support.

 **LaunchPad**

LaunchPad for *Reflect & Relate* offers videos and encourages self-assessment through adaptive quizzing. Go to **launchpadworks.com** to get access to:

 LearningCurve
Adaptive Quizzes

 Video clips that help you understand interpersonal communication

key terms

friendship,   353
communal friendships,   355
agentic friendships,   355
cross-category friendships,   356
identity support,   360
valued social identities,   360
friendship rules,   362
FWB relationships,   370

You can watch brief, illustrative videos of these terms and test your understanding of the concepts in LaunchPad.

key concepts

The Nature of Friendship

- Unlike family relationships, **friendships** are voluntary.
- Depending on the functions being fulfilled, friendships may be primarily **communal** or **agentic**.
- Age, culture, gender, and life situations all influence our view of friendship.
- While technology allows us to communicate with friends 24/7, our closest friends are often those that we spend time with online and off.

Types of Friendships

- We have many types of friends, but we often consider a smaller number our close and best friends. The latter are distinguished by providing unwavering **identity support** for our **valued social identities** over time.
- **Cross-category friendships**—cross-sex, cross-orientation, intercultural, and interethnic—are a powerful way to break down ingrouper and outgrouper perceptions.

Maintaining Friendships

- Across cultures, people agree on **friendship rules**, the basic principles that underlie the maintenance of successful friendships. Friends who follow these rules are more likely to remain friends than those who don't.
- Two of the most important maintenance strategies for friends are sharing activities and self-disclosure.

Friendship Challenges

- Friendship betrayal often leads to an overwhelming sense of relationship devaluation and loss.
- One of the greatest challenges friends face is geographic separation. Communication technologies can help such friends overcome distance by allowing for regular interaction and maintaining a sense of shared interests.
- Some people form sexual relationships with their friends, known as friends-with-benefits or **FWB relationships**. Both men and women enter these relationships to satisfy sexual needs. Most of these relationships fail, owing to unanticipated emotional challenges.

14 Relationships in the Workplace

In workplace relationships, the professional is profoundly personal.

Karin Cooper/Face the Nation/Getty Images News/Getty Images

"We are different; we are one."

For more than three decades they were intensely competitive coworkers who disagreed on nearly everything—yet worked collaboratively together.[1] He was pro-life, and she was pro-choice. She supported same-sex marriage, and he argued against it. And they weren't afraid to communicate their disputes openly. His legal opinion regarding the Affordable Care Act was "outlandish"; her opinion supporting the admission of women into the Virginia Military Institute (VMI) was "politics smuggled into law." When she confessed to having decided against her better judgment to have wine with dinner before the State of the Union address—leading her to fall asleep *during* it—he quipped, "That's the first intelligent thing you've done!" And yet they and their families spent every New Year's Eve together for 30 years—and when he died in 2016, she was grief-stricken. "We were best buddies," she said.

Supreme Court justices Ruth Bader Ginsburg and Antonin Scalia first worked together in the prestigious D.C. Circuit Court. They both previously had served as law professors, and this shared history drew them together. As Scalia noted, "We would read each other's opinions with a scholarly eye and offer suggestions on the writing. I would treat her like a colleague on the faculty." Their frequent interactions, and professional disputes, made the quality of their individual work better. For instance, with the VMI case, he gave her a copy of his arguments in advance, so she could

---

[1]This chapter opener uses information from Biskupic (2009), Carmon (2016), Cox (2020), National Public Radio (2016), and Scalia (2020).

prepare a better response. As she described, "He absolutely ruined my weekend! I took this very spicy dissent and tweaked my own arguments; but my opinion was ever so much better because of it."

As they spent more time working together, their bond deepened over numerous shared similarities. As Eugene Scalia, Antonin's son, describes, "They worked at the same place. They were both New Yorkers, close in age, and liked a lot of the same things: the law, teaching, travel, music and a meal with family and friends. They had a bond, I think, in that they both grew up as outsiders—to different degrees—she as a Jewish woman, he as a Catholic and Italian American." But beyond these points of commonality, there was enjoyment of each other's company. Ginsburg once said of Scalia, "As annoyed as you might be about his zinging dissent, he's so utterly charming, so amusing, so sometimes outrageous, you can't help but say, 'I'm glad that he's my friend and colleague.'"

Given their fierce dedication to their respective views, Ginsburg and Scalia were two of the most divisive and influential Supreme Court justices of recent decades. People with strong political leanings typically loved one and hated the other. But the two of *them* were able to bridge their differences to forge a profound workplace friendship, a fact honored by the 2015 opera *Scalia/Ginsburg*, featuring the song "We Are Different; We Are One." As Eugene Scalia explained following Ginsburg's death in 2020, "What we can learn from them—beyond how to be a friend—is how to welcome debate and differences. They had central roles in addressing some of the most divisive issues of the day. Not for a moment did one think the other should be condemned or ostracized. More than that, they believed that what they were doing—arriving at their own opinions thoughtfully and advancing them vigorously—was essential to the national good. With less debate, their friendship would have been diminished, and so, they believed, would our democracy."

We often think of our personal and professional lives as occupying separate spheres. Our personal lives are populated with "real" relationships: romantic partners, family members, and friends. Our work lives exist in a parallel universe of less meaningful interactions. But as the fierce and feisty friendship of Ruth Bader Ginsburg and Antonin Scalia illustrates, this division is a delusion. Our workplaces are systems of interpersonal relationships with peers, supervisors, and employees—relationships that often evolve into friendships (Sias et al., 2020). Close relationship development within the workplace is especially common among people who share high levels of professional interdependence—that is, coworkers with whom we repeatedly work on the same projects or tasks (Yakubovich & Burg, 2019). And we spend most of our adult waking hours working and spend more time interacting with coworkers than with any other type of relationship partner (Sias & Perry, 2004). This makes our workplace relationships at least as important as other interpersonal involvements. Indeed, workplace relationship health predicts both professional and personal outcomes: when our workplace communication and relationships are satisfying, we achieve more professionally and feel happier at home, and when our workplace communication and relationships slip into dysfunction, on-the-job productivity and relationships outside the workplace suffer (Myers, 2002).

In this chapter, we look at interpersonal communication and relationships in the workplace. You'll learn:

- How workplace relationships compare with other types of interpersonal relationships
- Tactics for fostering healthy relationships with peers at work
- Strategies for communicating competently with supervisors and employees
- Suggestions for coping with challenges to workplace relationships

Let's begin by describing the nature of workplace relationships, and examining the issues of organizational culture, networks, climate, and technology.

The Nature of Workplace Relationships

The influence of organizational culture, networks, climate, and technology

Whether it's a church, a branch of the military, a corporation, or a nonprofit charity, an organization exists and functions because coworkers communicate and form relationships with one another (Contractor & Grant, 1996). All the information sharing, decision making, and emotional and practical support that occur in the workplace do so in the context of coworker relationships (Sias et al., 2002). Consequently, interpersonal communication and relationships are an organization's lifeblood.

Any affiliation you have with a professional peer, supervisor, employee, or mentor can be considered a **workplace relationship**. These involvements differ along three dimensions: *organizational status, intimacy,* and *choice* (Sias & Perry, 2004). First, many organizations are structured hierarchically in terms of professional status, with people ranked higher or lower than others in organizational position and power. Thus, a defining feature of many workplace relationships is communication among people with different perspectives related to their positions within the organization. Second, workplace relationships vary in intimacy. Some remain work-focused, with communication largely restricted to work-related concerns. Others become deeply personal. Third, workplace relationships are defined by choice—the degree to which participants willingly engage in them. Although most of us don't get to handpick our coworkers, we do choose which coworkers we befriend.

Like all interpersonal involvements, workplace relationships provide us with both benefits and costs. On the plus side, workplace relationships provide us with practical and emotional support (Pillemer & Rothbard, 2018), and allow us to be better informed and better able to weather workplace stress, leading to greater job satisfaction (Sias et al., 2020). They can enhance our professional skills through the insights others provide, and increase the speed with which we rise through the organizational hierarchy (Sias & Perry, 2004). They also make work more enjoyable, bolster our commitment to the organization, improve morale, and decrease employee turnover (Sias & Cahill, 1998). On the negative side, workplace relationships can ignite disruptive and malicious gossip (Wu et al., 2016). Friendship cliques can arise that exclude certain coworkers, and if those cliques cross status boundaries, clique members who are in positions of authority can be accused of favoritism (Pillemer & Rothbard, 2018). When workplace romances end, the result often is increased conflict and reduced productivity (Verhoef & Terblanche, 2015). And in extreme cases,

self-reflection

Think of the relationships you have with people at work. What makes them more or less enjoyable? When you compare the benefits and drawbacks of your close workplace relationships, how does this affect your feelings about the organization?

workplace relationships can involve harassment, bullying, aggression, or other forms of mistreatment, increasing stress and decreasing both physical and mental health (Dhanani & LaPalme, 2019).

As we've emphasized throughout this book, interpersonal relationships are forged and maintained within the broader context of social networks and surrounding ethnic, gendered, religious, and socioeconomic class cultures and co-cultures. Workplace relationships are no exception. However, in addition to being shaped by all the previously mentioned forces, workplace relationships also are strongly influenced by each organization's unique culture, networks, climate, and technology.

THE CULTURE OF THE WORKPLACE

As with many teens growing up in the United States, Steve's first two jobs were in chain restaurants: six months at an ice cream parlor and five years at a pizza restaurant. The two workplaces couldn't have been more different. The ice cream parlor had a strict behavior code, and violations were grounds for termination. Managers snapped orders at employees and rarely socialized with them outside the workplace. Few people developed close friendships with coworkers. The pizza restaurant was the opposite. Workers socialized after hours, and supervisor–employee relationships were friendly. A sense of camaraderie permeated the restaurant, and management encouraged close friendships through outside activities, including a softball team and waterskiing parties.

In the same way that different cultures have unique traditions, each workplace possesses a distinct set of beliefs regarding how things are done and how people should behave, known as its **organizational culture** (Katz & Kahn, 1978). Organizational culture influences everything from job satisfaction and organizational commitment to service quality and staff turnover (Glisson & James, 2002). It also has a pronounced impact upon whether instances of sexual harassment will be tolerated or punished (Ford & Ivancic, 2020) and whether transgender, gender-diverse, and nonbinary workers will feel welcomed and supported (Huffman et al., 2020). An organization's culture derives from three sources, the first of which is *workplace values*: beliefs people share about work performance, dedication to the organization, and coworker relationships. For example, both places where Steve worked in his youth stressed the values of employee excellence and productivity. But the ice cream parlor discouraged friendships between coworkers, whereas the pizza restaurant encouraged such relationships. Kelly's first place of employment after college instilled a "work hard, play hard" culture such that hours on the job were very focused and productive, but the environment was playful, with friendly colleagues who often sang to the Beatles music blaring in the background. Other examples of workplace values include beliefs regarding corporate responsibility to the environment, commitment to stakeholders (customers, employees, business partners, shareholders, etc.), and worker integrity.

Workplace values create *workplace norms*—guidelines governing appropriate language use, interpersonal communication, and relationships (Eisenberg & Goodall, 2004). In each organization, expectations evolve regarding the frequency, tone, and type of communication. For instance, although most organizations still lack gender-identity-related communication policies (Jones, 2020), those that encourage or mandate use of gender-affirming pronouns and titles are perceived as more inclusive, creating greater job satisfaction among employees (Huffman et al., 2020).

Similarly, organizations that encourage all workers to actively challenge sexual, sexist, homophobic, and racist language create powerful norms that such behaviors are intolerable and that workers will have organizational support if or when such behaviors are perpetrated against them (Ford & Ivancic, 2020).

The final influence on an organization's culture is its policies and practices regarding *workplace artifacts*—the objects and structures that define the organization (Schein, 1985). Workplace artifacts include everything from the physical layout of your workspace to dress codes and even motivational items, such as hallway posters urging you to always perform at your best. Organizations also may have guidelines regarding personal workplace artifacts—that is, the degree to which workers can personalize their workspaces with meaningful objects of their own, like photos and other decorations. These types of displays are especially important for LGBTQ+ workers, who may display rainbow accessories or photos of themselves with their partners as a test of organizational acceptance and inclusion, prior to coming out in the workplace (Helens-Hart, 2017).

When you join an organization, you are socialized into its culture through formal and informal encounters with established coworkers (Miller, 1995). At the same time, although socialization into an organization's culture often is designed and experienced as a bonding process, it also can be marginalizing for co-cultural members entering a workplace dominated by people of privilege. For instance, women joining male-dominated workplaces often experience the socializing process as "chilling," in that it makes clear that they will be marked professionally as "other" and excluded from important information; and that their ideas may be rejected, their credentials ignored, and their credibility questioned (Hall & Gettings, 2020).

NETWORKS IN THE WORKPLACE

Just as each of us has social networks of acquaintances, friends, and family members linked through communication, workplaces also have systems of communication linkages, known as **organizational networks** (Miller, 1995). Organizational networks are defined by three characteristics: the nature of the information that flows through them, the modality or sensory channels through which the information flows, and the frequency and number of connections among people in a network, also known as *network density*.

In each organizational network, the types of information flowing through the network are diverse (Farace et al., 1977). In some parts of the network, participants exchange work-related information. For instance, people in product development may interact regularly with people in marketing to create the right advertising campaign for a new product. In other parts of the network, participants share personal information. The "rumor mill"—by which coworkers pass along gossip and speculate about one another's professional and personal lives—is an example.

The second characteristic is the modality or sensory channels through which people in workplaces exchange information. These include face-to-face encounters, phone conversations, videoconferences, social media posts, and text and email exchanges. When you share an office with someone, you communicate across many more sensory channels compared to if you work remotely and communicate only in a mediated fashion. Some networks may be **virtual networks**—groups of coworkers linked solely through video chat, email, social networking sites such as LinkedIn, or other online services. Virtual networks are increasingly prevalent in the wake of the 2020 COVID pandemic as more people opt to *telework* (substitute commuter travel with technology, such as working from home and communicating with coworkers via phone and computer). For example, prior to the pandemic, 3.6 percent of the U.S. workforce (5 million employees) spent at least half their time working from home, but when the pandemic struck, 97 percent of U.S. workers who were able to, changed to teleworking (Global Workplace Analytics, 2020).

Last, networks are defined by their density: how connected each member of the network is to other members. In dense networks, workers regularly interact with multiple network members. By contrast, members of loose networks may have contact with just one or two other members. Density is influenced by a variety of factors, including job requirements (some jobs simply don't allow for much interaction between network members), physical layout of the work space (whether network members are widely separated, clustered together, or working remotely with no physically shared space), and organizational culture (some workplaces encourage frequent interaction; others discourage it). However, two of the strongest factors are familiarity and intimacy: networks in which members have known one another for a long time and are personally close tend to be denser.

Organizational networks come in many forms. Some are formally defined by the organization—the supervisors to whom you report, the employees you oversee, the peers with whom you collaborate. Others are informal and are created by coworkers themselves. Sometimes **workplace cliques** emerge—dense networks of coworkers who share the same workplace values and broader life attitudes (Jones, 1999). Workplace cliques educate new employees about who they can trust and which networks they should belong to, helping people quickly assimilate into the organizational culture. They can enhance the productivity of an organization (Marion et al., 2016), and also provide information about how things work in the organization. For example, when the copier breaks down or you need to expedite a shipment, members of a workplace clique can provide you with the assistance you need. But cliques also have disadvantages. They can make workers who aren't members feel excluded, and create "information silos" that isolate nonmembers from important organizational knowledge (Pillemer & Rothbard, 2018). Such exclusion and isolation can be enhanced through the use of social media, as clique members create private online groups in which they share personal information as well as workplace gossip. Cliques also may espouse workplace values contrary to those advocated by the organization—priding themselves on being "rebels," or disparaging bosses behind their backs. Worse, they may encourage unethical workplace behavior, such as punching a friend's time card to cover up the fact that the friend is absent, or engaging in relational aggression (Crothers et al., 2009).

Regardless of the form that organizational networks take, they are the principal wellsprings from which people acquire their workplace information. As a consequence, it's vital to keep two things in mind. First, *the private is public in the workplace.* Because all workplace relationships occur within organizational networks, your communication and behavior will serve as material for discussion among network members, both online and off. Presume that everything you say and do *will* be shared throughout your organization, including what you communicate via social media.

Second, *the organizational networks to which you belong can strongly determine the kinds of opportunities—and obstacles—you'll encounter as you advance in your career.*

For this reason, it's important to build interpersonal ties with coworkers who are both respected and connected. Try to develop relationships with *organizational insiders*—workers who are reputable, knowledgeable, and connected to dense organizational networks. The coworkers you befriend will strongly determine your experiences in the organization.

ORGANIZATIONAL CLIMATES

Think about an organization with which you're currently involved as a paid worker, volunteer, or member. How would you describe the overall emotional tone of the place—that is, the way it *feels* to be there? Is it supportive, warm, and welcoming? Detached, cool, and unfriendly? Somewhere in between? This overarching emotional quality of a workplace is known as its **organizational climate** (Kreps, 1990). Organizational climate is created primarily through interpersonal communication—the amount of trust, openness, listening, and supportiveness present in the interactions between organizational members (Mohammed & Hussein, 2008).

At the broadest level, two types of organizational climates exist: defensive and supportive (Kreps, 1990). In a **defensive climate**, the environment is unfriendly, rigid, and unsupportive of workers' professional and personal needs. For example, supervisors may use communication as a way to strategically control others and to strictly enforce company hierarchy. Employees may resist change, be closed-minded toward new ideas or outside input, and negatively perceive any dissent. In contrast, workers in a **supportive climate** describe the workplace as warm, open, and cooperative. Workers communicate honestly, collaborate to solve problems, share credit, practice empathy, and encourage people to treat one another with respect, despite any imbalance in power.

One important and oft-overlooked feature that distinguishes supportive from defensive climates is the degree to which workplace *fun* is emphasized. Within supportive climate organizations, activities and events are created solely for worker enjoyment and socializing, and these activities have a positive impact on nearly every aspect of organizational life. Workplace fun has been documented as increasing job satisfaction, worker morale, pride in work, creativity, and service quality, while reducing absenteeism, anxiety, and burnout. Employees who perceive their managers as being more supportive of workplace fun are more emotionally attached to their organizations, and less likely to quit (Tews et al., 2014). Organizational climates are rarely purely defensive or supportive. Instead, most fall somewhere in between. In addition, organizations may have different climates within different units, depending on workers' personalities, job demands, and supervisor communication styles (Elçi & Alpkan, 2009). Research suggests that leaders fundamentally shape the climate of their employees, and that cohesive climates can be encouraged by leaders role-modeling expectations for behavior, and clearly articulating organizational practices and the reasons for such practices (Nishii & Paluch, 2018).

LaunchPad Video
launchpadworks.com

Defensive Climate
Watch this clip online to answer the questions below.

How did the coworkers in this video create a defensive climate? What influence do you think their workplace culture had on creating their organizational climate?
   Want to see more? Check out LaunchPad for a clip illustrating **supportive climate**.

Some companies encourage customs like "pajama day," which can help to build a supportive organizational climate and create a culture of happy, engaged workers. Chung Sung-Jun/Getty Images News/Getty Images

skills practice

Creating a Supportive Climate

Building supportiveness in the workplace

❶ *Encourage honest communication.* Workplace climates are most supportive when people view one another as honest and open.

❷ *Adopt a flexible mindset.* Be open to others' ideas, criticisms, and suggestions. Examine your own ideas for weaknesses. Avoid using absolutes ("This is the only option").

❸ *Collaborate rather than control.* Avoid trying to manipulate others. Instead, ask for their ideas and perspectives.

❹ *Describe challenges rather than assign blame.* When problems arise at work, talk about them in neutral terms rather than pointing fingers.

❺ *Offer concern rather than professional detachment.* When coworkers or employees seek your support on personal dilemmas, demonstrate empathy, respect, and understanding.

❻ *Emphasize equality.* Avoid pulling rank on people. When you have power over others, it's vital to treat them with respect.

As just one person in your organization, you obviously don't have sole control over the climate. Nevertheless, organizational climate is built from the ground up: it is the sum total of individuals' interpersonal behavior in the workplace. Consequently, everything you say and do in your workplace contributes to its climate.

TECHNOLOGY IN THE WORKPLACE

In most workplaces, nearly everyone uses video chat, texting, social media, and email to coordinate professional activities (Berry, 2006; Robertson & Kee, 2017). Such communication technologies provide substantial advantages over face-to-face and phone interactions, as they facilitate the ease and convenience with which people can work collaboratively as teams (Santuzzi & Barber, 2018). This is especially the case when complex decision making requires input from multiple employees who are geographically separated (Berry, 2006). For example, hosting meeting chatrooms online or posting to a common site ensures more active and equal participation than usually takes place during synchronous webcam or face-to-face meetings. People can contribute to the interaction without concern for interrupting or talking over others. The conversations are also more democratic: people in authority can't "stare down" or even "mute" those with whom they disagree, suppressing their input; and shy employees feel more comfortable contributing. In addition, asynchronous online discussions provide participants with freedom from time and geographic constraints. People can chime in on the conversation whenever they like over a period of days or even weeks, and participants can join or leave the discussion without having to physically move—an enormous benefit to those who are geographically distant. Online discussions are often more informative, detailed, and factual than synchronous conversations, as participants have the opportunity to fact-check the information in each of their comments before they post them. Keep these advantages in mind if you're in a position to guide such decision-making discussions.

But the biggest advantage of communication technologies within the workplace is that they *connect* workers in a relational fashion. Online chat has usurped gossiping in the break room or talking on the telephone as the leading way

▶ Many workers experience *workplace telepressure*—the expectation that they be engaged in checking messages or other work-related tasks at all times. Have you experienced workplace telepressure at a job? If so, what did you do?
Stefan Wermuth/Bloomberg/Getty Images

employees build and bolster interpersonal ties (Riedy & Wen, 2010). Technologies allow workers to form and maintain friendships with coworkers they previously would not have been able to befriend, including workers in other divisions of the company or other parts of the country or world (Quan-Haase et al., 2005). And these connections afforded by technology have additional workplace benefits. One study found that employees reported more job satisfaction when they spent more time interacting with colleagues on Facebook (Robertson & Kee, 2017), and another determined that when employees use social media for work purposes, such as to maintain contact with customers or find new contacts, they report more productivity (Leftheriotis & Giannakos, 2014).

Although communication technologies allow greater efficiency in connecting us to our workplaces and coworkers, they also have drawbacks. For instance, such technologies do provide faster transmission of critical workplace information, yet they allow for the rapid transfer of *irrelevant* information as well. Dealing with large amounts of incoming information is a time-consuming activity; consequently, as workplace communication has shifted to online messaging, the length of people's workdays has increased, as many of us now not only have to perform our jobs but also check, sort, and respond to all incoming work-relevant email, texts, and posts (Stich et al., 2018). What's more, although organizations frequently frame the embrace of new communication technologies as making things simpler and easier, many platforms, applications, and devices are anything but easy to use. Instead, complex user interfaces and instructions need to be learned and mastered—leading to additional work hours spent dealing with the logistical challenges of the technologies, rather than performing the tasks that are the principal focus of the job (Tarafdar et al., 2015). Even worse, companies are in constant competition with one another to be at the cutting edge of new and developing communication technologies, which means that many employees must navigate frequent upgrades as well as new devices and applications.

Perhaps the most negative outcome of workplace technologies isn't the time-sink of frequent tracking and reading of messages, or the challenge of adapting to new devices and applications; instead, it is the emotional drain of constantly being tethered to the workplace round-the-clock. This can increase stress, make professional burnout more likely, and reduce emotional and physical well-being. The pressure to always be connected to the workplace and to respond immediately to workplace communications—even during weekends and vacation days—is known as **workplace telepressure** (Barber & Santuzzi, 2015). Employees experiencing workplace telepressure are more likely to experience feelings of work overload, emotional fatigue, and dissatisfaction with their work–life balance (Grawitch et al., 2017). Workplace telepressure also results in high levels of physical and mental exhaustion and chronic sleep problems (Santuzzi & Barber, 2018).

What can be done to avoid the negative outcomes of workplace technologies? Communication scholars offer several suggestions (Stich et al., 2018). At the institutional level, organizations should educate their employees on the risks associated with telepressure. Regular surveys should audit employees' levels of telepressure and stress, and the results should then be used as the basis for collective discussions through peer support groups. If you are in a supervisory position, you should avoid sending emails or texts, or posting important information, outside of regular work hours; such behaviors create a culture of constant availability and an expectation that workers should respond immediately, even during their time off. Additionally, all workers—supervisors and employees alike—should encourage one another to

skills practice

Collaborating via Technology
Using technology to collaboratively meet organizational challenges

❶ Identify a challenge faced by your group or organization.

❷ Create an online discussion group or community related to this issue.

❸ Describe the problem in neutral terms, avoiding assignment of blame.

❹ Email or text everyone in your work unit, inviting them to post potential solutions.

❺ Encourage open and honest assessment of ideas from all participants.

⬆ Music producers Terry Lewis and James "Jimmy Jam" Harris have had remarkable success in working together as professional peers. What do you think are some of the benefits and complications of working closely with someone who is also a friend?
Rick Diamond/Getty Images Entertainment/Getty Images

📖 **LaunchPad** Video

launchpadworks.com

Professional Peers
Watch this clip online to answer the questions below.

What is the difference between being friendly with peers at work and being friends with coworkers? How does your communication reflect such differences? Do you develop the same type of peer relationships with face-to-face coworkers as with virtual ones? Why or why not?

understand and empathize with their colleagues, and to adjust their communication to reflect their colleagues' preferences. This includes not just when and what to communicate, but also the preferred modality.

Now that we've discussed the nature of workplace relationships, let's turn our attention to explore the relationships we have with our peers.

Peer Relationships

Peers provide personal and practical support

What do Usher, TLC, Boys II Men, and Mary J. Blige have in common with Gwen Stefani, Elton John, Janet Jackson, and Earth, Wind, & Fire? They've all performed songs written and produced by Terry Lewis and James "Jimmy Jam" Harris, *the* most successful musical production team in modern music history.[2] The two have collaborated to produce more than 40 number-one singles, over 100 gold and platinum albums, more than a dozen movie soundtracks, and even the music for the NBA All-Star Game. They've won five Grammies to date, and in October of 2020 they were signed by BMG to create their *own* albums in the future. But through all the fame and fortune they've achieved, the two still view each other primarily as musical coworkers and collaborators. After all, they've been friends since the early 1970s, when they both were students in the Upward Bound program at the University of Minnesota—and they've been professional partners since they both played in Prince's band in the 1980s. "The number one thing is that we don't do anything alone," notes Jimmy Jam. "We approach each project as equal partners."

Our most meaningful and intimate workplace relationships are those with our **professional peers**—employees holding positions of similar organizational status who have no formal authority over one another (Sias et al., 2020). Peers are the most important source of personal and practical support for employees in any type of organization, whether it's a bank, hospital, or band (Rawlins, 1992). This support yields a host of benefits, including buffering us from the negative emotional impacts that can arise from workplace crises (Charoensukmongkol & Phungsoonthorn, 2020), reducing our workplace stress and increasing our mental health (Goh et al., 2016), boosting our physical health (Wolff et al., 2016), and decreasing the likelihood that we will quit (Tews et al., 2019). Similar to Jimmy Jam and Terry Lewis, we also develop close peer relationships in the workplace (Sias et al., 2020). After all, our peer relationships are not simply professional; they're often intensely personal.

TYPES OF PEER RELATIONSHIPS

Although peer relationships strongly shape the quality of our work lives, not all peer relationships are the same (Fritz & Dillard, 1994). *Information peers* are equivalent-status coworkers with whom our communication is limited to work-related content.

---

[2]The information that follows is from Amorosi (2020), Johnson (2004), Kimpel (2010), and Williams (2018).

Information-peer relationships are typically created through assignment rather than choice, and as a result, they lack trust and intimacy. Although these relationships are common, especially in large corporations, many people view information peers as less open and less communicatively skilled than collegial or special peers (Myers et al., 1999).

Collegial peers are coworkers we consider friends. When we communicate with collegial peers, we talk about work and personal issues, we feel moderate levels of trust and intimacy toward these individuals, and we orient to them as "whole persons" rather than just professional colleagues (Sias et al., 2020). Scholars sometimes describe such relationships as "blended" because they incorporate elements of both professional and personal relationships (Bridge & Baxter, 1992).

Special peers are equivalent-status coworkers with whom we share very high levels of emotional support, career-related feedback, trust, self-disclosure, and friendship (Sias et al., 2002). The rarest type of peer relationship, special peers are considered best friends in the workplace.

Professional peer relationships can evolve from lesser to greater levels of intimacy over time. The first and most significant relationship transition is from information peer to collegial peer (Sias & Cahill, 1998). Workers who spend extended periods of time together on shared tasks, are placed in proximity with each other, or socialize together outside of the workplace inevitably form stronger bonds with each other (Yakubovich & Burg, 2019). However, sharing time and activities together is not enough to ensure that a coworker relationship will evolve from information peer to collegial peer. As with personal friendships, perceived similarity in interests, beliefs, and values are what decisively push a workplace relationship from acquaintanceship to friendship (Sias & Cahill, 1998).

The evolution of the relationship from information peer to collegial peer is similar for **virtual peers**—coworkers who communicate mainly through phone, email, video chat, and other communication technologies. For virtual peers, the progression from information peer to collegial peer hinges on how much time the peers spend interacting and working on shared tasks together. Given the familiarity that many modern workers have with communication technologies and the availability of such technologies in the workplace, it's commonplace for virtual peers to become virtual friends.

Not all collegial peers transition to special peers. Perceived similarity, shared time and tasks, and socializing are all important, but are not sufficient to push coworker friendships to the level of best friend (Sias & Cahill, 1998). Instead, the evolution of a coworker friendship to a higher state of intimacy is usually spurred by negative events in partners' personal lives (serious illness, marital discord) or serious work-related problems that require an exceptional level of social support.

MAINTAINING PEER RELATIONSHIPS

Like other interpersonal bonds, peer relationships remain healthy through the energy and effort you and your peers invest in maintenance. One important tactic that helps maintain your peer relationships is positivity, discussed in Chapters 11 and 12. A positive perspective and upbeat communication with your peers help offset the stress and demands everyone faces in the workplace. Practicing positivity in the workplace means communicating with your peers in a cheerful and optimistic fashion and doing unsolicited favors for them.

Openness also plays an important role. Openness means creating feelings of security and trust between you and your peers. You can create such feelings by

self-reflection

How many of your workplace peers do you consider friends rather than simply coworkers? Are there any you think of as best friends? How do your relationships with peers at work affect your feelings about your job and the organization?

▶ No matter your workplace setting, you can maintain your peer relationships by using positivity, openness, and assurances, and by remembering that peer relationships require a blend of personal and work conversational topics. michaeljung/Shutterstock

LaunchPad

Online Self-Quiz: Test Your Maintenance of Peer Relationships. To take this self-quiz, visit LaunchPad: **launchpadworks.com**

behaving in predictable, trustworthy, and ethical ways in your relationships with peers. This means following through on your promises, respecting confidences, and demonstrating honesty and integrity in both your personal and your professional behavior.

Two additional tactics will help you maintain your collegial- and special-peer relationships (Sias et al., 2002). Like assurances given to a romantic partner, assurances given to collegial and special peers help demonstrate your commitment to them. Because choice is what distinguishes close peer relationships from casual ones, a critical part of maintaining these relationships is routinely stressing to your collegial and special peers that your relationships are based on choice rather than professional assignment. This can be accomplished indirectly by inviting peers to join you in activities outside the workplace, which implies that you consider them friends and not just coworkers. More directly, you can straightforwardly tell collegial and special peers that you think of them primarily as friends.

Second, collegial- and special-peer relationships grow stronger when the people involved treat each other as whole human beings with unique qualities and do not strictly define each other simply as coworkers (Sias et al., 2020). Certainly, you will discuss work, but since your relationships with collegial and special peers are blended, you also will discuss your personal lives.

Another type of workplace relationship occurs between people with different levels of status, and we examine these mixed-status relationships next.

Mixed-Status Relationships

Communicating with supervisors and employees

Most organizations are hierarchical, with some people holding positions of power over others. Relationships between coworkers of different organizational status are called **mixed-status relationships**, and they provide the structural foundation on which most organizations are built (Farace et al., 1977). Mixed-status relationships take many forms, including trainer–trainee and mentor–protégé.

But when most of us think of mixed-status relationships, what leaps to mind are *supervisory relationships,* those in which one person outranks and supervises employees and has the formal authority to instruct and evaluate them (Lybarger et al., 2017). Most of these relationships are assigned rather than chosen.

Supervisory relationships are less likely than peer relationships to evolve into friendships because of the power imbalance (Zorn, 1995). In most friendships, people downplay any difference in status and emphasize their equality. Supervisors by definition have more power. They direct their employees' efforts, evaluate their performance, and make decisions regarding their pay and job security.

While some supervisors and employees can become friends, many organizations discourage or even forbid friendships between supervisors and their employees because it's assumed that such relationships will impair a supervisor's ability to objectively assess employees' work performance (Zorn, 1995). Research on organizational decision making supports this assumption. Managers are less likely to give negative feedback to employees they like than to those they dislike (Larson, 1984). This occurs for two reasons. First, we are reluctant to give friends who work under us negative feedback because of the relationship consequences that may ensue—our friend may become angry or accuse us of unfairness. Second, as we saw in Chapter 3, our perceptions of others are substantially biased by whether we like them or not. Consequently, if we're in a supervisory position, our affection for an employee friend may lead us to judge their performance more generously than others.

Now that we've briefly described mixed-status relationships, let's investigate two different forms of communication in these relationships.

MANAGING UP

Influencing people of higher organizational status to support our work-related needs and wants is achieved through **upward communication**—communication from employees to supervisors that is pursued with the desire to persuade. People feel more satisfied with their work lives when they believe that their supervisors listen and are responsive to their concerns (Eisenberg & Goodall, 2004).

The desire for upward communication often begins with a particular dilemma or desire that you feel needs to be expressed to your supervisor. Whether or not you voice these concerns upward, however, is largely determined by two factors: perceived safety and perceived efficacy (Mao & DeAndrea, 2019). In other words, you'll be more likely to communicate upward when you believe your job status and work relationships will not be negatively impacted by voicing your concern *and* you believe that expressing your concern will bring about the intended effects.

Many organizations provide their employees with technological channels—in the form of online or voice mail messaging systems—to anonymously engage in upward communication. However, such systems, though well intended, have limited effectiveness in bringing about actual organizational change, for two reasons. First, the very fact that messages must remain anonymous means that employees posting or leaving such messages must delete essential details such as the names of people involved, the relevant locations or work groups, and the dates and times of incidents, in order to protect their identities. Without these specifics, it's difficult for supervisors to know the exact nature of the problem, much less how to correct it. Additionally, managers often discount anonymous messages, assuming that the concern must not be credible if the message writer or caller doesn't want to be named (Mao & DeAndrea, 2019).

How well did the employee design his message according to the six suggested principles for advocacy? How would the employee revise his message for a supervisor who was a task-oriented listener, a relational listener, a critical listener, or an analytical listener?

Want to see more? Check out LaunchPad for clips illustrating **upward communication** and **downward communication**.

skills practice

Using Advocacy in Upward Communication
Sharpening your advocacy skills

❶ Identify a situation in which you might use advocacy to influence someone who has more power than you.

❷ Consider the person's communication and decision-making preferences.

❸ Create messages that embody advocacy principles.

❹ Assess whether your messages are compelling.

❺ Revisit your situation, but this time, imagine the person strongly disagrees with you.

❻ Generate new messages to counter possible objections.

❼ Choose the messages that will best help you advocate.

Organizational communication scholar Eric Eisenberg argues that the most effective form of upward communication is **advocacy** (Eisenberg & Goodall, 2004). Through advocacy, you learn your supervisor's communication preferences and how to design messages in ways that will appeal to them, and then convey your message directly to them. Advocacy is based on six principles. First, *plan before you pitch*. Most spontaneous appeals to supervisors ("Can I have a raise?" "Will you sign me up for that software course?") are rejected. To avoid this, take time to craft your request before you pitch it.

Second, *know why your supervisor should agree with you*. Your supervisor has the power to make decisions, so the burden is on you to present a compelling case. In your message, connect your goals to something your supervisor thinks is important. For example, "If you sign me up for this course, I'll be able to maintain our new database."

Third, *tailor your message*. Think about successful and unsuccessful attempts to influence your supervisor. Compare the different approaches you and other people have used, and consider their efficacy. Does your supervisor respond more favorably to statistics or to stories? To details or to generalities? Based on your supervisor's preferences, tailor your evidence and appeal accordingly.

Fourth, *know your supervisor's knowledge*. Many attempts at upward communication fail because employees present information at an inappropriate level. For example, they present their request in overly abstract terms, wrongly assuming that their supervisor is familiar with the subject. Or, they present their appeal in a simplistic form, inadvertently coming across as condescending. To avoid this, know your supervisor's knowledge of the subject before you broach it. You can find this out by talking to other workers who are familiar with your supervisor.

Fifth, *create coalitions before communicating*. Most arguments made by one person are unconvincing, particularly when presented by an employee to a supervisor. Try to strengthen your argument with support from others in your organization. Remember to present such information as a helpful and personal observation ("Just to make sure I wasn't completely off about the situation, I checked with Erika, Allen, and Will, and they all agreed") rather than as a threat to your supervisor's authority ("For your information, three other people feel the same way I do!"). Be sure to get approval beforehand from the people whose opinions you plan to cite. Some may not want their viewpoints referenced, and to use their sentiments as support for your arguments without their approval is highly unethical.

Lastly, *competently articulate your message*. You can plan and tailor a message all you want, but if you're unable to articulate it, your supervisor probably won't take it seriously. Before you talk with your supervisor, revisit the information on competent interpersonal communication described in Chapters 1 and 8 to brush up on your skills.

As a final note regarding upward communication, keep this general rule in mind: supervisors are more likely to listen to your concerns and grant your desires if they view you as a skilled communicator. Research documents that the top three communication skills employees most value are *relatability*, *documentation*, and *audience awareness*; and the communication behaviors they view most negatively are *deception*, *defensiveness*, and *aggression* (Coffelt & Smith, 2020). That is, supervisors hold in high regard employees who can network, build

self-QUIZ

Most Valued Workplace Communication Skills

Read each of the statements below, and choose the ones that you agree with. Then total your score to see how many of the most valued workplace communication skills you possess.

When communicating within the workplace, I routinely . . .

_____ do my best to put others at ease by being warm and friendly.

_____ try to use my communication to establish and build positive relationships.

_____ take careful notes on important information that is shared during the interaction.

_____ draw upon notes I've kept from previous interactions to solve problems that arise.

_____ genuinely try to understand others' perspectives.

_____ practice my active listening skills while others are speaking.

_____ adapt my communication to the preferences of others.

_____ approach others with a "you" attitude—placing their needs and wants before my own.

This self-quiz uses information from Coffelt & Smith (2020).

Scoring: 0–3: low skill; 4–5: moderate skill; 6–8: high skill

relationships, and put others at ease when interacting (relatability); who routinely record important workplace information in writing and then produce that documentation when needed to solve problems or assist customers (documentation); and who listen actively, seek genuine understanding of others' perspectives, adapt their communication to others' preferences, and have a "you" attitude (audience awareness). On the other hand, employees who have a history of being deceptive; who engage in aggressive behavior against other employees to get their way; and who are rigid, arrogant, and refuse to take responsibility for the errors they make are held in low regard (Coffelt & Smith, 2020). Thus, the success of your upward communication isn't just about the skill of your advocacy appeal—it's also about the long-term track record of communication behavior that you have established as an employee within your workplace in the weeks, months, and years preceding your current message.

COMMUNICATING WITH EMPLOYEES

When you communicate upward, you're typically trying to influence your supervisors. But when you are the supervisor, *you* have the influence. When you present a request or demand to your employees, you don't have to worry about using advocacy. You can simply tell them what to do and use whatever language you want. But should you?

Having formal authority in an organization gives you freedom in the messages you use when interacting with your employees, known as **downward communication**. With this freedom comes responsibility. Although some people in power positions exploit their freedom by bullying or harassing employees (as we'll discuss shortly), what distinguishes competent downward communication is the willingness of empowered people to communicate without relying on their power in order to appeal to employees in positive, empathic, respectful, and open ways.

A supervisor's downward communication shapes the morale and performance of all employees. James Hardy/PhotoAlto Agency RF Collections/Getty Images

self-reflection

Think about the most skilled supervisor you know. Which aspects of this supervisor's communication influence your perceptions of their competence? Openness? Ability to explain things? Honesty and integrity? Willingness to listen?

Competent Downward Communication A supervisor's communication sets the tone for their employees and for the organization. When a supervisor communicates competently, the effects radiate downward: employees are more motivated, more satisfied with their work, and more productive (Eisenberg & Goodall, 2004). Competent supervisors are seen as more caring and supportive, and as having better character (Lybarger et al., 2017); and employees who perceive supervisors as supportive experience less workplace stress and a greater sense of well-being as a result (Jia et al., 2017). But when a supervisor communicates incompetently, frustration and dissatisfaction build quickly. If you're a manager, you have not only organizational power and status but also the ability to shape the morale and performance of all of your workers, simply by how you interpersonally communicate with them.

Competent downward communication can be achieved by observing five principles (Eisenberg & Goodall, 2004). First, routinely and openly emphasize the importance of communication in workplace relationships with your employees. For example, some supervisors engage in both informal and formal interactions with their workers—hallway chats, impromptu office visits, weekly status updates, or team meetings. They also clearly and concisely explain instructions, performance expectations, and policies.

Second, listen empathically and actively. Active and empathic listening is viewed by both managers and employees as a key aspect of managerial competence (Jonsdottir & Fridriksdottir, 2020). To practice active listening as a manager with your employees, eliminate all distractions and interruptions when communicating with your workers; give them good eye contact while they are talking; ask questions and take notes; allow your employees to express their feelings and opinions without interruption or argument; and endeavor to keep your own preconceived opinions under control (Jonsdottir & Fridriksdottir, 2020). Strive to respond positively to your employees' attempts at upward communication rather than perceiving such attempts as a threat to power; and demonstrate a reasonable willingness to take fair and appropriate action in response to concerns they are expressing (Eisenberg & Goodall, 2004).

Third, when communicating wants and needs to your employees, frame these messages as polite requests ("Do you think you could . . .") or persuasive explanations ("Here's why we need to get this done in the next week . . ."). By contrast, incompetent downward communication involves using power to make threats ("Do this now or else!") and demands ("Take care of that customer immediately!").

Fourth, be sensitive to your employees' feelings. For instance, if constructive criticism is necessary, make it in private rather than in front of other workers. Keep such exchanges focused on behaviors that need to change rather than making judgments about the employee's character or worth: "John, I noticed that you arrived late to the last three staff meetings. I'm worried that late arrivals disrupt the meetings and cause us to lose time. What ideas do you have for ensuring that you get to meetings on time?"

Last, share relevant information with employees whenever possible. This includes notice of impending organizational changes as well as explanations about why the changes are coming. For example: "Our company hasn't been meeting its

focus on CULTURE

The Model Minority Myth

Karen Chan had worked in the finance department for seven years when a new supervisor was hired.[3] Karen was shocked when he talked about her ethnicity. "He would make comments like, 'I can always count on you to get the budget right, because I know Asians are good with numbers.'" His communication began to influence other department heads, who sought Karen's input on complicated financial questions. "I actually majored in English, and when I chose finance as a career, it wasn't because I was a quantitative expert. I knew I had an eye for detail, and I appreciated the foundation finance would provide for a long-term career in business."

Karen decided to confront her boss. She quickly learned that he was behaving out of ignorance. "He didn't mean to deliberately hurt me, but I didn't want him to continue doing it. I may want to make a switch to operations or marketing, and my boss's comments were cornering me into a finance career within the firm." They both agreed to communicate about these slips as they occurred.

Many Asian American people, like Karen Chan, are victims of the model minority myth—the belief that all members of certain immigrant groups are hardworking high achievers with special aptitudes for math, science, and engineering (Shams, 2020). The model minority myth is racist and, as Karen's story illustrates, can have real negative impacts. Writer Jane Hyun (2005) of the NAACP encourages workers who feel they are being stereotyped as model minorities to discuss the matter directly with their supervisors, much as Karen did. When you do, be sure to use "I" language and avoid "you" language (see Chapter 8)—for example, "I feel uncomfortable about this type of language" rather than "You make me uncomfortable when you say things like that." If, after talking with your supervisor, you still feel that your concerns are not being heard, consider reaching out to your human resources department or filing a complaint with the U.S. Equal Employment Opportunity Commission (EEOC).

discussion questions

- How does your culture shape your supervisor's downward communication with you?
- What impact does this communication have on your work? On your workplace satisfaction?

[3]Information regarding Karen Chan, including quotes, is from Hyun (2005).

forecasted revenues, so several units, including ours, are being sold to another company. We'll have an opportunity to accept jobs here or move to the company that's acquiring us. As soon as I know more about what this change means for all of us, I'll share that information."

Compliments and Criticism   Two challenges of downward communication are (1) how to effectively praise employees and (2) how to offer constructive criticism. Offering employees praise for their workplace accomplishments fosters a healthy organizational climate. Studies repeatedly show that employees rank "appreciation" and "supervisory recognition" at the top of their list of factors motivating them to work hard, and that feeling unappreciated at work is a leading cause of employee turnover (Forni, 2002).

Complimenting your workers is most effectively done when the compliments are focused on an employee's work—their achievements, expertise, attitude, cooperativeness, and so forth. Avoid compliments about personal matters, like an employee's appearance. Regardless of your intention, something as innocuous as complimenting the stylishness of a hairstyle or clothing objectifies that person and may make them feel uncomfortable and be perceived as inappropriate.

Praise is best presented privately rather than publicly, except in formal contexts, such as recognition dinners and award ceremonies. Many supervisors enjoy spontaneously singling out particular employees for praise in front of their coworkers ("Everyone, let's give Sam a round of applause—they led our unit in sales again this past month!"). These supervisors incorrectly believe that such praise improves morale, but it can do the opposite. When someone is publicly singled out in a context in which such recognition is unexpected, that person's status is elevated. This might be merited, but it could foster resentment and envy among the person's peers and ultimately undermine the organization's climate.

Of course, criticizing employees is no easier. Especially challenging is providing constructive criticism to high-achieving employees, who often have little experience receiving criticism and expect only praise (Field, 2005). But offering constructive criticism isn't as difficult as you might think. Instead, it requires you to draw on the many skills you have learned in previous chapters.

Begin by using your knowledge of emotion management from Chapter 4, remaining calm, kind, and understanding throughout the exchange. Open your interaction with positive remarks, and end your comments with similar commendations: "It was obvious you worked really hard on designing that presentation" or "This isn't the end of the world—just something I'd like you to work on for future presentations."

Second, follow the guidelines for competent interpersonal communication described in Chapter 1, and cooperative language detailed in Chapter 8. Informatively, honestly, and clearly identify the issue or behavior that concerns you, describing it neutrally rather than personalizing it or leveling accusations. For example, instead of saying, "You clearly don't realize how you came across," say, "I think the way you defended our team's work yesterday may not have been the most effective approach." Rather than "You shouldn't have gone in unprepared like that," say, "There seemed to be an expectation in the room for more precise data on projected sales."

Strive to experience and express empathy through perspective-taking and empathic concern (Chapter 3), showing that you understand how they may feel: "The same thing has happened to me before" rather than "I would never let something like that happen." Keep in mind how you have felt when receiving criticism from your supervisors, and adapt your communication accordingly.

Finally, avoid belaboring the error that has been made, and instead focus most of your talk time on ideas for avoiding such missteps in the future. Although you have the authority to dictate corrections, employees respond more favorably when supervisors negotiate solutions with them. Offer specific ideas, but frame them as suggestions, asking for their opinions. The goal of constructive criticism is not only to correct the errant behavior but also to create a mutual consensus with your employees.

Now that we share a firm understanding of best practices for communication upward and downward within an organization, let's conclude this chapter by reflecting on several different challenges we may face in the workplace.

Challenges to Workplace Relationships

Dealing with bullying, romance, and harassment

Before she returned to grad school and eventually became a professor, Kelly worked in business for several years. During her time with one company, Whitley was hired to be the interim regional director, but "interim" was quickly removed from her title. Her first day on the job, Whitley fired a respected division manager, and several more terminations quickly followed. Despite her new nickname—"Terminator"—Whitley disarmed people with her charm and energy, typically making strong positive first impressions. But behind the smile was someone who exploited power and micromanaged employees. She instituted new policies restricting employee freedom and creativity, telling all workers, "These are the only three areas you are going to focus on" for new business. She monitored administrative assistants, keeping track of the number of times phones rang before being answered, and punished those who didn't answer "quickly enough." Assistants were admonished by their direct supervisors to change where they walked outside during their breaks, so that Whitley wouldn't see them—as assistants were "forbidden to leave the building during work hours." She also played favorites, elevating the status and salaries of those who flattered her while demoting and demoralizing those who disagreed or questioned her decisions. When one worker dared to question a decision she had made during a company-wide meeting, Whitley called him into her office, reprimanded him, and threatened him with termination. Employees debated survival strategies: "Stand up and fight" or "Keep your head down and stay out of trouble." By the time Whitley left the company, the profits, rankings, and morale of the company had been hollowed out; many employees had left to join the competition and all of the divisional managers had been replaced.

Maintaining workplace relationships is hard. We must constantly juggle job demands, power issues, and intimacy, all while communicating in ways that are positive and professional (Sias et al., 2004). Yet as Kelly's experience navigating the abusive management of Whitley illustrates, sometimes even more intense challenges arise. Three of the most common, and difficult to manage, are workplace bullying, the development of romantic relationships with coworkers, and sexual harassment.

WORKPLACE BULLYING

In the course of your professional lives, many of you will experience situations similar to what Kelly experienced with Whitley. **Workplace bullying** is the repeated unethical and unfavorable treatment of one or more persons by others in the workplace (Boddy, 2011). Bullying occurs in a variety of ways, including shouting, swearing, spreading vicious rumors, destroying the target's property or work, and excessive criticism. It also is perpetrated through passive means, such as the silent treatment, exclusion from meetings and gatherings, and ignoring of requests (Tracy et al., 2006). In nearly one-fifth of cases, workplace bullying involves physical violence, including hitting, slapping, and shoving (Martin & LaVan, 2010). When bullying occurs online or via text messaging, it is known as *cyberbullying* (Kowalski et al., 2018). The most frequently reported forms of workplace cyberbullying are withholding or deleting important information sent via email, and spreading gossip or rumors through text messages, emails, and online posts (Privitera & Campbell, 2009). Perpetrators of workplace bullying usually combine several of these tactics to intimidate their victims. The most common forms are detailed in Table 14.1.

Workplace bullying is not the same thing as interpersonal conflict, negative criticism, or differing communication styles. Instead, what distinguishes bullying is the persistence and intensity of messages designed to devalue and demean the other person, despite their efforts to defend themselves. Workplace bullying also typically involves an organizational power or status difference between the persons involved. And although workplace bullies often target people based on gender or ethnicity, people also may be bullied based upon sexual orientation, disability, chronic illness, religion, or age (Tye-Williams et al., 2020). The possibility of workplace bullying is one reason LGBTQ+ workers often choose to not be "out" within the workplace (Sears & Mallory, 2014).

Workplace bullying has devastating effects on the target's physical and psychological health. Research documents that such bullying can lead to increases in smoking, alcohol consumption, drug abuse, sleep disruption, and chronic and cardiovascular diseases. People who are bullied in the workplace also are more likely to experience depression, post-traumatic stress disorder, and suicide (Bartlett & Bartlett, 2011). The associated costs to companies for workplace bullying are pronounced: they include disability and workers' compensation claims, lawsuits, low-quality work, reduced productivity, high staff turnover, increased absenteeism, and deteriorated customer relationships (Tracy et al., 2006).

Unfortunately, workplace bullying is common: about 19 percent of U.S. employees have experienced it or are currently experiencing it (Workplace Bullying Institute, n.d.). One reason that bullying is so widespread in the United States is that unlike in Canada, France, and Scandinavian countries, workplace bullying is technically *legal* in the United States. That is, unless targets can *prove* that the bully willfully intended to discriminate against them based upon protected class status under Title VII of the Civil Rights Act (e.g., race, gender, age, national origin)—and not for some other reason—their case is not actionable in court (Tye-Williams et al., 2020). Targets of bullying also are disinclined to share their stories of abuse with other people because they often aren't believed (Tracy et al., 2006). Furthermore, workplace bullies typically put on an act for their supervisors, behaving in a supportive fashion when they are being watched and being abusive when the boss is not around (Tracy et al., 2006). This was the case with Whitley, described previously: she was unfailingly friendly and upbeat with *her* supervisors, leading them to believe that she was a charismatic and inspirational leader.

table 14.1 Common Forms of Workplace Bullying

Form	Description
Isolation	Restrict employees' interaction with coworkers; isolate their work area from others; exclude them from group activities and offsite social gatherings
Control of important information	Prevent important information from reaching workers; provide false job-related information to them; block or delete their correspondence, email, telephone calls, or work assignments
Constraint of professional responsibilities	Assign workers to tasks that are useless, impossible, or absurd; intentionally leave them with nothing to do
Creation of dangerous work conditions	Distract workers during critical tasks to put them in peril; assign them tasks that endanger their health or safety; refuse to provide appropriate safety measures for their job
Verbal abuse	Make disdainful, ridiculing, and insulting remarks regarding workers' personal characteristics (appearance, intelligence, personality, etc.); spread rumors and lies about them
Destruction of professional reputation	Attack workers' professional performance; exaggerate the importance of their work errors; ignore or distort their correct decisions and achievements.

This table uses information from Escartín, Rodríguez-Carballeira, Zapf, Porrúa, and Martín-Peña (2009).

How can you cope with workplace bullying? Research has found that bullied workers typically cope in one of five ways (Lee et al., 2021). The first, and most common, is simply to ignore the bullying, staying calm and keeping focused on work. The second approach is to give in to the bullying and any demands that the bully makes. The result of such acquiescence, however, often is lower productivity and greater feelings of helplessness. Third, some bullied workers seek a new assignment, call in sick or take time off, or quit altogether and find another job. Of course, this is not an option for everyone, since most people depend on their income, and new job opportunities can be limited. The fourth coping strategy is to fight back against the bully with similar negative behaviors or look for other options to pursue revenge—an approach that oftentimes escalates rather than resolves the bullying. The final approach is to actively seek solutions by engaging in direct or indirect talks—either with the bully or with a supervisor or others in positions of authority. In private, point out which actions you feel are abusive and ask the bully to stop. Some bullies may back off when they are confronted. If the bully is not your direct supervisor, speak with your supervisor about the issue. Research suggests that managers play a key role in preventing workplace bullying, particularly when they are aware of the issue, address conflicts when they arise, and create a workplace culture that embodies support for organizational policy against workplace bullying (Woodrow & Guest, 2017).

WORKPLACE ROMANCES

A second challenge to workplace relationships is the development of romantic feelings for coworkers. The workplace is a natural venue for romantic attraction to unfold because of the constant proximity of coworkers, the time you spend together, the sense of unity and camaraderie that often exists within work teams, and the fact that people feel distanced from their problems at home and with their families (Verhoef & Terblanche, 2015). In a 2019 survey of more than 700 professionals, 58 percent reported having been involved in a workplace romance at some point in their careers (Vault Careers, 2019). Workplace romances typically occur among peers, although 29 percent of employees reported romantic relationships with a partner of higher status in the workplace, according to a survey of 4,000 U.S. employees (Chan-Serafin et al., 2017).

◗ The romantic tension and challenges experienced by Amy (America Ferrera) and Jonah (Ben Feldman) in *Superstore* demonstrate both the positives and downsides of workplace romance. UNIVERSAL TELEVISION/Album/Alamy

Workplace romances differ from romantic involvements outside of professional contexts (discussed in Chapter 11) in at least two ways. First, the partners must exercise caution regarding to whom they disclose their relationship information and what information they disclose, as the sharing of such information runs the risk of triggering gossip that could create negative professional consequences (Cowan & Horan, 2021). Consequently, privacy becomes a core concern within such relationships. Second, relationship decisions have professional, not just personal, consequences. For instance, partners who choose to form romantic involvements that cross organizational status lines—a supervisor and their employee, for example—often are trusted less and viewed as less credible by their colleagues, and this effect holds true for both same-sex and straight romances (Horan et al., 2019). In addition, if and when the relationship ends, a host of negative

self-
reflection

If you have had a workplace
romance, what were the
biggest challenges you faced?
How did you and your partner
meet these challenges? If you
haven't had a workplace
romance, what are your
perceptions of such romances?
Do you approve or disapprove
of them? How could they affect
your organization?

outcomes typically ensue, including reduced productivity, workplace gossip, and conflict with colleagues (Verhoef & Terblanche, 2015).

Historically, organizations have discouraged workplace romances, believing that they lead to favoritism, lack of worker motivation, decreased efficiency and productivity, and increased risk of sexual harassment lawsuits (Appelbaum et al., 2007). But many workplaces have begun to shift their views and policies, as research supports the idea that romantic involvement does not hurt worker productivity (Boyd, 2010). From the worker's perspective, workplace romance is typically viewed positively. Romantically involved workers are usually perceived by people in their organization as friendly and approachable (Hovick et al., 2003), and having romances in the workplace is seen as creating a positive work climate (Riach & Wilson, 2007). Relationship outcomes are often positive, too: married couples who work in the same location have a 50 percent *lower* divorce rate than those employed at different workplaces (Boyd, 2010).

Despite these positives, workplace romances face challenges, and these are especially pronounced for relationships that cross status lines (as noted earlier) and for women. For example, organizational leaders are more likely to discount the achievements of workers who have been or are currently involved in a cross-status romance and to deny them training opportunities and promotions (Chan-Serafin et al., 2017). And women are more likely than men to suffer unfavorable work evaluations based on romantic involvement, are judged more negatively by their colleagues following workplace romance breakups, and are more likely to be terminated by their companies for workplace affairs (Riach & Wilson, 2007).

How can you successfully overcome the challenge of maintaining a workplace romance should you become involved in one? First, leave your love at home, so to speak, and communicate with your partner in a strictly professional fashion during work hours. When romantic partners maintain a professional demeanor toward each other and communicate with all their coworkers in a consistent and positive fashion, the romance is usually ignored or even encouraged (Buzzanell, 1990).

Second, only use nonworkplace (private) email and social media to maintain your relationship. Messages exchanged in the workplace through organizational servers or chats should never contain intimate or controversial content. Although many workers use their business accounts for personal reasons, these messages are not secure, and anyone with the motivation and know-how can gain access to the messages you and your partner exchange.

SEXUAL HARASSMENT

In October 1991, Anita Hill testified before the U.S. Senate about the sexual harassment she claimed to have experienced when working for then–Supreme Court nominee Clarence Thomas. Though many women, and men, had experienced sexual harassment before this time, her testimony brought the issue to the forefront of public dialog. Conversations, once whispered between colleagues who did not know how to describe their experiences, grew in volume as people acquired the words and confidence to amplify their voices. Those with similar experiences—Kelly (the author) included—thought that this event, surely, would bring an end to sexual harassment. We were wrong.

The December 18, 2017, issue of *TIME* magazine heralded the "Silence Breakers" as their "Person" of the year. Pictured were Ashley Judd, Susan Fowler, Adama Iwu, Taylor Swift, and Isabel Pascual, who bravely came together to stand

Over 25 years after Anita Hill testified regarding her claims of sexual harassment while working for Clarence Thomas before he was appointed to the Supreme Court, hundreds of women, including Rose McGowan (pictured here) came forward as part of the #MeToo movement—originally launched by activist Tarana Burke (also pictured)—to bring sexual harassment back into the national conversation. Bettmann/ Getty Images; David McNew/Getty Images News/Getty Images; Aaron J. Thornton/ Getty Images Entertainment/Getty Images

up against the issue of sexual harassment, 25 years after Anita Hill had stood alone. Propelled by the power and speed of social media, thousands of voices united in support of the #MeToo movement, which had originally been started by activist Tarana Burke and was popularized in 2017 by actor Alyssa Milano. A culture of intolerance lost its foundation. The supporting pillars of whispers, minimizations, and denial of sexual harassment were cracked with the accusations of Anita Hill, and continue to weaken every time new policies are implemented, such as a federal initiative to protect women from sexual harassment by landlords (Lynch, 2018), and every time people are publicly held to account, as in the suspension of a Marine Corps general who minimized claims of sexual harassment under his command as "fake news" (Vanden Brook, 2018). Perhaps, now, we truly have cast a new cultural foundation, one where the next generation will not need to echo the chorus of voices currently chiming #MeToo.

The U.S. Equal Employment Opportunity Commission (EEOC) defines **sexual harassment** in the following way:

> Unwelcome sexual advances, requests for sexual favors, and other verbal or physical conduct of a sexual nature constitute sexual harassment when (1) this conduct explicitly or implicitly affects an individual's employment, (2) unreasonably interferes with an individual's work performance, or (3) creates an intimidating, hostile, or offensive work environment.

Two types of sexual harassment can occur in the workplace (EEOC, 1990). The first is *quid pro quo harassment*—or, "this for that"—when the submission or rejection of sexual advances is a condition of, or linked to decisions about, employment. An example of this would be a person in a supervisory position asking for or demanding sexual favors in return for professional advancement or protection from layoffs or other undesirable events (Gerdes, 1999). Much more prevalent than quid pro quo harassment, however, is a *hostile work environment*—when an intimidating, hostile, or offensive work environment is created because sexual conduct or gender-based hostility is perceived as so severe or pervasive that it disrupts a person's work performance (EEOC, 1990).

And sexual harassment in the workplace is indeed pervasive. One EEOC study indicates that "anywhere from 25% to 85% of women report having experienced sexual harassment in the workplace" (Golshan, 2017). Despite the prevalence, between 70 and 90 percent do not file a formal complaint (National Women's Law Center, 2016). This is a particular problem for women in low-wage occupations and traditionally male-dominated occupations, such as construction, medicine, and science. Furthermore, sexual harassment is not limited to the workplace. The Pew Research Center found that 59 percent of women and 27 percent of men have experienced unwanted sexual advances or verbal or physical harassment of a sexual nature in or outside of a work setting (Graf, 2018).

Sexual harassment creates an array of pronounced negative outcomes. In one of the largest analyses yet done of these outcomes, involving data from 41 studies involving nearly 70,000 participants, sexual harassment was found to substantially undermine both the physical and mental health of people who had experienced it, with the most impactful and frequent negative outcome being post-traumatic stress disorder (Willness et al., 2007). Targets of sexual harassment report also feeling angry, afraid, and depressed (Cochran et al., 1997). Like those targeted for workplace bullying, targets of sexual harassment are more likely to develop substance abuse and other health problems, including weight loss and sleep and stomach disorders (Clair, 1998). Within organizations in which women are consistently subjected to *bodily objectification*—in the form of messaging (both in-person and online) regarding their body type, physical attractiveness, and other aspects of appearance—a sense of *sexual harassment fatigue* can set in, whereby women develop a sense of futility regarding the utility of protesting harassment (Ford & Ivancic, 2020). And sexual harassment negatively impacts the workplace environment as well, being associated with both reduced workplace productivity and financial losses for the employers (NWLC, 2016).

Given the prevalence and significance of this problem, how can we use our interpersonal communication skills to deal with it? The EEOC states that it is helpful for the victim to inform the harasser directly that the conduct in question is unwelcome and must stop. Thus, instead of rationalizing or interpreting the behavior in a way that minimizes its seriousness, clearly state that you feel the behavior is inappropriate, it makes you uncomfortable, and it should not be repeated. Familiarize yourself with your organization's policies, reflecting both on how training is conducted and how it communicates organizational values. For example, are workshops conducted in face-to-face settings where middle managers and supervisors actively participate and support the training, or is it something that is completed individually in online training modules? The former conveys a stronger message to employees about the value placed on the organizational policy, while the latter does not (Roehling & Huang, 2018).

If you are experiencing sexual harassment and are unsure what to do, remember that there are a variety of resources available to you. Contact the Equal Employment Opportunity Commission. Go to www.eeoc.gov for detailed information on how to handle such situations, or call 1-800-669-4000 or the TTY phone number for those who are deaf or hard of hearing: 1-800-669-6820. Additional helpful information can be found at the National Women's Law Center (https://nwlc.org/); the Rape, Abuse and Incest National Network (https://www.rainn.org/); and the Stop Street Harassment Organization (http://www.stopstreetharassment.org/).

Workplace Relationships and Human Happiness

Happiness at work can affect other areas of our lives

In his book *The Pursuit of Happiness* (2002), psychologist David Myers comments on the role that workplace relationships play in his life:

> Through our work we identify with a *community*. My sense of community is rooted in the network of supportive friends who surround me on our department team, in the institution whose goals we embrace, and in the profession we call our own. (p. 130)

self-reflection

Would you continue working if you didn't need to? Why or why not? If you chose not to work, what consequences can you envision for your life? How would not having a job affect your sense of purpose? Your happiness?

For many of us, our motivation to work transcends the desire to bring home a paycheck. Although we need the money our jobs provide, we also want to feel that our work is meaningful and important. When asked, "Would you continue working, even if you inherited a huge fortune that made working unnecessary?" three out of four Americans answered "yes" (Eisenberg & Goodall, 2004). This isn't just an American value: people in nearly every industrialized nation report lower satisfaction with their lives if they're unemployed, regardless of their financial standing (Myers, 2002).

But it's not the work itself that fulfills us; it's the coupling of the professional with the personal, the creation of a coworker community. Day in and day out, we endure work stress and intense demands with those who surround us—our supervisors, employees, and peers. These people aren't just coworkers; they can be companions, friends, and sometimes even best friends or lovers. When these relationships are healthy, the effects spread to every part of our lives. We're happier in life and more productive on the job. Those around us find us more pleasant to work with, and the organization as a whole thrives. When it comes to workplace relationships, the professional is profoundly personal.

Through our work, we identify with a community.
Maskot/Getty Images

Dealing with Workplace Abuse

 LaunchPad For the best experience, complete all parts of this activity
in LaunchPad: **launchpadworks.com**

 Background

Workplace relationships and interactions always provide unanticipated challenges. But when supervisors abuse your trust in ways that are difficult to forgive, you must choose between maintaining peer friendships or preserving your own sense of honor. To consider how you might deal with such a situation, read the case study in Part 2; then, drawing on all you know about interpersonal communication, work through the problem-solving model in Part 3.

Visit LaunchPad to watch the video in Part 4 and assess your communication in Part 5.

2 Case Study

You take a job delivering pizzas to help pay for school. The restaurant has a supportive climate—workers are friendly and open. The delivery drivers in particular have a tight clique that they welcome you into, and you quickly become friends with several of them.

The only exception to the warmth of your new workplace is the manager, Elizabeth. She is controlling, manipulative, and dogmatic, and tries to run the restaurant "by the book." The drivers warn you to watch out for her, telling you, "She's really screwed people over before." But you get along with her fairly well because of your exemplary work performance and positive attitude.

The most important workplace rule for drivers is to never leave your money pouch unattended. The money pouch is the zippered bag into which you put all cash from sales. For safety's sake, drivers are supposed to deposit cash after every delivery run, but when things get hectic, drivers often forget—resulting in accumulated cash in the pouches.

One night you're on a run, but when a customer pays you, you discover you're missing your pouch. You hadn't deposited your money all night, and there was over $300 in it.

Arriving back at the store, you tell Elizabeth, and she says, "If it's lost, company policy requires that you cover the missing money from your next paycheck!" This means you're not going to be able to afford next month's rent, much less food and gas! You tear your car and the restaurant apart looking for the pouch, and soon the other drivers are helping you search, offering their support and sympathies. But to no avail: after an hour, the pouch is still missing. Sitting in despair, you begin to cry. Just then, Elizabeth walks up, and with a smirk, hands you your pouch. "You left it unattended on the delivery table earlier, so I hid it, to teach you a lesson!" You're stunned, humiliated, and furious! After months of exemplary work performance, why would she abuse you like that? Your first instinct is to quit in protest, even though you can't afford it. But quitting would hurt the other drivers— who would have to scramble to cover your shifts—and jeopardize your friendships with them. Should you stay, but confront Elizabeth? Or, just suck it up and say nothing? As you're pondering these options, Elizabeth says, "So, what lessons have you learned from this experience?"

3 Your Turn

Consider all you've learned thus far about interpersonal communication. Then work through the following five steps. Remember, there are no "right" answers, so think hard about what is the best choice! (P.S. Need help? See the *Helpful Concepts* list.)

step 1

Reflect on yourself. What are your thoughts and feelings in this situation? What attributions are you making about Elizabeth and her behavior? Are your attributions accurate? Why or why not?

step 2

Reflect on your partner. Using perspective-taking and empathic concern, put yourself in Elizabeth's shoes. Consider how she is thinking and feeling. How does she likely perceive you, and your behavior, in this situation?

step 3

Identify the optimal outcome. Think about all that has happened in this situation. Consider your feelings, those of Elizabeth, and the feelings of the other drivers. Given all these factors, what's the best, most constructive relationship outcome possible here? Be sure to consider not just what's best for *you*, but what's best for everyone else.

step 4

Locate the roadblocks. Taking into consideration your own thoughts and feelings, those of Elizabeth, and all that has happened in this situation, what's preventing you from achieving the optimal outcome?

step 5

Chart your course. What can you say and do to overcome the roadblocks and achieve your relationship outcome?

HELPFUL CONCEPTS

Workplace cliques, **382**
Organizational climate, **383**
Advocacy, **389**
Workplace bullying, **395**

4 The Other Side

Visit LaunchPad to watch a video in which Elizabeth tells her side of the case study story. As in many real-life situations, this is information to which you did not have access when you were initially crafting your response in Part 3. The video reminds us that even when we do our best to offer competent responses, there is always another side to the story that we need to consider.

5 Interpersonal Competence Self-Assessment

After watching the video, visit the Self-Assessment questions in LaunchPad. Think about the new information offered in Elizabeth's side of the story and all you've learned about interpersonal communication. Drawing on this knowledge, revisit your earlier responses in Part 3 and assess your interpersonal communication competence.

POSTSCRIPT

Karin Cooper/Face the Nation/Getty Images News/Getty Images

We began this chapter with the story of an unlikely yet enduring workplace relationship. Despite their vastly different viewpoints, Supreme Court justices Ruth Bader Ginsburg and Antonin Scalia were able to forge a productive collaboration for more than 30 years—and in the process, they became close friends.

Do you have a coworker you can count on to provide helpful insights? Is there someone whose companionship you so enjoy that you delight in spending time with them outside of the workplace as well as within it?

The friendship shared by Ginsburg and Scalia reminds us of the profound significance of workplace relationships and the professional and personal support they provide. But more important, as an aspirational lesson, is the unity the two of them achieved in the face of disagreement. To borrow from the opera written in their honor, when we're bound to others by a common mission—whether it's the preservation of justice or the successful production of quality work for an organization—*we may be different, but we are one.*

 **LaunchPad**

LaunchPad for Reflect & Relate offers videos and encourages self-assessment through adaptive quizzing. Go to **launchpadworks.com** to get access to:

 LearningCurve
Adaptive Quizzes

 Video clips that help you understand interpersonal communication

key terms

workplace relationship, 379
organizational culture, 380
organizational networks, 381
virtual networks, 381
workplace cliques, 382
organizational climate, 383
⊚ defensive climate, 383
⊚ supportive climate, 383
workplace telepressure, 385
⊚ professional peers, 386
virtual peers, 387
mixed-status relationships, 388
⊚ upward communication, 389
⊚ advocacy, 390
⊚ downward communication, 391
workplace bullying, 395
sexual harassment, 400

⊚ You can watch brief, illustrative videos of these terms and test your understanding of the concepts in LaunchPad.

key concepts

The Nature of Workplace Relationships

- Our **workplace relationships** are shaped by many forces. Two of the most powerful are **organizational culture** and **organizational networks**. Most workers learn their organization's culture during new employee socialization and by interacting with members of various networks.

- Organizational networks are the principal source of workplace information for most employees. **Virtual networks** also exist, particularly for workers who telecommute from home.

- When members of networks share common beliefs and personal values, they sometimes form **workplace cliques**. Cliques can provide useful insider information to new employees, but they can also be disruptive.

- The overall emotional tone of your organization, known as the **organizational climate**, can be rigid and cold in a **defensive climate**, open and warm in a **supportive climate**, or somewhere in between.

Peer Relationships

- Our closest workplace relationships are with our **professional peers**. Friendships between peers evolve from frequent interaction and common interests. The same is true for **virtual peers**.

Mixed-Status Relationships

- The primary interpersonal dynamic in **mixed-status relationships** is power. The difference in power makes forming friendships across status lines challenging.

- Much of **upward communication** is designed to gain influence. Although people use different tactics, the most effective is **advocacy**—designing a message that is specifically tailored to the viewpoints of your superior.

- When engaging in **downward communication**, it's important to communicate in positive, empathic, respectful, and open ways.

Challenges to Workplace Relationships

- **Workplace bullying** can occur in a variety of ways, including cyberbullying. Such bullying affects the target's physical and psychological health.

- Even though romances in the workplace are common, they offer both positives and challenges.

- **Sexual harassment** has devastating effects on victims.

acceptance: (p. 105) Your allowing emotions to naturally arise without damping or fanning them, and acknowledging that they are an inherent component of human nature, neither good nor bad.

accommodation: (p. 266) A way of handling conflict in which one person abandons their goals for the goals of another. For example, Louis gives in to Martel over where they should park their cars: "You can have the driveway. I'm tired of arguing about it."

actor-observer effect: (p. 68) A tendency to credit external forces as causes for our behaviors instead of internal factors. For instance, Leon says he snapped at a coworker because she was slow instead of blaming his own impatience.

adaptors: (p. 238) Touching gestures, often unconsciously made, that serve a physical or psychological purpose. For example, twirling hair while reading, jingling pocket change, and fingering jewelry may be gestures that provide comfort, signal anxiety, or are simply unconscious habits.

advocacy: (p. 390) Communication from a subordinate intended to influence a superior in an organization. For example, you convince your manager to try a new product line.

affect displays: (p. 246) Intentional or unintentional nonverbal behaviors that reveal actual or feigned emotions, such as a frown, a choked sob, or a smile intended to disguise fear.

agentic friendships: (p. 356) Friendships in which the parties are primarily focused on helping each other achieve practical goals, such as those among peers in a study group or colleagues at work.

aggressive-hostile touch: (p. 241) A touch designed to hurt and humiliate others, involving forms of physical violence like grabbing, slapping, and hitting.

aggressive listening: (p. 194) Listening in order to find an opportunity to attack or collect information to use against the speaker, such as when a father encourages his son to describe his ambitions just to ridicule the son's goals. (Also known as *ambushing*.)

algebraic impressions: (p. 78) Impressions of others that continually change as we add and subtract positive or negative information that we learn about them.

analytical listeners: (p. 189) Listeners who prefer to withhold their judgment until they have considered all the facts and sides of an issue.

anger: (p. 107) The negative primary emotion that occurs when you are blocked or interrupted from attaining an important goal by what you see as the improper action of an external agent.

appropriateness: (p. 15) A measure of communication competence that indicates the degree to which your communication matches the situational, relational, and cultural expectations regarding how people should communicate.

artifacts: (p. 244) Things we possess that influence how we see ourselves and that we use to express our identity to others. Jewelry, for instance, can indicate economic means, marital status, religious affiliation, style preferences, and taste.

attending: (p. 178) The second stage of the listening process in which a listener devotes attention to received information. For example, you may *hear* a radio but *attend* only when a favorite song comes on.

attention focus: (p. 105) Preventing unwanted emotions by intentionally devoting your attention only to aspects of an event or encounter that you know will not provoke those emotions. For example, you disregard your uncle's snide comments while forcing all your interest on your aunt's conversation.

attributional complexity: (p. 139) Acknowledging that other people's behaviors have complex causes that may reflect cultural differences.

attributions: (p. 65) Rationales we create to explain the comments or behaviors of others. For example, Ryan reasons that Jason's quietness in class means that Jason is shy.

avoidance: (p. 265) A way of handling conflict by ignoring it, pretending it isn't really happening, or communicating indirectly about the situation. For example, Martel hides behind the newspaper as Louis shouts, "Your car is blocking mine again. How many times do I have to ask you to park it to the side?" See also **skirting; sniping**.

avoiding: (p. 300) A relational stage in which one or both individuals in a couple try to distance themselves from each other physically. For example, Owen changes jobs to have an excuse to travel away from home frequently.

back-channel cues: (p. 182) Nonverbal and verbal responses that signal you've paid attention to and understood specific comments—for example, saying "Okay, got it" after someone details extensive driving directions, or nodding in agreement.

beautiful-is-good effect: (p. 293) A tendency for physical attractiveness to create the perception of competency and intelligence. For example, a witness is viewed favorably and seems credible because she is good-looking.

birds-of-a-feather effect: (p. 293) A tendency to be attracted to others if we perceive them as similar to ourselves.

blended emotions: (p. 98) Two or more primary emotions experienced at the same time. For instance, Melinda feels fear and anger when her daughter is not home by curfew.

bonding: (p. 298) A relational stage in which an official public ritual unites two people by the laws or customs of their culture. For example, Ruth marries Owen in her hometown church.

chilling effect: (p. 278) An outcome of physical violence in which individuals stop discussing relationship issues out of fear of their partner's negative reactions.

chronic hostility: (p. 107) A persistent state of simmering or barely suppressed anger and near-constant state of arousal and negative thinking.

circumscribing: (p. 300) A relational stage in which partners avoid talking about topics that produce conflict. For instance, whenever Owen mentions he's interested in moving, Ruth becomes upset and changes the subject.

co-cultural communication: (p. 126) A type of communication that members of co-cultures may engage in to assimilate into the dominant culture, get the dominant culture to accommodate their co-cultural identity, or separate themselves from it entirely.

Co-cultural Communication Theory: (p. 125) A theory that the people who have more power within a society determine the dominant culture.

co-cultures: (p. 126) Members of a society who don't conform to the dominant culture in terms of language, lifestyle, or even physical appearance.

cohabiting couples: (p. 327) Two unmarried adults who are involved romantically and live together with or without children.

collaboration: (p. 268) A way of handling conflict by treating it as a mutual problem-solving challenge. For example, Martel and Louis brainstorm ways to solve the problem they have with their shared parking area until they come up with an agreeable solution.

collectivistic cultures: (p. 131) Cultures that emphasize group identity, interpersonal harmony, and the well-being of ingroups. Collectivist cultures also value the importance of belonging to groups that look after members in exchange for loyalty. Contrast **individualistic cultures**.

commitment: (p. 290) A strong psychological attachment to a partner and an intention to continue the relationship long into the future.

communal friendships: (p. 355) Voluntary relationships focused on sharing time and activities together.

communication: (p. 3) The process through which people use messages to generate meanings within and across contexts, cultures, channels, and media.

communication accommodation theory: (p. 139) The idea that people are especially motivated to adapt their language when they seek social approval, wish to establish relationships with others, and view others' language use as appropriate.

communication apprehension: (p. 222) The fear or anxiety associated with interaction that keeps someone from being able to communicate cooperatively.

communication plans: (p. 222) Mental maps that describe exactly how communication encounters will unfold. For example, before calling to complain about her telephone bill, Marjorie mentally rehearses how she will explain her problem and what objections she might face.

Communication Privacy Management Theory: (p. 338) The idea that individuals create informational boundaries by choosing carefully the kind of private information they reveal and the people with whom they share it.

communication skills: (p. 15) Repeatable goal-directed behaviors and behavioral patterns that enable you to improve the quality of your interpersonal encounters and relationships. See also **appropriateness**.

companionate love: (p. 288) An intense form of liking defined by emotional investment and deeply intertwined lives.

competition: (p. 267) A way of handling conflict by an open and clear discussion of the goal clash that exists and the pursuit of one's own goals without regard for others' goals. For example, Martel and Louis yell back and forth about whose car should have the driveway parking spot and whose should be parked out front.

complementary relationships: (p. 261) Relationships characterized by an unequal balance of power, such as a marriage in which one spouse is the decision maker.

compromise: (p. 273) When, during a conflict, both parties change their goals to make them compatible. For example, though Matt wants to see the sci-fi thriller and Jane wants to see the new animated film, they agree to go to an adventure comedy.

conflict: (p. 257) The process that occurs when people perceive that they have incompatible goals or that someone is interfering in their ability to achieve their objectives.

conformity orientation: (p. 332) The degree to which family members believe communication should emphasize similarity or diversity in attitudes, beliefs, and values.

connotative meaning: (p. 208) Understanding of a word's meaning based on the situation and the shared knowledge between communication partners (i.e., not the dictionary definition). For instance, calling someone *slender* suggests something more positive than the word *skinny* or *scrawny* does, though all three words mean "underweight." Contrast **denotative meaning**.

consensual families: (p. 332) Families characterized by high levels of conformity and conversation orientation. For example, Dan's parents encourage their son to be open but also expect him to maintain family unity through agreement or obedience.

constitutive rules: (p. 203) Guidelines that define word meaning according to a particular language's vocabulary. For instance, "pencil" is *Bleistift* in German and *matita* in Italian.

contexts: (p. 4) Situations in which communication occurs. Context includes the physical locations, backgrounds, genders, ages, moods, and relationships of the communicators, as well as the time of day.

conversation orientation: (p. 331) The degree to which family members are encouraged to participate in unrestrained interaction about a wide array of topics.

Cooperative Principle: (p. 214) The idea that we should make our verbal messages as informative, honest, relevant, and clear as is required, given what the situation requires. For example, listening closely to your friend's problem with a coworker and then responding with support would demonstrate the Cooperative Principle; interrupting your friend to brag about your new laptop would not.

cooperative verbal communication: (p. 214) Producing messages that are understandable, taking active ownership for what you're saying by using "I" language, and making others feel included.

critical listeners: (p. 189) Listeners who focus their attention on the accuracy and consistency of what another person says.

cross-category friendships: (p. 356) Voluntary relationships that cross demographic lines.

culture: (p. 123) The established, coherent set of beliefs, attitudes, values, and practices shared by a large group of people.

cumulative annoyance: (p. 266) A buildup of repressed irritations that grows as the mental list of grievances we have against our partner grows. For example, Martel's anger about where Louis parks his car is a reaction to several other incidents in which Louis was inconsiderate.

deactivation: (p. 105) Preventing unwanted emotions by systematically desensitizing yourself to emotional experience. For example, Josh insulates himself with numbness after his wife's death.

deception: (p. 220) Deliberately using uninformative, untruthful, irrelevant, or vague language for the purpose of misleading others.

defensive climate: (p. 383) A workplace atmosphere that is unfriendly, rigid, or unsupportive of workers' professional and personal needs. Contrast **supportive climate**.

defensive communication: (p. 221) Impolite messages delivered in response to suggestions, criticism, or perceived slights. For instance, when Stacy asks Lena to slow down her driving, Lena snaps back, "I'm not going that fast. If you don't like the way I drive, ride with someone else."

demand-withdraw pattern: (p. 277) A way of handling conflict in which one partner in a relationship demands that their goals be met, and the other partner responds by withdrawing from the encounter.

denotative meaning: (p. 207) The literal, or dictionary, definition of a word. Contrast **connotative meaning**.

dialects: (p. 205) Variations on language rules shared by large groups or particular regions; this may include differences in vocabulary, grammar, and pronunciation. For example, in various regions of the United States, carbonated beverages are called *soda*, *pop*, or *Coke*.

differentiating: (p. 300) A relational stage in which the beliefs, attitudes, and values that distinguish you from your partner come to dominate your thoughts and communication. For example, Ruth and Owen argue over whose family they are going to visit for Thanksgiving and how much time each has spent fixing up the house.

dirty secrets: (p. 276) Truthful but destructive messages used deliberately to hurt someone during a conflict. For example, Judith tells her sister, "That boy you like—Craig? I heard him tell Elaine you laugh like a horse."

dismissive attachment: (p. 40) An attachment style in which individuals have low anxiety but high avoidance: they view close relationships as comparatively unimportant, instead prizing self-reliance.

display rules: (p. 134) Cultural norms about how people should and should not express emotion—that is, guidelines for when, where, and how to manage emotion displays appropriately. This includes specific aspects of nonverbal communication—how broadly you should smile, the appropriateness of shouting for joy in public, and so on.

domination: (p. 272) When one person gets their way in a conflict by influencing the other to engage in accommodation and abandon goals. For example, Jane wants to see the new animated film, but Matt refuses by saying that it is either his choice or no movie at all.

downward communication: (p. 391) Messages from a superior to subordinates. For example, the CEO of a company calls the regional managers together for a strategy session. Contrast **upward communication**.

dyadic: (p. 8) Communication involving only two people.

Dyadic Power Theory: (p. 261) The idea that people with only moderate power are most likely to use controlling communication.

eavesdropping: (p. 193) Intentionally listening in on private conversations.

effectiveness: (p. 16) The ability to use communication to accomplish interpersonal goals.

embarrassment: (p. 43) A feeling of shame, humiliation, and sadness that comes from losing face.

emblems: (p. 238) Gestures that symbolize a specific verbal meaning within a given culture, such as the "thumbs up" or the "V for victory" sign.

emotion: (p. 93) An intense reaction to an event that involves interpreting the meaning of the event, becoming physiologically aroused, labeling the experience as emotional, attempting to manage your reaction, and communicating this reaction in the form of emotional displays and disclosures.

emotional contagion: (p. 94) The rapid spreading of emotion from person to person, such as anger running through a mob.

emotional intelligence: (p. 102) The ability to accurately interpret your and others' emotions and use this information to manage emotions, communicate them competently, and solve relationship problems.

emotion management: (p. 104) Attempts to influence which emotions you have, when you have them, and how you experience and express them.

emotion-sharing: (p. 94) Disclosing your emotions to others.

empathy: (p. 81) Understanding of another person's perspective and awareness of their feelings in an attempt to identify with them. For instance, Gill doesn't agree with Mike's protest against the new policies at work, but he can see why Mike is worried and angry.

empathy mindset: (p. 82) Beliefs about whether empathy is something that can be developed and controlled.

encounter avoidance: (p. 105) Preventing unwanted emotions by keeping away from people, places, and activities likely to provoke them. For example, Jessica infuriates Roxanne, so Roxanne moves out of their shared apartment.

encounter structuring: (p. 105) Preventing unwanted emotions by intentionally avoiding discussion of difficult topics in encounters with others. For instance, Natalie and Julie avoid talking about living expenses because Natalie is jealous of Julie's income.

environment: (p. 244) A nonverbal code that represents the physical features of our surroundings.

equity: (p. 294) The balance of benefits and costs exchanged by you and the other person that determines whether a romantic relationship will take root (after attraction is established).

escalation: (p. 267) A dramatic rise in emotional intensity and increasingly negative communication during conflict, such as teasing that inflates to a heated exchange of insults.

ethics: (p. 17) The set of moral principles that guide our behavior toward others. Ethical communication consistently displays respect, kindness, and compassion.

ethnocentrism: (p. 139) The belief that your own culture's beliefs, attitudes, values, and practices are superior to those of all other cultures. For example, Americans, accustomed to lining up, who consider cultures that don't use waiting lines to be disorganized are displaying ethnocentrism. Contrast **world-mindedness**.

experimenting: (p. 298) A relational stage in which two people become acquainted by sharing factual or demographic information about themselves and making light conversation or small talk. For instance, after Ruth is introduced to Owen, they talk about their jobs and where they went to school, and they discover they both like jazz.

expertise currency: (p. 263) Power that comes from possessing specialized skills or knowledge, such as being able to use CPR if someone stops breathing.

extended family: (p. 327) A family type consisting of a group of people who are related to one another—such as aunts, uncles, cousins, or grandparents—and who live in the same household.

face: (p. 42) The self we allow others to see and know; the aspects of ourselves we choose to present publicly. For instance, you dress up and speak carefully for an important social occasion, though in private you're very casual.

family: (p. 325) A network of people who share their lives over long periods of time and are bound by marriage, blood, or commitment; who consider themselves as family; and who share a significant history and anticipated future of functioning in a family relationship.

family communication patterns: (p. 331) Interpersonal communication behaviors that reflect beliefs about how families should converse.

family privacy rules: (p. 339) The conditions governing what family members can talk about, how they can discuss such topics, and who should have access to family-relevant information.

family stories: (p. 328) Narratives of family events retold to bond family members. For example, Katie's mother often recounts how Katie was born on the day of a crippling blizzard.

fearful attachment: (p. 40) An attachment style in which individuals are high in both attachment anxiety and avoidance: they fear rejection and thus shun relationships, preferring to avoid the pain they believe is an inevitable part of intimacy.

feedback: (pp. 6, 182) Verbal and nonverbal messages that receivers use to indicate their reaction to communication, such as a frown or saying, "I disagree." See also **interactive communication model**.

feelings: (p. 95) Short-term emotional reactions to events that generate only limited arousal, such as the fleeting nostalgia you experience hearing a familiar song.

feminine cultural values: (p. 136) Values that emphasize compassion and cooperation—on caring for the weak and underprivileged and boosting the quality of life for all people.

fields of experience: (p. 6) Beliefs, attitudes, values, and experiences that each communicator brings to an interaction.

friendship: (p. 353) A voluntary relationship characterized by intimacy and liking.

friendship rules: (p. 362) General principles for appropriate communication and behavior within friendships, such as keeping a confidence and showing support.

friendship-warmth touch: (p. 241) A touch used to express liking for another person, such as an arm across another's shoulders, a victory slap between teammates, or playful jostling between friends.

functional-professional touch: (p. 241) A touch used to accomplish a task, such as a physical therapist positioning a client's arm or a dancer gripping his partner's waist for a lift.

fundamental attribution error: (p. 67) The tendency to attribute someone's behavior solely to their personality rather than to outside forces.

FWB relationships: (p. 370) Friendships negotiated to include sexual activity but not with the purpose of transforming the relationship into a romantic attachment.

gender: (pp. 20, 152) The composite of social, psychological, and cultural attributes generally associated with one sex or another.

gender fluid: (p. 150) A type of gender identity in which an individual does not identify as being either male or female, and their leanings toward one gender or another may fluctuate. See also **genderqueeer**.

gender identity: (p. 150) An individual's inner sense of being male, female, or an alternative gender.

gender polarization: (p. 149) A way of viewing and understanding gender which emphasizes a binary male-female construction of gender.

genderqueer: (p. 150) A type of gender identity in which an individual does not identify as being either male or female, and their leanings toward one gender or another may fluctuate. See also **gender fluid**.

gender roles: (p. 157) The shared expectations for conduct and behaviors that are deemed appropriate for men and women as taught by society. These roles tend to be rigid and further adhere to a binary structure.

Gestalt: (p. 76) A general sense of a person that's either positive or negative. See also **halo effect; horn effect**.

grief: (p. 111) Intense sadness that follows a substantial loss (such as the death of a loved one).

halo effect: (p. 77) A tendency to interpret anything another person says or does in a favorable light because you have a positive Gestalt of that person.

haptics: (p. 240) A nonverbal code that represents messages conveyed through touch. See also **friendship-warmth touch; functional-professional touch; love-intimacy touch; sexual-arousal touch; social-polite touch; aggressive-hostile touch**.

hearing: (p. 178) The sensory process of taking in and interpreting sound.

high-context cultures: (p. 133) Cultures that presume listeners share their viewpoints. People in such cultures talk indirectly, using hints to convey meaning. Vague, ambiguous language—and even silence—is often used, the presumption being that because individuals share the same contextual view, they automatically know what another person is trying to say. Contrast **low-context cultures**.

honesty: (p. 215) Truthful communication, without exaggeration or omission of relevant information. Failing to tell someone something can be as dishonest as an outright lie.

horn effect: (p. 78) A tendency to interpret anything another person says or does in a negative light because you have a negative Gestalt of that person.

identity support: (p. 360) Behaving in ways that convey understanding, acceptance, and support for a friend's valued social identities.

I-It: (p. 9) A type of perception and communication that occurs when you treat others as though they are objects that are there for your use and exploitation—for example, when you dismiss someone by saying, "I don't have time for your stupid questions. Figure it out yourself."

"I" language: (p. 216) Communication that uses the pronoun *I* in sentence construction to emphasize ownership of one's feelings, opinions, and beliefs—for example, "I'm frustrated because I think I'm doing more than you are on this project" instead of "You're really underperforming on this project." See also **"we" language; "you" language**.

illustrators: (p. 238) Gestures used to accent or illustrate a verbal message. For example, a fisherman holds his hands apart to show the size of his catch, or someone points emphatically at a door while saying, "Leave!"

immediacy: (p. 238) As expressed in your posture, the degree to which you find someone interesting and attractive.

impersonal communication: (p. 8) Messages that have negligible perceived impact on your thoughts, emotions, behaviors, or relationships, such as commenting about the television schedule or passing someone and saying, "How's it going?" without looking up.

implicit personality theories: (p. 75) Personal beliefs about different types of personalities and the ways in which traits cluster together. For instance, Bradley assumes that Will is a disorganized procrastinator because of Will's casual, friendly manner.

individualistic cultures: (p. 131) Cultures that value independence and personal achievement; individual goals over group or societal goals. Contrast **collectivistic cultures**.

ingroupers: (p. 70) People you consider fundamentally similar to yourself because of their interests, affiliations, or backgrounds. Contrast **outgroupers**.

initiating: (p. 297) A relational stage in which two people meet and form their first impressions of each other. For instance, Owen introduces himself in an email to Ruth after reading her profile on an online dating site, and she responds with her telephone number.

instrumental goals: (p. 14) Practical aims you want to achieve or tasks you want to accomplish through a particular interpersonal encounter.

integrating: (p. 298) A relational stage in which two people become a couple and begin to share an identity. For example, Ruth and Owen share an apartment together and spend time with each other's families.

integrative agreements: (p. 273) When, during a conflict, the two sides preserve and attain their goals by developing a creative solution to their problem. For example, because Matt and Jane can't agree on what film to see, they decide they'd both be happier going to a comedy club.

intensifying: (p. 298) A relational stage characterized by deeper self-disclosures, stronger attraction, and intimate communication. For example, Owen and Ruth have been dating for more than a year and talk with excitement about a future together.

interaction: (p. 4) A series of messages exchanged between people, whether face-to-face or online.

interactive communication model: (p. 5) A depiction of communication messages that are exchanged back and forth between a sender and a receiver and are influenced by feedback and the fields of experience of both communicators.

intercultural communication: (p. 24) The communication we engage in when we communicate with those belonging to a different culture.

intercultural competence: (p. 138) The ability to communicate appropriately, effectively, and ethically with people from diverse backgrounds.

interparental conflict: (p. 344) Overt, hostile interactions between parents in a household.

interpersonal communication: (p. 8) A dynamic form of communication between two (or more) people in which the messages exchanged significantly influence their thoughts, emotions, behaviors, and relationships.

interpersonal impressions: (p. 75) Ideas about who people are and how we feel about them. For instance, when Sarah and Georgia met, Georgia thought Sarah was unfriendly and conceited because she didn't say much.

interpersonal process model of intimacy: (p. 45) The idea that the closeness we feel toward others in our relationships is created through two things: self-disclosure and responsiveness of listeners to such disclosure.

interpretation: (p. 65) The stage of perception in which we assign meaning to the information we have selected. For instance, Randy thinks a man running down the

sidewalk hurries because he is late, but Shondra infers that the man is chasing someone.

intersectionality: (p. 128) Term coined by scholar Kimberlé Crenshaw to describe overlapping forms of oppression "greater than the sum of racism and sexism" (1989).

intimacy: (pp. 49, 248) A feeling of closeness and "union" that exists between us and our relationship partners.

intimacy currency: (p. 263) Power that comes from sharing a close bond with someone that no one else shares. For example, you can easily persuade a close friend to change her mind because she is fond of you.

intimate space: (p. 241) The narrowest proxemic zone—0 to 18 inches of space—between communicators.

intrapersonal communication: (p. 8) Communication involving only one person, such as talking to yourself.

I-Thou: (p. 9) A way to perceive a relationship based on embracing fundamental similarities that connect you to others, striving to see things from others' points of view, and communicating in ways that emphasize honesty and kindness.

jealousy: (pp. 98, 313) A protective reaction to a perceived threat to a valued relationship. For instance, Tyler is jealous when his girlfriend, Mary, flirts with Scott.

Jefferson strategy: (p. 108) A strategy to manage anger that involves counting slowly to 10 before responding to someone who says or does something that makes you angry. (The strategy was named after the third president of the United States.)

kinesics: (p. 237) A nonverbal code that represents messages communicated in visible body movements, such as facial expressions, body postures, gestures, and eye contact.

kitchen-sinking: (p. 259) A response to a conflict in which combatants hurl insults and accusations at each other that have very little to do with the original disagreement. For example, although Mary and Pat are arguing about the budget, Mary adds, "I'm sick of the mess you left in the garage and these papers all over the family room."

laissez-faire families: (p. 333) Families characterized by low levels of conformity and conversation orientation. For example, Samantha's parents prefer limited communication and encourage their daughter to make her own choices and decisions.

liking: (p. 287) A feeling of affection and respect typical of friendship.

linear communication model: (p. 5) A depiction of communication messages that flow in one direction from a starting point to an end point.

linguistic determinism: (p. 208) The view that the language we use defines the boundaries of our thinking.

linguistic relativity: (p. 209) The theory that languages create variations in the ways cultures perceive and think about the world.

listening: (p. 177) The five-stage process of receiving, attending to, understanding, responding to, and recalling sounds and visual images during interpersonal encounters.

listening functions: (p. 185) The five general purposes that listening serves: to comprehend, to discern, to analyze, to appreciate, and to support.

listening styles: (p. 189) Habitual patterns of listening behaviors, which reflect one's attitudes, beliefs, and predispositions about listening. See also **analytical listeners; critical listeners; relational listeners; task-oriented listeners.**

long-term memory: (p. 181) The part of your mind devoted to permanent information storage.

looking-glass self: (p. 33) Sociologist Charles Horton Cooley's idea that we define our self-concepts through thinking about how others see us. For example, a young girl who believes that others consider her poor in sports formulates an image of herself as uncoordinated even though she is a good dancer.

love-intimacy touch: (p. 241) A touch indicating deep emotional feeling, such as two romantic partners holding hands or two close friends embracing.

loving: (p. 287) An intense emotional commitment based on intimacy, caring, and attachment.

low-context cultures: (p. 134) Cultures in which people tend not to presume that others share their beliefs, attitudes, and values. They strive to be informative, clear, and direct in their communication. In such cultures, people make important information obvious, rather than hinting or implying. Contrast **high-context cultures.**

masculine cultural values: (p. 136) Values that include the accumulation of material wealth as an indicator of success, assertiveness, and personal achievement.

mask: (p. 42) The public self designed to strategically veil your private self—for example, putting on a happy face when you are sad or pretending to be confident while inside you feel shy or anxious.

matching: (p. 293) A tendency to be attracted to others whom we perceive to be at our own level of attractiveness. For example, Michael dates Jennifer because she is pretty but not unapproachably gorgeous.

mediated listening: (p. 188) Receiving, attending to, understanding, responding to, and recalling sounds and visual images through mediated, electronic, and social media channels.

mental bracketing: (p. 181) Systematically putting aside thoughts that aren't relevant to the interaction at hand if your attention wanders when listening—for example, by consciously dismissing your worries about an upcoming exam in order to focus on a customer's request at work.

mere exposure effect: (p. 292) A phenomenon in which you feel more attracted to those with whom you have frequent contact and less attracted to those with whom you interact rarely. For example, the more June sees of Tom, the more attracted to him she becomes.

message: (p. 4) The package of information transported during communication.

meta-communication: (p. 11) Verbal or nonverbal communication about communication—that is, messages that have communication as their central focus.

microaggressions: (p. 219) Communication stressors that negatively affect others, directed toward people who are members of underrepresented groups.

misunderstanding: (p. 215) Confusion resulting from the misperception of another's thoughts, feelings, or beliefs as expressed in the other individual's verbal communication.

mixed messages: (p. 232) Verbal and nonverbal behaviors that convey contradictory meanings, such as saying "I'm so happy for you" in a sarcastic tone of voice.

mixed-status relationships: (p. 388) Associations between coworkers at different levels of power and status in an organization, such as a manager and a salesclerk.

mnemonics: (p. 184) Devices that aid memory. For example, the mnemonic *Roy G. Biv* is commonly used to recall the order of the seven colors in the rainbow.

modalities: (p. 4) Forms of communication used for exchanging messages.

monochronic time orientation: (p. 137) A view of time as a precious resource that can be saved, spent, wasted, lost, or made up, and that can even run out. Contrast **polychronic time orientation.**

moods: (p. 95) Low-intensity states of mind that are not caused by particular events and typically last longer than emotions—for example, boredom, contentment, grouchiness, serenity.

naming: (p. 209) Creating linguistic symbols to represent people, objects, places, and ideas.

narcissistic listening: (p. 195) A self-absorbed approach to listening in which the listener redirects the conversation to their own interests. For example, Neil acts bored while Jack describes a recent ski trip, interrupting Jack and switching the topic to his own recent car purchase.

negativity effect: (p. 77) A tendency to place emphasis on the negative information we learn about others.

noise: (p. 5) Environmental factors that impede a message on the way to its destination.

nonbinary: (p. 150) A type of gender identity in which an individual does not identify with a dualistic distinction of gender as either man/male or woman/female.

nonverbal communication: (p. 231) The intentional or unintentional transmission of meaning through an individual's nonspoken physical and behavioral cues.

nonverbal communication codes: (p. 236) Different ways to transmit information nonverbally: artifacts, chronemics, environment, haptics, kinesics, physical appearance, proxemics, and vocalics.

nuclear family: (p. 327) A family type consisting of a wife, a husband, and their biological or adopted children.

organization: (p. 64) The step of perception in which we mentally structure selected sensory data into a coherent pattern.

organizational climate: (p. 383) The overarching emotional quality of a workplace environment. For example, employees might say their organization feels warm, frenetic, unfriendly, or serene.

organizational culture: (p. 380) A distinct set of beliefs about how things should be done and how people should behave.

organizational networks: (p. 381) Communication links among an organization's members, such as the nature, frequency, and ways information is exchanged. For example, you have weekly face-to-face status meetings with your boss or receive daily reminder emails from an assistant.

outgroupers: (p. 70) People you consider fundamentally different from you because of their interests, affiliations, or backgrounds. Contrast **ingroupers**.

paraphrasing: (p. 183) An active listening response that summarizes or restates others' comments after they have finished speaking.

parental favoritism: (p. 342) When one or both parents allocate an unfair amount of valuable resources to one child over others.

passion: (p. 110) A blended emotion of joy and surprise coupled with other positive feelings, such as excitement, amazement, and sexual attraction.

passionate love: (p. 287) A state of intense emotional and physical longing for union with another.

perception: (p. 63) The process of selecting, organizing, and interpreting information from our senses.

perception-checking: (p. 83) A five-step process to test your impressions of others and to avoid errors in judgment. It involves checking your punctuation, knowledge, attributions, perceptual influences, and impressions.

personal currency: (p. 263) Power that comes from personal characteristics that others admire, such as intelligence, physical beauty, charm, communication skill, or humor.

personal idioms: (p. 204) Words and phrases that have unique meanings to a particular relationship, such as pet names or private phrases with special meaning. For example, Uncle Henry was known for his practical jokes; now, years after his death, family members still refer to a practical joke as "pulling a Henry."

personality: (p. 73) An individual's characteristic way of thinking, feeling, and acting based on the traits they possess.

personal space: (p. 241) The proxemic zone that ranges from 18 inches to 4 feet of space between communicators. It is the spatial separation most often used in the United States for friendly conversation.

phubbing: (p. 16) Ignoring conversational partners during interactions by focusing instead on one's phone.

physical appearance: (p. 243) A nonverbal code that represents visual attributes such as body type, clothing, hair, and other physical features.

pluralistic families: (p. 332) Families characterized by low levels of conformity and high levels of conversation orientation. For example, Julie's parents encourage her to express herself freely, and when conflicts arise, they collaborate with her to resolve them.

polychronic time orientation: (p. 137) A flexible view of time in which harmonious interaction with others is more important than being on time or sticking to a schedule. Contrast **monochronic time orientation**.

positivity bias: (p. 77) A tendency for first impressions of others to be more positive than negative.

power: (pp. 238, 260) The ability to influence or control events and people.

power currency: (p. 262) Control over a resource that other people value. See also **expertise currency; intimacy currency; personal currency; resource currency; social network currency**.

power distance: (p. 132) The degree to which people in a culture view the unequal distribution of power as acceptable. For example, in some cultures, well-defined class distinctions limit interaction across class lines, but other cultures downplay status and privilege to foster a spirit of equality.

prejudice: (p. 128) A combination of negative beliefs, negative emotions, and a predisposition to behave negatively toward specific groups and their members.

preoccupied attachment: (p. 40) An attachment style in which individuals are high in anxiety and low in avoidance; they desire closeness but are plagued with fear of rejection.

primary emotions: (p. 98) Six emotions that involve unique and consistent behavioral displays across cultures: anger, disgust, fear, joy, sadness, and surprise.

professional peers: (p. 386) People who hold jobs at the same level of power and status as your own.

protective families: (p. 333) Families characterized by high levels of conformity and low levels of conversation orientation. For example, Brian's parents expect their son to be respectful, and they discourage family discussions.

proxemics: (p. 241) A nonverbal code for communication through physical distance. See also **intimate space; personal space; public space; social space**.

pseudo-conflict: (p. 266) A mistaken perception that a conflict exists when it doesn't. For example, Barbara thinks Anne is angry with her because Anne hasn't spoken to her all evening, but Anne is actually worried about a report from her physician.

pseudo-listening: (p. 193) Pretending to listen while preoccupied or bored.

public space: (p. 243) The widest proxemic zone. It ranges outward from 12 feet and is most appropriate for formal settings.

punctuation: (p. 64) A step during organization when you structure information you've selected into a chronological sequence that matches how you experienced the order of events. For example, Bobby claims his sister started the backseat argument, but she insists that he poked her first.

Rational Emotive Behavior Therapy (REBT): (p. 101) A therapy developed by psychologist Albert Ellis that helps neurotic patients systematically purge themselves of the tendency to think negative thoughts about themselves.

reactivity: (p. 267) A way of handling conflict by not pursuing conflict-related goals at all and communicating in an emotionally explosive and negative fashion instead.

reappraisal: (p. 105) Actively changing how you think about the meaning of emotion-eliciting situations so that their emotional impact is changed. For instance, though previously fearful of giving a speech, Luke reduces his anxiety by repeating positive affirmations and getting excited about the chance to share what he knows.

recalling: (p. 184) The fifth stage of the listening process in which a listener is able to remember information after it's received, attended to, understood, and responded to.

receiver: (p. 5) The individual for whom a message is intended or to whom it is delivered.

receiving: (p. 178) The first stage of the listening process in which a listener takes in information by seeing and hearing.

reciprocal liking: (p. 294) When the person we're attracted to makes it clear, through communication and other actions, that the attraction is mutual.

regulative rules: (p. 204) Guidelines that govern how we use language when we verbally communicate—that is, spelling and grammar as well as conversational usage. For example, we know how to respond correctly to a greeting, and we know that cursing in public is inappropriate.

regulators: (p. 238) Gestures used to control the exchange of conversational turns during interpersonal encounters—for example, averting eyes to avoid someone, or zipping up book bags as a class to signal to a professor that the lecture should end.

relational dialectics: (pp. 291, 337) Opposing tensions between ourselves and our feelings toward others that exist in interpersonal relationships, such as the tension between wishing to be completely honest with a partner yet not wanting to be hurtful.

relational intrusion: (p. 314) The violation of one's independence and privacy by a person who desires an intimate relationship.

relational listeners: (p. 189) People who view listening as an opportunity to build and maintain relationships with others.

relational maintenance: (p. 302) Communication and supportive behaviors partners use to sustain a desired relationship. They may show devotion by making time to talk, spending time together, and offering help or support to each other.

relationship goals: (p. 14) Goals of building, maintaining, or terminating relationships with others through interpersonal communication.

resource currency: (p. 262) Power that comes from controlling material items others want or need, such as money, food, or property.

resources for doing gender: (p. 154) Situations created by society, such as public restrooms, which teach differences by separating us according to a binary male-female construction of gender.

responding: (p. 182) The fourth stage of the listening process in which a listener communicates their attention and understanding—for example, by nodding or murmuring agreement.

romantic betrayal: (p. 310) An act that goes against expectations of a romantic relationship and, as a result, causes pain to a partner.

romantic relationship: (p. 289) An interpersonal involvement two people choose to enter into that is perceived as romantic by both. For instance, Louise is in love with Robert, and Robert returns her affections.

salience: (p. 64) The degree to which particular people or aspects of their communication attract our attention.

schemata: (p. 65) Mental structures that contain information defining the characteristics of various concepts (such as people, places, events), as well as how those characteristics are related to one another. We often use schemata when interpreting interpersonal communication. When Charlie describes his home as "retro," Amanda visualizes it before she even sees it.

secure attachment: (p. 39) An attachment style in which individuals are low on both anxiety and avoidance; they are comfortable with intimacy and seek close ties with others.

selection: (p. 64) The first step of perception in which we focus our attention on specific sensory data, such as sights, sounds, tastes, touches, or smells.

selective listening: (p. 192) Listening that takes in only those parts of a message that are immediately salient during an interpersonal encounter and dismisses the rest.

self: (p. 31) The evolving composite of who one is, including self-awareness, self-concept, and self-esteem.

self-awareness: (p. 31) The ability to view yourself as a unique person distinct from your surrounding environment and reflect on your thoughts, feelings, and behaviors.

self-concept: (p. 32) Your overall idea of who you are based on the beliefs, attitudes, and values you have about yourself.

self-concept clarity: (p. 33) The degree to which you have a clearly defined, consistent, and enduring sense of self.

self-disclosure: (p. 44) Revealing private information about yourself to others.

self-discrepancy theory: (p. 34) The idea that your self-esteem results from comparing two mental standards: your *ideal* self (the characteristics you want to possess based on your desires) and your *ought* self (the person others wish and expect you to be).

self-enhancement bias: (p. 74) The tendency to view our own unique traits more favorably than the unique traits of others.

self-esteem: (p. 34) The overall value, positive or negative, you assign to yourself.

self-fulfilling prophecies: (p. 33) Predictions about future encounters that lead us to behave in ways that ensure the interactions unfold as we predicted.

self-monitoring: (p. 31) The process of observing your own communication and the norms of the situation in order to make appropriate communication choices.

self-presentation goals: (p. 13) In interpersonal encounters, presenting yourself in certain ways so that others perceive you as being a particular type of person.

self-serving bias: (p. 68) A biased tendency to credit ourselves (internal factors) instead of external factors for our success. For instance, Ruth attributes the success of a project to her leadership qualities rather than to the dedicated efforts of her team.

selfie (p. 52) A positive photo of oneself taken by oneself.

sender: (p. 5) The individual who generates, packages, and delivers a message.

sensory channels: (p. 4) Perceptual pathways corresponding to our five senses: auditory (sound), visual (sight), tactile (touch), olfactory (scent), and oral (taste).

separation: (p. 272) A sudden withdrawal of one person from an encounter. For example, you walk away from an argument to cool off, or you angrily retreat to your room.

serial argument process model: (p. 277) The course that serial arguments take is determined by the goals individuals possess, the approaches they adopt for dealing with the conflict, and the consequent perception of whether or not the conflict is resolvable.

serial arguments: (p. 277) A series of unresolved disputes, all having to do with the same issue.

sex: (p. 150) A category assigned at birth determined by anatomical and biological traits, such as external genitalia, internal reproductive organs, hormones, and sex chromosomes. Sex categories are female, male, and intersex.

sexual-arousal touch: (p. 241) An intentional touch designed to physically stimulate another person.

sexual harassment: (p. 400) Unwelcome sexual advances, physical contact, or requests that render a workplace offensive or intimidating.

sexual orientation: (p. 21) Emotional, romantic, and/or sexual feelings toward other people.

short-term memory: (p. 181) The part of your mind that temporarily houses information while you seek to understand its meaning.

single-parent family: (p. 327) A household in which one adult has the sole responsibility to be the children's caregiver.

skirting: (p. 265) A way of avoiding conflict by changing the topic or joking about it. For example, Martel tries to evade Louis's criticism about where Martel parked his car by teasing, "I did you a favor. You walked twenty extra steps. Exercise is good for you."

sniping: (p. 265) A way of avoiding conflict by communicating in a negative fashion and then abandoning the encounter by physically leaving the scene or refusing to interact further, such as when Martel answers Louis's criticism about where he parked his car by insulting Louis and stomping out the door.

social comparison: (p. 32) Observing and assigning meaning to others' behaviors and then comparing their behavior to ours (when judging our own actions). For example, you might subtly check out how others are dressed at a party or how they scored on an exam to see if you compare favorably.

social exchange theory: (p. 294) The idea that you will be drawn to those you see as offering substantial benefits with few associated costs. For example, Meredith thinks Leonard is perfect for her because he is much more attentive and affectionate than her previous boyfriends and seems so easy to please.

social network currency: (p. 263) Power that comes from being linked with a network of friends, family, and acquaintances with substantial influence, such as being on a first-name basis with a sports celebrity.

social penetration theory: (p. 48) Altman and Taylor's model that you reveal information about yourself to others by peeling back or penetrating layers.

social-polite touch: (p. 241) A touch, such as a handshake, used to demonstrate social norms or culturally expected behaviors.

social space: (p. 243) The proxemic zone that ranges from 4 to 12 feet of space between communicators. It is the spatial separation most often used in the United States in the workplace and for conversations between acquaintances and strangers.

speech acts: (p. 210) The actions we perform with language, such as the question, "Is the antique clock in your window for sale?" and the reply, "Yes, let me get it out to show you."

spillover hypothesis: (p. 345) The idea that emotions, affect, and mood from the parental relationship "spill over" into the broader family, disrupting children's sense of emotional security.

stagnating: (p. 300) A relational stage in which communication comes to a standstill. For instance, day after day, Owen and Ruth speak only to ask if a bill has been paid or what is on television, without really listening to each other's answers.

stepfamily: (p. 327) A family type in which at least one of the adults has a child or children from a previous relationship.

stereotyping: (p. 78) Categorizing people into social groups and then evaluating them based on information we have in our schemata related to each group.

structural improvements: (p. 273) When people agree to change the basic rules or understandings that govern their relationship to prevent further conflict.

sudden-death statements: (p. 275) Messages, communicated at the height of a conflict, that suddenly declare the end of a relationship, even if that wasn't an option before— for example, "It's over. I never want to see you again."

supportive climate: (p. 383) A workplace atmosphere that is supportive, warm, and open. Contrast **defensive climate**.

supportive communication: (p. 113) Sharing messages that express emotional support and that offer personal assistance, such as extending your sympathy or listening to someone without judging.

suppression: (p. 104) Inhibiting thoughts, arousal, and outward behavioral displays of emotion. For example, Amanda stifles her anger, knowing it will kill her chances of receiving a good tip.

symbols: (p. 203) Items used to represent other things, ideas, or events. For example, the letters of the alphabet are symbols for specific sounds in English.

symmetrical relationships: (p. 261) Relationships characterized by an equal balance of power, such as a business partnership in which the partners co-own their company.

task-oriented listeners: (p. 189) People who view listening as transactional and prefer brief, to-the-point, and accurate messages.

terminating: (p. 300) A relational stage in which one or both partners end a relationship. For instance, Ruth asks Owen for a divorce once she realizes their marriage has deteriorated beyond salvation.

territoriality: (p. 243) The tendency to claim personal spaces as our own and define certain locations as areas we don't want others to invade without permission, such as spreading out personal items to claim the entire library table.

transactional communication model: (p. 6) A depiction of communication in which each participant equally influences the communication behavior of the other participants. For example, a salesperson who watches his customer's facial expression while describing a product is sending and receiving messages at the same time.

triangulation: (p. 340) Loyalty conflicts that arise when a coalition is formed, uniting one family member with another against a third family member.

trolls: (p. 194) Aggressive listeners who intentionally bait and attack others in online communication.

uncertainty avoidance: (p. 131) How cultures tolerate and accept unpredictability.

Uncertainty Reduction Theory: (p. 69) A theory explaining that the primary compulsion during initial encounters is to reduce uncertainty about our communication partners by gathering enough information about them that their communication becomes predictable and explainable.

understanding: (p. 181) The third stage of the listening process in which a listener interprets the meaning of another person's communication by comparing newly received information against past knowledge.

upward communication: (p. 389) Messages from a subordinate to a superior. For instance, a clerk notifies the department manager that inventory needs to be reordered. Contrast **downward communication**.

valued social identities: (p. 360) The aspects of your public self that you deem the most important in defining who you are—for example, musician, athlete, poet, dancer, teacher, or mother.

venting: (p. 105) Allowing emotions to dominate your thoughts and explosively expressing them, such as shrieking in happiness or storming into an office in a rage.

verbal aggression: (p. 218) The tendency to attack others' self-concepts—their appearance, behavior, or character—rather than their positions.

verbal communication: (p. 203) The exchange of spoken or written language with others during interactions.

virtual networks: (p. 382) Groups of coworkers linked solely through email, social networking sites, Skype, and other online services.

virtual peers: (p. 387) Coworkers who communicate mostly through phone, email, Skype, and other communication technologies.

vocalics: (p. 239) Vocal characteristics we use to communicate nonverbal messages, such as volume, pitch, rate, voice quality, vocalized sounds, and silence. For instance, a pause might signal discomfort, create tension, or be used to heighten drama.

voluntary kin family: (p. 327) A group of people who lack blood and legal kinship but who consider themselves "family."

warranting value: (p. 53) The degree to which online information is supported by other people and outside evidence.

wedging: (p. 313) When a person deliberately uses online communication—messages, photos, and posts—to try to insert themselves between romantic partners because they are interested in one of the partners.

"we" language: (p. 217) Communication that uses the pronoun *we* to emphasize inclusion—for example, "We need to decide what color to paint the living room" instead of "I need you to tell me what color paint you want for the living room." See also **"I" language; "you" language**.

workplace bullying: (p. 395) The repeated unethical and unfavorable treatment of one or more persons by others in the workplace.

workplace cliques: (p. 383) Dense networks of coworkers who share the same workplace values and broader life attitudes.

workplace relationships: (p. 379) Any affiliation you have with a professional peer, supervisor, subordinate, or mentor in a professional setting.

workplace telepressure: (p. 385) The pressure to always be connected to the workplace and to respond immediately to workplace communications, even during weekends and vacation days.

world-mindedness: (p. 138) The ability to practice and demonstrate acceptance and respect toward other cultures' beliefs, values, and customs. Contrast **ethnocentrism**.

"you" language: (p. 216) Communication that states or implies the pronoun *you* to place the focus of attention on blaming others—such as "You haven't done your share of the work on this project." Contrast **"I" language; "we" language**.

Zoom fatigue: (p. 235) Emotional and mental exhaustion experienced by a person on a video call.

Abel, J. (2020, February 7). 10 black trans* activists you should know. *Medium.* https://medium.com/tmi-consulting-inc/10-black-trans-activists-you-should-know-ec69464f66e9

Abramson, L., Uzefovsky, F., Toccaceli, V., & Knafo-Noam, A. (2020). The genetic and environmental origins of emotional and cognitive empathy: Review and meta-analyses of twin studies. *Neuroscience and Biobehavioral Reviews, 114,* 113–133. https://doi.org/10.1016/j.neubiorev.2020.03.023

Ackard, D. M., & Neumark-Sztainer, D. (2002). Date violence and date rape among adolescents: Associations with disordered eating behaviors and psychological health. *Child Abuse and Neglect, 26,* 455–473.

Adamson, A., & Jenson, V. (Directors). (2001). *Shrek* [Motion picture]. DreamWorks SKG.

Adegbola, O., Labador, A., & Oviedo, M. (2018). African students' identity negotiation and relational conflict management: Being "foreign", being "careful." *Journal of Intercultural Communication Research, 47*(6), 474–490. https://doi.org/10.1080/17475759.2018.1486876

Afifi, T. D. (2003). "Feeling caught" in stepfamilies: Managing boundary turbulence through appropriate communication privacy rules. *Journal of Social and Personal Relationships, 20*(6), 729–755.

Afifi, T. D., McManus, T., Hutchinson, S., & Baker, B. (2007). Parental divorce disclosures, the factors that prompt them, and their impact on parents' and adolescents' well-being. *Communication Monographs, 74,* 78–103.

Afifi, T. D., McManus, T., Steuber, K., & Coho, A. (2009). Verbal avoidance and dissatisfaction in intimate conflict situations. *Human Communication Research, 35,* 357–383.

Afifi, T. D., & Olson, L. (2005). The chilling effect and the pressure to conceal secrets in families. *Communication Monographs, 72,* 192–216.

Afifi, T. D., & Steuber, K. (2010). The cycle of concealment model. *Journal of Social and Personal Relationships, 27*(8), 1019–1034.

Afifi, W. A., Falato, W. L., & Weiner, J. L. (2001). Identity concerns following a severe relational transgression: The role of discovery method for the relational outcomes of infidelity. *Journal of Social and Personal Relationships, 18*(2), 291–308.

Allegrini, E. (2008, November 15). James Edgar's Santa Claus—the spirit of Christmas. *The Enterprise.* http://www.enterprisenews.com/article/20081116/News/311169851/?Start=1

Allport, G. W. (1954). *The nature of prejudice.* Addison-Wesley.

Aloia, L. S. (2020). Parent–child relationship satisfaction: The influence of family communication orientations and relational maintenance behaviors. *Family Journal: Counseling and Therapy for Couples and Families, 28*(1), 83–89. https://doi.org/10.1177/1066480719896561

Aloia, L. S., & High, A. C. (2020). Ameliorating the adverse consequences of verbal aggression: The buffering effect of esteem support on personal and relational outcomes. *Communication Reports, 33*(2), 55–67. https://doi.org/10.1080/08934215.2020.1741659

Aloia, L. S., & Worley, T. (2019). The role of family verbal aggression and taking conflict personally in romantic relationship complaint avoidance. *Communication Studies, 70*(2), 190–207. https://doi.org/10.1080/10510974.2018.1524777

Altman, I., & Taylor, D. A. (1973). *Social penetration: The development of interpersonal relationships.* Holt, Rinehart & Winston.

American Dialect Society. (2015). *2014 Word of the Year is "#blacklivesmatter."* https://www.americandialect.org/2014-word-of-the-year-is-blacklivesmatter

American Dialect Society. (2018). *"Fake news" is the 2017 American Dialect Society Word of the Year.* https://www.americandialect.org/category/words-of-the-year

American Psychological Association. (2012). Guidelines for psychological practice with lesbian, gay, and bisexual clients. *American Psychologist, 67*(1), 10–42. https://doi.org/10.1037/a0024659

American Psychological Association. (2013a). *National intimate partner and sexual violence survey: 2010 findings on victimization by sexual orientation: 541522013-001* [Data set]. https://doi.org/10.1037/e541522013-001

American Psychological Association. (2013b). College students' mental health is a growing concern, survey finds. *Monitor on Psychology, 44*(6), 13. https://www.apa.org/monitor/2013/06/college-students#:~:text=The%20survey%20also%20found%20that,clients%20were%20taking%20psychotropic%20medications

American Psychological Association. (2015a). *APA dictionary of psychology* (2nd ed.). Author.

American Psychological Association. (2015b). Guidelines for psychological practice with transgender and gender nonconforming people. *American Psychologist, 70*(9), 832–864. https://doi.org/10.1037/a00399006

American Psychological Association. (n.d.). Marriage & divorce. https://www.apa.org/topics/divorce#:~:text=They%20are%20also%20good%20for,subsequent%20marriages%20is%20even%20higher

American Psychological Association and National Association of School Psychologists. (2015). *Resolution on gender and sexual orientation diversity in children and adolescents in schools.* http://www.apa.org/about/policy/orientation-diversity.aspx

Amodio, D. M. (2014). The neuroscience of prejudice and stereotyping. *Nature Reviews Neuroscience, 15*(10), 670–682.

Amorosi, A. D. (2020). Grammy-winning production duo Jimmy Jam and Terry Lewis signs recording deal with BMG. *Variety.* https://variety.com/2020/music/news/jimmy-jam-terry-lewis-sign-recording-deal-bmg-1234810089/

Andersen, P. A. (1997). Cues of culture: The basis of intercultural differences in nonverbal communication. In L. A. Samovar & R. E. Porter (Eds.), *Intercultural communication: A reader* (8th ed., pp. 244–255). Wadsworth.

Andersen, P. A., Guerrero, L., & Jones, S. (2006). Nonverbal intimacy. In V. Manusov & M. J. Patterson (Eds.), *The SAGE Handbook of Nonverbal Communication* (pp. 259–277). SAGE.

Anderson, M., Vogels, E., & Turner, E. (2020, February 6). The virtues and downsides of online dating. *Pew Research Center.* https://www.pewresearch.org/internet/2020/02/06/the-virtues-and-downsides-of-online-dating/

Anderson, N. H. (1981). *Foundations of information integration theory.* Academic Press.

Andrews, Jennifer. Personal interview with authors, December 2014. Published with permission.

APA Online. (n.d.). *Just the facts about sexual orientation & youth: A primer for principals, educators, & school personnel.* http://www.apa.org/pi/lgbc/publications/justthefacts.html

Apatow, J., & Feig, P., & Mumolo, A., & Wiig, K. (2011). *Bridesmaids* [Motion picture]. Universal Pictures.

Apostolou, M., Keramari, D., Kagialis, A., & Sullman, M. (2020). Why people make friends: The nature of friendship. *Personal Relationships,* 1–15. https://doi.org/10.1111/pere.12352

Appelbaum, S. H., Marinescu, A., Klenin, J., & Bytautas, J. (2007). Fatal attractions: The mismanagement of workplace romance. *International Journal of Business Research, 7*(4), 31–43.

Arasaratnam, L. A. (2006). Further testing of a new model of intercultural communication competence. *Communication Research Reports, 23*, 93–99.

Archer, J. (2000). Sex differences in aggression between heterosexual partners: A meta-analytic review. *Psychological Bulletin, 126*, 651–680.

Argyle, M. (1969). *Social interaction.* Atherton Press.

Argyle, M., & Furnham, A. (1982). The ecology of relationships: Choice of situations as a function of relationship. *British Journal of Social Psychology, 21*, 259–262.

Argyle, M., & Henderson, M. (1984). The rules of friendship. *Journal of Social and Personal Relationships, 1*, 211–237.

Argyle, M., & Lu, L. (1990). Happiness and social skills. *Personality and Individual Differences, 11*, 1255–1261.

Aron, A., Fisher, H., Strong, G., Acevedo, B., Riela, S., & Tsapelas, I. (2008). Falling in love. In S. Sprecher, A. Wenzel, & J. Harvey (Eds.), *Handbook of relationship initiation* (pp. 315–336). Psychology Press.

Arriaga, X. B., & Agnew, C. R. (2001). Being committed: Affective, cognitive, and conative components of relationship commitment. *Personality and Social Psychology Bulletin, 27*, 1190–1203.

Artz, B., Goodall, A. H., & Oswald, A. J. (2018). Do women ask? *Industrial Relations: A Journal of Economy and Society, 57*(4), 611–636. https://doi.org/10.1111/irel.12214

Asada, K. J. K., Morrison, K., Hughes, M., & Fitzpatrick, S. (2003, May). *Is that what friends are for? Understanding the motivations, barriers, and emotions associated with friends with benefits relationships.* Paper presented at the International Communication Association Annual Meeting, San Diego, CA.

Asch, S. E. (1946). Forming impressions of personality. *Journal of Abnormal and Social Psychology, 41*, 258–290.

Aukett, R., Ritchie, J., & Mill, K. (1988). Gender differences in friendship patterns. *Sex Roles, 19*, 57–66.

Autry, R. (2020, September 12). U.S. Open women's final features Naomi Osaka's masks, Black hair and a bold cultural statement. *NBC News.* https://www.nbcnews.com/think/opinion/u-s-open-women-s-final-features-naomi-osaka-s-ncna1239914

Babcock, L., & Laschever, S. (2007). *Women don't ask.* Bantam.

Bakke, E. (2010). A model and measure of mobile communication competence. *Human Communication Research, 36*, 348–371.

Balderrama, A. (2010, May 6). Are you paying attention to your online reputation? Employers are. *The Work Buzz.* http://www.theworkbuzz.com/featured/online-reputation

Banas, J. A., Bessarabova, E., & Massey, Z. B. (2020). Meta-analysis on mediated contact and prejudice. *Human Communication Research, 46*(2–3), 120–160. https://doi.org/10.1093/hcr/hqaa004

Bane, R. (2010, August 12). How splintered is your attention? [Blog post]. http://www.baneofyourresistance.com/2010/08/12/how-splintered-is-your-attention-take-the-quiz-and-find-out

Baptiste, D. A., Jr. (1990). Therapeutic strategies with black-Hispanic families: Identity problems of a neglected minority. *Journal of Family Psychotherapy, 1*, 15–38.

Barber, L. K., & Santuzzi, A. M. (2015). Please respond ASAP: Workplace telepressure and employee recovery. *Journal of Occupational Health Psychology, 20*(2), 172–189. https://doi.org/10.1037/a0038278

Barker, L. L. (1971). *Listening behavior.* Prentice Hall.

Barker, L. L., & Watson, K. W. (2000). *Listen up.* St. Martin's Press.

Barker, V., & Ota, H. (2011). Mixi diary versus Facebook photos: Social networking site use among Japanese and Caucasian American females. *Journal of Intercultural Communication Research, 40*(1), 39–63.

Barnes, S. B. (2001). *Online connections: Internet interpersonal relationships.* Hampton Press.

Barnlund, D. C. (1975). *Private and public self in Japan and the United States.* Simul Press.

Barroso, A., Parker, K., & Bennett, J. (2020). As millennials near 40, they're approaching family life differently than previous generations. *Pew Research Center.* https://www.pewsocialtrends.org/2020/05/27/as-millennials-near-40-theyre-approaching-family-life-differently-than-previous-generations/

Barry, D. (2011, May 16). A sports executive leaves the safety of his shadow life. *New York Times.* https://www.nytimes.com/2011/05/16/sports/basketball/nba-executive-says-he-is-gay.html

Bartlett, J. E., & Bartlett, M. E. (2011). Workplace bullying: An integrative literature review. *Advances in Developing Human Resources, 13*(1), 69–84. https://doi.org/10.1177/1523422311410651

Baumgartner, S. E., van der Schuur, W. A., Lemmens, J. S., & te Poel, F. (2018). The relationship between media multitasking and attention problems in adolescents: Results of two longitudinal studies. *Human Communication Research, 44*(1), 3–30. https://doi.org/10.1111/hcre.12111

Baxter, L. A. (1990). Dialectical contradictions in relationship development. *Journal of Social and Personal Relationships, 7*, 69–88.

Baxter, L. A., Mazanec, M., Nicholson, J., Pittman, G., Smith, K., & West, L. (1997). Everyday loyalties and betrayals in personal relationships. *Journal of Social and Personal Relationships, 14*, 655–678.

Baym, N., Campbell, S. W., Horst, H., Kalyanaraman, S., Oliver, M. B., Rothenbuhler, E., Weber, R., & Miller, K. (2012). Communication theory and research in the age of new media: A conversation from the CM café. *Communication Monographs, 79*(2), 256–267.

Beach, W. A. (2002). Between dad and son: Initiating, delivering, and assimilating bad cancer news. *Health Communication, 14*, 271–298.

Merriam-Webster Dictionary. (n.d.). Bear. https://www.merriam-webster.com/dictionary/bear

Beck, J. (2015, October 22). How friendships change when you become an adult. *Atlantic.* https://www.theatlantic.com/health/archive/2015/10/how-friendships-change-over-time-in-adulthood/411466/

Becker, J. A. H., Ellevold, B., & Stamp, G. H. (2008). The creation of defensiveness in social interaction II: A model of defensive communication among romantic couples. *Communication Monographs, 75*(1), 86–110. https://doi.org/10.1080/03637750701885415

Becker, J. A. H., Johnson, A. J., Craig, E. A., Gilchrist, E. S., Haigh, M. M., & Lane, L. T. (2009). Friendships are flexible, not fragile: Turning points in geographically-close and long-distance friendships. *Journal of Social and Personal Relationships, 26*(4), 347–369.

Beer, J. S., John, O. P., Scabini, D., & Knight, R. T. (2006). Orbitofrontal cortex and social behavior: Integrating self-monitoring and emotion-cognition interactions. *Journal of Cognitive Neuroscience, 18*, 871–879.

Bell, F. (2008). Making you noise. *Nimrod International Journal: Memory: Lost and Found.*

Bell, R. A., Buerkel-Rothfuss, N. L., & Gore, K. E. (1987). Did you bring the yarmulke for the Cabbage Patch Kid? The idiomatic communication of young lovers. *Human Communication Research, 14*, 47–67.

Bem, S. L. (1995). Dismantling gender polarization and compulsory heterosexuality: Should we turn the volume down or up? *Journal of Sex Research, 32*, 329–334.

Bender, A., & Ingram, R. (2018). Connecting attachment style to resilience: Contributions of self-care and self-efficacy. *Personality and Individual Differences, 130*, 18–20. https://doi.org/10.1016/j.paid.2018.03.038

Bennett, S. H. (2003). *Radical pacifism: The War Resisters League and Gandhian nonviolence in America, 1915–1963.* Syracuse University Press.

Benoit, P. J., & Benoit, W. E. (1990). To argue or not to argue. In R. Trapp & J. Schuetz (Eds.), *Perspectives on argumentation: Essays in honor of Wayne Brockriede* (pp. 55–72). Waveland Press.

Berg, M., Fuchs, M., Wirkner, K., Loeffler, M., Engel, C., & Berger, T. (2017). The speaking voice in the general population: Normative data and associations to sociodemographic and lifestyle factors. *Journal of Voice, 31*(2). https://doi.org/10.1016/j.jvoice.2016.06.001

Berger, C. R., & Bradac, J. J. (1982). *Language and social knowledge: Uncertainty in interpersonal relations.* Edward Arnold.

Berger, C. R., & Calabrese, R. J. (1975). Some explorations in initial interaction and beyond: Toward a developmental theory of interpersonal communication. *Human Communication Research, 1,* 99–112. https://doi.org/10.1111/j.1468-2958.1975.tb00258.x

Berkowitz, L., & Harmon-Jones, E. (2004). Toward an understanding of the determinants of anger. *Emotion, 4,* 107–130.

Berry, G. R. (2006). Can computer-mediated asynchronous communication improve team processes and decision-making? *Journal of Business Communication, 43*(4), 344–366.

Berscheid, E. (2002). Emotion. In H. H. Kelley et al. (Eds.), *Close relationships* (2nd ed., pp. 110–168). Percheron Press.

Berscheid, E., & Peplau, L. A. (2002). The emerging science of relationships. In H. H. Kelley et al. (Eds.), *Close relationships* (2nd ed., pp. 1–19). Percheron Press.

Berscheid, E., & Regan, P. (2005). *The psychology of interpersonal relationships.* Pearson Education.

Berscheid, E., & Walster, E. (1978). *Interpersonal attraction* (2nd ed.). Addison-Wesley.

Bevan, J. L. (2014). Dyadic perceptions of goals, conflict strategies, and perceived resolvability in serial arguments. *Journal of Social and Personal Relationships, 31*(6), 773–795.

Bevan, J. L., Finan, A., & Kaminsky, A. (2008). Modeling serial arguments in close relationships: The serial argument process model. *Human Communication Research, 34,* 600–624.

Bian, L., Leslie, S.-J., & Cimpian, A. (2017). Gender stereotypes about intellectual ability emerge early and influence children's interests. *Science, 355,* 389–391.

Bianconi, L. (2002). *Culture and identity: Issues of authenticity in another value system.* Paper presented at the XII Sietar-EU Conference, Vienna, Austria.

Birdwhistell, R. L. (1970). *Kinesics and context: Essays on body motion communication.* University of Pennsylvania Press.

Biskupic, J. (2009, February 6). Scalia, Ginsburg strike a balance. *ABC News.* https://www.washingtonpost.com/posteverything/wp/2016/02/13/what-made-scalia-and-ginsburgs-friendship-work/

Bisson, M. A., & Levine, T. R. (2007). Negotiating a friend with benefits relationship. *Archives of Sexual Behavior, 38*(1), 66–73. https://doi.org/10.1007/s10508-007-9211-2

Błachnio, A., & Przepiorka, A. (2019). Be aware! If you start using Facebook problematically you will feel lonely: Phubbing, loneliness, self-esteem, and Facebook intrusion. A cross-sectional study. *Social Science Computer Review, 37*(2), 270–278. https://doi.org/10.1177/0894439318754490

Bleidorn, W., Arslan, R. C., Denissen, J. J. A., Rentfrow, P. J., Gebauer, J. E., Potter, J., & Gosling, S. D. (2016). Age and gender differences in self-esteem: A cross-cultural window. *Journal of Personality and Social Psychology, 111*(3), 396–410.

Bleiweis, R. (2020). Quick facts about the gender wage gap. *Center for American Progress.* https://www.americanprogress.org/issues/women/reports/2020/03/24/482141/quick-facts-gender-wage-gap/

Blum, R. W., Mmari, K., & Moreau, C. (2017). It begins at 10: How gender expectations shape early adolescence around the world. *Journal of Adolescent Health, 61,* S3–S4.

Bochner, S., & Hesketh, B. (1994). Power distance, individualism/collectivism, and job related attitudes in a culturally diverse work group. *Journal of Cross-Cultural Psychology, 25,* 233–257.

Boddy, C. R. (2011). Corporate psychopaths, bullying and unfair supervision in the workplace. *Journal of Business Ethics, 100,* 367–379.

Bodenhausen, G. V., Macrae, C. N., & Sherman, J. W. (1999). On the dialectics of discrimination: Dual processes in social stereotyping. In S. Chaiken & Y. Trope (Eds.), *Dual process theories in social psychology* (pp. 271–290). Guilford Press.

Bodhi, B., & Nanamoli, B. (1995). *The middle length discourse of the Buddha: A translation of the Majjhima Nikaya.* Wisdom Publications.

Bodie, G. D., Winter, J., Dupuis, D., & Tompkins, T. (2020). The echo listening profile: Initial validity evidence for a measure of four listening habits. *International Journal of Listening, 34*(3), 131–155. https://doi.org/10.1080/10904018.2019.1611433

Bodie, G. D., Worthington, D. L., & Gearhart, C. C. (2013). The Listening Styles Profile-Revised (LSP-R): A scale revision and evidence

for validity. *Communication Quarterly, 61*(1), 72–90. https://doi.org/10.1080/01463373.2012.720343

Bonilla-Zorita, G., Griffiths, M. D., & Kuss, D. J. (2020). Online dating and problematic use: A systematic review. *International Journal of Mental Health and Addiction.* https://doi.org/10.1007/s11469-020-00318-9

Bonus, J. A., Peebles, A., Mares, M.-L., & Sarmiento, I. G. (2018). Look on the bright side (of media effects): Pokémon Go as a catalyst for positive life experiences. *Media Psychology, 21*(2), 263–287. https://doi.org/10.1080/15213269.2017.1305280

Boren, C. (2017, August 8). Three girls' soccer players cut their hair short. Now they're accused of being boys. *Washington Post.* https://www.washingtonpost.com/news/early-lead/wp/2017/08/08/what-happens-with-three-girls-soccer-players-cut-their-hair-short-theyre-accused-of-being-boys/?noredirect=on&utm_term=.4730f36b048b

Bornstein, R. F. (1989). Exposure and affect: Overview and metaanalysis of research, 1968–1987. *Psychological Bulletin, 106,* 265–289.

Bornstein, R. F., & Craver-Lemley, C. (2004). Mere exposure effect. In R. F. Pohl (Ed.), *Cognitive illusions: A handbook on fallacies and biases in thinking, judgement, and memory* (pp. 215–234). Psychology Press.

Boursier, V., Gioia, F., & Griffiths, M. D. (2020). Do selfie-expectancies and social appearance anxiety predict adolescents' problematic social media use? *Computers in Human Behavior, 110,* 106395. https://doi.org/10.1016/j.chb.2020.106395

Bowlby, J. (1969). *Attachment and loss: Vol. 1. Attachment.* Basic Books.

Boyd, C. (2010). The debate over the prohibition of romance in the workplace. *Journal of Business Ethics, 97,* 325–338.

Boyer, C. R., & Galupo, M. P. (2018). Transgender friendship profiles: Patterns across gender identity and LGBT affiliation. *Gender Issues, 35*(3), 236–253. https://doi.org/10.1007/s12147-017-9199-4

Braithwaite, D. O., Bach, B. W., Baxter, L. A., DiVerniero, R., Hammonds, J. R., Hosek, A. M., ... Wolf, B. M. (2010). Constructing family: A typology of voluntary kin. *Journal of Social and Personal Relationships, 27*(3), 388–407. https://doi.org/10.1177/0265407510361615

Bregman, A., Golin, S. (Producers), Gondry, M. (Director), & Kaufman, C. (Writer). (2004). *Eternal sunshine of the spotless mind* [Motion picture]. Focus Features.

Brehm, S. S., Miller, R. S., Perlman, D., & Campbell, S. M. (2002). *Intimate relationships* (3rd ed.). McGraw-Hill.

Brend, R. (1975). Male-female intonation patterns in American English. In B. Thorne & N. Henley (Eds.), *Language and sex: Difference and dominance* (pp. 84–87). Newbury House.

Brewer, M. B. (1993). Social identity, distinctiveness, and in-group homogeneity. *Social Cognition, 11,* 150–164.

Brewer, M. B. (1999). The psychology of prejudice: Ingroup love or outgroup hate? *Journal of Social Issues, 55,* 429–444.

Brewer, M. B., & Campbell, D. T. (1976). *Ethnocentrism and intergroup attitudes: East African evidence.* SAGE.

Bridge, K., & Baxter, L. A. (1992). Blended relationships: Friends as work associates. *Western Journal of Communication, 56,* 200–225.

Brody, L. R., & Hall, J. A. (2000). Gender, emotion, and expression. In M. Lewis & J. M. Haviland (Eds.), *Handbook of emotions* (2nd ed., pp. 338–349). Guilford Press.

Brontë, E. (1995). *Wuthering Heights.* Oxford University Press. (Original work published 1848)

Brown, R. (1965). *Social psychology.* Free Press.

Brownhalls, J., Duffy, A., Eriksson, L., & Barlow, F. K. (2019). Reintroducing rationalization: A study of relational goal pursuit theory of intimate partner obsessive relational intrusion. *Journal of Interpersonal Violence.* https://doi.org/10.1177/0886260518822339

Bruess, C. J. S., & Pearson, J. C. (1993). "Sweet pea" and "pussy cat": An examination of idiom use and marital satisfaction over the life cycle. *Journal of Social and Personal Relationships, 10,* 609–615. https://doi.org/10.1177/0265407593104009

Bruner, F. (2018, February 6). The Internet thinks "lady-friendly" Doritos are in pretty bad taste. *TIME Magazine.* https://www.msn.com/en-nz/health/smartliving/the-internet-thinks-lady-friendly-doritos-are-in-pretty-bad-taste/ar-BBIKR1Y?li=AA2FZ8I

Bruner, J., & Taguiri, R. (1954). The perception of people. In G. Lindzey (Ed.), *Handbook of social psychology* (Vol. 1, pp. 601–633). Addison-Wesley.

Bruni, F. (2017, November 14). Danica Roem is really, really boring. *New York Times*. https://nyti.ms/2hzlsie

Buber, M. (1965). *The knowledge of man: A philosophy of the interhuman*. Harper & Row.

Bulfinch, T. (1985). *The golden age of myth and legend*. Bracken Books. (Original work published 1855)

Bunkers, S. S. (2010). The power and possibility in listening. *Nursing Science Quarterly, 23*(1), 22–27.

Burgoon, J. K., Buller, D. B., & Woodall, W. G. (1996). *Nonverbal communication: The unspoken dialogue* (2nd ed.). McGraw-Hill.

Burgoon, J. K., & Dunbar, N. E. (2000). An interactionist perspective on dominance-submission: Interpersonal dominance as a dynamic, situationally contingent social skill. *Communication Monographs, 67*, 96–121.

Burgoon, J. K., & Hoobler, G. D. (2002). Nonverbal signals. In M. L. Knapp & J. A. Daly (Eds.), *Handbook of interpersonal communication* (3rd ed., pp. 240–299). SAGE.

Burgoon, M. (1995). A kinder, gentler discipline: Feeling good about being mediocre. In B. R. Burleson (Ed.), *Communication yearbook* 18 (pp. 464–479). SAGE.

Burleson, B. R., & MacGeorge, E. L. (2002). Supportive communication. In M. L. Knapp & J. A. Daly (Eds.), *Handbook of interpersonal communication* (pp. 374–422). SAGE.

Burleson, B. R., & Samter, W. (1994). A social skills approach to relationship maintenance: How individual differences in communication skills affect the achievement of relationship functions. In D. J. Canary & L. Stafford (Eds.), *Communication and relational maintenance* (pp. 61–90). Academic Press.

Bushman, B. J. (2002). Does venting anger feed or extinguish the flame? Catharsis, rumination, distraction, anger, and aggressive responding. *Personality and Social Psychology Bulletin, 28*, 724–731.

Bushman, B. J., & Baumeister, R. F. (1998). Threatened egotism, narcissism, self-esteem, and direct and displaced aggression: Does self-love or self-hate lead to violence? *Journal of Personality and Social Psychology, 75*, 219–229.

Buss, D. M., Larsen, R. J., Westen, D., & Semmelroth, J. (1992). Sex differences in jealousy: Evolution, physiology, and psychology. *Psychological Science, 3*, 251–255.

Buss, D. M., Shackelford, T. K., Kirkpatrick, L. A., Choe, J. C., Lim, H. K., Hasegawa, M., . . . Bennett, K. (1999). Jealousy and the nature of beliefs about infidelity: Tests of competing hypotheses about sex differences in the United States, Korea, and Japan. *Personal Relationships, 6*, 125–150.

Buunk, B. P., Angleitner, A., Oubaid, V., & Buss, D. M. (1996). Sex differences in jealousy in evolutionary and cultural perspective: Tests from the Netherlands, Germany, and the United States. *Psychological Science, 7*, 359–363.

Buzzanell, P. (1990, November). *Managing workplace romance*. Paper presented at the Speech Communication Association Annual Meeting, Chicago, IL.

Cacioppo, J. T., Klein, D. J., Berntson, G. G., & Hatfield, E. (1993). The psychophysiology of emotion. In M. Lewis & J. M. Haviland (Eds.), *Handbook of emotions* (pp. 119–142). Guilford Press.

Caldwell, M. A., & Peplau, L. A. (1982). Sex differences in same-sex friendship. *Sex Roles, 8*, 721–732.

Cameron, D. (2009). A language in common. *Psychologist, 22*(7), 4.

Cameron, D. (2020). Language and gender: Mainstreaming and the persistence of patriarchy. *International Journal of the Sociology of Language, 2020*(263), 25–30. https://doi.org/10.1515/ijsl-2020-2078

Cameron, J. J., & Granger, S. (2019). Does self-esteem have an interpersonal imprint beyond self-reports? A meta-analysis of self-esteem and objective interpersonal indicators. *Personality and Social Psychology Review, 23*(1), 73–102.

Camirand, E., & Poulin, F. (2019). Changes in best friendship quality between adolescence and emerging adulthood: Considering the role of romantic involvement. *International Journal of Behavioral Development, 43*(3), 231–237. https://doi.org/10.1177/0165025418824995

Campbell, J. D., Trapnell, P. D., Heine, S. J., Katz, I. M., Lavallee, L. F., & Lehman, D. R. (1996). Self-concept clarity: Measurement, personality correlates, and cultural boundaries. *Journal of Personality and Social Psychology, 70*, 141–156.

Campbell, R. G., & Babrow, A. S. (2004). The role of empathy in responses to persuasive risk communication: Overcoming resistance to HIV prevention messages. *Health Communication, 16*, 159–182.

Canary, D. J. (2003). Managing interpersonal conflict: A model of events related to strategic choices. In J. O. Greene & B. R. Burleson (Eds.), *Handbook of communication and social interaction skills*. Erlbaum.

Canary, D. J., Emmers-Sommer, T. M., & Faulkner, S. (1997). *Sex and gender differences in personal relationships*. Guilford Press.

Canary, D. J., & Hause, K. S. (1993). Is there any reason to research sex differences in communication? *Communication Quarterly, 41*, 129–144.

Canary, D. J., & Zelley, E. (2000). Current research programs on relational maintenance behaviors. In M. E. Roloff (Ed.), *Communication yearbook* 23 (pp. 305–339). SAGE.

Carducci, B. J., & Zimbardo, P. G. (1995, November/December). Are you shy? *Psychology Today, 28*, 34–41.

Carlson, J. G., & Hatfield, E. (1992). *Psychology of emotion*. Harcourt Brace.

Carothers, B. J., & Reis, H. T. (2013). Men and women are from Earth: Examining the latent structure of gender. *Journal of Personality and Social Psychology, 104*(2), 385–407. https://doi.org/10.1037/a0030437

Carmon, I. (2016, February 13). What made the friendship between Scalia and Ginsburg work. *Washington Post*. https://www.washingtonpost.com/posteverything/wp/2016/02/13/what-made-scalia-and-ginsburgs-friendship-work/

Carpenter, C. J. (2012). Meta-analyses of sex differences in responses to sexual versus emotional infidelity: Men and women are more similar than different. *Psychology of Women Quarterly, 36*(1), 25–37. https://doi.org/10.1177/0361684311414537

Carr, N. (2010). *The shallows: What the Internet is doing to our brains*. W. W. Norton.

Castelli, L., Tomelleri, S., & Zogmaister, C. (2008). Implicit ingroup metafavoritism: Subtle preference for ingroup members displaying ingroup bias. *Personality and Social Psychology Bulletin, 34*(6), 807–818.

Caughlin, J. P. (2002). The demand/withdraw pattern of communication as a predictor of marital satisfaction over time: Unresolved issues and future directions. *Human Communication Research, 28*, 49–85.

Caughlin, J. P., & Vangelisti, A. L. (2000). An individual difference explanation of why married couples engage in demand/withdraw patterns of conflict. *Journal of Social and Personal Relationships, 17*, 523–551.

Centers for Disease Control and Prevention (CDC). (2020). Preventing intimate partner violence. https://www.cdc.gov/violenceprevention/intimatepartnerviolence/fastfact.html

Cerpas, N. (2002). *Variation in the display and experience of love between college Latino and non-Latino heterosexual romantic couples*. Ronald E. McNair Scholarship research report. University of California, Berkeley.

Chan, J. S. Y., Liu, G., Liang, D., Deng, K., Wu, J., & Yan, J. H. (2019). Special issue: Therapeutic benefits of physical activity for mood. A systematic review on the effects of exercise intensity, duration, and modality. *Journal of Psychology, 153*(1), 102–125. https://doi.org/10.1080/00223980.2018.1470487

Chandra-Mouli, V., Plesons, M., Adebayo, E., Amin, A., Avni, M., Kraft, J. M., . . . Malarcher, S. (2017). Implications of the Global Early Adolescent Study's formative research findings for action and for research. *Journal of Adolescent Health, 61*, S5–S9.

Chan-Serafin, S., Teo, L., Minbashian, A., Cheng, D., & Wang, L. (2017). The perils of dating your boss: The role of hierarchical workplace romance and sex on evaluators' career advancement decisions for lower status romance participants. *Journal of Social and Personal Relationships, 34,* 309–333.

Chaplin, T. M., Cole, P. M., & Zahn-Waxler, C. (2005). Parental socialization of emotion expression: Gender differences and relations to child adjustment. *Emotion, 5,* 80–88.

Chappell, B. (2017, June 22). Census finds a more diverse America, as whites lag growth. *NPR.* http://www.npr.org/sections/thetwo -way/2017/06/22/533926978/census-finds-a-more-diverse -america-as-whites-lag-growth

Charoensukmongkol, P., & Phungsoonthorn, T. (2020). The interaction effect of crisis communication and social support on the emotional exhaustion of university employees during the COVID-19 crisis. *International Journal of Business Communication.* https://doi.org /10.1177/2329488420953188

Chen, G.-M., & Chung, J. (1997). The "Five Asian Dragons": Management behaviors and organization communication. In L. A. Samovar & R. E. Porter (Eds.), *Intercultural communication: A reader* (pp. 317–328). Wadsworth.

Chen, G.-M., & Starosta, W. J. (2005). *Foundation of intercultural communication.* Allyn & Bacon.

Chesebro, J. L. (1999). The relationship between listening styles and conversational sensitivity. *Communication Research Reports, 16,* 233–238.

Chopik, W. J. (2017). Associations among relational values, support, health, and well-being across the adult lifespan. *Personal Relationships, 24,* 408–422. https://doi.org/10.1111/pere.12187

Chun, J., Lee, J., Kim, J., & Lee, S. (2020). An international systematic review of cyberbullying measurements. *Computers in Human Behavior, 113,* 106485. https://doi.org/10.1016/j.chb.2020.106485

Chung, J. H., Des Roches, C. M., Meunier, J., & Eavey, R. D. (2005). Evaluation of noise-induced hearing loss in young people using a web-based survey technique. *Pediatrics, 115,* 861–867.

Clair, R. P. (1998). *Organizing silence.* State University of New York Press.

Clark, E. M., Votaw, K. L. B., Harris, A. L., Hasan, M., & Fernandez, P. (2020). Unrequited love: The role of prior commitment, motivation to remain friends, and friendship maintenance. *Journal of Social Psychology, 160*(3), 293–309. https://doi.org/10.1080/00224545 .2019.1648234

Clark, R. A., & Delia, J. (1979). Topoi and rhetorical competence. *Quarterly Journal of Speech, 65,* 187–206.

Clayton, R. B. (2014). The third wheel: The impact of Twitter use on relationship infidelity and divorce. *Cyberpsychology, Behavior, and Social Networking, 17*(7), 425–430. https://doi.org/10.1089/cyber.2013.0570

Cleveland, J. N., Stockdale, M., & Murphy, K. R. (2000). *Women and men in organizations: Sex and gender issues at work.* Erlbaum.

Clopper, C. G., Conrey, B., & Pisoni, D. B. (2005). Effects of talker gender on dialect categorization. *Journal of Language and Social Psychology, 24*(2), 182–206. https://doi.org/10.1177/0261927X05275741

Cochran, C. C., Frazier, P. A., & Olson, A. M. (1997). Predictors of responses to unwanted sexual attention. *Psychology of Women Quarterly, 21,* 207–226.

Coffelt, T. A., & Smith, F. L. M. (2020). Exemplary and unacceptable workplace communication skills. *Business and Professional Communication Quarterly, 83*(4), 365–384. https://doi.org/10.1177 /2329490620946425

Cohn, D., & Passel, J. S. (2018). A record 64 million Americans live in multigenerational households. *Pew Research Center.* https://www .pewresearch.org/fact-tank/2018/04/05/a-record-64-million -americans-live-in-multigenerational-households/

Cole, M., & Cole, S. R. (1989). *The development of children.* W.H. Freeman.

Collins, N. L., & Feeney, B. C. (2004). An attachment theory perspective on closeness and intimacy. In D. J. Mashek & A. Aron (Eds.), *Handbook of closeness and intimacy* (pp. 163–187). Erlbaum.

Contractor, N. S., & Grant, S. (1996). The emergence of shared interpretations in organizations: A self-organizing systems perspective. In J. H. Watt & C. A. VanLear (Eds.), *Dynamic patterns in communication processes* (pp. 215–230). SAGE.

Cooley, C. H. (1902). *Human nature and the social order.* Scribner.

Cooper, A. N., Tao, C. T., Totenhagen, C. J., Randall, A. K., & Holley, S. R. (2020). Daily stress spillover and crossover: Moderating effects of difficulties in emotion regulation in same-sex couples. *Journal of Social and Personal Relationships, 37*(4), 1245–1267. https://doi.org /10.1177/0265407519891777

Costanzo, F. S., Markel, N. N., & Costanzo, R. R. (1969). Voice quality profile and perceived emotion. *Journal of Counseling Psychology, 16,* 267–270.

Coupland, N., Giles, H., & Wiemann, J. M. (Eds.). (1991). *Miscommunication and problematic talk.* SAGE.

Covarrubias, P. (2000). Of endearment and other terms of address: A Mexican perspective. In M. W. Lustig & J. Koestner (Eds.), *Among us: Essays on identity, belonging, and intercultural competence* (pp. 9–17). Longman.

Cowan, R. L., & Horan, S. M. (2021). Understanding information and communication technology use in workplace romance escalation and de-escalation. *International Journal of Business Communication, 58*(1), 55–78. https://doi.org/10.1177/2329488417731860

Cox, C. (2020, September 27). Fact check: It's true, Ginsburg and Scalia were close friends despite ideological differences. *USA Today.* https://www.usatoday.com/story/news/factcheck/2020/09/27 /fact-check-ruth-bader-ginsburg-antonin-scalia-were-close -friends/3518592001/

Crenshaw, K. (1989). Demarginalizing the intersection of race and sex: A black feminist critique of antidiscrimination doctrine, feminist theory and antiracist politics. *University of Chicago Legal Forum, 1989*(1), Article 8.

Crider, D. M., Willits, F. K., & Kanagy, C. L. (1991). Rurality and well-being during the middle years of life. *Social Indicators, 24,* 253–268.

Croes, E. A. J., Antheunis, M. L., Schouten, A. P., & Krahmer, E. J. (2019). Social attraction in video-mediated communication: The role of nonverbal affiliative behavior. *Journal of Social and Personal Relationships, 36*(4), 1210–1232.

Crosnoe, R., & Cavanagh, S. E. (2010). Families with children and adolescents: A review, critique, and future agenda. *Journal of Marriage and Family, 72,* 594–611.

Cross, S. E., & Madson, L. (1997). Models of the self: Self-construals and gender. *Psychological Bulletin, 122,* 5–37.

Crothers, L. M., Lipinski, J., & Minutolo, M. C. (2009). Cliques, rumors, and gossip by the water cooler: Female bullying in the workplace. *Psychologist-Manager Journal, 12,* 97–110.

Cruz, I. (2020). 10 teachers share their worst helicopter parent stories. *Did You Know?* https://didyouknowfacts.com/teacher-share -their-worst-helicopter-parent-experiences

Cunningham, M. (1988). Does happiness mean friendliness? Induced mood and heterosexual self-disclosure. *Personality and Social Psychology Bulletin, 14,* 283–297.

Cunningham, M. R., Shamblen, S. R., Barbee, A. P., & Ault, L. K. (2005). Social allergies in romantic relationships: Behavioral repetition, emotional sensitization, and dissatisfaction in dating couples. *Personal Relationships, 12*(2), 273–295. https://doi.org/10.1111 /j.1350-4126.2005.00115

Cupach, W. R., & Spitzberg, B. H. (1998). Obsessive relational intrusion and stalking. In B. H. Spitzberg & W. R. Cupach (Eds.), *The dark side of close relationships* (pp. 233–263). Erlbaum.

Cupach, W. R., & Spitzberg, B. H. (2004). *The dark side of relational pursuit: From attraction to obsession to stalking.* Erlbaum.

Custudio, J. (2002). The divine Ms. C.H.O.: Margaret Cho on her new stand-up movie, Lea Delaria, Joan Rivers, and the meaning of gay pride. *Montreal Mirror.* http://www.montrealmirror.com /ARCHIVES/2002/080102/divers7.html

Dainton, M., Zelley, E., & Langan, E. (2003). Maintaining friendships throughout the lifespan. In D. J. Canary & M. Dainton (Eds.), *Maintaining relationships through communication: Relational, contextual, and cultural variations* (pp. 79–102). Erlbaum.

Daly, J. (1975). *Listening and interpersonal evaluations.* Paper presented at the Central States Speech Association Annual Meeting, Kansas City, MO.

Daly, J. A., McCroskey, J. C., Ayres, J., Hopf, T., & Ayres, D. M. (Eds.). (2004). *Avoiding communication: Shyness, reticence, and communication apprehension* (3rd ed.). Hampton Press.

Daniels, D. (1986). Differential experiences of siblings in the same family as predictors of adolescent sibling personality differences. *Journal of Personality and Social Psychology, 51*(2), 339–346.

Darwin, H. (2020). Challenging the cisgender/transgender binary: Nonbinary people and the transgender label. *Gender & Society, 34*(3), 357–380. https://doi.org/10.1177/0891243220912256

David, M. E., & Roberts, J. A. (2017). Phubbed and alone: Phone snubbing, social exclusion, and attachment to social media. *Journal of the Association for Consumer Research, 2*(2), 155–163. https://doi.org/10.1086/690940

Davis, K. E., & Todd, M. L. (1985). Assessing friendship: Prototypes, paradigm cases, and relationship description. In S. Duck & D. Perlman (Eds.), *Understanding personal relationships: An interdisciplinary approach* (pp. 17–38). SAGE.

DeFranza, D., Mishra, H., & Mishra, A. (2020). How language shapes prejudice against women: An examination across 45 world languages. *Journal of Personality and Social Psychology, 119*(1), 7–22. https://doi.org/10.1037/pspa0000188

Delgado-Gaitan, C. (1993). Parenting in two generations of Mexican American families. *International Journal of Behavioral Development, 16*, 409–427.

Delia, J. G. (1972). Dialects and the effects of stereotypes on interpersonal attraction and cognitive processes in impression formation. *Quarterly Journal of Speech, 58*, 285–297.

Devine, P. G. (1989). Stereotypes and prejudice: Their automatic and controlled components. *Journal of Personality and Social Psychology, 56*, 5–18.

de Vries, B. (1996). The understanding of friendship: An adult life course perspective. In C. Magai & S. McFadden (Eds.), *Handbook of emotion, aging, and the life course* (pp. 249–268). Academic Press.

Dhanani, L. Y., & LaPalme, M. L. (2019). It's not personal: A review and theoretical integration of research on vicarious workplace mistreatment. *Journal of Management, 45*(6), 2322–2351. https://doi.org/10.1177/0149206318816162

Dindia, K., & Allen, M. (1992). Sex differences in self-disclosure: A meta-analysis. *Psychological Bulletin, 112*, 106–124.

Domingue, R., & Mollen, D. (2009). Attachment and conflict communication in adult romantic relationships. *Journal of Social and Personal Relationships, 26*, 678–696.

Donohue, W. A., & Kolt, R. (1992). *Managing interpersonal conflict.* SAGE.

Dovidio, J. F., Hewstone, M., Glick, P., & Esses, V. M. (2010). Prejudice, stereotyping, and discrimination: Theoretical and empirical overview. In J. F. Dovidio, M. Hewstone, P. Glick, & V. M. Esses (Eds.), *The SAGE Handbook of Prejudice, Stereotyping, and Discrimination* (pp. 3–28). https://doi.org/10.4135/9781446200919.n1

Dowd, M. (2018, February 3). *This is why Uma Thurman is angry: The actress is finally ready to talk about Harvey Weinstein.* https://www.nytimes.com/2018/02/03/opinion/sunday/this-is-why-uma-thurman-is-angry.html

Dreyer, A. S., Dreyer, C. A., & Davis, J. E. (1987). Individuality and mutuality in the language of families of field-dependent and field-independent children. *Journal of Genetic Psychology, 148*, 105–117.

Drobnick, R. (2017). 5 Ways men & women communicate differently. *Your Tango Experts for Psych Central.* https://psychcentral.com/blog/6-ways-men-and-women-communicate-differently/

Duan, C., & Hill, C. E. (1996). The current state of empathy research. *Journal of Counseling Psychology, 43*, 261–274.

Dunbar, N. E. (2004). Dyadic power theory: Constructing a communication-based theory of relational power. *Journal of Family Communication, 4*(3/4), 235–248.

Duncan, S., Jr., & Fiske, D. W. (1977). *Face-to-face interaction: Research, methods, and theory.* Wiley.

Dunleavy, K., & Booth-Butterfield, M. (2009). Idiomatic communication in the stages of coming together and falling apart. *Communication Quarterly, 57*(4), 416–432. https://doi.org/10.1080/01463370903320906

Dutton, L. B., & Winstead, B. A. (2006). Predicting unwanted pursuit: Attachment, relationship satisfaction, relationship alternatives, and break-up distress. *Journal of Social and Personal Relationships, 23*(4), 565–586.

Eagly, A. H., Ashmore, R. D., Makhijani, M. G., & Longo, L. C. (1991). What is beautiful is good, but . . .: A meta-analytic review of research on the physical attractiveness stereotype. *Psychological Bulletin, 110*, 109–128.

Eagly, A. H., & Wood, W. (2012). Social role theory. In P. A. M. Van Lange, A. W. Kruglanski, & E. T. Higgins (Eds.), *Handbook of theories of social psychology* (pp. 458–476). SAGE. https://doi.org/10.4135/9781446249222.n49

Eagly, A. H., Wood, W., & Diekman, A. B. (2000). Social role theory of sex differences and similarities: A current appraisal. In T. Eckes & H. M. Trautner (Eds.), *The developmental social psychology of gender* (pp. 123–174). Erlbaum.

Ebbeson, E., Duncan, B., & Konecni, V. (1975). Effects of content of verbal aggression on future verbal aggression: A field experiment. *Journal of Experimental Social Psychology, 11*, 192–204.

Ebrahimji, A. (2020, May 20). Female Fortune 500 CEOs reach an all-time high, but it's still a small percentage. *CNN.* https://www.cnn.com/2020/05/20/us/fortune-500-women-ceos-trnd/index.html

EducationData. (n.d.). International student enrollment statistics. https://educationdata.org/international-student-enrollment-statistics/

Eisenberg, E. M., & Goodall, H. L., Jr. (2004). *Organizational communication: Balancing creativity and constraint* (4th ed.). Bedford/St. Martin's.

Eisikovits, Z., & Buchbinder, E. (2000). *Locked in a violent embrace.* SAGE.

Ekman, P. (1972). Universals and cultural differences in facial expressions of emotion. In J. R. Cole (Ed.), *Nebraska Symposium on Motivation* (Vol. 19, pp. 207–283). University of Nebraska Press.

Ekman, P. (1976). Movements with precise meanings. *Journal of Communication, 26*, 14–26.

Ekman, P., & Friesen, W. V. (1969). The repertoire of nonverbal behavior: Categories, origins, usage, and coding. *Semiotica, 1*, 49–98.

Ekman, P., & Friesen, W. V. (1975). *Unmasking the face: A guide to recognizing emotions from facial clues.* Prentice-Hall.

El-Alayli, A., & Wynne, M. (2015). Whose personality is better, mine or my partner's? Self-enhancement bias in relationships. *Personal Relationships, 22*, 550–571. https://doi.org/10.1111/pere.12096

Elçi, M., & Alpkan, L. (2009). The impact of perceived organizational ethical climate on work satisfaction. *Journal of Business Ethics, 84*, 297–311.

Elliot, H. (2020, March 9). For Brenda Villa, the path to water polo glory began in the City of Commerce. *Los Angeles Times.* https://www.latimes.com/sports/story/2020-03-09/brenda-villa-water-polo

Ellis, A., & Dryden, W. (1997). *The practice of rational emotive behavior therapy.* Springer.

Ellison, N., Heino, R., & Gibbs, J. (2006). Managing impressions online: Self-presentation processes in the online dating environment. *Journal of Computer-Mediated Communication, 11*(2), article 2. http://jcmc.indiana.edu/vol11/issue2/ellison.html

Ellison, N. B., Steinfield, C., & Lampe, C. (2007). The benefits of Facebook "friends": Social capital and college students' use of online social network sites. *Journal of Computer-Mediated Communication, 12*(4), article 1. http://jcmc.indiana.edu/vol12/issue4/ellison.html

England, P., Levine, A., & Mishel, E. (2020, March 31). Progress toward gender equality in the United States has slowed or stalled. *PNAS, 117*(13). https://doi.org/10.1073/pnas.1918891117

Englehardt, E. E. (2001). Introduction to ethics in interpersonal communication. In E. E. Englehardt (Ed.), *Ethical issues in interpersonal communication: Friends, intimates, sexuality, marriage, and family* (pp. 1–27). Harcourt College.

The English language: Words borrowed from other languages. (n.d.). http://www.krysstal.com/borrow.html

Environmental Protection Agency. (2002, September). *Crosscultural communication.* http://www.epa.gov/superfund/community/pdfs/12ccc.pdf

Ermer, A. E., & Proulx, C. M. (2020). Social support and well-being among older adult married couples: A dyadic perspective. *Journal of Social and Personal Relationships, 37*(4), 1073–1091. https://doi.org/10.1177/0265407519886350

Escartín, J., Rodríguez-Carballeira, A., Zapf, D., Porrúa, C., & Martín-Peña, J. (2009). Perceived severity of various bullying behaviours at work and the relevance of exposure to bullying. *Work & Stress, 23*(3), 191–205.

Farace, R. V., Monge, P. R., & Russell, H. M. (1977). *Communicating and organizing.* Addison-Wesley.

Faus, S., Matas, A., & Elósegui, E. (2019). Music and regaining calm when faced with academic stress. *Cogent Arts & Humanities, 6*(1). https://doi.org/10.1080/23311983.2019.1634334

Feher, A., & Vernon, P. A. (2020). Looking beyond the Big Five: A selective review of alternatives to the Big Five model of personality. *Personality and Individual Differences,* 110002. https://doi.org/10.1016/j.paid.2020.110002

Fehr, B., Harasymchuk, C., & Sprecher, S. (2014). Compassionate love in romantic relationships: A review and some new findings. *Journal of Social and Personal Relationships, 31*(5), 575–600. https://doi.org/10.1177/0265407514533768

Fein, E., & Schneider, S. (1995). *The rules: Time-tested secrets for capturing the heart of Mr. Right.* Warner Books.

Feingold, A. (1988). Matching for attractiveness in romantic partners and same-sex friends: A meta-analysis and theoretical critique. *Psychological Bulletin, 104,* 226–235.

Felmlee, D., Orzechowicz, D., & Fortes, C. (2010). Fairy tales: Attraction and stereotypes in same-gender relationships. *Sex Roles, 62,* 226–240.

Felmlee, D. H. (2001). No couple is an island: A social network perspective on dyadic stability. *Social Forces, 79,* 1259–1287.

Fenigstein, A., Scheier, M. F., & Buss, A. H. (1975). Public and private self-consciousness: Assessment and theory. *Journal of Consulting and Clinical Psychology, 43,* 522–527.

Fiedler, K., Pampe, H., & Scherf, U. (1986). Mood and memory for tightly organized social information. *European Journal of Social Psychology, 16,* 149–165.

Field, A. (2005). Block that defense! Make sure your constructive criticism works. *Harvard Management Communication Letter, 2*(4), 3–5.

Field, A. E., Cheung, L., Wolf, A. M., Herzog, D. B., Gortmaker, S. L., & Colditz, G. A. (1999). Exposure to the mass media and weight concerns among girls. *Pediatrics, 103,* 6.

Fischer, A. H., Kret, M. E., & Broekens, J. (2018). Gender differences in emotion perception and self-reported emotional intelligence: A test of the emotion sensitivity hypothesis. *PLOS One.* https://doi.org/10.1371/journal.pone.0190712

Fischer, A. H., Rodriguez Mosquera, P. M., van Vianen, A. E. M., & Manstead, A. S. R. (2004). Gender and culture differences in emotion. *Emotion, 4,* 87–94.

Fischer, R., & Boer, D. (2011). What is more important for national well-being: Money or autonomy? A meta-analysis of well-being, burnout, and anxiety across 63 societies. *Journal of Personality and Social Psychology, 101*(1), 164–184. https://doi.org/10.1037/a0023663

Fisher, B. A. (1983). Differential effects of sexual composition and interactional context on interaction patterns in dyads. *Human Communication Research, 9,* 225–238.

Fischetti, M., & Christiansen, J. (2018, September 1). Only 150 of your Facebook contacts are real friends. *Scientific American.* https://doi.org/10.1038/scientificamerican0918-104

Fiske, S. T. (2018). Stereotype content: Warmth and competence endure. *Current Directions in Psychological Science, 27*(2), 67–73. https://doi.org/10.1177/0963721417738825

Fiske, S. T., Cuddy, A. J. C., Glick, P., & Xu, J. (2002). A model of (often mixed) stereotype content: Competence and warmth respectively follow from perceived status and competition. *Journal of Personality and Social Psychology, 82,* 878–902.

Fiske, S. T., & Taylor, S. E. (1991). *Social cognition* (2nd ed.). McGraw-Hill.

Fiske, S. T., & Taylor, S. E. (2017). *Social cognition: From brains to culture.* SAGE.

Fleischer, R. (Director), Reese, R., & Wernick, P. (Screenwriters). (2009). *Zombieland* [Motion picture]. Sony Pictures.

Floyd, K. (1999). All touches are not created equal: Effects of form and duration on observers' interpretations of an embrace. *Journal of Nonverbal Behavior, 23,* 283–299.

Floyd, K., & Burgoon, J. K. (1999). Reacting to nonverbal expressions of liking: A test of interaction adaptation theory. *Communication Monographs, 66,* 219–239.

Floyd, K., & Morman, M. T. (1999). The measurement of affectionate communication. *Communication Quarterly, 46,* 144–162.

Floyd, K., & Morman, M. T. (2005). Fathers' and sons' reports of fathers' affectionate communication: Implications of a naïve theory of affection. *Journal of Social and Personal Relationships, 22*(1), 99–109.

Foels, R., & Tomcho, T. J. (2009). Gender differences in interdependent self-construals: It's not the type of group, it's the way you see it. *Self and Identity, 8*(4), 396–417. https://doi.org/10.1080/15298860802391470

Ford, B. Q., Lam, P., John, O. P., & Mauss, I. B. (2018). The psychological health benefits of accepting negative emotions and thoughts: Laboratory, diary, and longitudinal evidence. *Journal of Personality and Social Psychology, 115*(6), 1075–1092.

Ford, J. L., & Ivancic, S. R. (2020). Surviving organizational tolerance of sexual harassment: An exploration of resilience, vulnerability, and harassment fatigue. *Journal of Applied Communication Research, 48*(2), 186–206. https://doi.org/10.1080/00909882.2020.1739317

Forgas, J. P. (2011a). She just doesn't look like a philosopher . . .? Affective influences on the halo effect in impression formation: Mood and halo effects. *European Journal of Social Psychology, 41*(7), 812–817. https://doi.org/10.1002/ejsp.842

Forgas, J. P. (2011b). Affective influences on self-disclosure: Mood effects on the intimacy and reciprocity of disclosing personal information. *Journal of Personality and Social Psychology, 100*(3), 449–461. https://doi.org/10.1037/a0021129

Forgas, J. P. (2019). Happy believers and sad skeptics? Affective influences on gullibility. *Current Directions in Psychological Science, 28*(3), 306–313. https://doi.org/10.1177/0963721419834543

Forgas, J. P., & Bower, G. H. (1987). Mood effects on person perception judgments. *Journal of Personality and Social Psychology, 53,* 53–60.

Forni, P. M. (2002). *Choosing civility: The twenty-five rules of considerate conduct.* St. Martin's Griffin.

Foss, S. K., Foss, K. A., & Trapp, R. (1991). *Contemporary perspectives in rhetoric* (2nd ed.). Waveland Press.

Fowler, C., & Gasiorek, J. (2017). Depressive symptoms, excessive reassurance seeking, and relationship maintenance. *Journal of Social and Personal Relationships, 34*(1) 91–113. https://doi.org/10.1177/0265407515624265

Fox, J., & Warber, K. M. (2014). Social networking sites in romantic relationships: Attachment, uncertainty, and partner surveillance on Facebook. *Cyberpsychology, Behavior, and Social Networking, 17*(1), 3–7. https://doi.org/10.1089/cyber.2012.0667

Franco, C. L., & Fugate, J. M. B. (2020). Emoji face renderings: Exploring the role emoji platform differences have on emotional interpretation. *Journal of Nonverbal Behavior, 44*(6), 301–328. https://doi.org/10.1007/s10919-019-00330-1

Frederick, D. A., & Fales, M. R. (2016). Upset over sexual versus emotional infidelity among gay, lesbian, bisexual, and heterosexual adults. *Archives of Sexual Behavior, 45*(1), 175–191. https://doi.org/10.1007/s10508-014-0409-9

Frey, W. H. (2020, July 1). The nation is diversifying even faster than predicted, according to new census data. *Brookings.* https://www.brookings.edu/research/new-census-data-shows-the-nation-is-diversifying-even-faster-than-predicted/

Frijda, N. H. (2005). Emotion experience. *Cognition and Emotion, 19,* 473–497.

Frisby, B. N., & Westerman, D. (2010). Rational actors: Channel selection and rational choices in romantic conflict episodes. *Journal of Social and Personal Relationships, 27*, 970–981.

Fritz, J. H., & Dillard, J. P. (1994, November). *The importance of peer relationships in organizational socialization.* Paper presented at the Speech Communication Association Annual Meeting, New Orleans, LA.

Frost, D. M. (2012). The narrative construction of intimacy and affect in relationship stories: Implications for relationship quality, stability, and mental health. *Journal of Social and Personal Relationships, 30*(3), 247–269. https://doi.org/10.1177/0265407512454463

Fuendeling, J. M. (1998). Affect regulation as a stylistic process within adult attachment. *Journal of Social and Personal Relationships, 15*, 291–322.

Furger, R. (1996). I'm okay, you're online. *PC World, 14*, 310–312.

Furman, W., & Simon, V. A. (1998). Advice from youth: Some lessons from the study of adolescent relationships. *Journal of Social and Personal Relationships, 15*, 723–739.

Furr, R. M., & Funder, D. C. (1998). A multimodal analysis of personal negativity. *Journal of Personality and Social Psychology, 74*, 1580–1591.

Gale, B. (1949, September). How to get a date. *Calling All Girls Magazine*, pp. 35, 70–71.

Galupo, M. P. (2009). Cross-category friendship patterns: Comparison of heterosexual and sexual minority adults. *Journal of Social and Personal Relationships, 26*(6–7), 811–831.

Galvin, K. M., Brommel, B. J., & Bylund, C. L. (2004). *Family communication: Cohesion and change* (6th ed.). Pearson Education.

Galyapina, V., Lebedeva, N., & Lepshokova, Z. (2020). Intercultural friendships, social identities and psychological well-being of ethnic minorities in different contexts. *Journal of Intercultural Communication Research, 49*(1), 86–105. https://doi.org/10.1080/17475759.2020.1713192

Gangestad, S. W., & Snyder, M. (2000). Self-monitoring: Appraisal and reappraisal. *Psychological Bulletin, 126*, 530–555.

Ganong, L., Coleman, M., Fine, M., & Martin, P. (1999). Stepparents' affinity-seeking and affinity-maintaining strategies with stepchildren. *Journal of Family Issues, 20*, 299–327.

Ganong, L. H., & Coleman, M. (1994). *Remarried family relationships.* SAGE.

Garcia, P., & Geisler, J. (1988). Sex and age/grade differences in adolescents' self-disclosure. *Perceptual and Motor Skills, 67*, 427–432.

Gareis, E., Goldman, J., & Merkin, R. (2019). Promoting intercultural friendship among college students. *Journal of International & Intercultural Communication, 12*(1), 1–22. https://doi.org/10.1080/17513057.2018.1502339

Gattario, K. H., Lindwall, M., & Frisén, A. (2020). Life after childhood bullying: Body image development and disordered eating in adulthood. *International Journal of Behavioral Development, 44*(3), 246–255. https://doi.org/10.1177/0165025419877971

Gaucher, D., Wood, J. V., Stinson, D. A., Forest, A. L., Holmes, J. G., & Logel, C. (2012). Perceived regard explains self-esteem differences in expressivity. *Personality and Social Psychology Bulletin, 38*(9) 1144–1156. https://doi.org/10.1177/0146167212445790

Geiger, A. W., & Livingston, G. (2019). 8 facts about love and marriage in America. *Pew Research Center.* https://www.pewresearch.org/fact-tank/2019/02/13/8-facts-about-love-and-marriage/

Geiman, K. L., & Greene, J. O. (2019). Listening and experiences of interpersonal transcendence. *Communication Studies, 70*(1), 114–128. https://doi.org/10.1080/10510974.2018.1492946

Gerdes, L. I. (1999). *Sexual harassment: Current controversies.* Greenhaven.

Gettings, J. (2005). *Civil disobedience: Black medalists raise fists for civil rights movement.* http://www.infoplease.com/spot/mm-mexicocity.html

Giannakakis, A. E., & Fritsche, I. (2011). Social identities, group norms, and threat: On the malleability of ingroup bias. *Personality and Social Psychology Bulletin, 37*(1), 82–93.

Gibbs, J. L., Ellison, N. B., & Heino, R. D. (2006). Self-presentation in online personals: The role of anticipated future interaction, self-disclosure, and perceived success in Internet dating. *Communication Research, 33*, 1–26.

Gibson, B., & Sachau, D. (2000). Sandbagging as a self-presentational style: Claiming to be less than you are. *Personality and Social Psychology Bulletin, 26*, 56–70.

Gifford, R., Ng, C. F., & Wilkinson, M. (1985). Nonverbal cues in the employment interview: Links between applicant qualities and interviewer judgments. *Journal of Applied Psychology, 70*, 729–736.

Giles, H., Coupland, N., & Coupland, J. (Eds.). (1991). *Contexts of accommodation: Developments in applied linguistics.* Cambridge University Press.

Giles, H., & Street, R. L. (1994). Communicator characteristics and behavior. In M. L. Knapp & G. R. Miller (Eds.), *Handbook of interpersonal communication* (2nd ed., pp. 103–161). SAGE.

Gillig, T. K., & Bighash, L. (2019). Gendered spaces, gendered friendship networks? Exploring the organizing patterns of LGBTQ youth. *International Journal of Communication, 13*, 4895–4916.

Gleason, L. B. (1989). *The development of language.* Merrill.

Glenn, D. (2010, February 28). Divided attention: In an age of classroom multitasking, scholars probe the nature of learning and memory. *Chronicle of Higher Education.* http://chronicle.com/article/Scholars-Turn-Their-Attention/63746/

Glick, P., & Fiske, S. T. (1996). The ambivalent sexism inventory: Differentiating hostile and benevolent sexism. *Journal of Personality and Social Psychology, 70*, 491–512.

Glisson, C., & James, L. R. (2002). The cross-level effects of culture and climate in human service teams. *Journal of Organizational Behavior, 23*, 767–794.

Global Workplace Analytics. (2018). *Latest telecommuting statistics.* http://globalworkplaceanalytics.com/telecommuting-statistics

Global Workplace Analytics. (2020, March 13). Latest work-at-home /telecommuting/mobile work/remote work statistics. *Global Workplace Analytics.* https://globalworkplaceanalytics.com/telecommuting-statistics

Goffman, E. (1955). On facework: An analysis of ritual elements in social interaction. *Psychiatry, 18*, 319–345.

Goffman, E. (1959). *The presentation of self in everyday life.* Doubleday Anchor Books.

Goffman, E. (1979). Footing. *Semiotica, 25*, 124–147.

Goh, J., Pfeffer, J., & Zenios, S. A. (2016). The relationship between workplace stressors and mortality and health costs in the United States. *Management Science, 62*(2), 608–628. https://doi.org/10.1287/mnsc.2014.2115

Goldberg, B. (2020, January 3). Singular "they" is voted Word of the Decade by U.S. linguists. *Reuters.* https://jp.reuters.com/article/us-usa-word-idUSKBN1Z21KF

Goldsmith, D. J., & Fulfs, P. A. (1999). "You just don't have the evidence": An analysis of claims and evidence in Deborah Tannen's *You just don't understand.* In M. E. Roloff (Ed.), *Communication yearbook 22* (pp. 1–49). Sage.

Goldstein, N. J., Vezich, I. S., & Shapiro, J. R. (2014). Perceived perspective taking: When others walk in our shoes. *Journal of Personality and Social Psychology, 106*(6), 941–960. https://doi.org/10.1037/a0036395

Goleman, D. (2006). *Social intelligence: The new science of human relationships.* Bantam Dell.

Goleman, D. (2007a, February 20). Flame first, think later: New clues to e-mail misbehavior. *New York Times.* https://www.nytimes.com/2007/02/20/health/psychology/20essa.html

Goleman, D. (2007b, August 24). Free won't: The marshmallow test revisited [Blog post]. http://danielgoleman.info/2007/free-wont-the-marshmallow-test-revisited/

Golish, T. D. (2000). Changes in closeness between adult children and their parents: A turning point analysis. *Communication Reports, 13*, 79–97.

Golish, T. D. (2003). Stepfamily communication strengths: Understanding the ties that bind. *Human Communication Research, 29*(1), 41–80.

Golshan, T. (2017, October 15). Study finds 75 percent of workplace harassment victims experienced retaliation when they spoke up. *Vox*. https://www.vox.com/identities/2017/10/15/16438750/weinstein-sexual-harassment-facts

Gong, X., Wong, N., & Wang, D. (2018). Are gender differences in emotion culturally universal? Comparison of emotional intensity between Chinese and German samples. *Journal of Cross-Cultural Psychology, 49*(6), 993–1005. https://doi.org/10.1177/0022022118768434

Goodman-Deane, J., Mieczakowski, A., Johnson, D., Goldhaber, T., & Clarkson, P. J. (2016). The impact of communication technologies on life and relationship satisfaction. *Computers in Human Behavior, 57*, 219–229. https://doi.org/10.1016/j.chb.2015.11.053

Goodsell, T. L., Bates, J. S., & Behnke, A. O. (2010). Fatherhood stories: Grandparents, grandchildren, and gender differences. *Journal of Social and Personal Relationships, 28*(1), 134–154.

Goodwin, C. (1981). *Conversational organization: Interaction between speakers and hearers.* Academic Press.

Gosling, S. D., Gaddis, S., & Vazire, S. (2007, March). *Personality impressions based on Facebook profiles.* Paper presented at the International Conference on Weblogs and Social Media (ICWSM), Boulder, CO.

Gottman, J. M., & Levenson, R. W. (2000). The timing of divorce: Predicting when a couple will divorce over a 14-year period. *Journal of Marriage and Family, 62*, 737–745.

Graf, N. (2018, April 4). Sexual harassment at work in the era of #MeToo. *Pew Research Center Social & Demographic Trends.* http://www.pewsocialtrends.org/2018/04/04/sexual-harassment-at-work-in-the-era-of-metoo/

Graham, J. M. (2011). Measuring love in romantic relationships: A meta-analysis. *Journal of Social and Personal Relationships, 28*(6), 748–771.

Grawitch, M. J., Werth, P. M., Palmer, S. N., Erb, K. R., & Lavigne, K. N. (2017). Self-imposed pressure or organizational norms? Further examination of the construct of workplace telepressure. *Stress and Health, 34*(2). https://doi.org/10.1002/smi.2792

Gray, J. (1992). *Men are from Mars, women are from Venus: A practical guide for improving communication and getting what you want in your relationships.* HarperCollins.

Greenwald, A. G., & Banaji, M. R. (1995). Implicit social cognition: Attitudes, self-esteem, and stereotypes. *Psychological Review, 102*(1), 4–27. https://doi.org/10.1037/0033-295X.102.1.4

Greenwald, A. G., Poehlman, T. A., Uhlmann, E. L., & Banaji, M. R. (2009). Understanding and using the Implicit Association Test: III. Meta-analysis of predictive validity. *Journal of Personality and Social Psychology, 97*(1), 17–41. https://doi.org/10.1037/a0015575

Grice, H. P. (1989). *Studies in the way of words.* Harvard University Press.

Gross, J. J., & John, O. P. (2002). Wise emotion regulation. In L. Feldman Barrett & P. Salovey (Eds.), *The wisdom in feeling: Psychological processes in emotional intelligence* (pp. 297–319). Guilford Press.

Gross, J. J., Richards, J. M., & John, O. P. (2006). Emotion regulation in everyday life. In D. K. Snyder, J. A. Simpson, & J. N. Hughes (Eds.), *Emotion regulation in couples and families: Pathways to dysfunction and health.* American Psychological Association.

Gudykunst, W. B., & Kim, Y. Y. (2003). *Communicating with strangers: An approach to intercultural communication* (4th ed.). McGraw-Hill.

Guerin, B. (1999). Children's intergroup attribution bias for liked and disliked peers. *Journal of Social Psychology, 139*, 583–589.

Guerrero, L. K., & Andersen, P. A. (1998). Jealousy experience and expression in romantic relationships. In P. A. Andersen & L. K. Guerrero (Eds.), *Handbook of communication and emotion* (pp. 155–188). Academic Press.

Gumperz, J. J., & Levinson, S. C. (Eds.). (1996). *Rethinking linguistic relativity.* Cambridge University Press.

Gurrentz, B. (2018). Living with an unmarried partner now common for young adults. *U.S. Census Bureau.* https://www.census.gov/library/stories/2018/11/cohabitaiton-is-up-marriage-is-down-for-young-adults.html#:~:text=Among%20those%20ages%2018

Gustavson, K., Røysamb, E., Borren, I., Torvik, F. A., & Karevold, E. (2016). Life satisfaction in close relationships: Findings from a longitudinal study. *Journal of Happiness Studies, 17*(3), 1293–1311. https://doi.org/10.1007/s10902-015-9643-7

Haas, S. M., & Stafford, L. (1998). An initial examination of maintenance behaviors in gay and lesbian relationships. *Journal of Social and Personal Relationships, 15*, 846–855.

Haas, S. M., & Stafford, L. (2005). Maintenance behaviors in same-sex and marital relationships: A matched sample comparison. *Journal of Family Communication, 5*, 43–60.

Haden, S. C., & Hojjat, M. (2006). Aggressive responses to betrayal: Type of relationship, victim's sex, and nature of aggression. *Journal of Social and Personal Relationships, 23*(1), 101–116.

Hafner, J. (2017, March 13). Gender reveals: Insanely popular—And also outdated? *USA Today.* https://www.usatoday.com/story/news/nation-now/2017/03/12/gender-reveals-gender-identity-cisgender/98535822/

Halatsis, P., & Christakis, N. (2009). The challenge of sexual attraction within heterosexuals' cross-sex friendship. *Journal of Social and Personal Relationships, 26*(6–7), 919–937.

Hall, E. D., & Gettings, P. E. (2020). Who is this little girl they hired to work here? Women's experiences of marginalizing communication in male-dominated workplaces. *Communication Monographs, 87*(4), 484–505. https://doi.org/10.1080/03637751.2020.1758736

Hall, E. T. (1966). A system of the notation of proxemics behavior. *American Anthropologist, 65*, 1003–1026.

Hall, E. T. (1976). *Beyond culture.* Anchor.

Hall, E. T. (1981). *The silent language.* Anchor/Doubleday.

Hall, E. T. (1983). *The dance of life: The other dimension of time.* Doubleday.

Hall, E. T. (1997a). Context and meaning. In L. A. Samovar & R. E. Porter (Eds.), *Intercultural communication: A reader* (pp. 45–53). Wadsworth.

Hall, E. T. (1997b). Monochronic and polychronic time. In L. A. Samovar & R. E. Porter (Eds.), *Intercultural communication: A reader* (8th ed., pp. 277–284). Wadsworth.

Hall, E. T., & Hall, M. R. (1987). *Understanding cultural differences.* Intercultural Press.

Hall, J. A. (2006). Nonverbal behavior, status, and gender: How do we understand their relations? *Psychology of Women Quarterly, 30*, 384–391.

Hall, J. A. (2011). Sex differences in friendship expectations: A meta-analysis. *Journal of Social and Personal Relationships, 28*, 723–747.

Hall, J. A., & Merolla, A. J. (2020). Connecting everyday talk and time alone to global well-being. *Human Communication Research, 46*, 86–111. https://doi.org/10.1093/hcr/hqz014

Halliwell, E., & Dittmar, H. (2006). Associations between appearance-related self-discrepancies and young women's and men's affect, body satisfaction, and emotional eating: A comparison of fixed-item and participant-generated self-discrepancies. *Personality and Social Psychology Bulletin, 32*, 447–458. https://doi.org/10.1177/0146167205284005

Hammer, M. R., Bennett, M. J., & Wiseman, R. (2003). Measuring intercultural sensitivity: The intercultural development inventory. *International Journal of Intercultural Relations, 27*, 421–443.

Hansen, G. L. (1985). Dating jealousy among college students. *Sex Roles, 12*, 713–721.

Hanson, K. (2019). Beauty "therapy": The emotional labor of commercialized listening in the salon industry. *International Journal of Listening, 33*(3), 148–153. https://doi.org/10.1080/10904018.2019.1634572

Harding, J. R. (2017, May). The poetics of *Hamilton*. *Babel: The Language Magazine*, pp. 10–15.

Harms, L. S. (1961). Listener judgments of status cues in speech. *Quarterly Journal of Speech, 47*, 164–168.

Harris, M. (2020, August 25). The actors with disabilities redefining representation. *New York Times.* https://www.nytimes.com/2020/08/25/t-magazine/actors-disability-theater-film-tv.html

Harrison, K. (2001). Ourselves, our bodies: Thin-ideal media, self-discrepancies, and eating disorder symptoms in adolescents. *Journal of Social and Clinical Psychology, 20*, 289–323.

Hassouri, P. (2020, September 8). What I learned as a parent of a transgender child. *New York Times.* https://www.nytimes.com /2020/09/08/well/family/transgender-child-parenting.html

Hatfield, E. (1983). Equity theory and research: An overview. In H. H. Blumberg, A. P. Hare, V. Kent, & M. Davies (Eds.), *Small groups and social interaction* (Vol. 2, pp. 401–412). Wiley.

Hatfield, E., Bensman, L., Thornton, P. D., & Rapson, R. L. (2014). New perspectives on emotional contagion: A review of classic and recent research on facial mimicry and contagion. *Interpersona, 8*(2), 159–179.

Hatfield, E., & Rapson, R. L. (1987). Passionate love: New directions in research. In W. H. Jones & D. Perlman (Eds.), *Advances in personal relationships* (Vol. 1, pp. 109–139). Jessica Kingsley.

Hatfield, E., Traupmann, J., & Sprecher, S. (1984). Older women's perceptions of their intimate relationships. *Journal of Social and Clinical Psychology, 2,* 108–124.

Hatfield, E., Traupmann, J., Sprecher, S., Utne, M., & Hay, M. (1985). Equity in close relationships. In W. Ickes (Ed.), *Compatible and incompatible relationships* (pp. 91–171). Springer-Verlag.

Hatfield, E. E., & Sprecher, S. (1986). *Mirror, mirror . . . the importance of looks in everyday life.* State University of New York Press.

Hauser, T. (2006). *Muhammad Ali: His life and times.* Simon & Schuster.

Hawkley, L. C., & Cacioppo, J. T. (2010). Loneliness matters: A theoretical and empirical review of consequences and mechanisms. *Annals of Behavioral Medicine, 40,* 218–227.

Hayashi, G. M., & Strickland, B. R. (1998). Long-term effects of parental divorce on love relationships: Divorce as attachment disruption. *Journal of Social and Personal Relationships, 15,* 23–38.

Hayes, J. G., & Metts, S. (2008). Managing the expression of emotion. *Western Journal of Communication, 72,* 374–396.

Hays, R. B. (1988). Friendship. In S. Duck (Ed.), *Handbook of personal relationships: Theory, research, and interventions* (pp. 391–408). Wiley.

Heider, F. (1958). *The psychology of interpersonal relations.* Wiley.

Heino, R. D., Ellison, N. B., & Gibbs, J. L. (2010). Relationshopping: Investigating the market metaphor in online dating. *Journal of Social and Personal Relationships, 27*(4), 427–447.

Heinz, M. (2018). Communicating while transgender: Apprehension, loneliness, and willingness to communicate in a Canadian sample. *SAGE Open, 8*(2), 2158244018777780. https://doi.org/10.1177 /2158244018777780

Helens-Hart, R. (2017). Females' (non)disclosure of minority sexual identities in the workplace from a communication privacy management perspective. *Communication Studies, 68*(5), 607–623. https://doi.org/10.1080/10510974.2017.1388827

Hemmings, K. H. (2008). *The descendants.* Random House.

Hendrick, C., & Hendrick, S. S. (1988). Lovers wear rose colored glasses. *Journal of Social and Personal Relationships, 5,* 161–183.

Hendrick, S. S., & Hendrick, C. (1992). *Romantic love.* SAGE.

Hendrick, S. S., & Hendrick, C. (2006). Measuring respect in close relationships. *Journal of Social and Personal Relationships, 23,* 881–899.

Henry, P. J., & Wetherell, G. (2017). Countries with greater gender equality have more positive attitudes and laws concerning lesbians and gay men. *Sex Roles, 77,* 523–532. https://doi.org/10.1007 /s11199-017-0744-0

Henry, N., Flynn, A., & Powell, A. (2020). Technology-facilitated domestic and sexual violence: A review. *Violence against Women, 26*(15–16), 1828–1854. https://doi.org/10.1177/1077801219875821

Heritage, J. C., & Watson, D. R. (1979). Formulations as conversational objectives. In G. Pathas (Ed.), *Everyday language: Studies in ethnomethodology.* Irvington.

Herrero, M., Martinez-Pampliega, A., & Alvarez, I. (2020). Family communication, adaptation to divorce and children's maladjustment: The moderating role of coparenting. *Journal of Family Communication, 20*(2), 114–128. https://doi.org/10.1080/15267431.2020.1723592

Hertwig, R., Davis, J. N., & Sulloway, F. J. (2002). Parental investment: How an equity motive can produce inequality. *Psychological Bulletin, 128,* 728–745.

Heslin, R. (1974, May). *Steps toward a taxonomy of touching.* Paper presented at the Midwestern Psychological Association Annual Meeting, Chicago, IL.

Hetherington, E. M. (1993). An overview of the Virginia longitudinal study of divorce and remarriage with a focus on early adolescence. *Journal of Family Psychology, 7,* 39–56.

Higgins, E. T. (1987). Self-discrepancy: A theory relating self and affect. *Psychological Review, 94,* 319–340.

Higgins, E. T., Klein, R., & Strauman, T. (1985). Self-concept discrepancy theory: A psychological model for distinguishing among different aspects of depression and anxiety. *Social Cognition, 3*(1), 51–76. https://doi.org/10.1521/soco.1985.3.1.51

Hill, C. T., Rubin, Z., & Peplau, L. A. (1976). Breakups before marriage: The end of 103 affairs. *Journal of Social Issues, 32,* 147–168.

Hodgins, H. S., & Belch, C. (2000). Interparental violence and nonverbal abilities. *Journal of Nonverbal Behavior, 24,* 3–24.

Hodgson, L. K., & Wertheim, E. H. (2007). Does good emotion management aid forgiving? Multiple dimensions of empathy, emotion management and forgiveness of self and others. *Journal of Social and Personal Relationships, 24*(6), 931–949.

Hofstede, G. (1991). *Cultures and organizations.* McGraw-Hill.

Hofstede, G. (2001). *Culture's consequences: Comparing values, behaviors, institutions, and organizations across nations* (2nd ed., pp. 79–123). SAGE.

Hofstede, G. (2009). *National cultural dimensions.* http://www.geert -hofstede.com/national-culture.html

Hohman, M. (2020, June 8). This "Mister Rogers" moment broke race barriers. It's just as powerful today. *TODAY.com.* https://www .today.com/popculture/how-mister-rogers-pool-moment-broke -race-barriers-t183635

Holt-Lunstad, J., Smith, T. B., & Layton, J. B. (2010). Social relationships and mortality risk: A meta-analytic review. *PLoS Med 7*(7), e1000316. https://doi.org/1-.1371/journal.pmed.1000316

Honeycutt, J. M. (1999). Typological differences in predicting marital happiness from oral history behaviors and imagined interactions. *Communication Monographs, 66,* 276–291.

Hong, S., Jahng, M. R., Lee, N., & Wise, K. R. (2020). Do you filter who you are? Excessive self-presentation, social cues, and user evaluations of Instagram selfies. *Computers in Human Behavior, 104,* 106159. https://doi.org/10.1016/j.chb.2019.106159

Horan, S. M., Cowan, R. L., & Carberry, E. G. (2019). Spillover effects: Communication involved with dissolved workplace romances. *Communication Studies, 70*(5), 564–581. https://doi.org/10.1080 /10510974.2019.1658613

Horne, C. F. (1917). *The sacred books and early literature of the East: Vol. II. Egypt.* Parke, Austin, & Lipscomb.

Horstman, H., Schrodt, P., Warner, B., Koerner, A. F., Maliski, R., Hays, A., & Colaner, C. (2018). Expanding the conceptual and empirical boundaries of family communication patterns: The development and validation of an expanded conformity orientation scale. *Communication Monographs, 85,* 157–180. https://doi.org/10.1080 /03637751.2018.1428354

Hovick, S. R. A., Meyers, R. A., & Timmerman, C. E. (2003). E-mail communication in workplace romantic relationships. *Communication Studies, 54,* 468–480.

Howard, P. E. N., Rainie, L., & Jones, S. (2001, November). Days and nights on the Internet: The impact of a diffusing technology. *American Behavioral Scientist, 45,* 383–405.

Huang, E. (2015). Bamboo-ceiling TV: The network tried to turn my memoir into a cornstarch sitcom and me into a mascot for America. I hated that. *New York Magazine.* http://www.vulture .com/2015/01/eddie-huang-fresh-off-the-boat-abc.html

Hudson, N. W., Lucas, R. E., & Donnellan, M. B. (2020). Are we happier with others? An investigation of the links between spending time with others and subjective well-being. *Journal of Personality and Social Psychology, 119*(3), 672–694. https://doi.org/10.1037 /pspp0000290

Hudson, N. W., Lucas, R. E., & Donnellan, M. B. (2020, March 23). Are we happier with others? An investigation of the links between spending time with others and subjective well-being. *Journal of Personality and Social Psychology*. Advance online publication. https://doi.org/10.1037/pspp0000290

Hudson, T. D. (2020, September 3). Interpersonalizing cultural difference: A grounded theory of the process of interracial friendship development and sustainment among college students. *Journal of Diversity in Higher Education*. https://doi.org/10.1037/dhe0000287

Huffman, A. H., Mills, M. J., Howes, S. S., & Albritton, M. D. (2020). Workplace support and affirming behaviors: Moving toward a transgender, gender diverse, and non-binary friendly workplace. *International Journal of Transgender Health*. Advance online publication. https://doi.org/10.1080/26895269.2020.1861575

Hughes, M., Morrison, K., & Asada, K. J. K. (2005). What's love got to do with it? Exploring the impact of maintenance rules, love attitudes, and network support on friends with benefits relationships. *Western Journal of Speech Communication, 69*, 49–66.

Hughes, M. E., Waite, L. J., Hawkley, L. C., & Cacioppo, J. T. (2004). A short scale for measuring loneliness in large surveys: Results from two population-based studies. *Research on Aging, 26*(6), 655–672.

Human Rights Campaign. (2020). *Glossary of terms*. https://www.hrc.org/resources/glossary-of-terms

Hunsinger, M., Isbell, L. M., & Clore, G. L. (2012). Sometimes happy people focus on the trees and sad people focus on the forest: Context-dependent effects of mood in impression formation. *Personality and Social Psychology Bulletin, 38*(2) 220–232.

Hunt, M. G., Marx, R., Lipson, C., & Young, J. (2018). No more FOMO: Limiting social media decreases loneliness and depression. *Journal of Social and Clinical Psychology, 37*(10), 751–768. https://doi.org/10.1521/jscp.2018.37.10.751

Hurley, D. (2005, April 19). Divorce rate: It's not as high as you think. *New York Times*, p. F7.

Hyde, J. S. (2005). The gender similarities hypothesis. *American Psychologist, 60*, 581–592.

Hyde, J. S., Bigler, R. S., Joel, D., Tate, C. C., & van Anders, S. M. (2019). The future of sex and gender in psychology: Five challenges to the gender binary. *American Psychologist, 74*(2), 171–193. https://doi.org/10.1037/amp0000307

Hyun, J. (2005). *Breaking the bamboo ceiling: Career strategies for Asians*. HarperCollins.

Imhof, M., & Janusik, L. A. (2006). Development and validation of the Imhof-Janusik listening concepts inventory to measure listening conceptualization differences between cultures. *Journal of Intercultural Communication Research, 35*(2), 79–98. https://doi.org/10.1080/17475750600909246

Infante, D. A. (1995). Teaching students to understand and control verbal aggression. *Communication Education, 44*, 51–63.

Infante, D. A., Chandler, T. A., & Rudd, J. E. (1989). Test of an argumentative skill deficiency model of interspousal violence. *Communication Monographs, 56*, 163–177.

Infante, D. A., Myers, S. A., & Burkel, R. A. (1994). Argument and verbal aggression in constructive and destructive family and organizational disagreements. *Western Journal of Communication, 58*, 73–84.

Infante, D. A., & Wigley, C. J. (1986). Verbal aggressiveness: An interpersonal model and measure. *Communication Monographs, 53*, 61–69.

InterACT. (2020, May 18). FAQ: What is intersex? https://interactadvocates.org/faq/#definition

Ivey, E. (2012). *The snow child*. Back Bay Books.

Jackson, D. C., Malmstadt, J. R., Larson, C. L., & Davidson, R. J. (2000). Suppression and enhancement of emotional responses to unpleasant pictures. *Psychophysiology, 37*, 515–522.

Jackson, M. (2008). *Distracted: The erosion of attention and the coming dark age*. Prometheus Books.

Jacobs, S. (1994). Language and interpersonal communication. In M. L. Knapp & G. R. Miller (Eds.), *Handbook of interpersonal communication* (2nd ed., pp. 199–228). SAGE.

Jacobs, S., Dawson, E. J., & Brashers, D. (1996). Information manipulation theory: A replication and assessment. *Communication Monographs, 63*, 70–82.

Janning, M., Gao, W., & Snyder, E. (2018). Constructing shared "space": Meaningfulness in long-distance romantic relationship communication formats. *Journal of Family Issues, 39*(5), 1281–1303. https://doi.org/10.1177/0192513X17698726

Janusik, L., & Imhof, M. (2016). Intercultural listening: Measuring listening concepts with the LCI-R. *International Journal of Listening, 31*(2), 80–97.

Janusik, L., & Imhof, M. (2017). Intercultural listening: Measuring listening concepts with the LCI-R. *International Journal of Listening, 31*, 80–97.

Janusik, L. A. (2007). Building listening theory: The validation of the conversational listening span. *Communication Studies, 58*(2), 139–156.

Jia, M., Cheng, J., & Hale, C. L. (2017). Workplace emotion and communication: Supervisor nonverbal immediacy, employees' emotion experience, and their communication motives. *Management Communication Quarterly, 31*(1), 69–87. https://doi.org/10.1177/0893318916650519

John, O. P., & Gross, J. J. (2004). Healthy and unhealthy emotion regulation: Personality processes, individual differences, and lifespan development. *Journal of Personality, 72*, 1301–1334.

Johnson, A. J., Haigh, M. M., Becker, J. A. H., Craig, E. A., & Wigley, S. (2008). College students' use of relational management strategies in email in long-distance and geographically close relationships. *Journal of Computer-Mediated Communication, 13*, 381–404.

Johnson, A. J., Wittenberg, E., Villagran, M. M., Mazur, M., & Villagran, P. (2003). Relational progression as a dialectic: Examining turning points in communication among friends. *Communication Monographs, 70*(3), 230–249.

Johnson, H. (2004, April 1). *Jimmy Jam: Three decades of hits; one seamless partnership*. http://mixonline.com/mag/audio_jimmy_jam

Joinson, A. N. (2001, March/April). Self-disclosure in computer-mediated communication: The role of self-awareness and visual anonymity. *European Journal of Social Psychology, 31*, 177–192.

Jones, D. C., Vigfusdottir, T. H., & Lee, Y. (2004). Body image and the appearance culture among adolescent girls and boys: An examination of friends' conversations, peer criticism, appearance magazines, and the internalization of appearance ideals. *Journal of Adolescent Research, 19*, 323–339.

Jones, P. T. (1996). *From his promise: A history of ALSAC and St. Jude Children's Research Hospital*. Guild Bindery Press.

Jones, S. E. (2020). Negotiating transgender identity at work: A movement to theorize a transgender standpoint epistemology. *Management Communication Quarterly, 34*(2), 251–278. https://doi.org/10.1177/0893318919898170

Jones, S. E., & LeBaron, C. D. (2002). Research on the relationship between verbal and nonverbal communication: Emerging integrations. *Journal of Communication, 52*, 499–521.

Jones, T. E. (1999). *If it's broken, you can fix it: Overcoming dysfunction in the workplace*. AMACOM Books.

Jones, W., Moore, D., Scratter, A., & Negel, L. (2001). Interpersonal transgression and betrayals. In R. M. Kowalski (Ed.), *Behaving badly: Aversive behavior in interpersonal relationships* (pp. 233–256). American Psychological Association.

Jones, W. H., & Burdette, M. P. (1994). Betrayal in relationships. In A. L. Weber & J. H. Harvey (Eds.), *Perspectives on close relationships* (pp. 243–262). Allyn & Bacon.

Jonsdottir, I. J., & Fridriksdottir, K. (2020). Active listening: Is it the forgotten dimension in managerial communication? *International Journal of Listening, 34*(3), 178–188. https://doi.org/10.1080/10904018.2019.1613156

Jourard, S. M. (1964). *The transparent self.* Van Nostrand Reinhold.

Joyner, K., Manning, W., & Prince, B. (2019). The qualities of same-sex and different-sex couples in young adulthood. *Journal of Marriage & Family, 81*(2), 487–505. https://doi.org/10.1111/jomf.12535

Juncoa, R., & Cotton, S. R. (2012). No A 4 U: The relationship between multitasking and academic performance. *Computers & Education, 59*(2), 505–514. https://doi.org/10.1016/j.compedu.2011.12.023

Kagawa, N., & McCornack, S. A. (2004, November). *Collectivistic Americans and individualistic Japanese: A cross-cultural comparison of parental understanding.* Paper presented at the National Communication Association Annual Meeting, Chicago, IL.

Kågesten, A., Gibbs, S., Blum, R. W., Moreau, C., Chandra-Mouli, V., Herbert, A., & Amin, A. (2016). Understanding factors that shape gender attitudes in early adolescence globally: A mixed-methods systematic review. *PLOS ONE, 11*(6), e0157805. https://doi.org/10.1371/journal.pone.0157805

Kaharit, K., Zachau, G., Eklof, M., Sandsjo, L., & Moller, C. (2003). Assessment of hearing and hearing disorders in rock/jazz musicians. *International Journal of Audiology, 42,* 279–288.

Kahneman, D. (1973). *Attention and effort.* Prentice Hall.

Kane, E. W. (2006). "No way my boys are going to be like that!": Parents' responses to children's gender nonconformity. *Gender & Society, 20,* 149–176. https://doi.org/10.1177/0891243205284276

Katz, D., & Kahn, R. (1978). *The social psychology of organizations* (2nd ed.). Wiley.

Katz, J. (1983). A theory of qualitative methodology. In R. M. Emerson (Ed.), *Contemporary field research: A collection of readings* (pp. 127–148). Waveland Press.

Katz, J., & Farrow, S. (2000). Discrepant self-views and young women's sexual and emotional adjustment. *Sex Roles, 42,* 781–805.

Keaton, S., & Worthington, D. L. (2018). Listening in mediated contexts: Introduction to a special issue. *International Journal of Listening, 32*(2), 65–68. https://doi.org/10.1080/10904018.2018.1439750

Keck, K. L., & Samp, J. A. (2007). The dynamic nature of goals and message production as revealed in a sequential analysis of conflict interactions. *Human Communication Research, 33,* 27–47.

Keesing, R. M. (1974). Theories of culture. *Annual Review of Anthropology, 3,* 73–97.

Kellas, J. K. (2005). Family ties: Communicating identity through jointly told family stories. *Communication Monographs, 72*(4), 365–389.

Kellas, J. K. (2018). Communicated narrative sense-making theory: Linking storytelling and well-being. In D. Braithewaite, E. Suter, & K. Floyd (Eds.), *Engaging theories in family communication* (2nd ed., pp. 62–74). Routledge.

Kellermann, K. (1989). The negativity effect in interaction: It's all in your point of view. *Human Communication Research, 16,* 147–183.

Kellermann, K. (1991). The conversation MOP: Progression through scenes in discourse. *Human Communication Research, 17,* 385–414.

Kelley, H. H., & Thibaut, J. W. (1978). *Interpersonal relations: A theory of interdependence.* Wiley.

Kelly, A. E., & McKillop, K. J. (1996). Consequences of revealing personal secrets. *Psychological Bulletin, 120,* 450–465.

Kelly, L., Miller-Ott, A. E., & Duran, R. L. (2017). Sports scores and intimate moments: An Expectancy Violations Theory approach to partner cellphone behaviors in adult romantic relationships. *Western Journal of Communication, 81*(5), 619–640. https://doi.org/10.1080/10570314.2017.1299206

Kennedy, H. R., Dalla, R. L., & Dreesman, S. (2018). "We are two of the lucky ones": Experiences with marriage and wellbeing for same-sex couples. *Journal of Homosexuality, 65*(9), 1207–1231. https://doi.org/10.1080/00918369.2017.1407612

Kettler, S. (2020, August 25). How Mister Rogers helped heal the nation after September 11. *Biography.com.* https://www.biography.com/news/mister-rogers-september-11-2001

Kimpel, D. (2010). *ASCAP Rhythm and Soul Heritage Award: Jimmy Jam & Terry Lewis.* http://www.ascap.com/eventsawards/awards/rsawards/2005/heritage.aspx

King, S. K. (2001). *Territoriality.* http://www.huna.org/html/territor.html

Klopf, D. W. (2001). *Intercultural encounters: The fundamentals of intercultural communication* (5th ed.). Morton.

Kluger, J. (2011, October 3). Playing favorites. *TIME Magazine.* http://www.time.com/time/magazine/article/0,9171,2094371,00.html

Knapp, M. (1984). *Interpersonal communication and human relationships.* Allyn & Bacon.

Knapp, M. L., & Hall, J. A. (2002). *Nonverbal communication in human interaction* (5th ed.). Wadsworth/Thomson Learning.

Knobloch, L. K. (2005). Evaluating a contextual model of responses to relational uncertainty increasing events: The role of intimacy, appraisals, and emotions. *Human Communication Research, 31*(1), 60–101.

Knutson, D., Koch, J. M., & Goldbach, C. (2019). Recommended terminology, pronouns, and documentation for work with transgender and non-binary populations. *Practice Innovations, 4*(4), 214–224. https://doi.org/10.1037/pri0000098

Koerner, A. F., & Fitzpatrick, M. A. (2002). Toward a theory of family communication. *Communication Theory, 12,* 70–91.

Koerner, A. F., & Fitzpatrick, M. A. (2006). Family communication patterns theory: A social cognitive approach. In D. O. Braithwaite & L. A. Baxter (Eds.), *Engaging theories in family communication: Multiple perspectives* (pp. 50–65). SAGE.

Koerner, S. S., Wallace, S., Lehman, S. J., & Raymond, M. (2002). Mother-to-daughter disclosure after divorce: A double-edged sword? *Journal of Child and Family Studies, 11,* 469–483.

Koss, M. (2017, August 5). No, they're not boys. But Madison soccer team endures criticism because players have short hair. *Milwaukee Journal Sentinel.* https://www.jsonline.com/story/news/2017/08/05/madison-girls-soccer-team-bristles-critics-who-say-players-boys/459741001/

Kostiuk, L. M., & Fouts, G. T. (2002). Understanding of emotions and emotion regulation in adolescent females with conduct problems: A qualitative analysis. *Qualitative Report, 7,* 1–10.

Kotzé, M., & Venter, I. (2011). Differences in emotional intelligence between effective and ineffective leaders in the public sector: An empirical study. *International Review of Administrative Sciences, 77*(2), 397–427.

Koval, P., Laham, S. M., Haslam, N., Bastian, B., & Whelan, J. A. (2012). Our flaws are more human than yours: Ingroup bias in humanizing negative characteristics. *Personality and Social Psychology Bulletin, 38*(3), 283–295.

Kowalski, R. M., Toth, A., & Morgan, M. (2018). Bullying and cyberbullying in adulthood and the workplace. *Journal of Social Psychology, 158,* 64–81.

Kowalski, R. M., Walker, S., Wilkinson, R., Queen, A., & Sharpe, B. (2003). Lying, cheating, complaining, and other aversive interpersonal behaviors: A narrative examination of the darker side of relationships. *Journal of Social and Personal Relationships, 20,* 471–490.

Kozan, M., & Ergin, C. (1998). Preference for third-party help in conflict management in the United States and Turkey. *Journal of Cross-Cultural Psychology, 29,* 525–539.

Krahé, B., & Papakonstantinou, L. (2020). Speaking like a man: Women's pitch as a cue for gender stereotyping. *Sex Roles, 82*(1738), 94–101. https://doi.org/10.1007/s11199-019-01041-z

Kramarae, C. (1981). *Women and men speaking: Frameworks for analysis.* Newbury House.

Kramer, S. (2019). U.S. has world's highest rate of children living in single-parent households. *Pew Research Center.* https://www.pewresearch.org/fact-tank/2019/12/12/u-s-children-more-likely-than-children-in-other-countries-to-live-with-just-one-parent/

Krause, J. (2001). *Properties of naturally produced clear speech at normal rates and implications for intelligibility enhancement* (Unpublished doctoral dissertation). Massachusetts Institute of Technology, Cambridge, MA.

Krauss, S., Orth, U., & Robins, R. W. (2020). Family environment and self-esteem development: A longitudinal study from age 10 to 16. *Journal of Personality and Social Psychology, 119*(2), 457–478.

Kreider, R. M. (2005). *Number, timing, and duration of marriages and divorces: 2001*. U.S. Census Bureau.

Kreps, G. L. (1990). *Organizational communication*. Longman.

Krishnakumar, A., Buehler, C., & Barber, B. K. (2003). Youth perceptions of interparental conflict, ineffective parenting, and youth problem behaviors in European-American and African-American families. *Journal of Social and Personal Relationships, 20*(2), 239–260.

Krusiewicz, E. S., & Wood, J. T. (2001). He was our child from the moment we walked in that room: Entrance stories of adoptive parents. *Journal of Social and Personal Relationships, 18*(6), 785–803.

Kubany, E. S., Richard, D. C., Bauer, G. B., & Muraoka, M. Y. (1992). Impact of assertive and accusatory communication of distress and anger: A verbal component analysis. *Aggressive Behavior, 18*, 337–347.

Kubota, J. T., & Ito, T. (2017). Rapid race perception despite individuation and accuracy goals. *Journal of Social Neuroscience, 12*(4). https://doi.org/10.1080/17470919.2016.1182585

Kugler, K. G., Reif, J. A. M., Kaschner, T., & Brodbeck, F. C. (2018). Gender differences in the initiation of negotiations: A meta-analysis. *Psychological Bulletin, 144*(2), 198–222. https://doi.org/10.1037/bul0000135

Kuhn, J. L. (2001). Toward an ecological humanistic psychology. *Journal of Humanistic Psychology, 41*, 9–24.

Kunecke, J., Wilhelm, O., & Sommer, W. (2017). Emotion recognition in nonverbal face-to-face communication. *Journal of Nonverbal Behavior, 41*(3), 221–238.

Kurdek, L. A. (2005). What do we know about gay and lesbian couples? *Current Directions in Psychological Science, 14*, 251–254.

Kurdek, L. A. (2008). Differences between partners from Black and White heterosexual dating couples in a path model of relational commitment. *Journal of Social and Personal Relationships, 25*, 51–70.

Kushlev, K., Hunter, J. F., Proulx, J., Pressman, S. D., & Dunn, E. (2019). Smartphones reduce smiles between strangers. *Computers in Human Behavior, 91*, 12–16. https://doi.org/10.1016/j.chb.2018.09.023

Kuss, D. J., & Griffiths, M. D. (2017). Social networking sites and addiction: Ten lessons learned. *International Journal of Environmental Research and Public Health, 14*(3), 311.

LaBelle, S., & Myers, S. A. (2016). The use of relational maintenance behaviors in sustained adult friendships. *Communication Research Reports, 33*(4), 310–316. https://doi.org/10.1080/08824096.2016.1224164

LaFollette, H., & Graham, G. (1986). Honesty and intimacy. *Journal of Social and Personal Relationships, 3*, 3–18.

LaForge, P. (2018, February 6). "Lady Doritos"? Pepsi wants a do-over. *New York Times*. https://www.nytimes.com/2018/02/06/business/lady-doritos-indra-nooyi.html

Lakoff, R. (1973). Language and woman's place. *Language in Society, 2*, 45–80.

Lane, C., Brundage, C. L., & Kreinin, T. (2017). Why we must invest in early adolescence: Early intervention, lasting impact. *Journal of Adolescent Health, 61*, S10–S11.

Langdridge, D., & Butt, T. (2004). The fundamental attribution error: A phenomenological critique. *British Journal of Social Psychology, 43*, 357–369.

Lapierre, M. A. (2020). Smartphones and loneliness in love: Testing links between smartphone engagement, loneliness, and relational health. *Psychology of Popular Media, 9*(2), 125–134. https://doi.org/10.1037/ppm0000230

Lareau, A. (2003). *Unequal childhoods: Class, race, and family life*. University of California Press.

Larsen, R. J., & Ketelaar, T. (1991). Personality and susceptibility to positive and negative emotional states. *Journal of Personality and Social Psychology, 61*, 132–140.

Larson, J. R. (1984). The performance feedback process: A preliminary model. *Organizational Behavior and Human Performance, 33*, 42–76.

Lasswell, H. D. (1948). The structure and function of communication in society. In L. Bryson (Ed.), *The communication of ideas* (pp. 32–51). Harper & Row.

Lausen, A., & Schacht, A. (2018). Gender differences in the recognition of vocal emotions. *Frontiers in Psychology, 9*(882), 1–22. https://doi.org/10.3389/fpsyg.2018.00882

Lavy, S., Mikulincer, M., Shaver, P. R., & Gillath, O. (2009). Intrusiveness in romantic relationships: A cross-cultural perspective on imbalances between proximity and autonomy. *Journal of Social and Personal Relationships, 26*(6–7), 989–1008.

Le, B., Korn, M. S., Crockett, E. E., & Loving, T. J. (2010). Missing you maintains us: Missing a romantic partner, commitment, relationship maintenance, and physical infidelity. *Journal of Social and Personal Relationships, 28*, 653–667.

Le, T. N., Straatman, L. V., Lea, J., & Westerberg, B. (2017). Current insights in noise-induced hearing loss: A literature review of the underlying mechanism, pathophysiology, asymmetry, and management options. *Journal of Otolaryngology: Head & Neck Surgery, 46*(1), 41. https://doi.org/10.1186/s40463-017-0219-x

Leaper, C., & Ayres, M. M. (2007). A meta-analytic review of gender variation in adults' language use: Talkativeness, affiliative speech, and assertive speech. *Personality and Social Psychology Review, 11*, 328–363.

Leaper, C., & Smith, T. E. (2004). A meta-analytic review of gender variations in children's language use: Talkativeness, affiliative speech, and assertive speech. *Developmental Psychology, 40*, 993–1027.

Leary, M. R. (2001). Toward a conceptualization of interpersonal rejection. In M. R. Leary (Ed.), *Interpersonal rejection* (pp. 3–20). Oxford University Press.

Leary, M. R., Gallagher, B., Fors, E., Buttermore, N., Baldwin, E., Kennedy, K., & Mills, A. (2003). The invalidity of disclaimers about the effects of social feedback on self-esteem. *Personality and Social Psychology Bulletin, 29*(5), 623–636. https://doi.org/10.1177/0146167203251530

Ledbetter, A. M., Griffin, A. E., & Sparks, G. G. (2007). Forecasting "friends forever": A longitudinal investigation of sustained closeness between best friends. *Personal Relationships, 14*, 343–350.

Lee, D. K. L., & Borah, P. (2020). Self-presentation on Instagram and friendship development among young adults: A moderated mediation model of media richness, perceived functionality, and openness. *Computers in Human Behavior, 103*, 57–66. https://doi.org/10.1016/j.chb.2019.09.017

Lee, J., Lim, J. J. C., & Heath, R. L. (2021). Coping with workplace bullying through NAVER: Effects of LMX relational concerns and cultural differences. *International Journal of Business Communication, 58*(1), 79–105. https://doi.org/10.1177/2329488417735649

Lee, J. A. (1973). *The colors of love: An exploration of the ways of loving*. New Press.

Lee-Flynn, S. C., Pomaki, G., DeLongis, A., Biesanz, J. C., & Puterman, E. (2011). Daily cognitive appraisals, daily affect, and long-term depressive symptoms: The role of self-esteem and self-concept clarity in the stress process. *Personality and Social Psychology Bulletin, 37*(2), 255–268. https://doi.org/10.1177/0146167210394204

Leftheriotis, I., & Giannakos, M. N. (2014). Using social media for work: Losing your time or improving your work? *Computers in Human Behavior, 31*, 134–142.

Lehrer, J. (2009, May 18). Don't! The secret of self-control. *New Yorker*. http://www.newyorker.com/reporting/2009/05/18/090518fa_fact_lehrer

Lemerise, E. A., & Dodge, K. A. (1993). The development of anger and hostile interactions. In M. Lewis and J. M. Haviland (Eds.), *Handbook of emotions* (pp. 537–546). Guilford Press.

Lenhart, A. (2015). Teens, technology and friendships. *Pew Research Center*. https://www.pewresearch.org/internet/2015/08/06/teens-technology-and-friendships/

Leubner, D., & Hinterberger, T. (2017). Reviewing the effectiveness of music interventions in treating depression. *Frontiers in Psychology, 8*, 1109. https://doi.org/10.3389/fpsyg.2017.01109

Lev-Ari, S., & Keysar, B. (2010). Why don't we believe non-native speakers? The influence of accent on credibility. *Journal of*

Experimental Social Psychology, 46, 1093–1096. https://doi.org /10.1016/j.jesp.2010.05.025

Levine, T. R., McCornack, S. A., & Baldwin Avery, P. (1992). Sex differences in emotional reactions to discovered deception. *Communication Quarterly, 40*, 289–296.

Levinson, S. C. (1985). *Pragmatics.* Cambridge University Press.

Lewellen, W. (2008, July 7). *Brenda Villa: The American saint of water polo. Women's Sports Foundation.* http://66.40.5.5/Content/Articles/Athletes /About-Athletes/B/Brenda-Villa-saint-of-Water-Polo.aspx

Li, Y., & Samp, J. A. (2019). Communication efficacy as a mechanism for the chilling effect on complaint avoidance: A cross-cultural comparison of American and Chinese romantic relationships. *Journal of Intercultural Communication, 49.*

Licoppe, C. (2003). Two modes of maintaining interpersonal relations through telephone: From the domestic to the mobile phone. In J. E. Katz (Ed.), *Machines that become us: The social context of personal communication technology* (pp. 171–185). Transaction.

Lippa, R. A. (2002). *Gender, nature, and nurture.* Erlbaum.

Lippmann, W. (1922). *Public opinion.* Harcourt Brace.

Liu, D., & Yang, C. (2016). Media niche of electronic communication channels in friendship: A meta-analysis. *Journal of Computer-Mediated Communication, 21*(6), 451–466. https://doi.org/10.1111 /jcc4.12175

Liu, M., Zhu, L., & Cionea, I. A. (2019). What makes some intercultural negotiations more difficult than others? Power distance and culture-role combinations. *Communication Research, 46*(4), 555–574. https://doi.org/10.1177/0093650216631096

Liw, L., & Han, S. Y. (2020). Coping as a moderator of self-discrepancies and psychological distress. *Counselling Psychology Quarterly*, 1–19. https://doi.org/10.1080/09515070.2020.1760208

Lopes, P. N., Salovey, P., Cote, S., & Beers, M. (2005). Emotion regulation abilities and the quality of social interaction. *Emotion, 5*, 113–118.

Lopez, G. (2017, July 27). Military to Trump: We won't ban transgender service members just because you tweeted about it. *Vox.* https:// www.vox.com/identities/2017/7/27/16050286/trump-transgender -military-ban

Ludden, D. (2017, July 30). Fact and fiction in mixed-race marriages. *Psychology Today.* https://www.psychologytoday.com/us/blog /talking-apes/201707/fact-and-fiction-in-mixed-race-marriages

Luft, J. (1970). *Group processes: An introduction to group dynamics* (2nd ed.). National Press Books.

Lui, P. P., & Quezada, L. (2019). Associations between microaggression and adjustment outcomes: A meta-analytic and narrative review. *Psychological Bulletin, 145*(1), 45–78. https://doi.org/10.1037/bul0000172

Lulofs, R. S., & Cahn, D. D. (2000). *Conflict: From theory to action* (2nd ed.). Allyn & Bacon.

Luscombe, B. (2010, November 18). Who needs marriage? A changing institution. *TIME Magazine.* http://www.time.com/time/magazine /article/0,9171,2032116,00.html

Lybarger, J. E., Rancer, A. S., & Lin, Y. (2017). Superior-employee communication in the workplace: Verbal aggression, nonverbal immediacy, and their joint effects on perceived superior credibility. *Communication Research Reports, 34*(2), 124–133. https://doi.org /10.1080/08824096.2016.1252909

Lydgate, C. (2017, March). Taking a fresh look at Hum 110: Turning a critical eye on the college's signature humanities course. *Reed Magazine, 96*(1).

Lynch, S. N. (2018, April 12). U.S. launches crackdown on sexual harassment in housing. *Reuters.* https://www.reuters.com/article /us-usa-justice-harassment/u-s-launches-crackdown-on-sexual -harassment-in-housing-idUSKBN1HJ2MU

MacCann, C., Jiang, Y., Brown, L. E. R., Double, K. S., Bucich, M., & Minbashian, A. (2020). Emotional intelligence predicts academic performance: A meta-analysis. *Psychological Bulletin, 146*(2), 150–186. https://doi.org/10.1037/bul0000219

Mack, K. (2020). She's a country girl all right: Rhiannon Giddens's powerful reclamation of country culture. *Journal of Popular Music Studies, 32*(2), 144–161. https://doi.org/10.1525/jpms.2020.32.2.144

Macrae, C. N., & Bodenhausen, G. V. (2001). Social cognition: Categorical person perception. *British Journal of Psychology, 92,* 239–255.

Ma-Kellams, C., Wang, M. C., & Cardiel, H. (2017). Attractiveness and relationship longevity: Beauty is not what it is cracked up to be. *Personal Relationships, 24,* 146–161. https://doi.org/10.1111/pere.12173

Malandro, L. A., & Barker, L. L. (1983). *Nonverbal communication.* Addison-Wesley.

Malcolm X. (1964). *Personal letter.* http://www.malcolm-x.org/docs /let_mecca.htm

Malis, R. S., & Roloff, M. E. (2006). Demand/withdraw patterns in serial arguments: Implications for well-being. *Human Communication Research, 32,* 198–216.

Mansson, D. H. (2020). Grandchildren's perceptions of grandparents' use of relational maintenance behaviors. *International Journal of Aging and Human Development, 91*(2), 127–148. https://doi.org /10.1177/0091415019852776

Mansson, D. H., & Sigurðardóttir, A. G. (2017). Trait affection given and received: A test of Hofstede's theoretical framework. *Journal of Intercultural Communication Research, 46*(2), 161–172. https:// doi.org/10.1080/17475759.2017.1292944

Mao, C. M., & DeAndrea, D. C. (2019). How anonymity and visibility affordances influence employees' decisions about voicing workplace concerns. *Management Communication Quarterly, 33*(2), 160–188. https://doi.org/10.1177/0893318918813202

Marganski, A., & Melander, L. (2018). Intimate partner violence victimization in the cyber and real world: Examining the extent of cyber aggression experiences and its association with in-person dating violence. *Journal of Interpersonal Violence, 33*(7), 1071–1095. https://doi.org/10.1177/0886260515614283

Marion, R., Christiansen, J., Klar, H. W., Schreiber, C., & Erdener, M. A. (2016). Informal leadership, interaction, cliques and productive capacity in organizations: A collectivist analysis. *Leadership Quarterly, 27,* 242–260.

Markey, P. M., & Markey, C. N. (2007). Romantic ideals, romantic obtainment, and relationship experiences: The complementarity of interpersonal traits among romantic partners. *Journal of Social and Personal Relationships, 24*(4), 517–533.

Marshall, E., Glazebrook, C., Robbins-Cherry, S., Nicholson, S., Thorne, N., & Arcelus, J. (2020). The quality and satisfaction of romantic relationships in transgender people: A systematic review of the literature. *International Journal of Transgender Health.* https://doi.org /10.1080/26895269.2020.1765446

Martin, W., & LaVan, H. (2010). Workplace bullying: A review of litigated cases. *Employee Responsibilities and Rights Journal, 22*(3), 175–194.

Martinez, N. (2017, October 10). Men vs. women: Communication styles explained. *The Huffington Post.* https://www.huffingtonpost.com /entry/men-vs-women-communication-styles-explained_us _59dc8d69e4b060f005fbd6ab

Martins, A., Pereira, M., Andrade, R., Dattilio, F. M., Narciso, I., & Canavarro, M. C. (2016). Infidelity in dating relationships: Gender-specific correlates of face-to-face and online extradyadic involvement. *Archives of Sexual Behavior, 45*(1), 193–205. https:// doi.org/10.1007/s10508-015-0576-3

Marwha, D., Halari, M., & Eliot, L. (2017). Meta-analysis reveals a lack of sexual dimorphism in human amygdala volume. *NeuroImage, 147,* 282. https://doi.org/10.1016/j.neuroimage.2016.12.021

Marzano, R. J., & Arredondo, D. E. (1996). *Tactics for thinking.* Mid Continent Regional Educational Laboratory.

Mashek, D. J., & Aron, A. (2004). *Handbook of closeness and intimacy.* Erlbaum.

Maslow, A. H. (1970). *Motivation and personality* (2nd ed.). Harper & Row.

Mason, T. B., Smith, K. E., Engwall, A., Lass, A., Mead, M., Sorby, M., Bjorlie, K., Strauman, T. J., & Wonderlich, S. (2019). Self-discrepancy theory as a transdiagnostic framework: A meta-analysis of self-discrepancy and psychopathology. *Psychological Bulletin, 145*(4), 372–389. https://doi.org/10.1037/bul0000186

Matlin, M., & Stang, D. (1978). *The Pollyanna principle: Selectivity in language, memory, and thought*. Schenkman.

Maunder, R. D., Day, S. C., & White, F. A. (2020). The benefit of contact for prejudice-prone individuals: The type of stigmatized outgroup matters. *Journal of Social Psychology, 160*(1), 92–104. https://doi.org/10.1080/00224545.2019.1601608

Mauss, I. B., Levenson, R. W., McCarter, L., Wilhelm, F. H., & Gross, J. J. (2005). The tie that binds: Coherence among emotion experience, behavior, and physiology. *Emotion, 5*, 175–190.

Mayer, J. D., & Salovey, P. (1997). What is emotional intelligence? In P. Salovey & J. D. Sluyter (Eds.), *Emotional development and emotional intelligence* (pp. 3–31). Basic Books.

Mayer, J. D., Salovey, P., & Caruso, D. R. (2004). Emotional intelligence: Theory, findings and implications. *Psychological Inquiry, 15*(3), 197–215.

Mazer, D. B., & Percival, E. F. (1989). Ideology or experience? The relationships among perceptions, attitudes, and experiences of sexual harassment in university students. *Sex Roles, 20*, 135–147.

Mazzeo, E. (2020, December 4). Disabled people finally get their holiday meet-cute in "Christmas Ever After." *Marie Claire.* https://www.marieclaire.com/culture/a34852227/christmas-ever-after-disability-representation/

McAleer, P., Todorov, A., & Belin, P. (2014). How do you say "Hello"? Personality impressions from brief novel voices. *PLOS One.* https://doi.org/10.1371/journal.pone.009077

McCarthy, M. H., Wood, J. V., & Holmes, J. G. (2017). Dispositional pathways to trust: Self-esteem and agreeableness interact to predict trust and negative emotional disclosure. *Journal of Personality and Social Psychology, 113*(1), 95–116.

McCornack, S. A. (1997). The generation of deceptive messages: Laying the groundwork for a viable theory of interpersonal deception. In J. O. Greene (Ed.), *Message production: Advances in communication theory* (pp. 91–126). Erlbaum.

McCornack, S. A. (2008). Information manipulation theory: Explaining how deception works. In L. A. Baxter & D. O. Braithwaite (Eds.), *Engaging theories in interpersonal communication: Multiple perspectives* (pp. 215–226). SAGE.

McCornack, S. A., & Husband, R. (1986, May). *The evolution of a long-term organizational conflict: A design logic approach.* Paper presented at the International Communication Association Annual Meeting, Chicago, IL.

McCornack, S. A., & Levine, T. R. (1990). When lies are uncovered: Emotional and relational outcomes of discovered deception. *Communication Monographs, 57*, 119–138.

McCrae, R. R. (2001). Trait psychology and culture. *Journal of Personality, 69*, 819–846.

McCrae, R. R., & Costa, P. T., Jr. (2001). A five-factor theory of personality. In L. A. Pervin and O. P. John (Eds.), *Handbook of personality: Theory and research* (2nd ed., pp. 139–153). Guilford Press.

McCrae, R. R., & Mõttus, R. (2019). What personality scales measure: A new psychometrics and its implications for theory and assessment. *Current Directions in Psychological Science, 28*(4), 415–420. https://doi.org/10.1177/0963721419849559

McCroskey, J. C., & Richmond, V. P. (1987). Willingness to communicate. In J. C. McCroskey & J. A. Daly (Eds.), *Personality and interpersonal communication* (pp. 129–156). SAGE.

McDuff, D., Girard, J. M., & Kaliouby, R. E. (2017). Large-scale observational evidence of cross-cultural differences in facial behavior. *Journal of Nonverbal Behavior, 41*(1), 1–19. https://doi.org/10.1007/s10919-016-0244-x

McDuff, D., Kodra, E., Kaliouby, Re., & LaFrance, M. (2017). A large-scale analysis of sex differences in facial expressions. *PLoS ONE 12*(4):e0173942. https://doi.org/10.1371/journal.pone.0173942.

McEwan, B., Babin Gallagher, B., & Farinelli, L. (2008, November). *The end of a friendship: Friendship dissolution reasons and methods.* Paper presented at the National Communication Association Annual Meeting, San Diego, CA.

McKasy, M. (2020). A discrete emotion with discrete effects: Effects of anger on depth of information processing. *Cognitive Processing, 21*, 555–573. https://doi.org/10.1007/s10339-020-00982-8

McLaren, R. M., & Sillars, A. (2020). Parent and adolescent conversations about hurt: How interaction patterns predict empathic accuracy and perceived understanding. *Communication Monographs.* https://doi.org/10.1080/03637751.2020.1722848

McLaughlin, M. L., & Cody, M. J. (1982). Awkward silences: Behavioral antecedents and consequences of the conversational lapse. *Human Communication Research, 8*, 299–316.

McNaughton, D., Hamlin, D., McCarthy, J., Head-Reeves, D., & Schreiner, M. (2007). Learning to listen: Teaching an active listening strategy to preservice education professionals. *Topics in Early Childhood Special Education, 27*(4), 223–231.

Mead, G. H. (1934). *Mind, self, and society.* University of Chicago Press.

Mehrabian, A. (1972). *Nonverbal communication.* Aldine.

Mehta, C., Hojjat, M., Smith, K. R., & Ayotte, B. J. (2017). Associations between gender segregation and gender identity in college students. *Sex Roles: A Journal of Research, 76*(11–12), 694–704. https://doi.org/10.1007/s11199-016-0685-z

Messerschmidt, J. W. (2009). "Doing gender": The impact and future of a salient sociological concept. *Gender & Society, 23*, 85–88. https://doi.org/10.1177/0891243208326253

Messman, S. J., Canary, D. J., & Hause, K. S. (2000). Motives to remain platonic, equity, and the use of maintenance strategies in opposite-sex friendships. *Journal of Social and Personal Relationships, 17*, 67–94.

Metin, U. B., Taris, T. W., & Peeters, M. C. W. (2016). Measuring procrastination at work and its associated workplace aspects. *Personality and Individual Differences, 101*, 254–263.

Metts, S., & Chronis, H. (1986, May). *Relational deception: An exploratory analysis.* Paper presented at the International Communication Association Annual Meeting, Chicago, IL.

Metts, S., & Planalp, S. (2002). Emotional communication. In M. L. Knapp & J. A. Daly (Eds.), *Handbook of interpersonal communication* (pp. 339–373). SAGE.

Mezulis, A. H., Abramson, L. Y., Hyde, J. S., & Hankin, B. L. (2004). Is there a universal positivity bias in attributions? A meta-analytic review of individual, developmental, and cultural differences in the self-serving attributional bias. *Psychological Bulletin, 130*(5), 711–747.

Michalos, A. C. (1991). *Global report on student well-being: Vol. 1. Life satisfaction and happiness.* Springer-Verlag.

Michaud, S. G., & Aynesworth, H. (1989). *The only living witness: A true account of homicidal insanity.* Signet.

Mickelson, K. D., Kessler, R. C., & Shaver, P. R. (1997). Adult attachment in a nationally representative sample. *Journal of Personality and Social Psychology, 73*, 1092–1106.

Mies, M. (1991). *Patriarchy and accumulation on a world scale: Women in the international division of labor.* Zed Books.

Miller, G. R., & Steinberg, M. (1975). *Between people: A new analysis of interpersonal communication.* Science Research Associates.

Miller, H., & Arnold, J. (2001). Breaking away from grounded identity: Women academics on the Web. *CyberPsychology and Behavior, 4*, 95–108.

Miller, K. (1995). *Organizational communication: Approaches and processes.* Wadsworth.

Miller, L., Hefner, V., & Scott, A. (2007, May). *Turning points in dyadic friendship development and termination.* Paper presented at the International Communication Association Annual Meeting, San Francisco, CA.

Miller, R. S. (2014). *Intimate relationships* (7th ed.). McGraw-Hill.

Miller, R. S., Perlman, D., & Brehm, S. S. (2007). Love. In R. S. Miller, D. Perlman, & S. S. Brehm (Eds.), *Intimate relationships* (chapter 8, pp. 244–275). McGraw-Hill.

Miller-Ott, A., & Kelly, L. (2015). The presence of cellphones in romantic partner face-to-face interactions: An Expectancy Violation

Theory approach. *Southern Communication Journal, 80*(4), 253–270. https://doi.org/10.1080/1041794X.2015.1055371

Millman, J. (1999, August 10). Brilliant careers: Fred Rogers. *Salon.com.* http://www.salon.com/1999/08/10/rogers_2/singleton/

Milne, A. A. (1926). *Winnie-the-Pooh.* E.P. Dutton.

Milne, A. A. (1928). *The house at Pooh corner.* E.P. Dutton.

Mister Rogers. (n.d.). *TVAcres.* http://www.tvacres.com/child_mrrogers.htm

Mjaavatn, P. E., Frostad, P., & Pijl, S.J. (2016). Adolescents: Differences in friendship patterns related to gender. *Issues in Educational Research, 26*(1), 45–64. http://www.iier.org.au/iier26/mjaavatn.pdf

Mohammed, R., & Hussein, A. (2008, August). *Communication climate and organizational performance.* Paper presented to the Eighth International Conference on Knowledge, Culture & Changes in Organizations, Cambridge University (UK).

Mongeau, P. A., Hale, J. L., & Alles, M. (1994). An experimental investigation of accounts and attributions following sexual infidelity. *Communication Monographs, 61,* 326–344.

Mongeau, P. A., Ramirez, A., & Vorrell, M. (2003, February). *Friends with benefits: Initial explorations of sexual, nonromantic relationships.* Paper presented at the Western Communication Association Annual Meeting, Salt Lake City, UT.

Mongeau, P. A., van Raalte, L. J., Bednarchik, L., & Generous, M. (2019). Investigating and extending variation among friends with benefits relationships: Relationship maintenance and social support. *Southern Communication Journal, 84*(5), 275–286. https://doi.org/10.1080/1041794X.2019.1641837

Monsour, M. (1992). Meanings of intimacy in cross- and same-sex friendships. *Journal of Social and Personal Relationships, 9,* 277–295.

Montagu, M. F. A. (1971). *Touching: The human significance of the skin.* Columbia University Press.

Montoya, R. M., & Horton, R. S. (2012). A meta-analytic investigation of the processes underlying the similarity-attraction effect. *Journal of Social and Personal Relationships, 30*(1), 64–94. https://doi.org/10.1177/0265407512452989

Montoya, R. M., Horton, R. S., & Kirchner, J. (2008). Is actual similarity necessary for attraction? A meta-analysis of actual and perceived similarity. *Journal of Social and Personal Relationships, 25,* 889–922.

Morrison, K., Lee, C. M., Wiedmaier, B., & Dibble, J. L. (2008, November). *The influence of MySpace and Facebook events on interpersonal relationships.* Paper presented at the National Communication Association Annual Meeting, San Diego, CA.

Morrison, K., & McCornack, S. A. (2011). *Studying attitudes toward LGBT persons in mid-Michigan: Challenges and goals.* Technical report presented at the Michigan Fairness Forum Annual Meeting, Lansing, MI.

Mosher, C., & Danoff-Burg, S. (2007). College students' life priorities: The influence of gender and gender-linked personality traits. *Gender Issues, 24*(2). https://doi.org/10.1007/s12147-007-9002-z

Mulac, A., Bradac, J. J., & Mann, S. K. (1985). Male/female language differences and attributional consequences in children's television. *Human Communication Research, 11,* 481–506.

Mulac, A., Giles, H., Bradac, J. J., & Palomares, N. A. (2013). The gender-linked language effect: An empirical test of a general process model. *Language Sciences, 38,* 22–31.

Mulac, A., Incontro, C. R., & James, M. R. (1985). Comparison of the gender-linked language effect and sex role stereotypes. *Journal of Personality and Social Psychology, 49,* 1098–1109.

Mumulo, A., & Wiig, K. (2011). *Bridesmaids* [Motion picture]. Universal Pictures.

Munro, K. (2002). Conflict in cyberspace: How to resolve conflict online. In J. Suler (Ed.), *The psychology of cyberspace.* http://www-usr.rider.edu/~suler/psycyber/conflict.html

Myers, D. (2015). Happiness. In D. Myers, *Psychology* (11th ed., pp. 479–486). Worth Publishers.

Myers, D. G. (2002). *The pursuit of happiness: Discovering the pathway to fulfillment, well-being, and enduring personal joy.* HarperCollins.

Myers, S. A., Knox, R. L., Pawlowski, D. R., & Ropog, B. L. (1999). Perceived communication openness and functional communication

skills among organizational peers. *Communication Reports, 12,* 71–83.

National Communication Association. (2017). *Credo for ethical communication.* https://www.natcom.org/sites/default/files/Public_Statement_Credo_for_Ethical_Communication_2017.pdf

National Institutes of Health. (2019). Noise-induced hearing loss. https://www.nidcd.nih.gov/health/noise-induced-hearing-loss

National Public Radio. (2016, February 15). Ginsburg and Scalia: "Best buddies." https://www.npr.org/2016/02/15/466848775/scalia-ginsburg-opera-commemorates-sparring-supreme-court-friendship

National Women's Law Center (2016, November). Workplace justice: Sexual harassment in the workplace [Fact sheet]. https://nwlc.org/resources/metoowhatnext-strengthening-workplace-sexual-harassment-protections-and-accountability/

Neuliep, J. W. (2002). Assessing the reliability and validity of the generalized ethnocentrism scale. *Journal of Intercultural Communication Research, 31,* 201–215.

Neuliep, J. W., & McCroskey, J. C. (1997). The development of a U.S. and generalized ethnocentrism scale. *Communication Research Reports, 14,* 385–398.

New Media and Marketing. (2017, August 22). *Men and women communicate differently.* http://www.newmediaandmarketing.com/men-women-communicate-differently/

Newport, F. (2014). The new era of communication among Americans. *Gallup Poll.* https://news.gallup.com/poll/179288/new-era-communication-americans.aspx

Ngabirano, A.-M. (2017, March 27). "Pink tax" forces women to pay more than men. *USA Today.* https://www.usatoday.com/story/money/business/2017/03/27/pink-tax-forces-women-pay-more-than-men/99462846/

Nicolau, E. (2020). For the hosts of Netflix's "Say I Do," it was "Love at First Sight": If you liked Queer Eye, this new reality show is for you. *Oprah Magazine.* https://www.oprahmag.com/entertainment/a33012792/netflix-say-i-do-hosts/

Nishii, L. H., & Paluch, R. M. (2018). Leaders as HR sensegivers: Four HR implementation behaviors that create strong HR systems. *Human Resource Management Review.* https://doi.org/10.1016/j.hrmr.2018.02.007

Nishiyama, K. (1971). Interpersonal persuasion in a vertical society. *Speech Monographs, 38,* 148–154.

Nofsinger, R. E. (1999). *Everyday conversation.* Waveland Press.

Ogolsky, B. G., & Bowers, J. R. (2012). A meta-analytic review of relationship maintenance and its correlates. *Journal of Social and Personal Relationships, 30*(3), 343–367. https://doi.org/10.1177/0265407512463338

Okdie, B. M., & Wirth, J. H. (2018). Can burdensome Facebook "friends" cause you pain? Self-reported pain as a motivation for exclusion. *Journal of Computer-Mediated Communication, 23*(6), 313–331. https://doi.org/10.1093/jcmc/zmy017

O'Keefe, B. J. (1988). The logic of message design. *Communication Monographs, 55,* 80–103.

O'Leary, K. D., & Vivian, D. (1990). Physical aggression in marriage. In F. D. Fincham & T. N. Bradbury (Eds.), *The psychology of marriage: Basic issues and applications* (pp. 323–348). Guilford Press.

Oetzel, J., Ting-Toomey, S., Matsumoto, T., Yokochi, Y., Pan, X., Takai, J., & Wilcox, R. (2001). Face and facework in conflict: A cross-cultural comparison of China, Germany, Japan, and the United States. *Communication Monographs, 68,* 235–258.

Ohbuchi, K., & Sato, K. (1994). Children's reactions to mitigating accounts: Apologies, excuses, and intentionality of harm. *Journal of Social Psychology, 134,* 5–17.

Olszanowski, M., Wróbel, M., & Hess, U. (2019). Mimicking and sharing emotions: A re-examination of the link between facial mimicry and emotional contagion. *Cognition and Emotion, 34*(2), 367–376. https://doi.org/10.1080/02699931.2019.1611543

Ophir, E., Nass, C. I., & Wagner, A. D. (2012). Cognitive control in media multitaskers. *Proceedings of the National Academy of Sciences.* http://www.pnas.org/content/106/37/15583

Orbe, M. P. (1998). *Constructing co-cultural theory: An explication of culture, power, and communication.* SAGE.

Orbe, M. P., & Roberts, T. L. (2012). Co-cultural theorizing: Foundations, applications & extensions. *Howard Journal of Communications, 23*(4), 293–311. https://doi.org/10.1080/10646175.2012.722838

Orth, U. (2018). The family environment in early childhood has a long-term effect on self-esteem: A longitudinal study from birth to age 27 years. *Journal of Personality and Social Psychology, 114*(4), 637–655. https://doi.org/10.1037/pspp0000143

Orth, U., Robins, R. W., Trzesniewski, K. H., Maes, J., & Schmitt, M. (2009). Low self-esteem is a risk factor for depressive symptoms from young adulthood to old age. *Journal of Abnormal Psychology, 118*, 472–478.

Osborne, L. (2013, May 26). Parents' anger as Disney turns brave girl into curvy princess. *Daily Mail.* http://www.dailymail.co.uk /tvshowbiz/article-2331417/Parents-anger-Disney-turns-Brave-girl -curvy-princess.html

Oxford English Dictionary. (2020). *New words list, June 2020.* https:// public.oed.com/updates/new-words-list-june-2020/

Oyamot, C. M., Fuglestad P. T., & Snyder, M. (2010). Balance of power and influence in relationships: The role of self-monitoring. *Journal of Social and Personal Relationships, 27*(1), 23–46. https://doi.org/10.1177/0265407509347302

Palmer, M. T., & Simmons, K. B. (1995). Communicating intentions through nonverbal behaviors: Conscious and nonconscious encoding of liking. *Human Communication Research, 22*, 128–160.

Palomares, N. A., & Derman, D. (2019). Topic avoidance, goal understanding, and relational perceptions: Experimental evidence. *Communication Research, 46*(6), 735–756. https://doi.org /10.1177/0093650216644649

Panteleeva, Y., Ceschi, G., Glowinski, D., Courvoisier, D. S., & Grandjean, D. (2018). Music for anxiety? Meta-analysis of anxiety reduction in non-clinical samples. *Psychology of Music, 46*(4), 473–487. https://doi.org/10.1177/0305735617712424

Park, H. S., & Guan, X. (2006). The effects of national culture and face concerns on intention to apologize: A comparison of the USA and China. *Journal of Intercultural Communication Research, 35*(3), 183–204.

Park, H. S., Levine, T. R., McCornack, S. A., Morrison, K., & Ferrara, M. (2002). How people really detect lies. *Communication Monographs, 69*, 144–157.

Parkinson, B., & Simons, G. (2012). Worry spreads: Interpersonal transfer of problem-related anxiety. *Cognition and Emotion, 26*(3), 462–479. https://doi.org/10.1080/02699931.2011.651101

Parkinson, B., Totterdell, P., Briner, R. B., & Reynolds, S. (1996). *Changing moods: The psychology of mood and mood regulation.* Longman.

Parks, M. R. (1994). Communicative competence and interpersonal control. In M. L. Knapp & G. R. Miller (Eds.), *Handbook of interpersonal communication* (2nd ed., pp. 589–620). SAGE.

Parks, M. R. (2007). Framing personal relationships. In *Personal relationships and personal networks* (pp. 1–23). Erlbaum.

Parks, M. R. (2007). *Personal relationships and personal networks.* Erlbaum.

Parks, M. R., & Adelman, M. B. (1983). Communication networks and the development of romantic relationships: An expansion of uncertainty reduction theory. *Human Communication Research, 10*, 55–79.

Parks, M. R., & Floyd, K. (1996). Making friends in cyberspace. *Journal of Communication, 46*, 80–97.

Patterson, B. R. (2007). Relationship development revisited: A preliminary look at communication in friendship over the lifespan. *Communication Research Reports, 24*(1), 29–37.

Patterson, M. L. (1988). Functions of nonverbal behavior in close relationships. In S. W. Duck (Ed.), *Handbook of personal relationships* (pp. 41–56). Wiley.

Patterson, M. L. (1995). A parallel process model of nonverbal communication. *Journal of Nonverbal Behavior, 19*, 3–29.

Paulson, M. (2015a, July 12). "Hamilton" heads to Broadway in a hip-hop retelling. *New York Times.* https://www.nytimes.com/2015/07/13 /theater/hamilton-heads-to-broadway-in-a-hip-hop-retelling .html?action=click&module=RelatedCoverage&pgtype= Article&region=Footer

Paulson, M. (2015b, August 12). Lin-Manuel Miranda, creator and star of "Hamilton," grew up on hip-hop and show tunes. *New York Times.* https://www.nytimes.com/2015/08/16/theater/lin-manuel -miranda-creator-and-star-of-hamilton-grew-up-on-hip-hop -and-show-tunes.html

Payne, M. J., & Sabourin, T. C. (1990). Argumentative skill deficiency and its relationship to quality of marriage. *Communication Research Reports, 7*, 121–124.

Peker, M., Booth, R. W., & Eke, A. (2018). Relationships among self-construal, gender, social dominance orientation, and interpersonal distance. *Journal of Applied Social Psychology, 48*(9), 494–505. https://doi.org/10.1111/jasp.12529

Pennebaker, J. W. (1997). *Opening up: The healing power of expressing emotions.* Guilford Press.

Pennington, N. (2009, November). *What it means to be a (Facebook) friend: Navigating friendship on social network sites.* Paper presented at the National Communication Association Annual Meeting, Chicago, IL.

Pennsylvania Dutch Country Welcome Center. (n.d.). *The Amish: FAQs.* http://www.padutch.com/atafaq.shtml

Perrin, A., & Anderson, M. (2019, April 10). Share of U.S. adults using social media, including Facebook, is mostly unchanged since 2018. *Pew Research Center FactTank.* https://www.pewresearch.org /fact-tank/2019/04/10/share-of-u-s-adults-using-social-media -including-facebook-is-mostly-unchanged-since-2018/

Persich, M. R., Krishnakumar, S., & Robinson, M. D. (2020). Are you a good friend? Assessing social relationship competence using situational judgments. *Personality and Social Psychology Bulletin, 46*(6), 913–926. https://doi.org/10.1177/0146167219880193

Pervin, L. A. (1993). Affect and personality. In M. Lewis & J. M. Haviland (Eds.), *Handbook of emotions* (pp. 301–311). Guilford Press.

Peterson, D. R. (2002). Conflict. In H. H. Kelley et al. (Eds.), *Close relationships* (2nd ed., pp. 360–396). Percheron Press.

Petit, S. (2017, October 23). Sam Smith opens up on gender-fluid identity: I feel just as much a woman as I am a man. *People.* https://people.com/bodies/sam-smith-opens-up-gender -fluid-identity-i-feel-just-as-much-a-woman-as-i-am-a-man/

Petronio, S. (2000). The boundaries of privacy: Praxis of everyday life. In S. Petronio (Ed.), *Balancing the secrets of private disclosures* (pp. 37–49). Erlbaum.

Petronio, S., & Caughlin, J. P. (2006). Communication privacy management theory: Understanding families. In D. O. Braithwaite & L. A. Baxter (Eds.), *Engaging theories in family communication: Multiple perspectives* (pp. 35–49). SAGE.

Petsko, C. D., & Bodenhausen, G. V. (2020). Multifarious person perception: How social perceivers manage the complexity of intersectional targets. *Social and Personality Psychology Compass, 14*(2). https://doi.org /10.1111/spc3.12518

Pew Research Center (2010). *Millennials: A portrait of generation next.* http://www.pewsocialtrends.org/files/2010/10/millennials -confident-connected-open-to-change.pdf

Pew Research Center. (2017, January 12). *Social media fact sheet.* http://www.pewinternet.org/fact-sheet/social-media/

PFLAG. (2020). *National glossary of terms.* https://pflag.org/glossary

Phillips, A. G., & Silvia, P. J. (2005). Self-awareness and the emotional consequences of self-discrepancies. *Personality and Social Psychology Bulletin, 31*, 703–713. https://doi.org/10.1177/0146167204271559

Phillips, S. P. (2005). Defining and measuring gender: A social determinant of health whose time has come. *International Journal for Equity in Health, 4*, 11. https://doi.org/10.1186/1475-9276-4-11

Pilarska, A. (2014). Self-construal as a mediator between identity structure and subjective well-being. *Current Psychology, 33*(2), 130–154. https://doi.org/10.1007/s12144-013-9202-5

Pillemer, J., & Rothbard, N. P. (2018). Friends without benefits: Understanding the dark sides of workplace friendship. *Academy of Management Review, 43*(4), 635–660. https://doi.org/10.5465/amr.2016.0309

Planalp, S., & Honeycutt, J. M. (1985). Events that increase uncertainty in personal relationships. *Human Communication Research, 11,* 593–604.

Plutchik, R. (1980). *Emotions: A psycho-evolutionary synthesis.* Harper & Row.

Plutchik, R. (1993). Emotions and their vicissitudes: Emotions and psychopathology. In M. Lewis & J. M. Haviland (Eds.), *Handbook of emotions* (pp. 53–66). Guilford Press.

Pocnet, C., Dupuis, M., Congard, A., & Jopp, D. (2017). Personality and its links to quality of life: Mediating effects of emotion regulation and self-efficacy beliefs. *Motivation and Emotion, 41*(2), 196–208. https://doi.org/10.1007/s11031-017-9603-0

Pollack, W. (1999). *Real boys: Rescuing our sons from the myths of boyhood.* Henry Holt.

Pomerantz, A. (1990). On the validity and generalizability of conversation analytic methods: Conversation analytic claims. *Communication Monographs, 57,* 231–235.

Portocarrero, F. F., Gonzalez, K., & Ekema-Agbaw, M. (2020). A meta-analytic review of the relationship between dispositional gratitude and well-being. *Personality and Individual Differences, 164.* https://doi.org/10.1016/j.paid.2020.110101

Pratto, F., Sidanius, J., Stallworth, L. M., & Malle, B. F. (1994). Social dominance orientation: A personality variable predicting social and political attitudes. *Journal of Personality and Social Psychology, 67*(4), 741–763. https://doi.org/10.1037/0022-3514.67.4.741

Primack, B. A., Karim, S. A., Shensa, A., Bowman, N., Knight, J., & Sidani, J. E. (2019). Positive and negative experiences on social media and perceived social isolation. *American Journal of Health Promotion, 33*(6), 859–868. https://doi.org/10.1177/0890117118824196

Privitera, C., & Campbell, M. A. (2009). Cyberbullying: The new face of workplace bullying? *Cyberpsychology & Behavior, 12*(4), 395–400.

Pruitt, D. G., & Carnevale, P. J. (1993). *Negotiation in social conflict.* Brooks-Cole.

Przepiorka, A., & Sobol-Kwapinska, M. (2020). People with positive time perspective are more grateful and happier: Gratitude mediates the relationship between time perspective and life satisfaction. *Journal of Happiness Studies, 22,* 113–126. https://doi.org/10.1007/s10902-020-00221-z

Przybylski, A. K., Murayama, K., DeHaan, C. R., & Gladwell, V. (2013). Motivational, emotional, and behavioral correlates of fear of missing out. *Computers in Human Behavior, 29,* 1814–1848.

Przybylski, A. K., & Weinstein, N. (2012). Can you connect with me now? How the presence of mobile communication technology influences face-to-face conversation quality. *Journal of Social and Personal Relationships, 30*(3), 237–246.

Quan-Haase, A., Cothrel, J., & Wellman, B. (2005). Instant messaging for collaboration: A case study of a high-tech firm. *Journal of Computer-Mediated Communication, 10.* http://jcmc.indiana.edu/vol10/issue4/quan-haase.html

Rabby, M. K. (1997, November). *Maintaining relationships via electronic mail.* Paper presented at the National Communication Association Annual Meeting, Chicago, IL.

Rainey, V. P. (2000, December). The potential for miscommunication using email as a source of communications. *Transactions of the Society for Design and Process Science, 4,* 21–43.

Ralph, B. C. W., Thomson, D. R., Cheyne, J. A., & Smilek, D. (2013). Media multitasking and failure of attention in everyday life. *Psychological Research, 78,* 661–669. https://doi.org/10.1007/s00426-013-0523-7

Ramasubramanian, S. (2010). Testing the cognitive-affective consistency model of intercultural attitudes: Do stereotypical perceptions influence prejudicial feelings? *Journal of Intercultural Communication Research, 39*(2), 105–121.

Ramírez-Sánchez, R. (2008). Marginalization from within: Expanding co-cultural theory through the experience of the Afro Punk. *Howard Journal of Communications, 19,* 89–104.

Rasmussen, E. E., & Densley, R. L. (2017). Girl in a country song: Gender roles and objectification of women in popular country music across 1990 to 2014. *Sex Roles, 76,* 188–201.

Rattrie, L. T. B., Kittler, M. G., & Paul, K. I. (2020). Culture, burnout, and engagement: A meta-analysis on national cultural values as moderators in JD-R theory. *Applied Psychology, 69*(1), 176–220. https://doi.org/10.1111/apps.12209

Rauscher, E. A., Schrodt, P., Campbell-Salome, G., & Freytag, J. (2020). The intergenerational transmission of family communication patterns: Inconsistencies in conversation and conformity orientations across two generations of family. *Journal of Family Communication, 20*(2), 97–113. https://doi.org/10.1080/15267431.2019.1683563

Rawlins, W. K. (1992). *Friendship matters: Communication, dialectics, and the life course.* Aldine de Gruyter.

Rawlins, W. K. (1994). Being there and growing apart: Sustaining friendships during adulthood. In D. J. Canary & L. Stafford (Eds.), *Communication and relational maintenance* (pp. 275–294). Emerald.

Redden, E. (2017, November 13). New international enrollments decline. *Inside Higher Ed.* https://www.insidehighered.com/news/2017/11/13/us-universities-report-declines-enrollments-new-international-students-study-abroad

Reeder, H. (2017). "He's like a brother": The social construction of satisfying cross-sex friendship roles. *Sexuality & Culture, 21*(1), 142–162. https://doi.org/10.1007/s12119-016-9387-5

Regan, P. C., Kocan, E. R., & Whitlock, T. (1998). Ain't love grand: A prototype analysis of the concept of romantic love. *Journal of Social and Personal Relationships, 15,* 411–420.

Reis, H. T., O'Keefe, S. D., & Lane, R. D. (2017). Fun is more fun when others are involved. *Journal of Positive Psychology, 12*(6), 547–557. https://doi.org/10.1080/17439760.2016.1221123

Reis, H. T., & Patrick, B. C. (1996). Attachment and intimacy: Component processes. In E. T. Higgins & A. W. Kruglanski (Eds.), *Social psychology: Handbook of basic principles* (pp. 523–563). Guilford Press.

Reis, H. T., & Shaver, P. (1988). Intimacy as an interpersonal process. In S. W. Duck (Ed.), *Handbook of personal relationships* (pp. 367–389). Wiley.

Riach, K., & Wilson, F. (2007). Don't screw the crew: Exploring the rules of engagement in organizational romance. *British Journal of Management, 18,* 79–92.

Richards, J. M., Butler, E. A., & Gross, J. J. (2003). Emotion regulation in romantic relationships: The cognitive consequences of concealing feelings. *Journal of Social and Personal Relationships, 20,* 599–620.

Ridge, R. D., & Berscheid, E. (1989, May). *On loving and being in love: A necessary distinction.* Paper presented at the Midwestern Psychological Association Annual Conference, Chicago, IL.

Riedy, M. K., & Wen, J. H. (2010). Electronic surveillance of Internet access in the American workplace: Implications for management. *Information & Communications Technology Law, 19*(1), 87–99.

Riela, S., Rodriguez, G., Aron, A., Xu, X., & Acevedo, B. P. (2010). Experiences of falling in love: Investigating culture, ethnicity, gender, and speed. *Journal of Social and Personal Relationships, 27,* 473–493.

Rintel, E. S., & Pittam, J. (1997). Strangers in a strange land: Interaction management on Internet relay chat. *Human Communication Research, 23,* 507–534.

Robertson, B. W., & Kee, K. F. (2017). Social media at work: The roles of job satisfaction, employment status, and Facebook use with co-workers. *Computers in Human Behavior, 70,* 191–196.

Robinson, S., Anderson, E., & White, A. (2018). The bromance: Undergraduate male friendships and the expansion of contemporary homosocial boundaries. *Sex Roles, 78,* 94–106.

Rochester Rising. (2018, September 18). Gender communication differences: What can we learn? https://rochesterrising.org/main/gender-communication-differences-what-can-we-learn

Rodrigues, L. N., & Kitzmann, K. M. (2007). Coping as a mediator between interparental conflict and adolescents' romantic attachment. *Journal of Social and Personal Relationships, 24*(3), 423–439.

Roehling, M. V., & Huang, J. (2018). Sexual harassment training effectiveness: An interdisciplinary review and call for research. *Journal of Organizational Behavior, 39,* 134–150.

Rohlfing, M. E. (1995). Doesn't anybody stay in one place anymore? An exploration of the under-studied phenomenon of long-distance relationships. In J. T. Wood & S. Duck (Eds.), *Under-studied relationships: Off the beaten track* (pp. 173–196). SAGE.

Roloff, M. E., & Soule, K. P. (2002). Interpersonal conflict: A review. In M. L. Knapp & J. A. Daly (Eds.), *Handbook of interpersonal communication* (3rd ed., pp. 475–528). SAGE.

Rosen, L. D., Carrier, L. M., & Cheever, N. A. (2013). Facebook and texting made me do it: Media-induced task-switching while studying. *Computers in Human Behavior, 29*, 948–958. https://doi.org/10.1016/j.chb.2012.12.001

Rosenfeld, H. M. (1987). Conversational control functions of nonverbal behavior. In A. W. Siegman & S. Feldstein (Eds.), *Nonverbal behavior and communication* (2nd ed., pp. 563–602). Erlbaum.

Rosenfeld, M. J., Thomas, R. J., & Hausen, S. (2019). Disintermediating your friends: How online dating in the United States displaces other ways of meeting. *Proceedings of the National Academy of Sciences, 116*(36), 17753–17758. https://doi.org/10.1073/pnas.1908630116

Rostosky, S. S., & Riggle, E. D. B. (2017). Same-sex couple relationship strengths: A review and synthesis of the empirical literature (2000–2016). *Psychology of Sexual Orientation and Gender Diversity, 4*, 1–13.

Rothman, J. (2014, December 24). The meaning of "culture." *New Yorker.* https://www.newyorker.com/books/joshua-rothman/meaning-culture

Rowatt, W. D., Cunningham, M. R., & Druen, P. B. (1998). Deception to get a date. *Personality and Social Psychology Bulletin, 24*, 1228–1242.

Rubin, L. B. (1996). Reflections on friendship. In K. M. Galvin & P. J. Cooper (Eds.), *Making connections: Readings in relational communication* (pp. 254–257). Roxbury.

Rubin, Z. (1973). *Liking and loving: An invitation to social psychology.* Holt, Rinehart & Winston.

Rubin, Z., Peplau, L. A., & Hill, C. T. (1981). Loving and leaving: Sex differences in romantic attachments. *Sex Roles, 7*, 821–835.

Rueter, M. A., & Koerner, A. F. (2008). The effect of family communication patterns on adopted adolescent adjustment. *Journal of Marriage and Family, 70*, 715–727.

Ruppel, E. K. (2014, July 9). Use of communication technologies in romantic relationships: Self-disclosure and the role of relationship development. *Journal of Social and Personal Relationships.* https://doi.org/10.1177/0265407514541075

Ruppel, E. K., Burke, T. J., & Cherney, M. R. (2018a). Channel complementarity and multiplexity in long-distance friends' patterns of communication technology use. *New Media & Society, 20*(4), 1564–1579. https://doi.org/10.1177/1461444817699995

Ruppel, E. K., Burke, T. J., Cherney, M. R., & Dinsmore D. R. (2018b). Social compensation and enhancement via mediated communication in the transition to college. *Human Communication Research, 44*(1), 58–79. https://doi.org/10.1093/hcr/hqx003

Rusbult, C. E. (1987). Responses to dissatisfaction in close relationships: The exit-voice-loyalty-neglect model. In D. Perlman & S. Duck (Eds.), *Intimate relationships: Development, dynamics, and deterioration* (pp. 209–237). SAGE.

Rusbult, C. E., Arriaga, X. B., & Agnew, C. R. (2001). Interdependence in close relationships. In G. J. O. Fletcher & M. S. Clark (Eds.), *Blackwell handbook of social psychology: Vol. 2. Interpersonal processes* (pp. 359–387). Blackwell.

Sabourin, T. C., Infante, D. A., & Rudd, J. E. (1993). Verbal aggression in marriages: A comparison of violent, distressed but nonviolent, and nondistressed couples. *Human Communication Research, 20*, 245–267.

Sahlstein, E. (2004). Relating at a distance: Negotiating being together and being apart in long-distance relationships. *Journal of Social and Personal Relationships, 21*, 689–702.

Sakiri, R. (2016, December 14). Twelve celebrities who broke gender roles, and HOW! *Optimism.* http://www.filtercopy.com/12-celebrities-who-broke-gender-roles-and-how-2473701094.html

Salovey, P., & Rodin, J. (1988). Coping with envy and jealousy. *Journal of Social and Clinical Psychology, 7*, 15–33.

Salpini, C. (2017, July 17). Study: 80% of Gen Z purchases influenced by social media. *Retail Dive.* https://www.retaildive.com/news/study-80-of-gen-z-purchases-influenced-by-social-media/447249/

Sander, L., & Bauman, O. (2020, May 19). Zoom fatigue is real: Here's why video calls are so draining. *Ideas.TED.com.* https://ideas.ted.com/zoom-fatigue-is-real-heres-why-video-calls-are-so-draining/

Santuzzi, A. M., & Barber, L. K. (2018). Workplace telepressure and worker well-being: The intervening role of psychological detachment. *Occupational Health Science, 2*, 337–363. https://doi.org/10.1007/s41542-018-0022-8

Saul, S. (2017, November 13). Fewer foreign students are coming to U.S., survey shows. *New York Times.* https://www.nytimes.com/2017/11/13/us/fewer-foreign-students-coming-to-us.html

Sauls, D., & Zeigler-Hill, V. (2020). The narcissistic experience of friendship: The roles of agentic and communal orientations toward friendship. *Journal of Social and Personal Relationships, 37*(10–11), 2693–2713. https://doi.org/10.1177/0265407520933685

Savicki, V., Kelley, M., & Oesterreich, E. (1999). Judgments of gender in computer-mediated communication. *Computers in Human Behavior, 15*, 185–194.

Scalia, E. (2020, September 19). What we can learn from Ginsburg's friendship with my father, Antonin Scalia. *Washington Post.* https://www.washingtonpost.com/opinions/eugene-scalia-rbg-friendship-oped/2020/09/19/35f7580c-faaa-11ea-a275-1a2c2d36e1f1_story.html

Scharp, K. M., Seiter, J. S., & Maughan, M. (2020). My Mom always tells that story to friends and relatives: Exploring the phenomenon of other-presentation. *Journal of Family Communication, 20*(2), 146–159. https://doi.org/10.1080/15267431.2020.1739689

Schein, E. H. (1985). *Organizational culture and leadership.* Jossey-Bass.

Scherer, K. R. (1974). Acoustic concomitants of emotional dimensions: Judging affect from synthesized tone sequences. In S. Weitz (Ed.), *Nonverbal communication: Readings with commentary* (pp. 105–111). Oxford University Press.

Scherer, K. R. (2001). Appraisal considered as a process of multilevel sequential checking. In K. R. Scherer, A. Schorr, & T. Johnstone (Eds.), *Appraisal processes in emotion* (pp. 92–120). Oxford University Press.

Schlaepfer, T. E., Harris, G. J., Tien, A. Y., Peng, L., Lee, S., & Pearlson, G. D. (1995). Structural differences in the cerebral cortex of healthy female and male subjects: A magnetic resonance imaging study. *Psychiatry Research, 61*, 129–135.

Schlegel, K., Palese, T., Schmid Mast, M., Rammsayer, T. H., Hall, J. A., & Murphy, N. A. (2020). A meta-analysis of the relationship between emotion recognition ability and intelligence. *Cognition and Emotion, 34*(2), 329–351. https://doi.org/10.1080/02699931.2019.1632801

Schmitt, D. P., & Buss, D. M. (2001). Human mate poaching: Tactics and temptations for infiltrating existing mateships. *Journal of Personality and Social Psychology, 80*, 894–917.

Schneider, C. S., & Kenny, D. A. (2000). Cross-sex friends who were once romantic partners: Are they platonic friends now? *Journal of Social and Personal Relationships, 17*(3), 451–466.

Schneider, F. M., & Hitzfeld, S. (2019). I ought to put down that phone but I phub nevertheless: Examining the predictors of phubbing behavior. *Social Science Computer Review.* https://doi.org/10.1177/0894439319882365

Schramm, W. (Ed.). (1954). *The process and effects of mass communication.* University of Illinois Press.

Schrodt, P. (2006). Development and validation of the Stepfamily Life Index. *Journal of Social and Personal Relationships, 23*(3), 427–444.

Schrodt, P., & Afifi, T. D. (2007). Communication processes that predict young adults' feelings of being caught and their associations with mental health and family satisfaction. *Communication Monographs, 74*(2), 200–228.

Schrodt, P., & Shimkowski, J. R. (2013). Feeling caught as a mediator of co-parental communication and young adult children's mental health and relational satisfaction with parents. *Journal of Social and Personal Relationships, 30*(8), 977–999. https://doi.org/10.1177/0265407513479213

Schroeder, K. M., & Liben, L. S. (2020). Felt pressure to conform to cultural gender roles: Correlates and consequences. *Sex Roles.* https://doi.org/10.1007/s11199-020-01155-9

Schumann, K., Zaki, J., & Dweck, C. S. (2014). Addressing the empathy deficit: Beliefs about the malleability of empathy predict effortful responses when empathy is challenging. *Journal of Personality and Social Psychology, 107*(3), 475–493. https://doi.org/10.1037/a0036738

Schwab, K., Crotti, R., Geiger, T., Ratcheva, V., & World Economic Forum. (2020). Global gender gap report 2020 insight report. *World Economic Forum.* http://www3.weforum.org/docs/WEF_GGGR_2020.pdf

Schwab, K., Samans, R., Zahidi, S., Leopold, T. A., Ratcheva, V., Hausmann, R., & D'Andrea Tyson, L. (2017). The Global Gender Gap Report 2017. *World Economic Forum.* https://www.weforum.org/reports/the-global-gender-gap-report-2017

Science Daily. (2017, January 17). *Mounting challenge to brain sex differences.* https://www.sciencedaily.com/releases/2017/01/170117135943.htm

Searle, J. R. (1965). What is a speech act? In M. Black (Ed.), *Philosophy in America* (pp. 221–239). Cornell University Press.

Searle, J. R. (1969). *Speech acts.* Cambridge University Press.

Searle, J. R. (1976). The classification of illocutionary acts. *Language in Society, 5,* 1–24.

Sears, B., & Mallory, C. (2014). Employment discrimination against LGBT people: Existence and impact. In C. M. Duffy & D. Visconti (Eds.), *Gender identity and sexual orientation discrimination in the workplace: A practical guide* (pp. 1–19). Bloomberg BNA.

Sebold, A. (2002). *The lovely bones.* Little, Brown.

Segrin, C., Burke, T. J., & Kauer, T. (2020). Overparenting is associated with perfectionism in parents of young adults. *Couple and Family Psychology: Research and Practice, 19*(30), 181–190. https://doi.org/10.1037/cfp0000143

Seiter, J. S., & Dutson, E. (2007). The effect of compliments on tipping behavior in hairstyling salons. *Journal of Applied Psychology, 37*(9), 1999–2007. https://doi.org/10.1111/j.1559-1816.2007.00247.x

Selkie, E., Adkins, V., Masters, E., Bajpai, A., & Shumer, D. (2020). Transgender adolescents' uses of social media for social support. *Journal of Adolescent Health, 66*(3), 275–280. https://doi.org/10.1016/j.jadohealth.2019.08.011

Seta, J. J., & Seta, C. E. (1993). Stereotypes and the generation of compensatory and noncompensatory expectancies of group members. *Personality and Social Psychology Bulletin, 19,* 722–731.

Shackelford, T. K., & Buss, D. M. (1997). Anticipation of marital dissolution as a consequence of spousal infidelity. *Journal of Social and Personal Relationships, 14,* 793–808.

Shams, T. (2020). Successful yet precarious: South Asian Muslim Americans, Islamophobia, and the model minority myth. *Sociological Perspectives, 63*(4), 653–669. https://doi.org/10.1177/0731121419895006

Shannon, C. E., & Weaver, W. (1949). *The mathematical theory of communication.* University of Illinois Press.

Shaver, P. R., Wu, S., & Schwartz, J. C. (1992). Cross-cultural similarities and differences in emotion and its representation. In M. S. Clark (Ed.), *Emotion* (pp. 175–212). SAGE.

Shechory Bitton, M., & Ben Shaul, D. (2013). Perceptions and attitudes to sexual harassment: An examination of sex differences and the sex composition of the harasser-target dyad. *Journal of Applied Social Psychology, 43,* 2136–2145.

Shedletsky, L. J., & Aitken, J. E. (2004). *Human communication on the Internet.* Pearson Education/Allyn & Bacon.

Shelton, J. N., Richeson, J. A., & Bergsieker, H. B. (2009). Interracial friendship development and attributional biases. *Journal of Social and Personal Relationships, 26*(2–3), 179–193.

Shelton, J. N., Trail, T. E., West, T. V., & Bergsieker, H. B. (2010). From strangers to friends: The interpersonal process model of intimacy in developing interracial friendships. *Journal of Social and Personal Relationships, 27*(1), 71–90.

Shensa, A., Sidani, J. E., Lin, L., Bowman, N., & Primack, B. A. (2016). Social media use and perceived emotional support among US young adults. *Journal of Community Health, 41*(3), 541–549.

Shoda, Y., Mischel, W., & Peake, P. K. (1990). Predicting adolescent cognitive and self-regulatory competencies from preschool delay of gratification: Identifying diagnostic conditions. *Developmental Psychology, 26*(6), 978–986.

Shweder, R. A. (1993). The cultural psychology of the emotions. In M. Lewis & J. M. Haviland (Eds.), *Handbook of emotions* (pp. 417–431). Guilford Press.

Sias, P. M., & Cahill, D. J. (1998). From co-workers to friends: The development of peer friendships in the workplace. *Western Journal of Communication, 62,* 273–300.

Sias, P. M., Drzewiecka, J. A., Meares, M., Bent, R., Konomi, Y., Ortega, M., & White, C. (2008). Intercultural friendship development. *Communication Reports, 21*(1), 1–13.

Sias, P. M., Heath, R. G., Perry, T., Silva, D., & Fix, B. (2004). Narratives of workplace friendship deterioration. *Journal of Social and Personal Relationships, 21*(3), 321–340.

Sias, P. M., Krone, K. J., & Jablin, F. M. (2002). An ecological systems perspective on workplace relationships. In M. L. Knapp & J. A. Daly (Eds.), *Handbook of interpersonal communication* (pp. 615–642). SAGE.

Sias, P. M., & Perry, T. (2004). Disengaging from workplace relationships: A research note. *Human Communication Research, 30,* 589–602.

Sias, P. M., Tsetsi, E., Woo, N., & Smith, A. D. (2020). With a little help from my friends: Perceived task interdependence, coworker communication, and workplace friendship. *Communication Studies, 71*(4), 528–549. https://doi.org/10.1080/10510974.2020.1749863

Sillars, A., & McLaren, R. M. (2015). Attribution in conflict. In C. R. Berger, M. E. Roloff, S. R. Wilson, J. P. Dillard, J. Caughlin, & D. Solomon (Eds.), *The international encyclopedia of interpersonal communication.* https://doi.org/10.1002/9781118540190.wbeic113

Sillars, A., Roberts, L. J., Leonard, K. E., & Dun, T. (2000). Cognition during marital conflict: The relationship of thought and talk. *Journal of Social and Personal Relationships, 17,* 479–502.

Sillars, A., Smith, T., & Koerner, A. (2010). Misattributions contributing to empathic (in)accuracy during parent–adolescent conflict discussions. *Journal of Social and Personal Relationships, 27*(6), 727–747.

Sillars, A. L. (1980). Attributions and communication in roommate conflicts. *Communication Monographs, 47,* 180–200.

Sillars, A. L., & Wilmot, W. W. (1994). Communication strategies in conflict and mediation. In J. Wiemann & J. Daly (Eds.), *Communicating strategically: Strategies in interpersonal communication* (pp. 163–190). Erlbaum.

Silver, L., Huang, C., & Taylor, K. (2019, August 22). In emerging economies, smartphone and social media users have broader social networks. *Pew Research Center.* https://www.pewresearch.org/internet/2019/08/22/in-emerging-economies-smartphone-and-social-media-users-have-broader-social-networks/

Silvera, D. H., Krull, D. S., & Sassler, M. A. (2002). Typhoid Pollyanna: The effect of category valence on retrieval order of positive and negative category members. *European Journal of Cognitive Psychology, 14,* 227–236.

Silversides, B. V. (1994). *The face pullers: Photographing native Canadians, 1871–1939.* Fifth House.

Silverstein, M., & Giarrusso, R. (2010). Aging and family life: A decade review. *Journal of Marriage and Family, 72,* 1039–1058.

Simonson, R. (2020). Revisit Lin-Manuel Miranda's interview about performing *The Hamilton Mixtape. Playbill.com.* https://www.playbill.com/article/playbill-brief-encounter-with-in-the-heights-and-hamilton-mixtape-songwriter-lin-manuel-miranda-com-186236

Smith, A., & Anderson, M. (2018). *Social media use in 2018.* www.pewinternet.org/2018/03/01/social-media-use-in-2018/

Smith, C. A., & Kirby, L. D. (2004). Appraisal as a pervasive determinant of anger. *Emotion, 4,* 133–138.

Smith, C. V., Lair, E. C., & O'Brien, S. M. (2019). Purposely stoic, accidentally alone? Self-monitoring moderates the relationship between emotion suppression and loneliness. *Personality and Individual Differences, 149,* 286–290.

Smith, G., & Anderson, K. J. (2005). Students' ratings of professors: The teaching style contingency for Latino/a professors. *Journal of Latinos and Education, 4,* 115–136.

Smith, J. S., LaFrance, M., Knol, K. H., Tellinghuisen, D. J., & Moes, P. (2015). Surprising smiles and unanticipated frowns: How emotion and status influence gender categorization. *Journal of Nonverbal Behavior, 39,* 115–130.

Smith, L., Heaven, P. C. L., & Ciarrochi, J. (2008). Trait emotional intelligence, conflict communication patterns, and relationship satisfaction. *Personality and Individual Differences, 44,* 1314–1325.

Smith, S. G., Zhang, X., Basile, K. C., Merrick, M. T., Wang, J., Kresnow, M., & Chen, J. (2018). *The national intimate partner and sexual violence survey (NISVS): 2015 data brief. Updated release.* National Center for Injury Prevention and Control, Centers for Disease Control and Prevention.

Snyder, M. (1974). Self-monitoring of expressive behavior. *Journal of Personality and Social Psychology, 30,* 526–537.

Social Media Week. (2017, April 20). *15 Stats on how Gen Z spends their time on social media and mobile messaging.* socialmediaweek.org/blog/2017

Solomon, D. H., & Samp, J. A. (1998). Power and problem appraisal: Perceptual foundations of the chilling effect in dating relationships. *Journal of Social and Personal Relationships, 15,* 191–209.

Soto, J. A., Levenson, R. W., & Ebling, R. (2005). Cultures of moderation and expression: Emotional experience, behavior, and physiology in Chinese Americans and Mexican Americans. *Emotion, 5,* 154–165.

Spears, R., Postmes, T., Lea, M., & Watt, S. E. (2001). A SIDE view of social influence. In J. P. Forgas & K. D. Williams (Eds.), *Social influence: Direct and indirect processes* (pp. 331–350). Psychology Press–Taylor and Francis Group.

Spender, D. (1984). Defining reality: A powerful tool. In C. Kramarae, M. Schultz, & W. O'Barr (Eds.), *Language and power* (pp. 195–205). SAGE.

Spender, D. (1990). *Man made language.* London: Pandora Press

Spitzberg, B. (1997). A model of intercultural communication competence. In L. A. Samovar & R. E. Porter (Eds.), *Intercultural communication: A reader* (pp. 379–391). Wadsworth.

Spitzberg, B. H., & Cupach, W. R. (1984). *Interpersonal communication competence.* SAGE.

Spitzberg, B. H., & Cupach, W. R. (2002). Interpersonal skills. In M. L. Knapp & J. A. Daly (Eds.), *Handbook of interpersonal communication* (3rd ed., pp. 564–611). SAGE.

Sprecher, S. (2001). A comparison of emotional consequences of and changes in equity over time using global and domain-specific measures of equity. *Journal of Social and Personal Relationships, 18,* 477–501.

Sprecher, S., & Metts, S. (1999). Romantic beliefs: Their influence on relationships and patterns of change over time. *Journal of Social and Personal Relationships, 16*(6), 834–851.

Stafford, L. (2003). Maintaining romantic relationships: A summary and analysis of one research program. In D. J. Canary & M. Dainton (Eds.), *Maintaining relationships through communication: Relational, contextual, and cultural variations* (pp. 51–77). Erlbaum.

Stafford, L. (2010). Measuring relationship maintenance behaviors: Critique and development of the revised relationship maintenance behavior scale. *Journal of Social and Personal Relationships, 28,* 278–303.

Stafford, L. (2020). Communal strength, exchange orientation, equity, and relational maintenance. *Journal of Social and Personal Relationships, 37*(8–9), 2345–2365. https://doi.org/10.1177/0265407520923741

Stafford, L., Dainton, M., & Haas, S. (2000). Measuring routine and strategic relational maintenance: Scale revision, sex versus gender roles, and the prediction of relational characteristics. *Communication Monographs, 67,* 306–323.

Stafford, L., & Merolla, A. J. (2007). Idealization, reunions, and stability in long-distance dating relationships. *Journal of Social and Personal Relationships, 24,* 37–54.

Stafford, L., Merolla, A. J., & Castle, J. (2006). When long-distance dating partners become geographically close. *Journal of Social and Personal Relationships, 23,* 901–919.

Standlee, A. (2019). Friendship and online filtering: The use of social media to construct offline social networks. *New Media & Society, 21*(3), 770–785. https://doi.org/10.1177/1461444818806844

Steinmetz, K. (2020, February 20). She coined the term "intersectionality" over 30 years ago. Here's what it means to her today. *Time.* https://time.com/5786710/kimberle-crenshaw-intersectionality/

Stewart, M. C., & Arnold, C. L. (2018). Defining social listening: recognizing an emerging dimension of listening. *International Journal of Listening, 32*(2), 85–100. https://doi.org/10.1080/10904018.2017.1330656

Stich, J., Tarafdar, M., & Cooper, C. L. (2018). Electronic communication in the workplace: Boon or bane? *Journal of Organizational Effectiveness: People and Performance, 5*(1), 98–106. https://doi.org/10.1108/JOEPP-05-2017-0046

Stiff, J. B., Dillard, J. P., Somera, L., Kim, H., & Sleight, C. (1988). Empathy, communication, and prosocial behavior. *Communication Monographs, 55,* 198–213.

Stimson, E. (1998, March). The real Mister Rogers: This Presbyterian minister is as genuinely nice in person as he is on TV. http://www.adventistreview.org/thisweek/story5.htm

Stocker, C. M., Gilligan, M., Klopack, E. T., Conger, K. J., Lanthier, R. P., Neppl, T. K., O'Neal, C. W., & Wickrama, K. A. S. (2020). Sibling relationships in older adulthood: Links with loneliness and well-being. *Journal of Family Psychology, 34*(2), 175–185. https://doi.org/10.1037/fam0000586

Stone, E. (2004). *Black sheep and kissing cousins: How our family stories shape us.* Transaction.

Storch, S. L., & Juarez-Paz, A. V. O. (2017). Family communication: Exploring the dynamics of listening with mobile devices. *International Journal of Listening, 32,* 115–126. https://doi.org/10.1080/10904018.2017.1330657

Storch, S. L., & Ortiz Juarez-Paz, A. V. (2018). Family communication: Exploring the dynamics of listening with mobile devices. *International Journal of Listening, 32*(2), 115–126. https://doi.org/10.1080/10904018.2017.1330657

Strauss, V. (2006, March 21). Putting parents in their place: Outside class. *Washington Post,* p. A08.

Streek, J. (1980). Speech acts in interaction: A critique of Searle. *Discourse Processes, 3,* 133–154.

Streek, J. (1993). Gesture as communication I: Its coordination with gaze and speech. *Communication Monographs, 60,* 275–299.

Suitor, J. J., Gilligan, M., Peng, S., Con, G., Rurka, M., & Pillemer, K. (2016). My pride and joy? Predicting favoritism and disfavoritism in mother-adult child relations. *Journal of Marriage and Family, 78,* 908–925. https://doi.org/10.1111/jomf.12288

Suitor, J. J., Sechrist, J., Plikuhn, M., Pardo, S. T., Gilligan, M., & Pillemer, K. (2009). The role of perceived maternal favoritism in sibling relations in midlife. *Journal of Marriage and Family, 71,* 1026–1038.

Suler, J. R. (2004). The online disinhibition effect. *CyberPsychology and Behavior, 7,* 321–326.

Sullivan, J. (2019, May 20). Rhiannon Giddens and what folk music means. *New Yorker.* https://www.newyorker.com/magazine/2019/05/20/rhiannon-giddens-and-what-folk-music-means

Sullivan, K. T., Riedstra, J., Arellano, B., Cardillo, B., Kalach, V., & Ram, A. (2020). Online communication and dating relationships: Effects of decreasing online communication on feelings of closeness and relationship satisfaction. *Journal of Social and Personal Relationships, 37*(8–9), 2409–2418. https://doi.org/10.1177/0265407520924707

Sumner, W. G. (1906). *Folkways.* Ginn.

Sung, Y., Lee, J. A., Kim, E., & Choi, S. M. (2016). Why we post selfies: Understanding motivations for posting pictures of oneself. *Personality and Individual Differences, 97,* 260–265.

Surra, C., & Hughes, D. (1997). Commitment processes in accounts of the development of premarital relationships. *Journal of Marriage and the Family, 59,* 5–21.

Szczygiel, D., & Mikolajczak, M. (2017). Why are people high in emotional intelligence happier? They make the most of their positive emotions. *Personality and Individual Differences, 117,* 177–181.

Tajmirriyahi, M., & Ickes, W. (2020). Self-concept clarity as a predictor of self-disclosure in romantic relationships. *Journal of Social and Personal Relationships, 37*(6), 1873–1891.

Tamir, M., & Robinson, M. D. (2007). The happy spotlight: Positive mood and selective attention to rewarding information. *Personality and Social Psychology Bulletin, 33,* 1124–1136. https://doi.org/10.1177/0146167207301030

Tannen, D. (1990, June 24). Sex, lies and conversation: Why is it so hard for men and women to talk to each other? *Washington Post.* https://www.washingtonpost.com/archive/opinions/1990/06/24/sex-lies-and-conversation/

Tannen, D. (2006). You just don't understand: Women and men in conversation. In E. Disch (Ed.), *Reconstructing gender: A multicultural anthology* (pp. 216–221). McGraw-Hill.

Tarafdar, M., D'Arcy, J., Turel, O., & Gupta, A. (2015). The dark side of information technology, *Sloan Management Review, 56*(2), 60–71.

Tardy, C., & Dindia, K. (1997). Self-disclosure. In O. Hargie (Ed.), *The handbook of communication skills.* Routledge.

Tardy, C. H. (2000). Self-disclosure and health: Revising Sidney Jourard's hypothesis. In S. Petronio (Ed.), *Balancing the secrets of private disclosures* (pp. 111–122). Erlbaum.

Tatum, S. (2018, March 23). White House announces policy to ban most transgender people from serving in military. *CNNPolitics.* https://www.cnn.com/2018/03/23/politics/transgender-white-house/index.html

Tavris, C. (1989). *Anger: The misunderstood emotion.* Touchstone Press.

Tay, L., & Diener, E. (2011). Needs and subjective well-being around the world. *Journal of Personality and Social Psychology, 101*(2), 354–365. https://doi.org/10.1037/a0023779

Technology.org. (2020, January 29). Millennials and Gen Z are more anxious than previous generations: Here's why. https://www.technology.org/2020/01/29/millennials-and-gen-z-are-more-anxious-than-previous-generations-heres-why/

Tews, M. J., Michel, J. W., & Allen, D. G. (2014). Fun and friends: The impact of workplace fun and constituent attachment on turnover in a hospitality context. *Human Relations, 67,* 923–946. https://doi.org/10.1177/0018726713508143

Tews, M. J., Michel, J. W., & Stafford, K. (2019). Abusive coworker treatment, coworker support, and employee turnover. *Journal of Leadership & Organizational Studies, 26*(4), 413–423. https://doi.org/10.1177/1548051818781812

Thayer, R. E., Newman, J. R., & McClain, T. M. (1994). Self-regulation of mood: Strategies for changing a bad mood, raising energy, and reducing tension. *Journal of Personality and Social Psychology, 67,* 910–925.

Thomas, D., & Davidson, B. (1991). *Make room for Danny.* G.P. Putnam's Sons.

Thomas, L. T., & Levine, T. R. (1994). Disentangling listening and verbal recall: Related but separate constructs? *Human Communication Research, 21,* 103–127.

Thorne, B. (1995). Girls and boys together . . . but mostly apart: Gender arrangements in elementary school. In M. S. Kimmel & M. A. Messner (Eds.), *Men's lives* (pp. 61–73). Allyn & Bacon.

Thottam, I. (n.d.). 10 online dating statistics you should know (U.S.). *eharmony.* https://www.eharmony.com/online-dating-statistics/

Tillema, T., Dijst, M., & Schwanen, T. (2010). Face-to-face and electronic communications in maintaining social networks: The influence of geographical and relational distance and of information content. *New Media & Society, 12*(6), 965–983.

Ting-Toomey, S. (1985). Toward a theory of conflict and culture. In W. B. Gudykunst, L. P. Stewart, & S. Ting-Toomey (Eds.), *Communication, culture, and organizational processes* (pp. 71–86). SAGE.

Ting-Toomey, S. (1997). Managing intercultural conflicts effectively. In L. A. Samovar & R. E. Porter (Eds.), *Intercultural communication: A reader* (pp. 392–403). Wadsworth.

Ting-Toomey, S. (1999). *Communicating across cultures.* Guilford Press.

Ting-Toomey, S. (2005). The matrix of face: An updated face-negotiation theory. In W. B. Gudykunst (Ed.), *Theorizing about intercultural communication* (pp. 211–234). SAGE.

Tippett, M. (1994). The face pullers [Review of the book *The face pullers,* by B. V. Silversides]. *Canadian Historical Review, 75,* 1–4.

Tovares, A. V. (2010). All in the family: Small stories and narrative construction of a shared family identity that includes pets. *Narrative Inquiry, 20*(1), 1–19.

Tracy, S. J., Lutgen-Sandvik, P., & Alberts, J. K. (2006). Nightmares, demons, and slaves: Exploring the painful metaphors of workplace bullying. *Management Communication Quarterly, 20*(2), 148–185.

Tran, P., Judge, M., & Kashima, Y. (2019). *Personal Relationships, 26,* 158–180. https://doi.org/10.1111/pere.12268

Trekels, J., & Eggermont, S. (2017). Beauty is good: The appearance culture, the internalization of appearance ideals, and dysfunctional appearance beliefs among tweens. *Human Communication Research, 43*(2), 173–192. https://doi.org/10.1111/hcre.12100

Twenge, J. M., Spitzberg, B. H., & Campbell, W. K. (2019). Less in-person social interaction with peers among U.S. adolescents in the 21st century and links to loneliness. *Journal of Social and Personal Relationships, 36*(6), 1892–1913. https://doi.org/10.1177/0265407519836170

Troyer, D., & Greitemeyer, T. (2018). The impact of attachment orientations on empathy in adults: Considering the mediating role of emotion regulation strategies and negative affectivity. *Personality and Individual Differences, 122,* 198–205.

Tsai, J. L., & Levenson, R. W. (1997). Cultural influences of emotional responding: Chinese American and European American dating couples during interpersonal conflict. *Journal of Cross-Cultural Psychology, 28,* 600–625.

Turkle, S. (1995). *Life on the screen: Identity in the age of the Internet.* Simon & Schuster.

Turner, J. C., Hogg, M. A., Oakes, P. J., Reicher, S. D., & Wetherell, M. S. (1987). *Rediscovering the social group: A self-categorization theory.* Basil Blackwell.

Twenge, J. M. (2017). *iGen: Why today's super-connected kids are growing up less rebellious, more tolerant, less happy—and completely unprepared for adulthood.* Simon & Schuster.

Tye-Williams, S., Carbo, J., D'Cruz, P., Hollis, L. P., Keashly, L., Mattice, C., & Tracy, S. J. (2020). Exploring workplace bullying from diverse perspectives: A *Journal of Applied Communication Research* forum. *Journal of Applied Communication Research, 48*(6), 637–653. https://doi.org/10.1080/00909882.2020.1830148

Umphrey, L. R., & Sherblom, J. C. (2018). The constitutive relationship of listening to hope, emotional intelligence, stress, and life satisfaction. *International Journal of Listening, 32*(1), 24–48. https://doi.org/10.1080/10904018.2017.1297237

Unger, R. K. (1979). Toward a redefinition of sex and gender. *American Psychologist, 34,* 1085–1094.

University of Rochester. (2013, February 1). *Men are from ~~Mars~~ Earth, women are from ~~Venus~~ Earth.* http://rochester.edu/news/show.php?id=5382

U.S. Census Bureau. (2012, May 17). *Most children younger than age 1 are minorities, Census Bureau reports.* http://www.census.gov/newsroom/releases/archives/population/cb12-90.html

U.S. Department of Defense. (2016). *Transgender policy.* https://www.defense.gov/News/Special-Reports/0616_transgender-policy/

U.S. Equal Employment Opportunity Commission (EEOC). (n.d.). *Facts about sexual harassment.* https://www.eeoc.gov/eeoc/publications/fs-sex.cfm

U.S. Equal Employment Opportunity Commission (EEOC). (1990, March 19). Policy guidance on current issues of sexual harassment. https://www.eeoc.gov/laws/guidance/policy-guidance-current-issues-sexual-harassment

Vallacher, R. R., Nowak, A., Froehlich, M., & Rockloff, M. (2002). The dynamics of self-evaluation. *Personality and Social Psychology Review, 6,* 370–379.

Vanden Brook, T. (2018, April 11). Marines suspend general who called allegations of sexual harassment "fake news." *USA Today*. https://www.usatoday.com/story/news/politics/2018/04/11/marines -suspend-general-who-called-allegations-sexual-harassment -fake-news/502788002/

Vangelisti, A. L., Crumley, L. P., & Baker, J. L. (1999). Family portraits: Stories as standards for family relationships. *Journal of Social and Personal Relationships, 16*(3), 335–368.

Vannier, S. A., & O'Sullivan, L. F. (2017). Passion, connection, and destiny: How romantic expectations help predict satisfaction and commitment in young adults' dating relationships. *Journal of Social and Personal Relationships, 34*(2), 235–257. https://doi.org /10.1177/0265407516631156

Vanorman, A., & Jacobsen, L. A. (2020). U.S. household composition shifts as the population grows older; more young adults live with parents. *Population Reference Bureau.* https://www.prb.org/u-s -household-composition-shifts-as-the-population-grows-older -more-young-adults-live-with-parents/#:~:text=By%202017%2C %20married%2Dcouple%20families,were%20married%20couples %20with%20children

Vault Careers. (2019, February 14). *Attention cubicle cupids: The 2019 office romance survey results are in!* https://www.vault.com/blogs /workplace-issues/2019-vault-office-romance-survey-results

Vazire, S., & Gosling, S. D. (2004). E-Perceptions: Personality impressions based on personal websites. *Journal of Personality and Social Psychology, 87,* 123–132.

Veale, D., Kinderman, P., Riley, S., & Lambrou, C. (2003). Self-discrepancy in body dysmorphic disorder. *British Journal of Clinical Psychology, 42,* 157–169.

Veenhoven, R. (2014). Informed pursuit of happiness: What we should know, do know, and can get to know. *Journal of Happiness Studies, 16*(4). https://doi.org/10.1007/s10902-014-9560-1

Velasquez, A. (2018). Parents' mobile relational maintenance in resource-constrained contexts: Barriers and facilitating access conditions. *New Media & Society, 20*(12), 4415–4435. https://doi.org /10.1177/1461444818774256

Venetis, M. K., Chernichky-Karcher, S., & Gettings, P. E. (2018). Disclosing mental illness information to a friend: Exploring how the disclosure decision-making model informs strategy selection. *Health Communication, 33*(6), 653–663. https://doi.org/10.1080 /10410236.2017.1294231

Vergoossen, H. P., Renström, E. A., Lindqvist, A., & Gustafsson Sendén, M. (2020). Four dimensions of criticism against gender-fair language. *Sex Roles: A Journal of Research, 83*(5–6), 328–337. https://doi.org/10.1007/s11199-019-01108-x

Verhoef, H., & Terblanche, L. (2015). The effect of dissolved workplace romances on the psychosocial functioning and productivity of the employees involved. *Social Work, 51,* 287–310. https://doi.org /10.15270/51-2-448

Vermeulen, A., Vandebosch, H., & Heirman, W. (2018). #Smiling, #venting, or both? Adolescents' social sharing of emotions on social media. *Computers in Human Behavior, 84,* 211–219. https://doi.org/10.1016 /j.chb.2018.02.022

Vespa, J., Medina, L., & Armstrong, D. M. (2020). Demographic turning points for the United States: Population projections for 2020 to 2060. *U.S. Census Bureau.* https://www.census.gov/content/dam /Census/library/publications/2020/demo/p25-1144.pdf

Vickery, A. J. (2018). Listening enables me to connect with others: Exploring college students' (mediated) listening metaphors. *International Journal of Listening, 32*(2), 69–84. https://doi.org/10.1080 /10904018.2018.1427587

Villaume, W. A., & Bodie, G. D. (2007). Discovering the listener within us: The impact of trait-like personality variables and communicator styles on preferences for listening style. *International Journal of Listening, 21,* 102–123.

Vogels, E. A. (2020, February 6). Ten facts about Americans and online dating. *Pew Research Center.* https://www.pewresearch.org/fact -tank/2020/02/06/10-facts-about-americans-and-online-dating/

Vogl-Bauer, S. (2003). Maintaining family relationships. In D. J. Canary & M. Dainton (Eds.), *Maintaining relationships through communication: Relational, contextual, and cultural variations* (pp. 31–50). Erlbaum.

Waldron, H. B., Turner, C. W., Alexander, J. F., & Barton, C. (1993). Coding defensive and supportive communications: Discriminant validity and subcategory convergence. *Journal of Family Psychology, 7,* 197–203.

Waldvogel, J. (2007). Greetings and closings in workplace email. *Journal of Computer-Mediated Communication, 12,* 122–143.

Wallace, P. (1999). *The psychology of the Internet.* Cambridge University Press.

Walsh, M., Millar, M., & Westfall, R. S. (2019). Sex differences in responses to emotional and sexual infidelity in dating relationships. *Journal of Individual Differences, 40*(2), 63–70. https://doi.org /10.1027/1614-0001/a000277

Wang, N., Roache, D. J., & Pusateri, K. B. (2019). Interconnection of multiple communication modes in long-distance dating relationships. *Western Journal of Communication, 83*(5), 600–623. https://doi.org/10.1080/10570314.2018.1552986

Walther, J. B., & Parks, M. R. (2002). Cues filtered out, cues filtered in: Computer-mediated communication and relationships. In M. L. Knapp & J. A. Daly (Eds.), *Handbook of interpersonal communication* (3rd ed., pp. 529–563). SAGE.

Walther, J. B., Van Der Heide, B., Hamel, L., & Schulman, H. (2008, May). *Self-generated versus other-generated statements and impressions in computer-mediated communication: A test of warranting theory using Facebook.* Paper presented at the International Communication Association Annual Meeting, Montreal, Canada.

Walther, J. B., Van Der Heide, B., Kim, S. Y., Westerman, D., & Tong, S. T. (2008). The role of friends' appearance and behavior on evaluations of individuals on Facebook: Are we known by the company we keep? *Human Communication Research, 34,* 28–49.

Wang, H., & Andersen, P. A. (2007, May). *Computer-mediated communication in relationship maintenance: An examination of self-disclosure in long-distance friendships.* Paper presented at the International Communication Association Annual Meeting, San Francisco, CA.

Warach, B., Josephs, L., & Gorman, B. S. (2019). Are cheaters sexual hypocrites? Sexual hypocrisy, the self-serving bias, and personality style. *Personality and Social Psychology Bulletin, 45*(10) 1499–1511. https://doi.org/10.1177/0146167219833392

Warr, P. B., & Payne, R. (1982). Experiences of strain and pleasure among British adults. *Social Science & Medicine, 16*(19), 1691–1697.

Waterman, A. (1984). *The psychology of individualism.* Praeger.

Watson, K. W., Barker, L. L., & Weaver, J. B., III. (1995). The listening styles profile (LSP-16): Development and validation of an instrument to assess four listening styles. *International Journal of Listening, 9,* 1–13.

Wattleton, Faye. (2008, May 5). *Eyes on Miley's bare back, not on the big picture.* http://ac360.blogs.cnn.com/2008/05/05/eyes-on -miley%E2%80%99s-bare-back-not-on-the-big-picture

Watzlawick, P., Beavin, J. H., & Jackson, D. D. (1967). *Pragmatics of human communication: A study of interactional patterns, pathologies, and paradoxes.* W.W. Norton.

We Are Social. (2019). *Digital in 2019 global overview.* https://wearesocial .com/it/blog/2019/01/digital-in-2019

Weger, H., & Emmett, M. C. (2009). Romantic intent, relationship uncertainty, and relationship maintenance in young adults' cross-sex friendships. *Journal of Social and Personal Relationships, 26*(6–7), 964–988.

Weigel, D. J., & Shrout, M. R. (2020). Suspicious minds: The psychological, physical and behavioral consequences of suspecting a partner's infidelity. *Journal of Social and Personal Relationships.* https://doi .org/10.1177/0265407520975851

Weinberg, N., Schmale, J. D., Uken, J., & Wessel, K. (1995). Computer-mediated support groups. *Social Work with Groups, 17,* 43–55.

Weisz, C., & Wood, L. F. (2005). Social identity support and friendship outcomes: A longitudinal study predicting who will be friends and best friends 4 years later. *Journal of Social and Personal Relationships, 22*(3), 416–432.

Welch, R. D., & Houser, M. E. (2010). Extending the four-category model of adult attachment: An interpersonal model of friendship attachment. *Journal of Social and Personal Relationships, 27*(3), 351–366.

Wells, G. L., Lindsay, R. C. L., & Tousignant, J. P. (1980). Effects of expert psychological advice on human performance in judging the validity of eyewitness testimony. *Law and Human Behavior, 4,* 275–285.

Wentzel, K. R., Jablansky, S., & Scalise, N. R. (2018). Do friendships afford academic benefits? A meta-analytic study. *Educational Psychology Review, 30*(4), 1241–1267. https://doi.org/10.1007/s10648-018-9447-5

West, C., & Zimmerman, D. H. (1987). Doing gender. *Gender & Society, 1,* 125–151.

West, C., & Zimmerman, D. H. (2009). Accounting for doing gender. *Gender and Society, 23,* 112–122. https://doi.org/10.1177/0891243208326529

Wheeless, L. R. (1978). A follow-up study of the relationships among trust, disclosure, and interpersonal solidarity. *Human Communication Research, 4,* 143–145.

White, A. E., Weinstein, E., & Selman, R. L. (2018). Adolescent friendship challenges in a digital context: Are new technologies game changers, amplifiers, or just a new medium? *Convergence, 24*(3), 269–288. https://doi.org/10.1177/1354856516678349

White, G. L. (1980). Physical attractiveness and courtship progress. *Journal of Personality and Social Psychology, 39,* 660–668.

Whitton, S. W., Godfrey, L. M., Crosby, S., & Newcomb, M. E. (2020). Romantic involvement and mental health in sexual and gender minority emerging adults assigned female at birth. *Journal of Social and Personal Relationships, 37*(4), 1340–1361.

Whorf, B. L. (1952). *Collected papers on metalinguistics.* Department of State, Foreign Service Institute.

Wiederman, M. W., & Hurd, C. (1999). Extradyadic involvement during dating. *Journal of Social and Personal Relationships, 16*(2), 265–274. https://doi.org/10.1177/0265407599162008

Wiederman, M. W., & Kendall, E. (1999). Evolution, sex, and jealousy: Investigation with a sample from Sweden. *Evolution and Human Behavior, 20,* 121–128.

Wieman, C., & Welsh, A. (2016). The connection between teaching methods and attributional errors. *Educational Psychology Review, 28,* 645–648. https://doi.org/10.1007/s10648-015-9317-3

Wiemann, J. M. (1977). Explication and test of a model of communicative competence. *Human Communication Research, 3,* 195–213.

Williams, C. (2018). The secret history of Jimmy Jam and Terry Lewis' iconic production catalog. *Okayplayer.* https://www.okayplayer.com/originals/jimmy-jam-terry-lewis-production-catalog-secret-history.html

Williams, S. L., LaDuke, S. L., Klik, K. A., & Hutsell, D. W. (2016). A paradox of support seeking and support response among gays and lesbians. *Personal Relationships, 23,* 296–310. https://doi.org/10.1111/pere.12127

Willis, J. T. (2014). Partner preferences across sexual orientations and biological sex. *Personal Relationships, 21*(1), 150–167. https://doi.org/10.1111/pere.12021

Willness, C. R., Steel, P., & Lee, K. (2007). The antecedents and consequences of workplace sexual harassment. *Personnel Psychology, 60,* 127–162. https://doi.org/10.1111/j.1744-6570.2007.00067.x

Wilmot, W. W., & Hocker, J. L. (2010). Interpersonal conflict (8th ed.). McGraw-Hill.

Winter, K., Scholl, A., & Sassenberg, K. (2020). A matter of flexibility: Changing outgroup attitudes through messages with negations. *Journal of Personality and Social Psychology, 120*(4), 956–976. https://doi.org/10.1037/pspi0000305

Winterson, J. (1993). *Written on the body.* Knopf.

Wolff, M. B., Gay, J. L., Wilson, M. G., DeJoy, D. M., & Vandenberg, R. J. (2016). Does organizational and coworker support moderate diabetes risk and job stress among employees? *American Journal of Health Promotion, 32*(4), 959–962. https://doi.org/10.1177/0890117116685802

Wolvin, A. D. (1987). *Culture as a listening variable.* Paper presented at the International Listening Association Summer Conference, Toronto, Canada.

Wolvin, A. D. (2010). Listening engagement: Intersecting theoretical perspectives. In A. D. Wolvin (Ed.), *Listening and human communication in the 21st century* (pp. 7–30). https://doi.org/10.1002/9781444314908.ch1

Wolvin, A., & Coakley, C. G. (1996). *Listening.* Brown & Benchmark.

Wood, J. T. (2015). *Gendered lives: Communication, gender, and culture.* Cengage Learning.

Wood, W., Rhodes, N., & Whelan, M. (1989). Sex differences in positive well-being: A consideration of emotional style and marital status. *Psychological Bulletin, 106,* 249–264.

Woodrow, C., & Guest, D. E. (2017). Leadership and approaches to the management of workplace bullying. *European Journal of Work and Organizational Psychology, 26,* 221–233.

Workplace Bullying Institute. (n.d.). *WBI U.S. workplace bullying survey, 2017.* https://workplacebullying.org/

World Economic Forum. (2019). Global gender gap report 2020 insight report. http://www3.weforum.org/docs/WEF_GGGR_2020.pdf

World Health Organization. (n.d.a). Definition and typology of violence. https://www.who.int/violenceprevention/approach/definition/en/

World Health Organization. (n.d.b). Ensuring an inclusive global health agenda for transgender people. https://doi.org/10.2471/BLT.16.183913

World Health Organization. (n.d.c). Social determinants of health: Women and gender equity. http://www.who.int/social_determinants/themes/womenandgender/en/

Wu, L., Birtch, T. A., Chiang, F. F. T., & Zhang, H. (2016). Perceptions of negative workplace gossip: A self-consistency theory framework. *Journal of Management, 44*(5), 1873–1898. https://doi.org/10.1177/0149206316632057

Wright, P. H. (1982). Men's friendships, women's friendships and the alleged inferiority of the latter. *Sex Roles, 8,* 1–20.

Wright, P. H. (1988). Interpreting research on gender differences in friendship: A case for moderation and a plea for caution. *Journal of Social and Personal Relationships, 5,* 367–373.

Wu, D. Y. H., & Tseng, W. (1985). Introduction: The characteristics of Chinese culture. In W. Tseng & D. Y. H. Wu (Eds.), *Chinese culture and mental health* (pp. 3–13). Academic Press.

Xie, X., Tang, X., Rapp, H., Tong, D., & Wang, P. (2020). Does forgiveness alleviate depression after being phubbed for emerging adults? The mediating role of self-esteem. *Computers in Human Behavior, 109,* 106362. https://doi.org/10.1016/j.chb.2020.106362

Yakubovich, V., & Burg, R. (2019). Friendship by assignment? From formal interdependence to informal relations in organizations. *Human Relations, 72*(6), 1013–1038. https://doi.org/10.1177/0018726718789479

Yoder, W., & Du Bois, S. N. (2020). Marital satisfaction is associated with health in long-distance relationships. *Family Journal: Counseling and Therapy for Couples and Families, 28*(2), 176–186. https://doi.org/10.1177/1066480720911609

Yoshie, M., & Sauter, D. A. (2019). Cultural norms influence nonverbal emotion communication: Japanese vocalizations of socially disengaging emotions. *Emotion, 20*(3), 513–517.

Zacchilli, T. L., Hendrick, C., & Hendrick, S. S. (2009). The romantic partner conflict scale: A new scale to measure relationship conflict. *Journal of Social and Personal Relationships, 26,* 1073–1096.

Zahn-Waxler, C. (2001). The development of empathy, guilt, and internalization of distress: Implications for gender differences in internalizing and externalizing problems. In R. Davidson (Ed.), *Anxiety, depression, and emotion: Wisconsin Symposium on Emotion* (Vol. 1, pp. 222–265). Oxford University Press.

Zell, E., Strickhouser, J. E., Lane, T. N., & Teeter, S. R. (2016). Mars, Venus, or Earth? Sexism and the exaggeration of psychological gender differences. *Sex Roles, 75,* 287–300.

Zhang, Q., Ting-Toomey, S., & Oetzel, J. G. (2014). Linking emotion to the conflict face-negotiation theory: A U.S.-China investigation of the mediating effects of anger, compassion, and guilt in interpersonal conflict. *Human Communication Research, 40*(3), 373–395. https://doi.org/10.1111/hcre.12029

Zhang, R. (2017). The stress-buffering effect of self-disclosure on Facebook: An examination of stressful life events, social support, and mental health among college students. *Computers in Human Behavior, 75,* 527–537.

Zimet, G. D., Dahlem, N. W., Zimet, S. G., & Farley, G. K. (1988). The multidimensional scale of perceived social support. *Journal of Personality Assessment, 52*(1), 30–41. https://doi.org/10.1207/s15327752jpa5201_2

Zimmer, B. (2016). *Hamilton* through the lens of language. *Slate.com.* https://slate.com/human-interest/2016/05/how-lin-manuel-mirandas-hamilton-foregrounds-the-pleasure-and-power-of-words.html

Zimmerman, E. (2020, June 18). What makes some people more resilient than others. *New York Times.*

Zorn, T. E. (1995). Bosses and buddies: Constructing and performing simultaneously hierarchical and close friendship relationships. In J. T. Wood & S. Duck (Eds.), *Under-studied relationships: Off the beaten track* (pp. 122–147). SAGE.

Zuckerman, M., Hodgins, H., & Miyake, K. (1990). The vocal attractiveness paradigm: Replication and elaboration. *Journal of Nonverbal Behavior, 14,* 97–112.

Zuckerman, M., Miyake, K., & Hodgins, H. S. (1991). Cross-channel effects of vocal and physical attractiveness and their implications for interpersonal perception. *Journal of Personality and Social Psychology, 60,* 545–554.

Acknowledgments

Page 17: National Communication Association Credo for Ethical Communication. Copyright © 1999 by the National Communication Association. Reprinted by permission of the National Communication Association.

Page 82: Quiz adapted from James B. Stiff, James Price Dillard, Lilnabeth Somera, Hyun Kim, and Carra Sleight (1988). "Empathy, communication and prosocial behavior," *Communication Monographs, 55*(2). Copyright © 1988.

Table 6.1: Reproduced with permission from American Psychological Association & National Association of School Psychologists. (2015). Resolution on Gender and Sexual Orientation Diversity in Children and Adolescents in Schools. Retrieved from https://www.apa.org/about/policy/orientation-diversity. Copyright © 2015 American Psychological Association. All rights reserved.

Table 6.2: The Pink Tax: Table showing price differences between men's and women's self-care products, excerpted from Candice Elliott, "The Pink Tax—The Cost of Being a Female Consumer," *Listen Money Matters,* https://www.listenmoneymatters.com/the-pink-tax/. Copyright © Listen Money Matters. Reprinted by permission.

Page 335: Francesca Bell, "Making You Noise." First appeared in Nimrod. Copyright © Francesca Bell. Used by permission of the author.

LaunchPad Videos

launchpadworks.com

- Over 90 video clips illustrate key interpersonal communication concepts.
- Videos marked with an asterisk appear as features in the margins of the text.